Lecture Notes in Computer Science

Edited by G. Goos and J. Hartmanis

338

Kumar (Eds.)

s of Software
and
Computer Science

une, India
88

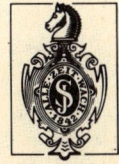

Springer-Verlag
Berlin Heidelberg New York London Paris Tokyo

Editorial Board
D. Barstow W. Brauer P. Brinch Hansen D. Gries D. Luckham
C. Moler A. Pnueli G. Seegmüller J. Stoer N. Wirth

Editors
Kesav V. Nori
Sanjeev Kumar
Tata Research Development and Design Centre
1, Mangaldas Road, Pune 411 001, India

CR Subject Classification (1987): D.3.1, F.1.3, F.2.2, F.3.2, F.4, H.2.0–1, I.2.3

ISBN 3-540-50517-2 Springer-Verlag Berlin Heidelberg New York
ISBN 0-387-50517-2 Springer-Verlag New York Berlin Heidelberg

This work is subject to copyright. All rights are reserved, whether the whole or part of the material is concerned, specifically the rights of translation, reprinting, re-use of illustrations, recitation, broadcasting, reproduction on microfilms or in other ways, and storage in data banks. Duplication of this publication or parts thereof is only permitted under the provisions of the German Copyright Law of September 9, 1965, in its version of June 24, 1985, and a copyright fee must always be paid. Violations fall under the prosecution act of the German Copyright Law.

© Springer-Verlag Berlin Heidelberg 1988
Printed in Germany

Printing and binding: Druckhaus Beltz, Hemsbach/Bergstr.
2145/3140-543210

Preface

The acceptance of the quality of the FST&TCS conferences by the international Computer Science research community is a source of much satisfaction to its organisers. This year, we received 129 submissions from authors from 21 countries. We also received tremendous support from the reviewers. The overall quality of the submissions was such that we had to turn away some papers which received good reviews, and would have been accepted at FST&TCS Conferences in the recent past. In all, 30 papers were accepted, of which 4 are in the short presentation category.

The success of this Conference has been largely due to the personal efforts of the members, past and present, of the Conference Advisory Committee and the Technical Programme Committee. The burden of finding secretarial support, as well as financial support, every year has fallen on a few located in the city where the Conference was held. A move to finding long term solutions to these problems is in progress, and, we hope, will be known in time for the organisation of the next conference.

Acknowledgements

On behalf of the Technical Programme Committee, we would like to place on record our sincere appreciation to

- the invited speakers;
- the authors of all submitted papers;
- the reviewers for their diligent help;
- TIFR, TRDDC, CDAC, DST, CMC, TCS, and Hinditron for their financial support;
- Dr. E. Bhagiratha Rao, Dean, IAT, for making available the venue, and extending organisational help;
- Lalita D'Netto, Dilshad Felfeli, Patricia Lobo, Sridhar Murthy, Sona Nanwani, and Yazdi Pajnigar, Shivaji Shelar for secretarial support;
- D Ganapathy, RV Godbole, Jai Kumar, Kishore Murthy, A Mahajani, P Mahesh, N Meenakshi, M Pavan Kumar, S Rajagopal, AG Ramesh, PV Ramesh, BS Reddy, GS Reddy, A Senthil Kumar, S Singhani, M Subramaniam, K Sudarshan, and R Venkatesh for helping us meet hard real-time schedules.

September 1988

Kesav V. Nori
Sanjeev Kumar

Conference Advisory Committee

D Bjørner (Denmark)
A Chandra (IBM Research)
B Chandrasekaran (Ohio State)
S Crespi Reghizzi (Milan)
Z Galil (Columbia)
D Gries (Cornell)
M Joseph (Warwick)
A Joshi (Pennsylvania)
U Montanari (Pisa)
A Nakamura (Hiroshima)
R Narasimhan (TIFR)
M Nivat (Paris)
R Parikh (New York)
S Rao Kosaraju (Johns Hopkins)
S Sahni (Minnesota)
W A Wulf (Virginia)

Programme Committee

A Bagchi (IIM Calcutta)
S Biswas (IIT Kanpur)
A Kumar (IIT Delhi)
S Kumar (TRDDC Pune)
C R Muthukrishnan (IIT Madras)
K V Nori (TRDDC Pune)
L M Patnaik (IISc Banglore)
H V Sahasrabuddhe (Poona University)
R Sangal (IIT Kanpur)
R K Shyamsunder (TIFR)
R Siromoney (Madras Christian College)
P S Thiagarajan (Matscience Madras)
C E Veni Madhavan (IISc Banglore)

List of Reviewers

P J Abisha, MCC, Madras
M Agarwal, IIT, Kanpur
V K Agarwal, ISRO, Bangalore
V Arvind, IIT, Delhi
D F Baca, Iowa State, Ames
J C M Baeten, Amsterdam
A Bagchi, IIM, Calcutta
R Bagrodia, Univ of California
A Balachandran, IIT, Bombay
S Balaji, ISRO, Bangalore
G Barua, IIT, Kanpur
B Bedres, Saarland, FRG
P Bellot, IBM-France
E Bevers, Leuven, Belgium
V P Bhatkar, C-DAC, Pune
G P Bhattacharjee, IIT, Kharagpur
B B Bhattacharya, ISI, Calcutta
S Biswas, IIT, Bombay
S Biswas, IIT, Kanpur
H A Blair, Syracuse Univ
N Blum, Saarland, FRG
A Bonarini, Milano, Italy
F J Brandenburg, Passau, FRG
D L Carvar, Louisiana State
R Chandrasekar, NCST, Bombay
A Cheese, Univ of Nottingham
W Chen, SUNY, Stony Brook
J Cheriyan, TIFR, Bombay
R K Chhotaray, REC, Rourkela
P M Chi, Academia Sinica, Beijing
A Ciepielewshi, ICOT, Tokyo
J L Clark, CSA, Singapore
B Courcelle, Talence, France
S Crespi-Reghizzi, Milano, Italy
K Culik II, Univ of S. Carolina
D D'Souza, RMIT, Melbourne
S Ben David, Technion, Haifa
U Dayal, Computer Corp of America
P Degano, Univ of Pisa
B Demoen, Leuven, Belgium
S Dhanabal, TCS, Delhi
A A Diwan, IIT, Bombay
P Dublish, IIT, Delhi
A G Duncan, GE, Schenectady
M Dutta, University of Guwahati
K Ephrasim, Technion, Haifa
M Fitting, CUNY, Brooklyn
L De Floriani, Genova, Italy
N Francez, Technion, Haifa
K Furukawa, ICOT
M Ganapathy, Stanford University
N Gehani, Bell Labs
K M George, Oklahoma State Univ
R Gerth, Eindhoven University
E Van Gestel, Leuven, Belgium
S Ghosh, Univ of Iowa
N S Gopalakrishnan, Pune

R Gorrieri, Univ of Pisa
A Goswami, Warwick University
G Gough, Eindhoven University
R Govindarajulu, REC, Warangal
C Haldar, IISc, Bangalore
R C Hansdah, IISc, Bangalore
R A Hartman, Iowa State, Ames
J Hartmann, Saarlandes, FRG
M Hedberg, Goteborg, Sweden
H Heller, München, FRG
M C Henson, Essex
G Hoeven, Enschede, Netherlands
M Hofri, Technion, Haifa
G Hotz, Univ of Saarland, FRG
G J Houben, Eindhoven University
M C Hsu, Computer Corp of America
W T Huang, Taipei, Taiwan
L Huimin, Academia Sinica, Beijing
O H Ibarra, Univ of Minnesota
R V Iyer, Washington State
K Jensen, Aarhus, Denmark
E W Johnson, SUNY, Stony Brook
M Joseph, Warwick
A K Joshi, Univ of Pennsylvania
M Kaminski, Technion, Haifa
T Kanamori, ICOT, Tokyo
P P Kanapathy, NUS, Singapore
K Kanchana, AIT, Bangkok
R Kannan, Carnegie-Mellon
S Kaplan, Hebrew Univ, Jerusalem
S Kapoor, IIT, Delhi
D Kapur, SUNY, Albany
H Karnick, IIT, Kanpur
G Kissin, Technion, Haifa
A Klapper, NE Univ, Boston
S C Kothari, Iowa State
E Kranakis, Amsterdam
H Kreowski, Bremen, FRG
M Pavan Kumar, TRDDC, Pune
S Kumar, TRDDC, Pune
A Lingas, Linkoping, Sweden
K Lodaya, Matscience, Madras
A Lord, Warwick
K Magel, N. Dakota State Univ
S M Mahajan, BARC, Bombay
M J Maher, IBM Yorktown Heights
S N Maheshwari, IIT, Delhi
A K Majumdar, IIT, Kharagpur
V M Malhotra, AIT, Bangkok
A D Marathe, TCS, Pune
K Marriott, Melbourne
T R Mathies, Carnegie-Mellon
R Mathur, BARC, Bombay
A D McGettrick, Glasgow
S Mitta, WIPRO, Bangalore
I Miyamoto, Univ of Hawaii
C K Mohan, SUNY, Stony Brook

P Molitor, Saarland, FRG
U Montanari, Univ of Pisa
E Mata Montero, Univ of Oregon
B N S Murthy, REC Surathakal
N Murthy, Pace University
V R K Murthy, Andhra Univ
C R Muthukrishnan, IIT, Madras
L Naish, Melbourne
A Nakamura, Hiroshima University
N K Nanda, AIT, Bangkok
P Narendran, GE, Schenectady
M Nivat, Paris
K V Nori, TRDDC, Pune
R L Norton, Poughkeepsie
P Ostermann, Bourgogne, France
A K Pal, IIM, Calcutta
S P Pal, IISc, Bangalore
P Pal Chaudhuri, IIT, Kharagpur
P Panangaden, Cornell Univ
P Pandaya, TIFR, Bombay
C Pandurangan, IIT, Madras
J Paredaens, Antwerp, Belgium
C Parent, Univ of Bourgogne
R Parikh, City Univ of New York
L M Patnaik, IISc, Bangalore
G Pelagatti, Milano, Italy
A Pettorossi, IASI-CNR, Italy
T V Prabhakar, IIT, Kanpur
K N Prakash, NCST, Bombay
K V S Prasad, Goteborg, Sweden
A Proskurowski, Univ of Oregon
G Pucci, Newcastle-upon-Tyne
A K Pujari, Osmania University
W V Puymbroeck, Bell Tel, Antwerp
P S Rajkumar, Keltron, Trivandrum
L N Rajaram, ESCPL, New Delhi
S Rajasekaran, Duke Univ, Durham
K S Rajasethupathy, TIFR, Bombay
S Rajopadhye, Univ of Oregon
R Ramanujam, Matscience, Madras
S Ramesh, Eindhoven University
S Upendra Rao, Andhra Univ
R Rastogi, BARC, Bombay
Rauch, Univ of Saarland, FRG
S S Ravi, SUNY at Albany
E Ravidran, IIT, Bombay
K Read, RMIT, Melbourne
T J Reynolds, Univ of Essex
D C Rine, George Mason Univ
A Rohra, Canon Inc, Japan
R Sadananda, AIT, Bangkok
H V Sahasrabuddhe, Pune University
S Sahni, Univ of Minnesota
R Sangal, IIT, Kanpur
A Sanyal, IIT, Bombay
A Saoudi, Univ of Paris

S N Sapre, Pune University
S Sarin, Computer Corp of America
M Sasi Kumar, NCST, Bombay
S Saxena, IIT, Delhi
R K Sen, IIT, Kharagpur
S Sen, Duke Univ, Durham
S Seth, Univ of Nebraska, Lincoln
D Shankar, Andhra Univ
S P Shonche, BARC, Bombay
S K Shrivastava, Newcastle
R K Shyamsunder, TIFR, Bombay
R Siromoney, MCC, Madras
G Slutzki, Iowa State, Ames
N Soundarajan, Ohio State Univ
S Spaccapietra, Univ of Bourgogne
U Sparman, Univ of Saarland, FRG
M A Sridhar, Univ of S. Carolina
S Sridharan, Hinditron, Bombay
Y N Srikant, IISc, Bangalore
P K Srimani, Southern Illinois
P Srinivas Kumar, IISc, Bangalore
M K Srivas, SUNY, Stony Brook
A Srivastava, Tektronix
R Stansifer, Purdue University
I A Stewart, Newcastle Upon Tyne
V S Subrahmaian, Syracuse Univ
K V Subrahmanyam, TIFR, Bombay
M Subramaniam, TRDDC, Pune
P S Subramanian, TIFR, Bombay
C R Subramanian, IISc, Bangalore
K G Subramanyam, MCC, Madras
S Sur_kolay, ISI, Calcutta
K Takeda, Univ of Hawaii
P S Thiagarajan, Matscience Madras
A K Tripathi, BHUIT, Varanasi
V Vazirani, Cornell Univ
C E Veni Madhavan, IISc, Bangalore
R Venkataraman, HAL, Bangalore
G Venkatesh, IIT, Bombay
B Vergauwen, Leuven, Belgium
R M Verma, SUNY, Stony Brook
K Vidyasankar, Memorial Univ
V Vinay, IISc, Bangalore
E Wagner, IBM Yorktown Heights
M Wand, NE Univ, Boston
Y R Wang, Texas A&I University
A Wasilewska, SUNY, Stony Brook
P Weijland, Amsterdam
E Welzl, Univ of Berlin, FRG
H Wen-Jing, Michigan State Univ
J F H Winkler, Siemens,München
H Yen, Iowa State, Ames
J Huai You, Alberta, Canada
S Zachos, CUNY, Brooklyn
C T Zahn, Scarsdale, New York
W Zimmermann, Karlsruhe, FRG

TABLE OF CONTENTS

Session 1 Invited Talk, chairperson: A Bagchi
Planar Point Location Revisited (A Guided Tour of a Decade of Research)   1
Franco P Preparata
(University of Illinois, Urbana-Champaign, USA)

Session 2 Algorithms, chairperson: Somenath Biswas
Computing a viewpoint of a set of points inside a polygon   18
Subir Kumar Ghosh (TIFR, Bombay)
Analysis of Preflow Push Algorithms for Maximum Network Flow   30
Joseph Cheriyan (TIFR, Bombay)
S N Maheshwari (Indian Institute of Technology, Delhi)
A New Linear Algorithm for the Two Path Problem on Chordal Graphs   49
S V Krishnan, C Pandu Rangan, S Seshadri
(Indian Institute of Technology, Madras)
Extending Planar Graph Algorithms to $K_{3,3}$-free Graphs   67
Samir Khuller (Cornell University, USA)

Session 3 Algorithms, chairperson: Anshul Kumar
Constant-Space String-Matching   80
Maxime Chrochemore (Université de Paris-Nord, France)
Inherent Nonslicibility of Rectangular Duals in VLSI Floorplanning   88
Susmita Sur-Kolay, Bhargab B Bhattacharya
(Indian Statistical Institute, Calcutta)
Path Planning with Local Information   108
Amitava Datta, Kamala Krithivasan
(Indian Institute of Technology, Madras)

Session 4 Algorithms, chairperson: C R Muthukrishnan
Linear Broadcast Routing   122
Ching-Tsun Chou (University of California, Los Angeles, USA)
Inder S Gopal (IBM TJ Watson Research Center, USA)   (Abstract)
Predicting Deadlock in Store-and-Forward Networks   123
Claudio Arbib (Universita di Roma, Italy)
Giuseppe F Italiano (Columbia University, USA)
Alessandro Panconesi (Cornell University, USA)

Session 5 Parallel algorithms, chairperson: H V Sahasrabuddhe
On Parallel Sorting and Addition with Concurrent Writes   143
Sanjeev Saxena, P C P Bhatt, V C Prasad
(Indian Institute of Technology, Delhi)

An Optimal Parallel Algorithm for Sorting Presorted Files Christos Levcopoulos, Ola Petersson (Linköping University, Sweden)	154
Superlinear Speedup in Parallel State-Space Search V Nageshwara Rao, Vipin Kumar (University of Texas, Austin, USA)	161

Session 6 Invited Talk, chairperson: R Siromoney
Minimal Ascending and Descending Tree Automata
Maurice Nivat (Paris University, France)
(not included)

Session 7 Complexity, chairperson: C E Veni Madhavan

Circuit Definitions of Nondeterministic Complexity Classes H Venkateswaran (Indian Institute of Science, Bangalore)	175
Non-Uniform Proof Systems: A New Framework to Describe Non-Uniform and Probabilistic Complexity Classes Jürgen Kämper (Universität Oldenburg, FRG)	193
Padding, Commitment and Self-reducibility Sanjeev N Khadilkar, Somenath Biswas (Indian Institute of Technology, Kanpur)	211
The Complexity of a Counting Finite-State Automaton Craig A Rich (California State Polytechnic Univ., Pomona, USA) Giora Slutzki (Iowa State University, Ames, USA)	225
A Hierarchy Theorem for PRAM-Based Complexity Classes Walter W Kirchherr, (San Jose State University, USA)	240

Session 8 Invited Talk, chairperson: R K Shyamsunder

A Natural Deduction treatment of Operational Semantics R Burstall (University of Edinburgh, UK) F Honsell (University of Turin, Italy)	250

Session 9 Semantics, chairperson: P S Thiagarajan

Uniformly Applicative Structures, A Theory of Computability and Polyadic Functions Patrick Bellot (IBM, France) V Jay (Universite Pierre et Marie Curie, Paris, France)	270
A Proof Technique for Register Atomicity Baruch Awerbuch (MIT, USA) Lefteris M Kirousis (University of Patras, Greece) Evangelos Kranakis, Paul M B Vitányi (Centrum voor Wiskunde en Informatica, Amsterdam, Netherlands)	286
Relation Level Semantics Jules Desharnais, Nazim H Madhavji (McGill University, Canada)	304
A Constructive Set Theory for Program Development Martin C Henson, Raymond Turner (University of Essex, England)	329

McCarthy's Amb Cannot Implement Fair Merge 348
Prakash Panangaden, Vasant Shanbhogue (Cornell University, USA)

Session 10 Invited Talk, chairperson: Kesav V Nori
GHC - A Language For a New Age of Parallel Programming 364
Koichi Furukawa, Kazunori Ueda (ICOT, Tokyo, Japan)

Session 11 Logic Prog. and Theorem Proving, chairperson: R Sangal
Accumulators: New Logic Variable Abstractions for Functional Languages 377
Keshav Pingali (Cornell University, USA)
Kattamuri Ekanadham (IBM TJ Watson Research Center, USA)
A Resolution Rule for Well-Formed Formulae 400
K S H S R Bhatta, Harish Karnick
(Indian Institute of Technology, Kanpur)
Algebraic and Operational Semantics of Positive/Negative Conditional Algebraic Specifications 419
Stéphane Kaplan (Hebrew University, Jerusalem, Israel)
Semi-Unification 435
Deepak Kapur (SUNY, Albany, USA)
David Musser (RPI, Troy, USA)
Paliath Narendran (General Electric, Schenectady, USA)
Jonathan Stillman (SUNY, Albany, USA)

Session 12 Databases and Knowledgebases, chairperson: L M Patnaik
A Method to Check Knowledge Base Consistency 455
Alain Beauvieux (IBM, France)
Knowledge Bases as Structured Theories 469
Jose Fiadeiro, Amilcar Sernadas, Cristina Sernadas
(INESC/IST, Portugal)
On Functional Independencies 487
Jürgen M Janas (Universität der Bundeswehr München, FRG)
A Generic Algorithm for Transaction Processing During Network Partitioning 509
Bharat Bhargava, Shirley Browne (Purdue University, USA)

Index 520

Planar Point Location Revisited
(A Guided Tour of a Decade of Research)[1]
Invited Paper

Franco P. Preparata
University of Illinois at Urbana-Champaign

Abstract

Point location is a fundamental primitive in Computational Geometry. In the plane it is stated as follows: Given a subdivision $\mathcal{R}$ of the plane and a query point q, determine the region of $\mathcal{R}$ containing q. We survey the work that has led to practical algorithms for the static version of the problem, and discuss current research on the corresponding dynamic algorithms.

1. Introduction

Point location, a fundamental primitive in Computational Geometry, has been the target of substantial research. The problem is stated as follows: Given a partition $\mathcal{R}$ of the d-dimensional Euclidean space E^d into a collection of cells and a query point $q \in E^d$, find the cell of $\mathcal{R}$ containing q. In the realm of geometric searching, point location is analogous to – and indeed it may be viewed as a generalization of – the classical dictionary problem for totally ordered sets: Given a set S of elements drawn from a totally ordered universal set U, and a query element $x \in U$, find the largest $y \in S$ such that $y \leq x$, if it exists. Thus, the dictionary problem can be recast as one-dimensional point location, where U is mapped to the real line and the abscissae in S partition U into cells that are intervals of the line (bounded or unbounded).

In the *repetitive mode* of operation, i.e., when the number of queries is arbitrarily large and each query is to be answered on-line, we allow preprocessing of S in order to improve the efficiency of the query operation. Within this approach, the classical solution of the dictionary problem consists of sorting the set S in order to use binary search to answer the query. The $O(\log |S|)$ execution time of the latter is also optimal for any solution based on comparisons, which trivially implies that an analogous lower bound holds in higher dimension.

With this motivation, it is natural to attempt a generalization to higher dimension of the algorithmic techniques for the one-dimensional case and immediately realize that the crucial property for the successful solution of the dictionary problem – total order – is absent in more than one dimension. If logarithmic – or polylogarithmic

---
[1] This work was supported in part by the Joint Services Electronics Program under Contract N00014-84-C-0149.

– search time is still the target, any eligible technique must be based on some conventional order artificially imposed either on the original cell partition or on some suitable modification of it. Indeed, all known efficient methods exhibit this feature or an equivalent one.

Of course, there are applications – as in statistics and communication theory – which need efficient point location in high-dimensional spaces, but the two- and three-dimensional cases are by far the most important ones for their obvious relevance to innumerable applications in engineering, geography, operations research, etc. As is typical of so many other areas of Computational Geometry, today we have a sufficient understanding of the two-dimensional case and we have begun tackling the three-dimensional problem. This guided tour, however, will be concerned exclusively with *planar* point location.

In two dimensions, the cell partition $\mathcal{R}$ is traditionally referred to as a *planar subdivision*. It typically consists of a collection of simple (bounded or unbounded) polygons whose sides are portions of straight lines, although this restriction is not essential. Therefore, it is customary to think of $\mathcal{R}$ as determined by a planar graph embedded in the plane with straight-line segments as edges (planar straight-line graph, or PSLG). We let n denote the number of vertices of this planar graph; by Euler's formula, the numbers of its edges and faces are both $O(n)$. In a comparison-based approach, the basic operation is necessarily of the form "$f(x,y) : 0$", for a suitable continuous function, f, which, in the case of PSLGs, is linear. Thus our most elementary primitive operation discriminates a (query) point with respect to a line.

In the repetitive mode of operation, the appropriate measures of performance are the query time $Q(n)$, the storage space $S(n)$ of the search data structure, and the time $P(n)$ spent to construct it (preprocessing time). It is also important to distinguish whether the subdivision is fixed or it is allowed to evolve (on-line) through the insertions/deletions of selected geometric constituents. The corresponding methods are called *static* and *dynamic*, respectively. In a dynamic method, the preprocessing time becomes irrelevant and is replaced by the appropriate update times.

Seeking a clue in the one-dimensional case, we recognize that the key for the successful dynamization of a dictionary (AVL trees, weight-balanced trees, red-black trees, etc.) is the presence of a total order easily maintained through insertions/deletions. The success in dynamizing a two-dimensional technique depends therefore upon our ability to efficiently maintain the artificial order on which the technique is based.

With this background, we shall now review the various methods, which shall be

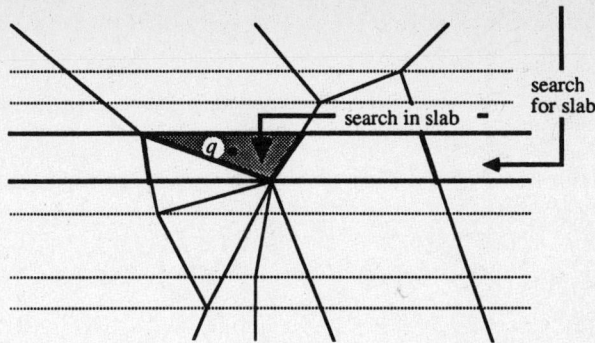

Figure 1: The slab method of Dobkin and Lipton applied to a given $\mathcal{R}$.

grouped on the basis of their conceptual affinity at the sacrifice of a strictly chronological presentation. We shall begin with the static methods.

2. Static implementations

2.1 Slab methods

The prototype in this group is the technique of Dobkin and Lipton [DL76]. Referring to Figure 1, an auxiliary subdivision $\mathcal{R}'$ is created by the set of horizontal lines passing by the vertices of $\mathcal{R}$ ($\mathcal{R}'$ consists of an ordered collection of horizontal "slabs"). The intersection of the slabs of $\mathcal{R}'$ with $\mathcal{R}$ provides the desired refinement of the original subdivision where each slab consists of an ordered collection of trapezoids. The conventional search order is the lexicographic order (slab, trapezoid), i.e., we first determine the slab and then the trapezoid (within *that* slab) containing the query point q. Thus two cascaded binary searches, running in total optimal time $O(\log n)$, achieve point location. This attractive query performance, however, is obtained at the expense of a high storage cost $O(n^2)$, since it is not hard to construct an instance where $\theta(n)$ edges may have representatives in $\theta(n)$ slabs.

This negative appraisal, however, is mitigated by two observations that reveal potential for improvement. First, "long" edges of $\mathcal{R}$ are likely to be responsible for the high storage cost, since they may be fragmented by several slabs; on the other hand, a long edge e may be a useful partitioning device of $\mathcal{R}$, since the horizontal slabs on either side of e form two independent structures. Second, the trapezoid sequences of two adjacent slabs are similar, since they differ only for the (small number of) trapezoids sharing the common vertex of the two slabs. This coherence suggests that

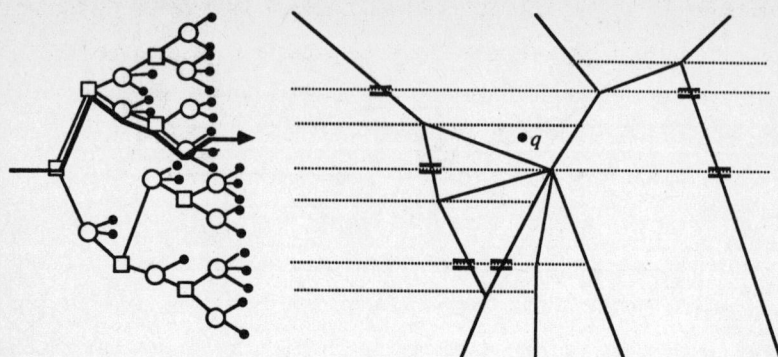

Figure 2: The trapezoid partition of $\mathcal{R}$ and the corresponding trapezoid tree. ∇-nodes are shown as boxes, O-nodes as circles.

only incremental changes in slab structure ought to be explicitly represented in the data structure.

The first observation leads to the trapezoid method of Preparata [P81]. A *trapezoid* τ is a portion of a horizontal strip contained between two nonhorizontal (not necessarily finite) segments crossing the strip (called *spanning* segments of the trapezoid). Note that the whole plane is also a trapezoid. Given a subdivision $\mathcal{R}$, the spanning segments of a trapezoid are always (portions of) edges of $\mathcal{R}$. The median of a trapezoid τ, $median(\tau)$, is the horizontal line passing by the median ordinate vertex of $\mathcal{R}$ among those belonging to the interior of τ. Starting from the trapezoid consisting of the entire plane (i.e., the whole, $\mathcal{R}$) the construction of the trapezoid partition of $\mathcal{R}$ is a recursive process specified as follows: If a nonempty trapezoid τ contains a spanning segment e in its interior, it is partitioned into two trapezoids τ_L and τ_R on either side of e; else, it contains at least one vertex of $\mathcal{R}$ in its interior and it is partitioned into two trapezoids τ_B and τ_T respectively below and above $median(\tau)$. This definition identifies two types of cuts, *vertical* cuts on spanning edges, and *horizontal* cuts on median lines. In the resulting search tree $\mathcal{T}$ (called *trapezoid tree*), these cuts respectively correspond to two distinct types of internal nodes, referred to as O-nodes and ∇-nodes (see Figure 2); the leaves of this tree correspond to the empty trapezoids of the partition. Vertical cuts take precedence over horizontal cuts; therefore a conventional total order is obtained for the search process, which is uniquely determined to within the specification of the sequence of consecutive vertical cuts of the same trapezoid. Answering the point-location query consists of traversing a root-to-leaf path in the previously described trapezoid tree (see again Figure 2).

To analyze the performance of the method, let the weight of a trapezoid be the number of vertices of $\mathcal{R}$ in its interior, and let a trapezoid tree be *irreducible* if it is associated with a trapezoid decomposed by a horizontal cut (and *reducible* otherwise). The trapezoid tree of a reducible trapezoid is weight-balanced, its leaves corresponding to irreducible trapezoid trees and its internal nodes to maximal sequences of spanning edges. The analysis shows that the trapezoid tree of an n-vertex $\mathcal{R}$ can be balanced to achieve depth at most $4 \log n$. This depth coincides with the worst-case query time, and not only is it asymptotically optimal, but it is also characterized by a "small constant" (a frequently overlooked feature in algorithmic analysis). This behavior, however, is obtained at some cost in storage, for it is easily realized that $\theta(n)$ edges may each be partitioned into $\theta(\log n)$ fragments, resulting in an attainable $\theta(n \log n)$ storage use. Thus, the technique is time-optimal but slightly suboptimal in space requirement, although its algorithmic simplicity and excellent experimental performance [EKA84] could make it the choice method in several applications (a reflection of the fact that asymptotic optimality is not always an absolute criterion).

The unexploited coherence between adjacent slabs in the original method of Dobkin and Lipton attracted the attention of Cole [C86] and, later, of Sarnak and Tarjan [ST86], who provided an optimal solution to the problem. Their approach views one dimension (in our case, the y-direction) as "time" so that we may think of the subdivision as being swept over by a horizontal line, maintaining at each instant the left-to-right sequence of the intersected edges (the so-called *sweep-line status* [PS85]). Keeping a copy of each distinct sequence of intersections is equivalent to keeping the full description of each slab, as in the original method. However, as the horizontal line sweeps over a vertex v of $\mathcal{R}$, the update of the sweep-line status involves *only* the edges incident on v. Thus, we may obtain access to any of the distinct sweep-line statuses by carrying out a plane sweep that performs the necessary updates at each vertex and by keeping a record of all such updates. This is the notion of *persistent* data structures, where – in the usual temporal fiction – updates occur only in the present, but accesses may occur also in the past; by contrast, the usual dynamic data structures, not exhibiting the access-in-the-past capability, are referred to as *ephemeral*. Note that in this approach a *static* two-dimensional point-location process is modelled by a *persistent* one-dimensional search process.

The sweep-line status is naturally represented as a binary search tree, whose leaves correspond to the intersected edges (thus, one such edge identifies a leaf-to-root path in the tree). As mentioned earlier, several types of dynamic balanced search trees are known: AVL, weight-balanced, and red-black (or 2-4). Red-black trees [GS78,T83] are particularly attractive, because rebalancing of their ephemeral version after an insertion/deletion involves $O(\log n)$ node label ("color") changes but only $O(1)$ rotations (i.e., only $O(1)$ pointer changes). In order to obtain the persistent version of red-black trees, it is sufficient to keep records of the tree nodes where changes occur. The most direct implementation consists of duplicating such nodes (*path copying*) and time-stamping the new edges, but it results in superlinear storage at the completion of the sweep over the entire planar graph (since $O(n)$ edges have been handled, each involving a path of length $O(\log n)$). An alternative implementation avoids copying the nodes of the search tree, but allows a node to have as many pointers as necessary. In other words, in this implementation the fictitious dimension "time" is represented by the fans of edges exiting the tree nodes. Since only $O(1)$ pointer changes are needed for each update, this results in linear storage; however, the price paid is an increase in query time, since, after m updates, $O(\log m)$ time may be spent at a node to decide which pointer to follow, thus resulting in $O(\log^2 n)$ worst-case query time. Sarnak and Tarjan devised an ingenious compromise between full path copying and no-node copying in order to achieve persistence. By bounding the admissible out-degree of each node and therefore introducing some node duplication, the existing tree structure is exploited to accommodate also the time dimension, resulting in a particularly attractive technique with optimal $O(n)$ storage and $O(\log n)$ query time.

2.2 Separating-chain methods

Substantially different from slab methods are those based on separating chains, whose prototype is an algorithm due to Lee and Preparata[LP77]. These techniques do not introduce artificial cuts to induce an order among the regions of $\mathcal{R}$, but use existing constituents of the subdivision, the separating chains, which we now define.

As usual, an edge (u, v) is a portion of a straight line, bounded or unbounded. A (polygonal) *chain* is a sequence $(e_i : e_i = (v_i v_{i+1}), i = 1, \ldots, p-1)$ of edges; it is *simple* if nonself-intersecting; it is *monotone* if its boundary is partitionable into two monotone chains. A subdivision $\mathcal{R}$ is *monotone* if each of its regions is a monotone polygon (we assume that no edge of $\mathcal{R}$ is horizontal). A *separating chain* σ (or, more succinctly, a *separator*) of a monotone subdivision $\mathcal{R}$ is a monotone chain consisting of edges of $\mathcal{R}$, whose extreme points are at infinity. Given two separators σ_1 and σ_2, σ_1 *is to the left* of σ_2 (denoted $\sigma_1 < \sigma_2$) if any horizontal line intersects σ_1 not to the right of σ_2. A *complete family of separators* Σ of $\mathcal{R}$ is a sequence $(\sigma_1, \sigma_2, \ldots, \sigma_t)$, with $\sigma_1 < \sigma_2 < \ldots < \sigma_t$, such that $\sigma_1 \cup \sigma_2 \cup \ldots \cup \sigma_t$ gives the underlying graph

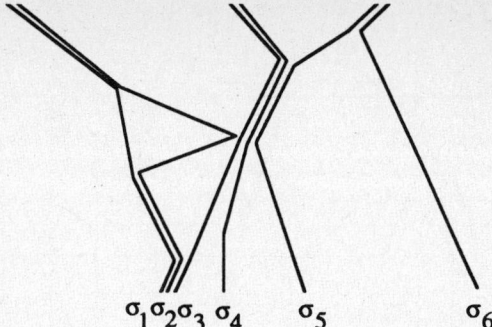

Figure 3: A complete family of separators for our running example.

of $\mathcal{R}$. A complete family of separators for our running example is given in Figure 3. It is known [LP77] that: (i) every monotone subdivision admits a (in general not unique) complete family of separators which is constructible in time $O(n \log n)$; (ii) an arbitrary subdivision with n vertices can be made monotone through the addition of $O(n)$ edges, also in time $O(n \log n)$.

A complete family of separators Σ determines a conventional order on the regions of $\mathcal{R}$, say, left-to-right on the separators, and, subordinately, bottom-to-top for the regions between consecutive separators. Thus Σ can be used to perform planar point location. Given an s-vertex separator σ, consider the planar subdivision whose underlying graph is just σ; by the slab method a one-dimensional search determines in time $O(\log s)$ on which side of σ a query point q lies. Using this *point-chain discrimination* as a primitive, a bisection search on Σ determines in time $O(\log^2 n)$ (the edges of) two consecutive separators between which q lies, i.e., it performs point location. Since Σ is used in a binary search, each separator σ is assigned to a node (briefly referred to as 'node σ') of a balanced binary search tree $\mathcal{T}$ (called *separator tree*). An edge e, however, need not be stored at the nodes of all separators sharing it. Since e belongs, in general, to a nonempty interval $(\sigma_i, \sigma_{i+1}, \ldots, \sigma_j)$ of separators, we just store it at the node of their common ancestor σ_k, where it can be met for the first time by the binary search process; e is called a *proper edge* of σ_k and *proper*(σ_k) denotes the set of proper edges of σ_k. Thus each edge is stored exactly once (yielding linear storage), and associated with a generic node σ of $\mathcal{T}$ there is a secondary one-dimensional data structure $T(\sigma)$. Structure $T(\sigma)$ represents a partition of the y-axis into a collection of intervals referred to as "edges" and "gaps", the former being the projections of the proper edges of σ. This organization is illustrated in Figure 4 for our running

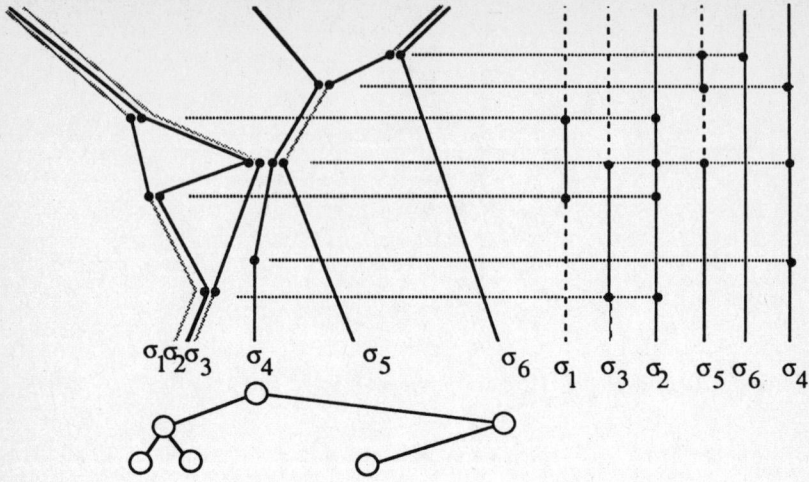

Figure 4: Topology of T and corresponding $proper(\sigma)$ for each separator σ (proper edges are shown solid). On the right we show the one-dimensional $T(\sigma)$'s.

example. In conclusion, comparing this technique with the original slab method of Dobkin and Lipton, linear storage has been achieved at the expense of an increase in query time from $O(\log n)$ to $O(\log^2 n)$.

It is not very difficult to identify the source of the above inefficiency. Indeed, each of the $O(\log n)$ point-chain discriminations (a one-dimensional search) executed in answering a query is performed on the *entire* range of ordinates. However, the admissible range for the ordinate $y(q)$ of the query point q generally shrinks as the search progresses, since it is confined to the intersection of the slabs spanned by the edges directly facing q in the point-chain discriminations performed so far. Unfortunately, no use of this accumulated knowledge is made by the original method. Capitalizing on this observation, Edelsbrunner, Guibas, and Stolfi [EGS86] proposed an elegant modification of the separating-chain method, where the secondary "data" structure $T(\sigma)$ of a node σ of the separator tree is coupled to that of each of its two children. This coupling is effected by a collection of "bridges", which partition the common y-range into "corridors", each containing $O(1)$ edge/gap intervals on the destination (child's) side. With this device, if the search process has located q within a given corridor at the father's side, location at the child's side can be accomplished in constant (rather than logarithmic) time. This is done by a suitable set of pointers that link each y-interval to the appropriate corridor containing it; after traversing the bridge, location at the child side is a march within the corridor. Notice that the bridge struc-

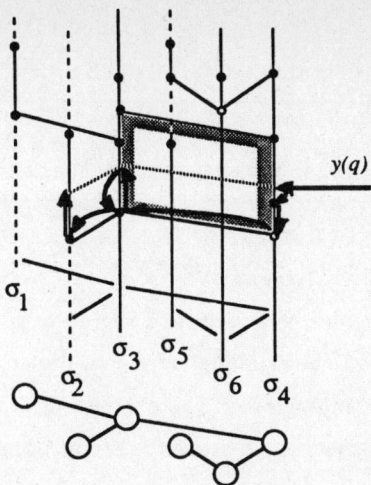

Figure 5: Bridged data structure with $k = 2$ for our running example. Original ordinates are shown as solid circles, propagated ones as hollow circles. A corridor from σ_4 to σ_2 is highlighted, and a search path is evidenced.

ture is simply a device to focus the search, which is still driven from parent to child by standard point-chain discriminations. Thus, in a balanced search tree, an $O(\log n)$ binary search is performed only at the node with no parent (the root), whereas the subsequent $O(\log n)$ point-chain discriminations cost each $O(1)$ time. The achieved query time is therefore optimal. What about storage? Suppose we have constructed the bridge structure for all nodes of the subtree rooted at σ, except for σ, and let $T'(\text{LSON}(\sigma))$ and $T'(\text{RSON}(\sigma))$ be the secondary structures of the two children of σ. To construct the modified $T'(\sigma)$, we extract with fixed period $k > 1$ a sample of ordinates from both $T'(\text{LSON}(\sigma))$, and $T'(\text{RSON}(\sigma))$, and add them to the original $T(\sigma)$. In Figure 5, we illustrate the modified data structure for our running example. This solution guarantees that each corridor contains at most k ordinates at the children sides; at the same time, the fact that only a proper fraction of ordinates is propagated from child to parent ensures that the overall storage use remains linear, as can be easily verified. This ingenious solution is a crisp example of a general methodology recently formalized as "fractional cascading" [CG86].

2.3 The triangulation refinement method

Whereas the methods described in the preceding sections are based on a conventional order imposed on the regions of $\mathcal{R}$ or on some refinement of it, in the method of Kirkpatrick [K83] (restricted to triangulated subdivisions) such an order is not as readily discernible. Here the primitive is inclusion in a triangle and thus it consists of three point-line discriminations. Given a triangulation $\mathcal{R}$, itself enclosed in a triangle t_0, we construct a sequence of triangulations $\mathcal{R}_h, \mathcal{R}_h - 1, \ldots, \mathcal{R}_1$ all with identical external boundary t_0 such that: (i) $\mathcal{R} = \mathcal{R}_h$; (ii) the number of vertices of $\mathcal{R}_i$ is strictly smaller than that of $\mathcal{R}_{i+1}(i = h - 1, \ldots 1)$ (and is 3 for $\mathcal{R}_1$); and (iii) each triangle of $\mathcal{R}_i$ intersects $O(1)$ triangles of $\mathcal{R}_{i+1}$. The nature of $(\mathcal{R}_h, \ldots, \mathcal{R}_1)$ justifies the denotation "triangulation refinement".

The data structure for the search is a directed acyclic graph, having a single source (the entire plane) and the triangles of $\mathcal{R}_h$ as destinations. The source has two pointers respectively to the interior and the exterior of t_0, and each t in $\mathcal{R}_i$ points to the triangles of $\mathcal{R}_{i+1}$ it intersects. The mechanism of point location is rather simple: if query point q has been located in triangle t of $\mathcal{R}_i$, then it can be located in $\mathcal{R}_{i+1}$ by brute-force testing for the inclusion of q in any of the $O(1)$ triangles of $\mathcal{R}_{i+1}$ having a nonempty intersection with t. Starting from $\mathcal{R}_1$ and advancing from $\mathcal{R}_i$ to $\mathcal{R}_{i+1}$, according to the illustrated mechanism, the search terminates at $\mathcal{R}_h$. The crux for efficiency is therefore that $h = O(\log n)$ (to achieve logarithmic query time) and that the number of vertices of $\mathcal{R}_i$ be at most a fraction $\alpha < 1$ of the corresponding number of $\mathcal{R}_{i+1}$. Indeed, denoting by ν_i the number of triangles of $\mathcal{R}_i$, each such triangle has at most K pointers to the triangles of $\mathcal{R}_{i+1}$ it intersects; thus the number S of pointers satisfies $S \leq \Sigma_{i=1}^{h-1} \nu_i K \leq \Sigma_{i=1}^{h-1} \nu_h \alpha^i K < \nu_h K \alpha/(1-\alpha) = O(n)$. Since each $\mathcal{R}_i$ is a planar graph, it has an independent set of vertices with bounded outdegree whose cardinality is at least a (small) fraction of ν_i; the removal of such internal vertices (and incident edges) and the re-triangulation of the resulting polygons achieves the transformation from $\mathcal{R}_{i+1}$ to $\mathcal{R}_i$, and the sequence $(\mathcal{R}_h, \ldots, \mathcal{R}_1)$ exhibits the desired properties.

This asymptotically optimal method, however, is not necessarily attractive from a practical viewpoint. Indeed, the above constant α is close to 1 both analytically [K83] and experimentally [EKA84], resulting in high multiplicative constants in the performance measures. This observation on the frequently unchallenged significance of asymptotic complexity should be contrasted with the complementary comments concerning the trapezoid method.

3. Dynamic implementations

Whereas our understanding of the static-mode problem has reached a mature stage, and among the available techniques there are some that are eminently practical, work on the dynamic-mode problem is a rather recent undertaking and much remains to be done. As to the performance measures, denoting by n the *current* size of $\mathcal{R}$, measures $S(n)$ and $Q(n)$ are fully relevant to dynamic algorithms, but they must be supplemented by the appropriate update times. From a practical standpoint, it is reasonable to accept higher cost for the updates than for the query (the query being the most frequent operation). The yet elusive goal of current research is a dynamic method with $S(n)$ and $Q(n)$ of the same order as those of their optimal static counterparts.

The set of supported updating operations must be such that an arbitrary subdivision of a given class may be assembled and disassembled using only operation from that set; in this case, we say that the set of updates is *adequate*.

3.1 Slab methods

Under the restriction that the vertices of $\mathcal{R}$ belong to a fixed finite sequence $(l_1, \ldots, l_N)$ of horizontal lines (ordered from bottom to top), dynamizations based on the notion of slab are possible. Indeed, the above restriction – assumed to hold throughout this section – suggests that the vertical spans of the edges of $\mathcal{R}$ can be dynamically handled by a segment-tree data structure.

Overmars[O85] proposed an algorithm where the search data structure has a primary component, consisting of a (fixed) segment tree $\mathcal{T}$ on the set of ordinates of $l_1, \ldots, l_N$; each node v of $\mathcal{T}$ points to a secondary structure, consisting of a balanced search tree that stores the edge fragments assigned to v in their left-to-right order. Associated with each edge fragment s is the name of the region of $\mathcal{R}$ immediately to the right of s. Due to the segment-tree mechanism, the data structure clearly uses space $O(n \log N)$. To locate a query point q in $\mathcal{R}$, we traverse the root-to-leaf path in $\mathcal{T}$ determined by the ordinate $y(q)$ (this corresponds to visiting a sequence of nested slabs); at each of the $\lceil \log N \rceil$ visited nodes, by means of an $O(\log n)$-time binary search in its secondary tree we determine the closest edge of $\mathcal{R}$ to the left of q; finally a run-off among these $O(\log N)$ edges completes the search, in total time $O(\log n \cdot \log N)$. Edge insertion is also quite simple and runs in the same time $O(\log n \cdot \log N)$, since the standard segment-tree fragmentation is followed by $O(\log N)$ insertions into secondary data structures; edge deletion is the reverse of insertion, although a simple trick achieves amortized time $O(\log N + \log n)$. The strengths of Overmars' approach are its simplicity and the absence of restrictions on the nature of the regions of $\mathcal{R}$; its weaknesses are its suboptimal performance (space and query time) and, of course,

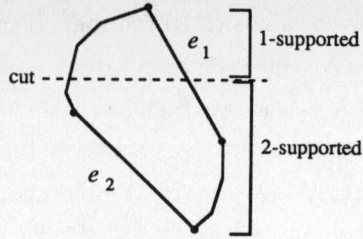

Figure 6: Illustration of the horizontal cut of a 2-supported polygon.

the restriction on the admissible vertex ordinates.[2]

The trapezoid method has been shown by Preparata and Tamassia[PT88b,T88] to be dynamizable in an uncomplicated – but certainly not obvious – way if $\mathcal{R}$ obeys the following condition: any polygon r of $\mathcal{R}$ is monotone and 2-*supported*, i.e., it has two edges e_1 and e_2 such that any horizontal line intersecting $\mathcal{R}$ intersects at least one of e_1 and e_2. (Analogously, r is 1-*supported* if it has one edge having the same vertical span as r itself.) This class of subdivisions is interesting because it obviously contains all triangulations; moreover, convex subdivisions can be handled by simply enforcing the condition of 2-supportedness. We have the property that of the two polygons resulting from cutting a given 2-supported polygon by means of a horizontal line at most one is 2-supported, and the other is always 1-supported (see Figure 6). We now illustrate how this property is crucial for the efficiency of the updates. An adequate repertory of updates consists of insertion/deletion of an edge, insertion/deletion of a vertex on an edge, and horizontal translation of a vertex. For brevity, we shall just consider the insertion of an edge e into a region r of $\mathcal{R}$. Edge e is partitioned by the underlying segment tree into $O(\log N)$ fragments, which define a collection of slabs (*allocation slabs*). We note: (i) Each fragment is to be inserted into a *target* trapezoid contained in the corresponding allocation slab; (ii) The allocation slabs partition r into a set of polygons of which at most one is 2-supported. It follows that all but one of the fragment insertions are straightforward operations, since in such case the fragment joins an existing sequence of spanning edges. In the singular case of the 2-supported polygon, the target trapezoid must undergo a substantial restructuring from being horizontally cut to being vertically cut. The analysis shows that, due to 2-supportedness, at most $O(\log N)$ nodes of

---

[2]Insertions/deletions of vertices can be supported by a somewhat heavy and and not very practical machinery, where $\mathcal{T}$ is realized as a weight-balanced tree, and the secondary structures are rebuilt at each rotation. The resulting update time is $O(\log^2 n)$, amortized.

the segment tree are involved in the restructuring, so that the entire edge insertion costs $O(\log n \cdot \log N)$ time. As regards query procedure and storage organization, the method is identical to static counterpart; thus we have $S(n) = O(n \log N)$, $Q(n) = O(\log n + \log N)$, and $O(\log n \cdot \log N)$ time for the insertions/deletions of edges and vertices (worst-case performances). Again, the restriction on the admissible vertex ordinates is a limitation of the method.

3.2 Separating chain methods

The separating chain approach is the foundation of two dynamic techniques developed recently.

The first is the still unpublished and only partially documented work of Fries and Mehlhorn[M84,FMN85,F85]. Its main strength is that no restriction is placed on the applicable subdivisions. Indeed, the separating chain method is extended to nonmonotone subdivisions, by developing a primitive of point-chain discrimination for nonmonotone chains. When the horizontal line passing by the query point q intersects chain σ in more than one point, the primitive must return the two edges of σ that bracket q. This complication, however, does not modify the asymptotic performance, which remains $O(\log n)$, yielding $Q(n) = O(\log^2 n)$ (worst-case). This structure is amenable to "semidynamic" behavior, i.e., the insertion of edges. Indeed, an edge e to be inserted splits a face whose boundary is contained in two consecutive separators σ_i and σ_{i+1}. Thus, a new separator σ containing edge e is easily constructed and the corresponding node is inserted into the separator tree $\mathcal{T}$ between σ_i and σ_{i+1}. Of course, the insertion of σ can throw $\mathcal{T}$ out of balance. Assuming that $\mathcal{T}$ is realized as a weight-balanced tree, it is shown in [M84] that $\mathcal{T}$ can be rebalanced and the secondary data structures updated in amortized time $O(\log^2 n)$.

Full dynamic behavior (i.e., the implementation of an adequate repertory of updates) for general subdivisions is claimed in [FMN85,F85]. This approach uses the more malleable monotone chains. For an arbitrary $\mathcal{R}$, it maintains a monotone refinement $\mathcal{R}^*$ of $\mathcal{R}$. Such refinement (a "normalization") of $\mathcal{R}$ has the property that any edge insertable into $\mathcal{R}$ cuts at most $O(\log n)$ edges of $\mathcal{R}^*$. Thus an edge insertion may involve the prior removal of at most $O(\log n)$ edges of $\mathcal{R}^*$ and the additional work necessary to restore the above crucial property. This approach is claimed to achieve the following performance: $S(n) = O(n)$, $Q(n) = O(\log^2 n)$ (worst-case), edge and vertex insertion/deletion in time $O(\log^4 n)$ (amortized).

A major difficulty encountered in dynamizing the separating chains method of

Lee-Preparata is the update of the secondary data structures after a rebalancing of the primary search tree (refer to Figure 4). Indeed, consider a pair of separator nodes σ_i and σ_j of $\mathcal{T}$ with $\sigma_i = FATHER(\sigma_j)$, which exchange their roles due to a rotation. The edges of $\sigma_j \cap proper(\sigma_i)$ must be reassigned from $proper(\sigma_i)$ to $proper(\sigma_j)$; since $proper(\sigma_i)$ may consist, in general, of several disjoint subchains, this update may use time $O(n)$. The structure of $\{proper(\sigma_i) : \sigma_i \in \Sigma\}$ is determined by the choice of Σ (which is not unique!) and of the root of the separator tree. If there is a Σ such that each $proper(\sigma_i)$ consists of a single chain, then dynamization appears possible. Indeed, in such case a rotation in $\mathcal{T}$ could be carried out in time $O(\log n)$, since the secondary structures are standard concatenable queues.

Preparata and Tamassia[PT88a] have shown that such a Σ indeed exists and is unique. We recall that an arbitrary Σ determines a conventional order on the regions of $\mathcal{R}$. However, a planar graph (and, therefore, any $\mathcal{R}$) possesses a natural order, whose underpinnings are the order-theoretic properties of planar lattices[KR75]. Specifically, given two regions r_1 and r_2 of $\mathcal{R}$, we define the following partial orders: (i) r_1 *is below* r_2 ($r_1 \uparrow r_2$), if there is a path in $\mathcal{R}$ from the top vertex of r_1 to the bottom vertex of r_2; (ii) r_1 *is to the left of* r_2 ($r_1 \rightarrow r_2$), if there is sequence of regions $r_1 = r'_1, r'_2, \ldots, r'_s = r_2$ such that r'_i and $r'_{i+1}(i = 0, \ldots, s-1)$ share an edge and r'_i is to the left of it. Partial orders "$\uparrow$" and "$\rightarrow$" are shown to be complementary, so that their union is the desired total order "$<$". Denoting with $(r_1, \ldots, r_p)$ the sequence of the regions of $\mathcal{R}$ in the order "$<$", we have a *unique* family of separators $\Sigma^* = (\sigma_1, \ldots, \sigma_{p-1})$, such that σ_i separates r_i and $r_{i+1}(i = 1, \ldots, p-1)$.

A monotone $\mathcal{R}$ is called *regular* if it contains no two regions r_1 and r_2 consecutive in "$<$" such that $r_1 \uparrow r_2$ ("vertically consecutive"). Regular subdivision are the target of our search, since it can be shown that, for each $\sigma_j \in \Sigma^*$, $proper(\sigma_j)$ consists of a single chain, as desired. Moreover, a generic monotone $\mathcal{R}$ can be viewed as regular if we simply generalize the notion of region to that of *cluster*, which is a maximal sequence of vertically consecutive regions of $\mathcal{R}$. The family Σ^* for our running example is shown in Figure 7. In a cluster, the paths joining two vertically consecutive regions is duplicated and is called a *channel*.

Suppose therefore that Σ^* has been chosen for a given monotone $\mathcal{R}$. The search data structure and the query algorithm are basically the same as those of its static counterpart. The remarkable feature of Σ^* is the drastic simplification of the operation of rotation at a node of $\mathcal{T}$, which is the key to dynamization. Our repertory of operations comprises insertion/deletion of a vertex, and insertion/deletion of a chain

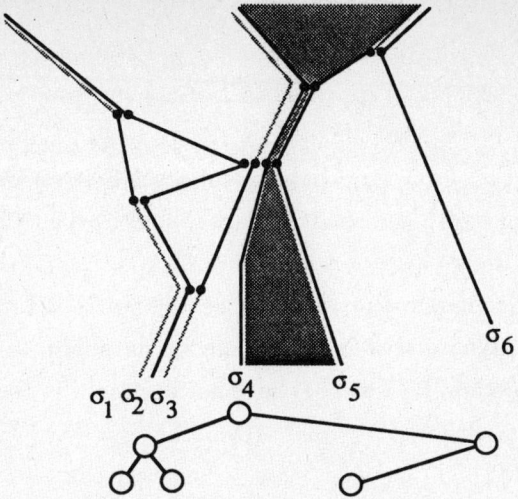

Figure 7: The family Σ^* for our example (compare it with Σ in Figure 4). The shading illustrates a cluster (notice the channel).

of edges between two vertices, under the condition that monotonicity be preserved. This repertory can be shown to be adequate. Handling of vertex updates if relatively simple, so we shall just consider edge updates, and, in particular, insertions. The analysis shows that the order of the regions of $\mathcal{R}$ resulting from the most complicated case of chain insertion is obtainable from the preceding one by disassembling $\mathcal{R}$ into $O(1)$ component subdivisions, to be subsequently reassembled. An individual operation of cutting/splicing a subdivision is simplified if the primary separator tree T is realized as a red-black tree. Indeed, it can be shown that in such implementation no more than $O(\log n)$ rotations are needed, resulting in total $O(\log^2 n)$ time, so that the update time is of the same order. In conclusion, for a monotone subdivision there is a data structure with $S(n) = O(n)$ and $Q(n) = O(\log^2 n)$, which allows for insertion/deletion of an edge in time $O(\log n)$ and insertion deletion of a k-edge chain in time $O(\log^2 n + k)$ (worst-case). Of course, the restriction to monotone subdivisions is a limitation of the method.

4. Chronology

The slab method of Dobkin and Lipton[DL76] appeared in manuscript form in 1975; in the following year, the space-optimal chain method of Lee and Preparata[LP77] was proposed. A theoretical breakthrough – not reported in this survey – was the asymptotically optimal technique of Lipton and Tarjan[LT77], based on the planar-separator theorem. Its enormous complications disqualified it as a practical method, but showed that optimal behavior was attainable and stimulated a keen interest. Indeed, Kirkpatrick's method[K83] appeared in manuscript form in 1979, more or less at the same time as the trapezoid method of Preparata[P81]. It was only in 1985 that the technique of Edelsbrunner, Guibas, and Stolfi[EGS86] was announced; it is essentially contemporary with the result of Sarnak and Tarjan[ST86].

Dynamic methods are an area of active research. Overmars' work[O85] appeared in 1985, in the same conference proceedings as the work of Fries, Mehlhorn, and Näher[FMN85]. The dynamizations of the monotone subdivision method[PT88b] and of the trapezoid method[PT88b,T88] have not appeared in the open literature at the time of this writing.

5. Acknowledgement

Insightful comments and suggestions of R. Tamassia are gratefully acknowledged.

References

[CG86] B.M. Chazelle and L.J. Guibas, "Fractional cascading: I. A data structuring technique," *Algorithmica*, vol. 1, pp. 133-162, 1986.

[C86] R. Cole, "Searching and storing similar list," *Journal of Algorithms*, vol. 7, n. 2, pp. 202-220; 1986.

[DL76] D.P. Dobkin and R.J. Lipton, "Multidimensional Searching Problems," *SIAM J. Computing* vol. 5, no. 2, pp. 181-186, 1976.

[EKA84] M. Edahiro, I. Kokubo, and T. Asano, "A New Point-Location Algorithm and its Practical Efficiency - Comparison with Existing Algorithms," *ACM Trans. on Graphics*, vol 3, no. 2, pp. 86-109, 1984.

[EGS86] H. Edelsbrunner, L.J. Guibas, and J. Stolfi, "Optimal Point Location in a Monotone Subdivision," *SIAM J. Computing*, vol. 15, no. 2, pp. 317-340, 1986.

[F85] O. Fries, "Zerlegung einer planaren Unterteilung der Ebene und ihre Anwendungen," M.S. Thesis, Inst. Angew. Math. and Inform., Univ. Saarlandes, Saarbrücken, Germany, 1985.

[FMN85] O. Fries, K. Mehlhorn, and S. Näher, "Dynamization of Geometric Data Structures," *Proc. ACM Symp. on Computational Geometry*, pp. 168-176, 1985.

[GS78] L.J. Guibas and R. Sedgewick, "A Dichromatic Framework for Balanced Trees," *Proc. 19th IEEE Symp. on Foundations of Computer Science*, pp. 8-21, 1978.

[K83] D.G. Kirkpatrick, "Optimal Search in Planar Subdivisions," *SIAM J. Computing*, vol. 12, no. 1, pp. 28-35, 1983.

[LP77] D.T. Lee and F.P. Preparata, "Location of a Point in a Planar Subdivision and its Applications," *SIAM J. Computing*, vol 6, no. 3, pp. 594-606, 1977.

[KR75] D. Kelly and I. Rival, "Planar Lattices," *Canadian J. Mathematics*, vol. 27, no. 3, pp. 636-665, 1975.

[LT77] R.J. Lipton and R.E. Tarjan, "Applications of a Planar Separator Theorem," *Proc. 18th IEEE Symp. on Foundations of Computer Science*, pp. 162-170, 1977.

[M84] K. Mehlhorn, *Data Structures and Algorithms 3: Multi-dimensional Searching and Computational Geometry*, Springer-Verlag, 1984.

[O85] M. Overmars, "Range Searching in a Set of Line Segments," *Proc. ACM Symp. on Computational Geometry*, pp. 177-185, 1985.

[P81] F.P. Preparata, "A New Approach to Planar Point Location," *SIAM J. Computing*, vol. 10, no. 3, pp. 473-483, 1981.

[PS85] F.P. Preparata and M.I. Shamos, *Computational Geometry*, Springer-Verlag, 1985.

[PT88a] F.P. Preparata and R. Tamassia, "Fully Dynamic Techniques for Point Location and Transitive Closure in Planar Structures," *Proc. 29th IEEE Symp. on Foundations of Computer Science*, 1988 (to appear).

[PT88b] F.P. Preparata and R. Tamassia, "Dynamic Planar Point Location with Optimal Query time," manuscript submitted for publication, 1988.

[ST86] N. Sarnak and R.E. Tarjan, "Planar Point Location Using Persistent Search Trees," *Communications ACM*, vol. 29, no. 7, pp. 669-679, 1986.

[T83] R.E. Tarjan, "Data Structures and Network Algorithms," *CBMS-NSF Regional Conference Series in Applied Mathematics*, vol. 44, Society for Industrial Applied Mathematics, 1983.

[T88] R. Tamassia, "Dynamic Data Structures for Two-dimensional Searching," Ph.D Thesis, University of Illinois; August 1988.

Computing a viewpoint of a set of points inside a polygon

Subir Kumar Ghosh
Computer Science Group
Tata Institute of Fundamental Research
Bombay 400005, INDIA

ABSTRACT

Given a set S of k points inside an n-sided simple polygon P, the problem is to find a point g of P, if it exists, such that all points of S are visible from g. Here we propose an algorithm for this problem that runs in O(n+k) time in the worst case and takes an O(nloglogn+klogn+klogk) time for preprocessing.

1. Introduction

The art gallery problem is to determine the minimum number of guards that are sufficient to *cover* or *see* every point in the interior of an art gallery room. The room can be viewed as a *simple polygon* P of n vertices and the guards are stationary points in P. Any point z of P is said to be *visible* from a guard g if the line segment joining z and g does not intersect the exterior of P. Note that if the line segment touches the boundary of P, they are still considered visible in P. The problem was posed by Klee [H76] and Chavatal [C75] proved that $\lfloor n/3 \rfloor$ guards are occasionally necessary and always sufficient to cover P. Fisk [F78] later gave a simple proof and based on this proof, Avis and Toussaint [AT81] developed an O(nlogn) time algorithm. For orthogonal polygons, where the edges are either horizontal or vertical, Kahn et al. [KKK83] have shown that $\lfloor n/4 \rfloor$ guards are always sufficient and sometimes necessary. O'Rourke [O83] later gave a simple proof of this result. Several O(nlogn) time algorithms have been proposed to decompose a orthogonal polygon into convex quadrilaterals [EOW84], [S82], [L85]. For an excellent survey of art gallery theorems and algorithms, see [O87].

Usually the guards may be placed anywhere inside the polygon. If the guards are restricted to the vertices of the polygon, we call them *point guards*. If there is no restriction, the guards are referred to as *point guards*. If the guards are mobile, i.e., able to patrol along an edge of P, O'Rourke [OR83] has shown that $\lfloor n/4 \rfloor$ *edge guards* are necessary and sufficient.

The minimum guard problem is to find the minimum number of guards that can see every point in the interior of a given simple polygon. O'Rourke and Supowit [OS83] have

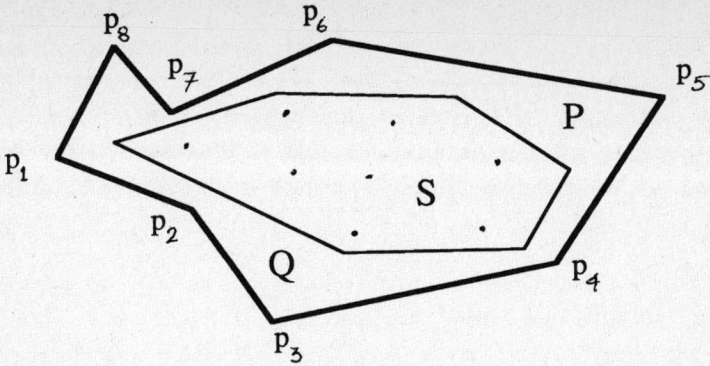

Figure 1

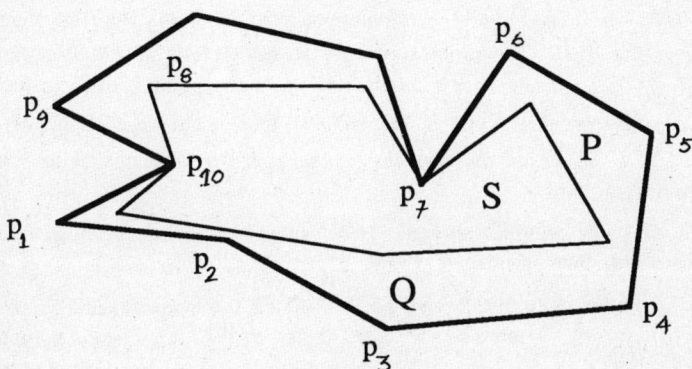

Figure 2

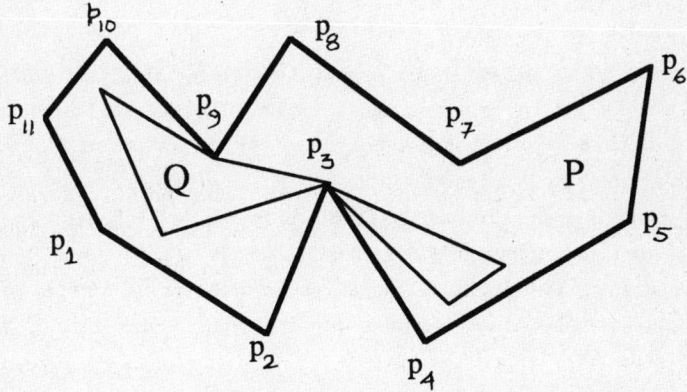

Figure 3

shown that the minimum vertex, point and edge guard problems for polygon with holes are NP-hard. Even in the case of polygons without holes, the minimum vertex, point and edge guard problems are NP-hard [LL86]. Ghosh [G86] proposed approximation algorithms for the minimum vertex and edge guard problems for polygons with or without holes. The approximation algorithms run in $O(n^5 \log n)$ time and yield solutions which can be at most $O(\log n)$ times the optimal solutions. Here we address another variation of the art gallery problem.

Suppose there are sculptures in an art gallery and we wish to place the minimum number of guards inside the art gallery such that every sculpture can be seen at least from one guard. The art gallary can be viewed as a simple pologon P and the sculptures are the points inside P. So the problem reduces to the following. Given a polygon P and a set of points $S=(s_1,s_2,...,s_k)$ inside P, the problem is to find a minimal set of points $G=(g_1,g_2,...,g_j)$ such that every point s_i of S is visible at least from a point g_m of G. It follows directly from the proof of Lee and Lin [LL86] that this problem is also NP-hard. Here we consider a special case of this problem for $|G|=1$. The problem can be stated as follows. Given a polygon P and a set of points $S=(s_1,s_2,...,s_k)$ inside P, the problem is to find a point g of P (called a viewpoint), if it exists, such that every point s_i of S is visible from g. This was originally posed by H. ElGingy. If a point s_i of S lies on the segment joining g and s_j, where s_j is in S and s_i is not s_j, s_j is still considered visible from g.

We assume that the simple polygon P is given as a counterclockwise sequence of vertices $p_1,p_2,...,p_n$ with their respective x and y coordinates. The symbol P is used to denote the region of the plane enclosed by P and bd(P) denotes the boundary of P. We also assume that points $s_1,s_2,...,s_k$ of S are given with their respective x and y coordinates. The preprocessing step of our algorithm is to compute a polygon Q from P and S such that Q satisfies the following properties.
(1) Q lies totally inside P.
(2) All points of S lie inside Q.
(3) The perimeter of Q is the minimum.
Note that the vertices of Q are either the points of S (Figure 1) or the points of S and the vertices of P (Figure 2). Let Q_s be the set of all vertices of Q that are the points of S. It is not hard to show that if there exists a viewpoint that can see all vertices of Q_s, then all points of S are also visible from the viewpoint. Sklansky et al. [SCH72] developed an $O(nk)$ time algorithm for computing Q. Toussaint [T86] proposed a subquadratic algorithm for computing Q that runs in $O(n \log \log n + k \log n + k \log k)$ time. In what follows, we assume that Q is given as an input along with P and S, and all points of S are the vertices of Q. In the next section, we propose an $O(n+k)$ time algorithm for computing a viewpoint of S. In Section 3, we conclude the paper with a few remarks.

2. An algorithm for computing a viewpoint

We assume that the polygon Q is given as a counterclockwise sequence of vertices $q_1,q_2,...,q_m$ with their respective x and y coordinates. The symbol Q is used to denotethe

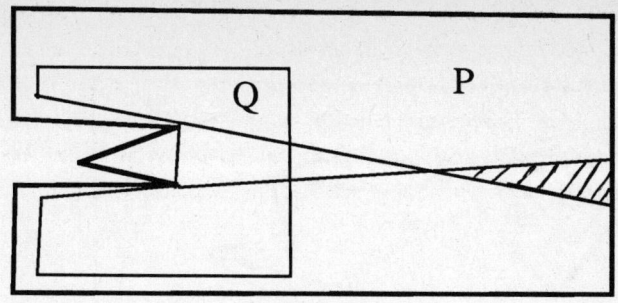

Figure 4

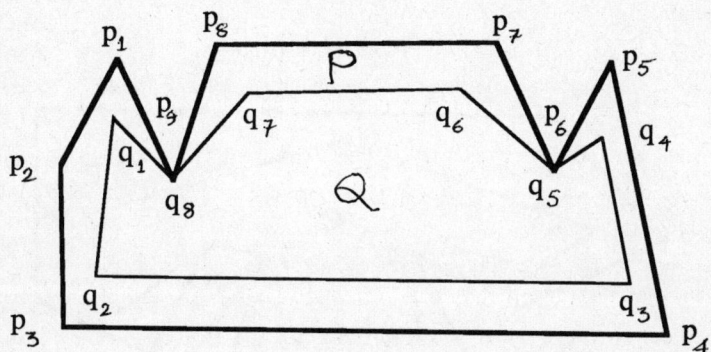

Figure 5

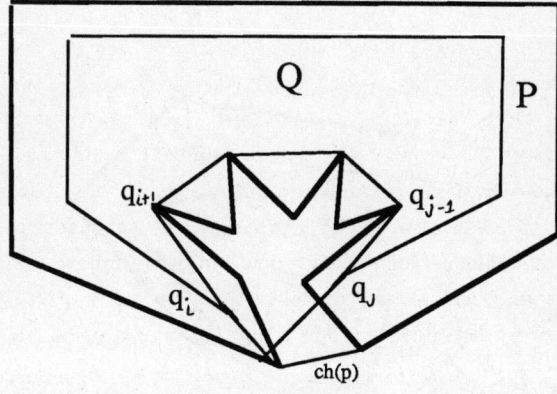

Figure 6

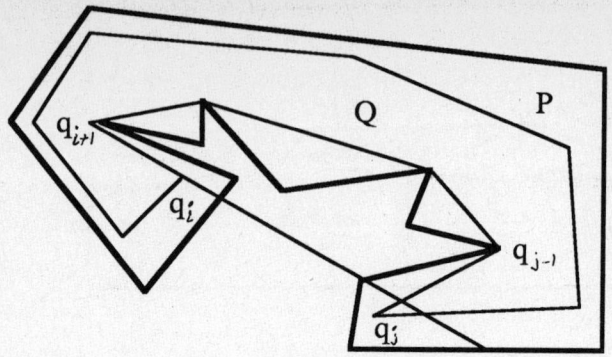

Figure 7

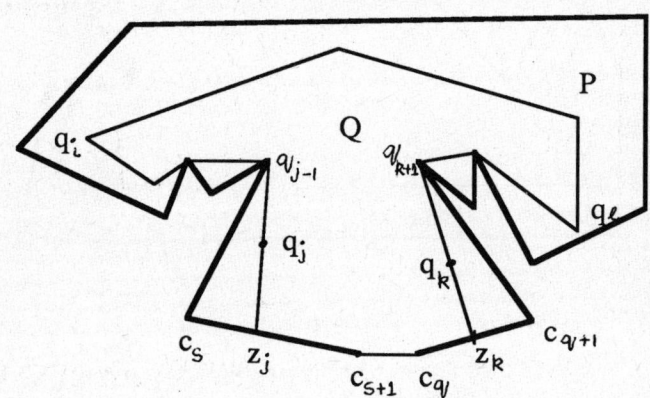

Figure 8

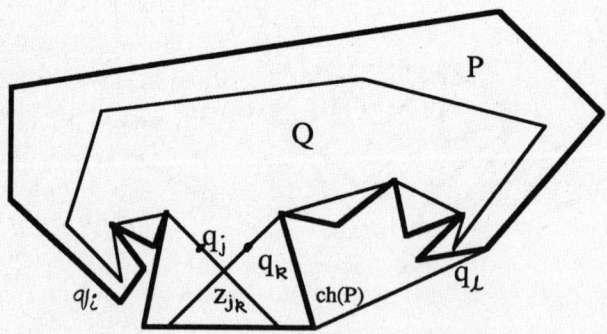

Figure 9

region of P enclosed by Q and bd(Q) denotes the boundary of Q. Q is said to be a *star-shaped polygon* if there exists a region K of Q such that Q is totally visible from all points of K. K is called the *kernel* of Q. If Q is a star-shaped polygon, any point of the kernel of Q is a viewpoint of S. The linear time algorithm of Lee and Preparata [LP79] for computing the kernel of a simple polygon can be used to test whether Q is a star-shaped polygon. Note that if Q is a degenerated polygon (Figure 3), we assume that the kernel of Q is empty. If Q is not a star-shaped polygon, it may be the case that a viewpoint lies outside Q but inside P as shown in Figure 4.

Let $hp(q_iq_{i+1})$ denote the region of the plane lying to the left of the line containing q_i and q_{i+1}, where the direction of the line is from q_i to q_{i+1}. If the internal angle of Q at q_i or q_{i+1} is reflex, it can be seen that any viewpoint that can see both q_i and q_{i+1} must lie in $hp(q_iq_{i+1})$. Similarly we define $hp(p_ip_j)$. Let ch(P) denote the convex hull of P. Since a viewpoint must lie inside P, it must also lie inside ch(P) and therefore, it lies in $hp(p_ip_j)$ for every edges of ch(P). Now we define two sets H_q and H_c as follows.

$H_q = \{hp(q_iq_{i+1}) |$ the internal angle of Q at q_i or q_{i+1} is reflex$\}$.

$H_c = \{hp(p_ip_j) | p_ip_j$ is an edge of ch(P) where p_j is the next counterclockwise vertex of p_i on the boundary of ch(P)$\}$.

In Figure 5, $H_q = \{hp(q_8q_1), hp(q_7q_8), hp(q_5,q_6), hp(q_4q_5)\}$ and $H_c = \{hp(p_8p_1), hp(p_1p_2), hp(p_2p_3), hp(p_3p_4), hp(p_4p_5), hp(p_5p_7), hp(p_7p_8)\}$. Let H be the union of H_q and H_c. We wish to compute the intersection region R of H. If R is empty, there is no viewpoint of S in P, as stated in the following lemma.

Lemma 1: If the intersection region R of H is empty, there is no viewpoint of S in P.

Proof: The proof is omitted in this version.

Now we compute R from H. If we consider H as an arbitrary set of half-planes, we can compute R in $O(|H|\log|H|)$ time by the algorithm of Shamos [S78] for computing the intersection of half-planes. However, we compute R in $O(|H|)$ time as follows. We construct a polygon CP such that R is the kernel of CP and the boundary of CP consists of some edges of Q and ch(P). For every edge q_iq_{i+1} of Q, we remove q_iq_{i+1} from Q, if the internal angles of Q at q_i and q_{i+1} are convex. This operation splits bd(Q) into chains. Note that every edge that has induced a half-plane in H_q belongs to one of the chains of Q. Let $(q_i,q_{i+1},...,q_j)$ be one such chain of Q and we denote it as $dchain(q_i,q_j)$. Let $ext(q_{i+1},q_i)$ denote the extension of q_iq_{i+1} from q_i to the boundary of ch(P). If $ext(q_{i+1},q_i)$ intersects $ext(q_{j-1},q_j)$ (Figure 6), then R is empty. If $ext(q_{i+1},q_i)$ or $ext(q_{j-1},q_j)$ intersects dchain (q_i,q_j) (Figure 7), R is also empty. So we assume that the extensions of a dchain do not intersect each other or the dechain itself. Now we connect the dchains to form the boundary of CP. Let $dchain(q_i,q_j)$ and $dchain(q_k,q_l)$ be two consequtive dchains and edges from q_j and q_k are deleted edges of Q (Figure 8). Let z_j and z_k be the meeting points of $ext(q_{j-1},q_j)$ and $ext(q_{k+1},q_k)$ with the boundary of ch(P) respectively. Let $(c_1,c_2,...,c_u)$ be the counterclockwise sequence of vertices of ch(P). Let z_j and z_k lie on c_sc_{s+1} and c_qc_{q+1} respectively where s<q. So the boundary of CP in counterclockwise order from q_i to q_l consists of

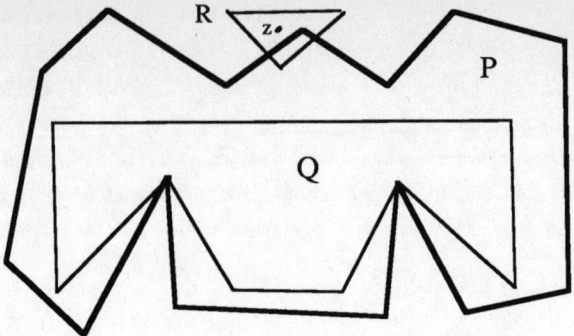

Figure 10

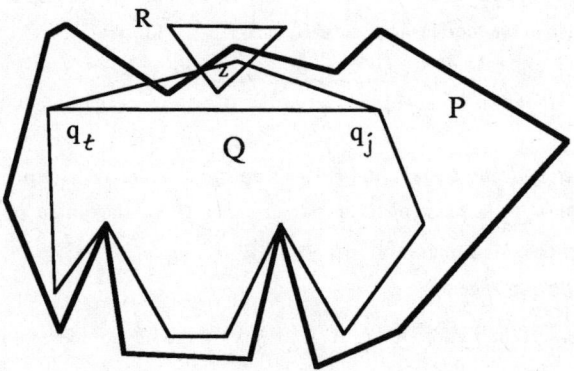

Figure 11

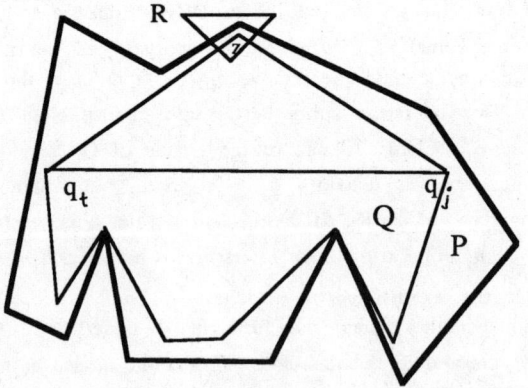

Figure 12

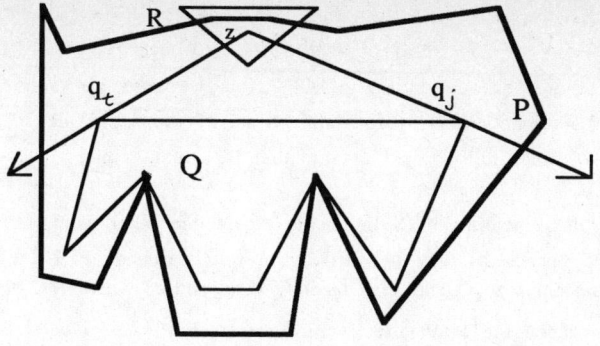

Figure 13

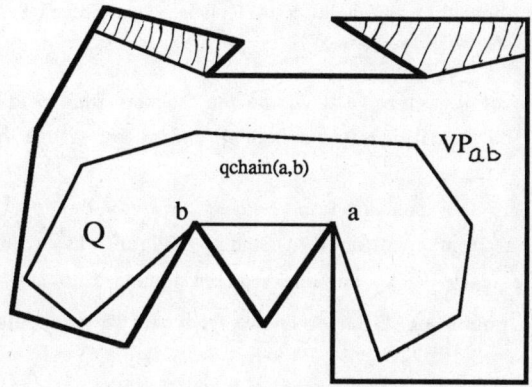

Figure 14

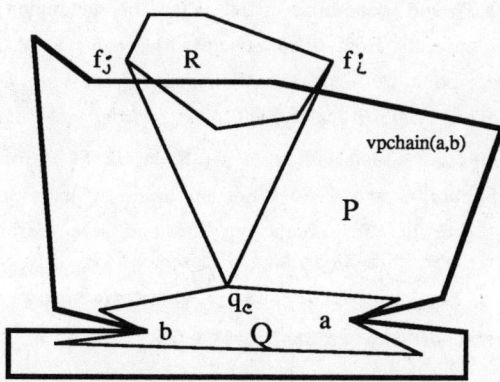

Figure 15

$q_i,q_{i+1},...,q_j,z_j,c_{s+1},...,c_q,z_k,q_k,...,q_l$. If q_jz_j intersects q_kz_k at a point z_{jk}, the boundary of CP in counterclockwise order from q_i to q_l consists of $q_i,...,q_j,z_{jk},q_k,...,q_l$ (Figure 9). Thus we connect the dchains to form the boundary of CP. Now we compute the kernel of CP by the algorithm of Lee and Preparata [LP79] in linear time. If the kernel R is empty, there is no viewpoint of S in P. In what follows, we assume that R is not empty.

We know that all viewpoints of S lie inside R. On the other hand, all points of R need not be viewpoints of S because R may lie partially or totally outside P. Let z be a point of R. We draw two tangents from z to Q and they meet Q at q_j and q_t where j<t. Now we have the following three cases depending upon the position of z in P.

Case 1: z lies outside P (Figure 10).
Case 2: z lies inside P, q_j or q_t is not visible from z (Figure 11).
Case 3: z lies inside P, q_j and q_t are visible from z (Figure 12).

In the following lemma, we show that any point z in R is a viewpoint of S if and only if z lies inside P and both q_j and q_t are visible from z.

Lemma 2: Let z be a point of R. Let zq_j and zq_t be the tangents from z to Q. The point z is a viewpoint of S if and only if z lies inside P and both q_j and q_t are visible from z.

Proof: Since zq_j and zq_t are the tangents from z to Q, every vertex of Q lies in the wedge formed by two rays drawn from z through q_t and q_j (Figure 13). Since bd(P) does not intersect zq_j or zq_t, they lie inside P. So the line segment joining z to any point of Q does not intersect bd(P). Hence all points of Q are visible from z. The converse is trivially true. Q.E.D.

Let zq_j and zq_t be the tangents from a point z of R to Q. Let qchain(q_j,q_t) denote the portion of bd(Q) from q_j to q_t in counterclockwise order. Since z belongs to R, no vertex of qchain(q_j,q_t) is a vertex of P. Let a and b the vertices of both P and Q such that q_j and q_t belong to qchain(a,b) and none of the vertices of P belong to qchain(a,b). Let pchain(p_i,p_l) denote the portion of bd(P) from p_i to p_l in counterclockwise order. Let P_{ab} be the region of P bounded between pchain(a,b) and qchain(a,b). Let VP_{ab} be the region of P_{ab} such that for every point u of VP_{ab}, both tangents from u to qchain(a,b) lie inside P_{ab}. Note that no point v of (P_{ab}-VP_{ab}) can be a viewpoint of S since both tangents from v to Q do not lie inside P. VP_{ab} is known as the *complete* visibility polygon of P_{ab} from qchain(a,b) (Figure 14). A polygon M is said to be *completely* visible from a set K inside M if for every point w of M and v of K, line segment joining w and v does not intersect the exterior of M. Ghosh[GH86] has proposed a linear time algorithm for computing the complete visibility polygon from a set inside the polygon and we use this algorithm to compute VP_{ab}. It can be seen that every point z lying in R as well as VP_{ab} satisfies Lemma 2 and therefore, z is a viewpoint of S. Using the linear time algorithm of Ghosh [G84], we detect a point of intersection of R and VP_{ab} as follows.

Let $(f_1,f_2,...,f_r)$ be a clockwise sequence of corner points of R. Without loss of generality, we assume that qchain(a,b)=(a,q_c,b). We draw tangents from q_c to R and they meet R at f_i and f_j where i<j. Let vpchain(a,b) denote the subset of pchain(a,b) that is completely visible from qchain(a,b). If vpchain(a,b) does not intersect $q_c f_i$, f_i is a viewpoint of S. So we assume that vpchain(a,b) has intersected both $q_c f_i$ and $q_c f_j$ (Figure 15). Let fchain(f_i,f_j) denote the set of corner points from f_i to f_j in clockwise order. Since R is a convex region, the corner points of fchain(f_i,f_j) are in sorted angular order with respect to q_c. Since q_c is a star-point of VP_{ab}, the vertices of vpchain(a,b) are in sorted order with respect to q_c. If we draw rays from q_c through every vertex of vpchain(a,b) and every corner points of fchain(f_i, f_j), they divide the plane into wedges. In every wedge, there is an edge of vpchain(a,b) and an edge of fchain(f_i,f_j). We check the intersection between the pair of edges in each wedge by traversing wedges from a to b in sorted angular order (Figure 15). If we detect an intersection between vpchain(a,b) and fchain(f_i,f_j), we report an intersection point of the chains as a viewpoint of S. Now we formally state our algorithm *Find-viewpoint* for computing a viewpoint of S from P and Q.

Algorithm   Find-viewpoint
begin /*view is a boolean variable, initially set to true*/
    compute the kernel of Q by the algorithm of Lee and Preparata [LP79];
    if the kernel of Q is not empty **then** g:=a point of the kernel **else**
    begin compute ch(P) by the algorithm of Graham and Yao [GY83]; initialize CP to Q;
        for i=1 to m **do**
            if the internal angles at q_i and q_{i+1} are convex **then** remove $q_i q_{i+1}$ from CP;
        repeat
            move to the next dchain(q_i,q_j);
            if ext(q_{i+1},q_i) intersects ext(q_{j-1},q_j) **then** view:=False **else**
            if ext(q_{i+1},q_i) or ext(q_{j-1},q_j) intersects dchain(q_i,q_j) **then** view:=False
        until (view=False **or** all dchains are considered);
        if view **then**
        begin for any two consecutive dchain(q_i,q_j) and dchain(q_t,q_l)
            if ext(q_{j-1},q_j) intersects ext(q_{t+1},q_t) **then** insert the intersection point in CP
                between q_j and q_t
            else /*Let ext(q_{j-1},q_j) and ext(q_{t-1},q_t) meet the boundary of ch(P)
                at z_j and z_t respectively*/
            insert all the vertices of ch(P) between z_i and z_t in CP between q_j and q_t;
            compute the kernel R of CP by the algorithm of Lee and Preparata [LP79];
            if R is empty **then** view:=False **else**
            begin draw two tangents to Q from a point z of R and they meet Q at q_j and q_t;
                find pchain (a,b) and qchain(a,b) where qchain(a,b) contains q_j and q_t;
                Compute the completely visible boundary vpchain(a,b) of pchain(a,b) from qchain(a,b) by the algorithm of Ghosh [GH86]; draw two tangents from q_c of qchain(a,b) to R;/*Let two tangents meet R at f_i and f_j*/
                if vpchain(a,b) does not intersect $q_c f_i$ **then** g:=f_i
                else if vpchain(a,b) does not intersect $q_c f_j$ **then** g:=f_j **else**
                    begin check the intersection between vpchain(a,b) and fchain(f_i,f_j) by the
                        algorithm of Ghosh[G84];
                        if an intersection is found **then** g:=an intersection point **else** view:=False;
                    end;
            end;
        end;
    end;
    if view **then report** "g is a viewpoint of S" **else report** "There is no viewpoint of S"
end.

Theorem 1: Algorithm *Find-viewpoint* correctly finds a viewpoint of S from the given P and Q in O(n+k) time, where |S|=k, |Q|=m and |P|=n.

Proof: The correctness of the algorithm follows from Lemmas 1 and 2. Now we analyze the time complexity of the algorithm. Computing the kernel of Q takes O(m) time. Computing the convex hull of P takes O(n) time. By traversing the boundary of ch(P) and dchains in counterclockwise order, polygon CP can be computed in O(n+m) time. Computing the kernel of CP takes O(n+m) time. Computing vchain(a,b) from qchain(a,b) takes O(n+m) time. Detecting an intersection between vpchain(a,b) and fchain(f_i,f_j) takes O(n+m) time. Since m is less than n+k, the overall time complexity of the algorithm is O(n+k). **Q.E.D**.

3. Concluding remarks

We have proposed an efficient algorithm for computing a viewpoint of a given set S of points inside a simple polygon P. If the given set S is a set of line segments rather than points, the problem reduces to the following problem. Given a set S of disjoint line segments inside a polygon P, the problem is to find a point z of P, if it exists, such that every segment of S is totally or partially visible from z. Our approach does not seem to work for this problem and it will be interesting to design an efficient algorithm for the same.

Acknowledgements

I gratefully acknowledge the helpful comments and suggestions of Joseph O'Rourke and Subhash Suri in production of this paper. This work was done when the author visited the Johns Hopkins University and was supported by NSF Grant DCR83-51468 and a grant from IBM.

References

[AT81] D. Avis and G. T. Toussaint, " An efficient algorithm for decomposing a polygon into star-shaped polygons", *Pattern Recognition*, vol. 13, pp. 395-398, 1981.

[C75] V. Chvatal, "A combinatorial theorem in plane geometry", *Journal of Combinatorial Theory*, Series B, vol. 18, pp. 39-41, 1975.

[EOW84] H. Edelsbrunner, J. O'Rourke and E. Welzl, "Stationing guards in rectilinear art galleries", *Computer Vision, Graphics, Image Processing*, vol. 27, pp. 167-176, 1984.

[F78] S. Fisk, "A short proof of Chavatal's watchman theorem", *Journal of Combinatorial Theory*, Series B, vol. 24, pp. 374, 1978.

[G84] S. K. Ghosh, "A linear time algorithm for determining the intersection type of two star polygons", *Lecture Notes in Computer Science*, no. 181, pp. 317-330, Springer-Verlag, 1984.

[G86] S. K. Ghosh, "Approximation algorithms for art gallery problems", Technical Report no. JHU/EECS-86/15, Department of Electrical Engineering and Computer Science, The Johns Hopkins University, 1986.

[GH86] S. K. Ghosh, "Computing the visibility polygon from a convex set", Technical report no. CAR-TR-246, Center for Automation Research, University of Maryland, 1986.

[GY83] R. L. Graham anf F. F. Yao, "Finding the convex hull of a simple polygon", *Journal of Algorithms*, vol. 4, pp. 324-331, 1983.

[H79] R. Honsberger, Mathematical games II, Mathematical Associations for America, 1979.

[KKK83] J. Kahn, M. Klawe and D. Kleitman, "Traditional galleries require few watchmen", *SIAM Journal on Algebraic and Discrete Methods*, vol. 4, pp. 194-206, 1983.

[L85] A. Lubiw, "Decomposing polygons into covex quadrilaterals", *Proceedings of the ACM Symposium on Computational Geometry*, pp. 97-106, 1985.

[LL86] D. T. Lee and A. K. Lin, "Computational complexity of art gallery problems", *IEEE Transactions on Information Theory*, vol. IT-32, pp. 276-282, 1986.

[LP79] D. T. Lee and F. P. Preparata, "An optimal algorithm for finding the kernel of a polygon", *Journal of the ACM*, vol. 26, pp. 415-421, 1979.

[O83] J. O'Rourke, "An alternate proof of the rectilinear art gallery theorem", *Journal of Geometry*, vol. 211, pp.118-130, 1983.

[O87] J. O'Rourke, Art gallery theorems and algorithms, Oxford University press, 1987.

[OR83] J. O'Rourke, "Galleries need fewer mobile guards: A variation on Chavatal's theorem", *Geometricae Dedicata*, vol. 14, pp. 273-283, 1983.

[OS83] J. O'Rourke and K. Supowit, "Some NP-hard polygon decomposition problems", *IEEE Transactions on Information Theory*, vol. IT-29, pp. 181-190, 1983.

[S78] M. I. Shamos, Computational Geometry, Ph. D. Thesis, Yale University, 1978.

[S82] J. Sack, "An O(nlogn) algorithm for decomposing simple rectilinear polygons into convex quadrilaterals", *Proceedings of 20th Allerton Conference*, pp. 64-74, 1982.

[SCH72] J. Sklansky, R. L. Chazin and B. J. Hansen, "Minimum-perimeter polygons of digitized silhouettes", *IEEE Transactions on Computers*, vol. C-21, pp. 260-268, 1972.

[T86] G. T. Toussaint, "An optimal algorithm for computing the relative convex hull of a set of points in a polygon", *Signal Processing III: Theories and Applications*, I. T. Young et al. (editors), North-Holland, 1986.

ANALYSIS OF PREFLOW PUSH ALGORITHMS
FOR MAXIMUM NETWORK FLOW

J.Cheriyan
Computer Science Group
Tata Institute of Fundamental
Research
Colaba, Bombay 400 005, INDIA.

S.N.Maheshwari
Department of Computer Science
and Engineering
Indian Institute of Technology
New Delhi 110 016, INDIA.

Abstract. We study the class of preflow push algorithms recently introduced by Goldberg and Tarjan for solving the maximum network flow problem on a weighted digraph $G(V,E)$. We improve Goldberg and Tarjan's $O(n^3)$ time bound for the maximum distance preflow push algorithm to $O(n^2\sqrt{m})$ and show that this bound is tight by constructing a parametrized worst case network. We then develop the maximal excess preflow push algorithm and show that it achieves a bound of $O(n^2\sqrt{m})$ pushes. Based on this we develop a maximum network flow algorithm for the synchronous distributed model of computation that uses at most $O(n^2\sqrt{m})$ messages and $O(n^2)$ time, thereby improving upon the best previously known algorithms for this model.

1.Introduction

The maximum network flow problem is one of the most important problems in the area of combinatorial optimization. The problem is as follows.

Let $G(V,E)$ be a weighted digraph with two distinguished vertices, a source s and a sink t, and a positive real valued capacity $c(v \rightarrow w)$ on every edge $v \rightarrow w$. (For convenience define $c(v \rightarrow w)=0$ if $v \rightarrow w$ is not an edge.) A flow on G is a real valued function f on vertex pairs having the following two properties

1. Capacity constraint: $f(v \rightarrow w) \leq c(v \rightarrow w)$ for all vertex pairs v,w.

2. Flow conservation: $\sum_u f(u \to v) = \sum_w f(v \to w)$ for every vertex v other than s and t.

The value $|f|$ of a flow is the net flow into the sink, $\sum_v f(v \to t) - \sum_w f(t \to w)$. The maximum network flow problem is to find a flow of maximum value. We shall use n to denote the number of vertices of G and m to denote the number of edges of G.

Recently, Goldberg and Tarjan in "A new approach to the maximum flow problem" [GT], introduced a class of algorithms called <u>preflow push algorithms</u>. A preflow push algorithm consists of a general scheme together with a rule (or heuristic) for selecting a vertex having flow excess. A <u>Pushing Step</u> is applied to the selected vertex. Different algorithms can be obtained by using different rules. The most important attribute of a preflow push algorithm is the number of Pushing Steps performed by it since this is what determines the time complexity of the algorithm.

In this paper we are interested in studying preflow push algorithms. The main motivating factor is the intrinsic appeal of simple heuristics (for selecting a vertex on which to apply a Pushing Step) that lead to surprisingly good performance. Further, preflow push algorithms are not dependent on centralized resources and so work very well in distributed models of computation. We emphasize that our goal here is not to obtain the fastest sequential maximum network flow algorithm, but rather to give improved time bounds for two simple algorithms. The improved analysis leads to an improved algorithm for the synchronous distributed model of computation.

Goldberg and Tarjan showed that two of these algorithms, namely, the round robin preflow push algorithm and the maximum distance preflow push algorithm perform $O(n^3)$ pushes and so achieve an $O(n^3)$ time bound. (We mention that Goldberg and Tarjan improved the round robin preflow push algorithm to $O(nm(\log n^2/m))$ by using the dynamic trees data structure. This is asymptotically the fastest known algorithm.)

We first show that the actual time bound for the maximum distance preflow push algorithm is $O(n^2\sqrt{m})$. Although this is $O(n^3)$ for dense graphs, it is $O(n^{2.5})$ for sparse graphs. Our analysis is based on ideas used before by Cherkasky [Ch] and Galil [Ga1] to analyze their respective maximum network flow algorithms. We then show that this bound is tight by constructing a parametrized worst case network. Given n and m, $600 \leq n \leq m/3$, this network has at most n vertices and m edges, and the maximum distance preflow push algorithm requires $\Omega(n^2\sqrt{m})$ pushes on it. Our construction uses techniques introduced by Galil [Ga2] to construct a parametrized worst case network for many of the earlier maximum network flow algorithms. We then develop the maximal excess preflow push algorithm which combines the best features of the round robin preflow push algorithm and the maximum distance preflow push algorithm. We are able to show that this algorithm performs at most $O(n^2\sqrt{m})$ pushes and we also have a parametrized worst case network on which this algorithm requires $\Omega(n^2\sqrt{m})$ pushes.

The maximal excess preflow push algorithm leads us to a maximum network flow algorithm for the synchronous distributed model of computation that uses at most $O(n^2\sqrt{m})$ messages and $O(n^2)$ time. This improves upon the $O(n^3)$ messages and $O(n^2)$ time algorithms of Awerbuch [Aw] and Goldberg and Tarjan [GT]. Recently, Marberg and Gafni [MG] have developed a maximum flow algorithm for the asynchronous distributed model of computation that uses $O(n^2\sqrt{m})$ messages and $O(n^2\sqrt{m})$ time. Clearly, this gives an algorithm for the synchronous distributed model of computation that uses $O(n^2\sqrt{m})$ messages and $O(n^2\sqrt{m})$ time. Although our distributed algorithm works only for the synchronous model notice that our time bound is better than that of [MG] for this model.

Section 2 has the $O(n^2\sqrt{m})$ bound for the maximum distance preflow push algorithm and Section 3 has the parametrized worst case network showing that this bound is tight. Section 4 considers the maximal excess preflow push algorithm. The synchronous distributed algorithm is developed in Section 5.

A brief introduction to preflow push algorithms follows, together with a few definitions and preliminary results. Further details may be found in Goldberg and Tarjan [GT], and Goldberg [Go].

A preflow push algorithm computes a maximum flow in a given network by manipulating a preflow f on the network. A preflow is a real valued function on vertex pairs satisfying the capacity constraint, (1), as well as the following weaker form of the conservation constraint, (2).

3. Every vertex v in V-{s} has net incoming flow greater than or equal to zero, $\sum_u f(u \to v) \geq \sum_w f(v \to w)$.

The flow excess e(v) of a vertex is defined to be the net flow into v, $\sum_u f(u \to v) - \sum_w f(v \to w)$. The residual capacity of an edge v→w with respect to a preflow f is given by $r(v \to w) = c(v \to w) - f(v \to w) + f(w \to v)$. The residual graph with respect to a preflow f has vertex set V and has an edge v→w iff r(v→w) is greater than zero. The algorithm also maintains a distance labelling for each vertex v, where d(v) is the length of the shortest path from v to the sink t in the residual graph with respect to the current preflow. (Such a distance labelling is called "exact", and in Section 3 we assume that the distance labelling is exact although preflow push algorithms also work with approximate distance labels.) At each iteration of the algorithm a vertex, say v, with (positive) flow excess is selected, and its excess is sent closer to the sink by making use of the distance labels of v and its neighbours in the residual graph. If the flow excess cannot be sent to vertices with smaller distance labels then the distance label of v is increased. An outline of the algorithm follows.

BEGIN
preprocess: Let the initial preflow f be equal to the edge capacity on each edge emanating from the source and zero on all other edges. Let d(s)=n and compute d(v) for all other vertices by doing a backward bfs starting from t.
WHILE there is a vertex v in V-{s,t} with e(v)>0 DO
    BEGIN
    select: Select a vertex v in V-{s,t} with e(v)>0;
    push: WHILE e(v)>0 and there is an edge v→w with d(v)=d(w)+1
        and r(v→w)>0 DO
        Send min{ r(v→w),e(v) } units of flow from v to w and
        update e(v), e(w), r(v→w) and r(w→v) accordingly;

```
            IF there is no edge v→w with d(v)=d(w)+1 and r(v→w)>0  THEN
               BEGIN
               relabel: Replace d(v) by 1+min{ d(w) | r(v→w)>0 };
               Propagate the relabel backwards in the  residual  graph
               with  respect to the current preflow, i.e., if there is
               a  vertex  u   with  d(u)=d(v)+1  and  v is the unique
               successor of u at  distance d(v) then relabel u, and so
               on;
               END;
            END;
      END;
```

Notice that if after a Relabelling Step at vertex v the distance label d(v) becomes greater than n-1 then all paths from v to the sink are saturated. When this happens the remaining flow excess is pushed back along shortest available paths to the source.

The correctness and termination of any preflow push algorithm that is based on the general scheme above is proved by Goldberg and Tarjan by using the max flow min cut theorem (the interested reader is referred to [GT]).

An outgoing edge from vertex v is called eligible if it lies on a shortest path from v to t in the present residual graph. A push along edge v→w is called saturating if the resulting preflow of v→w equals its capacity, otherwise the push is called nonsaturating. Let us say that a push on an edge v→w is a nonzeroing push if this is the first push on v→w after either v or w is relabelled. Notice that when a Pushing Step (i.e., the inner while loop) terminates then the last push, say along edge v→w, may have been nonsaturating. In this case v→w becomes the current edge of v. The importance of the current edge is that the next time v is chosen for a Pushing Step, the current edge is the first edge on which a push is done, provided it is still eligible.

It is easy to see that at any step of the algorithm the current edges, one edge outgoing from each vertex, form a spanning tree rooted at the sink, t, with the edges of the tree directed towards the root. (If some vertices have no current edge we have a forest rather than a   tree.   However, this makes no difference.) A flow excess at vertex v is called a **maximal excess** if the subtree rooted at v has no other flow excesses.

Over the whole algorithm there may be $O(n)$ nonzeroing pushes on an edge v→w (since each of v and w is relabelled at most n times) and hence the total number of nonzeroing pushes is $O(nm)$. Likewise, the total number of saturating pushes is $O(nm)$. The number of Relabelling Steps is $O(n^2)$, and it can be shown that the total time spent in Relabelling Steps is $O(nm)$. It follows that the time bound of any preflow push algorithm is determined by the number of nonsaturating pushes, since the time spent in the other steps is $O(nm)$. Goldberg and Tarjan [GT] showed that there is a naive upper bound of $O(n^2m)$ on the number of pushes performed by any preflow push algorithm and hence any preflow push algorithm runs in $O(n^2m)$ time.

Several particular algorithms can be obtained from the general scheme above depending on the rule used in the Select Step.

The **round robin preflow push algorithm** maintains all vertices with flow excess in a FIFO queue. In the Select Step it chooses the vertex at the front of the queue and applies a Pushing Step to it; if this results in flow excesses at any new vertices then these new vertices are added to the rear of the queue.

The **maximum distance preflow push algorithm** selects a vertex having flow excess that is furthest from the sink in each Select Step. In other words, if we let $d_{max} = \max\{ d(v) \mid e(v) > 0 \}$ then a vertex v with $d(v) = d_{max}$ and $e(v) > 0$ is selected.

Let MAXCAP denote the maximum of the capacities of the edges emanating from the source. In the following, we sometimes say that an edge has infinite capacity. This should be interpreted as m*MAXCAP or more. We shall occasionally regard a flow excess as a "physical entity" that is originated by either a saturating push or a nonzeroing push.

2. $O(n^2\sqrt{m})$ bound for the maximum distance preflow push algorithm

In order to determine the number of nonsaturating pushes required by the maximum distance preflow push algorithm we divide the computation into phases. A <u>phase</u> consists of all pushes which occur between two consecutive Relabelling Steps. Notice that during a phase the flow excesses that are most distant from the sink are pushed down one level at a time.

Recall that d_{max} is the distance of the furthest flow excess from the sink at any step of the algorithm. Notice that the total increase in d_{max} over the whole algorithm sums to $O(n^2)$ because each increase is caused by some vertex updating its distance label during a Relabelling Step. The <u>length</u>, l_i, of phase i, is defined to be the difference between d_{max} at the start of the phase and d_{max} at the end of the phase. Goldberg and Tarjan showed that the sum of the lengths of all phases, $\sum_i l_i$, is $O(n^2)$. This follows because $\sum_i l_i$ is just the total decrease in d_{max} over the whole algorithm, and hence is bounded by $O(n)$ plus the total increase in d_{max}.

We need the notion of <u>originating edge</u> of a maximal excess, in order to improve the time bound below $O(n^3)$. Consider any step of the algorithm. Starting from a maximal excess at a vertex v, (i.e. the current edge subtree rooted at v has no other flow excesses) we can backtrace along a path of current edges till we reach an edge, say x→y, such that the last push along x→y was either a saturating push or a nonzeroing push. This edge is called the originating edge of the flow excess at v. The path of current edges from x→y to v is called a <u>trajectory</u>.

During a phase each nonsaturating push leaves behind a current edge. At the end of the phase these current edges constitute a forest, since each vertex has at most one outgoing edge. We partition these current edges among trajectories that are vertex disjoint, except possibly for the end vertices of some trajectories. We shall account for the nonsaturating pushes by the originating edges of these trajectories.

<u>Theorem 1.</u> The maximum distance preflow push algorithm does at most $O(n^2\sqrt{m})$ nonsaturating pushes, and its time bound is $O(n^2\sqrt{m})$.
<u>PROOF.</u> We partition the nonsaturating pushes into two kinds of pushes and show that over the whole algorithm there are $O(n^2\sqrt{m})$ pushes of each kind.

The nonsaturating pushes that occur along a trajectory within a distance of $n/\sqrt{m}$ from the originating edge of the trajectory are called <u>short trajectory pushes</u>, and the remaining pushes that occur along a trajectory at a distance greater than $n/\sqrt{m}$ from the originating edge are called <u>long trajectory pushes</u>.

It is easily seen that over the whole algorithm there are $O(n^2\sqrt{m})$ short trajectory pushes because each trajectory starts with either a saturating push or a nonzeroing push and over the whole algorithm the total number of saturating pushes and nonzeroing pushes is $O(nm)$.

The long trajectory pushes are accounted for as follows. Observe that during any phase the trajectories are vertex disjoint and hence the number of "long" trajectories (i.e. longer than $n/\sqrt{m}$) is at most $\sqrt{m}$. Thus the number of long trajectory pushes in a phase of length l_i is at most $\sqrt{m}l_i$. Summed over all phases this is $O(n^2\sqrt{m})$.

The algorithm maintains all vertices having flow excess in a data structure so that it can easily choose the maximum distance vertex. This can be done at a cost of $O(1)$ per chosen vertex by using a list based buckets data structure. The theorem follows. ▯

3. Parametrized worst case network for the maximum distance preflow push algorithm

Given n and m, $600 \leq n \leq m/3$, we construct a network having at most n vertices and m edges on which the maximum distance preflow push algorithm performs $\Omega(n^2\sqrt{m})$ pushes. We first introduce some gadgets that are used in the network. The following convention will be used when we draw a figure for a gadget or a network. The direction of each edge is given by the direction in which the edge is traversed by a shortest path from s to t through that edge. The capacity of some of the edges are shown in the figures. If the capacity of an edge is not shown then it is supposed to have ∞ (infinite) capacity. The exact capacity of an ∞-capacity edge does not matter provided it is at least m*MAXCAP.

Gadget A (Figure 1a) is a path with telescoping edge capacities. When the maximum distance preflow push algorithm is run on this, it gives rise to a Relabelling Step whenever flow is pushed into an edge of capacity $c*i$. Thus a sequence of $L/2$ flow excesses is sent into the subnetwork $G´$ (Figure 1b). Putting together W copies of gadget A we get gadget B (Figure 2a), which sends a sequence of $W*L/2$ flow excesses into subnetwork $G´$ (Figure 2b).

Gadget C (Figure 3) causes the distance of the central vertex u from the sink to increase in jumps of $\ell´$ as a sequence of flow excesses of value $c´$ is pushed into u. Note that each edge emanating from u has capacity $c´$, and the path has infinite bottleneck capacity.

Gadget D (Figure 4) is a collection of W paths, each path having length L and having infinite bottleneck capacity. Each edge emanating from vertex p has capacity $c"$. If a flow excess of value $c"*W$ is pushed into p it gives rise to $W*L$ nonsaturating pushes along the collection of paths.

Gadget E (Figure 5) is obtained by putting together two copies D_1, D_2 of gadget D and two copies C_1, C_2 of gadget C, along with some additional edges between the tails of paths in D_1 and the tails of paths in D_2. These additional edges constitute a complete bipartite graph $K_{w,w}$ with W^2 edges, and each edge has capacity $c"$. In gadgets C_1 and C_2 there are $L/2$ edges emanating from the central vertices u_1 and u_2 respectively, where each edge has capacity $c´$. The value of $\ell´$ is taken to be a small constant. The gadget D_1 is located $\ell´/2$ levels higher (with respect to distance from the sink) than gadget D_2.

If a sequence of W flow excesses, each of value $c"*W$, is pushed into vertex p_1 then each of these flow excesses is routed through one of the vertices x_i and gives rise to $W*L$ nonsaturating pushes in gadget D_2. This sequence of flow excesses causes the first edge in gadget C_2 to saturate (we take $c´=c"*W^2$ for ensuring this) and thus raises the level of gadget D_2 by $\ell´$. Now, a sequence of W flow excesses, each of value $c"*W$, is pushed into vertex p_2. Again each of these flow excesses gives rise to $W*L$ nonsaturating pushes in gadget D_1. This process of alternately sending a sequence of flow excesses into p_1 and p_2 can be repeated $L/2$ times, till the gadgets

C_1 and C_2 are completely saturated.

We can obtain an $O(n^2)$ worst case network by putting together a copy of gadget E and two copies B_1, B_2 of gadget B, and properly offsetting the two copies of gadget B. The values of the parameters W and L have to be chosen so that W*L is $O(n)$; for example we could use $W=O(\sqrt{m})$ and $L=O(n/\sqrt{m})$. The $O(n^2\sqrt{m})$ worst case network is somewhat more complicated and is given in Figure 6.

The additional gadgets C_3 and C_4, which are copies of gadget C having bottleneck edge capacities equal to one, are needed to repeatedly use gadgets B_1 and B_2 $O(n/L)$ times, by reversing flows through these gadgets periodically. A "period" starts by moving flow excess from vertex g to b_1 and b_2. Then gadgets B_1 and B_2 are used to send sequences of W flow excesses alternately to vertices p_1 and p_2 of gadget E. Finally, all the flow excess accumulates at vertex z. The next push saturates the current edge of gadget C_3 and raises the level of z by (12L+2d), where d is a small constant. This causes the flow to be reversed through gadgets B_1, B_2 and E. All this flow eventually accumulates at vertex g. The next push causes the level of g to increase by (12L+2d). This completes one "period". The number of "periods" is W/8 since there are W/8 edges emanating from the central vertices of gadgets C_3 and C_4.

Notice that some edge capacities in the worst case network have been offset by γ. This is done to compensate for the one unit of "leakage flow" per "period" in gadgets C_3 and C_4, respectively.

Taking appropriate values for the parameters, we have $W=\sqrt{m}/8$ and $L=n/\sqrt{m}$. Also, we take $\ell=8$ and $d=6$. Thus we have the following fact.

<u>Fact 1.</u> There is a parametrized network on which the maximum distance preflow push algorithm requires $\Omega(n^2\sqrt{m})$ nonsaturating pushes, and hence this algorithm requires at least $\Omega(n^2\sqrt{m})$ time. ▯

4. Maximal excess preflow push algorithm

Notice that the maximum distance preflow push algorithm and the round robin preflow push algorithm are able to improve upon the naive bound of $O(n^2m)$ for preflow push algorithms because they effectively exploit the mechanism of coalescing flow excesses. In this section we investigate how far this idea of coalescing flow excesses can be carried. Another motivation is to obtain an algorithm that is more amenable to the distributed computation model than the maximum distance preflow push algorithm.

The flow excesses can be coalesced together by pushing as many flow excesses as possible in the round robin order while still retaining the desirable feature of the maximum distance preflow push algorithm, namely, a nonmaximal excess is never pushed. This suggests the following rule. "Push all maximal excesses in the round robin order." In what follows, we ignore the data structure overheads required to implement the above rule.

The analysis given in Theorem 1 does not apply to the maximal excess preflow push algorithm because a vertex v may do several nonsaturating pushes during a single phase (recall that a phase consists of all pushes between two consecutive Relabelling Steps). However, we can still obtain an $O(n^2\sqrt{m})$ bound on the number of pushes by using an approach similar to that in Theorem 1.

<u>Theorem 2.</u> The maximal excess preflow push algorithm performs at most $O(n^2\sqrt{m})$ nonsaturating pushes.
<u>PROOF.</u> We partition the nonsaturating pushes into short trajectory pushes and long trajectory pushes, as in the proof of Theorem 1. It is easily seen that over the whole algorithm there are $O(n^2\sqrt{m})$ short trajectory pushes.

The number of long trajectory pushes is shown to be $O(n^2\sqrt{m})$ as follows. We assume that the algorithm operates in "clock pulses" where during one "clock pulse" Pushing Steps are simultaneously performed on all maximal excesses. (Note that if the algorithm is implemented using a FIFO queue then a "clock pulse" corresponds to one pass over the queue.) It is easily seen that there are $O(n^2)$ "clock pulses" over the whole algorithm because during each "clock pulse" d_{max} (defined in Section 1) either decreases by one or increases, and the total decrease in d_{max} over the whole algorithm is $O(n^2)$ and likewise for the total increase in d_{max}.

Now we make the crucial observation that at any "clock pulse" the trajectories of all maximal excesses are vertex disjoint; otherwise, if the trajectories of two flow excesses overlap then either the two flow excesses have coalesced or one of the flow excesses is nonmaximal. It follows that at any "clock pulse" the number of long trajectory pushes is at most $\sqrt{m}$ because the number of maximal excesses having "long" trajectories (i.e. longer than $n/\sqrt{m}$) is at most $\sqrt{m}$. Hence, over the whole algorithm the number of long trajectory pushes is $O(n^2\sqrt{m})$. The theorem follows. ▯

There is a parametrized worst case network on which the maximal excess preflow push algorithm requires $\Omega(n^2\sqrt{m})$ pushes. This network is obtained from the network in Section 3 by replacing gadgets B_1 and B_2 by new gadgets. We omit the details of the network. This gives us Fact 2.

Fact 2. There is a parametrized worst case network on which the maximal excess preflow push algorithm requires $\Omega(n^2\sqrt{m})$ pushes. ▯

5. A distributed maximum network flow algorithm

In this section we develop a maximum network flow algorithm for the synchronous distributed model of computation that uses at most $O(n^2\sqrt{m})$ messages and $O(n^2)$ time. This is a multiprocessor model with no shared memory. The graph underlying the network is realized as a processor network with one processor located at each vertex and all interprocessor communication occurs along the (bidirectional) edges of the graph. The processors are <u>synchronized</u>. The time required by each processor for its local computations is assumed to be negligible. The resource bounds of interest are the number of messages used by the algorithm and the total time taken (i.e. the number of clock pulses used). We shall only use messages of length $O((\log n) + (\log MAXCAP))$ bits.

The obvious approach of simulating the centralized maximum distance preflow push algorithm fails because a pair of flow excesses at the same distance level may be arbitrarily (i.e. $O(n)$) far apart, and so the number of messages required for just activating all flow excesses at the same distance level would sum to more than $O(n^2\sqrt{m})$ over the whole algorithm.

Instead, we shall base our algorithm on the proof of Theorem 2. A <u>push message</u> is a message used by the algorithm to indicate the pushing of flow along some edge. Each flow excess keeps track of its originating edge and the distance it has moved since leaving the originating edge. (Recall from Section 1 that we may regard a flow excess as a physical entity.) A flow excess moves freely as long as its distance from its originating edge does not exceed $n/\sqrt{m}$.

Recall from Theorem 2 that at each "clock pulse" the number of long trajectory pushes (i.e., nonsaturating pushes that occur along trajectories at a distance greater than $n/\sqrt{m}$ from the respective originating edges) is at most $\sqrt{m}$ because the "long" trajectories are vertex disjoint and so there are at most $\sqrt{m}$ maximal excesses that have "long" trajectories. In order to ensure that "long" trajectories in the distributed algorithm are vertex disjoint each flow excess moves in <u>stages</u>. During stage i a flow excess moves for a distance of at most $(2^i n/\sqrt{m})$, i.e., it undergoes at most $(2^i n/\sqrt{m})$ nonsaturating pushes. When it has moved this distance it stops and checks whether its trajectory is overlapped by the trajectory of some other flow excess. For this purpose it sends a <u>probe message</u> backwards along its trajectory all the way to its originating edge. The originating edge echoes back the probe message along the trajectory to the flow excess. Upon receiving the echoed probe message the flow excess enters stage i+1 and resumes its movement. Of course, if a probe message is intercepted by a different flow excess then the probe message is immediately destroyed.

<u>Theorem 3.</u> The above synchronous distributed algorithm for the maximum network flow problem uses at most $O(n^2\sqrt{m})$ messages and $O(n^2)$ time.

PROOF. The number of clock pulses used by the algorithm is shown to be $O(n^2)$ by using an argument similar to that in Theorem 2. It can be seen that the maximum time taken by a flow excess to move a distance L is 5L, provided that its probe message has not been destroyed. This follows because for $L=(2^i-1)*n/\sqrt{m}$ the time taken by a flow excess to move this distance is $L+(2^{i+2}-2i-4)*n/\sqrt{m}$. Also, recall that the total decrease in dmax over the whole algorithm is $O(n^2)$ and likewise for the total increase in dmax. It follows from this that the number of clock pulses is $O(n^2)$.

Now consider the number of messages used by the algorithm. The number of push messages and probe messages used in stage zero and stage one, summed over all flow excesses originated in the algorithm, is at most $(11n/\sqrt{m})*(2nm)$ which is $O(n^2\sqrt{m})$.

<u>Claim.</u> The number of stage i push messages at each clock pulse, summed over all i, i>1, is $O(\sqrt{m})$.

The $O(n^2\sqrt{m})$ bound on the number of messages would follow from the claim, because the total number of clock pulses is $O(n^2)$ and the number of probe messages is at most four times the number of push messages.

The claim is proved by associating with each stage i, i>1, push message (at each clock pulse) a subpath of its trajectory having at least $(2^i-2)*n/\sqrt{m}$ vertices such that for distinct stage i push messages the associated subpaths are vertex disjoint.

Let f_1 and f_2 be two flow excesses such that they give rise to two stage i, i>1, push messages that are transmitted at the same clock pulse. Suppose that the trajectories of f_1 and f_2 overlap since otherwise there is nothing to prove. Assume that f_1 was originated earlier. Clearly, at any vertex v common to both trajectories, the (echoed) probe message which initiates stage i for f_1 precedes the push message for f_2. Let t be the time at which the probe message for f_1 passes through v, and let d be the distance from v to the originating edge of f_1.

It can be seen that stage i for f_1 comes to an end at most $((2^i-1)*n/\sqrt{m})-d+(2^i*n/\sqrt{m})$ clock pulses after t. Similarly, stage i for f_2 can start only $2*(2^i-1)*n/\sqrt{m}$ clock pulses after t. Thus d is at most $n/\sqrt{m}$ since stage i push messages for f_1 and f_2 are transmitted at the same clock pulse.

Let p_1 denote f_1's trajectory at the end of stage (i-1), and likewise for p_2. It can be seen that the suffix of p_1 obtained by deleting f_1's trajectory at the end of stage zero is vertex disjoint from the similar suffix of p_2. Hence, the number of stage i, i>1, push messages transmitted at any clock pulse is at most $\sqrt{m}/(2^i-2)$, and the claim follows. ▯

References

[Aw] B.Awerbuch, "Reducing complexities of the distributed max-flow and breadth-first-search algorithms by means of network synchronization", Networks 15(1985), 425-437.

[Ch] B.V.Cherkasky, "Algorithm of construction of maximal flow in networks with complexity of $O(V^2\sqrt{E})$ operations", Mathematical Methods of Solution of Economical Problems 7(1977), 112.

[D] E.A.Dinic, "Algorithm for solution of a problem of maximum flow in networks with power estimation", Soviet Math. Doklady 11(1980), 1277- 1280.

[Ga1] Z.Galil, "An $O(V^{5/3}E^{2/3})$ algorithm for the maximal flow problem", Acta Informatica 14(1980), 221-242.

[Ga2] Z.Galil, "On the theoretical efficiency of various network flow algorithms", Theoretical Computer Science 14(1981) 103-111.

[Go] A.V.Goldberg, "Efficient graph algorithms for sequential and parallel computers", Ph.D. Thesis, MIT/LCS/TR-374, Feb 1987.

[GT] A.V.Goldberg and R.E.Tarjan, "A new approach to the maximum flow problem", Proc. 18th Annual ACM Symp. on Theory of Computing (1986).

[MG] J.M.Marberg and E.Gafni, "An $O(n^2m^{1/2})$ distributed max-flow algorithm", Proc. International Conference on Parallel Processing, 1987.

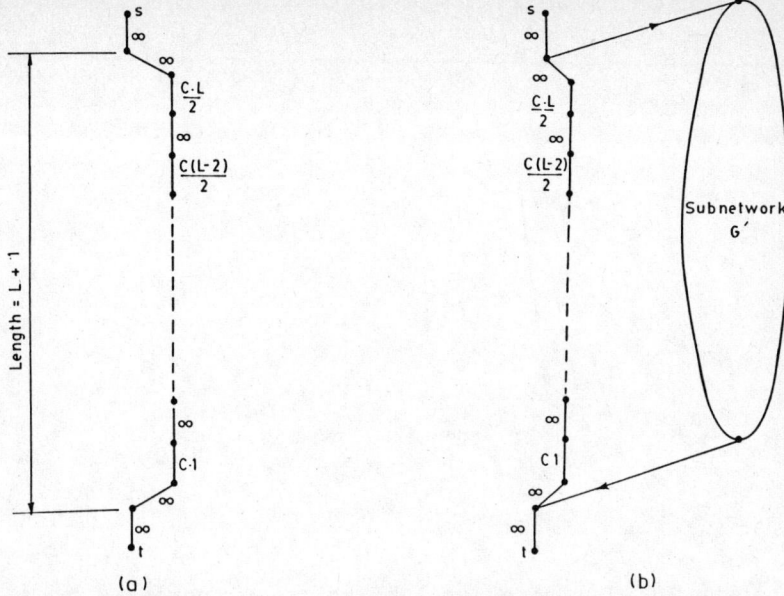

Figure 1. (a) Gadget A. (b) Gadget A being used to send a sequence of L/2 flow excesses into G´. Relevant edge capacities are indicated.

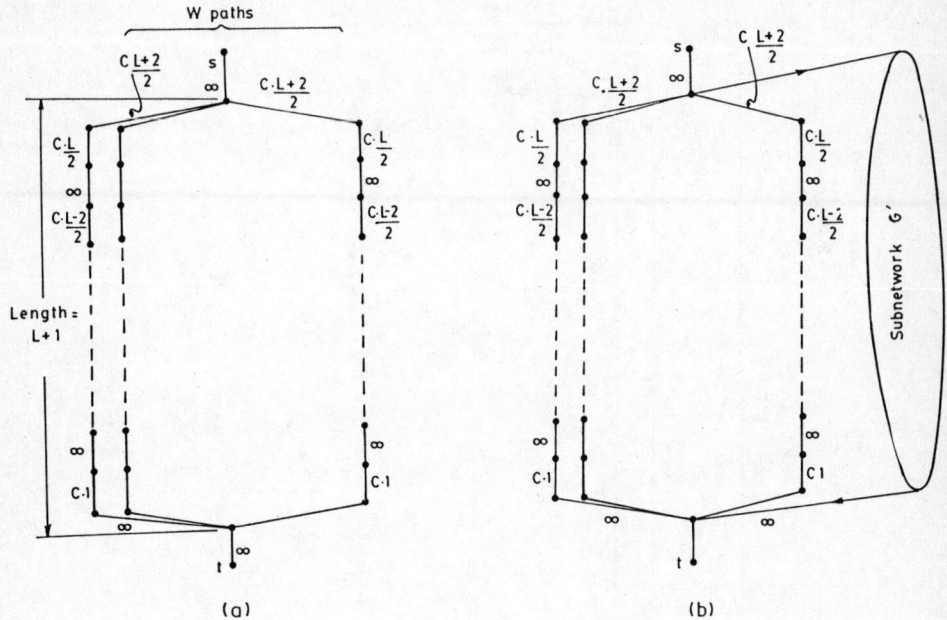

Figure 2. (a) Gadget B. (b) Gadget B being used to send a sequence of W*L/2 flow excesses into G´.

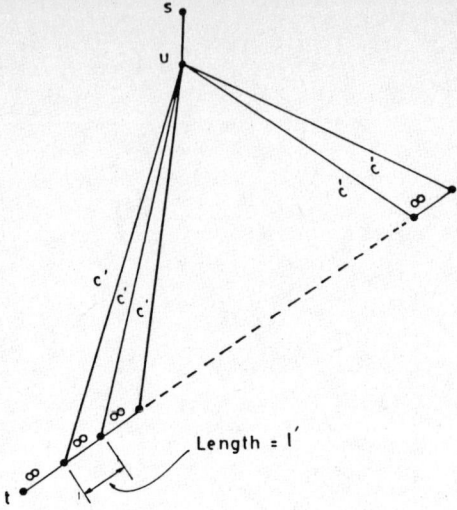

Figure 3. Gadget C. Distance label of vertex u increases by l' each time a flow excess of value c' is pushed in at u.

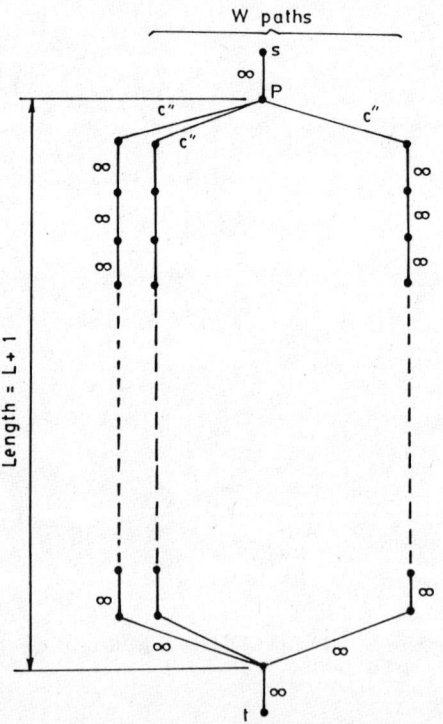

Figure 4. Gadget D. W*L nonsaturating pushes occur in the gadget each time a flow excess of value $c''*W$ is pushed in at p.

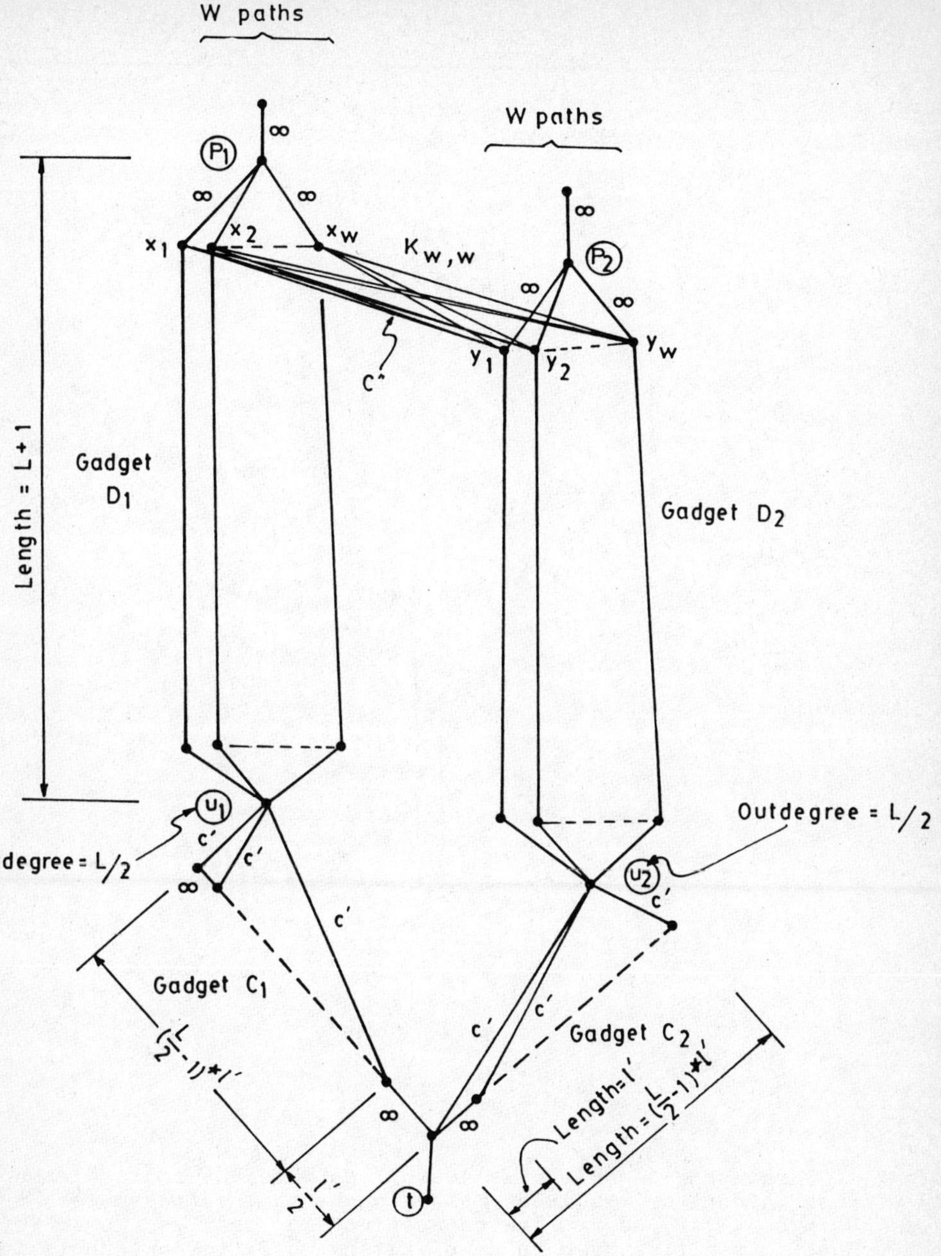

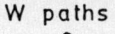

Figure 5. Gadget E. If a sequence of W flow excesses, each of value c"*W, is pushed in at p_1 then each flow excess causes W*L nonsaturating pushes in Gadget D_2. Finally, the current edge of vertex u_2 is saturated and the distance label of u_2 increases by ℓ. The parameters are $L=n/\sqrt{m}$, $W=\sqrt{m}/8$, $\ell=8$, $c'=c"*W^2$.

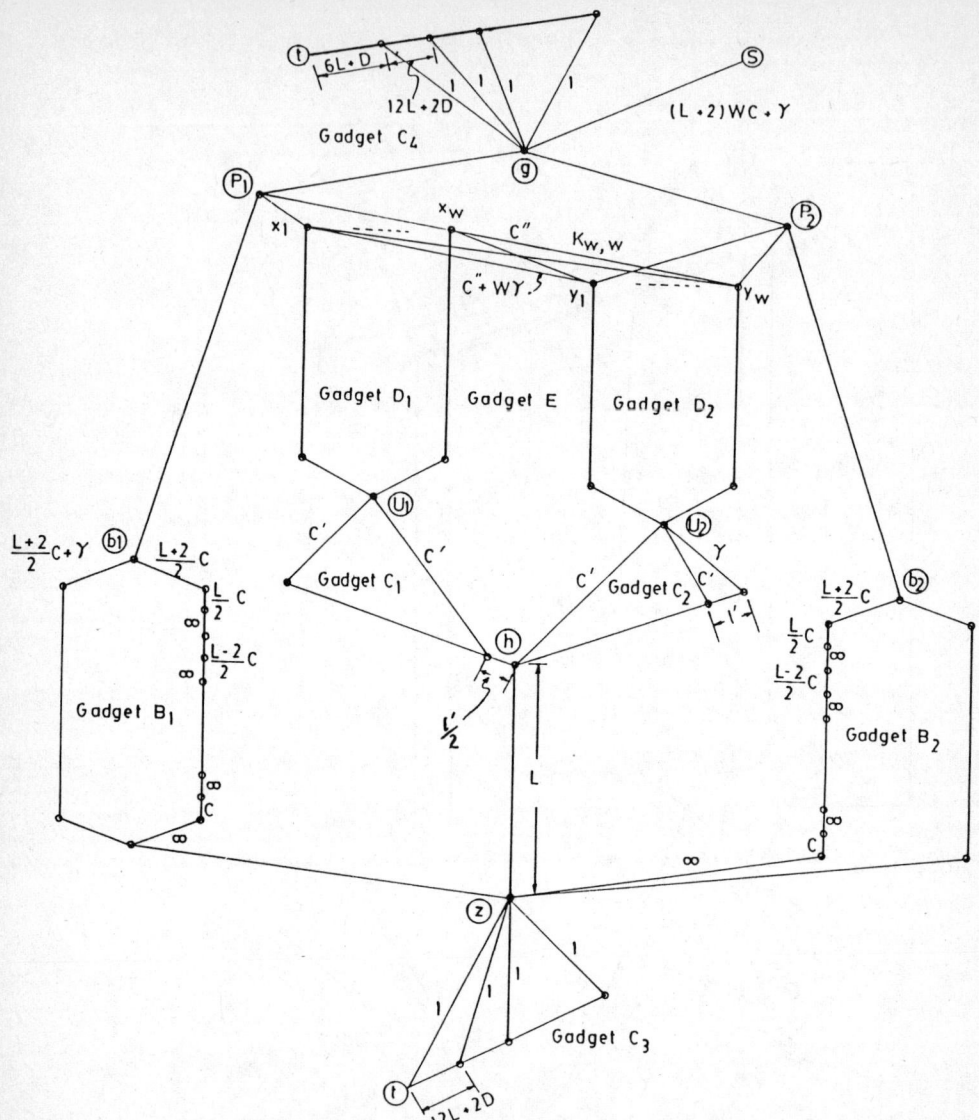

Figure 6. Parametrized worst case network on which maximum distance preflow push algorithm requires $\Omega(n^2\sqrt{m})$ pushes. The parameters are $L=n/\sqrt{m}$, $W=\sqrt{m}/8$, $l'=8$, $d=6$. The capacities are $c=c''*W$, $c'=c''*W^2$, $c''=4W^2$. Some capacities have to be offset by $\gamma=2W$ to compensate for leakage flows in Gadgets C_3 and C_4. All edges in $K_{w,w}$ have capacity c'' except one edge that has capacity $c''+\gamma*W$.

A NEW LINEAR ALGORITHM FOR THE TWO PATH PROBLEM ON CHORDAL GRAPHS

S.V.Krishnan , C.Pandu Rangan, S.Seshadri
Department of Computer Science and Engineering
Indian Institute Of Technology , Madras-600036

ABSTRACT : Let G= (V,E) be a finite undirected graph with four distinguished vertices s , t , u , v .The two path problem (TPP) is to determine whether there exist two vertex disjoint paths connecting s with t and u with v and to find such paths if they exist.

In this paper , a simple and efficient algorithm for TPP restricted to 2-connected chordal graphs is given.The reduction of TPP for a general chordal graph to the TPP for a 2-connected chordal graph is outlined.

1.INTRODUCTION : Given an undirected graph G=(V,E) and four distinguished vertices s,t,u, and v , the two path problem (henceforth TPP)is to find two vertex disjoint paths $P_1(s,t)$ from s to t and $P_2(u,v)$ from u to v.This problem may arise as a transportation network problem and in printed circuits routing [3].

An $O(n*|E|)$ algorithm for the TPP for a general undirected graph was reported in [6]. In [6] a complicated reduction process is used to obtain a solution of TPP of an arbitrary graph from the solutions of its tri-connected components. It is customary to present a solution for a class of tri-connected graphs satisfying a certain property and generalising this solution for all graphs satisfying that property.

For instance , an O(n) algorithm for TPP for 3-connected planar graphs was presented first by [4] and later a much simpler algorithm of O(n) by Ramprasad and Pandu Rangan [5]. For the class of 3-connected chordal graphs an $O(|E|)$ algorithm was presented in [4]. It is an extremely simple algorithm , but the sheer complexity of the reduction process involved in obtaining the solution for TPP on a general chordal graph has motivated us to investigate the problem from a new angle.

We will first show how the solution of TPP for a biconnected chordal graph can elegantly and easily be used to obtain the solution for TPP for an arbitrary chordal graph. Later we present a much simpler and more natural algorithm for TPP on a biconnected chordal graph. Also our algorithm runs in optimal $O(|E|)$ time.

We will employ the notion of bridges (introduced by Tutte) to design our algorithm. Like the depth first search tree the bridges offer clean solutions to a variety of graph problems. The graph viewed as a suitable circuit or a path together with a collection of its bridges offer some new insight into its structure.

PRELIMINARIES

DEFINITION 1.1: A graph is said to be chordal if and only if every cycle of length greater than 3 has a chord.

THEOREM 1.2: [2] A graph is chordal if and only if a minimal seperating set for any pair of non-adjacent vertices is a clique (complete graph).

If P is a path from vertex s to vertex t then the whole path will be represented as P[s,t]. If x and y are two vertices on P, then P[x,y] denotes the subpath of P from x to y (both inclusive); P]x,y] denotes the subpath excluding x but including y; P[x,y[denotes the subpath including x but excluding y and P]x,y[denotes the subpath excluding both x and y.

Note that if in the above we say P[y,x] we mean the subpath from y to x along P (here the edges are traversed in the opposite direction as compared to P[x,y]).

If P_1 and P_2 are two paths from x to z and from z to y respectively and if P_1 and P_2 are vertex disjoint except for z then the concatenation of P_1 and P_2 is denoted by $P_1[x,z] * P_2[z,y]$.

DEFINITION 1.3 : A vertex of attachment of a subgraph H of a graph G is a vertex of H that is incident in G with some edge not belonging to H.

DEFINITION 1.4 : BRIDGES : Let J be a fixed subgraph of G. A subgraph G_1 of G is said to be J-detached in G , if all its vertices of attachment in G are in J. We define a bridge of J as any subgraph B that satisfies the three following conditions :
  1. B is not a subgraph of J.
  2. B is **J**-detached in **G**.
  3. No proper subgraph of B satisfies (1) and (2).

The set of vertices of attachments of a bridge B of a subgraph J in G is denoted by $W(G,B) = \{v_1, v_2, \ldots v_k\}$. $w(G,B)$ will stand for the cardinality of the set $W(G,B)$.

DEFINITION 1.5 : Let J be as defined in definition 1.4. An edge [u,v] of G not belonging to J but having both ends in J is said to be a <u>DEGENERATE BRIDGE</u>.

Let G' be the subgraph obtained by deleting the vertices of J and all their incident edges. Let C be any connected component of G'. Let B be the subgraph of G obtained from C by adjoining to it each edge of G having one end in J and one end in C and also the ends(vertices) of these edges that are in J. B satisfies the conditions to be a bridge. Such a bridge is called <u>PROPER</u>. The component C of G' is called the nucleus of B and denoted as N(B). The nucleus of a degenerate bridge is the empty graph.

DEFINITION 1.6 : Let J be a subgraph of G. Let B be a bridge of J. Let x and y be attachments of B. A <u>CROSS-CUT</u> from x to y through B is a path between x and y such that none of its internal vertices are in J and all its edges are in B. Such a cross-cut is denoted by $cc_B[x,Y]$. The vertices x and y are called the end vertices of the cross-cut. A P-crosscut is one both of whose end vertices are in P. A Q-crosscut is similarly defined. A PQ-crosscut is one which has one end vertex on P and the other on Q.

DEFINITION 1.7 : Let G be an undirected biconnected graph with two distinguished vertices s and t with two internally vertex disjoint paths P[s,t] and Q[s,t].

Now consider the cycle $J = P \cup Q$ of G formed by P and Q. The bridges of J are classified as follows :

<u>PQ-BRIDGE</u> : A bridge of J with at least one vertex of attachment on P]s,t[and at least one vertex of attachment on Q]s,t[is called a PQ-Bridge.

<u>P-BRIDGE</u> : A bridge with at least one vertex of attachment on P]s,t[and none on Q]s,t[is called a P-bridge.

<u>Q-BRIDGE</u> : A bridge with at least one vertex of attachment on Q]s,t[and none on P]s,t[is called a Q-bridge.

<u>st-BRIDGE</u> : A bridge with only s and t as vertices of attachments is called an st-bridge.

DEFINITION 1.8 : Let J be as defined in Definition 1.7. For any bridge B, $s_P(B)$ denotes the vertex of attachment of B on P which is nearest along P to s and $t_P(B)$ denotes the vertex of attachment of B on P which is nearest along P to t, if such vertices exist. Similarly $s_Q(B)$ and $t_Q(B)$ are defined whenever they exist.

DEFINITION 1.9 : A vertex x on P is said to be under a bridge B if x is on $P[s_P(B),t_P(B)]$. It is properly under a bridge B if it is on $P]s_P(B),t_P(B)[$. A vertex x is said to be under a P-crosscut $cc_B(y,z)$ if x is in $P[y,z]$. It is strictly under the same crosscut if it is in $P]y,z[$.

DEFINITION 1.10 : Two cross-cuts $cc_B(a,c)$ and $cc_B(b,d)$ are said to <u>interlace</u> if a, b, c and d occur in that order in J, where J is as in definition 1.7.

DEFINITION 1.11 : Let G = (V, E) be a graph. The block graph T= (V',E') of the graph G is an undirected bipartite graph with the set of vertices V' corresponding to the biconnected components (green) and the seperation vertices (blue). The edges are drawn only between green and blue vertices. An edge is drawn from x (green) to y(blue) if and only if the biconnected component corresponding to x contains the cut vertex corresponding to y. It is easy to show that the block graph is indeed a tree.

We use a boolean variable TPP which is set to true if and only if there exists two vertex disjoint paths from s to t and from u to v. Otherwise we set TPP to false.

2. TPP FOR A GENERAL CHORDAL GRAPH

In this section we will show how the TPP for any arbitrary chordal graph can be reduced to the TPP for biconnected chordal graph.

LEMMA 2.1 : If the TPP can be solved for any biconnected chordal graph then it can be solved for any general chordal graph.

PROOF :

Let G=(V,E) be an arbitrary chordal graph.

Consider the block graph T = (V',E') of G.

We define the vertex C_s in T as follows : If s is a separation vertex, then C_s is the blue vertex corresponding to s. If not, then C_s is the green vertex corresponding to the biconnected component containing s. Similarly C_t, C_u and C_v are defined.

Let P_{st} and P_{uv} denote the paths from C_s to C_t and from C_u to C_v respectively in T. Note that every path from s to t will have to pass through every blue vertex on P_{st} and some of the internal vertices of every green vertex on P_{st} in T and through no other vertex of G.

There are three cases to consider.

CASE I : P_{st} and P_{uv} are vertex disjoint. TPP is true from the above observation.

CASE II : P_{st} and P_{uv} have at least one blue vertex in common and let z be the corresponding cut vertex of G. In this case every path from s to t and from u to v will have to pass through z and hence TPP is false.

CASE III : P_{st} and P_{uv} have exactly one green vertex in common. Note that there cannot be a path between any two green vertices which does not pass through a blue vertex. Hence we consider the case where P_{st} and P_{uv} have exactly one green vertex in common. The problem reduces to that of finding two vertex disjoint paths in the common biconnected component C_B from a to c and b to d as shown in fig 1 which by assumption can be solved.   Q.E.D.

3.TPP FOR A BICONNECTED CHORDAL GRAPH

From the lemma of the previous section it is enough if we consider a biconnected chordal graph G. We shall now eliminate a trivial case by the following lemma whose proof is fairly obvious.

LEMMA 3.1 : Let s and t be adjacent to each other .If there is a path from u to v in G - {s,t} then the TPP is true. Otherwise TPP is false.

From lemma 3.1 , we can assume that the vertices s , t and u, v are such that neither pair is adjacent.

Let C' = P' U Q' be an arbitrary cycle passing through s and t. This cycle may have some degenerate P' and Q' bridges. Consider the subgraph G(P') of G induced by the vertices of P'. Consider a chordless path from s to t in G(P') and let it be P. Let Q be similarly defined. Let C = P U Q be the resulting cycle. From now onwards we will consider only the cycle C and the chordless paths P and Q as defined above.

LEMMA 3.2 : The cycle C defined above does not have any degenerate P or Q bridges.

PROOF : Follows from the construction of P and Q.   Q.E.D.

LEMMA 3.3 : Every P or Q bridge should have exactly two vertices of attachments and the vertices of attachment must be adjacent.

PROOF : As G is biconnected , every bridge B must have at least two vertices of attachment. Let B be a P-bridge. The set S = W(G,B) is a separating set for a vertex in N(B) and a vertex not in B. A minimal separating set M which is a subset of S contains both $s_P(B)$ and $t_P(B)$. So , by theorem 1.2 , $s_P(B)$ and $t_P(B)$ are adjacent. As P is chordless they are adjacent along P and hence B has only two vertices of attachments.   Q.E.D.

COROLLARY 3.4 : Two P (Q) bridges can have at most two vertices of attachments in common. If they have exactly one vertex of attachment in common , say y, then x , y and z are consecutive vertices on P (Q) where x and z are the remaining vertices of attachment of the two different bridges respectively.

LEMMA 3.5 : Let B be a proper PQ-bridge . Then every vertex on P]$s_P(B), t_P(B)$[is a vertex of attachment of B and similarly every vertex on Q]$s_Q(B), t_Q(B)$[is a vertex of attachment of B.

PROOF : Consider an arbitrary vertex x on P]$s_P(B), t_P(B)$[. Let y_1 be the vertex of attachment of B nearest to x on P[$s_P(B), x$] and y_2 be the vertex of attachment of B nearest to x on P[$x, t_P(B)$]. Assume that x is not a vertex of attachment. Then y_1 and y_2 are distinct. Let $cc_B(y_1, y_2)$ be the shortest crosscut through B. Consider the cycle P[y_1, y_2] U $cc_B(y_1, y_2)$ = C_1. (fig. 2).P[y_1, y_2] and $cc_B(y_1, y_2)$ are chordless Also , no vertex in P]y_1, y_2[is adjacent to an interior vertex in $cc_B(y_1, y_2)$. Hence C_1 is chordless . Also C_1 has at least four vertices. But this means that the graph is not chordal - a contradiction. Q.E.D.

In fact we can say even more. The following lemma provides greater insight into the structure of bridges in a biconnected chordal graph.

LEMMA 3.6 : Every vertex on P]s,t[or Q]s,t[is a vertex of attachment of some degenerate PQ-bridge.

PROOF : Assume that a vertex x on P]s,t[is not incident on any degenerate bridge. Consider the shortest cycle C1 containing x. As P and Q are chordless, C1 contains the two vertices adjacent along P and at least one vertex on Q. So C1 is a chordless cycle of length at least four - a contradiction to definition 1.1. Q.E.D.

LEMMA 3.7: The cycle C consists only of P-bridges, Q-bridges and PQ-bridges.

PROOF :The only other possibility is an st-bridge. If an st-bridge exists then s and t form a minimal seperating set for any vertex inside the st-bridge and a vertex on P. By theorem 1.2, s and t will be adjacent. But as we have already assumed that they are not adjacent, there can be no st-bridge. Q.E.D.

DEFINITION 3.8 : Since every vertex is a vertex of attachment of a degenerate PQ-bridge, for any vertex x on Q we can talk of $lm_P(x)$ and $rm_P(x)$ which are defined as follows :

$lm_P(x)$ = y such that y is the vertex nearest to s along P among the vertices of attachments on P of degenerate PQ-bridges incident on x.

$rm_P(x) = y$ such that y is the vertex nearest to t along P among the vertices of attachments on P of degenerate PQ-bridges incident on x.

We can define $lm_Q(x)$ and $rm_Q(x)$ as vertices nearest to s and t along P among the vertices of attachments of degenerate PQ-bridges incident on x where x is a vertex on P. If x is on P then only $lm_Q(x)$ and $rm_Q(x)$ make sense and so when it is obvious we drop the subscript P and Q.

DEFINITION 3.9 : We define the notions of "left" and "right" which apply only to the vertices on P and Q. A vertex x is said to lie to the left of y if x lies on P[s,y] (assuming x and y are on P). A vertex x is said to be to the right of y if x lies on P[y,t]. We can similarly define for vertices x and y lying on Q also. Note that by definition x is to the left of x and also to the right of x.

We can define "strictly to the left" as follows : x is strictly to the left of y if x lies on P[s,y[. "Strictly to the right" can also be similarly defined.

LEMMA 3.10 : If x is any vertex strictly to the left of y then rm(y) is to the right of rm(x).

PROOF : Assume x and y are on Q. The case when x and y are on P can be similarly proved.

If possible assume that rm(x) is strictly to the right of rm(y) (See figure 3). Let z be the vertex on Q]s,y[such that rm(z) is to the right of rm(z') where z' is any vertex on Q]s,y[. Obviously rm(z) is strictly to the right of rm(y) because of our assumption.

Consider the seperating set S consisting of all the vertices on P]s,rm(z)] and y for the pair of vertices s and t. Now consider a minimal seperating set M(M is a subset of S). It must contain y and rm(z) because if it does not contain rm(z) then there is a path Q[s,z]*(z,rm(z))*P[rm(z),t] and if it does not contain y then there is a path from s to t through Q. So, by lemma 1.2, rm(z) is adjacent to y which contradicts our assumption. So rm(z) cannot be strictly to the right of rm(y) and this implies that rm(y) is to the right of rm(x). Q.E.D.

LEMMA 3.11 : If x is any vertex strictly to the right of y then lm(y) is to the left of lm(x).

PROOF : Similar to lemma 3.10.

LEMMA 3.12 : For any proper PQ-bridge B, $s_P(B)$ and $s_Q(B)$ are adjacent as also $t_P(B)$ and $t_Q(B)$.

PROOF : (See figure 4) Consider a vertex in the nucleus of B and the vertex s. The set S = W(G,B) is a seperating set for these two vertices. But any minimal seperating set M(M is a subset of S) must contain $s_P(B)$ and $s_Q(B)$. So, by lemma 1.2, they are adjacent. The proof for adjacency of $t_P(B)$ and $t_Q(B)$ is similar.   Q.E.D.

LEMMA 3.13: Every vertex on $P[s_P(B),t_P(B)]$ $(Q[s_Q(B),t_Q(B)])$ is adjacent to x where x is the only attachment of B on Q(P) .

PROOF : Consider the cycle $(x,s_P(B),*P[s_P(B),t_P(B)]*(t_P(B),x)$. If it is of length of at least four then it has to have a chord which will have to be from x to a vertex y on $P]s_P(B),t_P(B)[$. So we now have two cycles each containing edge(x,y). If they are of length at least four then same argument holds good for this also. **Q.E.D.**

LEMMA 3.14 : For any proper PQ-bridge B with at least two vertices of attachments on P and at least two vertices of attachments on Q at least one of the following is true :-

   1) There is a degenerate PQ-bridge from $s_p(B)$ to y where y is on $Q]s_Q(B),t_Q(B)]$.

   2) There is a degenerate PQ-bridge from $s_Q(B)$ to y where y is on $P]s_P(B),t_P(B)]$.

A similar result is also true for $t_P(B)$ and $t_Q(B)$.

PROOF : Let a and b be the vertices adjacent to $s_P(B)$ and $s_Q(B)$ respectively and under B. If the lemma is not true , there will be a chordless cycle of length at least four containing a , b , $s_P(B)$ and $s_Q(B)$ - a contradiction to definition 1.1.   **Q.E.D.**

DEFINITION 3.15 : (See fig 5) If x and y are two vertices on Q such that x is strictly to the left of y and lm(y) is strictly to the left of rm(x) then x and y are said to <u>CROSSOVER</u>.

LEMMA 3.16 :Let z be any vertex on Q]x,y[. If x and y crossover then

   1. x and z crossover.

   2. y and z crossover.

PROOF :(See fig 6)Since z is strictly to the right of x , rm(z) is to the right of rm(x) by lemma 3.10. Therefore rm(z) is strictly to the right of lm(y). Hence z and y crossover. Similarly we can prove that x and z crossover.   Q.E.D.

   Now we consider a case by case analysis according to the positions of vertices u and v in graph G. Since the arguments are symmetrical between the paths P and Q and also between u and v we will have the following cases:

CASE 1 :(Type 1 graph) u and v are on P-bridges or on P.

CASE 2 :(Type 2 graph) u and v are on the nuclei of PQ-bridges(the PQ-bridges may be same or different).

CASE 3 :(Type 3 graph) u is on a P-bridge(or path P) and v is on the nucleus of a PQ-bridge.

In the above three cases TPP is true. The path from s to t can use Q while the path from u to v can use P and the appropriate bridges.

CASE 4 :(Type 4 graph) u is on P and v is on Q

{Note: If u is on a P-bridge B1 or v is on a Q-bridge B2, the path from u to v has to necessarily pass through one of the two vertices of attachments of both B1 and B2. Also the path from s to t cannot use any of the vertices of B1 or B2. So, to find the path from u to v is equivalent to finding a path between the vertices of attachments of bridges B1 and B2. So we replace u and v by the appropriate vertices of attachments of B1 and B2 and solve the TPP. There may be at most four combinations of these vertices of attachments that have to be checked.}

CASE 4.a :(Type 4.a graph) u is properly under a PQ-bridge B.

In this case TPP is true. The path from s to t can be taken as $P[s, s_P(B)] * cc_B(s_P(B), t_P(B)) * P[t_P(B), t]$. By lemma 3.6 there is a degenerate PQ-bridge incident on u. Using this we can reach Q, from where we can reach v. (fig.7)

CASE 4.b :(Type 4.b graph) u and v are such that u is to the left of $s_P(B)$ and v is to the right of $t_Q(B)$, of a proper PQ-bridge B with at least two vertices of attachments on each of P and Q. There is also a symmetric case. In this case TPP is true. Now by lemma 3.14 there is a degenerate PQ-bridge from $s_P(B)$ to y, where y is on $Q]s_Q(B), t_Q(B)]$ or from $s_Q(B)$ to z, where z is on $P]s_P(B), t_P(B)]$. In former case take path from s to t as $Q[s, s_Q(B)] * cc_B[s_Q(B), t_P(B)] * P[t_P(B)], t]$ and the path from u to v as $P[u, s_P(B)] * (s_P(B), y) * Q[y, v]$. We can get two disjoint paths similarly in the latter case also.

CASE 4.c :(Type 4.c graph) Cases 4.a and 4.b are not satisfied.

Without loss of generality assume that rm(u) is to the left of v (fig.9). If not, either v is in between rm(u) and lm(u) or v is strictly to the left of lm(u). In the former case, (fig.10) by lemma 3.13, u will be adjacent to v, which can be dealt with seperately as discussed earlier. In the latter case (fig. 11), rm(v) is strictly to the left of u and this is a symmetric case with respect to P and Q and u and v.

CASE 4.c.1 :(Type 4.c.1 graph) There is a pair x, y on Q such that
   i) x and y crossover.
   ii) x is strictly to the left of v and y.
   iii) rm(x) is strictly to the the right of u.   In this case TPP is true. For the path from s to t take $Q[s,x] * (x, rm(x)) *$

P[rm(x),t]. For the path from u to v take P[u,lm(y)] * (lm(y),y) * Q[y,v] (fig.12).
(Note : There is a symmetrical case when x and y are on P such that
   i) x and y crossover.
  ii) x is strictly to the left of u and y.
 iii) rm(x) is strictly to the the right of v.
     In this case also TPP is true and similar disjoint paths can be given.)

DEFINITION 3.17 :

   We define two functions pred : V(P) -> V(P) and succ : V(P) -> V(P) where V(P) refers to the vertices on P.
   If x is on P]s,t], then pred(x) is the vertex strictly to the left of x and adjacent to x on P.
   pred(s) = s.
   If x is on P[s,t[then succ(x) is the vertex strictly to the right of x and adjacent to x on P.
   succ(t) = t.
   The pred and succ functions can be similarly defined for vertices of Q as well.

LEMMA 3.18 : If there exists a x as in case 4.c.1 , then there exists a x' which satisfies properties of x as in case 4.c.1 and it lies to the right of pred(rm(u)) on Q.

PROOF :

   If x lies on Q[pred(rm(u)),t[,then x' = x.
   If not x is strictly to the left of pred(rm(u)) , but rm(x) is strictly to the right of u. So, by lemma 3.10 rm(pred(rm(u))) is strictly to the right of u. Now we can take x' = pred(rm(u)) and y = rm(u). It can be verified that they satisfy case 4.c.1. Q.E.D.

   From now onwards we will assume the x in case 4.c.1 to be to the right of pred(rm(u)) , if it exists.

LEMMA 3.19 : If there exists a y satisfying conditions of case 4.c.1, then there will exist a y' which satisfies the properties of y as in case 4.c.1 and y' lies on Q[rm(u),v].

PROOF :

   y' has to be to strictly to the right of x. Hence by lemma 3.18 a y' can be found which is strictly to the right of pred(rm(u)).
   If y lies on Q[rm(u),v] , we are done as y = y'.
   If not , y is strictly to the right of v , and by a similar argument as in lemma 3.18 we can show that y' = v.   Q.E.D.

   From now onwards we can assume that the pair x and y lie on Q[pred(rm(u)),v] if they exist.

LEMMA 3.20 : If there exist x and y satisfying conditions of case 4.c.1 then there will exist two adjacent vertices x' and y' on Q[pred(rm(u)),v] satisfying the same properties.
PROOF :
If x and y are adjacent we are done. Otherwise consider pred(y) and y to be x' and y'. It can be seen that they satisfy conditions of case 4.c.1.   Q.E.D.
So , from now onwards it is enough if we look for two adjacent vertices on Q[pred(rm(u)),v] , for the pairs x and y.
CASE 4.c.2 :(Type 4.c.2 graph) There is no pair x and y satisfying conditions of case 4.c.1.

Since we have already assumed for case 4.c that rm(u) is to the left of v without loss of generality it is enough to consider that case alone.

Note that any path from s to t not containing u and v cannot use P or Q alone. Such a path , if it exists has to keep alternating between P and Q. Also it can be seen that usage of P and Q bridges is redundant.
LEMMA 3.21 : If TPP is true , then case 4.c.2 is not satisfied.
PROOF : Let P_{st} = path from s to t and P_{uv} = path from u to v. P_{st} has to go from the left of u or v to the right of u or v to bypass u and v. This is done in four ways :
Case 1: from strictly to the left of u to strictly to the right of u. This means that u is strictly under a PQ-bridge B - case 4.a.
Case 2: from strictly to the left of v to strictly to the right of v. This requires v to be strictly under a PQ-bridge B - case 4.a.
Case 3: from strictly to the left of v to strictly to the right of u. This requires a PQ-crosscut through a PQ-bridge B. Let its end vertices be x on Q and y on P. We will assume that P or Q crosscuts are used only if the subpath of P or Q contains a vertex of the other path.

If B has at least two vertices of attachments on both P and Q , then depending on the positions of $t_Q(B)$ and $s_P(B)$, either case 4.a or case 4.b is satisfied.

If not , let B have only one vertex of attachment on P . Then a degenerate bridge will be incident on both x and y which cannot be used by P_{uv}. So , we will assume that the bridge used for this crosscut is a degenerate bridge A.

Now P_{uv} has to go from strictly to the left of x or y to strictly to the right of x or y. This can be done in three ways.
Case 3.a : From strictly to left of y to strictly to right of x. A

cross-cut through a PQ-bridge is to be used. If this has only one attachment on P or Q , then from lemma 3.13 , there will be a degenerate PQ-bridge incident to both the end vertices of the cross-cut.So case 4.c.1 will be satisfied. If this cross-cut is through the nucleus of a proper PQ-bridge with at least two attachments on both P and Q , then depending on the positions of $s_P(B)$, $t_P(B)$, and $s_Q(B)$, case 4.a or 4.b or 4.c.1 will satisfied. (If $t_P(B)$ is to the left of u, then the degenerate bridge connecting $t_P(B)$ to $t_Q(B)$ gives rise to a crossover.)

Case 3.b: From strictly to left of x to strictly to right of x. In this case a Q-crosscut D is used. If the bridge used say B1 , has at least two attachments on both P and Q , then one of cases 4.a , 4.b, 4.c.1 is satisfied depending on the positions of $s_P(B)$, $t_P(B)$, and $s_Q(B)$. Now consider the crosscuts in the paths P_{uv} and P_{st}. Partition them in such a way that if two crosscuts interlace than they are in the same partition. Let partition P1 contain A. Partition the Q-crosscuts of P1 using the same realtion. Let partition P2 of P1 contain D. If one of these crosscuts in P2 uses a PQ-bridge with at least two vertices of attachments on both P and Q , then the PQ-bridge which has its attachments nearest to x will help satisfy case 4.a , 4.b or 4.c.1. Now assume that such bridges do not exist. If a PQ-bridge used by a crosscut of P2 has only one attachment y" on P , where y" <> y , then case 4.c.1 will be satisfied. So , assume that every crosscut in P2 is in a PQ-bridge with only one attachment on P wich is y. Let a and b be the vertices nearest to s and to t respectively of the vertices of P2 which are on Q. The subgraph Z = P2 U Q]a,b[has portions of both P_{st} and P_{uv}. So , there must be four distinct vertices , two each on P_{st} and P_{uv} , which are nearest to Z and on C. Two of these four vertices must be on Q as otherwise, the property of a and b will be contradicted. Both of them must be end vertices of PQ-crosscuts which interlace with some crosscut in P2. One of them could be A. The othermust have a vertex other than y as its end vertex on P.By a similar argument as in the beginning of this paragraph , we can show that one of cases 4.a , 4.b or 4.c.1 will be satisfied.

Case 3.c : From strictly to left of y to strictly to right of y. Proof similar to case 3.b.

Case 4 : from strictly to the left of u to strictly to the right of v. Proof similar to case 3.

As case 4.c.2 is not satisfied in any of the cases, the lemma is true.   Q.E.D.

DEFINITION 3.23 : In a rooted tree for any pair of vertices x and y , LCA(x,y) is defined to be the first common vertex between the two paths from x to the root and y to the root .

OBSERVATION 3.24 : In a rooted tree two paths P_{uv} and P_{st} from u to v and from s to t respectively are vertex disjoint if and only if LCA(u,v) does not lie on P_{st} and LCA(s,t) does not lie on P_{uv} .

4. IMPLEMENTATION :

For a biconnected graph , the implementation involves the following. First we have to check s and t adjacency and u and v adjacency. If s and t are adjacent then we have to check if there is a path from u to v in G - {s,t}. If u and v are adjacent then we have to check if there is a path from s to t in G - {u,v}. This can be done in $O(|E|)$ time. If neither pair is adjacent , then we need to find an arbitrary cycle containing s and t. This can be done in $O(|E|)$ time using the algorithm in [1]. To find C requires finding two chordless paths P and Q from s to t which can be done in $O(|E|)$ time. The vertices of the paths P and Q are ordered from s to t. We can find the bridges of C using any algorithm for connected components. We can also find their attachments on P and Q and identify their type - P, Q or PQ. Simultaneously , we can identify the positions of u and v. All this can be done in $O(|E|)$ time. So testing for cases 1,2,3 and 4 as well as for cases 4.a and 4.b can be done in $O(|E|)$ time. Looking through the adjacency lists of the vertices on P and Q we can find the lm's and rm's of all these vertices in $O(|E|)$ time. By theorem 3.20 , we have to check for crossover between adjacent vertices on Q[pred(rm(u)),vv] This will take at most $O(|V|)$ time. (We must also check for the symmetric case on P.). If case 4.c.1 is not satisfied , case 4.c.2 is satisfied. So the algorithm takes $O(|E|)$ time.

For a general graph , we have to form the block graph T. This involves finding biconnected components which can be done in $O(|E|)$ time. The cases I,II and III as in lemma 2.1 can be differentiated in $O(|E|)$ time using preorder numbering. (This follows from observation 3.24.) . If G satisfies case III , then the as the TPP for biconnected graph can be solved in $O(|E|)$ time , the TPP for the entire graph can be solved in $O(|E|)$ time.

5. CONCLUSION:
The TPP for a general graph is $O(n*e)$ while as we have seen the same problem can be solved in linear time for the class of chordal graphs. This just goes to show that a problem restricted to a certain class can be solved much more efficiently. Also the bridges of

a biconnected chordal graph for the circuit considered by us seems to have certain interesting structural properties which could be used to solve other problems related to chordal graphs.

REFERENCES:

1. Ebert,J., A Linear Disjoint Path Algorithm, Proceedings WG82, Munich : Hanser Verlag (1982) 37 -45.

2. Golumbic,M.C., Algorithmic Graph Theory and Perfect Graphs , Academic Press 1980.

3. Ohtsuki,T., The two disjoint path problem and wire routing design,   Graph Theory and Algorithms (Eds. Saito,N. and Nishizeki,T.)   Springer 108 (1980) 207 - 216.

4. Perl,Y. and Shiloach,Y., Finding two disjoint paths between two pairs of vertices in a graph , Journal of ACM , 25 (1978) 1 - 9.

5. Ramprasad,P.B. and Pandu Rangan,C., A new linear algorithm for the   two path problem on planar graphs   (To appear).

6. Shiloach,Y., A polynomial solution to the undirected two path problem , Journal of ACM , 27 (1980) 445-456.

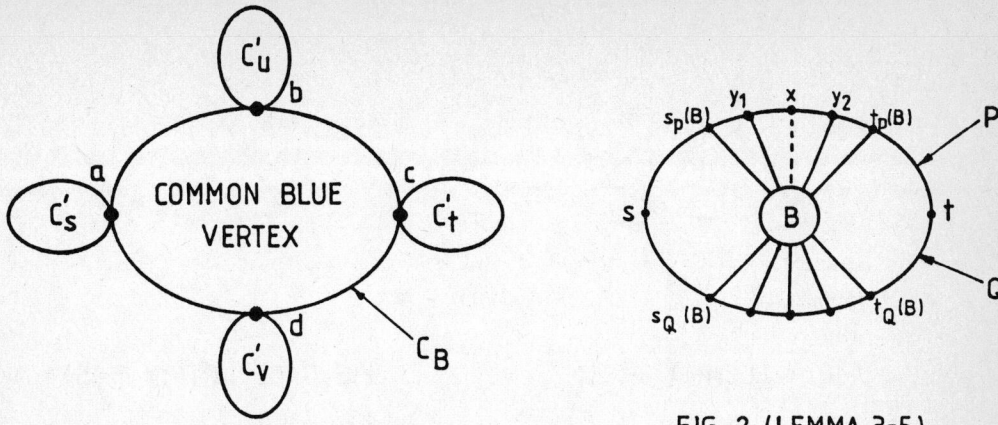

C'_s, C'_t, C'_u and C'_v lie on the paths P_{st} and P_{uv}

FIG. 1. (LEMMA 2-1)

FIG. 2. (LEMMA 3-5)

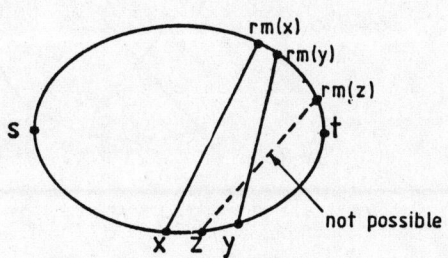

FIG. 3. (LEMMA 3-10)

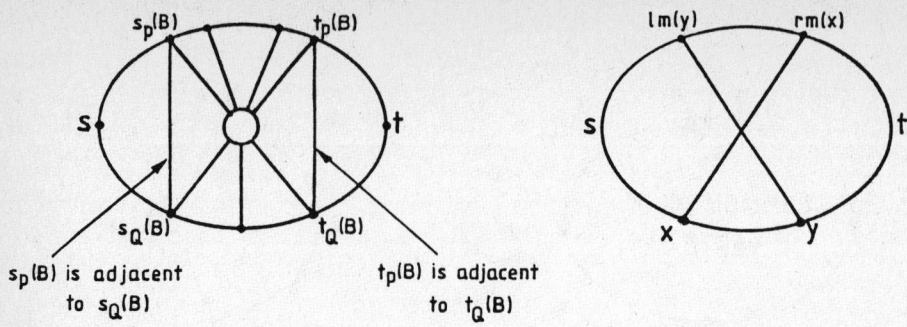

FIG. 4. (LEMMA 3-12)

FIG. 5 (DEFINITION 3-15)

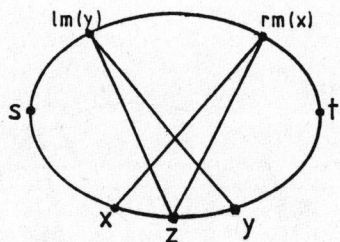

FIG. 6. (LEMMA 3-16)

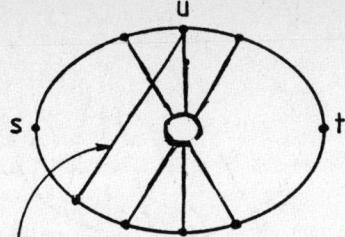

Degenerate PQ-bridge used for path from U to V.

FIG. 7. (CASE 4-a)

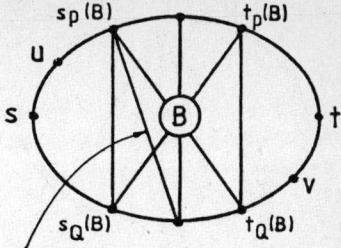

Degenerate PQ-bridge used for path from U to V.

FIG. 8. (CASE 4-b)

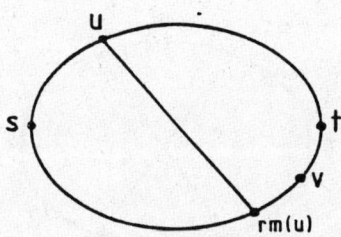

FIG. 9.

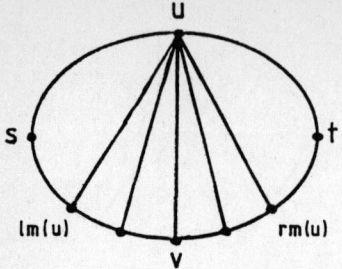
FIG. 10.

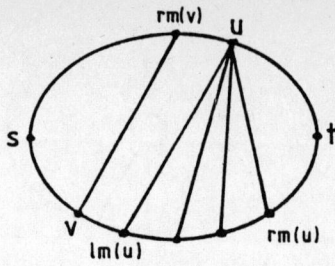
FIG. 11.

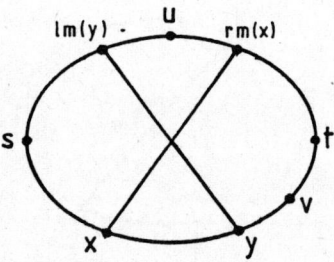
FIG. 12. (CASE 4·c·1)

Extending Planar Graph Algorithms to $K_{3,3}$-free Graphs

Samir Khuller [*]
Computer Science Department, Cornell University,
Ithaca, NY 14853.

Abstract

For several problems, restricting attention to special classes of graphs has yielded better algorithms. In particular, restricting to planar graphs yields efficient parallel algorithms for several graph problems. In this paper we extend these algorithms to $K_{3,3}$-free graphs, showing that the restriction of planarity is not important. The three problems dealt with are : graph coloring, depth first search and maximal independent sets. As a corollary we show that $K_{3,3}$-free graphs are five colorable (this bound is tight).

1 Introduction

For several graph-theoretic problems, solutions are known only for special classes of graphs and not for general graphs. For example, it is an open question if finding a depth first search tree (from now on referred to as DFS) for general graphs is in the complexity class NC (the class of problems which can be solved in polylog time with polynomially many processors). However, an NC algorithm is known for the case of planar graphs [XiYe 88]. A parallel algorithm has been developed for DFS on general graphs [AgAn 87] using randomization, showing the problem to be in the class Random NC.

A natural question is: is planarity fundamentally important in getting fast parallel algorithms for these problems ? Planar graphs have been characterized by Kuratowski's theorem in terms of the forbidden homeomorphs K_5 and $K_{3,3}$. We give a negative answer to the above question by extending several planar graph NC algorithms to $K_{3,3}$-free graphs (i.e. graphs not containing any subgraph homeomorphic to $K_{3,3}$).

[*]supported by NSF grant DCR 85 52938 and PYI matching funds from AT&T Bell Labs.

The problem of coloring a graph has attracted a lot of attention and study. The problem is defined as follows: given a graph $G(V,E)$, obtain a k-coloring for the graph (where k is an integer) such that each node is assigned a color and no two adjacent nodes have the same color. No more than k colors should be used. In particular find a function $f : V \to \{1,2,..,k\}$ such that f(u) $\neq$ f(v) whenever (u,v) $\in E$.

It has been shown by [GPS 87] how to five color a planar graph in parallel. Using their algorithm we develop a five coloring NC algorithm for $K_{3,3}$-free graphs. Our algorithm runs in time $O(log^2 n)$ and uses $O(n)$ processors. The sequential complexity of our algorithm is $O(n)$. As a corollary we show that $K_{3,3}$-free graphs are five colorable (this bound is tight since K_5 requires exactly five colors). The corresponding tight bound for coloring planar graphs was an open problem for many years until it was proven by [ApHa 77] by a complicated case analysis that every planar graph is four colorable. Notice the relative ease of proving the tight bound for $K_{3,3}$-free graphs. The four coloring of a planar graph can be obtained by a polynomial time algorithm (implied by the proof in [ApHa 77]), although it is an open question if this four coloring can be obtained in NC.

We also show how to find a *Maximal Independent Set* in $K_{3,3}$-free graphs. Luby's algorithm for MIS takes $O(log^2 n)$ time but uses $O(n^3)$ processors. For planar graphs it has been shown in [XinH 87] that only $O(n)$ processors are sufficient to achieve the same running time We develop a MIS algorithm for $K_{3,3}$-free graphs. Our algorithm runs in $O(log^2 n)$ time using $O(n)$ processors.

Smith [Smit 86] discovered a deterministic NC algorithm to find the DFS tree in planar graphs in $O(log^3 n)$ time using $O(n^4)$ processors. The result was improved by [XiYe 88] to show that for planar graphs, the problem can be solved in $O(log^2 n)$ time by using only $O(n)$ processors. The main idea of the algorithm lies in obtaining a separating cycle in the planar graph using Miller's algorithm [Mill 86]. In this paper it is shown how to decompose $K_{3,3}$-free graphs by finding a separating cycle in them. Using this separating cycle and ideas from [XiYe 88] it is relatively easy to construct a DFS tree in the graph. The algorithm takes $O(log^3 n)$ time and uses $O(n)$ processors.

Our algorithms are based on a special characterization of $K_{3,3}$-free graphs obtained by Vazirani in [Vaz 87]. This decomposition was used in [Vaz 87] to show that the problem of counting the number of perfect matchings in $K_{3,3}$-free graphs is in NC.

The model of computation assumed is the CRCW (Concurrent Read Concurrent Write) PRAM model. The model consists of a number of identical processors and a common globally shared memory In each time unit, a processor can read from a memory cell, perform an arithmetic or logical computation and write into a memory cell. Both concurrent reads and concurrent writes into the same memory cell by different processors are permitted. If a write conflict occurs, an arbitrary processor succeeds.

2 Terminology and Background

Let $G(V, E)$ denote a simple undirected graph. Let c_v denote the color of vertex v. A *legal coloring* of the graph is an assignment of colors to the vertices such that no two adjacent vertices have the same color. A set of vertices I, is said to be independent if no two of them are adjacent. Let $N(v)$ denote the set of vertices which are adjacent to vertex v. Let $\{a, b\}$ be a pair of vertices in a biconnected simple graph G. Suppose the edges of G are divided into equivalence classes $E_1, ..., E_n$ such that two edges which lie on a common path not containing any vertex of $\{a, b\}$ except as an endpoint are in the same class. The classes E_i are called the *separation classes* of G with respect to $\{a, b\}$. If there are at least two separation classes, then $\{a, b\}$ is a *separation pair* of G unless there are exactly two separation classes, and one class consists of a single edge.

If G is biconnected such that no pair $\{a, b\}$ is a separation pair of G, then G is *triconnected*. Let $\{a, b\}$ be a separation pair of G. Let the separation classes of G with respect to $\{a, b\}$ be $E_1, ..., E_n$. Let $E' = \cup_{i=1}^{k} E_i$ and $E'' = \cup_{i=k+1}^{n} E_i$ be such that $|E'| \geq 2$, $|E''| \geq 2$. Let $G_1 = (V(E'), E' \cup \{(a, b)\})$, $G_2 = (V(E''), E'' \cup \{(a, b)\})$.

The Graphs G_1 and G_2 are called the *split* graphs of G with respect to $\{a, b\}$. Replacing a graph G by two split graphs is called *splitting* G. A new edge (a,b) called a *virtual edge* is added in the split components if such an edge (a,b) is not already present in the graph G. Suppose G is split, the split graphs are split, and so on, until no more splits are possible (each remaining graph is triconnected). The graphs constructed in this way are called the *split components* of G.

A planar embedding of a planar graph G is a drawing of G in the plane such that no two edges intersect with each other in the drawing. A *Depth First Spanning tree* is a spanning tree T in G if and only if all edges which are not edges in T are between a pair of nodes, one of which is an ancestor of the other in the tree (assuming the tree has been rooted at a particular vertex).

NC^k is defined to be the class of problems which can be solved in $O(log^k n)$ time using polynomially many processors.

3 Decomposition of $K_{3,3}$-free graphs

The heart of the parallel algorithms lie in a special decomposition of $K_{3,3}$-free graphs. This decomposition is made possible by a theorem due to [Vaz 87], which is based on the following lemma due to Hall in [Hall 43] (see also [Asan 85]).

Lemma 1 (Hall) *Each triconnected component of a $K_{3,3}$-free graph is either planar or exactly the graph K_5.*

Let G be a $K_{3,3}$-free graph. First obtain the decomposition of G into triconnected components. Then keep merging two planar components if they share a pair of vertices. The components obtained in the end will either be planar pieces or $K_5's$ (merging two planar components keeps them planar). We call these components *pieces*. In [Vaz 87] it is shown that the pieces are invariants of the graph and do not depend on the order in which these components are merged. Pairs of vertices shared by two or more pieces are called *connecting pairs*. Two connecting pairs have at most one vertex in common. Each connecting pair is also a separating pair.

Theorem 1 (Vazirani) *There is a unique decomposition of a $K_{3,3}$-free graph into pieces. Let P be the set of pieces and C the set of connecting pairs of such a decomposition. Construct a new graph H on the vertex set $P \cup C$. If a connecting pair c is contained in a piece p then there is an edge (p,c) in H. The graph H is a tree.*

Root the tree H at a K_5 piece and call the root T_r. Now we define the decomposition tree T (also called a tree of pieces) as having its vertex set P. We put an edge from P_1 to P_2 if in the rooted tree H, P_1 and P_2 share a connecting pair c_1 with P_1 being an ancestor of P_2.

We can assume that G is biconnected since if not, we can find the biconnected components and solve the problem for each biconnected component independently. Then it is an easy task to put the solutions together using similar ideas to the ones presented in this paper.

4 The Coloring Algorithm

The first step in the algorithm is to obtain the decomposition of the graph into its triconnected components. This can be easily done by using the parallel algorithm of [MiRa 87]. The components can be checked for planarity using the algorithm in [KlRe 86] and the planar and K_5 pieces can thus be identified. Each piece in the tree can now be colored independently in parallel.
For the
 (i) Planar pieces : use the algorithm in [GPS 87].
 (ii) K_5 pieces : give each vertex a different color.

The colors are assumed to be drawn from the set $\{1, 2, 3, 4, 5\}$ and each vertex is given a color c_v. The next step is to "put" these colors together. Each piece in the tree T, has a unique path from the root T_r (K_5 piece). Each piece has many connecting pairs incident on it, but only one which separates it from its parent piece in the tree. Call this connecting pair the *parent connecting pair*. Each piece (except for the root T_r) has a unique parent connecting pair. We first describe the sequential algorithm to "put" the color's together and then show how it can be parallelized.

Definition 1 $cflip(c_1, u, H)$:
The color-flip operation (cflip) exchanges the colors of vertices colored c_u with the vertices colored c_1 in the piece H.

Definition 2 $cmatch(H_1, H_2)$: If H_1 and H_2 are two pieces sharing a parent connecting pair (u,v) (H_1 being the parent of H_2 in the tree T rooted at T_r). In H_1 the color's of u and v are c_u' and c_v'. In H_2 the color's are c_u and c_v.
Cmatch does the following two operations in sequence : $cflip(c_u', u, H_2)$; $cflip(c_v', v, H_2)$.

The operation ensures that the new color's of u and v in H_2 are c_u' and c_v'. Thus the piece $H_1 \cup H_2$ maintains a proper graph coloring.

Lemma 2 *If a graph G has a valid coloring, performing a $cflip(c,u,G)$ maintains the graph coloring as a valid one.*

Proof: Consider any two vertices v_1 and v_2 such that $(v_1, v_2) \in E$. Now there are various cases to consider:

i) cflip did not change the color of v_1 or v_2 since $c_{v1} \neq c_{v2}$ initially, after the cflip $c_{v1} \neq c_{v2}$.

ii) color of v_1 changed if c_{v1} was initially c (case for c_u is identical), then $c_{v2} \neq c$. If $c_{v2} = c_u$ then the new colors of c_{v1} and c_{v2} are c_u and c respectively.

iii) both colors changed if both have the same new colors, then both must have had the same old colors (c or c_u) which is not possible. $\square$

The next step is to "match" the colors of all the pieces. We use the fact that the decomposition of G has a tree structure (on the pieces). Direct all the edges away from the root T_r. If $H_1 \to p$ and $p \to H_2$ are the two edges in the directed tree (p is a connecting pair (u,v)), then the piece H_2 is a 'son' of the piece H_1. In order to match the colors of the two pieces we do a $cmatch(H_1, H_2)$ operation. This causes a change in the colors of piece H_2. The piece $H_1 \cup H_2$ now has a valid coloring. This change of colors will also be carried over to all the descendents of H_2 by doing $cmatch(H_2, H_k)$ operations when H_k is a child of H_2. We can thus piece the entire graph back together from its decomposition, ensuring that the coloring remains a valid one.

Thus T_r fixes its color and the rest of the pieces adjust their colors level by level in the tree T. This is the sequential algorithm for obtaining a five coloring for G.

Now we show how to parallelize the color matchings between pieces which was done level by level on the tree T in the sequential algorithm. Note that, on a graph G the cflip operation can be done in constant time on a PRAM by using only $O(n)$ processors with one processor for each vertex. Thus the Cmatch operation can also be done in constant time in parallel.

In the rooted tree T, the new colors of each piece T_i are determined by the colors of the pieces on the unique path from T_i to the root T_r. After rooting the tree at T_r, assign levels to each node T_i.

$$level(T_i) = \begin{cases} 1 & \text{if } T_i = T_r \\ 1 + level(parent(T_i)) & \text{otherwise} \end{cases}$$

The *depth* of the tree T is defined to be Max(level(T_i)) over all nodes T_i of the tree T.

Let $OddT = \{T_i \mid level(T_i) \text{ is odd }\}$. OddT is essentially the set of pieces having an odd level in the tree T.

Now for each $T_i \in$ OddT and $T_j \in$ Children(T_i) do a Cmatch(T_i,T_j) operation. This takes constant time using $O(n)$ processors. Now merge all the $T_j \in$ Children(T_i) pieces with T_i.

Thus all the nodes at an even level in the tree get merged with their parent nodes, to yield a new tree T^1 from $T^0(T)$.

Obviously depth(T^1) = $\lceil$ depth(T^0)/2 $\rceil$.

The Cmatch ensures that when a node and all of its children get merged, the colors of the children are appropriately flipped to achieve a valid coloring for the new merged piece $T_i \cup$ Children(T_i) ($T_i \in$ OddT). Now perform the above Cmatch and Merging step on the new decomposition tree T^1 to get tree T^2. In $O(log\ n)$ steps the entire tree T, will be reduced to a single node with a valid coloring. Thus the entire graph can be colored in $O(log\ n)$ time once all the planar pieces have been colored.

Summarizing the steps of the Algorithm:

1) Obtain the triconnected components of G and from this obtain the decomposition tree T, after merging adjacent planar pieces.

2) Root the tree at an arbitrary K_5 piece and direct all edges towards their parents in the rooted tree.

3) Color each planar and K_5 piece independently.

4) Put all the colors together doing the Cmatch operations between adjacent pieces and keep shrinking the decomposition tree until we achieve a valid coloring for the

entire graph.

ANALYSIS:

Analysis for the Parallel Algorithm:

The algorithm of [MiRa 87] takes $O(log^2 n)$ time and $O(n)$ processors. Planarity checking takes time $O(log^2 n)$ and $O(n)$ processors using the algorithm by [KlRe 86]. The coloring algorithm [GPS 87] takes $O(log\ n\ log^* n)$ time and $O(n)$ processors.

Finding the decomposition tree of pieces and obtaining the rooted tree of pieces can be done in $O(log^2 n)$ time using only $O(n)$ processors by finding a DFS tree rooted at the vertex chosen as the root [XiYe 88]. The parities of the nodes in the decomposition tree can be computed by a standard pointer jumping technique. Matching up all the colors can easily be done in $O(log\ n)$ time with $O(n)$ processors. Thus the entire parallel algorithm runs in $O(log^2 n)$ time with $O(n)$ processors.

Analysis for the Sequential Algorithm:

If we use the algorithm of [ChNS 81] to color all the planar pieces of the decomposition tree T we can achieve a running time of $O(n)$. Since the triconnected components can be obtained by [HoTa 73] in $O(n)$ time and planarity checking can also be done in $O(n)$ time using [HoTa 74]. Obtaining the tree of pieces and rooting it is a relatively easy task and takes no more that $O(n)$ time. Performing the color matchings level by level in the tree also takes $O(n)$ time. Thus a five coloring of a $K_{3,3}$-free graph can be obtained in $O(n)$ time.

We have therefore proved the following:

Theorem 2 *Every $K_{3,3}$-free graph is five colorable and there is an NC^2 algorithm to obtain the five coloring using only $O(n)$ processors.*

Remark: It should be noted that the bound of five colors is tight, since K_5 is a $K_{3,3}$-free graph which needs exactly five colors for a valid coloring.

5 Depth First Search

Let C be a simple cycle in a graph G. Removal of the vertices on the cycle C, decomposes the graph into connected components. If no connected component of the graph contains more than $\frac{2}{3}n$ vertices, C is called a *separating cycle* of G. The DFS algorithm for planar graphs in [XiYe 88] relies on the fact that all planar graphs have a separating cycle which can be obtained very fast in parallel as shown in [Mill 86]. In fact Miller showed that a separating cycle of size $O(\sqrt{n})$ always exists and can be obtained in NC. To solve the DFS problem the length of the cycle is not important, allowing us to construct a cycle of arbitrary length more efficiently. The separating cycle allows us to decompose the graph and find a DFS tree on the smaller pieces recursively as shown in [XiYe 88]. To find the DFS tree of G rooted at vertex r, we obtain a separating cycle C for the graph. Now find a path P_{rx} from r to any node x on C such that no other vertex of C is on P_{rx}. Let y be one of the neighbours of x on C. Consider a path P_{ry} from r to y going through x and all around the cycle C. Suppose $G - P_{ry}$ is the union of connected components $\{G_i\}$. Let e be an edge of G. We call e a *touching edge* of G_i if one end vertex of e is in P_{ry} and the other end is in G_i. A touching edge of G_i is called an *essential touching edge* if there does not exist another touching edge e' of G_i which touches P_{ry} at a point further (in P_{ry}) from r than the point at which e touches P_{ry}. Let e_i be an essential touching edge (if there are many such, pick one) of G_i and let x_i be the end vertex of e_i in G_i. Suppose T_i is the DFS tree of G_i rooted at x_i. It is shown in [Smit 86] that the union of P_{ry}, $\{e_i\}$ and $\{T_i\}$ forms a DFS tree for the graph G.

Here we show that all $K_{3,3}$-free graphs have a separating cycle which can be found in parallel, allowing us to find a DFS tree on $K_{3,3}$-free graphs in parallel.

To show how to construct the separating cycle in the $K_{3,3}$-free graph in parallel we first state the following lemma.

Lemma 3 *Let T be a tree and each node $v_i \in T$ have a nonnegative weight w_i. Define $W = \sum_{v_i \in T} w_i$. Then there exists a vertex v in T, such that every connected component of $T-v$ has total weight $\leq \frac{2}{3}W$. v is called a* separating vertex *for the tree.*

Proof: See [Mehl 84]. □

Theorem 3 *Every $K_{3,3}$-free graph has a separating cycle which can be obtained in NC^2 using only $O(n)$ processors.*

Proof: Consider the decomposition tree T of the graph G. To each node T_i assign a weight $w_i = $ number of vertices in piece T_i. Now using the above lemma find the separating vertex for the decomposition tree. Call this piece (vertex in tree T) T_p. We need to find a cycle within the piece T_p whose removal breaks up the graph into connected components each of which is no larger than $\frac{2}{3}n$. Note that, we may not be able to disconnect all the triconnected components hanging off from the piece T_p. The only components which get disconnected are the ones which have their connecting pairs on the cycle, the others get into one of two groups: Interior group and Exterior group. The triconnected components in each group may remain connected to one another. We need to consider two cases:
(i) T_p is a K_5 piece.

Choose C to be the cycle consisting of all the five vertices in the K_5 piece. Some of the edges (a,b) on the cycle may be virtual edges, with a piece hanging off from the connecting pair (a,b). In which case we can find a path from a to b in the piece hanging off and splice it into the cycle C, replacing the virtual edge (a,b). Each connected component formed is a subgraph of the connected component corresponding to the connected component formed in the tree T on removal of the vertex T_p. Since T_p was a separating vertex each connected component has fewer than $\frac{2}{3}n$ vertices.

(ii) T_p is a planar piece.

Consider every connecting pair (u,v) in T_p. Removal of (u,v) from the graph yields at least two connected components. Let n_{uv} be the sum of the number of vertices in all the connected components formed except for the component containing the piece T_p. Introduce n_{uv} new nodes on the virtual edge (u,v) in T_p. The total number of vertices in the graph with the new nodes added is still n. Introduction of the new vertices preserves planarity of the graph. In the resulting planar graph find a separating cycle C (using Miller's parallel algorithm). Each group of nodes added on an edge will either be removed (being on the cycle), belong to the Interior group or the Exterior group. In the case that the new group of nodes added on the virtual edge are on the cycle C, we delete all the nodes on the virtual edge from the cycle and find a path in the component hanging off from the connecting pair (u,v). This yields more connected components on deletion of the vertices on the path (each of which is bounded in size by $\frac{2}{3}n$). Although the cycle will not contain as many vertices as before (we deleted n_{uv} vertices and may have added fewer when splicing with a path) the total sizes of the Interior and Exterior group remain unchanged. Some new components get formed due to deletion of the path from the component hanging off the virtual edge which was chosen as part of the cycle C. All these components are bounded in size by $\frac{2}{3}n$ since T_p was a separating vertex in the tree T. The sizes of the connected components formed are less than the sizes of the connected components in the graph with the new vertices after deletion of the cycle C. The separating cycle in this graph ensures that the sizes of the connected components in the Interior and Exterior groups are bounded by $\frac{2}{3}n$.

The decomposition tree can be obtained in time $O(log^2 n)$ with $O(n)$ processors (shown in the analysis for five coloring). Using the planar graph DFS algorithm we can root the tree in the same time using only a linear number of processors. To compute the separating vertex of the tree we use the RAKE and COMPRESS operations in [MiRe 85]. These operations allow us to propogate information very easily from the leaf nodes to the root of the tree. Using these two operations we can compute the sizes of the connected components formed when a vertex is removed from the tree (this can be done in $O(log\ n)$ time using only $O(n)$ processors for all the vertices in the tree). Once the sizes of the components formed are known it is easy to identify (in parallel) a separating vertex. If the separating vertex is a K_5 piece, then we can trivially identify a five cycle, replace the virtual edges by splicing in paths (which can be found in $O(log\ n)$ time with $O(n)$ processors as in [XiYe 88]). If the piece is planar we find a separating cycle using Miller's algorithm [Mill 86], which takes time $O(log\ n)$ and $O(n)$ processors if we do not care about the length of the separating cycle. Thus the separating cycle for the $K_{3,3}$-free graph can be obtained in $O(log^2 n)$ time using only $O(n)$ processors. □

Obtaining the DFS tree for the graph by using this separating cycle adds a factor of $O(log\ n)$ to the running time since we need to solve the problem recursively on smaller subgraphs, yielding a running time of $O(log^3 n)$ using $O(n)$ processors.

We have therefore proved the following:

Theorem 4 *The Depth First Spanning Tree problem for $K_{3,3}$-free graphs is in NC^3 and uses only $O(n)$ processors.*

6 Maximal Independent Sets

The construction of a MIS on these graphs relies on first obtaining the decomposition tree of the graph (as obtained for coloring). The essential idea is to find Maximal Independent Sets for each piece and then combine these sets together to produce a MIS for the entire graph. The difficulty arises in handling cases when the vertices of a connecting pair belonging to many pieces, are in the MIS's for some of the pieces and not in the MIS's for the others. As before, root the decomposition tree at some vertex T_r. Each piece has a parent connecting pair (u,v). There are four possibilities:
1) u and v are in the MIS (only if they do not have a real edge)
2) u is in the MIS and v is not
3) v is in the MIS and u is not
4) both u and v are not in the MIS
Essentially we need to construct four MIS's for each piece, one for each of the above cases (this is done by forcing the vertices either into the set or out of it, then constructing a MIS on the rest of the piece). Call the MIS's corresponding to each of the above cases A,B,C,D respectively. A K_5 piece is a constant sized piece and we can easily construct a MIS for it considering only the real edges. For constructing a MIS on the planar piece use the algorithm by [XinH 87].

Now consider the following tree of macro nodes. Each macro node denotes a piece in the decomposition of the graph. Each macronode T_i contains four nodes in it, namely $T_i^A, T_i^B, T_i^C, T_i^D$. Each node within a macronode denotes a MIS for the corresponding piece. Let $X, Y \in \{A, B, C, D\}$. In the tree, we put an edge (directed) from T_i^X to T_j^Y if T_i is the parent of T_j in the macro node tree and the MIS's corresponding to X and Y "agree" in their containment of u and v (where (u,v) is the parent connecting pair of T_j. More formally, $(u \in T_i^X \Leftrightarrow u \in T_j^Y$ and $v \in T_i^X \Leftrightarrow v \in T_j^Y)$ iff there is an edge (directed) from T_i^X to T_j^Y. We can arbitrarily pick one of the nodes in T_r as the chosen MIS for piece T_r and call it T_r^A.

To construct a MIS for the entire graph, we chose all the MIS's T_i^U if there is a directed path from T_r^A to T_i^U. By a pointer jumping technique it is possible to determine for every node if there is a path to it from the root node in $O(log^2 n)$ time with $O(n)$ processors. It is easy to show by induction on the levels of the macro node tree, that in every macro node only one node gets selected as the chosen MIS for that piece. The basic idea is to keep compressing the tree by merging its odd and even level macro nodes. We add an edge from $T_i^X to T_k^Z$ if there is an edge from $T_i^X to T_j^Y$ and an edge from $T_j^Y to T_k^Z$ (T_i and T_k are at even levels in the macro node tree, level(T_k)= level(T_i) + 2). The operation keeps halving the height of the tree at each step and at the end of $O(log\ n)$ steps, all nodes at level = $\frac{depth}{2^k}$ for k=0,1,2,..,$log\ depth$ which have a path from the root node have been identified. Now we can recursively solve the problem for the parts of the tree formed by deleting the nodes (call these selected nodes) at levels which have been identified as having paths from the root to them. We need to find paths from the selected nodes to the other nodes in the trees rooted at the selected nodes, which is done recursively using the same algorithm.

ANALYSIS:
Constructing the decomposition tree, rooting it and finding out all the MIS's for the pieces takes time $O(log^2 n)$ using the algorithm by [XinH 87] and $O(n)$ processors. The pointer jumping technique as shown above takes time $O(log^2 n)$ with $O(n)$ processors (the extra $O(logn)$ factor comes due the recursive step). Hence a MIS for the entire graph takes $O(log^2 n)$ time using only $O(n)$ processors.

We have therefore proved the following:

Theorem 5 *The Maximal Independent Set problem for $K_{3,3}$-free graphs is in NC^2 and uses $O(n)$ processors.*

7 Acknowledgements

I would like to thank Vijay Vazirani for ideas, discussions and encouragement without whom this work would not have been possible. Thanks also to Esther Arkin,

Rafael Hassin and Joseph Mitchell for commenting on earlier drafts of the paper.

References

[AgAn 87] A.Aggarwal and R.J.Anderson, 'A Random NC algorithm for depth first search', *Proceedings of STOC conference*, (1987), pp 325-334.

[ApHa 77] K.Appel and W.Haken, 'Every planar map is four-colorable', *Illinois Journal of Maths*, 21 (1977), pp 429-567.

[Asan 85] T.Asano, 'An approach to the subgraph homeomorphism problem', *Theoretical Computer Science*, 38 (1985), pp 249-267.

[ChNS 81] N.Chiba, T.Nishizeki and N.Saito, 'A linear algorithm for five coloring a planar graph', *Graph Theory and Algorithms, LNCS*, Vol 108 (Springer, Berlin 1981), pp 9-19.

[GPS 87] A.Goldberg, S.Plotkin and G.Shannon, 'Parallel symmetry breaking in sparse graphs', *Proceedings of STOC conference*, (1987), pp 315-325.

[Hall 43] D.W.Hall, 'A note on primitive skew curves', *Bull. Amer. Math. Soc.*, 49 (1943), pp 935-937.

[HoTa 73] J.E.Hopcroft and R.E.Tarjan, 'Dividing a graph into triconnected components', *SIAM Journal of Computing*, 2:3, Sept (1973), pp 135-158.

[HoTa 74] J.E.Hopcroft and R.E.Tarjan, 'Efficient planarity testing', *Journal of the Assoc for Comp Mach*, 21, (1974), pp 549-568.

[KlRe 86] P.N.Klein and J.H.Reif, 'An Efficient parallel algorithm for planarity', *Proceedings of FOCS conference*, (1986), pp 465-477.

[Mehl 84] K.Mehlhorn, 'Graph algorithms and NP-Completeness', *Springer Verlag*, (1984).

[Mill 86] G.L.Miller, 'Finding small simple separators for 2-connected planar graphs', *Journal of Computer and System Sciences*, 32 (1986), pp 265-279.

[MiRa 87] G.L.Miller and V.Ramachandran, 'A New graph triconnectivity algorithm and its Parallelization', *Proceedings of STOC conference*, (1987), pp 335-344.

[MiRe 85] G.L.Miller and J.Reif, 'Parallel tree contraction and its applications', *Proceedings of FOCS conference*, (1985), pp 478-489.

[Smit 86] J.Smith, 'Parallel algorithms for depth first searches I:Planar Graphs', *SIAM Journal of Computing*, 15, (1986), pp 814-830.

[Vaz 87] V.V.Vazirani, 'NC Algorithms for computing the number of perfect matchings in $K_{3,3}$ free graphs and related problems', to appear in *Information and Computation*.

[XinH 87] X.He, 'A nearly optimal parallel algorithm for constructing maximal independent sets in planar graphs', *to appear*.

[XiYe 88] X.He and Y.Yesha, 'A nearly optimal parallel algorithm for constructing depth first spanning trees in planar graphs', *SIAM Journal of Computing*, vol 17, no 3, June (1988).

Constant-Space String-Matching*.

Maxime Crochemore
Université de Paris-Nord
avenue J-B Clément
F - 93430 VILLETANEUSE

Abstract. We present a string-matching algorithm with the following properties: it is linear in time with a small multiplicative constant during all its phases; it processes the searched text with constant memory space in addition to the string.

1. Introduction.

String-matching is the simplest case of pattern recognition. It consists in locating all the occurrences of a *word* (or *pattern*) inside another word, called the *text*. Both words are supposed to be sequences of letters from the same alphabet.

String-matching algorithms are interesting for their own, but they are often included in wider software tools. For instance, identification of patterns in images lead to string-matching questions when their contours are encoded into words. More generally, all formal systems handling strings of symbols involve parsing phases to recognize certain patterns. Regular expression is one of the techniques to specify simple patterns [26]. It certainly leads to practicable algorithms available under most operating systems or edition tools especially with Unix, but these algorithms are far less efficient than classical solutions to string-matching.

Solutions to string-matching can be divided into two families. In the first one the text is considered as fixed whereas the word is variable. This situation occurs when the text is a dictionary, for example. The basic solution of that sort is due to Weiner who introduced the notion of position trees [29]. It is a kind of index which as been improved in different ways (see [21], [5], [10]).

For the second family of solutions to string-matching, it is the word that is fixed. The two most famous and efficient string-matching algorithms of this family have been designed by Knuth, Morris & Pratt [18] and Boyer & Moore [7]. They have been subject to several studies, improvements or extensions (see [1], [11], [13-16], [22], [23], [25], [28]). A variation to the initial problem happens when approximate patterns are considered (see [20], [27]). String-matching is also close to detection of repetitions in strings (see [3], [10], [17], [25]). In fact, the

---

* This work has been supported by PRC Math.-Info.

study of regularities in strings is a part of the analysis of string-matching algorithms.

In this paper, we present an algorithm which is a slight improvement of the algorithm of [11]. The algorithm starts with a first phase during which the *word* alone is processed. Then, the *text* is searched during a second phase.

String-matching algorithms commonly achieve a linear time complexity by memorizing informations about the word. To do so, they need a memory space proportional to the length of the pattern. And thus, they have to manage dynamic memory. The first property of our algorithm is that it requires only constant additional memory space during all its phases. From that viewpoint it can be compared to the one of [15].

The number of letter comparisons done by the algorithm of [18] is $2n$ in worst case, if n is the length of the pattern. It is n, in the best case. These two quantities are respectively $2n$ and n/m, if pattern has length m, for sophisticated improvements of the algorithm of [7] (see [13], [2]). The second main property of our algorithm is that it shares the maximal number of letter comparisons with the above algorithms. The minimal number of letter comparisons it requires is $2n/m$.

The algorithm can be considered as intermediate between algorithms of [18] and [7]. It makes use of a deep theorem on words known as the crittical factorization theorem which relates local and global periods of a word (see [19]).

During its first phase the algorithm computes the smallest period of the pattern, in some situations. The computation suceeds when this period is not too great. The question remains whether there exists an algorithm computing the smallest period of a word in linear time with constant extra memory space.

2. Critical factorization.

We consider a finite alphabet A. Let A^* be the set of words on the alphabet A. The empty word is denoted by ε. We denote by $|x|$ the length of the word x and thus $|\varepsilon| = 0$. Concatenation of two words u and v of A^* is noted uv and if $x = uv$ the pair (u, v) is said a **factorization** of x. The word u is called a **prefix** of x and v is called a **suffix** of x. A prefix of v is called a **factor** of x, and its position in x is $|u|$.

Let x be a nonempty word. The ith letter of x is noted $x[i]$. We say that an integer p is a **period** of x if

$$x[i] = x[i+p]$$

whenever both sides are defined. In other terms, p is a period of x if two letters at distance p always coincide. We designate by $p(x)$ the smallest period of x and call it "the" period of x.

Given a factorization (u,v) of x, the **repetition** at (u,v) is the minimal length of a nonempty word w such that

(i) w is a suffix of u or conversely u is a suffix of w, and

(ii) w is a prefix of v or conversely v is a prefix of w.

It is denoted by $r(u,v)$. One has always the inequalities $1 \leq r(u,v) \leq |x|$. More accurately, one may verify that

$$r(u,v) \leq p(x).$$

A factorization (u,v) of x such that $r(u,v) = p(x)$ is called a **critical factorization** of x. For instance, the word

$$x = abaabaa$$

has period 3. It has three critical factorizations, namely

$$(ab, aabaa), (abaa, baa), (abaab, aa).$$

The following result is due to Cesari, Vincent and Duval (see [19] for precise references).

Critical Factorization Theorem. Each nonempty word has at least one critical factorization.

There exist several available proofs of this result. All of them lead to a more precise result asserting the existence of a critical factorization with a cutpoint in each factor of length equal to the period of x.

A weak version of the theorem occurs if one makes the additional assumption that the inequality

$$3\,p(x) \leq |x|$$

holds. Indeed, in this case, one may write

$$x = ywwz$$

where $|w| = p(x)$ and w is chosen minimal among its cyclic shifts. This means, by definition, that w is a Lyndon word (see [19]). One can prove that a Lyndon word has no nonempty prefix equals to one of its suffix. Consequently the factorization

$$(yw, wz)$$

is critical. This version is the argument used in [15] to build a string-matching algorithm using restricted memory space.

The existence of a critical factorization may be proved by considering alphabetical orderings. Each order $\leq$ on the alphabet A extends to an **alphabetical ordering** (also noted $\leq$) on the set A^*. It is defined as usual by $x \leq y$ if either x is a prefix of y or

$$x = fag,\ y = fbh$$

with a,b two letters such that $a < b$.

Let $\leq$ be an alphabetical ordering on A^*. We denote by $\lesssim$ the alphabetical ordering obtained by reverting the order $\leq$ on A.

Theorem. Let x be a word on A. Let v (resp. v') be the maximal suffix of x according to the ordering $\leq$ (resp. $\lesssim$). Let $x = uv = u'v'$. Then, if $|u| \geq |u'|$, (u,v) is a critical factorization of x. Otherwise (u', v') is a critical factorization of x.

The critical factorization (u, v) the theorem provides is such that the length of u is less than the period of x. As an example, the theorem produces the factorization $(ab, aabaa)$ for the word $x = abaabaa$.

A consequence of the previous theorem is that the computation of a critical factorization relies on the localization of maximal suffixes. Several algorithms exist to solve this problem (see [6], [12], [24]). One is given in figure 1 as a function which returns the position of the maximal suffix of its input. It uses only constant extra memory space (five integers if |x| is included) and its time linearity can be proved by showing that the sum $i+j+k$ strictly increases at each step of the "while" loop, from 2 up to $2|x|$ at most.

Time complexity. The maximal number of letter comparisons done by function "maximal suffix" on input x is $2|x|$.

```
function maximal suffix (x);
        i <-- 0;  j <-- 1;  k <-- 1;  p <-- 1;
        while (j + k ≤ |x|) do
        {       a <-- x[i + k];  b <-- x[j + k];
                if ( a < b ) then
                {       i <-- j;  j <-- j + 1;  k <-- 1;  p <-- 1; }
                if ( a = b ) then
                {       if ( k ≠ p ) then { k <-- k + 1; }
                        else { j <-- j + p;  k <-- 1; }}
                if ( a > b ) then
                {       j <-- j + k;  k <-- 1;  p <-- j - i; }
        }
        return ( i );
end function
```

figure 1. Localization of a maximal suffix.

3. Constant-space algorithm

The algorithm presented in this section competes with those of [18] and [7]. It shares their efficiency in time, but requires only constant extra space while the others need linear space.

To find out the occurrences of a word x inside a text t, both algorithms of [18] and [7] search the text t from left to right. But the former scans the word x from left to right while the latter scans it in the reverse direction. The main feature of our algorithm is that it starts to scan the word x at a cutpoint of a critical factorization (u, v). It is conceptually divided into two steps. During the first step, part v of the factorization is first scanned from left to right. Then, when an occurrence of v is found in t, the second step begins. The algorithm then checks whether u occurs before the occurrence of v by scanning u from right to left. As far as we know, the algorithm in [15] was the first to proceed that way. It uses a factorization (u, v) of x which roughly satisfies: at most one prefix of v is a cube.

The string-matching algorithm is shown in figure 2. It assumes that (u, v) is a critical factorization of x such that $|u|$ is less than $p(x)$, the period of x. Such a factorization can be deduced from theorem 1 of section 2. We now explain the role of the variable l. After a mismatch is found or an occurrence of x is discovered and the word x is shifted to the right. When the shift is compatible with the period of x a prefix of x still matches the text t. The variable l memorizes the length of that prefix.

The correctness of procedure "match" in figure 2 relies on several properties of critical factorizations that are summarized below.

Proposition. Let (u, v) be a critical factorization of a word x of A^*.
(a)   If yu is a prefix of x, $p(x)$ divides $|y|$.
(b)   If w and yw are prefixes of x and $p(x) \leq |w|$, $p(x)$ divides $|y|$.
(c)   If w is a prefix of v, z is a suffix of w and wz is a suffix of uw (in this situation w overlaps the cutpoint of the factorization), $p(x)$ divides $|z|$.

The time complexity of algorithm in figure 2 is linear in the length of the text. One can prove that letter comparisons done during the first step strictly increase the value of $position+i$ which varies from $|u|+1$ to $|t|$ in the worst case. At the second step, word x is shifted $p(x)$ places to the right. Since, by assumption, the length of u is less than $p(x)$, comparisons done during next second steps are done on different letters of t. Then at most $|t|$ letter comparisons are done at each step.

Time complexity. The maximum number of letter comparisons during a run of procedure "match" on inputs x and t is $2|t|$.

```
procedure match ( x, t );
    position <-- 0;   l <-- 0;
    while ( position + |x| ≤ |t| ) do
    {      i <-- max( |u|, l) + 1;
           while ( i ≤ |x| and x[i] = t[position + i] ) do
                i <-- i + 1;
           if ( i ≤ |x| ) then
           {      position <-- position + max(i-|u|, l-p(x)+1);
                  l <-- 0; }
           else
           {      j <-- |u|;
                  while ( j > s and x[j] = t[position +j] ) do
                       j <-- j - 1;
                  if ( j = l ) then output(x occurs at position);
                  position <-- position + p(x);
                  l <-- |x| - p(x); }
    }
end procedure
```

figure 2. Constant-space string-matching algorithm.

The precomputation of the period $p(x)$ can be done in linear time by any of the classical methods, such as the algorithm of [18]. But, those solutions needs $O(|x|)$ memory space. In order to keep the extra memory space bounded, another solution is proposed.

The entire algorithm distinguishes two cases whether the period is small or not. As a consequence of property (a) of the above proposition, figure 3 shows a function which computes $p(x)$ or a lower bound of it. Now, if that function produces the exact period $p(x)$, the procedure "match" of figure 2 is applied. In the other situation one may observe that $p(x)$ is greater than half the length of x. A modified procedure "match" is applied in which variable l is eliminated and $|x|/2$ shifts are substituted to the $p(x)$ shifts of the original procedure. The time complexity proposition remains true.

The so modified string-matching algorithm, including the preprocessing of the x, is linear in the sum of the lengths of the word x and the text t. All phases of the process only require bounded extra space.

```
function small period (x);
    let (u, v) be a critical factorization of x computed with the help
    of function "maximal suffix";
    period p(v) is the final value of p in function "maximal suffix";
    if (|u|≤|x|/2 and u suffix of v[1]...v[p(v)]) then
        return (the period of x is p(v))
    else
        return (the period of x is greater than max(|u|,|v|))
end function
```

figure 3. Constant-space computation of small periods.

4. References

[1] A.V. AHO & M.J. CORASICK, Efficient string matching : An aid to bibliographic search, *Comm. ACM* **18** (1975) 333-340.

[2] A. APOSTOLICO & R. GIANCARLO, The Boyer-Moore-Galil searching strategies revisited, *SIAM J. Comput.* **15**, 1 (1986) 98-105.

[3] A. APOSTOLICO & F.P. PREPARATA, Optimal off-line detection of repetitionsin a string, *Theoret. Comput. Sci.* **22** (1983) 297-315.

[4] D.R. BEAN, A. EHRENFEUCHT & G.F. McNULTY, Avoidable patterns in strings of symbols, *Pacific J. Math.* **85** (1979) 261-294.

[5] A. BLUMER, J. BLUMER, A. EHRENFEUCHT, D. HAUSSLER, M.T. CHEN & J. SEIFERAS, The smallest automaton recognizing the subwords of a text, *Theoret. Comput. Sci.* **40**, 1 (1985) 31-56.

[6] K.S. BOOTH, Lexicographically least circular substrings, *Inform. Process. Lett.* **10**, 4, 5 (1980) 240-242.

[7] R.S. BOYER & J.S. MOORE, A fast string searching algorithm, *Comm. ACM* **20** (1977) 762-772.

[8] Y. CESARI & M. VINCENT, Une caractérisation des mots périodiques, *C.R. Acad.Sc.* t.**286**, série A (1978) 1175.

[9] C. CHOFFRUT & M.P. SCHÜTZENBERGER, Counting with rationnal functions, to appear in *Theoret. Comput. Sci.* (1988).

[10] M. CROCHEMORE, Transducers and repetitions, *Theoret. Comput. Sci.* **45** (1986) 63-86.

[11] M. CROCHEMORE & D. PERRIN, Pattern matching in strings, to appear in *J. Assoc. Comput. Mach.* (1988).

[12] J.P. DUVAL, Factorizing Words over an Ordered Alphabet, *J. Algorithms* **4** (1983) 363-381.

[13] Z. GALIL, On improving the most case running time of the Boyer-Moore string-matching algorithm, *Comm. ACM* **22**, 9 (1979) 505-508.

[14] Z. GALIL, String Matching in real time, *J. Assoc. Comput. Mach.* **28**, 1 (1981) 134-149.

[15] Z. GALIL & J. SEIFERAS, Time Space Optimal String Matching, *J. Comput. Syst. Sci.* **26** (1983) 280-294.

[16] L.J. GUIBAS & A.M. ODLYSKO, A new proof of the linearity of the Boyer-Moore string searching algorithm, in: (Proc. 18 th Annual IEEE Symposium on Fundations of Computer Science (1977)) 189-195.

[17] R.M. KARP, R.E. MILLER & A.L. ROSENBERG, Rapid identification of repeated patterns in strings, trees, and arrays,in: (*ACM Symposium on Theory of Computing*, Vol. **4**, ACM, New York (1972)) 125-136.

[18] D.E. KNUTH, J.H. MORRIS & V.R. PRATT, Fast pattern matching in strings, *SIAM J. Comput.* **6**, 2 (1977) 323-350.

[19] LOTHAIRE, *Combinatorics on Words*, Addison-Wesley, Reading, Mass., 1982.

[20] G.M. LANDAU & U. VISHKIN, Efficient string matching with k differences, Technical Report 186, Courant Institute of Mathematical Sciences, New York University (1985).

[21] E.M. MCCREIGHT, A space-economical suffix tree construction algorithms, *J. Assoc. Comput. Mach.* **28**, 2 (1976) 262-272.

[22] R.L. RIVEST, On the worst-case behavior of string-searching algorithms, *SIAM J. Comput.* **6**, 4 (1977) 669-674.

[23] W. RYTTER, A correct preprocessing algorithm for Boyer-Moore string-searching, *SIAM J. Comput.* **9**, 3 (1980) 509-512.

[24] V. SHILOACH, Fast canonization of circular strings, *J. Algorithms* **2** (1981) 107-121.

[25] A.O. SLISENKO, Detection of periodicities and string-matching in real-time, *J. of Soviet Mathematics* **22**, 3 (1983) 1316-1387.

[26] K. THOMPSON, Regular expression search algorithm, *Comm. ACM* **11** (1968) 419-442.

[27] E. UKKONEN, Finding Approximate Patterns in Strings, *J.Algorithms* **6** (1985) 132-137.

[28] U. VISHKIN, Optimal parallel pattern matching in strings, in: (Proc. 12th ICALP, Lecture Notes in Computer Science **194**, Springer-Verlag (1985)) 497-508.

[29] P. WEINER, Linear pattern matching algorithms, *IEEE Symposium on Switching and Automata Theory*, Vol. **14**, IEEE, New York (1972)) 1-11.

INHERENT NONSLICIBILITY OF RECTANGULAR DUALS IN VLSI FLOORPLANNING

Susmita Sur-Kolay and Bhargab B. Bhattacharya

Electronics Unit, Indian Statistical Institute,
Calcutta - 700 035.

Abstract: This paper addresses a crucial question in VLSI floorplanning by rectangular dualization method: for any planar graph having a rectangular dual, does there exist a slicible dual? A minimum counterexample is presented and the concept of inherent nonslicibility is introduced. The problem of transforming a given nonslicible floorplan to a slicible one with change in shapes of a minimal subset of modules, is then formulated and a heuristic algorithm is proposed. The algorithm has a time complexity of $O(n)$, where n is the number of modules in the floorplan.

Keywords: VLSI layout, floorplanning, plane triangulated graphs, rectangular duals, slicing structures, algorithms.

1. Introduction

In hierarchical VLSI circuit layout [HK86], a set of rectangular functional modules and their topological neighbourhood relation based on the logic design of the circuit, is given; the problem of allocation of positions to these modules on the chip is known as floorplanning. If the dimensions of the modules are fixed, then we have the traditional problem of module placement. Floorplanning problem is the generalised version of the placement problem; the modules can assume any shape permitted by given constraints specifying area and a range of aspect ratios. Parameters such as area, perimeter or aspect ratio of the chip are usually optimised. It has been established [La80] that the placement problem is NP-complete.

With rapid rise in the scale of integration in chips, several automated layout design systems have been developed. Most of the earlier systems [Ri82], [OHM85] were based on placement followed by interconnection methodology. The floorplan technique has been found to produce better designs [Ot82], [DK86] because flexibility in the shape of modules emulates the human designer's freedom to redistribute the internal components of a module. Well established floorplan techniques use the concept of rectangular dual of a planar graph representing the topological neighbourhood of the modules. Special types of floorplans called slicings are preferred for their computational ease.

In this paper, we answer the following fundamental theoretical question which has been baffling floorplan designers from the inception of this technique: does an arbitrary planar graph having a rectangular dual, always have a slicible dual? A minimum counterexample which negates the possibility, is presented. This leads us to define a class of planar graphs which have inherently nonslicible rectangular duals. Since slicible duals provide many advantages in the VLSI design process, we consider the possibility of transforming a nonslicible floorplan to a slicible one with a minimum sacrifice of some design constraints. We then propose a polynomial time greedy heuristic which transforms a given nonslicible floorplan to a slicible one by altering the shapes of some modules.

2. Preliminaries and Definitions

For graph-theoretic terminologies used without definition in this paper, we refer the reader to [Ha69]. A **floorplan** is essentially a **rectangle dissection,** which is a subdivision of an enveloping rectangle by horizontal (parallel to x-axis) and vertical (parallel to y-axis) line segments into a finite number of indivisible non-overlapping rectangles. The indivisible non-overlapping rectangles correspond to the functional modules in the floorplan (Fig. 1a). The horizontal or vertical line segments defining the rectangle dissection, are called **cutlines** or simply **cuts.** It can be shown easily that a floorplan with n cuts has exactly n+1 modules. For simplicity sake, we follow the frequently used standard convention that two perpendicular cuts can meet but not cross. In other words, the intersection of cuts forms T-junctions only. A cross (`+') junction can be treated as a conjunction of two adjacent T-junctions.

A floorplan is said to be **slicible**, or a **slicing**, if it is a rectangular dissection that can be obtained by recursively dividing rectangles into smaller rectangles until each non-overlapping rectangle is indivisible and corresponds to a module. Slicible floorplans are also called **slicing structures.** A floorplan may or may not be slicible (Figs. 1a & 1b resp.)

Given a floorplan F, a **rectangular graph** $R = (V,E)$, represents the adjacency of modules in F. Each vertex in V corresponds to a distinct module in F and there is an undirected edge (u,v) in E iff the module corresponding to vertex u and that corresponding to vertex v are

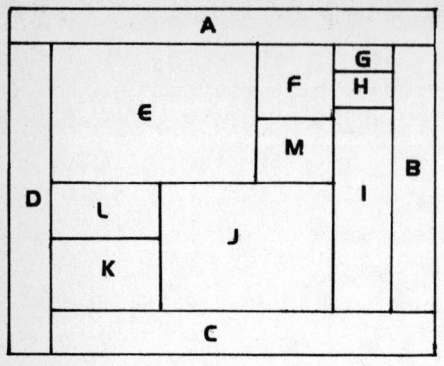
(a) Slicible Floorplan

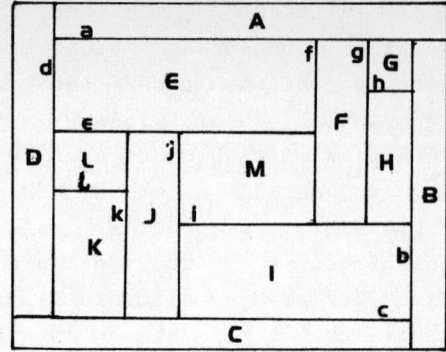
(b) Nonslicible Floorplan

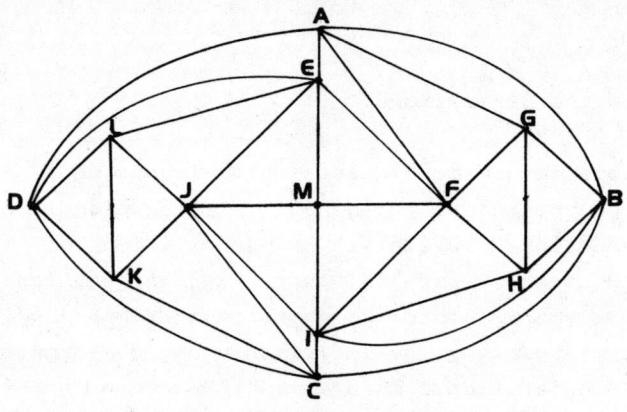
(c) Rectangular Graph

Fig. 1

adjacent (i.e. share a common boundary). For example, Fig. 1c shows the rectangular graph for the floorplan shown in Fig. 1a.

It is easy to see that for a given floorplan a unique rectangular graph always exists. By definition, a rectangular floorplan is embedded on a plane which implies that its rectangular graph is a **plane graph** [Ha69]. The assumption about all intersections except the corners of F being T-junctions leads to the fact that all the internal faces of R are bounded by three edges. Thus, a rectangular graph is a <u>plane triangulated graph</u>. Plane triangulated graphs depicting adjacency of modules are also known as neighbourhood graphs.

Given an n-vertex plane triangulated graph G, its **rectangular dual** RD consists of n non-overlapping rectangles where each vertex i in G corresponds to a distinct rectangle in RD, an edge (i,j) in G demands the adjacency of rectangles i and j in RD, and the boundary of RD is also rectangular. The rectangular dual of G, if it exists, corresponds to a valid rectangular floorplan where the rectangles represent the modules of the floorplan. Since all faces of G are triangles, no more than three rectangular faces in the rectangular dual of G meet at a point. This means that the floorplan has only T-junctions and no cross junctions.

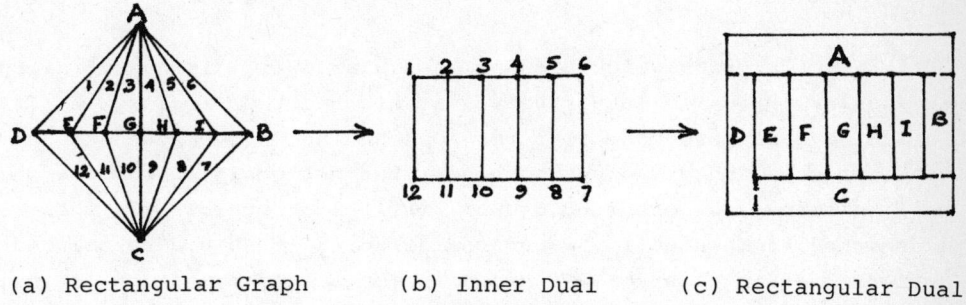

(a) Rectangular Graph   (b) Inner Dual   (c) Rectangular Dual

Fig. 2

A rectilinear embedding of a plane graph is an embedding in which all the edges of the graph are either horizontal or vertical. A cycle in the graph is embedded as a rectilinear polygon. Given a plane triangulated graph G, its **inner dual** D, is a rectilinear embedding of the geometric dual [Ha69] of G, excluding the vertex corresponding to the exterior face of G, such that each internal face of D is bounded by four or more edges and embedded as a rectangle. All the internal vertices of D have degree 3. Thus we can obtain (Fig. 2) the rectangular dual of G by placing the inner dual of G within an enveloping rectangle (since the exterior face of G is not reflected in D), and projecting each degree 2 (resp. degree 1) vertex of D onto the side (resp. two sides) of the enveloping rectangle nearest to it.

Some plane triangulated graphs (Fig. 1c) may have more than one rectangular dual (Figs. 1a, 1b) whereas others may not have any (Fig. 3). A triangle of a plane triangulated graph G, which is not a boundary of a face, is called a **complex triangle**. It has been shown in [KK85], [LL84] that one of the necessary conditions for G to have a rectangular dual is that G has no complex triangles. Such a graph is a **properly triangulated plane (PTP)** graph [BS86]. The necessary and sufficient conditions under which a PTP graph G, has a rectangular dual, were established in [KK85].

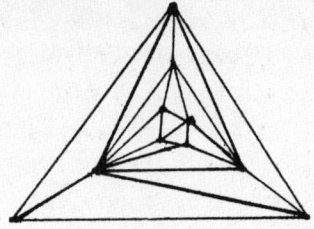

Fig. 3   Complex triangle in plane triangulated graph

Remark: A PTP graph which has a rectangular dual, is by definition a rectangular graph. Intuitively, a biconnected rectangular graph should have no more than four vertices having degree 2 and these, if at all present, should appear on the outermost cycle. From now on, we shall assume a biconnected graph; if it is otherwise, then each biconnected component is to be considered. It should be pointed out that the definition of PTP graph is implicitly based on a unique embedding of the graph on a plane. This follows from the 2-connectedness of plane graphs [Ha69].

To summarize the steps of floorplanning phase [HSM82] of circuit layout, first a planar subgraph is obtained from the logical network of the circuit by deleting a minimum number of edges or a set of edges with minimum total weight. This problem has been proven to be NP-complete [GJ79]. Second, this planar graph is triangulated, which can be done in linear time. Third, all complex triangles are eliminated from the plane triangulated graph, and there is no polynomial time optimum algorithm or a NP-completeness proof [TKS86] for this. Finally, a rectangular dual of this PTP graph is constructed, if it exists. A linear time algorithm to check existence of rectangular dual for a given planar triangulated graph is given in [BS87]. Efficient algorithms for constructing a rectangular dual have been developed in [KK84], [LL84], [BS86].

3. Slicible Floorplans

Several investigators have advocated that in top-down hierarchical circuit design, slicing structures have several advantages over general nonslicing ones. Slicible floorplans can be represented by elegant data structures such as series-parallel polar graphs [Ot82], slicing trees [Ot83], normalized Polish postfix expressions [WL86]. These types of floorplans are computationally easier to deal with because they allow a natural partition of the design into partially independent subproblems, hence divide-and-conquer strategy succeeds.

The problem of optimal orientations of modules is solvable in polynomial time for a slicible floorplan but remains NP-complete in the strong sense for general floorplans [St83]. Otten [Ot83] has developed a polynomial time algorithm for constructing a slicible floorplan, given the topology of recursive slicings in the form of a slicing tree. Another approach to floorplanning using simulated annealing has been proposed in [WL86]; only slicing structures are considered in the search space to speed up convergence significantly. Slicing facilitates not only floorplanning but also wiring. Optimal wiring of a single net in a slicing structure, minimizing the overall area instead of wire length, can be done in $O(n\log n)$ time [LSW87]. It seems that this problem is far more complicated in the general case.

A graph-theoretic characterisation of a slicible floorplan has been given in [SS83]. It is based on the concept of a channel graph where a channel in a floorplan is a cutline. By the convention of T-junctions only, no two channels overlap. If two perpendicular channels c and d intersect at a point p, then p is an endpoint of either c or d, but not both; the one of which p is an endpoint is called the **base** of the T-junction and the other is called the **crosspiece**. The two parts of the crosspiece channel on either side of the junction are called **arms**.

A **channel graph** of a floorplan is a directed graph $C = (V,A)$ where there is a distinct vertex in V for each channel and there is an arc (d,c) from d to c in A iff there is a T-junction of which d is the base and c is the crosspiece. The channel graph of the floorplan shown in Fig 1b is given in Fig. 4a.

Note that a channel graph is planar. The outdegree of any vertex is at most 2 because a channel has two endpoints, so it can be the base of atmost two T-junctions. There is no restriction however on the indegree of vertices in channel graph. Two crucial theorems were proved in [SS83].

4-cycle Theorem [SS83]: A channel graph has a directed cycle iff it has a cycle of length 4.

Slicing Theorem [SS83]: A channel graph of a floorplan is acyclic iff the floorplan is a slicible floorplan.

We can deduce from the Slicing Theorem that if a floorplan is nonslicible, its channel graph C, has a directed cycle, and then by the 4-cycle Theorem, C has a directed 4-cycle. So by detecting directed 4-cycles in the channel graph of a given floorplan, we can recognize whether the floorplan is nonslicible. There are two possible arrangements of channels in a floorplan which produce

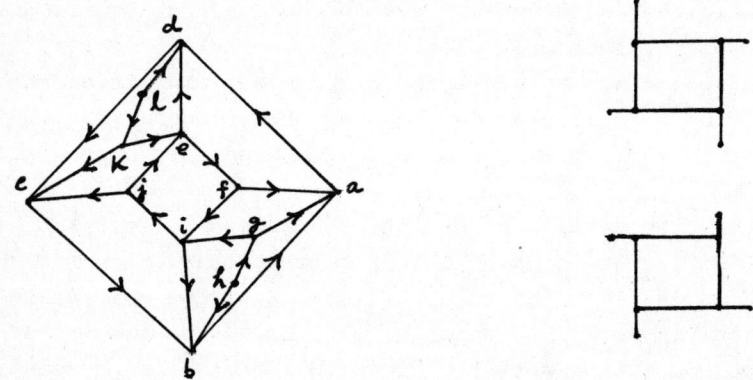

(a) Channel graph of floorplan in Fig. 1b   (b) Two possible arrangements of channels causing nonslicibility

Fig. 4

directed 4-cycles in the channel graph (Fig. 4b). We shall make use of this fact in our algorithm presented in Section 5. Prior to that, in the next section we take up the question of existence of a slicible dual of a given rectangular graph.

4. Inherent Nonslicibility

Given a rectangular graph R, its rectangular dual is guaranteed to exist by definition. The dual may not be unique. It may be the case that both slicible (Fig. 1a) and nonslicible (Fig.1b) duals exist for a given R (Fig. 1c). A natural question that comes up is whether a slicible floorplan exists for every rectangular graph. In the previous section, the criterion for slicibility of a given floorplan was outlined. We are interested in the converse question, i.e. the criterion of slicibility of a given rectangular graph, because in practice, it is this graph which is specified to a floorplanner.

Definition: A rectangular graph is **inherently nonslicible** if there exists no slicible rectangular dual of it, consequently no slicible floorplan.

Before we present the main theorem on inherent nonslicibility, we need a lemma concerning rectilinear embedding. A corner of a rectilinear polygon (Fig. 5) is a vertex v, where the two edges of the polygon which are incident on v, form an interior angle of either +90 or -90 degrees (i.e. 270 degrees); the first type of corner is a convex corner and the second type a concave corner. A rectilinear polygon is simple if all its corners are distinct.

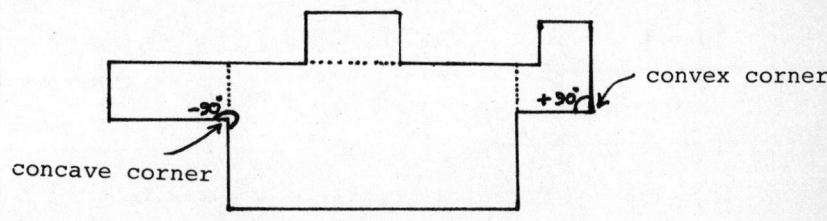

Fig. 5 Rectilinear Polygon

Lemma: If any simple rectilinear polygon has j convex corners and k concave corners, then j is at least 4, k = j-4 and j+k is even.

Proof: The sum of all interior angles at the corners of a rectilinear polygon is always 360 degrees; hence we must have 4 more convex corners than concave ones. Thus, j is at least 4 and k = j - 4. Since we consider simple polygons, a concave corner always has an adjacent convex one. For the second part, j+k = 2j-4, which is always even. A rectilinear polygon has even number of corners. QED

Theorem 1: There exists an inherently nonslicible graph N, having 9 vertices.

Proof: Consider a graph N, (Fig. 6a) having 9 vertices and 20 edges. All its internal faces are triangles and the exterior face has 4 edges. It is biconnected, has no complex triangles and has exactly four vertices of degree 2. Hence N is a rectangular graph. The rectangularity of N is also apparent from the existence of its floorplan (Fig. 6d).

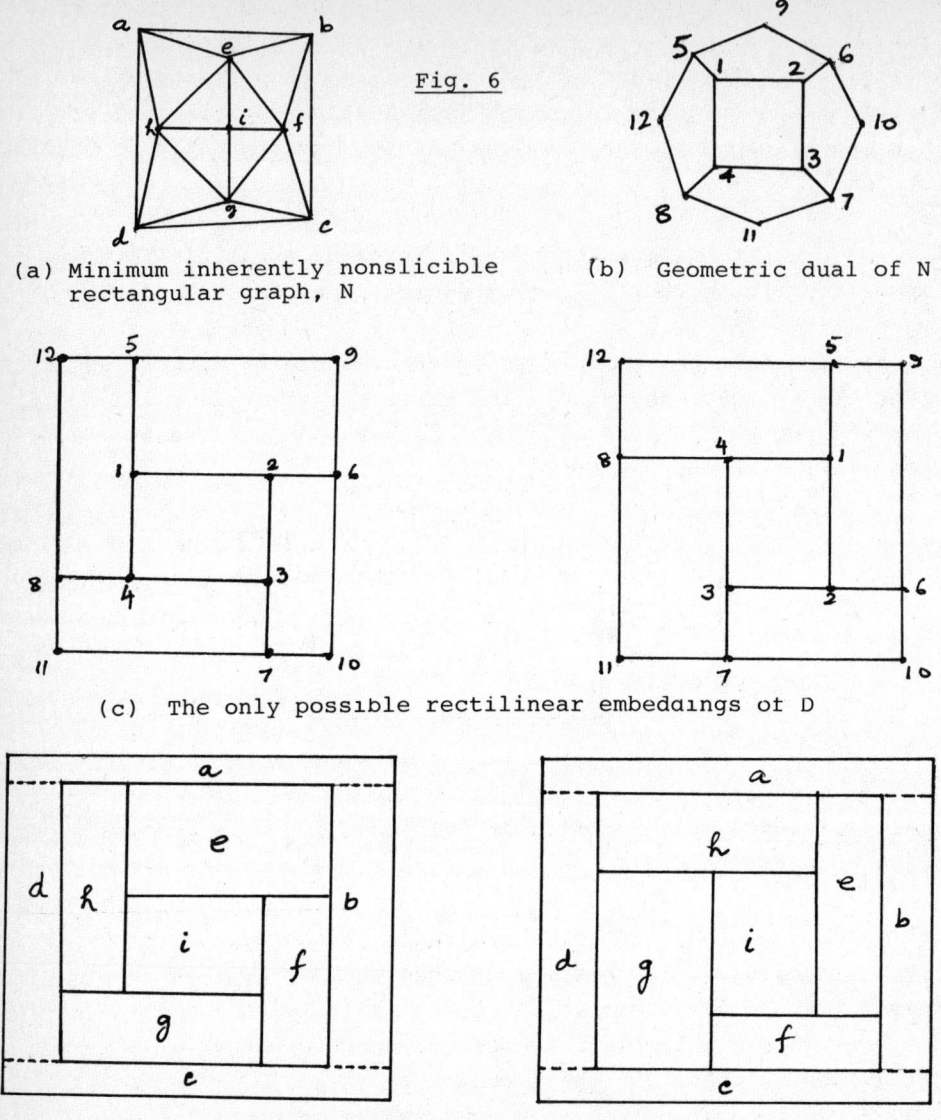

Fig. 6

(a) Minimum inherently nonslicible rectangular graph, N

(b) Geometric dual of N

(c) The only possible rectilinear embeddings of D

(d) Rectangular duals of N

The geometric dual of N, without a vertex for the exterior face, has 12 vertices, and 16 edges (Fig. 6b). It has an innermost cycle $I = \{1,2,3,4\}$, and an outermost cycle $O = \{5,9,6,10,7,11,8,12\}$; there are also four interior faces each bounded by five edges. In O, vertices 5,6,7,8 have degree 3 and the other four have degree 2. Since N is rectangular, this geometric dual is embeddable rectilinearly, i.e. an inner dual D exists. In D, all faces including O should appear as rectilinear polygons.

Let us consider the rectilinear embedding of the cycle O first. Note that all the degree 3 vertices on O have two neighbouring vertices on O and the third one is an internal vertex of D. If a degree 3 vertex on O is a corner in its rectilinear embedding, then it has to be a concave corner (Fig. 5). Similarly, if a degree 2 vertex on this cycle is a corner, then it can only be a convex corner. Since D has only four degree 2 vertices, all four must be convex corners. D has j = 4, so by the Lemma above $k = j - 4 = 0$. Therefore, none of the degree 3 vertices are corners and the embedding of O is a rectangle.

Finally, the cycle I having exactly four vertices must be embedded as a rectangle. This can be embedded in one of the two ways, since the sides of this rectangle must be parallel to those of the rectangle corresponding to O. If the four edges in the path {6,2,1,4,8} were all parallel forming a cut, then the cycle I with exactly four edges cannot be embedded as a rectangle because two of its adjacent edges are parallel. If the sequence of three edges (5,1),(1,4),(4,8) were all parallel, then the cycle {12,5,1,4,8} of 5 edges cannot be embedded as a rectangle. The only possible rectangular embeddings of D are shown in Fig. 6c.

For completeness sake, the rectangular dual or the floorplan has an enveloping rectangle in which this dual D, is placed rectilinearly and only T-junctions are allowed. Line segments from the four convex degree 2 corners of O are extended towards the enveloping rectangle. Each convex corner can be extended outwards only and in one of two ways. Hence, the resultant rectangular dual and the corresponding floorplan (Fig. 6d) for N is always nonslicible. QED

We define a **maximal rectangular graph (MRG)** as a rectangular graph to which no edge can be added without violating rectangularity. It can be shown easily that for all $n \geq 4$, a MRG of n vertices and $3n-7$ edges can be constructed such that it has exactly four edges in its exterior face. Note that a maximal planar graph of n vertices has $3n-6$ edges [Ha69]. The inherently nonslicible graph N, is a MRG of 9 vertices and 20 (= 3.9 - 7) edges. Incidentally, a MRG of n vertices is not unique. For all $n \geq 4$, there exists a MRG with $3n-7$ edges which has a slicible dual (Fig. 2a). Moreover, $3n-7$ is the maximum number of edges in a MRG of n vertices, because there are MRGs of n vertices with fewer edges, e.g. an n-wheel having $2n-2$ edges.

Theorem 2: N is a minimum (in the number of vertices and edges) inherently nonslicible rectangular graph.

Proof: By using Euler's theorem for planar graphs, a MRG of n vertices and $3n-7$ edges has $(3n-7) - n + 2 = 2n - 5$ faces. So, it has $2n-6$ interior faces, and all are triangles. Thus, its geometric inner dual has $2n - 6$ vertices.

To ensure nonslicibility, we need an arrangement of cuts similar to Fig. 4b as derived from the Slicibility Theorem. In the inner dual, this needs 8 vertices. Four more vertices are required for the corners of a rectangle enclosing this arrangement so that all other choices of orienting the edges in the interior faces are ruled out. This accounts for the necessity of a minimum of 12 vertices in the dual. From $2n-6 =12$, we get $n=9$. Hence 9 is the minimum number of vertices in any inherently nonslicible rectangular graph.

Let us assume that there is an inherently nonslicible rectangular graph of 9 vertices which has fewer than 20 edges. In that case, it will have fewer than $2.9-6 =12$ interior faces and so fewer than 12 vertices in the dual. But a dual with less than 12 vertices cannot be nonslicible. Therefore, a minimum inherently nonslicible rectangular graph must have 9 vertices and 20 edges. The graph N satisfies this. QED

Corollary: Any rectangular graph with 8 or fewer vertices has a slicible floorplan.

Conjecture: The minimum rectangular graph which is inherently nonslicible is unique.

This minimum inherently nonslicible graph N, is 4-chromatic. We investigated whether there is any link between inherent nonslicibility and the chromatic number of rectangular graphs. Since all planar graphs are 4-colorable, rectangular graphs being plane triangulated, must be either 3-chromatic or 4-chromatic. We could not however, find a 3-chromatic rectangular graph, which has no slicible dual. The converse is not true either, as there are many 4-chromatic, slicible rectangular graphs. One may hypothesize that the inherently nonslicible graphs are 4-chromatic.

5. Transforming Nonslicing to Slicing

In the VLSI design cycle, the floorplanning i.e., the rectangular dualization process from the given neighbourhood graph of modules, plays an important role. Algorithms such as [BS86] for constructing rectangular dual of a neighbourhood graph produce a dual, if it exists. While constructing the dual, no special attention is paid by the existing algorithms to find a slicible dual, even if it is possible to create one. In the automated design process, we can end up with a nonslicible floorplan either due to the indifference of the dual-construction algorithm or due to the fact that the rectangular graph specified as input was inherently nonslicible. This issue brings us to the question of transforming a nonslicible floorplan to a slicible one with as little sacrifice as possible.

5.1 Algorithm Overview

A floorplan is transformed by introducing a geometrical perturbation. Intuitively, if there is a module blocking a through cut, we alter its aspect ratio to extend the cut (channel) towards the boundary so that a proper slicing is obtained. We have adopted the notion of a perturbation being the rotation of a T-junction by a right angle. The two channels, which formed the base and the crosspiece of the T-junction, interchange their roles. The former crosspiece is shortened, i.e. one of its two arms is deleted, while the former base is extended. This is reflected as a change in the aspect ratios of some of the modules whose boundaries are part of the T-junction (Fig. 7).

The representation of the floorplan on which our algorithm is based, is the channel graph C described in Section 3. Any nonslicibility of the given floorplan is depicted as the existence of at least one directed 4-cycle in its channel graph. So, the goal is to transform a given channel graph with cycles (henceforth, by cycles we always mean directed 4-cycles) into an acyclic one in as few steps as possible and hence achieve fast convergence. A directed cycle can be broken by reversing the direction of one of its arcs. Each T-junction in the floorplan, except the ones on its boundary, is represented in C by an arc.

Let c and d denote the base and the crosspiece respectively of the T-junction which is rotated. In C, there is an arc from vertex c to vertex d.   Rotation of this T-junction causes c and d to interchange roles and therefore the arc in C is reversed from d to c. At the same time, while an outgoing arc from d is deleted, a new outgoing arc from c is inserted in C.   If there were other channels forming bases of T-junctions, with the arm of channel d which has been deleted as the common crosspiece, then the corresponding arcs to vertex d from each of the vertices corresponding to those channels are deleted from C. In the perturbed floorplan, those channels have to be extended to meet the nearest perpendicular channel.   New arcs corresponding to these new T-junctions formed are inserted.   Thus new cycles may be created, and   then new arcs inserted must appear in these new cycles. However, these new cycles must include the vertex c (Fig. 7d); in other words, no new cycle which is vertex disjoint with the cycles broken after rotating a T-junction, can be created.

Since C is a planar graph, any arc in it can occur in at most two cycles.   Reversal of an arc which is common to two cycles, destroys both cycles in one step. Furthermore, deletion of one or more arcs due to rotation of a T-junction, may break one or more additional cycles in which they appear. Several important properties of these cycles are summarised in the next Proposition.

<u>Proposition 1</u>:
(a) At most four cycles of a channel graph can share a vertex.

(b) All four cycles sharing a vertex of a channel graph can be broken by reversing a single arc, and exactly one new cycle is created.

(c) If three cycles share a vertex of a channel graph, then all three can be broken by reversing a single arc and at most one new cycle is created.

(d) By reversing a single arc of a cycle in a channel graph, at most two new cycles can be created.

(e) When one arm of d is deleted from the floorplan, no additional cycle is created in C solely due to extensions of those channels which formed bases of T-junctions with the deleted arm of d as a common crosspiece.

The proposition is illustrated in Figs. 7 - 9. The proof is simple, mainly based on planarity of C and that the outdegree of any vertex is at most 2. The details are omitted due to space limitations.

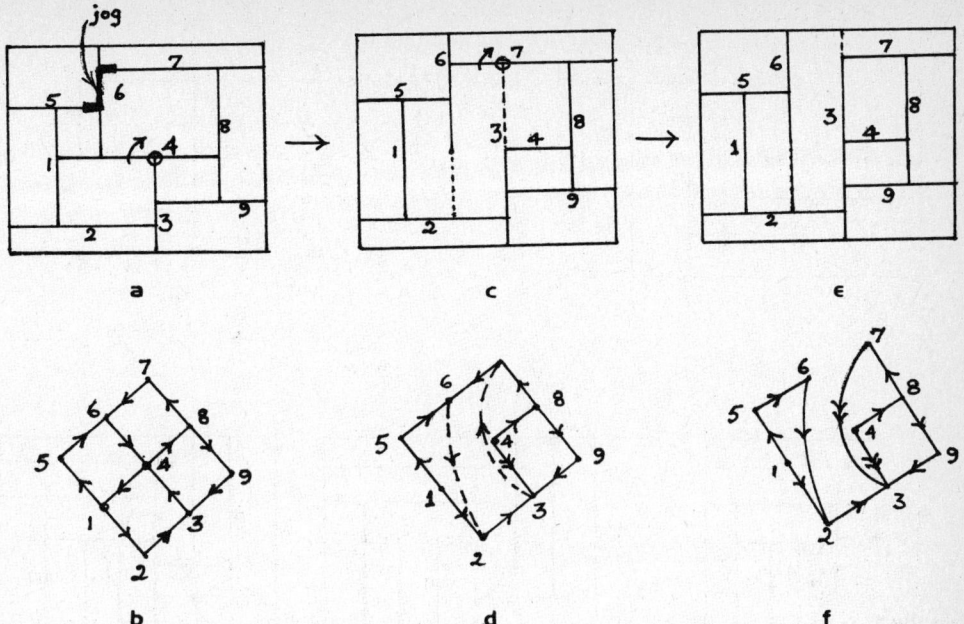

Fig. 7 Illustration of Proposition 1(b) [Floorplans and corresponding channel graphs]

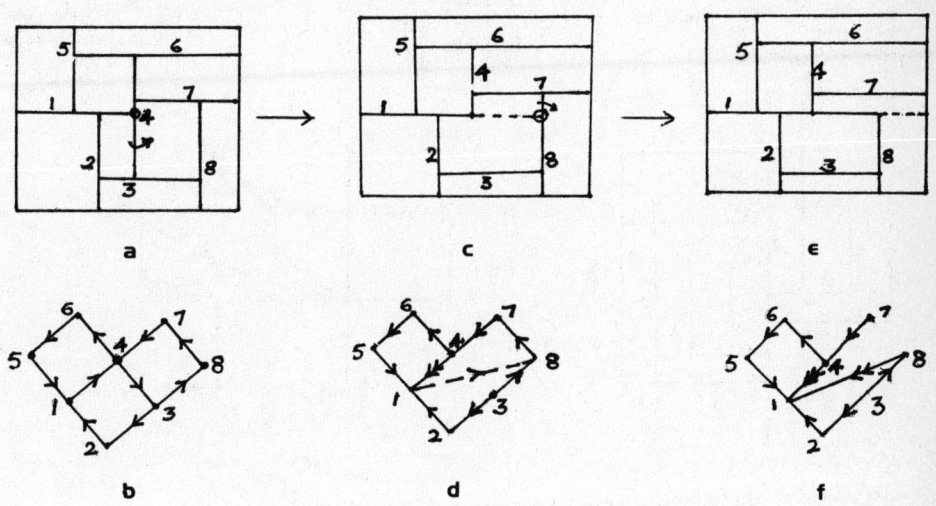

Fig. 8 Illustration of Proposition 1(c)

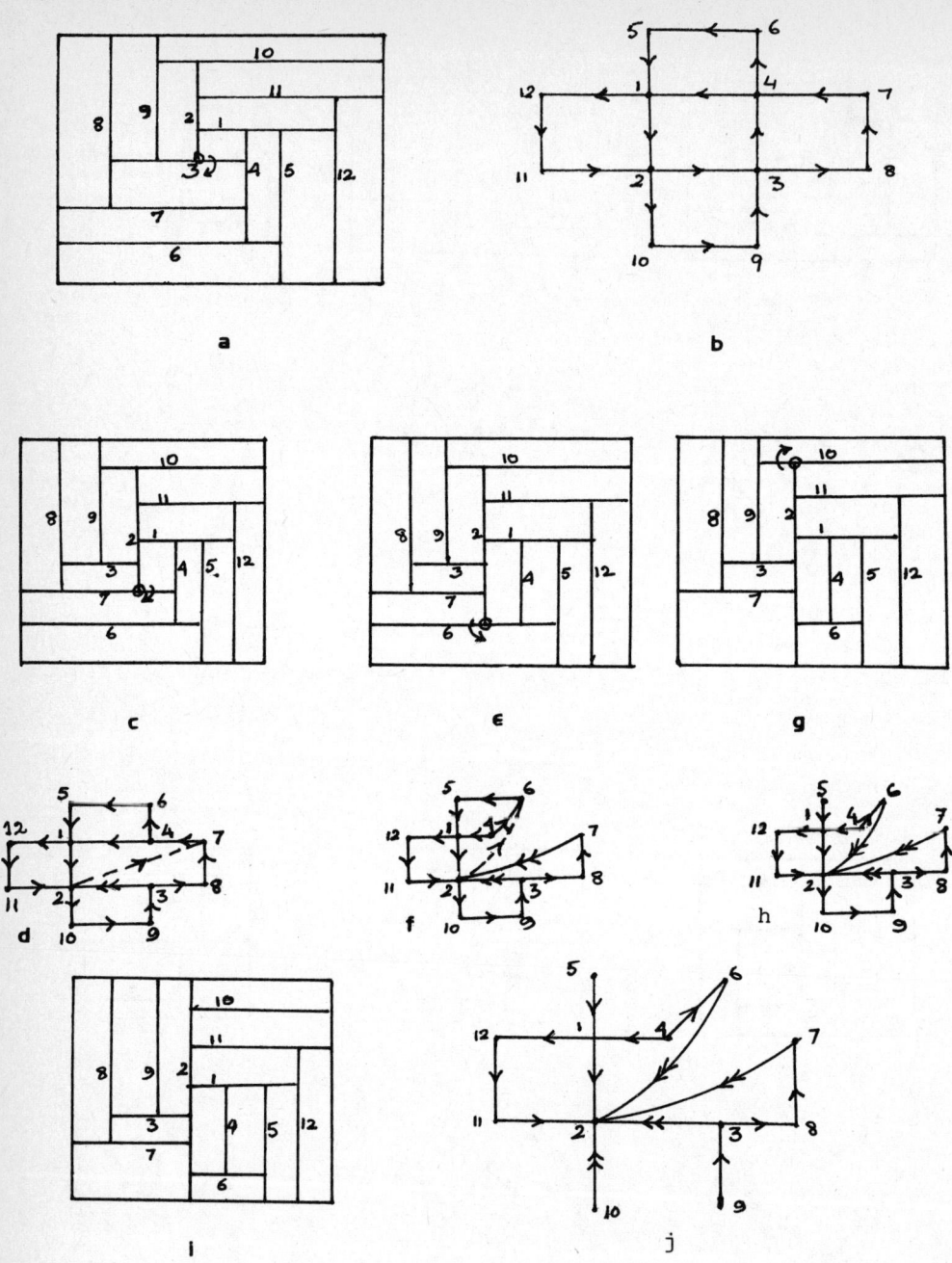

Fig. 9   Illustration of Proposition 1(d)

To each arc appearing in a cycle in the channel graph, we can associate a figure-of-merit called **gain**, which is defined as follows:

Gain due to an arc reversal = (# cycles broken) - (# new cycles created).

By Proposition 1(a), 1(b) and 1(d), the maximum value of the gain is +3 and the minimum gain is -1. This gain function guides the choice of the arc to be reversed. At any stage of the algorithm, a vertex v which occurs in maximum number of cycles is chosen, and the arc with one end at this vertex and whose reversal maximises the gain, is chosen. All the cycles containing v are thus broken and then another cluster of cycles around another vertex is processed. An implicit decision is involved in the rotation, namely which of the two arms of the crosspiece of the T-junction under consideration is to be deleted (Fig. 7a). If the value of gain for an arc is the same with deletion of either arm, then the rule of thumb is to delete the arm which forms crosspieces of fewer T-junctions. The rationale behind this is that the shapes of fewer modules are altered.

A T-junction which has been rotated once, is not rotated again later on. This prevents oscillations in the algorithm and ensures termination. Once the arc to be reversed has been decided upon, the database for the floorplan is updated to reflect the rotation of the corresponding T-junction.

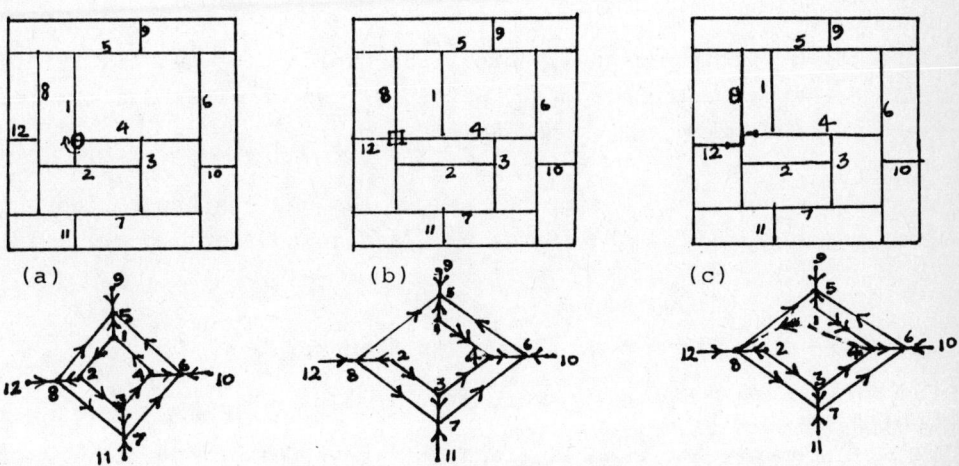

Fig. 10   Handling cross junctions created

There is yet another issue to be handled. After rotating a T-junction, the extending channel c will intersect a perpendicular cut, thereby forming a new T-junction. If this new junction happens to abut with an existing one to form a cross junction, then we deliberately introduce a skew between the two junctions and retain both of them. Formation of such cross junctions (Fig. 10) has to be detected by referring to the coordinates of the T-junctions in question. No additional cycles can be created due to skew.

5.2 Algorithm Description

Algorithm: NONSLICING-TO-SLICING
Input: A nonslicing floorplan and its channel graph $C = (V,A)$.
Output: A slicing floorplan with near-minimum number of T-junctions altered.
Method:

Step 1 Initialise by unmarking all arcs in C. For all v in V, find all directed 4-cycles in C containing v and set cyc-list(v) to this list of cycles; put v in bucket B_m and set $B(v)$ to m, where m is the size of its cyc-list. (By Proposition 1(a), m can be 1, 2, 3 or 4). Set m ← 4.

Step 2 If B_m is empty, then go to Step 5, else pick any vertex v from it.

Step 3 Using Proposition 1, break the cycles in cyc-list(v) by reversing that incoming arc of v, say (u,v), which gives maximum gain. In case of ties, choose any one. ROTATE(u,v).

Step 4 If there are one or two new cycles containing u (not in present cyc-list(u)), then set v ← u and go to Step 3, else go to Step 2.

Step 5 m ← m-1. If m > 0, then go to Step 2, else Stop.

Algorithm: ROTATE(t,h)
Input: Floorplan, its channel graph and arc (t,h).
Output: Updated floorplan and its channel graph.
Method:
Update floorplan after rotation of corresponding T-junction. Update

C, i.e. reverse arc (t,h) and delete and insert arcs accordingly. Mark reversed arc (h,t). For all vertices w which shared one or more cycles with h, delete the cycles shared with h from cyc-list(w). Depending on new size of cyc-list(w), move w to appropriate bucket and update B(w). Clear cyc-list(h). Detect cross-junctions created in floorplan after the rotation of T-junction corresponding to arc (u,v). If any, introduce skew in floorplan.

5.3 Complexity

If a floorplan has n modules, then the number of channels is n-1. In the worst case, its channel graph has O(n) cycles. The minimum gain of any arc in a cycle is -1; once this occurs, it is monotonically non-decreasing due to the greedy approach of choosing the arc with maximum gain each time. This implies that at worst the number of cycles can double. Searching for all directed 4-cycles passing through a particular vertex in C (where maximum outdegree is 2), requires constant time using breadth-first. Gain is computed using Proposition-1 and it takes constant time. The routine ROTATE does local updating around a T-junction and is again a constant time operation. Finally, any T-junction is not rotated more than once. Thus with efficient data structures, each of the steps takes constant time and there are O(n) iterations. Therefore, the algorithm terminates in linear time. The correctness is ensured by the absence of any cycles in the channnel graph at termination.

This algorithm cannot guarantee minimality of the number of T-junctions rotated. At the initialisation step, we have a planar digraph with a number of directed cycles. The problem of finding a minimum set of arcs covering all its cycles is an instance of Feedback Arc Set Problem [GJ79] and is solvable in polynomial time. But our problem is an adaptive, hence more complicated, because breaking one cycle affects other cycles, as well as creates new cycles. Next, the problem of finding a minimum subset of vertices covering all cycles in the planar channel digraph is an instance of Feedback Vertex Set Problem. This is NP-complete in general [GJ79], but there is no known proof of NP-completeness for this special case. Moreover, the gain heuristic does not capture the globally best possible choice at each step.

6. Conclusions

We introduced the notion of inherent nonslicibility of rectangular duals in this paper. Layout designers keep interconnection patterns in mind while specifying the topological neighbourhood relation for functional modules. But these specifications might inadvertently incur inherent nonslicibility, which might lead to inefficiencies associated with a nonslicible floorplan. We presented a minimum inherently nonslicible rectangular graph. Currently, we are working on the necessary and sufficient conditions for inherently nonslicible rectangular graphs, which will thereby lead to a recognition algorithm. This will be accompanied with a dual construction algorithm which guarantees a slicible dual, if one exists.

Given a nonslicible floorplan, our linear-time algorithm transforms it to a slicible floorplan with changes in shapes of some modules. Since the heuristic does not assure minimality, an improved version is being developed. The idea is to straighten any jog (as in Fig. 7a) on a cut for which the corresponding vertex in the channel graph appears in directed 4-cycles, and then the algorithm proposed here is run. In practice, a range of areas and a range of aspect ratios are specified for each module. The algorithm described in this paper does not consider this. The improved version will take this into account.

Acknowledgement: The authors would like to thank the anonymous referees for their constructive comments. One of the authors (B.B.B.) is grateful to Professors S. C. Seth and J. S. Deogun of the University of Nebraska-Lincoln, USA for many helpful discussions.

References:

[BS86] Bhasker, J. & S. Sahni, "A Linear Algorithm to find a Rectangular Dual of a Planar Triangulated Graph," Proc. 23rd Design Automation Conference, June 1986, pp. 108-114.

[BS87] Bhasker, J. & S.Sahni, "A Linear Time Algorithm to Check for the Existence of a Rectangular Dual of a Planar Triangulated Graph," Networks, Vol. 17, 1987, pp. 307-317.

[DK86] Dai, W.M. & E.S. Kuh, "Hierarchical Floor Planning for Building Block Layout," Proc. ICCAD, 1986, pp.454-457.

[Ha69] Harary, F., Graph Theory, Addison-Wesley Publishing Co., Reading, 1969.

[HSM82] Heller, W. R., G. Sorkin & K. Maling, "The Planar Package

Planner for System Designers," Proc. 19th Design Automation Conference, 1982, pp.253-260.

[HK86] Hu, T.C., & E.S. Kuh, "Thoery and Concepts of Circuit Layout," Theory and Design of VLSI Layout, IEEE Press, 1986, pp. 3-18.

[GJ79] Garey, M. R. & D. S. Johnson, Computers and Intractability: A Guide to the Theory of NP-completeness, W.H. Freeman & Co., 1979.

[KK84] Kozminski, K. & E. Kinnen, "An Algorithm for Finding a Rectangular Dual of a Planar Graph for Use in Area Planning for VLSI Integrated Circuits," Proc. 21st Design Automation Conference, June 1984, pp. 655-656.

[KK85] Kozminski, K. & E. Kinnen, "Rectangular Dual of Planar Graphs," Networks, Vol. 15, No. 2, 1985, pp. 145-157.

[La80] LaPaugh, A.S., "Algorithms for Integrated Circuit Layout: An Analytic Approach," Ph.D. Thesis, M.I.T., 1980.

[LL84] Leinwand, S. M., & Y.T. Lai, "An Algorithm for building Rectangular Floor-plans," Proc. 21st Design Automation Conference, 1984, pp. 663-664.

[LSW87] Luk, W. K., P. Sipala & C.K. Wong, "Minimum-area Wiring for Slicing Structures," IEEE Trans. on Computers, Vol. C-36, No.6, June 1987, pp. 745-760.

[Ot82a] Otten, R.H.J.M., "Automatic Floorplan Design," Proc. 19th Design Automation Conference, 1982, pp. 261-267.

[Ot82b] Otten, R.H.J.M., "Layout Structures," Proc. Large Scale Systems Symp. (IEEE), 1982, pp. 349-353.

[Ot83] Otten, R.H.J.M., "Efficient Floorplan Optimization," Proc. ICCD, 1983, pp. 499-502.

[OHM85] Ousterhout, J., G. Hamachi, R. Mayo, W.Scott & G. Taylor, "The MAGIC VLSI Layout System," IEEE Design and Test, Feb. 1985.

[Ri82] Rivest, R.L.,"The PI (Placement and Interconnect) System," Proc. 19th Design Automation Conference, June 1982, pp. 475-481.

[St83] Stockmeyer, L.J., "Optimal Orientations of Cells in Slicing Floorplan designs," Information and Control, Vol. 57, 1983, pp. 91-101.

[SS83] Supowit, K.J. & E.F. Slutz, "Placement Algorithms for Custom VLSI," Proc. 20th Design Automation Conference, June 1983, pp. 164-170.

[TKS86] Tsukiyama, S., K. Koike & I. Shirakawa, "An Algorithm to eliminate All Complex Triangles in a Maximal Planar Graph for use in VLSI Floor-plan," Proc. Intl. Symposium on Circuits and Systems (IEEE), 1986, pp. 321-324.

[WL86] Wong, D.F. & C.L. Liu, "A New Algorithm for Floorplan Design," Proc. 23rd Design Automation Conference, June 1986, pp. 101-107.

PATH PLANNING WITH LOCAL INFORMATION

Amitava Datta and Kamala Krithivasan,
Department of Computer Science and Engineering,
Indian Institute of Technology, Madras - 600 036, India.

ABSTRACT

We consider the problem of path-planning for a point mobile automaton in the presence of unknown obstacles in a two dimensional space. We present an algorithm which has better worst case complexity than that of Lumelsky and Stepanov [4], which is the best known at present.

1. INTRODUCTION

Recently there is lot of interest in finding the path in which an object can move in the presence of obstacles. The current research on robot path planning can be classified into two basic classes depending on which of the following models is being used. In the first model, called path planning with complete information (popular term is 'the piano movers problem'), perfect information about the obstacles is assumed [5,6]. Because full information is assumed, the whole operation of path planning is a one-time, off-line operation. In the second model, called path planning with incomplete information, an element of uncertainty about the environment is present. The moving object has only some local information. The attraction of the model of path planning with incomplete information is in the possibility of naturally introducing a powerful notion of feedback control and thus transforming the operation of path planning into a continuous on-line process.

Works related to the second model have primarily come from

studies on autonomous vehicle navigation [2,3,7] and maze search problems [1]. One problem about this model is that, because of the dynamic character of the incoming information, the path cannot be pre-planned. So, we cannot expect to get globally optimal solutions. The performance of the algorithm has to be evaluated by comparing with other existing or theoretically feasible algorithms, or how optimal they are locally or how resonable they look from human traveller standpoint.

In [4], the authors consider a mobile automaton moving in a two dimensional plane. Every time the automaton encounters an obstacle, it can turn only left or right along the obstacle boundary. The main goal of that work was to design provable robot path planning algorithms and to minimize the resources of the automaton. They have presented two algorithms and a third which is a combination of the first two and discussed their complexity.

In this paper we improve upon their algorithms. We present an algorithm which has the same average complexity as the best achieved by theirs but a much better worst case complexity. The only additional information we assume is that the automaton has one register to sense its direction. When it reaches a point on the obstacle boundary, it can decide whether it reached there from left or right or from outside the obstacle boundary.

In the next section, we present the model of computation and some definitions. In section 3, we briefly review the algorithms of Lumelsky and Stepanov [4]. In section 4, we present our algorithm, proving its correctness and discussing the complexity. The paper ends with a concluding remark in section 5.

2. BASIC DEFINITIONS

The model considered in this paper consists of two parts - the environment and the automaton.

ENVIRONMENT : The environment is a plane with obstacles and the two points Start(S) and Target(T) in it. Each obstacle is a closed curve of finite length, such that, a straight line intersects an obstacle at a finite number of points. Obstacles do not touch each other. So, a point on an obstacle belongs to that obstacle only. Number of obstacles is locally finite. This means that a disc of finite radius intersects a finite number of obstacles. The set of obstacles is not necessarily finite.

AUTOMATON : The mobile automaton (MA) is a point. So, it can pass through an opening of any size. The only information available to MA is (1) its current coordinates, (2) the coordinates of the target and (3) the fact of contacting an obstacle. So, the direction and the distance of the target is always known. The automaton has a sense of direction. At a point on an obstacle boundary, it can distinguish between left and right direction. When it reaches a point on an obstacle, it can decide whether it came from left or right or from outside the obstacle boundary. The memory and computing capabilities of the automaton is limited. It has a few words of memory and a few registers. MA can perform three actions, move towards the target along the straight line (Start,Target), move around an obstacle and stop.

DEFINITIONS : While moving along the straight line (Start,Target) and towards the target, MA defines a *hit point* when it hits an obstacle at a point H^i. While moving along an obstacle boundary, MA defines a *leave point* when it meets the line (Start,Target) at a point L^i and the line (L^i,Target) does not cross the obstacle boundary at L^i. When the line (Start,Target) touches an obstacle tangentially, no hit or leave point is registered. Starting from a hit point, MA may traverse the obstacle boundary towards left or right, depending upon certain conditions. A scene is called an *in-position* scene, if (1) either the Start or the Target or both are inside the convex hull of an obstacle and (2) if the line (Start,Target) crosses an obstacle boundary at least once. In an *out-position* scene, neither the Start nor the Target is inside the convex hull of an obstacle.

The following terms and notations are used :
D is the Eucledian distance from the start to the target. d(A,B) is the distance between any two points A and B. d(Start,Target) = D. d(A,Target) is written in short as d(A).
P is the total length of the path generated by MA in its walk from the Start to the Target.
p_i is the perimeter of the ith obstacle met by MA.

3. EARLIER WORK

In this section, we briefly discuss the algorithms in [4]. Due to the unpredictable nature of the obstacles, they have introduced the notion of path length as a measure of complexity of such algorithms. The model presented in [4] is the one used for the present work and has been discussed in the previous section. The only difference in our model is that, the local direction of traversal may change depending on certain conditions. But, in the model presented in [4], the local direction of traversal is fixed and always it is either right or left. They have given a lower bound and three algorithms for the path planning problem. These are discussed below. For proof and details of the algorithms, the reader is referred to [4].

The lower bound : For any path-planning problem satisfying the assumptions of the model, any (however large) $P > 0$, any (however small) $D > 0$, and any (however small) $d > 0$, there exists a scene for which the algorithm will generate a path of length P, and
$$P > D + \sum_i p_i - d,$$
where D is the distance between the points Start and Target, and p_i are the perimeters of the obstacles intersecting the disc of radius D centered at the target.

The first algorithm (Bug1) : While executing this algorithm, the point mobile automaton (MA) takes a cautious approach. During its walk from the point Start towards Target, it may hit some obstacle O_i. It registers a hit point H^i and goes completely around the obstacle along its boundary once. At each point on the obstacle boundary, MA calculates the distance of the target and stores the minimum distance. When it comes back to H^i, it goes back to the point of minimum distance (P) on the obstacle boundary and either takes off along the line (P,Target) or stops if the target is unreachable. The average and worst case behaviour of the algorithm is same. The length of the generated path will never exceed the limit
$$P = D + 1.5 \sum_i p_i.$$
Where p_i refers to the perimeters of the obstacles intersecting the disc of radius D centered at the target.

The second algorithm (Bug2): Under Bug2, whenever MA hits an obstacle, it takes a prespecified local direction and moves along the obstacle boundary. Whenever it reaches a point P on the obstacle such that P lies on the line (Start,Target) and the line (P,Target) does not cross the obstacle boundary at the point P, it takes off along the line (Start,Target). When all the obstacles are convex, the path produced by MA in the worst case is : $P = D + \sum_i p_i$ and on the average $P = D + 0.5 \sum_i p_i$,

where D is the distance (Start,Target) and p_i refers to the perimeters of the obstacles intersecting the line (Start,Target). But for arbitrary obstacles, the performance of Bug2 may be much worse. For in-position scenes, it can generate a path as large as $P = D + \sum_i (n_i p_i / 2)$, where n_i is the number of intersections between the straight line (Start,Target) and the ith obstacle.

The third algorithm (Bug M1) : This is a combination of the two previous algorithms. For convex obstacles, it takes the approach of Bug2 and whenever there is a chance of multiple local cycles, it switches over to Bug1 and takes a cautious approach. Under this algorithm, MA may cross a particular point on an obstacle boundary at most thrice. So, the path generated will not exceed the limit:
$$P = D + 3 \sum_i p_i.$$

4. THE ALGORITHM

The algorithm is executed at any point of a continuous path executed by the automaton. The goal is to generate a path from Start to Target. In the process of doing so, the automaton either reaches the point Target or declares it as unreachable. MA can meet the same obstacle more than once and it cannot distinguish an obstacle from another. The index j is used to indicate the jth occurance of a hit or a leave point. The point Start is the 0th leave point L^0. A pair of consecutive hit and leave points will have the same index(H^j, L^j). There are three registers: R_H, R_{dir} and R_L. R_H is used to store the current hit point. R_{dir} stores the current direction of traversal of the obstacle boundary as decided by the automaton. The content of R_{dir} can be left or right. If the automaton meets the straight line (Start,Target) at a point P outside the interval (Start,Target) and on the same side of the point Start, the coordinates of the furthest (from Start) such point P is stored in the register R_L.
The Algorithm is described in the following steps:

1. From the point L^{j-1}, move along the straight line (Start,Target) until one of the following occurs:
   a. The target is reached. The procedure stops.
   b. An obstacle is encountered and a hit point H^j is defined. Set, $R_H = H^j$ and R_{dir} = left. Goto step 2.
2. Follow the obstacle boundary in the direction specified in R_{dir} until one of the following occurs:
   a. The target is reached, the procedure stops.
   b. The line (Start,Target) is met at a point Q such that $d(Q) < d(H^j)$ and the line (Q,Target) does not cross the current obstacle at the point Q. Define the leave point $L^j = Q$. $j=j+1$. Goto step 1.
   c. The line (Start,Target) is met at a point Q such that $d(Q) > d(H^j)$ and the line (Q,Target) does not cross the current obstacle at the point Q. Two cases may arise :
      i. R_{dir} = left. If $d(Q) > d(Start)$ and $d(Q,Start) > d(R_L,Start)$, set $R_L = Q$. Goto step 3.
      ii. R_{dir} = right. Goto step 4.
   d. The point H^j is reached from the right side. The target is unreachable. The procedure stops.
3. Follow the line (Q,Target). Two cases may arise:
   a. The obstacle boundary is met at a point P such that, $d(P) > d(H^j)$. Goto step 2.
   b. The obstacle boundary is met at the point H^j. Set R_{dir} = right. Goto step 2.
4. Follow the obstacle boundary in the direction specified in R_{dir}, until one of the following occurs:
   a. The line (Start,Target) is met at a point Q outside the interval (Start,Target). Two cases may arise:
      i. $R_L = Q$. The target is unreachable.
      ii. R_L is not equal to Q. Goto step 2.
   b. The line (Start,Target) is met at a point Q such that $d(Q) < d(H^j)$. Goto step 1.
   c. The target is reached. The procedure stops.

Characteristics of the algorithm

Lemma 1. MA meets only a finite number of obstacles on its way to the target.

Proof : The straight line segments of the path executed by MA are the lines connecting a leave point L^{j-1} and the next hit point H^j. These line segments are always within a circle of radius D (the distance between Start and Target). This follows from step 2.b. of the algorithm, i,e. $d(L^j) < d(H^j) < d(L^{j-1})$.... A circle of radius D can intersect only a finite number of obstacles and so, the lemma follows.

Corollary : The only obstacles met by MA are those which intersect the straight line (Start,Target).

The above lemma ensures the convergence of the algorithm.

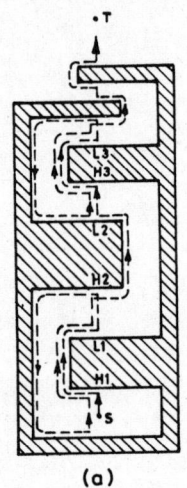 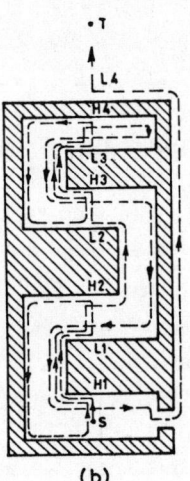

Figure 1. (a) Path of the automaton for an in-position scene. (b) Possible worst case path for an in-position scene.

Lemma 2. For a particular hit point H^j, it can be reached from outside the obstacle surface for a second time (i,e. step 3b.) and $R_H = H^j$, only if H^j is inside the convex hull of the obstacle (Figure 1a).

Proof : For convex obstacles, the proof is trivial. The path from Start to Target can never come back to a hit point before registering a leave point. Since the obstacles do not touch each other, $d(H^i) > d(L^i) > d(H^{i+1}) > \ldots$. So, once the automaton leaves the ith obstacle, it cannot come back to it.

For arbitrary obstacles, suppose a hit point H^j is outside the convex hull of an obstacle O_j. So, there is no point P on this obstacle such that, P lies on the line (Start,Target) and the line joining H^j and P does not intersect the obstacle boundary. So, if the path hits the point H^j for a second time from outside the obstacle surface, it should come from some other obstacle O_j. The automaton must have registered a leave point L^k and corresponding hit point H^k on the obstacle O_j. So, $R_H = H^k$.

Corollary : For a hit point H^j outside the convex hull of an obstacle, it can be reached for a second time only from its right side (step 2d.) and R_{dir} will never be set to right.

Lemma 3. After registering a hit point and while traversing an obstacle, the automaton can meet the line (Start,Target) outside the interval (Start,Target) and nearer to the point Start, if Start is within the convex hull of the same obstacle.

Proof : The obstacle should have two points on the line (Start,Target) and the point Start should be in between them. Hence Start is within the convex hull of the obstacle.

Lemma 4. When the automaton traverses in the right direction from a hit point H^j (step 4), it does not retrace the path previously traversed, except for the path segments between two consecutive hit and leave points ($H^i L^i$).

Proof : From steps 2c and 3, it is clear that, during left traversal, the automaton does not cross over to the right side of the line (Start,Target).

The automaton encounters the condition of this lemma if H^j is within the convex hull of the obstacle(from lemma 2). So, during the right traversal, the automaton may cross the line (Start,Target) several times. Whenever it reaches a leave point(L^i), it traverses the line segment $L^i H^i$ and turns right from the point H^i. When it reaches a point P on the line (Start,Target) outside the interval (Start,Target) and nearer to Start and $R_L = P$, it declares that target is unreachable (step 4a). So, the only common path segments between left and right traversal are the line segments between consecutive hit and leave points.

Lemma 5 : While traversing left, when the automaton registers a hit point, it can come back to it only once more.

Proof : The automaton can reach a hit point H^j either from the right or from outside the obstacle boundary. It cannot reach a point from left during left traversal. If it reaches the point from the right, the algorithm stops (step 2d) (Figure 2b). According to lemma 2, it can reach H^j from outside the obstacle boundary if H^j is within the convex hull of the obstacle. Suppose, MA reaches H^j for the second time during left traversal from some other hit point H^k which is the current hit point, that is, $R_H = H^k$. Now, it will retrace the path from H^j and ultimately reach H^k from outside the obstacle surface. So, right traversal will start from H^k. In its right traversal, MA may register a new leave point L^k, otherwise it is trapped. The path from H^k to L^k goes along the obstacle boundary. Consider some other hit point H^l such that $d(H^l) < d(L^k)$. During left traversal from H^l, MA will reach the point L^k before H^k. From L^k, it will take off along the line (L^k,Target). So, it will not reach H^k. If MA has to reach H^i during some left traversal, it has to go through H^k. Hence, H^i can be reached at most twice during left traversal.

Corollary 1. During left traversal of an obstacle, the path segments between consecutive hit and leave points and the straight line segments of the line (Start,Target) may be traversed at most twice. All other parts of the obstacle boundary on the left side of the line (Start,Target) are traversed only once.

Corollary 2. MA divides the obstacle boundary on the left side of the line (Start,Target) in disjoint parts (Figure 1b).

Tests for target reachability :

The automaton detects that the target is unreachable in two places in the algorithm, step 2.d and 4.a.i.

Step 2.d : Starting from the hit point H^j and continuing in its left traversal, it comes back to H^j from the right without registering another leave point L^j. This means that the automaton cannot take off from the obstacle towards the target. The target is trapped inside the obstacle. So, the target is unreachable (Figure 2b).

Step 4.a.i : Starting from the hit point H^j and continuing in its right traversal, it meets the line (Start,Target) outside the interval (Start,Target) and nearer to Start. Let this point be P and R_L = P. This situation occurs when Start is within the convex hull of the obstacle. At this point, the automaton decides that the target is unreachable, because the start point is trapped.

Suppose the automaton continues in its right traversal across the line (Start,Target). Since, the obstacles do not touch each other and the line (Start,Target) intersects the obstacle at a finite number of points, there are two possibilities:

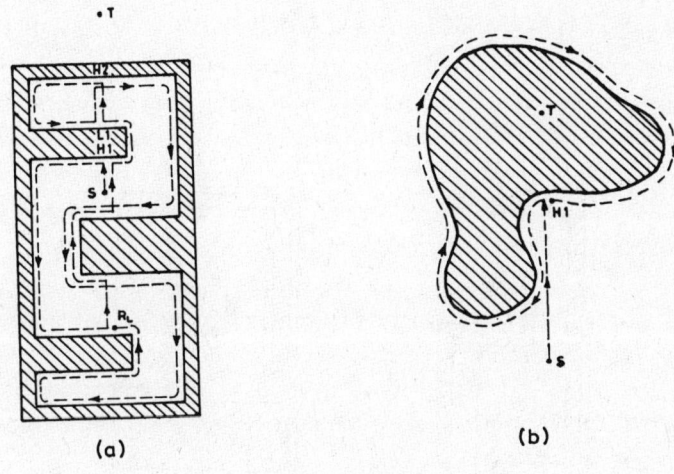

Figure 2. (a) Path of the automaton when the source is trapped. R_L is the point upto which the automaton goes during right traversal.
(b) Path of the automaton when the target is trapped.

Case 1. The automaton in its right traversal meets the line (Start,Target) at a point H^k and $d(H^k) < d(Start)$. The point H^k was a hit point in the left traversal of the automaton. So, in its left traversal, the automaton has explored the obstacle surface between H^k and P and there was no escape point. Otherwise, it would have escaped from the inside in the left traversal itself and the present situation would never occur.

Case 2. The automaton meets the line (Start,Target) at a point Q such that, d(Q) > d(Start). This means that the automaton has escaped from the inside. So, there is an opening in the obstacle boundary and it goes along the point Y. Consider the point just opposite Y, i,e. X. Starting from X if we go along the inside of the obstacle, we will reach at some point H^k which is a previous hit point. So, in its left traversal, it has explored the left side from H^k. If there was such an opening, it would have escaped in the left traversal itself. Hence, this case cannot occur.

So, without continuing its right traversal, the automaton decides that the target is unreachable (Figure 2a).

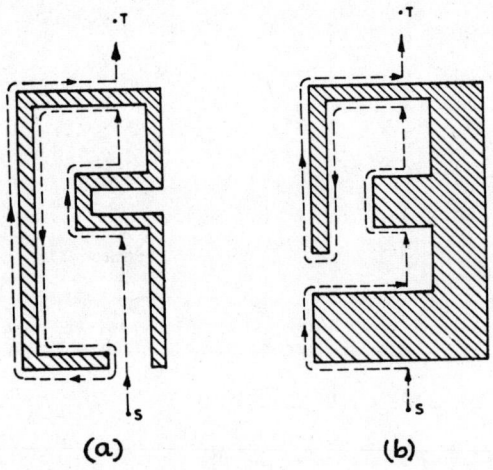

Figure 3. Paths of the automaton in case of out-position scenes.

Theorem 1. MA does not pass any point of an obstacle boundary more than once for out-position scenes.

Proof: From lemma 4 and lemma 5, it is clear that the only path segments on the obstacle boundary MA can traverse more than once are those between consecutive hit and leave points (H^iL^i). We prove that, for out-position scenes, such repeated traversal is not possible.

A hit point H^j can be reached for a second time either from outside the obstacle boundary in the left traversal or during right traversal. Moreover, the hit point should be inside the convex hull of the obstacle (lemma 2). Consider an obstacle O_i. MA can register a hit point inside the convex hull of O_i in two ways. In the first case, it may directly hit a point H^i within O_i (Figure 3a). H^i is the first hit point on the path of MA on the obstacle O_i. There is a chance of multiple traversal, if MA reaches a point L^j on the line (Start,Target) within O_i such that $d(L^j) > d(H^i)$ or it reaches a point on (Start,Target) outside the interval (Start,Target). The second case is possible only for an in- position case (lemma 3). So, we do not consider this possibility. Suppose it reaches a point L^j such that $d(L^j) > d(H^i)$. Then, there is a corresponding hit point for L^j, i,e. H^j. MA would have reached H^j before reaching H^i. But we have assumed that H^i is the first hit point within O_i. A contradiction arises and MA cannot reach a point L^j on the line (Start,Target) within O_i such that $d(L^j) > d(H^i)$.

In the second case, MA may hit a point outside the convex hull of O_i and go inside O_i during left traversal (Figure 3b). So, there is an opening along the left semiplane of the obstacle boundary through which MA goes inside (the line (Start,Target) divides O_i in two half planes). Again, MA will register some leave point L^i and the corresponding hit point H^{i+1} inside O_i. MA cannot come back to some other point L^k due to the previous argument. Suppose, MA comes back to L^i during left traversal. Then, there is no opening along the obstacle boundary between H^{i+1} and L^i on the left side of the line (Start,Target). This is again a contradiction. Since, MA came inside O_i through such an opening.

Corollary : If all the obstacles in the scene are convex, there cannot be any in-position scene and in the worst case,
the path generated by MA is $P = D + \sum_i p_i$. Where p_i are the perimeters of the obstacles intersecting the line (Start,Target). This is actually the lower limit mentioned in [4]. On the average,
$$P = D + 0.5 \sum_i p_i.$$
For a random distribution of convex obstacles, MA will traverse only half of the obstacle boundaries on the average.

Theorem 2. The length of the path generated by MA never exceeds the limit (for an in-position scene) :
$$P = D + \sum_i p_i + \sum_i d_i + 2 \sum_i H^i L^i.$$

Where, D is the distance (Start,Target), p_i are the perimeters of the obstacles intersecting the straight line (Start,Target), d_i are the staright line segments of the line (Start,Target) within an obstacle between a leave point L^i and the next hit point H^{i+1}. And $H^i L^i$ are the obstacle boundaries between a hit point and the corresponding leave point within an obstacle.

Proof : From Theorem 1, multiple traversal of path may happen for in-position scenes only. From lemma 5, $H^i L^i$ and d_i can be traversed at most twice during left traversal. From lemma 4, $H^i L^i$ can be traversed at most once during right traversal. All other parts of the obstacle boundary are traversed at most once. One $H^i L^i$ is absorbed in perimeter p_i and similarly, one d_i is absorbed in D. So, we are left with :
$$P = D + \sum_i p_i + \sum_i d_i + 2 \sum_i H^i L^i.$$

The segments of obstacle boundaries denoted as $\sum_i H^i L^i$, are always less than $\sum_i p_i$. Since $H^i L^i$ are only parts of the perimeter of an obstacle. Consider the line segments d_i. For a particular d_i, there is a path between the end points of d_i along the obstacle boundary and the length of this path is greater than d_i. So, in all,
$$\sum_i d_i + 2\sum_i H^i L^i < 2 \sum_i p_i.$$
Though the exact differnce between $\sum_i d_i + 2 \sum_i H^i L^i$ and $2 \sum_i p_i$ will vary from case to case, in many cases $\sum_i d_i + 2 \sum_i H^i L^i$ will be only a fraction of $2 \sum_i p_i$. So, the total path generated is much less than $D + 3 \sum_i p_i$ in most cases.

5. CONCLUSION

The introduction of some extra capability in the automaton, namely the sense of direction, improves the performance of the path planning algorithms. It will be interesting to see whether within the same model we can improve the performance still further. The path planning problem in presence of three dimensional obstacles is little studied. It is not known whether the same concepts are applicable in the three dimensional case as well. We are presently trying to investigate along these directions.

REFERENCES

1. H. Abelson and A. diSessa, Turtle Geometry, MIT Press, Cambridge, MA, 1980.
2. B. Bullock, D.Keirsey, J.Mitchell, T. Nussmeier, and D. Tseng, Autonomous Vehicle Control: an overview of the Hughes project, Proceedings of the IEEE Computer Society Conference "Trends and Applications, 1983: Automating Intelligent Behaviour", Gaithersburg, MD, 1983.
3. D.M. Kersey, E. Koch, J. Mckisson, A.M. Meystel, and J.S.B. Mitchell, Algorithm of navigation for a mobile robot, Proceedings of the International Conference on Robotics, Atlanta, GA, 1984.
4. V.J. Lumelsky and A.A. Stepanov, Path-planning strategies for a point mobile automaton moving amidst unknown obstacles of arbitrary shape, Algorithmica, 2(1987), 403-430.
5. J.T. Schwartz and M. Sharir, On the "piano movers" problem : I. The case of a two dimensional rigid polygonal body moving amidst polygonal barriers, Comm. Pure Appl. Math., 36(1983), 345-398.
6. J.T. Schwartz and M. Sharir, On the "piano movers" problem : II. General techniques for computing topological properties of real algebraic manifolds, Adv. in Appl. Math., 4(1983), 298-351.
7. A.M. Thompson, The navigation system of the JPL robot, Proceedings of the Fifth Joint International Conference on Artificial Intelligence, Cambridge, MA, 1977.

Linear Broadcast Routing

Ching-Tsun Chou
Computer Science Department
University of California, Los Angeles
Los Angeles, CA 90024

Inder S. Gopal
IBM T.J. Watson Research Center
Yorktown Heights, New York 10598

ABSTRACT

In this paper we examine the problem of performing broadcasts in networks where the messages are constrained to follow linear paths. Many high speed networks where routing is done in specialized hardware have this characteristic. We show that the general problem is NP-complete but find a polynomial time approximation algorithm which is guaranteed to provide a solution which is within twice of optimal. We also suggest some generalizations of this work and propose several open problems.

Predicting deadlock
in Store-and-Forward Networks
by
Claudio Arbib [1,5], *Giuseppe F. Italiano* [2,4], *Alessandro Panconesi* [3]

Abstract

Aim of this paper is to study the complexity of the Deadlock-Safety problem for Store-and-Forward networks. The following results are shown: 1. the problem is in general NP-complete, even for tree-like networks. It is still NP-complete for various "simple" topologies (including bipartite, grid and two-terminals series-parallel graphs) when each vertex buffer is of unit capacity; 2. the problem is solvable in PTIME for 1-buffer tree-like networks.

1. Introduction

A *Store-and-Forward Network* (in short *SF-Network*) can be represented as an undirected graph $G=(V,E)$, where the vertices stand for processors and the edges for communication links.

When necessary, the notation is completed by a function $b : V \to \mathbb{Z}^+$, associating with each vertex v_i the number b_i of buffers available at that vertex [13]. When $b_i=k$ for each vertex v_i, the network is usually called a *k-network* [2]. We prefer to denote in such a way a network with the *max* b_i for $i \in V$ equal to k (in particular, every *1*-network has a single buffer per vertex). The function b defines the *buffer configuration* of the network.

A *route* $R_p = \{v_1, v_2, ..., v_d\}$ is a directed, acyclic path in G associated with each packet p. Such routes can be either assumed as fixed a-priori or not [7]. In the latter case we are only given the pair $<v_1, v_d>$, which is called the *source-destination pair* of p.

A packet in the network is subject to the following *network moves*:

1. Generation. A vertex v creates a packet which is placed in an empty buffer of v.

---

[1] Dipartimento di Elettronica, Universita' di Roma "Tor Vergata", 00173 Roma, Italy.
[2] Department of Computer Science, Columbia University, New York, NY 10027, USA.
[3] Department of Computer Science, Cornell University, Ithaca, NY 14850, USA.
[4] On leave from Dipartimento di Informatica e Sistemistica, Universita' di Roma "La Sapienza", Roma, Italy.
[5] To whom correspondence should be addressed.

2. *Passing*. A vertex v transfers a packet in one of its buffers to an empty buffer of vertex w, provided that (v,w) is an edge and the route of the packet has w following v. The buffer of v holding the packet becomes empty.

3. *Consumption*. A packet in a buffer of v, such that the destination of the packet is v, is removed from that buffer, and the buffer is made empty.

The network moves are performed by means of a *flow control procedure* (from now on, *fcp*). Several classes of *fcp's* may be considered, depending on which moves are allowed [13]: in particular, an *fcp* is *unrestricted* if the only requirement for a vertex v_i to accept a packet is that v_i has at least one empty buffer.

Each of the previous moves causes a transition from a certain *state of the network* to another. By definition, the state of the network at time t_k is a mapping associating with each packet the vertex it occupies at t_k. Let P_k denotes the set of packets standing in the network at time t_k and $\sigma_k : P_k \to V$ be such a mapping. Clearly, P_k depends on the time considered: to give a more synthetic definition, we have to slighty modify the network topology so to avoid such a dependance.

Let us therefore introduce extra-nodes s_p and d_p, respectively linked to the source and the destination of each packet p (see figure 1.1) and working as mailboxes for respectively the producer and the consumer of the message. In the new network, each packet always occupies a buffer and the number of packets standing in the network is not time-dependent: consequently, the only move which can be performed is *passing*. We can therefore set $\sigma_k(p) = s_p$ if, at time t_k, p is still to be generated and $\sigma_k(p) = d_p$ if it has been consumed. A packet p is referred to as *active* at time t_k if $\sigma_k(p) \neq d_p$. The mapping σ_k completely defines the *state of the network* at time t_k.

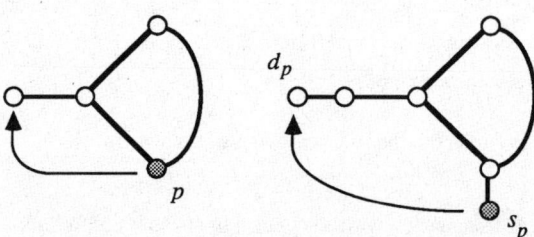

Fig. 1.1: An SF-network transformation in order to consider only *passing* moves.

A state σ_i *includes* a state σ_k if $\sigma_i(p) \neq s_p$ preceeds $\sigma_k(p) \neq d_p$ along the route R_p for each packet p. A serie $\{\sigma_k\}$ of states is *monothonic* if σ_i includes σ_j for $i < j$. An *fcp* is *monothonic* if the serie of states it produces is monothonic. In the following, we shall consider only monothonic *fcp*'s.

A state σ_k is a *deadlock state* if one or more packets can never reach their destination, no matter what sequence of moves is performed (see for example figure 1.2).

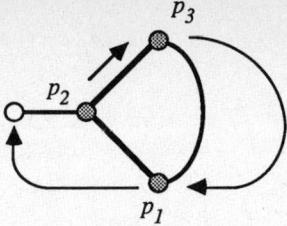

Fig. 1.2: An SF-network in a deadlock state.

An *SF-Network* G is said to be *bound to deadlock* (or *deadlock-bound*) in a state σ_k if one of the following conditions holds

(i) σ_k is a deadlock state;

(ii) for each allowed move, G is bound to deadlock in σ_{k+1}.

In other words, when an *SF-Network* is bound to deadlock, a deadlock will necessarily occur within a finite number of moves, regardless of the *fcp* used (see figure 1.3.a). Clearly, when a network is bound to deadlock in a state σ_k, it is also bound to deadlock in any state σ_i including σ_k. *SF-Networks* which are not bound to deadlock in a certain state are called *deadlock-safe* in that state.

An *SF-Network* is *exposed to deadlock* (or *deadlock-exposed*) if the *fcp* may perform moves causing a deadlock state [13]. Notice that deadlock-exposed *SF-Networks* are not necessarily bound to deadlock (see figure 1.3.b: a solving strategy is that of homing p_3, then p_2 and finally p_1; if we home p_3 and then try to home p_1, we cause a deadlock state). Actually, the deadlock-exposure is a characteristic of the network depending on the *fcp* type and on the buffer configuration.

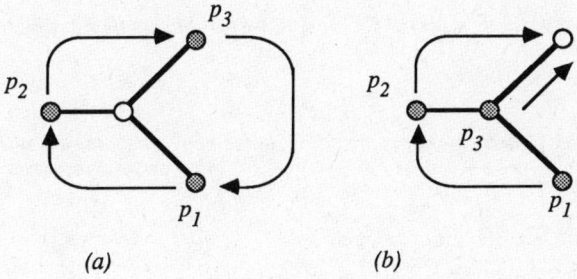

Fig. 1.3: A deadlock-bound state (a) and a deadlock-exposed SF-network (b).

A packet is referred to as *free* if all the vertices in its route have at least one empty buffer. An SF-Network is said to be *greedy-solvable* if (see also fig. 1.3.b)

(i)   it contains no packets, or

(ii)   there exists at least one free packet p and after its removal the network is again greedy-solvable.

In other words, a network is greedy-solvable if the following greedy algorithm is a flow control procedure which makes all the packets be delivered to destination:

> **procedure** GREEDY
>> **begin**
>>> **while** a free packet p exists
>>> **do** move p home
>>
>> **end** GREEDY.

In the literature, many attention has been devoted to the design of efficient flow control procedures for preventing deadlock states in *SF-Networks* [2,3,4,5,9,10,12,14]. The approach proposed by Toueg and Steiglitz in [13] is rather that of trying to recognize deadlock-exposed networks and leads to the definition of the following *deadlock-exposure* problems:

(P1) Given an SF-Network G and a set of routes in G, is the network exposed to deadlock?

(P2) Given an SF-Network G and a set of source-destination pairs in G, is there a corresponding set of routes in G such that the network is not exposed to deadlock?

The Authors characterize the complexity of both problems with respect to the flow control procedure adopted. In most cases, the problems turn out to be NP-complete or even NP-hard.

The approach we consider here is that of looking at the *deadlock-safety* problems corresponding to *(P1)* and *(P2)*, namely:

(P3) Given an SF-Network G and a set of routes in G, is the network deadlock-safe (i.e., not bound to deadlock)?

(P4) Given an SF-Network G and a set of source-destination pairs in G, is there a corresponding set of routes in G such that the network is not bound to deadlock?

We shall first concern ourselves with the case of *1*-networks, i.e. networks with only one buffer per vertex. In this framework, we shall see in Section 2 that problems *(P3)* and *(P4)* are NP-complete for general *1*-networks and remain NP-complete even for simple classes of graphs, such as bipartite graphs, grid graphs (and therefore planar graphs), and two-terminals series-parallelel *(TTSP)* graphs.

On the other hand, we shall see that both problems are polynomially solvable for tree-like networks (Section 4). In this case, two algorithms for checking whether a tree-like *1*-network with n vertices, m edges and p packets is bound to deadlock are proposed. The former has time and space complexity $O(pn)$, while the latter requires $O(nlog(n))$ time and $O(n)$ space. As a consequence, the former behaves favorably in networks with very few packets, while the latter is competitive when at least $log(n)$ packets are in the network.

Due to the complexity of problems *(P3)* and *(P4)* in the case of general *1*-networks, we devoted Section 3 to the following simpler problems, which seem to provide useful information when no answer about the deadlock safety of a given network is available in polynomial time.

(P5) Given an SF-Network G and a set of routes in G, is the network greedy-solvable?

(P6) Given an SF-Network G and a set of source-destination pairs in G, is there a corresponding set of routes such that the network is greedy-solvable?

Problems *(P5)* and *(P6)* are shown to be polynomially solvable for *1*-networks. More in detail, we present algorithms for solving *(P5)* in $O(pn)$ time and space, and *(P6)* in $O(n+mlog(n))$ time and $O(m+n)$ space, on a *1*-network with m edges, n vertices and $p \leq n$ packets. As a side result, we shall prove that problems *(P3)*, *(P4)*, *(P5)* and *(P6)* are completely equivalent in the case of tree-like *1*-networks.

Finally, in the case of *k*-networks with $k \geq 3$, problems *(P3)* and *(P4)* are proved to be still NP-complete. In this case, however, a tree-like topology is proved to lead in general to no simplifications.

2. Some complexity results

In this Section we give some negative results about the complexity of problems *(P3)* and *(P4)* (see Introduction). The first theorem is a general result of NP-completeness for *(P3)* and *(P4)* on *k*-networks: it shows that, when $k \geq 3$, both problems are NP-complete even for tree-like networks (Theorem 2.1). On the other hand we shall see that, in the general case, no simplifications are produced if we limit our attention to *1*-networks. Furthermore, this negative result holds for particular network topologies (Corollaries 2.1 and 2.2, Theorems 2.3, 2.4 and 2.5).

THEOREM 2.1 *Problems (P3) and (P4) on a tree-like k-network are NP-complete for $k \geq 3$.*

PROOF First, observe that both *(P3)* and *(P4)* are in NP: in fact, the lenght of any instance can be assumed linear in the number n of nodes of the network plus the number p of source-destination pairs. Since routes have no cycles by definition, it follows that the feasibility of an *fcp* (i.e. of a solution) can be checked in $O(pn)$.

The demonstration of completeness will be carried out referring to *(P4)* only: the completeness of *(P3)* will in fact follow from observing that, on tree-like networks, a source-destination pair identifies a route. We shall prove the NP-completeness of *(P4)* by reduction to *3-Satisfiability*, trying to associate a particular network T_F with each conjunctive normal form instance **F** of *3-SAT*, in such a way that T_F is deadlock-bound if and only if **F** is unsatisfiable. Let then $\mathbf{F} = \mathbf{F}_1,...,\mathbf{F}_m$ be a CNF *3-SAT* instance with literals l_{ij}, $j=1,2,3$, for each clause $\mathbf{F}_i$ in **F**, and let $x_1,...,x_n$ be the variables (complemented or not) occurring in **F**. The topology of T_F is shown in fig. 2.1.a.

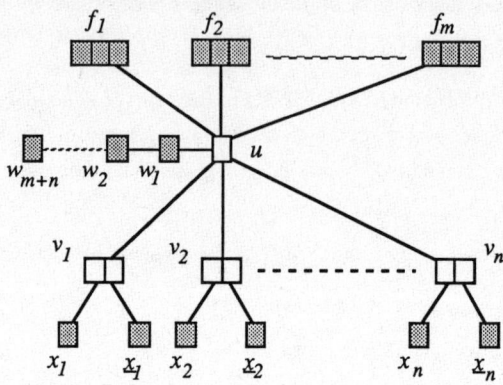

fig.2.1.a - Topology of the SF-network T_F associated with the CNF formula **F**

We have:

a central vertex u (the root) with one buffer, which is linked to

m 3-buffered vertices $f_1,...,f_m$, one for each clause in **F**, plus

n 2-buffered vertices $v_1,...,v_n$, one for each variable occurring in **F**, plus

an (m+n)-chain consisting of $(m+n)$ 1-buffered vertices $w_1,...,w_{m+n}$.

Also, each vertex v_k is linked to a pair $\{x_k, \underline{x}_k\}$ of 1-buffered vertices, for $k=1,...,n$. Clearly, the described instance of *(P4)* can be associated with **F** in $O(m+n)$ time.

At time t_o, four different kinds of packets (indicated with shaded vertices in fig. 2.1.a) are standing in the network, for a total amount of $(4m + 3n)$ packets. A function σ_o defines the state of the network at t_o as shown in tab. 2.1:

packet	σ_o (packet)
p_{ij}	the jth buffer of f_i
r_i	w_i
q_k	x_k
$\underline{q}_k$	$\underline{x}_k$

Tab. 2.1: The state of T_F at time t_o.

The following source-destination pairs are associated with each packet :

if $l_{ij} = x_k$ then $<f_i, x_k>$ else $<f_i, \underline{x}_k>$ for packets p_{ij}
if $i \leq m$ then $<w_i, f_i>$ else $<w_i, v_{i-m}>$ for packets r_i
$<x_k, w_{m+n}>$ for packets q_k
$<\underline{x}_k, w_{m+n}>$ for packets $\underline{q}_k$

Two packets p_{ij} and p_{hk} with destinations respectively x_q and $\underline{x}_q$ are said to have *clashing destinations*. Observe that, whenever the destinations of a pair of p_{ij} clash, a deadlock-bound state is liable to occur since a situation like the one depicted in fig. 2.1.b is produced (remind that a route is not allowed to touch the same vertex more than once).

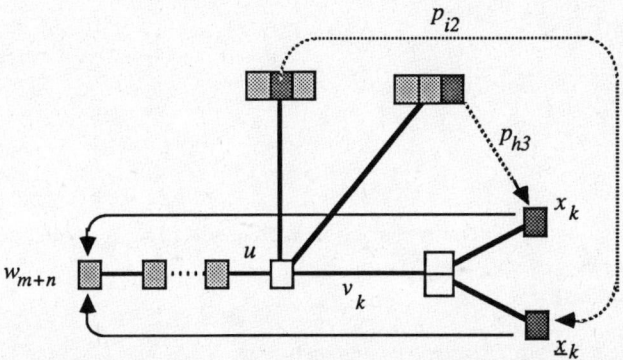

fig. 2.1.b - A deadlock-bound state may occur when the destination of p_{ij} clashes with that of p_{hk} (the routes of type p packets are indicated with dotted lines; the routes of type r packets are not indicated).

Assume now **F** unsatisfiable. This means that, for any given truth assignment τ, there is a clause at least, say F_i, which is not satisfied, i.e. no variable occurring in F_i is set to the appropriate value which makes the corresponding literal true. In terms of our network T_F, this means that there is at least one vertex f_i such that all the packets p_{ij} it contains at time t_o have a clashing destination with other packets of the same type. Hence, by the above observation, σ_o is a deadlock-bound state.

Conversely, assume **F** satisfiable and let D denote the set of the variables indexes which are set to "true" in a satisfying truth assignment. Then T_F is not bound to deadlock, since the following *fcp* can be used to home all the packets:

procedure FLOW_1 (*D*: set_of_indexes)
    begin
        for k in D
        do move q_k into v_k;
        for k not in D
        do move $\underline{q}_k$ into v_k;
                There still is a free buffer for each vertex v_k: packets associated with satisfied literals can be homed through them.
        for $i := 1$ **to** m
        do begin
            choose l_{ij} such that
                $l_{ij} = x_k$, k in D
        or $l_{ij} = \sim x_k$, k not in D;

```
            move p_ij home (resp. x_k or x̱_k);
      end;
                              At least one buffer for each vertex f_i, v_i is now free. Thus,
                              each packet r_i can be homed.
      for i := 1 to m
      do  move r_i intof_i;
      for i := m+1 to n
      do  move r_i intov_{i-m};
                              The buffer of each vertex w_i is free. Hence, packets q_k and q̱_k
                              can be homed.
      for k := 1 to n
      do  begin
                move q_k into w_m;
                move q̱_k into w_m
          end

end FLOW_1.
```

Q.E.D.

It can be proved that both problems remain NP-complete when $k=1$ for each buffer; as for problem (P4), we have the following

THEOREM 2.2 *Problem (P4) is NP-complete on 1-networks.*

PROOF We have only to apply the arguments of Theorem 2.1 to the 1-network drawn in fig. 2.2.a, trivially derived by the network T_F of fig. 2.1.a. We still have four kinds of packets, with the same source-destination pairs as above except for packets p_{ij}, the source of which are nodes l_{ij} (instead of f_i).

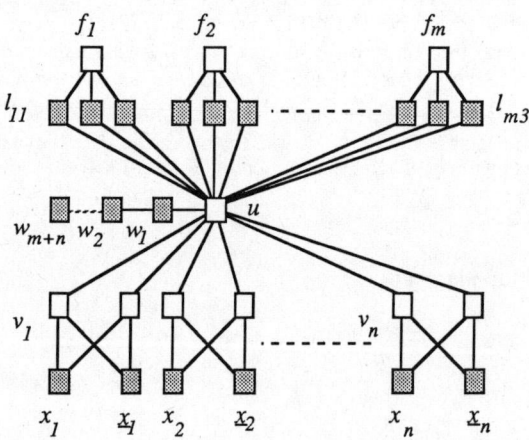

fig. 2.2.a - The 1-network derived by the k-network of fig. 2.1.a

Q.E.D.

It should be noticed that the *1*-network used to demonstrate the NP-completeness of *(P4)* does not have a general topology: in fact, the graph drawn in fig. 2.2.a is bipartite (in particular, it is a *q*-layered graph, with $q=max\{4,m\}$) and planar. Hence we have:

COROLLARY 2.1 *Problem (P4) on 1-networks isomorphic to a bipartite graph is NP-complete.*

COROLLARY 2.2 *Problem (P4) on 1-networks isomorphic to a planar graph is NP-complete.*

One could wonder whether the same result would apply to problem *(P3)* and, if so, if particular classes of planar graphs exist in which *(P3)* can be solved in polynomial time. Interesting sample classes could be those of *two terminals series parallel graphs* (in short, *TTSP graphs*) [8] and *grid graphs*.

Unfortunately, we have the following negative results:

THEOREM 2.3 *Problem (P3) is NP-complete on 1-networks isomorphic to TTSP graphs.*

PROOF The proof is given again by reduction from 3-Satisfiability. Let us associate each clause $\mathbf{F}_i$ in $\mathbf{F}$ with a graph F_i defined as follows:

F_i: $V(F_i) = \{l_{ij}, a_{ij}, b_{ij} : j=1,2,3\} \cup \{u_{i1}, u_{i2}\}$
$E(F_i) = \{(l_{ij}, a_{ij}), (l_{ij}, b_{ij}) : j=1,2,3\} \cup \{(a_{ij}, a_{ij+1}), (b_{ij}, b_{ij+1}) : j = 1,2\} \cup$
$\cup \{(a_{i1}, u_{i1}), (u_{i1}, u_{i2}), (u_{i2}, b_{i1})\}$

for $i = 1,...,m$ (see fig. 2.3.a). Let us also associate each variable x_k with the following graph X_k:

X_k: $V(X_k) = \{x_k, \underline{x}_k, v_k\}$
$E(X_k) = \{(x_k, v_k), (\underline{x}_k, v_k)\}$

for k = 1,...,n. Furthermore, let us consider an s-chain C, defined as

C: $V(C) = \{w_1,...,w_s\}$
$E(C) = \{(w_1, w_2),...,(w_{s-1}, w_s)\}$

with $s \geq 9m$.

To obtain the SF-Network G associated with $\mathbf{F}$, we must connect the graphs F_i, X_k and C as follows:

G: $V(G) = \quad V(F_1) \cup V(F_2) \cup ... \cup V(F_m) \cup$
$\cup V(X_1) \cup V(X_2) \cup ... \cup V(X_n) \cup V(C)$

$E(G) = \quad E(F_1) \cup E(F_2) \cup ... \cup E(F_m) \cup$
$\cup E(X_1) \cup E(X_2) \cup ... \cup E(X_n) \cup E(C) \cup$
$\cup \{(a_{11}, x_k), (a_{11}, \underline{x}_k) : k = 1,...,n\} \cup$
$\cup \{(v_k, b_{11}) : k = 1,...,n\} \cup$
$\cup \{(w_1, b_{11}), (b_{13}, b_{21}),...,(b_{m-1.3}, b_{m1}),$
$(a_{13}, a_{21}),...,(a_{m-1.3}, a_{m1})\}$

(see fig. 2.3.b). Notice that the F_i's are nested in a chinese box - like way and that G turns out to be a *TTSP* graph.

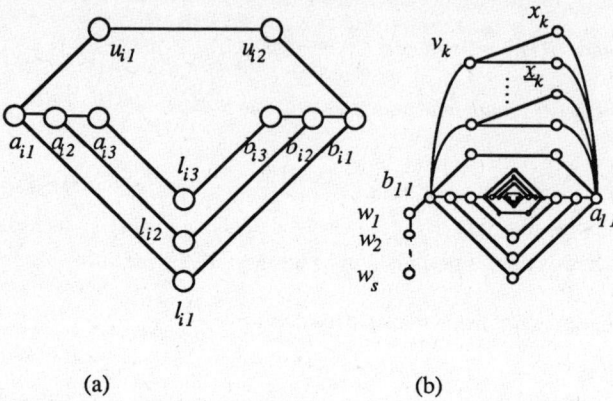

(a)   (b)

fig. 2.3.a) The graph F_i associated with the clause F_i; b) The whole network.

As in Theorem 2.1, let us consider four different packet types with associated routes:

1. $R_p = \{l_{ij}, b_{ij}, b_{ij-1}, \ldots, b_{i1}, u_{i2}, u_{i1}, a_{i1}, a_{i-1.3}, a_{i-1.2}, \ldots, a_{11}, d\}$

    with $\quad d = x_k$ if $l_{ij} = x_k$
    and $\quad d = \underline{x}_k$ if $l_{ij} = \sim x_k$ $\qquad$ for $p = p_{ij}$ (see fig. 2.3.c)

2. $R_p = \{x_k, v_k, b_{11}, w_1, \ldots, w_s\}$ $\qquad$ for $p = q_k$

3. $R_p = \{\underline{x}_k, v_k, b_{11}, w_1, \ldots, w_s\}$ $\qquad$ for $p = \underline{q}_k$

4. $R_p = \{w_h, \ldots, w_1, b_{11}, l_{11}, a_{11}, a_{12}, l_{12}, b_{12}, b_{13}, l_{13}, a_{13}, a_{21}, l_{21}, b_{21}, \ldots$
    $\ldots, b_{m3}, l_{m3}, a_{m3}\}$

    $\qquad\qquad\qquad\qquad\qquad\qquad\qquad\qquad$ for $p = r_h$ (m even, see fig. 2.3.d)

Observe that the routes of packets r_h touch all the vertices of G but u_{i1} and u_{i2}, $i=1,\ldots,m$, for a total amount of $18m=2s$ vertices. In other words, u_{i1} and u_{i2} are the only vertices which can be used as parking areas for packets p_{ij} associated with non-satisfiable literals. Since no more than two such vertices are available for each clause, one packet p_{ij} at least in F_i, $i=1,\ldots,m$, must be homed before any r_h reaches its destination. The conclusions are similar to those of Theorem 2.1,

$\qquad\qquad\qquad\qquad\qquad\qquad\qquad\qquad\qquad\qquad\qquad\qquad\qquad\qquad$ Q.E.D.

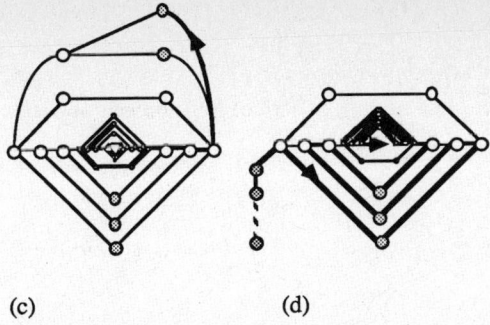

Fig. 2.3.c) The route to be followed by packets p_{ij} .and d) r_h.

As a direct consequence, a similar, negative result can be derived:

THEOREM 2.4 *Problem (P3) is NP-complete on 1-networks isomorphic to bipartite graphs.*

PROOF The network G constructed to prove Theorem 2.2 can be modified by duplicating the vertices l_{ij} into l_{ij}' and l_{ij}'', introducing then a corresponding pair of packets for each of them and finally adding two places to the parking area u_{i1}, u_{i2} (see fig. 2.4.a; consistently, a literal $l_{ij} = x_k$ ($\sim x_k$) is satisfied iff both the associated packets p_{ij}' and p_{ij}'' are homed at x_k ($\underline{x}_k$)). Also, set $p = 12m$. As shown in the figure, the resulting graph is 2-colorable,

Q.E.D.

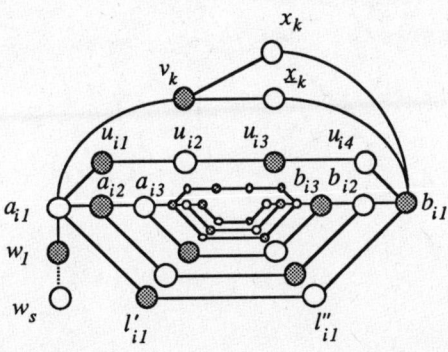

Fig. 2.4.a: An SF-network isomorphic to a bipartite *TTSP* graph.

Finally, the same result can be derived for *grid graphs* (a planar graph G is called a grid graph if there is a positive integer n such that G is a partial subgraph of the $n \times n$ grid):

THEOREM 2.5 *Problem (P3) is NP-complete on 1-networks isomorphic to grid graphs.*

For the sake of shortness, the proof is omitted.

The remainder of the paper is devoted to set some positive results. In particular, we shall see that, on tree-like 1-networks, both problems considered here are polynomially solvable.

3. Greedy-solvability of 1-networks

In this section we shall describe polynomial algorithms for deciding whether a *1*-network is greedy-solvable, either in the case of a fixed routing procedure or in the other case in which the routes are not a-priori fixed.

Suppose we are given a network with n vertices, one buffer per vertex and p packets, each one with a given route. If a packet p_i is in the buffer of a vertex belonging to the route of a packet p_j, we shall say that p_i *hampers* p_j. A *cycle of packets* is a sequence of packets $\{p_0, p_1, ..., p_k\}$ such that $p_0 = p_k$ and p_i hampers p_{i-1}, $1 \leq i \leq k$. A cycle of packets is said to be *simple* if it does not contain other cycles of packets. The *rank* of a cycle of packets is the number of different edges of the network involved in the cycle.

EXAMPLE 3.1 *Figure 3.1 shows a simple cycle of packets of rank 5. Packets are denoted by shaded vertices, while bold lines indicate the edges involved in the cycle.*

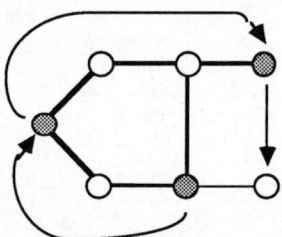

Fig. 3.1: A cycles of packets with rank 5.

The following theorem gives a necessary and sufficient condition for a given *1*-network to be greedy-solvable.

THEOREM 3.1 *A 1-network G with a fixed routing procedure is greedy-solvable if and only if it does not contain cycles of packets.*

PROOF We proceed by induction on the number of packets in the network.
Networks with no packets are trivially both greedy-solvable and without cycles of packets. Assume now that the theorem holds for *1*-networks with $r \geq 0$ packets and consider any *1*-network G in a state σ with $r+1$ packets. If G is greedy-solvable in σ, then at least one free packet p_k exists. Denote by σ' the new state in which G will be after the removal of p_k. In such a state, G will contain exactly r packets and

will be again greedy-solvable. As a consequence of the inductive hypothesis, G will be without cycles of packets in σ' and therefore in σ. On the other hand, the same argument could be repeated for proving the if-part of the induction step,

Q.E.D.

As a straightforward consequence of Theorem 3.1, one could check whether a 1-network is greedy-solvable by simply testing the presence of a cycle of packets. In order to make this test easier, let us associate with each 1-network in a given state a directed graph G_p, referred to as the *Packet Graph* and defined as follows:

For each packet p_k in the 1-network, $k=1,...,p$, there is a chain of length l_k in G_p, where l_k is the length of the route of p_k. These p disjoint chains are completed by introducing n nodes n_i, $i=1,...,n$, corresponding to the vertices v_i of the 1-network and

(i) one arc from the node n_i to the first node of the chain c_j, if the packet p_j has its source in v_i;

(ii) one arc from a node in c_k (corresponding to a vertex v_h in the 1-network) to n_h, if v_h belongs to the route of p_k and is also the source of another packet.

EXAMPLE 3.2 *Figure 3.2 it is shows the 1-network of fig. 3.1 (with an added packet) together with the corresponding Packet Graph.*

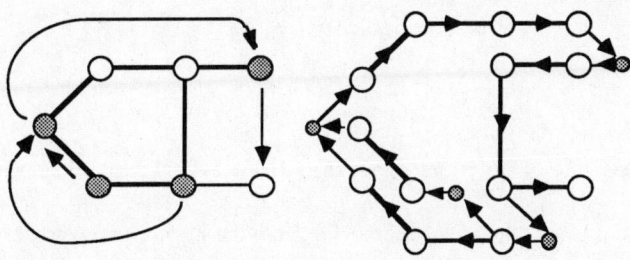

Fig. 3.2: A 1-network and the associated Packet Graph.

As a consequence of this definition, there is a one-to-one correspondence between cycles of packets in a 1-network and cycles in the associated Packet Graph. Thus, one could check whether a 1-network is greedy-solvable by building the corresponding Packet Graph G_p and then finding out whether it contains a cycle. The Packet Graph G_p can be constructed in $O(pn)$ time and requires $O(pn)$ space, where n denotes the number of vertices and p the number of packets in the 1-network. Since to detect the presence of a cycle in G_p requires in turn $O(pn)$ time (see for example [11]), we have the following theorem:

THEOREM 3.2 *It is possible to check whether a 1-network with n vertices and p packets with a-priori fixed routes is greedy-solvable in O(pn) time and O(pn) space.*

PROOF It is an immediate consequence of the above discussion,

$$Q.E.D.$$

The above described algorithm cannot be applied if the routes are not a-priori fixed, since no Packet Graph can be individuated. In that case, the greedy-solvability of a network may be checked as follows.

Before describing the algorithm, we need some preliminary terminology. For each vertex v in the network $G=(V,E)$, let us introduce the following notations:

$$N(v) = \{u \in V \mid (u,v) \in E\}$$

$$S(v) = \{u \in V \mid \exists \text{ a packet with source destination pair } (u,v)\}$$

In other words, $N(v)$ contains all the neighbors of v in the network, while $S(v)$ contains all the vertices which are sources of packets with destination v.

The following lemma, the simple proof of which has been omitted, characterizes the overall size of these sets.

LEMMA 3.1 *For any network $G=(V,E)$ with n vertices, m edges and p packets,*

$$\sum_{v \in V} |N(v)| \leq 2m$$

$$\sum_{v \in V} |S(v)| \leq p$$

If a vertex v is the source of any packet p_i, we shall denote by $d(v)$ the destination of p_i.

The algorithm is based on the idea of removing from the network the vertices with a non-empty buffer. The remaining vertices are organized by maintaining the connected components of the resulting network. By doing so it follows that, if $d(v)$ and any vertex in $N(v)$ are in the same connected component, then there is at least one free route from v to $d(v)$, and hence the packet in v may be delivered to its destination. For this reason, for any vertex v with a non-empty buffer we shall say that $d(v)$ is a *mate* of any vertex in $N(v)$, and viceversa any vertex in $N(v)$ is a *mate* of $d(v)$. Once the packet with source in v has been delivered, the buffer at v is empty and the new connected components must therefore be recomputed by taking into account the vertex v and all the edges incident on it.

We are now able to give a high level description of the algorithm:

Algorithm SOLVABILITY

Step 1 Compute $N(v)$, $S(v)$, $d(v)$ for each vertex v in the network.

Step 2 Remove from the network the vertices with an empty buffer.

Step 3 Check whether there are two mate vertices in the same connected component (which allow to deliver a packet p_i). If not, go to step 5.

Step 4 Deliver the packet p_i. Insert the source of p_i in the graph, together with its incident edges. Go to step 3.

Step 5 If all the packets in the original network have been delivered, then return *yes*. Otherwise, return *no*.

A naïve implementation of the algorithm SOLVABILITY will lead to the following bounds:

THEOREM 3.3 *It is possible to check whether a 1-network with m edges, n vertices and $p \leq n$ packets (whose routes are not fixed a priori) is greedy-solvable in $O((m+n)p^2)$ time and $O(m+n)$ space.*

PROOF Step 1, as well as step 2, can be performed in $O(m+n)$ time [11]. In particular, they are both executed at most once. The test at step 3 may be carried out by checking, for any vertex v which is source of a packet, whether $d(v)$ is in the same component of one of its mates in $N(v)$. This can be done in time $O(m+n)$, thus implying an $O((m+n)p)$ bound whenever step 3 is executed. Step 4 can require $O(n)$ time, while step 5 may be accomplished in constant time. Hence, the overall complexity of the algorithm is dominated by step 3 and step 4, which may be executed at most p times. This leads to an $O((m+n)p^2)$ time. The space required is $O(m+n)$.

Q.E.D.

A more sophisticated and efficient version of this algorithm is based on a different implementation of steps 3 and 4.

In this approach, the connected components are maintained on-line as sets in which *unions between sets* (when a vertex is reintroduced into the graph) and *find* operations (for testing whether two mates are in the same connected component) are allowed. For this purpose, we can make use of a data structure for the set union problem [1], in which different sets are maintained as rooted trees of height one. In such trees, the leaves are the vertices in a connected component, while the root contains a label which identifies the set. Such a label is referred to as the *name* of the set. The name of each set may for instance be any vertex of the corresponding component. Each edge in a tree is a directed arc from a leaf to a root.

When a *find(x)* has to be performed, the leaf corresponding to x is first accessed. Then, the pointer to the root is followed and the name of the component is returned. With this technique, one is able to check in constant time whether two vertices belong to the same component.

The reintroduction of a vertex the packet of which has been delivered to its destination entails the merging of two or more different components, i.e. the union of the corresponding sets. When performing such a union operation, we make all the leaves in the smaller set be children of the root of the larger one, arbitrarily breaking a tie. Also, for each leaf v we moved, we check whether

(i) for each vertex x in $N(v)$, $d(x)$ is in the new component which v has been moved to;

(ii) for each vertex y in $S(v)$, there is any vertex z in $N(y)$ in the new component which v has been moved to.

This test is necessary because, in case i), by moving v we created a new possibility for a packet in $x \in N(v)$ to be delivered, while in case ii) a packet with destination v may now be delivered.

We are now able to improve the efficiency of the algorithm SOLVABILITY.

THEOREM 3.4 *It is possible to check whether a 1-network with m edges, n vertices and $p \leq n$ packets, with routes not a-priori fixed, is greedy-solvable in $O(n+m\log(n))$ time and $O(m+n)$ space.*

PROOF Since the connected components of a graph can be computed in $O(m+n)$ time, this is also the overall complexity of steps 1, 2 and 5. If steps 3 and 4 are implemented as above, a number of n union operations between disjoint sets is required at most. Whenever a vertex v is moved from a component to another, at most

$$|N(v)| + \sum_{y \in S(v)} |N(y)|$$

of such operations are performed. Since a *find* operation can be accomplished in constant time, this is also the cost charged to a vertex each time it is moved. Whenever a vertex is moved from a set, it is moved into a set which is at least twice as large as before. Thus, no vertex v can be moved more than $log(n)$ times during the n union operations, and the total cost charged to v is

$$(|N(v)| + \sum_{y \in S(v)} |N(y)|) \log(n)$$

The total cost of steps 3 and 4 is obtained by adding up the costs charged to the vertices

$$\sum_{v \in V} (|N(v)| + \sum_{y \in S(v)} |N(y)|) \log(n)$$

Considering that, by Lemma 3.1,

$$\sum_{v \in V} |N(v)| \leq 4m$$

$$\sum_{v \in V} \sum_{y \in S(v)} |N(y)| \leq \sum_{y \in V} N(y) \leq 4m$$

the time complexity of the algorithm follows to be $O(n+m\log(n))$. The space required is still $O(m+n)$.

Q.E.D.

4. The deadlock safety problem on tree-like networks

Suppose we are given a tree-like network T with n vertices, one buffer per vertex and $p \leq n$ packets, each with a given source-destination pair. As noticed in Section 2, every pair of vertices of T univocally individuates a path (in particular, any source-destination pair denotes a route). As a consequence, problems *(P3)* and *(P5)* trivially coincide respectively with *(P4)* and *(P6)* in case of tree-like networks.

In order to characterizie deadlock-bound tree-like networks, we need the following preliminary result.

LEMMA 4.1 *Let $T=(V,E)$ be a tree-like 1-network containing a cycle of packets $C=\{p_0,p_1,...,p_s\}$. For every edge (x,y) in E involved in the cycle C, there are at least two packets in C with routes traversing (x,y) in opposite directions.*

PROOF Let (x,y) be any edge involved in $C=\{p_0,p_1,...,p_s\}$. This implies that at least one packet exists which needs to traverse (x,y). Denote it by p_i *($1 \leq i \leq s$)* and, without loss of generality, assume that it must traverse (x,y) from x to y. If the edge (x,y) is removed from T, T will be splitted into two subtrees: T_x (containing x) and T_y (containing y). Since the routes are acyclic, the source of p_i is in T_x while its destination is in T_y. By definition of cycle of packets, there must be now a packet in C which has to traverse (x,y) from y to x, i.e. in an direction opposite to that of p_i.

Q.E.D.

We are now able to prove the following theorem:

THEOREM 4.1 *A tree-like 1-network T is bound to deadlock in a given state σ if and only if σ admits at least one cycle of packets.*

PROOF *If-part.* We proceed by induction on the rank of the cycle of packets.
States with cycles of packets of rank *1* are bound to deadlock since the two packets in the cycle are clearly deadlocked. Suppose now that all the states with cycles of packets of rank at most $r \geq 1$ let T be deadlock-bound. Let $C=\{p_0,p_1,...,p_s\}$ with $p_0=p_s$ be any cycle of packets of rank $r+1$ contained in a state σ_j of T. We shall restrict ourselves to a state σ_h which contains only the packets in the cycle and we shall prove that T is bound to deadlock in σ_h. Since σ_h is included in σ_j, if the network is bound to deadlock in σ_h, then it will be bound to deadlock also in σ_j.

If C is not simple, then it contains a simple cycle of rank at most r. For the inductive hypothesis, T will be bound to deadlock in σ_h.

If C is simple, then at least one packet p_i *($1 \leq i \leq s$)* must exist in the state σ_h which is allowed to move, otherwise C would contain a cycle of rank 1 and therefore it would not be simple. Let x and y be respectively the second and the third vertex in the route of p_i and let us move p_i into x. The edge (x,y) is clearly in C and thus, by Lemma 4.1, there exists a packet p_k *($1 \leq k \leq s$ and $k \neq i$)* the route of which contains the edge (x,y) traversed from y to x. As p_k is blocked by p_i in the new situation, a new cycle $\{p_i,p_{i+1},...,p_k,p_i\}$ *($1 \leq k \leq s$ and $k \neq i$)* of rank at most r is created in σ_{h+1} and therefore, by the inductive hypothesis, T is bound to deadlock in σ_{h+1}. Since this argument can be repeated for each allowed move in σ_h, T is bound to deadlock in σ_h.

Only-if-part. Assume by contradiction that the network is bound to deadlock but there are no cycles of packets. In this case, at least one packet must be free. If this packet is delivered to its destination and removed from the network, there will not be cycles of packets again. By repeating this argument, we shall find a sequence of passing and consumption moves which allows to deliver all the packets in the network, clearly contradicting the hypothesis that the network is bound to deadlock.

Q.E.D.

As an immediate consequence of Theorem 4.1 and 3.1, the following corollary can be stated:

COROLLARY 4.1 *A tree-like 1-network T is bound to deadlock in a given state if and only if it is not greedy-solvable.*

Notice that, as a first consequence of Corollary 4.1, problems *(P3), (P4), (P5)* and *(P6)* are completely equivalent in case of tree-like networks. Furthermore, the algorithms proposed in the previous section for detecting the greedy-solvability of a given *1*-network could be used for deciding whether a tree-like network is bound to deadlock. This remark gives rise to the following theorems.

THEOREM 4.2 *It is possible to check whether a given tree-like 1-network with n vertices and $p \leq n$ packets is bound to deadlock in O(pn) time and space.*

PROOF In case of trees, every source-destination pair univocally corresponds to a route and henceforth a fixed routing procedure is always implicitly given. Then, the thesis follows immediately from Corollary 4.1 and Theorem 3.2.

Q.E.D.

THEOREM 4.3 *It is possible to check whether a given tree-like 1-network with n vertices is bound to deadlock in O(nlog(n)) time and O(n) space.*

PROOF It is a straightforward consequence of Corollary 4.1 and Theorem 3.4, in which it has been taken into account that tree-like networks with *n* vertices have exactly *n-1* edges.

Q.E.D.

As a consequence of these two theorems, two algorithms for solving deadlock safety problems on tree-like networks have been implicitly given. They are based on quite different ideas and give rise to different performances.

The former (Theorem 4.2) detects the presence of cycle of packets, and seems to be more suitable for networks with very few packets (i.e., $p < log(n)$), while the latter (Theorem 4.3) tries to check the greedy-solvability of the network and may conveniently be used in the other cases.

5. Conclusions

In this paper, we considered the following problem:

Given an SF-network G in a given state σ at time t, find a flow control procedure (if one) to deliver to destination all the packets which are in the network at t.

We showed that, unless P=NP, no polynomially bound algorithm exists to solve the version of this problem in which the biggest node in the network contains at least three buffers and the network topology is a tree. On the other hand, if we limit our attention to tree-like *1*-networks, the problem turns out to be solvable in polynomial time. In particular, we gave two algorithms with time bounds respectively $O(pn)$ and $O(nlog(n))$, where p is the number of packets and n the number of nodes in the network. Analogies with the set ordering problem seem to indicate that, when $p \leq nlog(n)$, $O(nlog(n))$ is likely to be also a lower bound.

The complexity analysis we carried out seems to suggest that what makes the problem easy to solve in the case of tree-like *1*-networks is the stronger property of trees, i.e. acyclicity. In fact, weaker properties like planarity, or being a bipartite graph, (both owned as well by trees) lead to NP-complete versions of the problem, both when the packet routing is a-priori given and when it is not. In the case of fixed routing, we tried also to investigate the complexity of particular classes of problem instances on planar graphs (Grid graphs, *TTSP* graphs) which are interesting from the applications viewpoint. The related negative results we found seem to confirm our conjecture linking a high complexity of the problem with network topologies presenting cycles.

The problem complexity could suggest to consider an opposite viewpoint, corresponding to the following approach:

> Given a flow control procedure Ω, find all the SF-networks G in a state σ such that Ω is able to deliver to destination all the packets.

This problem can be shown to be easily solvable for flow control procedure with given characteristics. In particular, a *greedy fcp*, which attempts to home all the packets by delivering to destination only the free ones, is by definition successful only on the so-called *greedy-solvable networks*. We exhibited two polynomially bound algorithms for checking whether a network is greedy-solvable, either in the case of a fixed routing procedure or in the other case in which the routes are not a-priori fixed. Further investigations might lead to polynomial characterizations of networks which can be solved by more sophisticated *fcp*'s.

References

[1] A.V. Aho, J.E. Hopcroft, J.D. Ullman, *The design and analysis of computer algorithms*, Addison-Wesley, Reading, 1974.

[2] J. Blazewicz, D.P. Bovet, G. Gambosi, "Deadlock-resistant flow control procedures for Store-and-Forward networks", *IEEE Trans. on Comm., COM-32* (1984), 884-887.

[3] J. Blazewicz, J. Brzezinski, G. Gambosi, "Time-stamps approach to Store-and-Forward deadlock prevention", *IEEE Trans. on Comm., COM-35* (1987), 490-495.

[4] G. Bongiovanni, D.P. Bovet, "Minimal deadlock-free Store-and-forward communication networks", *Networks 17* (1987), 187-200.

[5]   D.P. Bovet, G. Gambosi, D.A. Menasce, "Detection and removal of deadlocks in Store-and-Forward communication networks", *Performance '84*.

[6]   R.C. Holt, "Some deadlock properties of computer systems", *ACM Comp. Surv., 4, no. 3*, (1972), pp. 178-196.

[7]   L. Kleinrock, *Queuing Systems*, vol. II : computer applications, John Wiley, New York, 1976.

[8]   E.L. Lawler, *Combinatorial Optimization: Networks and Matroids*, Holt, Rinehart and Winston, New York, 1976.

[9]   P.M. Merlin, P.J. Schweitzer, "Deadlock avoidance in Store-and-Forward networks I : Store-and-Forward deadlock", *IEEE Trans. on Comm., COM-28 n. 3* (1980), 345-354.

[10] P.M. Merlin, P.J. Schweitzer, "Deadlock avoidance in Store-and-Forward networks II : other deadlock types", *IEEE Trans. on Comm., COM-28 n. 3* (1980), 355-360.

[11] R.E. Tarjan, "Depth-first search and linear graph algorithms", *SIAM J. Comput. 2* (1972), 146-160.

[12] S. Toueg, "Deadlock- and livelock- free packet switching networks", *Proc. ACM STOC* (1980), 94-108.

[13] S. Toueg, K. Steiglitz, "Some complexity results in the design of deadlock-free packet switching networks", *SIAM J. Comput. 10* (1981), 702-712.

[14] S. Toueg, J.D. Ullman, "Deadlock-free packet switching networks", Proc. ACM STOC (1979), 89-98.

Acknowledgement

The authors wish to thank Daniel P. Bovet for having pointed out the problem to them.

ON PARALLEL SORTING AND ADDITION WITH CONCURRENT WRITES

Sanjeev Saxena , P.C.P.Bhatt   and   V.C.Prasad
Computer Science and Engineering,   Electrical Engineering,
Indian Institute of Technology, Delhi, New Delhi 110016, India.

ABSTRACT

In this paper, following results are obtained :

1. N numbers of m bits can be added in time $O(\lg N/\lg(\lg N)+\lg m)$ with $O(\ (m*N^{1-(c/\lg\lg N)})*(\lg\lg N/\lg^2 N)\ +\ (N*\lg\lg N/\lg N)\ )$ processors. Here, c is some pre-assigned constant ($\lg N$ is $\lg_2 N$).

2. $O(N\ \lg\lg N/\lg N)$ processors are sufficient to add $O(N^{c/\lg\lg N})$ bit numbers in $\Theta(\lg N/\lg\lg N)$ time. Thus, the algorithm achieves optimal (linear) speed-up.

3. An algorithm to add N-bit numbers in $O(\lg N/\lg\lg N)$ time if all bits of a number can be set independently in parallel.

4. With $N^{1+(1/\lg\lg N)}$ processors it is possible to sort in $\Theta(\lg N/\lg\lg N)$ time.

5. N numbers can be sorted in $O(\lg N/\lg\lg M)$ time using $O(N*M)$ processors (if $\lg M/\lg\lg M \geq \lg\lg N$).

1. INTRODUCTION

Parallel processing offers an interesting alternative to super-computing for a large class of problems. In this paper we consider the problem of adding and sorting N numbers in parallel. $O(\lg N)$ time parallel solutions for these problems are well known. We discuss the problem for sorting and adding in $o(\lg N)$ time on CRCW shared memory model of parallel computers.

In shared memory Single Instruction Multiple Data (SIMD) model, all processors execute the same program and communicate amongst themselves by reading and writing in the shared memory. In Concurrent Read Concurrent Write (CRCW) model, more than one processor can simultaneously read from the same memory location. More than one processor can simultaneously attempt to write in the same location, but only one of them actually succeeds.

The CRCW model is very useful for studying inherent parallelism present in a problem. It is independent of technological fan-in limitations. Moreover, algorithms requiring $t(n)$ time on CRCW model require $O(t(n)*\lg n)$ time on Exclusive Read Exclusive Write Model (simultaneously reads or writes from same memory location are not allowed) and $O(t(n)*\lg^2 n)$ time on hypercube.

Kruskal et.al.[KRS85] have shown that N numbers can be added in $O(\lg N)$ time with N processors on EREW model. Cole and Vishkin [CV87] have described an algorithm for adding N $O(\lg N)$ bit long numbers in $O(\lg N / \lg(\lg N))$ time with $(N*\lg(\lg N) / \lg N)$ processors on CRCW model. Reif[R85] has obtained the same bounds for smaller sized numbers on the same model. A similar algorithm for circuits with same time bounds is also discussed in Chandra et.al.[CSV84]. However, circuits correspond to non-uniform PRAMs[SV84]. In non-uniform PRAM each processor can have a different program and the program depends on the size of the input. Thus, their results do not carry over to (uniform) CRCW computers (by CRCW we mean uniform CRCW unless stated otherwise).

In this paper it is shown that, even significantly larger numbers, which may require up to $N^{c/\lg\lg N}$ bits, can also be added in $O(\lg N/\lg\lg N)$ time with $O(N \lg\lg N/\lg N)$ processors on CRCW model, for any constant c(cor 2.1). The algorithm achieves linear speed up. Li and Yesha[LY86] claim that they have an addition algorithm for $O(N^{1/\lg\lg N})$ bit numbers in $O(\lg N/\lg\lg N)$ time. However, they have not indicated the number of processors required (but, it is polynomial).

The results obtained here are the best possible as Li and Yesha[LY86] have shown that numbers larger than $N^{c/\lg\lg N}$, (c not constant) cannot be added in $O(\lg N/\lg\lg N)$ time even with $O(N^k)$ processors, for any constant k (they have proved a lower bound of min(lg n,lg b), for b-bit numbers). We also study processor-time trade-offs when $1 \leq c(n)=c \leq k*\lg\lg N$ (theorem 2). The upper bound on time matches the lower bound of Li and Yesha[LY86].

We also show that it is possible to beat Li and Yesha's bound on a slightly different model. Beame[B88] gives a combinatorial (non-constructive) argument to say that it can be. We give a formal (constructive) algorithm for this purpose.

Algorithms for sorting N numbers in $O(\lg N)$ time with $O(N)$ processors are well known [AKS83,C86]. Previously, Cook et.al.[CDR86] have shown that sorting requires $\Theta(\lg N)$ time in the absence of concurrent writes. In this paper we show that on CRCW model, with $O(N*M)$ processors it is possible to sort in $O(\lg N/\lg\lg M)$ time (theorem 3), the lower bound for comparison based sorting is $\Omega(\lg N/\lg\lg N + \lg N/\lg M))$ (cor 2.1). In particular with $N^{1+(1/\lg\lg N)}$ processors it is possible to sort in $O(\lg N/\lg\lg N)$ time (cor 3.1).

The general problem of parallel M-way merge sort is also considered. **The generic algorithm presented here matches or betters (upto a constant multiplicative factor) all known algorithms for parallel sorting for number of processors ranging from linear in N to exponential in N.**

These results are a generalization of results discussed in [SBP87].

2. MAIN RESULTS

We begin by describing the following lower bound reduction.

Theorem 1:(Lower Bound) Any deterministic parallel algorithm requires at least $\Omega(\lg N / \lg(\lg N))$ time to sort N numbers with polynomial number of processors (even single bit numbers).

Proof: Given an instance of parity, sorting the input in decreasing order places all ones before zeros. N processors can determine in O(1) time the processor number, say k, at which the sorted output changes from one to zero. Parity can be found from the least significant bit of k. Hastad [H86] and Beame and Hastad [BH87] have shown that parity requires $\Omega(\lg N/\lg\lg N)$ time. The lower bound for sorting clearly follows. ∎

Azar and Vishkin [AV87] have shown that sorting N numbers by comparison on comparision tree-model, with $p \geq N$ processors requires $\Omega(\lg N/\lg(1+(p/N)))$ comparision rounds. The same lower bound holds for all PRAM models. Hence, we have,

Cor 1.1: Lower bound for comparison based sorting of N numbers with N*M processors on CRCW model is $\Omega(\lg N/\lg\lg N + \lg N/\lg M))$, $M \geq 2$. ∎

Theorem 2:(Tight Upper Bound for Addition) N numbers of b bits each can be added in parallel on CRCW model in time $O(\lg N/\lg(\lg N)+\lg b)$ with $(b*N^{1-(c/\lg\lg N)})*(\lg\lg N/\lg^2 N)$ + $(N*\lg\lg N/\lg N)$ processors. processors. Here, c is any arbitrary constant.

Proof: Form $N_1 = N*(\lg\lg N/\lg N)$ groups of $\lg N/\lg\lg N$ numbers, assign a processor to each group and find the group sum sequentially in $O(\lg N/\lg(\lg N))$ time. N_1 numbers are left. Then form $X = N_1/(N^{c/\lg\lg N})$ groups of $(N^{c/\lg\lg N})$ numbers each, find the group sum in $O(\lg(N^{c/\lg\lg N})) = O(\lg N/\lg\lg N)$ time with $(N^{c/\lg\lg N})$ processors per group using the algorithm due to Kruskal et.al[KRS85].

After this step X numbers of at most $\lg(\lg N/\lg\lg N)$ + $\lg((N^{c/\lg\lg N})) + b + 1 \leq 2*b$ bits are left (for $b \geq \lg N$).

Divide X numbers into at most (2*b/lg X) pieces, each piece of lg X bits, namely, the trailing lg X bits, the next least significant lg X bits and so on (Xb/lgX processors can do this).

For $1 \leq i \leq (2*b/\lg X)$, compute the sum for the ith set of pieces using Cole and Vishkin's algorithm[CV87]. This takes $O(\lg X/\lg\lg X) < O(\lg N/\lg\lg N)$ time with $(X \lg\lg X/\lg X)*(2b/\lg X) < X*(2b/\lg X)$ processors. But

$X*b = b*(N*\lg\lg N/\lg N)/N^{(c/\lg\lg N)}$

$= (b*N^{1-(c/\lg\lg N)})*(\lg\lg N/\lg N)$.

The pieces can be combined two at a time in O(lg b) time with b processors. The theorem thus follows. ∎

Note 1: It is assumed that two b bit numbers can be added in O(1) time (the word size is b).

Note 2: Li and Yesha [LY86] have shown that addition of N, b bit numbers requires $\Omega(\min(\lg N, \lg b))$ time, and Hastad[H86] and Beame and Hastad [BH87] have shown that adding even one bit numbers requires $\Omega(\lg N/\lg\lg N)$ time with polynomial processors hence the bound in theorem 2 is tight.

Note 3: The assumption made in note 1 is not un-realistic. For, the sum of two N bit numbers can be obtained in O(1) time using a polynomial number of processors.

Let the bits of two N bit numbers be in BIT[1,*] and BIT[2,*] then their sum can be found in O(1) time with polynomial processors as follows (algorithm for circuit is given in [CSV84]).

1. for I:= 0 to N-1 do

   parbegin

   GENERATE[I] := BIT[1,I] $\wedge$ BIT[2,I] ;

   PROPOGATE[I] := BIT[1,I] $\oplus$ BIT[2,I] ;

parend

2. for I:= 0 to N-1 do

   parbegin

   A[I]:= 1 ; MAX[I] := N ; CARRY[I]:= 1 ; /* initialize */

   for J:= 0 to I-1 do and for K := J+1 to I-1 do

   parbegin

   if (GENERATE[J] < GENERATE[K]) or

   (GENERATE[J] = GENERATE[K] = 1) then A[J]:= 0 ;

   parend ;

   for J:=0 to I-1 **parbegin** if A[J] = 1 then MAX[I]:=J **parend** ;

   for J:= MAX[I]+1 to I-1 do

   parbegin if PROPOGATE[J] = 0 then CARRY[I]:= 0 **parend** ;

   SUM[I] := BIT[1,I] $\oplus$ BIT[2,I] $\oplus$ CARRY[I] /* XOR the bits */

   parend /* SUM contains bits of sum */

<u>Cor 2.1</u>:(<u>Linear Speed Up</u>) N numbers of $b \leq N^{c/\lg\lg N}$ bits can be added in parallel on CRCW model in time $\Theta(\lg N/\lg\lg N)$ with $N*\lg\lg N/\lg N$ processors. Here, c is any arbitrary constant.

<u>Theorem 3</u>:(<u>Trade-offs for sorting</u>) N arbitrary numbers can be sorted in parallel with $(N*M)*(\lg\lg M/\lg M)$ processors in time $O(\lg N/\lg\lg M)$ on CRCW PRAM, where $M \leq N$ and $\lg M/\lg\lg M \geq \Omega(\lg\lg N)$.

<u>Proof</u>(M-way merge sort): Define the rank of item X with respect to the sorted list L, as the number of items of list L smaller than X.

If L_1 and L_2 are two sorted lists, then the ranks of all elements of L_1 with respect to elements of L_2, i.e cross-ranks, can be obtained by merging them. If i^{th} item of L_1 is in j^{th} position in the merged list, then, its rank with respect to L_2 is simply j-i.

Two lists of N elements can be merged in $O(p*\lg\lg N)$ time with $N/(p*\lg\lg N)$ processors [BH85,K83]. Thus two lists of M^k elements can be merged in $O(\lg M/\lg\lg M)$ time with $O(M^k*\lg\lg M/\lg M)$ processors.

In M-way merge sort, each item is initially in a separate list. In each round M lists are merged. Thus after k^{th} round, $N/(M^{k-1})$ lists are left. Hence sorting is complete after lg N/lg M rounds.

M-way merge is performed by forming groups of M lists and finding cross-ranks with respect to lists in that group. Position in the merged list is obtained by adding all M cross-ranks.

In k^{th} round, there are at most M^{k-1} elements in each of $N/(M^{k-1})$ lists. Since each list is merged with at most M lists, the number of processors required, for merging in O(lg M/lglg M) time, is $(N/(M^{k-1}))*(M)*(M^{k-1}$ lglg M/lg M) = N*M*lglg M/lg M.

M numbers less than N (of O(lg N) bits) can be added in O(lg M/lglg M) time with M*lglg M/lg M processors (cor 2.1, by hypothesis, $M^{1/lglg\ M} \geq$ lg N). Total number of processors used is N*M*lglg M/lg M.

Since each round requires O(lg M/lglg M) time and there are lg N/lg M rounds, the result follows. ∎

Note : The word size necessary is O(lg N) bits only as ranks do not exceed N.

Cor 3.1:(Fastest Algorithm) N numbers can be sorted in parallel in Θ(lg N/lglg N) time with $O(N^{1+(1/lglg\ N)})$ processors on CRCW model. ∎

Further, from the proof of theorem 3, the following corollary follows.

Cor 3.2: N numbers can be sorted in parallel in time O((lg N/lg M)*(time for adding M lg N bit numbers with M processors +
lglg N))

using O(NM) processors on CRCW model. ∎

Using techniques similar to that used by Cole [C87], it may be possible to find cross ranks in O(1) time. Thus, it may be possible to drop lglg N term in Cor 3.2. But, as adding M, lg N bit numbers requires Ω(min(lglg N, lg M)) time[LY86], the saving obtained by the above corollary is not significant, unless lg M < lglg N, in which case the algorithm requires $O(\lg N)$ time. In other words M-way merge sort runs in $O(\lg N)$ time for $M \leq O(\lg^{O(1)} N)$.

<u>Cor 3.3</u>: N arbitrary numbers can be sorted in parallel with $N*(M^{1-c/\lg\lg M} * \lg\lg M)*(\lg N/\lg^2 M)$ processors in time $O((\lg N*\lg\lg N)/\lg M)$ on CRCW PRAM, where $\Omega(\lg^{O(1)} N) \leq M$ and $\lg M/\lg\lg M \leq O(\lg\lg N)$.

Proof : The proof follows from theorem 2. ▮

<u>Lemma 4.1</u>: N numbers each of $O(\lg N)$ bits can be added with 2^M processors, $M = N^e$ in $O(1)$ time.

Proof: Cole and Vishkin [CV87] have shown that n numbers of m bits can be added with $(n*2^{mn})$ processors in $O(1)$ time. If the numbers are divided in groups of $n = M^{0.5}$ numbers, then as $(n*2^{\lg N*n}) < 2^M$, numbers in each group can be added in $O(1)$ time. And, N/n numbers are left, these can again be added in $O(1)$ time as before. The process requires $O(\lg N/\lg n) = O(2*\lg N/\lg M) = O(1)$ steps. As $M = N^e$, the lemma follows. ▮

<u>Theorem 4</u>: N arbitrary numbers can be sorted in parallel with 2^M processors, $M = N^k$, in $O(1)$ time on CRCW PRAM.

Proof : The first step of the algorithm given below uses $O(N^2)$ processors and the second step uses lemma above, with $e = k/2$ for finding the sum, SUM (clearly, $N < 2^M$, $M = N^e$). Both steps require $O(1)$ time.

1. for I:= 1 to N and for J:=1 to N do

   parbegin

   if ((INPUT[I] < INPUT[J]) or ((INPUT[I]=INPUT[J]) and (I$\geq$J))

   then FLAG[I,J]:=1 else FLAG[I,J]:=0;

   parend;

2. for I:= 1 to N do

   parbegin

   POSITION[I]:=SUM(FLAG[I,1],...,FLAG[I,N]);

   OUTPUT[POSITION[I]]:=INPUT[I] ;

parend ;

end ;   ∎

Remark: Note that in theorem 4, the factor, $O(\lg N/\lg\lg M) = O(1)$.

We next use the bit packing technique of Chandra et.al.[CSV84] to obtain a faster algorithm for the parallel computer model in which all the bits of a number can be set independently in parallel. This condition is clearly true for circuits.

Theorem 5: N numbers of $M \leq N$ bits can be added in $\lg N/\lg\lg N$ time with polynomial processors.

Proof: Let the N numbers of M bits be in array A, then the following algorithm can be used to find the sum.

1. Find the sum of bits in BITSUM[0..M-1] using the algorithm given in [CV87,R85].

2. for I:=0 to M-1 and J:=0 to $\lfloor \lg(\text{BITSUM}[I]) \rfloor$

   parbegin /* prepare for packing bits in lg N numbers */

   B[I mod($\lfloor 1+\lg N \rfloor$),J+I]:= BITSUM[I] $\wedge$ (0,...,0,1,0,...,1);

   parend ; /* 1 is in J^{th} place */

3. for I:=0 to lg N and J:=0 to M+$\lfloor \lg(N) \rfloor$ -1

   parbegin

   PACKEDBITS[I:J]:= B[I,J] /* copy bit B[I,J] in J^{th} bit of

                                                PACKEDBITS[I] */

   parend ;

4. Use Normal Parallel Algorithm for adding lg N numbers of O(N) bits in O(lglg(N)) time with polynomial number of processors.

The result clearly follows. ∎

Remark 1: Theorem 5 shows that Li and Yesha's[LY86] lower time bound of $\Omega(\lg N)$ for adding O(N) bit numbers on CRCW PRAM is not valid if all bits of a number can be set independently in parallel and for circuits. Thus, these models are stronger than CRCW PRAMs. Recently Immerman [I87] has shown that algorithms requiring O(lg N) time on bounded fan-in model can be simulated in O(lg N/lglg N) time on the models in which lg N shift can be done in O(1) time. This provides an alternate proof of theorem 5.

3. CONCLUSION

The upper bounds for addition matches the corresponding lower bound, thus the gap is closed. Moreover, the algorithm achieves optimal (linear) speed up for numbers having upto $O(N^{O(1)/lglg\ N})$ bits.

It appears, that addition may be the bottle neck in parallel sorting. The bound O(lg N/lglg M) for sorting with O(NM) processors is valid for a very large range of M. We thus believe, and conjecture, this to be the lower bound. Moreover, all known parallel algorithms for sorting, with O(NM) processors require O(lg N/lglg M) time (starting from constant M to exponential M).

ACKNOWLEDGEMENT : We thank referees for their helpful comments and suggestions.

REFERENCES

[AKS83] M.Ajtai, J.Komlos and E.Szemeredi, An O(nlog n) Sorting network, Proc 15th ACM Symposium on Theory of Computing (1983) , 1-9 .

[AV87] Y.Azar and U.Vishkin, Tight comparison bounds on the complexity of parallel sorting, SIAM J Computing, 16 (1987), 458-464.

[B88] P.Beame, Limits on the power of Concurrent write machines, Info and Contr, 76, (1988) 13-28.

[BH87] P.Beame and J.Hastad(1987), Optimal Bounds for Decision Problems on the CRCW PRAM, Proc 19th annual ACM Symp on theory of Computing, 83-93.

[BH85] A.Borodin and J.E.Hopcroft, Routing, Merging and Sorting on

Parallel Models of Computation, J. Computer System Sc, 30 (1985), 130-145.

[CSV84] A.K.Chandra, L.Stockmeyer and U.Vishkin, Constant Depth Reducibility, SIAM J Computing, 13 (1984), 423-439.

[C86] R.Cole, Parallel Merge Sort, Proc 27th IEEE Annual Symp on Foundations of computer Science (1986), 511-516.

[CV87] R.Cole and U.Vishkin, Faster Optimal Parallel Prefix Sums and list Ranking, Ultra Computer Note #117 & Computer Sc Tech Rept #227, New York University, Feb 1987.

[CDR86] S.Cook, C.Dwork and R.Reischuk, Upper and lower time bounds for Parallel Random Access Machines without Simultaneous writes, SIAM J Computing, 15 (1986), 87-97.

[H86] Hastad J, Almost optimal lower bounds for small depth circuits, Proc 18th ACM Symp Theory of Computing (1986), 6-20.

[I87] N.Immerman, Expressibility as a Complexity Measure : Results and Directions, Manuscript, 1987.

[K83] C.P.Kruskal, Searching, Merging and Sorting in Parallel Computation, IEEE trans Computer, C-32 (1983), 942-946.

[KRS85] C.P.Kruskal, L.Rudolph and M.Snir, The power of Parallel Prefix, IEEE trans Computer, C-34 (1985), 965-968.

[LY86] M.Li and Y.C.Yesha, New lower bounds for parallel computations, Proc 18th ACM Symposium on Theory of Computing (1986), 177-187.

[R85] J.F.Rief, An Optimal Algorithm for Integer Sorting, Proc 26th IEEE Annual Symp on Foundations of Computer Sc (1985), 496-504.

[SBP87] S.Saxena, P.C.P.Bhatt and V.C.Prasad, Fastest Possible Parallel Sorting and Addition Algorithms with polynomial number of processors, CSI communications, Dec 1987, 34-35.

[SV84] L.Stockmeyer and U.Vishkin, Simulation of Parallel Random Access Machines by Circuits, SIAM J Comput, 13 (1984), 409-422.

AN OPTIMAL PARALLEL ALGORITHM FOR SORTING PRESORTED FILES

Christos Levcopoulos
Ola Petersson
Department of Computer and Information Science
Linköping University, S-581 83 Linköping, Sweden

Abstract: We present a cost optimal parallel algorithm for sorting presorted files. The measure of presortedness we consider is the number of inversions in the input file. The algorithm sorts a file of length n, with $O(mn)$ inversions, in $O(\log n(\log^* n - \log^* m))$ time, provided $O(\frac{n \log m}{\log n \cdot (\log^* n - \log^* m)})$ processors are available, in the EREW PRAM model. This is the first PRAM sorting algorithm which is cost optimal, with respect to the number of inversions. Our method uses a new approach, which can also be used to derive a simple sequential sorting algorithm, which is efficient with respect to the number of inversions.

1. Introduction

Sequential algorithms for sorting presorted files have received a lot of attention (see e.g. Mehlhorn [8,9], Cook and Kim [4], Dijkstra [5], Mannila [7] and Estivill-Castro and Wood [6]). The term presortedness was coined by Mehlhorn [8], who used the number of inversions in the file as a measure. Mehlhorn [9] gave an $O(n + n \log(\frac{F}{n}))$ time algorithm, which we will refer to as A-Sort, for sorting a file of length n, with F inversions, which is optimal. Mannila [7] formalized the concept of presortedness and also gave optimal algorithms with respect to several other measures. Cook and Kim [4] have studied the problem empirically.

Optimal parallel algorithms, which do not utilize presortedness, have been known since 1983, when Ajtai, Kolmos and Szemeredi [1] gave an $O(n \log n)$ sorting network, which can be simulated by an EREW PRAM (Exclusive Read Exclusive Write Parallel Random Access Machine). The running time of the algorithm was $O(\log n)$; however the constant was huge. In 1986 Cole [3] gave a parallel implementation of Merge Sort, which sorts n elements in time $O(\log n)$, by using $O(n)$ processors, in the EREW PRAM model. Cole's algorithm, which we will refer to as Parallel Merge Sort, did not have such a large constant of proportionality.

Parallel algorithms for presorted files, in contrast, have not been so deeply studied. We provide the first cost optimal parallel sorting algorithm, with respect to the number of inversions, in any PRAM model. The model used is the weakest among the different PRAM's, i.e. the EREW PRAM. The algorithm sorts a file of length n, with $O(mn)$ inversions in time $O(\log n(\log^* n - \log^* m))$ by using $O(\frac{n \log m}{\log n \cdot (\log^* n - \log^* m)})$ processors on an EREW PRAM, which is cost optimal.(Increasing the number of processors by a factor p yields a reduction in running time to $O(\log n(\log^* n - \log^* m - \log^* p))$).

The algorithm actually consists of two algorithms, Algorithm A and Algorithm B, which are similar. In both algorithms we first divide the input sequence into subsequences, of equal length. We sort each subsequence, permute them, remove elements causing inversions, sort the removed elements and finally merge. The difference between the two algorithms is that in Algorithm A we have enough processors to perform the above steps in a straightforward way, while in Algorithm B we use Algorithm A as a subroutine. The algorithm uses both Parallel Merge Sort [3] and A-Sort [9] as subroutines.

By using our technique it is possible to design new sequential sorting algorithms, which are efficient with respect to the number of inversions, without using any complicated data structures (see Section 5).

The rest of the paper is organized as follows. In Section 2 we state the definitions. Section 3 and Section 4 contain the presentation and analysis of Algorithm A and Algorithm B, respectively. In Section 5 we discuss the results and outline some possible extensions.

2. Preliminaries

Let $S = \langle x_1, \ldots, x_n \rangle$ be a *sequence* of length n of elements x_i from some linear order, that is, for all $i, j \in \{1, \ldots, n\}$, $x_i \leq x_j$ or $x_j \leq x_i$. If $S = \langle x_1, \ldots, x_n \rangle$ and $S' = \langle y_1, \ldots, y_m \rangle$ are two sequences their *catenation* is denoted SS' and is defined as $\langle x_1, \ldots, x_n, y_1, \ldots, y_m \rangle$. The *length* of a sequence, S, is denoted $|S|$ and the *cardinality* of a set, A, is denoted $|A|$. We call S', $|S'| = m$, a *subsequence* of $S = \langle x_1, \ldots, x_n \rangle$ if there is an i, $1 \leq i \leq n - m + 1$, such that $S' = \langle x_i, \ldots, x_{i+m-1} \rangle$. The number of *inversions* in a sequence S, $|S| = n$, is denoted $Inv(S)$ and defined as $Inv(S) = |\{(i,j) \mid 1 \leq i < j \leq n \text{ and } x_i > x_j\}|$.

We use the following notation:
$\log x = max\{1, \log_2 x\}$
$\log^{(1)} x = \log x$
$\log^{(i)} x = \log \log^{(i-1)} x$
$\log^* x = min\{i \mid \log^{(i)} x \leq 1\}$
$2 \uparrow\uparrow 1 = 2$
$2 \uparrow\uparrow i = 2^{(2\uparrow\uparrow(i-1))}$

3. Algorithm A

Let $S = \langle x_1, \ldots, x_n \rangle$ be the sequence to be sorted, let mn be the number of inversions in S, and let $P = O(\frac{n \log m}{\log n})$ be the number of processors available. Algorithm A is applied if $m \geq \log^{\frac{1}{4}} n$ and works as follows.

1. Divide S into consecutive subsequences S_i, $1 \leq i \leq \lceil \frac{n}{l} \rceil$, of length $l = min\{n, (max\{m, \log n\})^3\}$ and sort each S_i.
2. Sort the medians of the subsequences.
3. Permute the subsequences such that the medians are sorted.
4. For each pair of subsequences S_i and S_{i+1}, $1 \leq i < \lceil \frac{n}{l} \rceil$, remove the same number of elements from the end of S_i as from the front of S_{i+1}, such that
   (i) $S_i S_{i+1}$ is sorted, and
   (ii) if we remove fewer elements $S_i S_{i+1}$ is not sorted
5. Sort the removed elements.
6. Merge S (the sorted elements left in S) with the removed elements.

Analysis and details of Algorithm A

We show that each step takes time no more than $O(\log n)$ if $P = O(\frac{n \log m}{\log n})$ processors are available.

1. Distributing the processors evenly gives us $\Theta(\frac{l \cdot \log m}{\log n})$ processors per subsequence. Using Parallel Merge Sort we can sort each S_i in time $O(\frac{\log n \log l}{\log m})$, which is $O(\log n)$.
2. Since the number of medians is less than the number of processors they can be sorted in time $O(\log n)$.
3. This step can trivially be done in $O(\log n)$, since we have less than $\log n$ elements per processor.
4. Assign one processor to each pair of subsequences, S_i and S_{i+1}. Each processor can determine the elements which shall be removed from the end of S_i and from the front of S_{i+1}, by performing an exponential and binary search (see Mehlhorn [9]), backward in S_i and forward in S_{i+1}. This search takes time $O(\log l)$, which is $O(\log n)$. Using known methods we can remove the elements and compact the remaining sequence in time $O(\log n)$.
5. We first make the following observation :

Observation 1: The number of inversions cannot have increased during the earlier steps.

How many elements can there be that were removed during step 4? Let d_i, $1 \leq i < \lceil \frac{n}{l} \rceil$, be the number of elements which were removed to make $S_i S_{i+1}$ a sorted sequence, during step 4. Since each d_i elements cause $\Omega(d_i^2)$ inversions, and by Observation 1, we get the inequality $\sum_{i=1}^{\lceil \frac{n}{l} \rceil - 1} d_i^2 \leq mn$. The number of removed elements, $\sum_{i=1}^{\lceil \frac{n}{l} \rceil - 1} d_i$, is maximized, without violating the above inequality, if all d_i's are equal to d or to $d+1$, for some integer d. We get $(\lceil \frac{n}{l} \rceil - 1) \cdot d^2 \leq mn$ and, hence, $d \leq \sqrt{\frac{m \cdot n}{\lceil n/l \rceil - 1}}$. Therefore, the maximal number of removed elements is bounded by $(\lceil \frac{n}{l} \rceil - 1) \cdot d \leq \frac{n\sqrt{m}}{\sqrt{l}}$. As in step 2, the number of elements is not greater than the number of processors, and can hence be sorted in time $O(\log n)$.

6. Bilardi and Nicolau [2] have shown that merging two sorted sequences, of length at most n, can be done in time $O(\log n)$ using $O(n/\log n)$ processors in the EREW PRAM model.

4. Algorithm B

The idea of Algorithm B, which is for the case when $m < \log^{1/4} n$, is almost the same as in Algorithm A. The exceptions are that in step 1 we set $l = \sqrt{\log n}$ and use another method for sorting the subsequences. In step 2 and step 5 we use Algorithm A to sort. We first give an $O(\log n(\log^* n - \log^* m))$ time, $O(\frac{n \log m}{\log n})$ processor, algorithm and then show how to reduce the number of processors to $O(\frac{n \log m}{\log n \cdot (\log^* n - \log^* m)})$.

The details of step 1 are as follows. We do not have enough processors to distribute them evenly and directly sort each subsequence within the requested time bound, $O(\log n(\log^* n - \log^* m))$. Let c_1 be a constant, such that A-Sort [9] sorts every sequence of length n, with $m \cdot n$ inversions, in $c_1 \cdot n \cdot \log m$ steps. Step 1, of Algorithm B, consists of $\log^* n - \log^* m - 1$ passes, each taking time $O(\log n)$. The processors are distributed evenly among the unsorted subsequences. In the first pass each processor runs $c_1 \sqrt{\log n} \cdot 2 \log m$ steps of A-Sort on each subsequence. It does not necessary sort them all but spends the same amount of time on each subsequence, such that the total time spent is $\Theta(\log n)$. In each of the following passes i, $2 \leq i \leq \log^* n - \log^* m - 1$ we proceed as follows. First we redistribute the processors evenly among the subsequences that are not yet sorted, then each processor applies $c_1 \cdot \sqrt{\log n} \cdot (2 \uparrow\uparrow (i-1))^{\log m}$ steps of A-Sort on each one of its subsequences. Again, it does not necessarily sort them all, but performs the same number of steps on each subsequence, such that the total time spent is $\Theta(\log n)$.

Analysis of Algorithm B

We show that each step, except step 1, takes time $O(\log n)$ if $P = O(\frac{n \log m}{\log n})$ processors are available. Step 1 will be shown to take time $O(\log n(\log^* n - \log^* m))$.

1. To see why $\log^* n - \log^* m - 1$ passes are enough, observe the following. In the first pass we run $c_1 \sqrt{\log n} \cdot 2 \log m$ steps of A-Sort on each subsequence. Let X_1 be the number of subsequences which are not in sorted order after the first pass. Each of these X_1 subsequences must have had more than $\sqrt{\log n} \cdot m^2$ inversions, otherwise they would have been sorted. Hence, we get the inequality $X_1 \sqrt{\log n} \cdot m^2 \leq mn$, from which we conclude that $X_1 \leq \frac{n}{m\sqrt{\log n}}$. Now, after redistributing the processors, in the second pass we can spend time $\Omega(\sqrt{\log n} \cdot m \cdot \log m)$ on each subsequence so we run

$c_1\sqrt{\log n} \cdot m$ steps of A-Sort on each subsequence. In the third pass we can spend at least $\Omega(\sqrt{\log n} \cdot 2^m)$ and so on. In the $\log^* n - \log^* m - 1$:th pass we can spend at least $\Omega(\sqrt{\log n} \cdot \log \log n)$ time on each subsequence, which is enough to sort it, independently of the number of inversions.

2. We have enough processors to apply Algorithm A to sort the medians. To see this set $n' = \frac{n}{\sqrt{\log n}}$, that is the number of medians to be sorted. If we rewrite P in terms of n' we get the inequality $P \geq \frac{n'}{\log n'}\sqrt{\log n'}$. Let m' be a number such that the number of inversions among the medians is $m'n'$. The number of inversions is bounded by $mn = n'\sqrt{\log n'} \cdot m < n' \cdot \log^{3/4} n'$, so we get $m' < \log^{3/4} n'$. Since the inequality $P \geq \frac{n' \cdot \log m'}{\log n'}$ holds, and since $\sqrt{\log n} \geq \frac{1}{4} \log \log n'$ for sufficiently large n', Algorithm A can be applied to sort the medians in time $O(\log n') = O(\log n)$.

3. This step can, as was the case for Algorithm A, be done in time $O(\log n)$ since we have less than $\log n$ elements per processor.

4. The same argument as for Algorithm A applies. Hence, it can be done in time $O(\log n)$.

5. By the same argument as in the analysis for Algorithm A we conclude that the number of removed elements $n' \leq \frac{n\sqrt{m}}{\sqrt{l}} < \frac{n}{\log^{1/8} n}$. If $n' \leq \frac{n}{\log n}$ we can use Parallel Merge Sort [3] to sort the removed elements in time $O(\log n)$. Otherwise we can apply Algorithm A. To see this rewrite P in terms of n'; we get the inequality $P > \frac{n'}{\log n'} \cdot \log^{1/8} n'$. Let m' be a number such that the number of inversions among the removed elements is $m'n'$. The number of inversions is, by Observation 1, bounded by $mn \leq m \cdot n' \log n' < n' \cdot \log^{5/4} n'$, from which we conclude that $m' < \log^{5/4} n'$. Since we have at least $\frac{n'}{\log n'} \cdot \log m'$ processors, and since $\log^{1/8} n' \geq \frac{1}{4} \log \log n'$ for sufficiently large n', Algorithm A can be applied to sort the n' elements in time $O(\log n') = O(\log n)$.

6. As in Algorithm A the merging is done in time $O(\log n)$.

Together Algorithm A and Algorithm B imply that we can sort a sequence S, $|S| = n$, with $O(nm)$ inversions in time $O(\log n(\log^* n - \log^* m))$ if $P = O(\frac{n \log m}{\log n})$ processors are available. Next, we show how to transform this into an optimal algorithm, by reducing the number of processors. We show

Theorem: Let S be a sequence of n elements, with $O(mn)$ inversions. Given $P = O(\frac{n \log m}{\log n(\log^* n - \log^* m)})$ processors, S can be sorted in time $O(\log n(\log^* n - \log^* m))$ in the EREW PRAM model, which is optimal.

Proof: In Algorithm A, $\log^* n - \log^* m$ is a constant, since $m \geq \log^{1/4} n$. Hence, Algorithm A needs no changes to run in time $O(\log n)$ by using $P = O(\frac{n \log m}{\log n(\log^* n - \log^* m)})$ processors. In Algorithm B, however, $\log^* n - \log^* m$ is no longer a constant. The only critical step in Algorithm B is the first one. (The other steps can easily be shown to run in time $O(\log n(\log^* n - \log^* m))$ by slowing down everything by a factor $\log^* n - \log^* m$). The idea is to first use time $O(\log n(\log^* n - \log^* m))$ to sort all but $\frac{n}{\sqrt{\log n}} \cdot (\log^* n - \log^* m)$ subsequences and then apply the method of step 1, given for Algorithm B above, to sort the remaining unsorted subsequences in time $O(\log n(\log^* n - \log^* m))$. An optimal sequential algorithm with respect to the number of inversions, for sorting all but $\frac{n}{\sqrt{\log n (\log^* n - \log^* m)}}$ subsequences would perform $c \cdot n \log m$ operations. The following is a parallelization of such an algorithm which performs no more than $2 \cdot c \cdot n \log m$ operations, and is what we do in the first stage of step 1.

Distribute the processors evenly;
while each processor has at least $\frac{\sqrt{\log n}}{\log m}$ subsequences **do begin**
  repeat in parallel
    Each processor picks any of its subsequences and starts sorting it;
    When finished it picks another of its subsequences and starts sorting;
  until $\log n$ time is used;
  in parallel do
    Each processor completes the sorting of the subsequence it was working
      on (if any) when it was interrupted;
  Redistribute the processors evenly;
end; {*while*}

Since each processor has at least $\frac{\sqrt{\log n}}{\log m}$ subsequences, that is $\frac{\log n}{\log m}$ elements, and since we can spend $O(\log m)$ time on each element, it follows that no processor is ever idle during the repeat-loop, except possibly during $O(\log m)$ time for each element it has been working on. Hence, the processors are performing relevant sorting work all the time except for at most $O(n \log m)$ operations. Since $O(n \log m)$ operations are sufficient for doing the work and since we use $O(\frac{n \log m}{\log n(\log^* n - \log^* m)})$ processors, the running time is $O(\log n(\log^* n - \log^* m))$. The remaining unsorted subsequences can be sorted within the same time bound by using the method described in step 1, of Algorithm B above.

5. Final Comments

We have presented the first PRAM sorting algorithm which is cost optimal with respect to the number of inversions in the input file. If the number of inversions, $m \cdot n$, is known in advance then we allocate the appropriate number of processors and sort optimally. On the other hand, if we are given P processors we compute k such that $P = O(\frac{n \log k}{\log n(\log^* n - \log^* k)})$ and assume that $m = k$. If $k \geq \log^{\frac{1}{4}} n$ we run the first four steps of Algorithm A. If, in step 5, the number of removed elements is not greater than the number of processors the last two steps are performed and the sorting is completed. Otherwise we restart the algorithm and assume that $m = k^2$. Again, the first four steps are run and if there are too many elements left we assume that $m = k^4$ and so on. If $k < \log^{\frac{1}{4}} n$ the first step of Algorithm B is run repeatedly, with $m = k, k^2, k^4, k^8$ and so on, until all subsequences are sorted, or until $m \geq \log^{\frac{1}{4}} n$ in which case we start Algorithm A, as described above. If the number of inversions in the input sequence is at least $k \cdot n$, i.e. $k \leq m$, the last iteration takes time $O(\frac{\log m}{\log k} \cdot \log n(\log^* n - \log^* k))$ and the sum of the time taken by all other iterations is dominated by the last one. Hence, the running time is optimal, that is $O(\frac{n \log m}{P})$. Otherwise, if the number of inversions is $< k \cdot n$, P can be written as $P = O(p \cdot \frac{n \log m}{\log n(\log^* n - \log^* m)})$ and as mentioned in Section 1 the running time will be $O(\log n(\log^* n - \log^* m - \log^* p))$.

If the number of inversions is fairly large, say $n \log^{\Omega(1)} n$, Algorithm A is applied to sort the file optimally. By using the method described above, for the case when m is not known in advance, it is easily seen that Algorithm A can be implemented sequentially to run optimally if the number of inversions is $n \log^{\Omega(1)} n$, without using any complicated data structures, such as those used in A-Sort [9]. If the number of inversions is fewer it will run in time $O(n \log \log n)$.

We are currently working on designing parallel algorithms which utilize other measures of presortedness.

REFERENCES

[1] M.Ajtai, J.Komlos, E.Szemeredi, "An $O(n \log n)$ sorting network", Combinatorica 3, 1983, 1-19.
[2] G.Bilardi, A.Nicolau, "Adaptive Bitonic Sorting: An optimal parallel algorithm for shared memory models", to appear in SIAM Journal on Computing.
[3] R.Cole, "Parallel Merge Sort", 27th FOCS, 1986, 511-516.
[4] C.R.Cook, D.J.Kim, "Best sorting algorithms for nearly sorted lists", Comm. of the ACM 23-11, 1980, 620-624.
[5] E.W.Dijkstra, "Smoothsort, an alternative to sorting in situ", Science of Computer Programming 1, 1982, 223-233.
[6] V.Estivill-Castro, D.Wood, "A new measure of presortedness", Research Report CS-87-58, 1987, Waterloo.
[7] H.Mannila, "Measures of presortedness and optimal sorting algorithms", ICALP 1984, 324-336.
[8] K.Mehlhorn, "Sorting presorted files", 4th GI Conference on Theoretical Computer Science, Springer Verlag, 1979, 199-212.
[9] K.Mehlhorn, "Data Structures and Algorithms 1: Sorting and Searching", Springer Verlag, 1984, 217-228.

Superlinear Speedup in Parallel State-Space Search

V. Nageshwara Rao and Vipin Kumar*

Department of Computer Sciences,
University of Texas at Austin,
Austin, Texas 78712

Abstract

When N processors perform depth-first search on disjoint parts of a state space tree to find a solution, the speedup can be superlinear (i.e., $> N$) or sublinear (i.e., $< N$) depending upon when a solution is first encountered in the space by one of the processors. It may appear that on the average, the speedup would be either linear or sublinear. Using an analytical model, we show that if the search space has more than one solution and if these solutions are randomly distributed in a relatively small region of the search space, then the average speedup in parallel depth-first search can be superlinear. If all the solutions (one or more) are uniformly distributed over the whole search space, then the average speedup is linear. This model is validated by our experiments on synthetic state-space trees and the 15-puzzle problem. The same model predicts average superlinear speedup in parallel best-first branch-and-bound algorithms on suitable problems.

1 Introduction

Consider the problem of finding a solution in a state-space tree containing one or more solutions [3,22,21]. Depth-first search (DFS) is a widely used technique for solving such problems[7,22]. A number of parallel formulations of depth-first search have been developed by various researchers [18,10,6,1,17,11]. In one such formulation[10], N processors concurrently perform depth-first search in disjoint parts of a state-space tree to find a solution in the search space. The parts of the state-space searched by different processors are determined dynamically, and are roughly of equal sizes. Since only one solution is needed, the search terminates whenever any of the processors encounters a solution. Depending upon when a solution is first encountered in the space by the processors, the speedup can be superlinear (i.e., $> N$) or sublinear (i.e., $< N$)[1]. This phenomenon of speedup being greater than N on N processors in isolated executions of parallel depth-first search has been reported by many researchers [6,18,17,1,25]. The speedup can differ greatly from one execution to another, as the actual parts of the search space searched by different processors are determined dynamically, and can be different for different executions. Hence

---

*This work was supported by Army Research Office grant # DAAG29-84-K-0060 to the Artificial Intelligence Laboratory, and Office of Naval Research Grant N00014-86-K-0763 to the computer science department at the University of Texas at Austin.

[1]This phenomenon is also referred to as 'speedup anomalies'.

for some execution sequences, the parallel version may find a solution by visiting fewer nodes than the sequential version (giving superlinear speedup), and for others it may find a solution only after visiting more nodes (giving sublinear speedup). It may appear that on the average the speedup would be either linear or sublinear. Using an analytical model, we show that if the search space has more than one solution and if these solutions are uniformly distributed in a relatively small (randomly located) region of the search space, then the average speedup in parallel depth-first search can be superlinear. If all of the solutions (one or more) are uniformly distributed over the whole search space, then the average speedup is linear. This model is validated by our experiments on synthetic state-space trees modelling the hackers problem[24] and the 15-puzzle problem[21]. For some instances of 15-puzzle with this property, the average speedup was found to be as much as 17 for 9 processors. Our model also predicts average superlinear speedup in parallel best-first branch-and-bound algorithms on suitable problems.

Section 2 gives a brief review of parallel depth-first search. Section 3 presents assumptions and definitions used in the analysis, and introduces a model for the analysis of speedup in parallel depth-first search. Experimental results on synthetic trees and 15-puzzle instances are presented in Section 4. Section 5 discusses the relevance of the model to best-first branch-and-bound. Section 6 discusses related research. Conclusions follow in Section 7.

2 Review of Parallel Depth-First search

There are many different parallel formulations of depth-first search[1,8,18,2,13], suitable for execution on asynchronous MIMD multiprocessors. The formulation discussed here is the most commonly used formulation[17,18,11]. In this formulation, the search space is split into many disjoint parts and each part is assigned to one of the processors. More than one part may be assigned to one processor. The splitting of the search space may be done statically before hand [13] or may be performed dynamically [18,17,1]. In dynamic splitting whenever a processor completes search on the part assigned to it, it requests a busy processor for work. The busy processor splits its search space into two pieces and gives a piece of its work to the requesting processor. When a solution is found by any processor, all of them quit. If the search space is finite and has no solutions, then eventually all the processors would run out of work, and the (parallel) search will terminate without finding any solution.

3 A Model for the Analysis of Speedup in Parallel DFS

3.1 Assumptions and Definitions

We study a simple model of parallel depth-first search of a complete binary tree of M leaf nodes, with static partitioning of the tree among N processors. Each processor gets a contiguous part (of size $\frac{M}{N}$) of the search space for itself. Solutions occur among the leaf nodes. We assume that the solutions are distributed uniformly in a randomly located region. Such an assumption is valid in problems for which no good heuristic is available to direct the search.[2] For simplicity we assume

---

[2]If a good heuristic is available, then it will be difficult to obtain even linear speedup. The heuristic would cause the solutions to migrate to the left part of the tree, where they will be quickly found by the sequential depth-first search.

that the number of nodes in any subtree of the search tree (generated by DFS) is proportional to the number of leaves in that subtree. Hence amount of work done in a search can be estimated by the number of leaf nodes visited. Sequential and parallel depth-first search stop after finding one solution.

1. Problem size M: is the size of the search space (in number of leaf nodes).

2. Number of processors N : is the number of processors being used to run parallel DFS.

3. Number of Solutions α : is the number of solutions in the search space.

4. Solution region r : is the region of the search horizon which contains all the solutions. We assume that the solutions are uniformly distributed in the region r. The symbol r is also used to denote the size of the region containing the solution nodes. When the solutions occur uniformly distributed over entire search space, $r = M$. Fig. 1 schematically shows an example of a search tree being searched by four processors.

5. Nodes expanded W_N: is the average of the total number of nodes visited by N processors before one of the processors finds a solution. In our experiments, this average is taken over a large number of executions of parallel depth-first search on a problem instance. In each execution, successors of nodes are ordered randomly. W_1 is the average number of nodes expanded by sequential depth-first search.

6. Running time T_N: is the average execution time on N processors. T_1 is the sequential execution time.

7. Speedup S : is the ratio $\frac{T_1}{T_N}$. For the experiments discussed in this paper the overheads of parallel depth-first search used are negligible. Hence the execution time of a processor (in the sequential as well as parallel case) is proportional to the number of nodes expanded. Therefore,

$$Speedup\ S \simeq \frac{W_1}{W_N} \star N$$

8. Efficiency E: is the speedup divided by N. E denotes the effective utilization of computing resources.

$$E = \frac{S}{N}$$
$$\simeq \frac{W_1}{W_N * N}$$

In Section 3.2, we analyze the amount of work done by sequential depth-first search and by parallel depth-first search. We derive formulas relating W_N to number of processors and distribution of solutions for depth-first search and for parallel depth-first search. In the Section 3.3, these formulas are used to compute speedup and efficiency. Although we are able to derive the formulas for W_N only under certain restrictive conditions, we are still able to explain the results of Section 4.

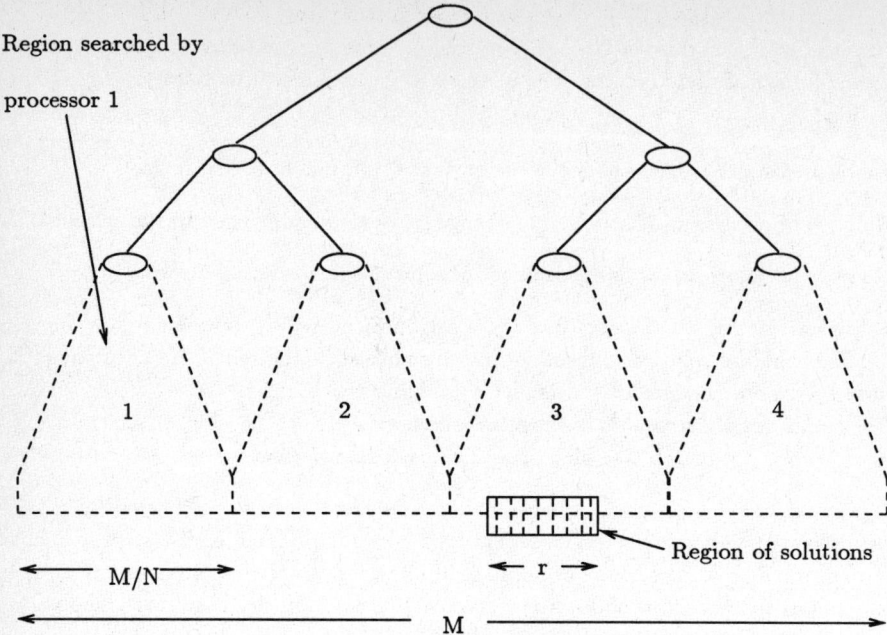

Figure 1: Example of a search tree being searched by four processors.

3.2 Average work done by depth-first search

3.2.1 Single processor performing DFS

When one processor performs depth-first search on a space with uniform distribution of α solutions over the entire space M,

$$Work\ done\ W_1 = \frac{M}{\alpha + 1}$$

This follows from the following analysis. When α out of M nodes are chosen to be goal nodes at random, the mean number of leaf nodes visited by a single processor searching left to right is the expected value of the minimum of the indices of the solution nodes. Expected value of min of the indices

$$= \frac{1}{^M C_\alpha}(1 \star {^{M-1}C_{\alpha-1}} + 2 \star {^{M-2}C_{\alpha-1}} + \cdots + (N - \alpha + 1) \star {^{\alpha-1}C_{\alpha-1}})$$

We have

$$\sum_{i=0}^{i=N} {^i C_M} = {^{N+1} C_{M+1}}$$

$$and\ {^N C_M} = 0\ if\ N < M$$

Hence

$$Work\ done\ W_1 = \frac{1}{^M C_\alpha}(\sum_{i=0}^{i=M-1} {^i C_{\alpha-1}} + \sum_{i=0}^{i=M-2} {^i C_{\alpha-1}} + \cdots + \sum_{i=0}^{i=0} {^i C_{\alpha-1}})$$

$$= \frac{1}{^M C_\alpha} \sum_{i=0}^{i=M} {}^i C_\alpha$$

$$= \frac{^{M+1} C_{\alpha+1}}{^M C_\alpha}$$

$$= \frac{M+1}{\alpha+1}$$

$$\simeq \frac{M}{\alpha+1} \; for \; large \; M$$

Now we consider the more general case in which α solutions are distributed uniformly in a region r, and the region r occurs at a random location in the search horizon. (Clearly, if $r = M$, then we get the previous case in which α solutions are distributed uniformly in the entire search horizon.) The starting point of the region r is any where between 0 and $M - r$. Once search reaches the region, it searches for 1 solution in region r containing α solutions. Hence,

$$Work \; done \; W_1 \simeq \frac{1}{2}(M-r) + \frac{r}{\alpha+1} \quad (1)$$

3.2.2 Multiple processors performing PDFS

Here we consider the case in which N processors search a space of size M in parallel. As before, α solutions are distributed uniformly in a region r, and the region r occurs at a random location in the search horizon. We have two cases, one when $r \leq \frac{M}{N}$, and the other when $r \geq \frac{M}{N}$.

When $r \leq \frac{M}{N}$, we only compute W_N for the case in which one of the processors has the solution region entirely in its search space while the other processors do not have any solution in their search spaces. In this case, one of the processors searches a space of size $\frac{M}{N}$ with a solution region of size r. Assuming that all processors work at uniform speed, the work done by N processors in parallel equals N times the work done by a single processor searching on a space of size $\frac{M}{N}$ with the region r randomly distributed with in this space.

Therefore

$$Work \; done \; W_N = N(\frac{1}{2}(\frac{M}{N}-r) + \frac{r}{\alpha+1}) \quad (2)$$

When $r \geq \frac{M}{N}$, we only analyze the simple case in which r is a multiple of $\frac{M}{N}$ (i.e., $r = k\frac{M}{N}$), and k processors have α solutions uniformly distributed in their search space, while the rest have no solutions in their search space. If $k = 1$, then the work done by N processors in parallel equals N times the work done by a single processor searching on a space of size $\frac{M}{N}$ with α solutions distributed uniformly in its space.

Therefore

$$Work \; done \; W_N \simeq N(\frac{\frac{M}{N}}{\alpha+1}) = \frac{M}{\alpha+1} \quad (3)$$

The above equation holds even if $k > 1$, provided $\alpha \ll \frac{M}{N}$ (which is generally the case) for the following reason. When $\alpha \ll \frac{M}{N}$, the probability of two or more processors finding a solution at the same time becomes low. In parallel search, k nodes are visited in each step by the 'k processors' and there are α solutions in all, uniformly distributed in $\frac{M}{N}$ steps without repetitions. This situation is similar to a single processor searching for α solutions uniformly distributed in its search space of size $\frac{M}{N}$. Therefore the processors require $\frac{\frac{M}{N}}{\alpha+1}$ steps to find a solution.

3.3 Efficiency of Parallel Depth-First Search

We study the efficiency of parallel DFS in the following three cases.

- Uniform distribution of a single solution in the search space.
- Uniform distribution of multiple solutions in the search space.
- Non-uniform distribution of multiple solutions in the search space.

3.3.1 Uniform distribution of a single solution in the search space

In this case, $\alpha = 1$ and $r = M$. Using equations 1 and 3, we have

$$Average\ work\ done\ by\ sequential\ DFS\ \ W_1 = \frac{M}{2}$$

$$Average\ work\ done\ by\ parallel\ DFS\ \ W_N = \frac{M}{1+1}$$

$$Efficiency\ of\ parallel\ DFS\ \ E = \frac{W_1}{W_N} = 1$$

Thus if one solution is uniformly distributed in the search space, then parallel DFS only obtains linear speedup on the average.

3.3.2 Uniform distribution of multiple solutions in the Search Space

In this case again, we have $r = M$. Using equations 1 and 3, we have

$$W_1 = \frac{M}{\alpha + 1}$$

$$W_N = \frac{M}{\alpha + 1}$$

$$E = 1$$

Thus the speedup remains linear, because the absolute amount of average work done by both sequential and parallel depth-first search goes down by the same amount when α is increased.

3.3.3 Non uniform distribution of multiple solutions

In section 3.2.2, we have computed W_N only for two restrictive cases: (i) $r = k\frac{M}{N}$ for some positive integer k, and k processors have α solutions uniformly distributed in their search space; (ii) $r \leq \frac{M}{N}$, and the solution region falls within one processor's search space. In the first case, by Equation 3 we have

$$W_N = \frac{M}{\alpha + 1}$$

In the second case, by Equation 2 we have

$$W_N = N(\frac{1}{2}(\frac{M}{N} - r) + \frac{r}{\alpha + 1})$$

As we decrease r from M to $\frac{M}{N}$ (in the multiples of $\frac{M}{N}$) and then from $\frac{M}{N}$ to α (continuously), we see that the value of W_N remains at $\frac{M}{\alpha+1}$ until $r = \frac{M}{N}$ and then increases to $\frac{M}{2}$. On the other hand from Equation 1, the work done in sequential depth-first search increases from $\frac{M}{\alpha+1}$ to $\frac{M}{2}$. Hence we have a region of values for r where we get superlinear speedup.

We obtain maximum efficiency when $r = \frac{M}{N}$.

$$Maximum\ Efficiency = \frac{\frac{1}{2}(M - \frac{M}{N}) + \frac{\frac{M}{N}}{\alpha+1}}{\frac{M}{\alpha+1}}$$

$$= \frac{\alpha+1}{2} - \frac{\alpha-1}{2N}$$

$$\simeq \frac{\alpha+1}{2}\ (for\ large\ N)$$

This analysis suggests that superlinear speedup occurs in depth-first search when the the size of the region of solutions is comparable to the size of the search space of each processor $\frac{M}{N}$ and there are multiple solutions. When the region of solutions is very small compared to $\frac{M}{N}$, the speedup is linear. The speedup is also linear when solutions are uniformly distributed over the entire search space.

4 Experimental Results

We analyzed the performance of parallel DFS in two problems. The first one is the search of an abstract binary tree (of depth 16) and the other is the classical 15-puzzle problem[21]. In both the problems, parallel DFS technique described in [18,19] was used. This scheme uses dynamic splitting of the search space; experiments with both of the problems deviate from the model, as the solution region may be scattered over many processors.

The binary tree search problem models the hacker's problem[24]. It involves searching a complete binary tree in which some of the leaf nodes are solution nodes. The path to the solution node represents the correct password among the various binary sequences of a fixed length. This problem was chosen in order to be able to directly manipulate the size of the solution region r and the density of solutions ρ. We implemented a program on Sequent Balance 21000 multiprocessor and experimented with different cases for up to 16 processors. In order to get mean values of T_N and W_N, each experiment was repeated at least 100 times. The experiments analyzing superlinear speedup for large N were repeated more often. Fig. 2 shows a plot of efficiency of parallel depth-first search versus number of processors for the case in which solutions are distributed uniformly in the entire search space. The different plots are for different solution densities. The absolute amount of work done in both sequential and parallel depth-first search varies inversely with α (the number of solutions) as predicted by equations 1 and 3 (this information is not shown in Fig. 2).

Fig. 3 shows efficiency of parallel depth-first search versus number of processors for the case in which all the solutions are distributed (uniformly) in a region r. In order to randomize the location of the solution region, each experiment involved searching the tree with the solution region starting at a randomly chosen location. Different plots are for different ratios of r to M with fixed α (=4). As prediced by Equation 1, for small values of r, the sequential depth-first search searches approximately half the space. Notice that when $\frac{r}{M} = \frac{1}{8}$, peak efficiency is obtained for 8-10 processors and when $\frac{r}{M} = \frac{1}{16}$ efficiency increases up to 16 processors. Peak efficiency is not as high as predicted by our analysis because the solution region is not confined to one processor

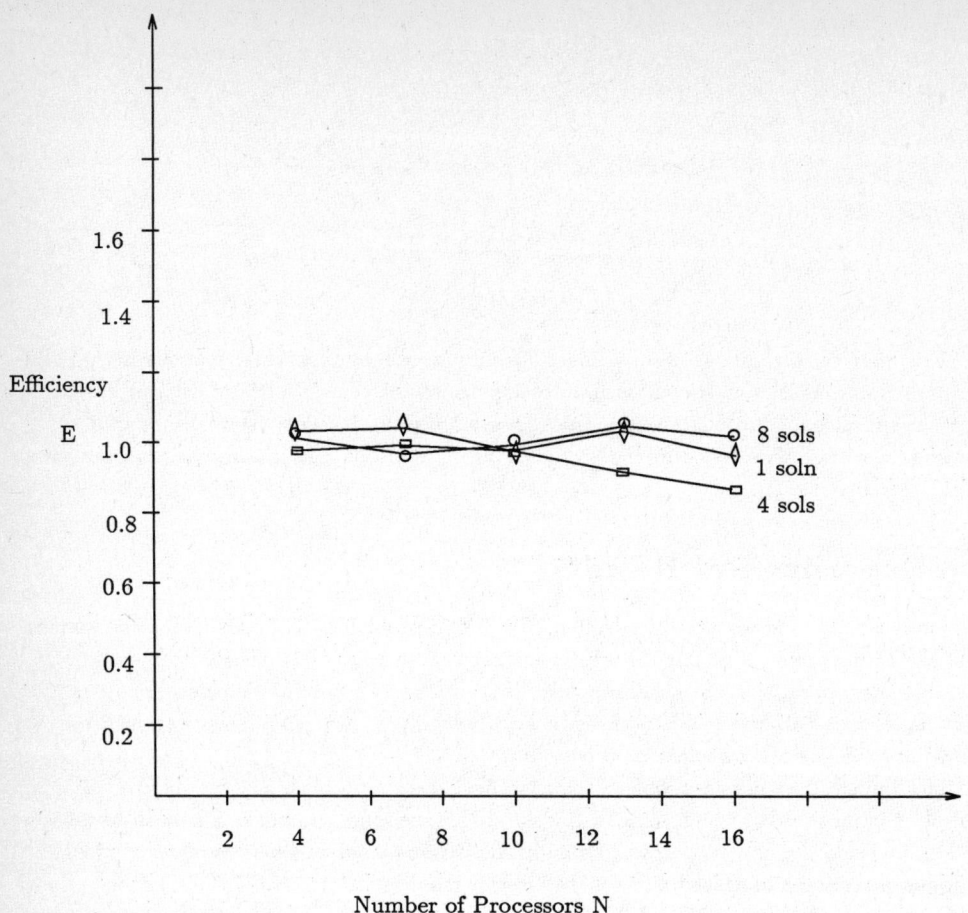

Figure 2: Efficiency vs number of processors for various solutions densities with uniform distribution. The number of solutions is given next to the curves.

(as assumed in the analysis). Since the search space is divided dynamically, the solution region may be shared by many processors. However it appears that some processors were able to get a reasonable distribution of solutions which resulted in the superlinear speedup. Note that the peak speedup is smaller for the ratio $\frac{r}{M} = \frac{1}{16}$ than for the ratio $\frac{r}{M} = \frac{1}{8}$. One possible explanation for this is that as $\frac{r}{M}$ decreases, the solution region becomes narrower which makes it harder for any of the processors to get a reasonable part of the overall solution region. This suggests that if the ratio $\frac{r}{M}$ is decreased to a very small number (e.g., $\frac{1}{256}$), then the peak efficiency would not be much higher than 1. Thus it appears that the superlinear speedup is likely only for a small number of processors.

The 15-puzzle problem was used to experiment with a search space bounded by a heuristic. These experiments were performed on the BBN Butterfly parallel processor for up to 9 processors. The experiments involved instances of the 15-puzzle with single solution, uniform distribution of multiple solutions, and non-uniform distribution of multiple solutions. A bounded depth-first

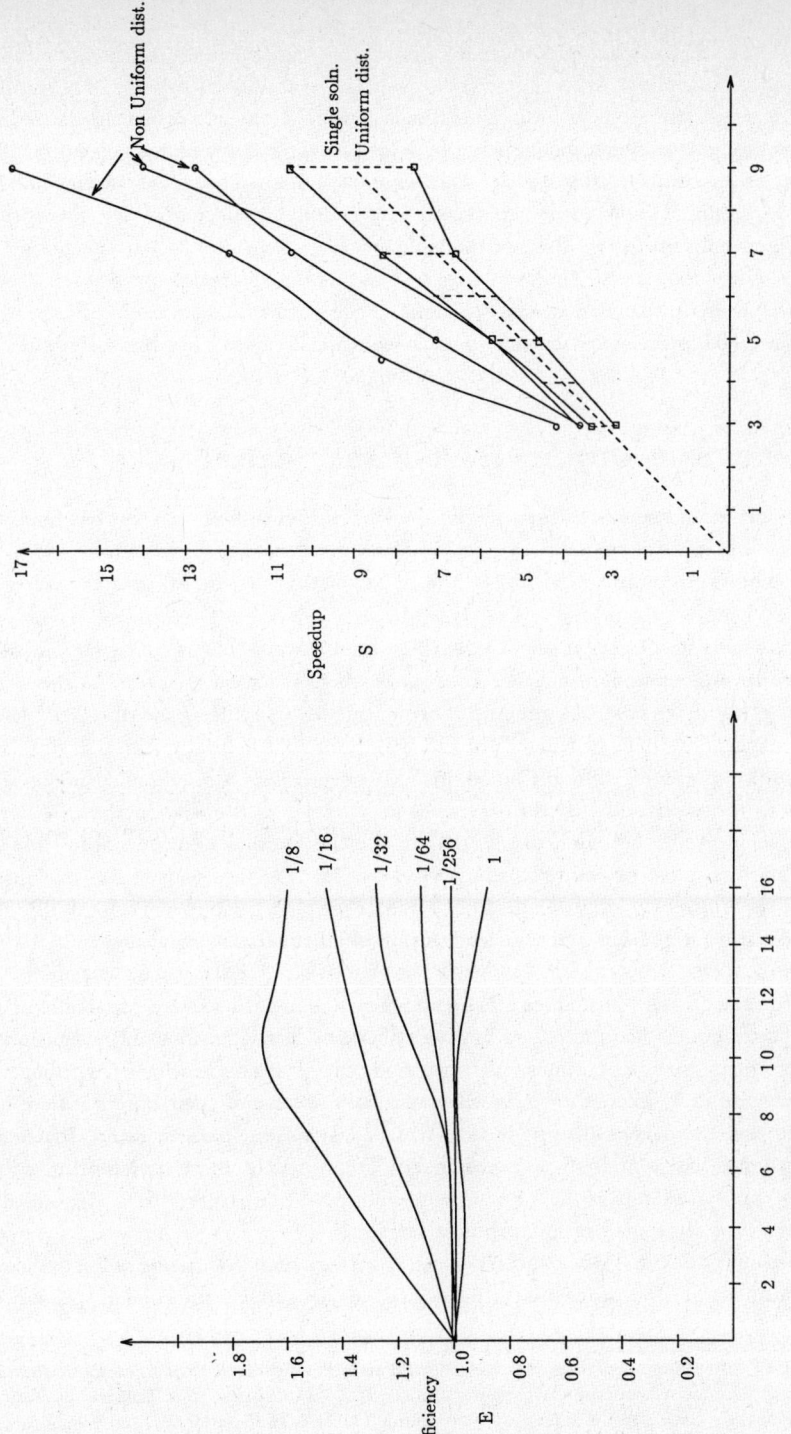

Figure 3: Efficiency vs number of processors for different values of region of solutions. An efficiency greater than 1 indicates superlinear speedup.

Figure 4: Experiments on 15-puzzle.

search was used to limit the search space. Both the sequential and parallel DFS perform the search in a random order - the alternatives at each node in the search tree are randomly ordered for traversal.[3] The average timings for sequential and parallel search were obtained by running each experiment 100 times (for every 15-puzzle instance). Fig. 4 shows the average speedups obtained. The instances with uniform distribution of solutions show a near linear speedup. The maximum deviation of speedup is indicated by the banded region. The width of the banded region is is expected to reduce if a lot more repetitions (say a 1000 for every instance) were tried. The instances with non-uniform distribution of multiple solutions give superlinear speedups.

Both of these experiments confirm the predictions of the model. Superlinear speedup occurs in parallel depth-first search whenever many solutions occur within a restricted region of the search space. Linear speedup occurs when one or more solutions occur uniformly distributed in the search space.

5 Superlinear Speedup in Best-First Search

So far we discussed the phenomenon of superlinear speedup in depth-first search. Our analysis also predicts average superlinear speedup in parallel (best-first) branch-and-bound (B&B) for certain kinds of problems. As discussed in [7,20], the A* algorithm [21] for state-space search is a best-first B&B algorithm.

In B&B/A*, if the heuristic function is consistent[21], then the cost of the nodes expanded in successive iterations never goes down (it either goes up or stays the same). Let V_i be the set of nodes expanded by A* after the cost has gone up i^{th} time but before it has gone up $i+1^{th}$ time. Clearly the cost of each node in V_i (for any i) is the same, and the heuristic function does not provide any discrimination among different nodes in V_i. V_0 represents the expanded nodes that have the same cost as the start node. If the cost goes up L times in the search, then V_L is the set of nodes expanded whose cost is the same as that of the the optimal solution. Note that the heuristic functions used in most of the problems solved by B&B/A* are consistent. For many such problems (e.g., the Vertex Cover problem, the 15-puzzle problem), V_i grows very rapidly. For these problems, nodes in V_L represent a very large fraction of all the nodes expanded by A*. (For the instances of Vertex Cover Problem and 15-puzzle that we tried, V_L constitute more than 70% of the total nodes expanded by A*[9].) Since all the nodes in V_L have the same cost, the heuristic function does not provide any discrimination between these nodes. Consider the execution of B&B search after cost has gone up L times. When a node in V_L is selected for expansion, and some of its successors are in V_L (i.e., they have the same cost as that of their parent), then one of these is expanded and the others are put on a list of nodes to be expanded later. Hence A* essentially performs depth-first search of the nodes in V_L. Conceptually, the parallel formulations of best-first B&B/A* presented in [9,16,12] divide the search space represented by V_L dynamically and expand nodes in these subspaces in a depth-first fashion.

Hence if the solution nodes in V_L are located close together, and fall in the search space of one of (or a small number of) the processors, then again we can expect superlinear speedup on the average.

---

[3]It might seem that DFS with random ordering of successors would perform much worse than ordered DFS in which successors are ordered according to a heuristic). Experience with the IDA* algorithm on the 15-puzzle problem [5] indicates that the use of the Manhattan distance heuristic for ordering (which is the best known admissible heuristic for 15-puzzle) does not make depth-first search any better. This is contrary to general expectation.

6 Related Research

Monien et al.[17] studied a parallel formulation of depth-first search for solving the satisfiability problem. In this formulation, each processor tries to prove the satisfiability of a different subformula of the input formula. Due to the nature of the satisfiability problem, each of these subformulas leads to a search space with a different average density of solutions. Monien developed an abstract model to show that these differing solution densities are responsible for the average superlinear speedup. Our model is related to this model, as location of solutions in a part of the space indirectly causes difference in the solution densities of the regions searched by different processors.

If the search space is searched in a random fashion, then the number of nodes expanded before a solution is found is a random variable (let's call it T(1)). One very simple parallel formulation[15,2] of depth-first search is to let the same search space be searched by many processors independently until one of the processors finds a solution[4]. The total number of nodes expanded by a processor in this formulation is again a random variable (let's call it T(N)). Clearly, $T(N) = \min\{V_1,...,V_N\}$, where each V_i is a random variable. If the average value of T(N) is less than $\frac{1}{N}$ times T(1), then also we can expect superlinear speedup[15,2,5]. For certain distributions of T(1), this happens to be the case[15]. For example, if the probability of finding a solution at any level of the state-space tree is the same, then T(1) has this property[5]. Clearly, for these cases, our parallel formulation (in which different processors search different parts of the search space) would also exhibit superlinear speedup on the average. But for the distributions discussed in this paper, speedup using this simple parallel formulation is not superlinear (see [2]).

It is also possible to obtain superlinear speedup if simple depth-first search (without its incorporation in the IDA* algorithm) is used to find an optimal path in a state-space graph or tree. In this case, the search continues even after finding the first solution. Whenever a search branch is encountered that has worse cost than the best solution found so far, it is terminated. Search ends when the whole space is exhausted. (Note that this kind of search is very different from that done by IDA*, in which each iteration is a simple depth-first search for **one** solution in a cost-bounded space.) In this case, the efficiency depends greatly on finding a good solution early in the search tree which could be used later to prune other branches. If many processors search the space simultaneously, then the probability of finding a good solution early in the search increases. This can cause superlinear speedups on the average. This phenomenon was investigated by Imai, et. al.[1]. Here the presence of super-linear speedup is not surprising at all, as for finding an optimal solution, "best-first" search methods (and the iterative-deepening method) are strictly better. The parallel version of depth-first search for this case tries to approximate best-first search, hence does better than the sequential depth-first search. On the other hand, for finding a solution in the state-space tree, depth-first search is not dominated by a "best-first" search (or by any other) method.

The possibility of anomalies in speedup in parallel best-first B&B algorithms has been investigated by many researchers[12,14,23]. Lai and Sahni[12] show that it is possible to obtain arbitrarily large speedups on certain abstract state-space trees. Based upon their experience with the traveling salesperson problem and the knapsack problem, they conclude that such behavior is unlikely in real problems. Quinn and Deo[23] note that speedup anomalies are unlikely 'unless

---

[4]Note that our parallel formulation of DFS will always perform better than this simple parallel formulation, as in our formulation there is no duplication of work.

there are a large number of subproblems with the same lower bound as the solution cost' (in our terminology, unless V_N is large). Our analysis shows that if V_N is large and if the goals are distributed uniformly, then on the average the speedup will only be linear. But if V_N is large and the goal nodes are located in a relatively small region, then superlinear speedup should be observed.

7 Concluding Remarks

The research reported in this paper was motivated by our earlier work on a parallel implementation of the IDA* algorithm.[18] Even though, IDA* is the best known sequential algorithm for solving the 15-puzzle (i.e., for finding a shortest sequence of moves between two configurations of the puzzle)[4], we were surprised to obtain superlinear speedups on the average on randomly chosen 15-puzzle instances[5]. Our first reaction was to assume that our sample size was too small, and that for big enough sample size, the average speedup would become sublinear. We were later encouraged by Monien's analysis of the superlinear speedup in the satisfiability problem to perform a similar analysis for the 15-puzzle.

Although the model presented here is rather artificial, it is adequate to explain the superlinear speedups in parallel depth-first search of search spaces containing a few goal nodes located in a small part of the search space. If all the goal nodes are spread uniformly over the search space, then the model predicts and our experimental results confirm that the average speedup is linear. The model also predicts superlinear speedup on the average even in parallel A*/B&B algorithms for certain kinds of problems. We expect the phenomenon of close location of many goal nodes to occur in many natural problems, as good nongoal nodes in the state space usually lead to many goal nodes (which would be located in a relatively small region of the state-space tree). For example, in the n-queens problem, a good partial assignment of queens leads to many goal nodes, whereas a bad partial assignment leads to no goal nodes[2]. Not surprisingly, researchers have observed superlinear speedup in some n-queen instances[25].

Acknowledgements: The authors would like to thank Rich Korf and Sartaj Sahni for helpful comments on an earlier draft of this paper. Some of the experiments were done on a Balance 21000 multiprocessor owned by Sequent Computer Corporation.

References

[1] M. Imai, Y. Yoshida, and T. Fukumura. A parallel searching scheme for multiprocessor systems and its application to combinatorial problems. In *IJCAI*, pages 416–418, 1979.

[2] Virendra K. Janakiram, Dharma P. Agrawal, and Ram Mehrotra. Randomized parallel algorithms for prolog programs and backtracking applications. In *Proceedings of International conference on Parallel Processing*, pages 278–281, 1987.

---

[5] the speedup was averaged over many problem instances, and each problem instance was solved many times using the parallel formulation

[3] Laveen Kanal and Vipin Kumar (editors). *Search in Artificial Intelligence*. Springer-Verlag, New York, 1988(in press).

[4] R.E. Korf. Depth-first iterative-deepening: an optimal admissible tree search. *Artificial Intelligence*, 27:97–109, 1985. Also a chapter in 'Search and Artificial Intelligence',Vipin Kumar and Laveen Kanal Eds, Springer-Verlag,1987(to appear).

[5] Richard Korf. Personal communication. In *the Univ. of California at Los Angeles*, 1988.

[6] W. Kornfeld. The use of parallelism to implement a heuristic search. In *IJCAI*, pages 575–580, 1981.

[7] Vipin Kumar. Depth-first search. In Stuart C. Shapiro, editor, *Encyclopaedia of Artificial Intelligence: Vol 2*, pages 1004–1005, John Wiley and Sons, Inc., New York, 1987.

[8] Vipin Kumar and Laveen N. Kanal. Parallel branch-and-bound formulations for and/or tree search. *IEEE Transactions on Pattern Analysis and Machine Intelligence*, PAMI-6, November 84.

[9] Vipin Kumar, K. Ramesh, and V. Nageshwara Rao. Parallel heuristic search of state-space graphs: a summary of results. In *Proceedings of the 1988 National Conference on Artificial Intelligence*, August 1988. Also AI Lab Tech. Report 88-70, University of Texas at Austin, March 88.

[10] Vipin Kumar and V. Nageshwara Rao. Parallel depth-first search, part II: analysis. *International Journal of Parallel Programming*, 16 (6), 1987.

[11] Kouichi Kumon, Hideo Masuzawa, and Akihiro Itashaki. Kabu-wake: a new parallel inference method and its evaluation. In *Digest of papers - IEEE Computer Society International Conference*, pages 168–172, 1986.

[12] T. H. Lai and Sartaj Sahni. Anomalies in parallel branch and bound algorithms. *Communications of the ACM*, 594–602, 1984.

[13] Guo-Jie Li and Benjamin W. Wah. *Computational Efficiency of Parallel Approximate Branch-and-Bound Algorithms*. Technical Report TR-84-6, Purdue University, School of Electrical Engineering, FEBRUARY 84.

[14] Guo-Jie Li and Benjamin W. Wah. Coping with anomalies in parallel branch-and-bound algorithms. *IEEE Trans on Computers*, C-35, June 1986.

[15] R. Mehrotra and E. Gehringer. Superlinear speedup through randomized algorithms. In *Proceedings of International conference on Parallel Processing*, pages 291–300, 1985.

[16] Joseph Mohan. Experience with two parallel programs solving the traveling salesman problem. In *Proceedings of International conference on Parallel Processing*, pages 191–193, 1983.

[17] B. Monien, E. Spekenmeyer, and O. Vornberger. *Superlinear Speedup for Parallel Backtracking*. Technical Report 30, Univ. of Paderborn, FRG, 1986.

[18] V. Nageshwara Rao, V. Kumar, and K. Ramesh. A parallel implementation of iterative-deepening-a*. In *AAAI*, pages 878–882, 1987. Also AI Lab TR 87-46, University of Texas at Austin, January 87.

[19] V. Nageshwara Rao and Vipin Kumar. Parallel depth-first search, part I: implementation. *International Journal of Parallel Programming*, 16 (6), 1987.

[20] D.S. Nau, V. Kumar, and L. Kanal. General branch-and-bound and its relation to a* and ao*. *Artificial Intelligence*, 23, 1984.

[21] Nils J. Nilsson. *Principles of Artificial Intelligence*. Tioga Press, 1980.

[22] Judea Pearl. *Heuristics - Intelligent Search Strategies for Computer Problem Solving*. Addison-Wesley, Reading, MA, 1984.

[23] Michael J. Quinn and Narsingh Deo. An upper bound for the speedup of parallel branch-and-bound algorithms. *BIT*, 6,No 1, March 1986.

[24] H. Stone and P. Sipala. The average complexity of depth-first search with backtracking and cutoff. *IBM Journal of Research and Development*, May 1986.

[25] Peter Tinker. Performance and pragmaticsof an OR-parallel logic programming system. *International Journal of Parallel Programming*, ?, 1988.

Circuit Definitions of Nondeterministic Complexity Classes[1]

H. Venkateswaran
Department of Computer Science and Automation
Indian Institute of Science, Bangalore-560 012, INDIA

Abstract

We consider restictions on Boolean circuits and use them to obtain new uniform circuit characterizations of nondeterministic space and time classes.We also obtain characterizations of counting classes based on nondeterministic time bounded computations on the arithmetic circuit model. It is shown how the notion of semi-unboundedness unifies the definitions of many natural complexity classes.

1 Introduction

Uniform Boolean circuits have provided a very useful framework to study some of the important issues that arise in Turing machine based complexity theory. Close connections have been established between complexity classes based on uniform circuits with those based on the machine model [1,5,9,10,12]. In one direction, complexity classes defined using the circuit model have been characterized using the machine model. NC is a well known example of such a complexity class defined using the uniform Boolean circuit model [9] that has been characterized using the alternating Turing machine model by Ruzzo [12]. In the other direction, traditional complexity classes based on the machine model have been characterized in the circuit model. The definition of the class P using Boolean circuits [7,10] is probably the first such result. Other results of this nature are the characterizations in the circuit model of the classes AC^1 [13] and LOGCFL [14]. The results by Ruzzo [12] also make it possible to obtain circuit characterizations of complexity classes defined using alternating Turing machines. The work reported here extends these results to characterize classes defined using nondeterministic Turing machines.

First, we consider restrictions of Boolean circuits and use them to characterize nondeterministic space and time classes. This includes a characterization of nondeterministic time classes on the semi-unbounded fan-in circuit model.Semi-unbounded

---
[1] This material is based upon work supported by the National Science Foundation under grant CCR-8711749. This work was done while the author was at the school of Information and Computer Science, Georgia Institute of Technology, Atlanta, Georgia 30332-0280, USA.

fan-in circuits, which are Boolean circuits in which the AND gats have bounded fan-in, have been previously used to define the class LOGCFL [14]. We define skew circuits as Boolean circuits in which all but one input of every AND gate are circuit inputs and use them to characterize nondeterministic space and time classes. Nondeterministic space is defined in terms of the size of such circuits and nondeterministic time is shown to correspond to the depth of these circuits. This should be contrasted with the well known correspondences between deterministic time and Boolean circuit size [10] and between nondeterministic space and Boolean circuit depth [1].

Second, we use the monotone arithmetic circuit model to characterize counting classes based on nondeterministic time bounded computations. Monotone arithmetic circuits are arithmetic circuits over the domain of non-negative integers and which use only the addition and multiplication operations. An interesting consequence of this characterization is the definition of the well known counting class #P as the set of functions computed by uniform families of monotone arithmetic circuits that have polynomial depth and polynomial degree. The degree measure here refers to the algebraic degree of the polynomial associated with the circuit.

Some of the appealing features of the characterization results in this paper are listed below.

* The circuit characterizations of NP presented here are, to our knowledge, the first uniform circuit characterizations of this important complexity class. Of particular interest is the definition of NP as the class of languages accepted by uniform families of semi-unbounded fan-in circuits of exponential size and log depth. This provides a framework to study some interesting questions about the class NP. Recently, Borodin et al. [2] proved that if a language is accepted by a family of semi-unbounded fan-in circuits of size $Z(n)$ and depth $D(n)$, then its complement is accepted by a family of semi-unbounded fan-in circuits of size polynomial in $Z(n)$ and depth $O(D(n)+\log Z(n))$. Their result does not apply directly to NP, since it only shows that CO-NP is accepted by semi-unbounded fan-in circuits of exponential size and polynomial depth. But, it does raise a relevant question: are classes accepted by size Z and depth $O(\log Z)$ semi-unbounded fan-in circuits closed under complement? It is known that the classes accepted by size Z and depth $o(\log n)$ semi-unbounded fan-in circuits are not closed under complement [14]. Another complexity question pertaining to NP that can be phrased in this model is its relationship with the other classes definable using semi-unbounded fan-in circuits. Thus, for instance, the separation between NP and LOGCFL now becomes a question of the relative power of exponential size and polynomial size semi-unbounded fan-in circuits of logarithmic depth.

* The skew Boolean circuits provide a model to rephrase many of the famous separation questions among complexity classes. Thus the relationship between P and NLOG translates into the question of the relative power of polynomial size Boolean circuits and polynomial size skew Boolean circuits. The P versus PSPACE question becomes a question of the relative power of polynomial size Boolean circuits and exponential size skew Boolean circuits.

* The arithmetic characterization of #P presented here is the first alternative characterization of this class. In this framework, the famous open question about the relationship between #P and NP gets translated into the question of the relationship between monotone arithmetic circuits and Boolean circuits.

* These characterizations also make it possible to identify appropriate circuit value problems that are complete for each of these complexity classes.

* The semi-unbounded circuit model seems useful to capture the definitions of many nondeterministic complexity classes (see table 1).

This paper is organized as follows. Section 1.1 contains some preliminary definitions. Boolean circuit characterizations of nondeterministic space and time classes are in section 2. A characterization of nondeterministic time that follows as a simple consequence of known results is presented in section 3. A Monotone arithmetic circuit characterization of counting classes that are based on nondeterministic time bounded computations is presented in section 4.

1.1 Preliminaries

Boolean Circuits: A Boolean circuit G_n with n inputs is a finite acyclic directed graph with vertices having indegree zero or two and labelled as follows. Vertices of indegree zero are labelled from the set $\{0, 1, x_1, x_2, \ldots, x_n, \bar{x}_1, \bar{x}_2, \ldots, \bar{x}_n\}$. All other vertices (also called gates) are labelled either AND or OR. It should be noted that not including negation gates in the definition of a Boolean circuit is done with no loss of generality. Vertices with outdegree zero are called outputs. The evaluation of G_n on inputs of length n is defined in the standard way. Typically, only circuits with one output vertex will be considered. This makes it convenient to consider circuits as language acceptors.

The size $C(G_n)$ of a circuit G_n is the number of edges in G_n. The depth of a vertex v in a circuit is the length of a longest path from any input to v. The depth of a circuit is the depth of its output vertex.

The language L_n accepted by a Boolean circuit G_n is the set of all length n strings on which G_n evaluates to one.

A family of circuits is a sequence $\{G_n / n=0,1,2,\ldots\}$, where the n-th circuit G_n has n inputs. The language L accepted by a family $\{G_n\}$ of circuits is defined as the union over all $n \geq 0$ of L_n, where L_n is the language accepted by the n-th member G_n of the family.

Skew Boolean Circuits: Let G be a Boolean circuit. An AND gate v in G is said to be a skew gate if it has at most one input that is not an input of G. Without loss of generality, we will assume that all but one of its inputs are inputs to the circuit G. We will refer to the input of v that is not an input to G as a non-skew input of v. The circuit G is said to be a skew cricuit if all AND gates in it are skew gates. A family $\{G_n\}$ of Boolean circuits is said to be a skew circuit family if all its members are skew circuits.

Semi-Unbounded Fan-in Boolean Circuits: A family of Boolean circuits is said to have semi-unbounded fan-in if there exists a positive constant c such that for any circuit in the family, the OR gates in the circuit can have unbounded fan-in and all the AND gates have fan-in at most c.

Semi-Unbounded Alternating Turing Machines: An alternating Turing machine is semi-unbounded if there are no two consecutive universal configurations along any path in the computation tree of the machine. Without loss of generality, we will assume that every universal configuration of a semi-unbounded alternating Turing machine has exactly two existential configurations as immediate successors.

Uniformity: We will use the following notion of uniformity, called U_D-uniformity, defined by Ruzzo [12]. Define the direct connection language L_{DC} of a family of Boolean circuits to be the set of strings of the form <n,g,y> such that either (i) g and y are gate names and y is an input of the gate g, or (ii) g is a gate name and y is the type of the gate g, that is, y is one of AND or OR or an input to G_n or its negation. A family $\{G_n\}$ of Boolean circuits of size C(n) is said to be uniform if the corresponding direct connection language can be recognized by a deterministic Turing machine in time $O(\log C(n))$.

For the space characterization results in section 2, it would have been sufficient to consider log space unfiormity defined by Borodin and Cook [3]. But a stronger uniformity condition is needed for the time characterization results to avoid the possibility of having a uniformity machine that is more powerful than the class being characterized. Such will be the case, for instance, in theorem 7 if we have used log-space uniformity since NTIME(T(n)) DSPACE($T^{O(1)}(n)$).

Accepting Substrees [15]: The notion of an accepting subtree of a Boolean circuit given an input on which it evaluates to one is analogous to the notion of accepting subtress of machines.

Let B be a Boolean circuit, and let T(B) be its tree equivalent. (The tree-equivalent of a graph is obtained by replicating vertices whose outdegree is greater than one until the resulting graph is a tree). Let x be an input which B evaluates to one. An accepting subtree H of the circuit B on input x is a subtree of T(B) defined as follows:

* H includes the output gate,

* for any AND gave v included in H, all the immediate predecessors of v in T(B) are included as its immediate predecessors in H,

* for any OR gate v included in H, exactly one immediate predecessor of v in T(B) is included as its only immediate predecessor in H, and

* any input vertex of T(B) included in H has value one as determined by the input x.

It is easy to verify the fact that the circuit B evaluates to one given the input x if and only if there is an accepting subtree of T(B) on input x.

Tree-Size [15]: The tree-size measure for Boolean circuits can now be defined analogous to the tree-size measure for alternating Turing machines [12].

The circuit B_n is said to have tree-size $Z(n)$ if, for every input x accepted by B_n, there exists an accepting subtree with at most $Z(n)$ vertices.

Degree: We define the degree of a circuit to be the algebraic degree of the polynomial computed by the circuit. Thus, the constants have degree zero, the circuit inputs have degree one, the degree of an OR vertex is the maximum of the degrees of its inputs, and the degree of an AND vertex is the sum of the degrees of its inputs.

The following lemma [14], whose proof is by induction on the depth of a vertex in the circuit, establishes a relationship between the measures degree and tree-size for Boolean circuits.

Lemma 1 Let $D(n), Z(n)$, and $d(n)$ be the degree, tree-size, and depth respectively of a Boolean circuit B_n. Then,

$$Z(n) \leq D(n)d(n)+1$$

2 Characterizations of Space and Time Classes

This section contains the characterizations of nondeterministic space and time classes in terms of skew circuits and semi-unbounded fan-in circuits. Theorem 6 relates simultaneous space and time bounded nondeterministic classes to simultaneous size and depth bounded skew circuits. In this respect, it is similar to the result of Ruzzo [12] relating simultaneous space and time bounded alternating classes to simultaneous size and depth bounded circuits. However, the correspondence between the time and depth bounds in theorem 6 is only within a polynomial as opposed to the correspondence within a constant factor between circuit depth and alternating time shown by Ruzzo [12].

In the proof lemma 3 below, we choose to use the alternating Turing machine model instead of directly constructing a semi-unbounded circuit corresponding to a skew circuit. This is done to simplify the proof since we can use known simulation techniques. It also provides a new characterization of nondeterministic time on the alternating Turing machine model (see theorem 9). The correspondence between the machine and circuit models will be established through a sequence of lemmas.

Lemma 2 For $S(n)=\Omega(\log n)$, $T(n)=\Omega(n)$, and $S(n) \leq T(n)$,
$$\text{NSPACE,TIME}(S(n),T(n)) \subseteq \text{Uniform Skew Circuit SIZE,DEPTH-}(2^{O(S(n))},T(n)).$$

Proof: Let L be accepted by a nondeterministic Turing machine M in $S(n)$ space and $T(n)$ time. The construction of a circuit family G_n that accepts the same language as M can be done using standard techniques [12,14]. For the sake of completeness, we will outline below the construction of G_n, the n-th member of this family.

The configurations of M can be classified into two types: existential and read. We will assume that M is determinisstic while reading inputs.

For $0 \leq t \leq T(n)$, and configuration c of M using space $S(n)$, there is a gate in the circuit in one of the following forms: $[t,c]$, or $[t,c,i]$, or $[t,c,i,b]$, where $0 \leq i \leq n$ is an integer and b is either zero or one. The first component t in a gate name is used to avoid cycles in the circuit. The type of gate of the form $[t,c]$ ($[t,c,i]$, $[t,c,i,b]$) is OR (OR, AND respectively).

Let c_I be the initial configuration of M. The output gate is $[0,c_I]$.

The inputs of a gate are constructed as follows. Consider a gate $[t,c]$ corresponding to a non-read configuration c of the machine. If $t+1 > T(n)$, it has only one input, namely the constant zero. Otherwise, its inputs are constructed from the set D of all configurations reachable by M in one move from c. There will be one input corresponding to each d in D. For any d in D, if d uses space $\geq S(n)$, then the corresponding input is the constant zero. For all other d in D, there are two cases. If d is an existential configuration the corresponding input is the gate [t+1,d] and its inputs are constructed recursively. If d is read configuration in which M reads the ith symbol, the corresponding input is an OR gate [t+1,d,i] with two inputs: [t+1,d,i,0] and [t+1,d,i,1]. The gate [t+1,d,i,0] is an AND gate with two inputs: a constant one (zero) if the ith input has value zero (respectively, one), and the gate [t+2,e], where e is the configuration to which M moves from the read configuration d, if the ith input read has value zero. The inputs of the gate [t+2,e] are constructed recursively. The gate [t+1,d,i,1] is constructed in an analogous fashion.

It is clear from the construction of G_n above that it is a skew circuit. The only AND gates constructed correspond to the read configurations of M. It is easy to show that $\{G_n\}$ accepts the same language as M. The size of the resulting circuit is $2^{O(S(n))}$. Its depth is $T(n)$.

It can be verified that the direct connection language of $\{G_n\}$ can be recognized by a deterministic Turing machine using $O(S(n))$ time, thus showing that the circuit family $\{G_n\}$ in uniform.

Lemma 3 For $S(n)=\Omega(\log n), T(n)=\Omega(n)$, and $S(n) \leq T(n)$
Uniform Skew Circuit SIZE,DEPTH($2^{O(S(n))}$,T(n)) $\subseteq$ Uniform Semi-Unbounded Circuit SIZE,DEPTH($2^{O(S(n))}$,log T(n)).

Proof: Let $\{G_n\}$ be a uniform family of skew circuits with the given size and depth bounds. Then $\{G_n\}$ has tree-size that is polynomial in $T(n)$. An alternating Turing machine M that simulates G_n on an input x of length n can be constructed as in the simulation by Ruzzo [12] of a space and tree-size bounded alternating Turing machine by a space and time bounded alternating Turing machine. The machine M is semi-unbounded and uses space $O(S(n))$, alternations $O(\log T(n))$, and time $T^{O(1)}(n)$. Let the time used by M be $T'(n)=T^a(n)$ for some constant $a \geq 1$. Furthermore, M is in a normal form such that only one input symbol is read along any path of the machine's computation tree. A uniform family $\{H_n\}$ of semi-unbounded fan-in circuits, with size $2^{O(S(n))}$ and depth $O(\log T(n))$, that accepts the same language as M can be constructed by adapting known techniques [14]. The basic idea of the construction is to make as inputs to an OR (AND) gate all non-existential (non-universal) configurations of M reachable through only existential (universal) configurations.

We will outline the construction of the n-th member H_n of this family. The configurations of M are assumed to be one of the following three types: existential, universal, and read.

Let $D(n) = \lceil \log_2 T'(n) \rceil$.

Gates in the circuit H_n are all the form [c], or [d'], or [c,d], or [s,c,d], or [s,c,d,e], where $0 \leq s \leq D(n)$, and c,d and e are all configurations of M. The output gate of H_n is $[r_0]$, where r_0 is the initial configuration of M. In general, the type of a gate of the form [c] is OR (AND) if the type of the configuration c is existential (respectively, universal). Given a gate [c], its inputs are defined as follows.

Case 1: [c] is an OR gate. Its inputs are gates [c,d] for all configurations d that are not existential. Each of the gates [c,d] is an AND gate and it has two inputs [0,c,d] and [d'] defined as follows.

* The gate [0,c,d] is the output of an D(n) depth semi-unbounded fan-in circuit that checks that in M the configuration d is reachable from the configuration c using only existential configurations of M. The following is a description of such a reachability circuit [14].

Given a gate [s,c,d] with $0 \leq s \leq D(n)$, the goal is to describe a subcircuit of which this gate is the output, such that the subcircuit checks that c is reachable from d in G_n using a path of at most $2^{D(n)-s}$ OR gates (see also the construction by Borodin [1]).

If d is an immediate predecessor of c in G_n, then [s,c,d] is the constant one. Otherwise, if $s+1 > D(n)$, then [s,c,d] is the constant zero. Otherwise, the gate [s,c,d] is an OR gate. Its inputs are gates [s+1,c,d,e] for all OR gates e in G_n. Each of the gates [s+1,c,d,e] is an AND gate, and it has two inputs [s+1,c,e] and [s+1,e,d]. These two subcircuits are constructed recursively.

* The gate [d'] is an OR gate with a single input [d] defined as follows. If d is a read configuration with a,i on its index tape, then [d] is the i-th input to H_n. Otherwise, d is a universal configuration. Then [d] is an AND gate. Its inputs are constructed recursively.

Case 2: [c] is an AND gate. Let d_1, d_2 be the existential configurations of M that immediately succeds the configuration C. The inputs to [C] are the OR gates $[d_1]$ and $[d_2]$. The inputs to these two OR gates are constructed recursively.

The circuit H_n has size $2^{O(S(n))}$ and depth $O(\log T(n))$. Note that the OR gates in H_n may have exponential fan-in whereas the fan-in of the AND gates is bounded by a constant. It is easy to show that G_n and H_n accept the same language. It is also straightforward to check that the direct connection language for the circuit family $\{H_n\}$ can be recognized by a deterministic Turing machine in time $O(S(n))$.

Lemma 4 For $S(n)=\Omega(\log n)$, $T(n)=\Omega(n)$, and $S(n) \leq T(n)$,
Uniform Semi-Unbounded Circuit SIZE,DEPTH($2^{O(S(n))}$, $\log T(n)) \subseteq$ NSPACE, TIME($S(n) \log T(n)$, $T^{O(1)}(n)$).

Proof: This follows from the simulation of semi-unbounded fan-in circuits by nondeterministic auxiliary pushdown automata by Venkateswaran [14]. In this case, we are interested in the space and time used in the simulation.

Let L be accepted by $\{G_n\}$, a uniform family of semi-unbounded fan-in circuits with size $2^{O(S(n))}$ and depth $O(\log T(n))$. Given x of length n, a nondeterministic machine M checks whether the circuit evaluates to one on x by doing a depth-first evaluation. The machine M maintains a stack to do the circuit evaluation.

M begins the simulation with the output gate r_0. Given a gate v and its type, M checks that v evaluates to one on x as follows. Let $C(v)$ denote the configuration of M as it begins checking the gate v.

Case 1: v is an OR gate. M existentially guesses one of its true inputs u and its type and verifies with the uniformity machine that the guesses are correct. it then recursively checks that the gate u evaluates to one.

Case 2: v is an AND gate. Then it has a constant number, say k, inputs. M existentially guesses these inputs, say, $v_1, \ldots, v_k$, and their types and verifies with the uniformity machine that the guesses are correct. M then pushes the gates $v_2, \ldots, v_k$ onto the stack. Along with a gate its type is also pushed onto the stack. M then recursively checks that v_1 evaluates to one.

Case 3: v is an input to the circuit. If its value is zero, M rejects. Suppose v has value one. M makes its final pop move and accepts if the stack is empty. Otherwise, M pops a gate u and its type from the stack and recursively checks that u evaluates to one.

For correctness, it can be shown, by induction, that the output r_0 of the circuit G_n evaluates to one on input x if and only if M accepts starting from $C(r_0)$ and an empty stack [14].

It can be verified that M uses space $O(S(n) \log T(n))$ and time $T^{O(1)}(n)$.

In the proof of lemma 4 above, the space used for the stack can be completely avoided if the circuits being simulated are skew circuits. This observation leads immediately to the following lemma:

Lemma 5 For $S(n)=\Omega(\log n), T(n)=\Omega(n)$, and $S(n) \leq T(n)$,
Uniform Skew Circuit SIZE,DEPTH$(2^{O(S(n))}, T^{O(1)}(n)) \subseteq$ NSPACE,TIME$(S(n), T^{O(1)}(n))$.

Lemmas 2 and 5 yield the following theorem:

Theorem 6 For $S(n)=\Omega(\log n), T(n)=\Omega(n)$, and $S(n)$ $T(n)$,
NSPACE,TIME$(S(n), T^{O(1)}(n))$ = Uniform Skew Circuit SIZE,DEPTH$(2^{O(S(n))}, T^{O(1)}(n))$.

The following characterizations of nondeterministic time using skew circuits and semi-unbounded fan-in circuits are now immediate from lemmas 2, 3, and 4.

Theorem 7 For $T(n)=\Omega(n)$, the following complexity classes are equal:

1. NTIME$(T^{O(1)}(n))$

2. Uniform Skew Circuit DEPTH$(T^{O(1)}(n))$

3. Uniform Semi-Unbounded Circuit SIZE,DEPTH$(2^{O(T(n))}, \log T(n))$

As interesting consequences of theorems 6 and 7, we obtain the following Boolean circuit characterizations of the classes NLOG, PSPACE, and NP.

Corollary 8 1. NLOG = Uniform Skew Circuit Size$(n^{O(1)})$
2. PSPACE = Uniform Skew Circuit SIZE$(2^{n^{O(1)}})$.
3. NP = Uniform Skew Circuit DEPTH$(n^{O(1)})$.
4. NP = Uniform Semi-Unbounded Circuit SIZE,DEPTH$(2^{n^{O(1)}}, \log n)$.

3 Other Characterizations of Nondeterministic Time

There are some circuit characterizations of nondeterministic time that follow as simple consequences of known results. We will present here one such characterization using the depth and degree measures for Boolean circuits. The characterization results in section 4 of counting classes based on nondeterministic time bounded computations are suggested by this characterization.

The proof of theorem 9 below can be reconstructed from the results of Ruzzo[11,12] and the correspondence between degree and tree-size (see lemma 1).

Theorem 9 For $T(n)= \Omega(n)$, the complexity class NTIME$(T^{O(1)}(n))$ is the same as the class Uniform Circuit DEPTH,DEGREE$(T^{O(1)}(n), T^{O(1)}(n))$.

Thus, for instance, NP has the following characterization in terms of degree and depth of Boolean Circuits:

Corollary 10 NP = Uniform Circuit DEPTH,DEGREE($n^{O(1)}, n^{O(1)}$).

The Boolean circuit characterization of NP in Corollary 10 should be compared with the following bounded fan-in Boolean circuit characterizations of PSPACE[1,12]:

PSPACE = Uniform Circuit DEPTH($n^{O(1)}$)
= Uniform Circuit DEPTH,DEGREE($n^{O(1)}, 2^{n^{O(1)}}$).

4 Montone Arithmeic Circuits and Counting Classes

This section contains the characterizations of counting classes based on nondeterministic time bounded computations on the montone arithmetic circuit model (defined below). As a corollary, we obtain a characterization of class #P on this model.

4.1 Definitions

It wil be convenient to consider Boolean circuits in which every AND gate has exactly two inputs.

Montone Arithmetic Circuits: These are defined just as Boolean circuits (see section 1.1), except that the gates compute the integer sum and integer product of their inputs instead of computing the OR and AND functions. Although the results in this section, especially lemma 13, can be strengthened to handle n bit nonnegative integers as inputs to the circuit, it suffices to consider only single bit inputs.

Uniformity: For defining uniformity, we now require that, in the direct connection language, the left and right inputs of an AND gate can be identified.

Define the direct connection language of a family $\{G_n\}$ of Boolean circuits to be the set of strings of the form <n,g,y,p> such that either (i) g is an OR gate and y is an input of g, or (ii) g is a AND gate and y is a left (right) input of g if p is L (respectively, R), or (iii) g is a gate name and y is the type of the gate g. A family $\{G_n\}$ of Boolean circuits of size C(n) is said to be uniform if the corresponding direct connection language can be recognized by a deterministic Turing machine in time O(log C(n)).

The uniformity condition for monotone arithmetic circuits is defined exactly as for Boolean circuits with PLUS (MULT) gates replaced for OR (respectively, AND) gates.

Degree: The degree measure for monotone arithmetic circuits is defined analogous to Boolean circuits (see section 1.1). Thus, the constants have degree zero, the circuit inputs have degree one, the degree of a PLUS vertex is the maximum of the degrees of its inputs, and the degree of a MULT vertex is the sum of the degrees of its inputs.

Notations: Let N denote the set of natural numbers. A function $f: \{0,1\}^* \to N$ is in # Uniform Circuit SIZE,DEPTH,DEGREE(Z(n),d(n),D(n)) if and only if there exists a uniform family $\{G_n\}$ of Boolean circuits of size $O(Z(n))$, depth $O(d(n))$, and degree $O(D(n))$ such that for all strings x of length n, f(x) is the number of accepting subtrees of G_n on input x.

The other counting classes are defined in a similar fashion.

4.2 The Characterization Results

The following fact can be used to set up a correspondence between Boolean and monotone arithmetic circuits. The proof of this fact is a direct consequence of the definition of an accepting subtree of a Boolean circuit (see secion 1.1).

Fact 11 Let B be Boolean circuit that evaluates to one an input x. Given x as an input, the number of accepting subtrees of B rooted at an OR (AND) gate v is the sum (respectively, product) of the number of accepting subtrees of B rooted at the inputs of v.

It may be noted that lemmas 12,13, and 14 below are stronger statements than needed to prove the main results of this section, namely lemma 15 and theorem 16.

Lemma 12 Let B be a Boolean circuit of size Z, depth d, and degree D. Then three exists an arithmtic circuit A of size Z, depth d, and degree D such that B has p accepting subtrees on an input x on which it evaluates to one if and only if A has value p on input x.

Proof Sketch: Given a Boolean circuit B, let the arithmetic circuit A be obtained by replacing all the OR (AND) gates of B by PLUS (respectively, MULT) gates. Then the conclusion follows by using fact 11.

Lemma 13 Let A be a monotone arithmetic circuit of size Z, depth d, and degree D with n inputs from $\{0,1\}$. Then there exists a Boolean circuit B of size Z, depth d, and degree D such that A has value p if and only if B has p accepting subtrees given this input.

Proof Sketch: Given a monotone arithmetic circuit A, consider the Boolean circuit B constructed from A by replacing all PLUS (MULT) gates by OR (respectively,

AND) gates. The proof then follows by a simple inductive argument.

The circuits involved in the lemmas 12 and 13 above can be made uniform thereby showing the following correspondence between monotone arithmetic and Boolean circuits.

Lemma 14 For $Z(n), D(n) = \Omega(n)$

$\#$Uniform Circuit SIZE,DEPTH,DEGREE$(Z^{O(1)}(n), d(n), D(n))=$ Uniform Monotone Arithmetic Circuit SIZE,DEPTH,DEGREE-$(Z^{O(1)}(n), d(n), D(n))$.

Lemma 15 below establishes the correspondence between the number of accepting paths in nondeterministic Turing machines and the number of accepting subtrees of Boolean circuits.

Lemma 15 For $T(n) = \Omega(n)$,
$\#$NTIME$(T^{O(1)}(n))$ = $\#$Uniform Circuit DEPTH,DEGREE$(T^{O(1)}(n), T^{O(1)}(n))$.

Proof: Let M be a nondeterministic Turing machine that runs in time $T(n)$. By theorem 7, there is a uniform family $\{B_n\}$ of $O(T(n))$ depth bounded skew circuits that accepts the same language as M. It can be verified that the degree of B_n is $O(T(n))$. We claim that M has p accepting paths on an input x of length n if and only if B_n has p accepting subtrees.

We will assume that M is deterministic while reading its inputs, and that the immediate successor of a read configuration is an existential configuration. Let x be an input of length n accepted by M. Then B_n evaluates to one on x. We will show that there is a bijective function that maps the accepting paths in the computation tree of M on input x with the accepting subtrees of B_n on input x.

Let p be an accepting path of M on input x. The starting vertex of p is labelled by the initial configuration c_I of M. Consider the following subtree $A(p)$ of B_n on input x. The root of $A(p)$ is the output gate $[0, c_I]$ of B_n. In general, the construction proceeds as follows. For the t-th vertex of p labelled with an existential configuration c, pick the corresponding gate $[t,c]$ of B_n. The configuration d that immediately succeeds c along p is either an existential configuration or a read configuration. If d is an existential configuration pick as the input of the gate $[t,c]$ its input labelled $[t+1,d]$. Suppose d is a read configuration in which M reads the i-th input symbol and moves to an existential configuration $e(f)$ if the i-th input is zero (rspectively, one). Consider the case when the i-th input symbol is zero. (The construction in the case when the i-th input symbol is one is analogous). Then d has the configuration e as its immediate successor along p. Pick the gate [t+1,d,i] as the input of the gate [t,c], the AND gate [t+1,d,i,0] as the input of [t+1,d,i], and the gate [t+2,e] as the input of the gate [t+1,d,i,0]. It is easy to see that A(p) is an accepting subtree of B_n on input x.

The mapping described above from accepting paths of M on input x to accepting subtrees of B_n on input x is well-defined. It can be verified that it is also bijective function.

Conversely, let B_n be a uniform family of Boolean circuits of depth $T^{O(1)}(n)$ and degree $T^{O(1)}(n)$. Let M be a nondeterministic Turing machine that simulates B_n of an input x of length n in a depth-first fashion as in the proof of lemma 4. The one difference here is the need to ensure that the simulation of an AND gate maintains the correspondence between the number of accepting paths of the machine and the number of accepting subtrees of the circuit. Let C(v) denote the configuration of M as it begins checking the gate v.

In simulating an AND gate v, M does the following. It guesses the right input, say v_2, of v, verifies with the uniformity machine that the guess is correct, and pushes v_2 onto the stack. It then guesses the left input, say v_1, of v, verifies with the uniformity machine that the guess is correct, and verifies that v_1 evaluates to one. This will guarantee that there is a single accepting patn segment from the configuration C(v) to the configuration $C(v_1)$.

It can be shown that M has p accepting paths on x if and only if B_n has p accepting subtrees on input x.

By lemma 1, the tree-size of B_n is $T^{O(1)}(n)$. Since B_n has size at most exponential in $T^{O(1)}(n)$, it follows, as in the simulation of lemma 4, that M uses time $T^{O(1)}(n)$.

Lemmas 14 and 15 together imply the following theorem:

Theorem 16 For $T(n)=\Omega(n)$,
$$\#NTIME(T^{O(1)}(n))=$$
Uniform Monotone Arithmetic Circuit DEPTH, DEGREE($T^{O(1)}, T^{O(1)}(n)$).

As a special case of the above theorem, we obtain the following new characterization of the important counting class #P:

Corollary 17 #P = Uniform Monotone Arithmetic Circuit DEPTH,DEGREE($n^{O(1)}, n^{O(1)}$).

4.3 Some Consequences

The results in this section lead to some interesting consequences. We will present two of these below.

Unique SAT: The Unique SAT problem is defined as follows [8]: Given an instance of SAT, does it have a unique solution? As another interesting corollary of theorem 16, we can identify an arithmetic circuit value problem that is equivalent to the Unique SAT problem.

Let M be a fixed uniformity machine for a family $\{G_n\}$ of monotone arithmetic circuits of polynomial depth and polynomial degree. Given as input n and an n bit vector x, the MVCPI problem is to determine whether the circuit G_n evaluates to one on input x.

Corollary 18 There is a log space transformation from Unique SAT to MCVPI and vice versa.

New NP-Complete Problems: Theorem 16 suggests a new arithmetic circuit value problem that is complete for NP. Let M be a fixed uniformity machine for a family $\{G_n\}$ of monotone arithmetic circuits of polynomial depth and polynomial degree. Given as input n and an n bit vector x, the MCVP problem is to determine whether the circuit G_n evaluates to a non-zero value on input x.

Proposition 19 The MCVP problem is NP-complete.

5 Conclusion

This work provides a circuit framework in which some well-known open problems of complexity theory can be studied. We considered two constraints on the Boolean circuit model, namely skewness and semi-unboundedness, and used it to define nondeterministic space and time complexity classes. We also considered monotone arithmetic circuits to define counting classes based on non-deterministic time.

The known uniform Boolean circuit characterizations of classes between LOGCFL and PSPACE are summarized in table 1 (the definitions of the classes LOGCFL and P in this table use log-space uniformity). It should not be too difficult to construct entries for classes above PSPACE.

As a consequence of these characterizations, we can define for each of these complexity classes a Boolean circuit value problem that is a natural complete problem for the class. For example, the following circuit value problem is NP-complete. Let M be a fixed uniformity machine for a family $\{G_n\}$ of Boolean circuits of polynomial depth and polynomial degree. Given as input n and an n bit vector x, the problem is the determine whether the circuit G_n evaluates to one on input x.

We will conclude with a few remarks about the relevance of the semi-unboundedness notion for questions in complexity theory.

One can define an analogue of the polynomial time hierachy using semi-unbounded alternating Turing machines. Then, by theorem 9, NP is the class languages accepted by polynomial time semiunbounded alternating Turing machines using O(log-n) alternations. This is interesting because it shows that with the constraint of semi-unboundedness O(log-n) alternations is in NP, whereas without this constraint, even constant alternations is not known to be in NP.

OR fan-in	AND fan-in	SIZE	DEPTH	DEGREE	CLASS
$n^{O(1)}$/bounded	$n^{O(1)}$/bounded	$n^{O(1)}$		$n^{O(1)}$	LOGCFL
$n^{O(1)}$	bounded	$n^{O(1)}$	$\log n$		LOGCFL
$n^{O(1)}$	$n^{O(1)}$	$n^{O(1)}$	$\log n$		AC^1
$n^{O(1)}$/bounded	$n^{O(1)}$/bounded	$n^{O(1)}$			P
$2^{n^{O(1)}}$	bounded	$2^{n^{O(1)}}$	$\log n$		NP
$2^{n^{O(1)}}$/bounded	$2^{n^{O(1)}}$/bounded	$2^{n^{O(1)}}$	$n^{O(1)}$	$n^{O(1)}$	NP
$2^{n^{O(1)}}$/bounded	$2^{n^{O(1)}}$/bounded	$2^{n^{O(1)}}$		$2^{n^{O(1)}}$	PSPACE
$2^{n^{O(1)}}$/bounded	$2^{n^{O(1)}}$/bounded	$2^{n^{O(1)}}$	$n^{O(1)}$		PSPACE

Table 1: Circuit Definitions of Complexity Classes

Finally, it can be seen from table 1 that many of the well-known space and time complexity classes have definitions in terms of semi-unbounded fan-in circuits. Thus, for instance, the following are definitions of some well known classes using the semi-unbounded fan-in circuit model:

LOGCFL = Uniform Semi-Unbounded Circuit SIZE,DEPTH($n^{O(1)}$, $\log n$)
P   = Uniform Semi-Unbounded Circuit SIZE,DEPTH($n^{O(1)}$, $n^{O(1)}$)
NP   = Uniform Semi-Unbounded Circuit SIZE,DEPTH($2^{n^{O(1)}}$, $\log n$)
PSPACE = Uniform Semi-unbounded Circuit SIZE,DEPTH($2^{n^{O(1)}}$, $n^{O(1)}$).

Acknowledgements

I am grateful to Martin Tompa for useful discussions. My thanks are due to Larry Ruzzo whose work on alternating Turing machines and Boolean circuits was a source of inpsiration for the results reported here. I am also thankful to Gary Peterson for his comments.

References

[1] Borodin, A., On Relating Time and Space to Size and Depth, SIAM Journal of Computing **6**, (1977), 733-743.

[2] Borodin, A., S.A. Cook, P.W. Dymond, W.L. Ruzzo, and M. Tompa, Two Applications of Complementation via Inductive Counting, University of Washington Technical Report 87-10-01, October 1987.

[3] Cook, S.A., Deterministic CFL's are accepted simultaneously in polynomial time and log squared space, Proc. 11th Annual ACM Symposium on Theory of Computing, (1979), 338-345.

[4] Cook, S.A., A Taxonomy of Problems with Fast Parallel Algorithms, Information and Control **64**, 1-3 (Jan/Feb/Mar 1985), 2-22.

[5] Dymond, P.W. and S.A. Cook, Hardware Complexity and Parallel Computation, Proc. 21st Annual Symposium on Foundations of Computer Science, Toronnto, 1980.

[6] Goldschlager, L.M., The Monotone and Planar Circuit Value Problems are log space Complete for P, SIGACT News **9**, 2, 1977, 25-29.

[7] Ladner, R.E., The Circuit Value Problem is log space Complete for P, SIGACT News **7**, 1, 1975, 18-20.

[8] Papadimitriou, C.H., M. Yannakakis, The Complexity of Facets (and some Facets of Complexity), Journal of Computer and System Science **28**, (1984), 244-259.

[9] Pippenger, N., On Simultaneous Resource Bounds, Proc. 20th Annual Symposium on Foundations of Computer Science, Puerto Rico, 1979.

[10] Pippenger, N., and M.J. Fischer, Relations among Complexity Measures, Journal of the Association for Computing Machinery **26**, (1979), 361-381.

[11] Ruzzo, W.L., Tree-Size Bounded Alternation, Journal of Computer and System Sciences **20**, (1980), 218-235.

[12] Ruzzo, W.L., On Uniform Circuit Complexity, Journal of Computer and System Sciences **22**, (1981), 365-383.

[13] Stockmeyer, L. and U. Vishkin, Simulation of Parallel Random Acces Machines by Circuits, SIAM Journal of Computing **13**, (1984), 409-422.

[14] Venkateswaran, H., Properties that Characterize LOGCFL, Proc. 19th Annual ACM Symposium on Theory of Computing, (1987), 141-150.

[15] Venkateswaran, H. and M. Tompa, A New Pebble Game that Characterizes Parallel Complexity Classes, Proc. 27th Annual Symposium on Foundations of Computer Science, Toronto, 1986.

Non-Uniform Proof Systems: A New Framework to Describe Non-Uniform and Probabilistic Complexity Classes.

Jürgen Kämper
Universität Oldenburg, Fachbereich Informatik
Postfach 2503, D-2900 Oldenburg

Abstract. The concept of non-uniform proof systems is introduced. This notion allows a uniform description of non-uniform complexity classes [10], probabilistic classes (e.g. BPP [8,15,27,32], AM [2,3]) and language classes defined by simultaneous non-uniform and nondeterministic time bounds. Non-uniform proof systems provide a better understanding of many results concerning these classes, particularly their connections to uniform complexity measures. We give an uniform approach to lowness results [19,20] for various complexity classes. For instance, we show that co-NP/Poly $\cap$ NP is contained in the third level of the low hierarchy and that, NP $\subseteq$ (NP $\cap$ co-NP)/Poly implies that the polynomial time hierarchy collapses to its second level (see also [1]). Finally, some evidence is given that the low hierarchy cannot be extended beyond its third level by the current techniques.

0. Introduction

Motivated by the still unsolved P-NP-question, various concepts of polynomial time computations have been investigated. Our work is centered on three of the most succesful of them:

1. Non-uniform complexity theory deals with functions limiting the growth rate of descriptions of the finite initial subsets of languages. To formalize this complexity measure in a polynomial setting various concepts have been developed: circuits of polynomial size, polynomially time bounded Turing machines with polynomial advices, and polynomial time oracle Turing machines using sparse sets as their oracle languages. All these models describe the same language class, called P/Poly [10]. They have become an important tool in complexity theory through many results establishing connections to uniform complexity classes. Of particular interest are connections having the form "If a fixed set A has small non-uniform complexity, then there follow some statements concerning Turing-machine complexity", e.g.: If NP is included in P/Poly, then the polynomial time hierarchy collapses to its second level [10]. This result gives evidence that the non-uniform complexity measure P/Poly describes only a fragment of NP.

2. In recent years many attempts have been made to attack intractable problems, for which no deterministic polynomial time algorithm is known, by probabilistic algorithms or by approximation algorithms. Probabilistic algorithms lead to classes as BPP and R (for a broad discussion see [8,15,27,31,32]). Related to probabilistic complexity measures is the class AM, defined by Arthur-Merlin games (with 2 rounds) [2,3]. Approximation algorithms can be divided in "almost correct" algorithms leading to the class P-close [30] and "almost fast" algorithms leading to the class APT [17]. It can easily be seen that P-close and APT are subclasses of P/Poly (see e.g. [20]). By iterating probabilistic algorithms and using quantifier simulation techniques, also connections between probabilistic complexity classes and non-uniform measures have been established (see e.g. [24]).

3. Chandra, Kozen and Stockmeyer introduced alternating Turing machines as a generalization of nondeterministic Turing machines [7]. In the case of nondeterministic machines, a single configuration α can reach several configurations $\beta_1, \beta_2, ..., \beta_k$. The configuration α leads to acceptance iff, at least one successor β_i leads to acceptance. In addition to these "existential branches", alternating machines can also make "universal branches". Then, α leads to acceptance iff all the successors β_i lead to acceptance. Polynomially time bounded, alternating Turing machines accept the class PSPACE which contain all sets recognized by deterministic Turing machines using polynomial space. The power of this computation model can be restricted by allowing only a constant number of alternations between "existential" and "universal branches". Thereby, we get a characterization of the polynomial time hierarchy PH: The k-th levels, Σ^p_k and Π^p_k, contain all languages recognized by polynomially time bounded, alternating Turing machines with k alternations starting with an existential or an universal branch, respectively. Originally, Stockmeyer [28] defined the polynomial hierarchy using the concepts of polynomially length bounded quantifiers and nondeterministic, polynomial time oracle machines.

The low and high hierarchies from Schöning [19] reflect the polynomial time hierarchy on NP-sets. A set L in NP belongs to the k-th level L^p_k of the low hierarchy iff, $\Sigma^p_n(L) \subseteq \Sigma^p_n$. L belongs to the k-th level H^p_k of the high hierarchy iff, $\Sigma^p_{n+1} \subseteq \Sigma^p(L)$. Thus, if L is low then, with respect to the operator Σ^p_n, L does not encode any information, but if L is high, then L encodes the power of an additional, polynomially length bounded quantifier. It is easy to see that, the polynomial time hierarchy collapses iff there is a set being both, low and high. The restrictions of non-uniform classes (P/Poly), probabilistic classes (R, BPP) and language classes defined by approximation algorithms (APT, P-Close) to NP-sets are included in some levels of the low hierarchy (for an overview see [20]). Therefore, these concepts describe only fragments of the class NP unless the polynomial time hierarchy collapses. Recently, Schöning [21] has shown that the problem "GraphIsomorphism" belongs to the second level of the low hierarchy.

Non-uniform proof systems are a new concept to obtain the main results of the above mentioned areas in a very homogeneous manner. To explain this model we first formalize non-uniform complexity measures using the notion of advices [10]: Let Σ be the fixed alphabet {0,1} and let <.,.> be a pairing function. For a set I and a string u over Σ, I_u

denotes the language: $I_u = \{x \in \Sigma^* \mid <x,u> \in I\}$. $I^{\leq n}$ consists of all strings from I which are bounded in their length by n. For a language class C, let C/Poly be the class of all sets A, for which there are a set $I \in C$ and a polynomial p such that, for all $n \in |N$ it exists an advice u of length p(n) with: $A^{\leq n} = I_u^{\leq n}$. With other words, using polynomially length bounded advices which depend only on the length of the considered string, the set A can very easily be reduced to the set I, namely by the pairing function <.,.>. The set I interprets the advices as descriptions of the finite initial subsets of A. Therefore, we call I an interpretation set. The fundamental idea of this paper is to comprehend special sets of advices, which describe the language A correctly with regard to the interpretation set, as the second component of our model. Notice that, for any $n \in |N$ these sets contain at least one advice of appropriate length, namely of length p(n) (where p is a polynomial). The described sets are called proof sets, and they allow to investigate the complexity of recognizing correct advices. Moreover, they are helpful to describe various complexity classes and thereby, to obtain results concerning these classes uniformely. For two language classes C_1 and C_2, C_1-C_2-PSL [Proof System Language] includes all sets A for which there is a proof system with an interpretation set from C_1 and a proof set from C_2.

In Section 1 we establish our notation, whereas Section 2 contains the exact definition of non-uniform proof systems and some easy results concerning this concept. It turns out that non-uniform complexity classes can be described in our terms by using proof sets of unlimited complexity [e.g.: P/Poly = P-P_Σ-PSL, where P_Σ denotes the class of all languages over Σ].

Section 3 locates languages from NP for which there are proof systems with an interpretation set from co-NP and a proof set from the polynomial time hierarchy inside the low hierarchy [(co-NP)-Σ^P_k-PSL $\cap$ NP $\subseteq L^P_k$]. Using an observation from Section 2 [co-NP/Poly $\cap$ NP $\subseteq$ (co-NP)-Π^P_2-PSL], this main theorem is strong enough to prove that the class co-NP/Poly $\cap$ NP is included in the third level of the low hierarchy. This strengthens results from Balcazar, Book and Schöning [5,6] and from Yap [29].

Two interesting types of non-uniform proof systems are investigated in Section 4: In a secure proof system with an interpretation set I advices u not belonging to the proof set can lead to errors only in one direction: strings not belonging to the considered language A are rejected by I when using u as its advice, i.e. $I_u^{\leq n} \subseteq A^{\leq n}$. C_1-C_2-SPSL [Secure Proof System Language] denotes the class of all languages for which there is a secure proof system with an interpretation set from C_1 and a proof set from C_2. Dense proof systems are characterized by the property that their proof sets include a majority of all advices of appropriate length (1/2 + δ, where δ is independent of the length of the considered advices). We denote the class of all languages having a dense proof system with an interpretation set from C_1 and a proof set from C_2 by C_1-C_2-DPSL [Dense Proof System Language]. Classes characterized by proof systems being both, dense and secure, are denoted by an expression of the form C_1-C_2-SDPSL.

We show that, for secure proof systems the complexity of recognizing correct advices can be bounded in the complexity of interpreting these advices, i.e. C-P_Σ-SPSL = C-$\Pi^P_1(C)$-SPSL. Similiar, for all $k \geq 1$, Π^P_k-P_Σ-SPSL $\cap \Sigma^P_k = \Pi^P_k$-$\Pi^P_k$-PSL $\cap \Sigma^P_k$.

This proposition and our main theorem from Section 3 prove that P-P$_\Sigma$-SPSL and also (co-NP)-P$_\Sigma$-SPSL $\cap$ NP are included in the second level of the low hierarchy. Moreover, we show that proof systems for disjunctive self-reducible languages can always be transformed into secure proof systems [C$_1$-C$_2$-PSL $\cap$ DSR $\subseteq$ P(C$_1$)-C$_2$-SPSL, where DSR is the class of all disjunctive self-reducible sets]. We conclude that the polynomial time hierarchy collapses to its second level if the class (NP $\cap$ co-NP)/Poly contains NP. This result, which was independently observed by Abadi, Feigenbaum and Kilian [1], extends a theorem from Karp and Lipton [10].

Dense proof systems are used to describe probabilistic complexity classes [e.g.: BPP = P-P$_\Sigma$-DPSL, AM = NP-P$_\Sigma$-DPSL], and proof systems being both, dense and secure, are used for the description of probabilistic classes with one-sided error [e.g.: R = P-P$_\Sigma$-SDPSL]. This requires only the well known techniques of iterating probabilistic algorithms and quantifier simulation. Applying a theorem from Schöning [24], we get that, in some cases dense proof systems can be transformed into secure proof systems [if co-C is closed under NP$_{pos}$-reductions then, C-P$_\Sigma$-DPSL $\subseteq$ C-P$_\Sigma$-SDPSL]. From this result the lowness of some probabilistic classes follows.

As shown in sections 3 and 4 all language classes known to belong to the low hierarchy can be characterized by proof systems with interpretation sets from co-NP. Moreover, in all cases these classes could be located in one of the first three levels of the low hierarchy. In Section 5 we show that for k $\geq$ 3, proof systems with an interpretation set from the k-th level of the low hierarchy capture only NP-sets from the same level [LP$_k$-P$_\Sigma$-PSL $\cap$ NP = L^k_p]. This shows that polynomial advices do not augment the power of the higher levels. Hence, it seems that non-uniform complexity measures cannot be used to extend the low hierarchy beyond its third level.

1. Preliminaries

It is assumed that the reader is familiar with the basic concepts of complexity theory. Here, only our notation is established. For exact definitions see [20].

All the sets in this work are languages over the fixed alphabet Σ = {0,1}. For a string w $\in$ Σ^*, let |w| be its length. ε denotes the empty string. For a set A and an n $\geq$ 0, define A$^{=n}$ = {x $\in$ A | |x| = n}, A$^{\leq n}$ = {x $\in$ A | |x| $\leq$ n}, and A$^-$ = {x $\in$ Σ^* | x $\notin$ A}. ||S|| denotes the cardinality of the set S. Let P$_\Sigma$ be the class of all languages over Σ. The join of two sets A and B is A $\oplus$ B = {0x | x $\in$ A} $\cup$ {1x | x $\in$ B}, and the join of two language classes C$_1$ and C$_2$ is C1 $\oplus$ C2 = {L $\in$ P$_\Sigma$ | ($\exists$ L$_1$ $\in$ C$_1$) ($\exists$ L$_2$ $\in$ C$_2$) : L = L$_1$ $\oplus$ L$_2$}. For a class C let co-C be the class of complements of sets in C, co-C = {A $\in$ P$_\Sigma$ | A$^-$ $\in$ C}.

Let L(T) be the set accepted by Turing machine T, and let L(M,A) be the language accepted by oracle Turing machine M when using A as its oracle set. The classes of the polynomial time hierarchy and their relativized versions are denoted as usual.

Let Sparse denote the class of all languages for which some polynomial p exists such that for all n, ||L$^{\leq n}$|| $\leq$ p(n). Tally contains all sets over the one letter alphabet {0}.

$\leq^P_m$ ($\leq^P_T$) denotes the polynomial time many-one (Turing) reducibility. Let Q_k denote the quantifier $\exists$ if k is odd, and the quantifier $\forall$ if k is even. Let $<.,.>$ be a pairing function. This function and its inverses should be computable in polynomial time. For all k > 2 and for all $y_1, y_2,...,y_k \in \Sigma^*$, let $<y_1,y_2,...,y_k>$ denote the string $<y_1,<y_2,...,y_k>>$. Poly denotes the class of all polynomials. Let SAT be the set of all satisfiable Boolean formulas.

2. Definitions and Elementary Results

In this section we formally define the concept of non-uniform proof systems and prove some easy results being helpful in the succeeding investigations. In the theory of non-uniform complexity measures for the decision wether a string u belongs to a language A some additional information is used. This advice depends only on the length of u. To formalize this notion, we follow Karp and Lipton [10]:

<u>Definition 2.1.</u>   For a set $I \in P_\Sigma$ and a string $u \in \Sigma^*$, let $I_u = \{x \in \Sigma^* \mid <x,u> \in I\}$. For a language class C and a class of functions F from $\mathbb{N}$ to $\mathbb{N}$, define C/F as the class of sets A for which there are a language $I \in C$ and a function $f \in F$ such that,
$(\forall n \in \mathbb{N})(\exists u \in \Sigma^{=f(n)}): A^{\leq n} = I_u^{\leq n}$.

In [10] it is only demanded that the length of the advices is bounded by the function f, whereas the above definition requires that the function f describes exactly the length of advices. If the considered function class F contains only time constructible functions and if the language class C is closed under $\leq^P_m$-reducibility then both are equivalent. Observe that the class of all polynomials and all levels from the polynomial time hierarchy satisfy these conditions.

Non-uniform complexity measures can be characterized also by oracle Turing-machines using sparse or tally sets as their oracle languages (see [20]), e.g.: P/Poly = P(Sparse), NP/Poly = NP(Sparse), co-NP/Poly = co-NP(Sparse). Pippenger [18] shows that P/Poly contains all languages having polynomial size circuits, and Schöning [23] gives a characterization of NP/Poly by polynomial size generators. An analogous result for co-NP/Poly can be obtained by equipping circuits with universal quantifiers instead of the existential quantifiers of generators.

The set I in definition 2.1 interpretes the advices as descriptions of finite initial subsets of the language A. Therefore, we call this set an interpretation set. Let B' be the set of all advices which are correct with regard to the interpretation set I, i.e.
$B' = \{<0^n,u> \mid n \in \mathbb{N}; u \in \Sigma^{=f(n)}; A^{\leq n} = I_u^{\leq n}\}$
Then, B' may contain many advices $<0^n,u>$ for some $n \in \mathbb{N}$. Definition 2.1 only demands that for all $n \in \mathbb{N}$, B' includes at least one advice $<0^n,u>$. In order to recognize the set A using the interpretation set I this requirement suffices. The fundamental idea of this paper is to consider subsets of B' which contain at least one advice for any $n \in \mathbb{N}$.

We call such a subset of B' a proof set. Note that recognition of A by the interpretation set I can be based on any proof set in place of B'. Therefore, the notion of proof sets allows an investigation of the complexity of recognizing correct advices. Note that subsets of B' may be much easier to compute than B'.

Definition 2.2. For a function $f : |N \to |N$ a set $B \subseteq \{<0^n,u> \mid n \in |N; u \in \Sigma^{=f(n)}\}$ is called an **f-set**. Let $I \in P_\Sigma$ be a set, let $f : |N \to |N$ be a function, and let B be an f-set. (I,B,f) is a **(non-uniform) proof system** for a language A iff,

(2.1) $(\forall n \in |N) (\exists u \in \Sigma^{=f(n)}) : <0^n,u> \in B$, and

(2.2) $(\forall n \in |N) (\forall u \in \Sigma^{=f(n)}) : <0^n,u> \in B \Rightarrow A^{\leq n} = I_u^{\leq n}$.

The first (second / third) component of a non-uniform proof system is called **interpretation set (proof set / length function)**.

Note that the conditions (2.1) and (2.2) guarantee that the proof set contains an advice for any length of strings, and that all elements of the proof set are correct with regard to the interpretation set, respectively.

The power of non-uniform proof systems depends on the complexities of the interpretation sets and the proof sets, and the rate of growth of the length functions. Note that for any language A there is a proof system with an interpretation set from P and a length function growing exponentially, since the finite initial subsets of A can be encoded very easily by advices of exponential length. We limit ourselves to length functions growing polynomially.

Definition 2.3. Let C_1 and C_2 be language classes. A proof system (I,B,f) is called a C_1-C_2 **proof system** iff, $I \in C_1$ & $B \in C_2$ & $f \in$ Poly. C_1-C_2-**PSL** denotes the class of languages for which there are C_1-C_2 proof systems.

This definition subsumes that of non-uniform complexity classes: For any language class C, C/Poly = C-P_Σ-PSL. Therefore, non-uniform classes can be described by proof systems which do not limit the complexity of recognizing correct advices. The following instances of this equation will be of particular interest:
P/Poly = P-P_Σ-PSL, NP/Poly = NP-P_Σ-PSL, and co-NP/Poly = (co-NP)-P_Σ-PSL.

The succeeding relations among proof systems are easy consequences of our definitions. For all language classes C_1, C_2, C_3 and C_4,

(2.3) co-(C_1-C_2-PSL) = (co-C_1)-C_2-PSL,

(2.4) $C_1 \subseteq C_3$ & $C_2 \subseteq C_4$ => C_1-C_2-PSL $\subseteq$ C_3-C_4-PSL, and

(2.5) (C_1-C_2-PSL) $\cup$ (C_3-C_2-PSL) = ($C_1 \cup C_3$)-C_2-PSL.

Moreover, for C_1 closed under $\leq^P_m$-reductions and for C_2 containing any p-set B (for any polynomial p) which satisfies (2.1),

(2.6) $C_1 \subseteq C_1$-C_2-PSL.

We next observe that in certain cases the complexity of proof sets can be decreased without reducing the power of the proof systems.

Proposition 2.4. For all language classes C being closed under $\leq^P_m$-reductions,
$$(\forall k \geq 1) : C\text{-}\Sigma^P_k\text{-PSL} = C\text{-}\Pi^P_{k-1}\text{-PSL}.$$

Proof: For a proof of the not trivial inclusion let (I,B,p) be a $C\text{-}\Sigma^P_k$ proof system for a given language A. Since $B \in \Sigma^P_k$ and B is a p-set there are a polynomial q and a set B' from Π^P_{k-1} such that, $B = \{<0^n,u> \mid n \in \mathbb{N}; u \in \Sigma^{=p(n)}; (\exists y \in \Sigma^{=q(n)}) : <0^n,u,y> \in B'\}$. B' can be extended to a $C\text{-}\Pi^P_{k-1}$ proof system (I',B',p') for the language A by letting $I'=\{<x,u,y> \mid <x,u> \in I\}$ and choosing p' in an appropriate way. •

The proof of the above proposition actually shows that for any classes C_1 and C_2 which are closed under $\leq^P_m$-reducibility, $C_1\text{-}C_2\text{-PSL} = C_1\text{-}CL_\exists(C_2)\text{-PSL}$. Here $CL_\exists(C_2)$ denotes the closure of C_2 under polynomially bounded existential quantifiers. In paticular, for C_1 closed under $\leq^P_m$-reducibility, $C_1\text{-}P(C_2)\text{-PSL} = C_1\text{-}NP(C_2)\text{-PSL}$.

Limiting the complexities of computing correct advices and of interpreting advices of course limits the complexity of the describable languages. In particular, sets belonging to the polynomial time hierarchy are only able to constitute proof systems for languages of this hierarchy.

Proposition 2.5. $(\forall k, l \geq 0) : \Sigma^P_k\text{-}\Sigma^P_l\text{-PSL} \subseteq \Sigma^P_{\max\{k,l\}}$

Proof: Suppose, $A \in \Sigma^P_k\text{-}\Sigma^P_l\text{-PSL}$, and let (I,B,p) be a $\Sigma^P_k\text{-}\Sigma^P_l$ proof system for A. Then, $A = \{x \in \Sigma^* \mid (\exists u \in \Sigma^{=p(|x|)}) : <0^{|x|},u> \in B \ \& \ <x,u> \in I\}$. Hence, $A \in \Sigma^P_{\max\{k,l\}}$. •

By (2.6), for all $l \geq 0$, and all $k \geq l$, also the inverse direction of the above proposition holds. The next proposition shows that the complexity of computing correct advices can be bounded in the complexity of interpreting these advices and the complexity of the described language.

Proposition 2.6. For all language classes C_1 and C_2,
$$C_1\text{-}P_\Sigma\text{-PSL} \cap C_2 = C_1\text{-}\Pi^P_1(C_1 \oplus C_2)\text{-PSL} \cap C_2.$$

Proof: For a proof of the not trivial inclusion let (I,B,p) be a $C_1\text{-}P_\Sigma$ proof system for a given language $A \in C_2$. The set B' is constructed as a completion of B:
$$B' = \{<0^n,u> \mid n \in \mathbb{N}; u \in \Sigma^{=p(n)}; (\forall x \in \Sigma^{\leq n}) : <x,u> \in I <=> x \in A\}.$$
(I,B',p) is a $C_1\text{-}\Pi^P_1(C_1 \oplus C_2)$ proof system for the language A. •

In the following the above proposition will be helpful for proving lowness of several language classes. In particular the succeeding instances will be required:

(2.7) $\Pi^P_1/\text{Poly} \cap NP = \Pi^P_1\text{-}\Pi^P_2\text{-PSL} \cap NP$,

and for all $C \subseteq P_\Sigma$,

(2.8) $P/\text{Poly} \cap C = P\text{-}\Pi^P_1(C)\text{-PSL} \cap C$.

3. Non-Uniform Proof Systems and the Low Hierarchy

Schöning [19] introduced the low and high hierarchies as follows:

Definition 3.1. For each $k \geq 0$, LP_k contains a language $A \in NP$ iff $\Sigma P_k(A) \subseteq \Sigma P_k$, and HP_k contains a language $A \in NP$ iff $\Sigma P_{k+1} \subseteq \Sigma P_k(A)$.

For a detailed discussion of these concepts see [14,19,20]. There, also the following proposition is proved.

Proposition 3.2.
i) $(\forall k \geq 0) : LP_k \subseteq LP_{k+1}$ & $HP_k \subseteq HP_{k+1}$
ii) $LP_0 = P$ & $LP_1 = NP \cap \text{co-NP}$
iii) $HP_0 = \{A \in P_\Sigma \mid A \text{ is } \leq^p_T\text{-complete for NP}\}$ &
$HP_1 = \{A \in P_\Sigma \mid A \text{ is } \leq^{sn}_T\text{-complete for NP}\}$
iv) $(\forall k \geq 0) : LP_k \cap HP_k \neq \emptyset \iff \Sigma P_k = \Sigma P_{k+1}$

Here, $\leq^{sn}_T$ denotes the polynomial time, strong nondeterministic Turing reducibility [16]. Many other notions of NP-completeness (using nondeterministic, probabilistic or circuit reducibilities) are also included in some levels of the high hierarchy. This fact and part iv of the preceding proposition give the handle to prove polynomial hierarchy collapsing results: if some set being NP-complete with regard to one of the above mentioned reducibilities were low then the polynomial time hierarchy collapses. On the other hand, there are many classes and languages known to be low. They cannot be NP-complete unless the polynomial time hierarchy collapses.

We show now, that sets from NP for which there are proof systems with an interpretation set from co-NP and a proof set from the polynomial time hierarchy belong to the low hierarchy.

Theorem 3.3. $(\forall k \geq 1) : \Pi P_1\text{-}\Sigma P_k\text{-PSL} \cap NP \subseteq LP_k$

Proof: By proposition 2.4, we have to show, $(\forall k \geq 1) : \Pi P_1\text{-}\Pi P_{k-1}\text{-PSL} \cap NP \subseteq LP_k$. We distinguish three cases.

case 1: k = 1 Suppose, $A \in \Pi P_1\text{-P-PSL} \cap NP$. By (2.3), $A \in \text{co-}(NP\text{-P-PSL}) \cap NP$. From proposition 2.5 we get, $A \in \text{co-NP} \cap NP$. Hence, by proposition 3.2, $A \in LP_1$.

case 2: k ≥ 2 and k is even Let $A \in \Pi P_1\text{-}\Pi P_{k-1}\text{-PSL} \cap NP$, and $L \in \Sigma P_k(A)$. Then there are 1) a $\Pi P_1\text{-}\Pi P_{k-1}$ proof system (I,B,p) for A,
2) a set $D \in P$, and a polynomial q such that $A = \{x \in \Sigma^* \mid (\exists z \in \Sigma^{\leq q(|x|)}): <x,z> \in D\}$,
3) a set $E \in P$ and a polynomial q' such that, $(\forall n \in \mathbb{N}) (\forall x \in \Sigma^{\leq n})$
$(\forall u \in \Sigma^{=p(n)}) : [<x,u> \in I \iff (\forall z' \in \Sigma^{\leq q'(n)}) : <x,u,z'> \in E]$,

and 4) a polynomial time oracle machine M, and a polynomial q" such that,
$$L = \{ x \in \Sigma^* \mid (\exists y_1 \in \Sigma^{\leq q''(|x|)}) (\forall y_2 \in \Sigma^{\leq q''(|x|)})...(\forall y_k \in \Sigma^{\leq q''(|x|)}) :$$
$$<x,y_1,y_2,...,y_k> \in L(M,A)\}.$$

Let r be a polynomial such that for all $n \in |N$, $r(n)$ bounds the number and the length of oracle queries of M on an input of the form $<x,y_1,...,y_k>$ where $x \in \Sigma^{\leq n}$ and $|y_i| \leq q''(n)$. We constructe a deterministic, polynomially time bounded Turing machine T that, on an input of the form $<x,y_1,...,y_k,z_1,...,z_{r(|x|)},z'_1,...,z'_{r(|x|)},u>$ operates like M on input $<x,y_1,...,y_k>$ where the i-th oracle query "s ∈ A?" of M is simulated in such a way that:

    1) the answer "yes" is assumed if $<s,z_i> \in D$,

    2) the answer "no" is assumed if $<s,z_i> \notin D$ and $<s,u,z'_i> \notin E$,

and 3) the machine T stopps accepting its input if $<s,z_i> \notin D$ and $<s,u,z'_i> \in E$.

In a sense, T simulates the machine M correctly. This is the statement of the following claim.

<u>Claim:</u> For all $n \in |N$, all $x \in \Sigma^{\leq n}$, all $<0^{r(n)},u> \in B$, and all $y_1,...,y_k \in \Sigma^{\leq q''(n)}$,
$$<x,y_1,...,y_k> \in L(M,A) \iff (\forall z_1,...,z_{r(n)} \in \Sigma^{\leq q(r(n))}) (\forall z'_1,...,z'_{r(n)} \in \Sigma^{\leq q'(r(n))})$$
$$<x,y_1,...,y_k,z_1,...,z_{r(n)},z'_1,...,z'_{r(n)},u> \in L(T).$$

<u>Proof of the claim:</u> For fixed $n \in |N$, $x \in \Sigma^{\leq n}$, $<0^{r(n)},u> \in B$, and $y_1,...,y_k \in \Sigma^{\leq q''(n)}$ the claim follows easily from two observations:

1) For all $z_1,...,z_{r(n)} \in \Sigma^{\leq q(r(n))}$ and all $z'_1,...,z'_{r(n)} \in \Sigma^{\leq q'(r(n))}$, on input $<x,y_1,...,y_k,z_1,...z_{r(n)},z'_1,...,z'_{r(n)},u>$ the machine T does not simulate the wrong answer to any oracle query "s ∈ A ?" of M on input $<x,y_1,...,y_k>$. If the input does not allow to determine whether s belongs to A then the machine T stopps accepting its input. This proves the direction "=>".

2) There are strings $z_1,...,z_{r(n)} \in \Sigma^{\leq q(r(n))}$ and $z'_1,...,z'_{r(n)} \in \Sigma^{\leq q'(r(n))}$ such that, on input $<x,y_1,...,y_k,z_1,...,z_{r(n)},z'_1,...,z'_{r(n)},u>$ the machine T is able to answer all oracle queries of M on input $<x,y_1,...,y_k>$ correctly, and so to simulate the machine M on this input completely. This proves direction "<=".

By this claim we get that the language L can be characterized as follows:
$$L = \{ x \in \Sigma^* \mid (\exists y_1 \in \Sigma^{\leq q''(|x|)}) (\exists u \in \Sigma^{=p(r(|x|))}) :$$
        1) $<0^{r(|x|)},u> \in B$ and

    and 2) $(\forall y_2 \in \Sigma^{\leq q''(|x|)}) (\exists y_3 \in \Sigma^{\leq q''(|x|)})...(\forall y_k \in \Sigma^{\leq q''(|x|)})$
$$(\forall z_1,...,z_{r(|x|)} \in \Sigma^{\leq q(r(|x|))}) (\forall z'_1,...,z'_{r(|x|)} \in \Sigma^{\leq q'(r(|x|))}):$$
$$<x,y_1,...,y_k,z_1,...,z_{r(|x|)},z'_1,...,z'_{r(|x|)},u> \in L(T) \}\}$$

By the facts $L(T) \in P$ and $B \in \Pi P_{k-1}$ it follows, $L \in \Sigma P_k$. Hence, $A \in LP_k$.

<u>case 3: $k \geq 3$ and k is odd</u>   We only point out the both main differences to case 2.

1) If the machine T is not able to determine wether a string for which the machine M queries its oracle belongs to A then T rejects the input instead of accepting it.

2) In the concluding characterization of the language L the strings $z_1,...,z_{r(|x|)}$ and $z'_1,...,z'_{r(|x|)}$ are guessed by existential quantifiers instead of universal quantifiers.

The further argumentation can be adapted very easily.

Consequently, all possible cases are proved. •

Later we will see that this theorem is strong enough to prove the most known results concerning the lowness of language classes. Using (2.7) we get a new result.

<u>Corollary 3.4.</u>   co-NP/Poly $\cap$ NP $\subseteq$ L^P_3

Therefore, if there is a high set in co-NP/Poly $\cap$ NP then the polynomial time hierarchy collapses. The above Corollary strengthens two results in the literature: P/Poly $\cap$ NP $\subseteq$ L^P_3 [5,6], and co-NP/Poly $\supseteq$ NP => PH = Σ^P_3 [29].

4. Properties of Non-Uniform Proof Systems

4.1. Secure Proof Systems

Definition 2.2 demands the correctness of the interpretation set only for advices belonging to the proof set. In this section the behaviour of the interpretation set with regard to all possible advices is considered. The interpretation sets of secure proof systems make errors only in one direction.

<u>Definition 4.1.1.</u>   A proof system (I,B,p) for a set A is called **secure** iff,
$$(\forall n \in |N) (\forall u \in \Sigma^{=p(n)}) : A^{\leq n} \supseteq I_u^{\leq n}.$$
Let C_1 and C_2 be language classes. **C_1-C_2-SPSL** denotes the class of sets $A \subseteq \Sigma^*$ for which there are secure C_1-C_2 proof systems.

The above defined property of proof systems will be very important for the succeeding investigations: We will show that, for secure proof systems the complexity of recognizing correct advices can be bounded very sharply. This will imply that (co-NP)-P_Σ-SPSL $\cap$ NP is contained in the second level of the low hierarchy. Later we will see that this class subsumes all the other classes known to belong to this level of the low hierarchy [e.g.: co-AM $\cap$ NP]. Moreover, we will show that proof systems for disjunctive self-reducible sets can always be transformed into secure proof systems. Thereby we will get the result, (co-NP $\cap$ NP)/Poly $\supseteq$ NP => PH = Σ^P_2.

The notion of secure proof systems will be helpful also for the descriptions of probabilistic classes with one-sided error [e.g.: R]. In [9] secure proof systems with interpretation sets from P are investigated very extensively. There it is shown that this class contains exactly those languages which have a short NP-description [22]. Moreover a characterization of this class by a restricted Turing-reducibility to sparse sets is given. This reducibility is equivalent to the notion of one-sided helping [11].

Observe that the statements (2.4), (2.5) and (2.6) hold for the classes of definition 4.1.1 in an analogous way. For secure proof systems proposition 2.5 can be improved.

<u>Proposition 4.1.2.</u> $(\forall k \geq 1) : \Sigma^P_k$-$P_\Sigma$-SPSL $= \Sigma^P_k$

Proof: For a proof of the not trivial inclusion let (I,B,p) be a secure Σ^P_k-P_Σ proof system for a given language A. The succeeding characterization of A proofs that this set belongs to Σ^P_k. $A = \{x \in \Sigma^* \mid (\exists u \in \Sigma^{=p(|x|)}) : <x,u> \in I\}$ •

The characterization of the language A in the preceding proof shows that secure proof systems lead to language classes which are a combination of non-uniform and nondeterministic complexity classes: There are advices of polynomial length which describe the finite initial subsets of A, and in order to reduce A to I these advices can be guessed by existential quantifiers. Now, we will show that the language class (co-NP)-P_Σ-SPSL $\cap$ NP is included in the second level of the low hierarchy. For that we have to improve proposition 2.6 for secure proof systems.

Proposition 4.1.3.
i) For each language class C, C-P_Σ-SPSL = C-Π^P_1(C)-SPSL
ii) $(\forall k \geq 1) : \Pi^P_k$-$P_\Sigma$-SPSL $\cap \Sigma^P_k = \Pi^P_k$-$\Pi^P_k$-PSL $\cap \Sigma^P_k$

Proof: Let (I,B,p) be a secure proof system for a language A. Then, the completion of the proof set - compare proof of proposition 2.6. - can be characterized as follows:
ad i) B' = $\{<0^n,u> \mid u \in \Sigma^{=p(n)}; (\forall u' \in \Sigma^{=p(n)}) (\forall x \in \Sigma^{\leq n}) : <x,u'> \in I => <x,u> \in I\}$
ad ii) B' = $\{<0^n,u> \mid u \in \Sigma^{=p(n)}; (\forall x \in \Sigma^{\leq n}) : x \notin A$ oder $<x,u> \in I\}$
Using these constructions the inclusions of the left sides in the right sides follow easily. For part i, the other direction is trivial. Therefore, it remains to prove the inclusion of the right side in the left side for part ii. Let (I,B,p) be a Π^P_k-Π^P_k proof system for any language A. We define, I' = $\{<x,u> \mid <x,u> \in I$ & $[\exists n \geq |x|: u \in \Sigma^{=p(n)}$ & $<0^n,u> \in B]\}$. As one can easily check, (I',B,p) is a secure proof system for A and, I' $\in \Pi^P_k$. Hence, A $\in \Pi^P_k$-Π^P_k-SPSL.•

Together with theorem 3.3, part ii of this proposition shows that the class (co-NP)-P_Σ-SPSL $\cap$ NP is contained in the second level of the low hierarchy.

Corollary 4.1.4. Π^P_1-P_Σ-SPSL $\cap$ NP $\subseteq L^P_2$

In [9] it is shown that the classes Sparse $\cap$ NP, APT $\cap$ NP and P-Selective $\cap$ NP (for definitions see e.g. [20]) are subclasses of P-P_Σ-SPSL. From this and the above corollary the known lowness results for these classes follow. Proof Systems for sets being disjunctive self-reducible can always be transformed into secure proof systems. To formalize this result we apply a notion of disjunctive self-reducibility defined in [4].

Definition 4.1.5. A set A is **self-reducible** iff there exists a deterministic polynomial time oracle machine M such that A = L(M,A), and on any input x only strings from $\Sigma^{<|x|}$ are queried to the oracle. It is **disjunctive self-reducible** iff it is self-reducible, and the machine witnessing this fact accepts its input whenever the oracle answers positively to any of the queries. **DSR** includes all sets being disjunctive self-reducible.

In [12] the inclusion DSR $\subseteq$ NP is shown. SAT is a member of the class DSR. The required oracle machine is based on the following observation: a Boolean formula u that has a variable x is satisfiable iff, at least one of the both formulas, which are obtained from u by assigning a value to x, is satisfiable. Note that Boolean formulas can be encoded in such a way that assigning values to variables decreases the length of the formulas. The following theorem holds also for some generalizations of the above defined notion (see e.g. [4,12]), but definition 4.1.5 suffices for our purposes.

Theorem 4.1.6. For all languages A $\in$ DSR, and all proof system (I,B,p) for A there is a set I' $\in$ P(I) such that (I',B,p) is a secure proof system for A.

Proof: Let A be a disjunctive self-reducible set, say via machine M, and let (I,B,p) be a proof system for A. We construct a deterministic oracle machine M' such that (L(M',I),B,p) is a secure proof system for A. On input <x,u>, M' operates as follows:
  Simulate the machine M on input x replacing each oracle query of M for some string s by a query for <s,u> until one of the following cases occurs:
  case 1: The machine M stops.
  In this case accept the input <x,u> iff the machine M accepts the input x.
  case2 : An oracle query <s,u> is answered positively.
  In this case accept the input <x,u> iff the string <s,u> is accepted by this algorithm.
It is easy to see that the machine M' is polynomially time bounded. The both following claims can be proved very easily by induction on the length of x [9]. They show that (L(M',I),B,p) is a secure proof system for the language A. This completes the proof.
Claim 1: ($\forall$ x, u $\in$ Σ^*) : <x,u> $\in$ L(M',I) => x $\in$ A.
Claim 2: ($\forall$ n $\in$ |N) ($\forall$ <0^n,u> $\in$ B) ($\forall$ x $\in$ $\Sigma^{\leq n}$) : <x,u> $\in$ L(M',I) <=> x $\in$ A. •

Using proposition 4.1.3 and the disjunctive self-reducibility of any NP-complete set (e.g. SAT), there are some applications of the preceding theorem. (For a proof see [9]).

Corollary 4.1.7.
  i) DSR $\cap$ P/Poly $\subseteq$ P-Π^p_1-SPSL
  ii) DSR $\cap$ (NP $\cap$ co-NP)/Poly $\subseteq$ Π^p_1-Π^p_1-PSL
  iii) NP $\subseteq$ (NP $\cap$ co-NP)/Poly => PH = Σ^p_2

Part III improves the known result P/Poly $\supseteq$ NP => PH = Σ^p_2 from Karp and Lipton [10] and was independently observed by Abadi, Feigenbaum and Kilian [1].

4.2. Dense Proof Sytems

In this section we will characterize probabilistic complexity classes in terms of our notion. Schöning [24] defines probabilistic ("Monte Carlo") classes as follows:

<u>Definition 4.2.1.</u> Let C be any language class. **BPC** denotes the class of all languages A such that for some $B \in C$, some $\delta > 0$, some polynomial p, all $n \in \mathbb{N}$, and all inputs x from $\Sigma^{=n}$, $\| \{ y \in \Sigma^{=p(n)} \mid <x,y> \in B <=> x \in A \} \| > (1/2 + \delta) * 2^{p(n)}$.
RC denotes the class of all languages A such that for some $B \in C$, some $\delta > 0$, some polynomial p, all $n \in \mathbb{N}$, and all inputs $x \in \Sigma^{=n}$,
    1) $x \in A \Rightarrow \| \{ y \in \Sigma^{=p(n)} \mid <x,y> \in B \} \| > \delta * 2^{p(n)}$,
and 2) $x \notin A \Rightarrow (\forall y \in \Sigma^{*}) : <x,y> \notin B$.

To describe the classes of this definition by non-uniform proof systems, we have to analyze the density of proof sets.

<u>Definition 4.2.2.</u>   A proof system (I,B,p) is called **dense** iff,
$$(\exists \delta > 0)(\forall n \in \mathbb{N}) : \| B \cap \{ <0^n,u> \mid u \in \Sigma^{=p(n)} \} \| > (1/2 + \delta) * 2^{p(n)}.$$
Let C_1 and C_2 be language classes. C_1-C_2-**DPSL** denotes the class of all sets which have dense C_1-C_2 proof systems. C_1-C_2-**SDPSL** includes all languages which have C_1-C_2 proof systems being both, secure and dense.

The statements (2.4) and (2.5) hold for dense proof systems and for proof systems being both, secure and dense, in an analogous way. For dense proof systems also (2.3) holds. In order to relate dense proof systems to "Monte Carlo" classes we require the notion of positive reducibility [26]. Recall that, for a set A $P_{pos}(A)$ [$NP_{pos}(A)$] denotes the class of all languages B for which there is a deterministic [nondeterministic], polynomially time bounded oracle machine M such that, B = L(M,A), and for all sets C and D, $C \supseteq D \Rightarrow L(M,C) \supseteq L(M,D)$. In [9] the succeeding theorem is proved using the known techniques of iterating probabilistic algorithms and quantifier simulation (compare [24]).

<u>Theorem 4.2.3.</u>   For all language classes C being closed under P_{pos}-reductions,
            BPC = C-P_Σ-DPSL and RC = C-P_Σ-SDPSL.

In [26] it is shown that all classes of the polynomial time hierarchy are closed under P_{pos}-reductions. This fact and the preceding theorem show that probabilistic complexity classes can be described in terms of our notions, e.g.:
(**R** :=) RP = P-P_Σ-SDPSL   BPP = P-P_Σ-DPSL
(**AM** :=) BPNP = NP-P_Σ-DPSL   co-AM = co-(NP-P_Σ-DPSL) = (co-NP)-P_Σ-DPSL
For a broad discussion of the above classes see [2,3,8,15,27,31,32]. In the succeeding we will obtain some results concerning probabilistic complexity classes using the notion of dense proof systems.

From the above characterizations of the classes BPP and R, theorem 4.1.6 and the disjunctive self-reducibility of the NP-complete set SAT a result from KO [13] follows:

BPP $\supseteq$ NP => R = NP

The complexity of the proof set of dense proof systems can be bounded in the complexity of the interpretation set. This result improves proposition 2.6 for this type of proof systems. (For a proof which bases on a lemma from [20] see [9].)

<u>Theorem 4.2.4.</u> For all language classes C being closed under P_{pos}-reductions,
$$C\text{-}P_\Sigma\text{-DPSL} \subseteq C\text{-}\Pi^P_1(C)\text{-PSL}.$$

One instance of this result is of particular interest: BPP = P-P_Σ-DPSL $\subseteq$ P-Π^P_1-PSL. By proposition 2.5, and the fact that BPP is closed under complement, the known result "BPP $\subseteq \Sigma^P_2 \cap \Pi^P_2$" [15,27] follows. By theorem 3.3 we get, BPP $\cap$ NP $\subseteq L^P_2$. - Note that analogous results follow also for the class BP(NP $\cap$ co-NP). - We continue with an astonishing link between dense and secure proof systems: (For a proof of the following theorem which bases on a result from [24] see [9].)

<u>Theorem 4.2.5.</u> Let C be a language class closed under $\leq^P_m$-reductions for which it holds, co-C = NP$_{pos}$(co-C). Then, C-P_Σ-DPSL $\subseteq$ C-P_Σ-SDPSL.

It is unknown whether the equation (P-P_Σ-SDPSL =) R =?= BPP (= P-P_Σ-DPSL) holds. From the above theorem, and the fact that the classes Σ^P_k (k $\geq$ 1) are closed under NP$_{pos}$-reductions [26] we get that the analogous question for interpretation sets from Π^P_k (k $\geq$ 1) can be answered positively, i.e.: Π^P_k-P_Σ-SDPSL = Π^P_k-P_Σ-DPSL. Using this equation, theorem 4.2.3 and corollary 4.1.4 we get the recently proved result that the class co-AM $\cap$ NP is included in the second level of the low hierarchy [21].

5. Non-uniform proof systems with interpretation sets from the low hierarchy

In section 3 we have located languages from NP for which there exist proof systems with interpretation sets from co-NP inside the low hierarchy. Using this main theorem, in section 4 we have developed the known lowness results in our framework. The following figure summarizes the obtained inclusions among the considered classes restricted to NP:

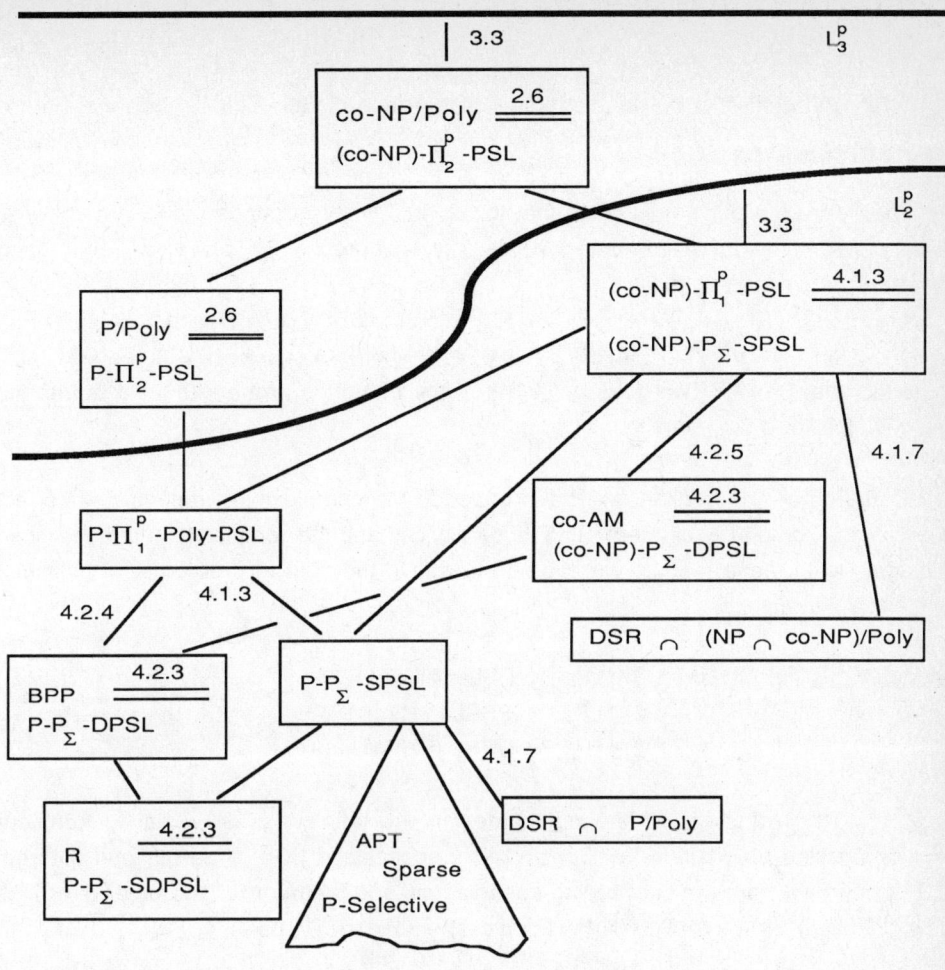

Figure 1: Inclusion structure of low sets in NP

We conclude our investigations of non-uniform proof systems by considering systems with low interpretation sets. We will show that, for a language A from NP such a proof system exists only if A is low itself. First we restrict our investigations to proof sets from the polynomial time hierarchy. The proof of the succeeding theorem exploits ideas which we have used already in the proof of theorem 3.3.

<u>Theorem 5.1.</u> $(\forall k \geq 1) : L^p_k\text{-}\Sigma^p_k\text{-PSL} \cap NP = L^p_k$

<u>Proof:</u> For a proof of the not trivial inclusion let $A \in L^p_k\text{-}\Sigma^p_k\text{-PSL}$, and let (I,B,p) be a $L^p_k\text{-}\Sigma^p_k$ proof system for A. We have to show, $\Sigma^p_k(A) \subseteq \Sigma^p_k$. Fix $L \in \Sigma^p_k(A)$. Then there are a polynomially time bounded oracle machine M and a polynomial q such that:

$$L = \{ x \in \Sigma^* \mid \quad (\exists y_1 \in \Sigma^{\leq q(|x|)}) (\forall y_2 \in \Sigma^{\leq q(|x|)}) \ldots (Q_k y_k \in \Sigma^{\leq q(|x|)}) :$$
$$<x, y_1, y_2, \ldots, y_k> \in L(M,A) \}$$

Let M' be a deterministic, polynomial time oracle Turing machine that, on an input of the form $<x,y_1,y_2,\ldots,y_k,u>$ behaves like M on input $<x,y_1,y_2,\ldots,y_k>$ with the following exception: Any oracle query "s ∈ A ?" of M is replaced by the query "$<s,u> \in I$?". Moreover, let r be a polynomial such that for all $n \in \mathbb{N}$, $r(n)$ bounds the length of oracle queries of M on an input of the form $<x,y_1,y_2,\ldots,y_k>$ where $x \in \Sigma^{\leq n}$ and $y_i \in \Sigma^{\leq q(n)}$. Then L can be characterized as follows:

$$L = \{ x \in \Sigma^* \mid (\exists y_1 \in \Sigma^{\leq q(|x|)}) (\exists u \in \Sigma^{=p(r(|x|))}) : <0^{r(|x|)}, u> \in B \text{ and}$$
$$[(\forall y_2 \in \Sigma^{\leq q(|x|)}) \ldots (Q_k y_k \in \Sigma^{\leq q(|x|)}) : <x, y_1, y_2, \ldots, y_k, u> \in L(M', I)] \}$$

By the fact that $B \in \Sigma^P_k$ we get $L \in \Sigma^P_k(I)$. Since I belongs to the k-th level of the low hierarchy, it follows $L \in \Sigma^P_k$. ∎

In the preceding sections we have bounded the complexity of recognizing correct advices in the complexity of interpreting these advices and the complexity of the described language. Using these results, we extend the above theorem to proof sets of unlimited complexity.

<u>Theorem 5.2.</u>
   i) $(\forall k \geq 3) : L^P_k\text{-}P_\Sigma\text{-PSL} \cap NP = L^P_k$
   ii) $(\forall k \geq 2) : L^P_k\text{-}P_\Sigma\text{-SPSL} \cap NP = L^P_k$
   iii) $(\forall k \geq 2) : L^P_k\text{-}P_\Sigma\text{-DPSL} \cap NP = L^P_k$

<u>Proof:</u> The inclusions of the right sides in the left sides follow easily from our definitions. Using proposition 2.6 (for part i), proposition 4.1.3 (for part ii) and theorem 4.2.4 (for part iii), from the succeeding observations and theorem 5.1 the other directions follow.   ad i) $(\forall k \geq 3): \Pi^P_1(NP \oplus L^P_k) \subseteq \Pi^P_2(L^P_k) \subseteq \Sigma^P_k(L^P_k) \subseteq \Sigma^P_k$
ad ii) $(\forall k \geq 2): \Pi^P_1(L^P_k) \subseteq \Sigma^P_k(L^P_k) \subseteq \Sigma^P_k$
ad iii) All levels from the low hierarchie are closed under P_{pos}-reducibility and,
$(\forall k \geq 2): \Pi^P_1(L^P_k) \subseteq \Sigma^P_k(L^P_k) \subseteq \Sigma^P_k$ ∎

This theorem shows that polynomially length bounded advices do not augment the power of the higher levels of the low hierarchy. Hence, it seems that non-uniform complexity measures cannot be an appropriate technique to extend this hierarchy beyond its third level. New techniques will be required to proof lowness results concerning higher levels.

6. Conclusions

We have used the new concept of non-uniform proof systems as a framework for the study of various complexity classes. Non-uniform classes can be described directly in terms of this notion. For the study of probabilistic classes an analysis of the density of proof sets is necessary. Demanding that interpretation sets make errors only in one direction, it is possible to describe probabilistic classes with one-sided error and classes defined by simultaneous non-uniform and nondeterministic time bounds. This homogeneous description allows a better understanding of the relationships between the considered classes, and also between these classes and uniform complexity measures.

We have obtained the known lowness results from our main theorem and an inclusion structure of the considered classes. Moreover, we have shown that for any $k \geq 3$, polynomially length bounded advices do not augment the power of the k-th level of the low hierarchy. This result gives evidence that new techniques will be required to obtain lowness results concerning higher levels.

References

[1] M. Abadi, J. Feigenbaum and J. Kilian, On hiding information from an oracle, in: Proc. 19th ACM STOC (1987) 195 - 203.
[2] L. Babai, Arthur-Merlin games: a randomized proof system and a short hierarchy of complexity classes, manuscript, 1986.
[3] L. Babai, Trading group theory for randomness, in: Proc. 17th ACM STOC (1985) 421 - 429.
[4] J.L. Balcazar, Self-reducibility, in: Proc. 4th STACS, Lecture Notes in Computer Science **247** (Springer, Berlin, 1986) 136 - 147.
[5] J.L. Balcazar, R.V. Book and U. Schöning, Sparse oracles, lowness, and highness, in: Proc. 11th Intern. Sympos. Math. Foundations of Comput. Sci. , Lecture Notes in Computer Science **176** (Springer, Berlin, 1984) 185 - 193.
[6] J.L. Balcazar, R.V. Book and U. Schöning, Sparse sets, lowness, and highness, SIAM Journ. Comput. **15** (1986) 739 -747.
[7] A.K. Chandra, D.C. Kozen and L.J. Stockmeyer, Alternation, Journal of the ACM **28** (1981) 114 - 133.
[8] J.Gill, Computational complexity of probabilistic complexity classes, SIAM Journ. Comput. **6** (1977) 675 - 695.
[9] J.Kämper, Non-uniform proof systems: A new framework to describe non-uniform and probabilistic complexity classes, Bericht **3/87**, Universität Oldenburg, 1987.
[10] R.M. Karp and R.J. Lipton, Some connections between nonuniform and uniform complexity classes, in: Proc. 12th ACM STOC (1980) 302 - 309.
[11] K. Ko, On helping by robust oracle machines, in: Proc. Structure in Complexity Theory Conf. (1987) 182 - 190.
[12] K. Ko, On self-reducibility and weak p-selectivity, J. Comput. Syst. Sci. **26** (1983) 209 - 221.
[13] K. Ko, Some obversations on the probabilistic algorithms and NP-hard problems, Inform. Proc. Lett.**14** (1983) 39 - 43.

[14] K. Ko and U. Schöning, On circuit-size complexity and the low hierarchy in NP, SIAM Journ. Comput. **14** (1985) 41 - 51.

[15] C. Lautemann, BPP and the polynomial hierarchy, Inform. Proc. Lett. **14** (1983) 215 - 217.

[16] T.J. Long, Strong nondeterministic polynomial-time reducibilities, Theor. Comput. Sci. **21** (1982) 1 - 25.

[17] A. Meyer and M. Paterson, With what frequency are apparently intractable problems difficult?, MIT/LCS/TM-**126**, Lab. for Computer Science, MIT, Cambridge, Mass., 1979.

[18] N. Pippenger, On simultaneous resource bounds, in: Proc. 20th IEEE Symp. Foundations of Computer Science (1979) 307 - 311.

[19] U. Schöning, A low and a high hierarchy within NP, J. Comput. Syst. Sci. **27** (1983) 14 - 28.

[20] U. Schöning, Complexity and Structure, Lecture Notes in Computer Science **211** (Springer, Berlin, 1986).

[21] U. Schöning, Graph isomorphism is in the low hierarchy, in: Proc. 4th STACS, Lecture Notes in Computer Science **247** (Springer, Berlin, 1986) 114 - 124.

[22] U. Schöning, Netzwerkkomplexität, probabilistische Algorithmen und Relativierungen, Habilitationsschrift, Universität Stuttgart, 1985.

[23] U. Schöning, On small generators, Theor. Comput. Sci. **34** (1984) 337 - 341.

[24] U. Schöning, Probabilistic complexity classes and lowness, in: Proc. Structure in Complexity Theory Conf. (1987) 2 - 8.

[25] A.L. Selman, P-selective sets, tally languages, and the behaviour of polynomial time reducibilities on NP, Math. Systems Theory **13** (1979) 55 - 65.

[26] A.L. Selman, Reductions on NP and p-selective sets, Theor. Comput. Sci. **19** (1982) 287 - 304.

[27] M. Sipser, A complexity theoretic approach to randomness, in: Proc. 15th ACM STOC (1983) 330 - 335.

[28] L.J. Stockmeyer, The polynomial-time hierarchy, Theor. Comput. Sci. **3** (1977) 1 - 22.

[29] C.K. Yap, Some consequences of non-uniform conditions on uniform classes, Theor. Comput. Sci. **26** (1983) 287 - 300.

[30] Y. Yesha, On certain polynomial-time truth-table reducibilities of complete sets to sparse sets, SIAM Journ. Comput. **12** (1983) 411 - 425.

[31] S. Zachos, Probabilistic quantifiers, adversaries, and complexity classes, in: Proc. Structure in Complexity Theory Conf. , Lecture Notes in Computer Science **223** (Springer, Berlin, 1986) 383 - 400.

[32] S. Zachos and H. Heller, A decisive characterization of BPP, Inform. and Contr. **69** (1986) 125 -135.

Padding, Commitment and Self-reducibility

Sanjeev N. Khadilkar
Somenath Biswas
Dept. of Computer Science and Engineering,
I.I.T. Kanpur - 208016, INDIA.

1. Introduction

We introduce in this paper a property called commitability which is exhibited by many sets in NP including all $\leq_m^P$-complete ones. What we have attempted to capture in commitability is a common enough phenomenon and may be illustrated in the context of the language of Hamiltonian graphs as follows. Given a graph G, and a set E_1 of edges of G, it is not difficult to obtain another graph H such that H is Hamiltonian iff G has a Hamiltonian circuit that includes all edges in E_1. Thus, for this NP language, our ´commitment´ towards a kind of ´solution´ (in looking for a Hamiltonian circuit that includes E_1 entirely) can be reflected in the membership question of the language itself. We give the formal definition of commitability in Section 3.

The main reason why commitability may be considered interesting is because of its relation to disjunctive self-reducibility, d-self-reducibility for short. Commitability is a more extensive property than d-self-reducibility: we show that every d-self-reducible set is commitable. Yet, commitability captures an important aspect of d-self-reducibility which has been used variously, e.g. in [Be78, F79, M80, Se86]. In a certain sense, therefore this new notion is a generalization of d-self-reducibility.

Two other notions are of relevance here: padding and kernel constructibility. (The latter captures a form of self-reducibility weaker than d-self-reducibility). We prove some connecting results, e.g. we show that every paddable set is kernel constructible and that if a set is both paddable and commitable, then it is also d-self-reducible.

This paper is organized as follows. Section 2 details the preliminaries. Section 3 introduces commitability and proves some basic results about this concept. Section 4 gives some connecting results. In Section 5, we show how commitability manages to retain an important structural aspect of d-self-reducibility. Concluding remarks are given in Section 6.

2. Preliminaries

The notion of padding in the context of polynomial time was introduced by Berman and Hartmanis [BH77].

Definition 1: A set A is said to be **paddable** if there exist polynomial time computable functions S_A, D_A^1 and D_A^2 such that

$(\forall x,y) [S_A(x,y) \in A \text{ iff } x \in A]$,

$(\forall x,y) [D_A^1(S_A(x,y)) = x]$,

$(\forall x,y) [D_A^2(S_A(x,y)) = y]$.

In the original definition [BH77] for paddability, existence of D_A^1 was not insisted upon. However, as noted by Mahaney and Young [MY85], existence of D_A^1 follows from the other two functions.

Berman and Hartmanis [BH77] also introduced the notion of p-isomorphism which is very helpful in showing structural similarities of sets in NP.

Definition 2: Two sets $A \subseteq \Sigma^*$, $B \subseteq \Gamma^*$ are said to be **p-isomorphic** if there exists a bijection f from Σ^* to Γ^* such that f is a $\leq_m^P$-reduction of A to B and f^{-1} is a $\leq_m^P$-reduction of B to A where both f and f^{-1} are polynomial time computable.

The important fact connecting paddability and p-isomorphism is given by the following theorem:

Theorem 3: [BH77,MY85] If two sets A,B satisfy

(i) $A \leq_m^P B$ and $B \leq_m^P A$ and

(ii) Both A and B are paddable,

then A and B are p-isomorphic.

The notion of self-reducibility, a property found in many natural NP sets, has been investigated in many contexts, see e.g. [MP79], [Sc81], [Se86], [Ba87]. Here we shall use disjunctive self-reducibility, d-self-reducibility for short.

Definition 4: [MP79,Se86,Ba87] A set A is d-self-reducible if there is a deterministic polynomial time oracle Turing machine M, such that A = L(M,A), (that is, the language accepted by M with A as the oracle set is A itself) with M satisfying the following:

(i) On input x, M either does not query the oracle at all, or if it does, then x is in A iff any of the queried strings is in A.

(ii) On input x, M can query only those strings which are strictly less than x in an a priori fixed partial order $\sqsubset$, where $\sqsubset$ satisfies:

(a) It is decidable in polynomial time whether or not $y \sqsubset z$ is true,

(b) Every strictly decreasing chain is finite, and is bounded in length by p of the length of its maximum element in the partial order, and

(c) If $y \sqsubset z$ then $|y| \leq q(|z|)$,

p(.) and q(.) being fixed polynomials.

The following shows why the above concept is interesting in the context of NP. See e.g. [Se86].

Proposition 5: [Se86] Every set in P is d-self-reducible. Every d-self-reducible set is in NP. All known natural NP-complete sets are d-self-reducible.

We shall need another concept, called kernel constructibility. This also attempts to capture the self-reducibility phenomenon, but in a weaker form than d-self-reducibility.

Definition 6: [AB83,A87] A set A is **kernel constructible** if there is a PTIME set K_A and a PTIME verifiable relation R_A where

(i) $K_A \subseteq A$.

(ii) For all x and y, if $x \in A$ and $x R_A y$ then $y \in A$.

(iii) For all $x \in A - K_A$, there exist $y_1, y_2, \ldots y_n$ such that $y_1 \in K_A$, $y_1 R_A y_2$, $y_2 R_A y_3$, $\ldots y_{n-1} R_A y_n$, $y_n R_A x$ and each $|y_i|$ and n is less than or equal to $q(|x|)$, for some fixed polynomial $q(.)$.

K_A and R_A are called a **kernel** and a **constructing relation** for A respectively.

It can be easily shown that

Proposition 7: Every d-self-reducible set is kernel constructible.

3. Commitability

In the rest of the paper we assume a fixed alphabet $\Sigma = \{0,1\}$, unless otherwise specified.

For every set A in NP, by definition, there exists a polynomial time verifiable relation R_A such that

$$x \in A \text{ iff } (\exists y) [\ |y| \leq p(|x|) \land x R_A y\ ]$$

where $p(.)$ is some fixed polynomial. The string y is called a **witness** of x that sees x in A in the context of the relation R_A. R_A is called a **defining relation** for the NP set A.

Clearly, one can trivially modify R_A to $\bar{R_A}$, such that

$$x \in A \text{ iff } (\exists y) [\ |y| \leq p(|x|) \land (y = e \lor y = 0\Sigma^*) \land x \bar{R_A} y\ ].$$

Thus, without loss of generality, one can assume that every NP set A has a defining relation R_A such that none of the witnesses with respect to R_A for elements of A begins with a 1. We call such a relation an **eligible relation** and the corresponding witnesses **eligible witnesses**.

Definition 8: A set A in NP with an eligible defining relation R_A is

said to be **commitable** if there exists a polynomial time computable function C_A, $C_A: \Sigma^* \times \Sigma^* \longrightarrow \Sigma^*$, such that
($\forall x,y$) [$C_A(x,y) \in A$ iff either y is a witness of x with respect to the eligible relation R_A <u>or</u> y0 is a prefix of a witness of x with respect to the eligible relation R_A].

(Some reasons for defining commitability in the above manner are discussed in a note in Section 4 after the proof of Theorem 12.)

Commitability is a natural phenomenon in very many NP sets. Consider, for example, SAT, the set of satisfiable propositional formulae in conjunctive normal form. A witness of a member x of SAT can be taken to be a bit string that codes a satisfying truth assignment to x; the ith bit of the witness is 0 if the ith variable (of the set of variables occurring in x) is set false in the satisfying truth assignment, otherwise it is 1. Now, any binary string u may be regarded as a commitment for an instance x, in the sense that one is looking for a witness v for x such that u is a prefix of v. SAT can be regarded as commitable since this commitment can be reflected in the membership question of SAT itself; we can obtain an instance y of SAT such that y is in SAT iff u is a prefix of some witness of x. (y can be obtained from x and u by substituting in x the truth values of the partial assignment specified by u and then performing trivial simplifications. We are assuming that $|u| \leq n$, where n is the number of variables occurring in x.). We can obtain a commitment function for SAT as per Definition 8 that would first check if u is of the form 0v, then generate instance y from x and a commitment of v0, along the lines discussed above. Thus,

Proposition 9: SAT is commitable.

Many other sets in NP, both complete and otherwise, can be shown with equal ease to be commitable. A non-trivial result is that the set ISO of pairs of isomorphic graphs is commitable. This can be obtained by using the idea that Schnorr used to demonstrate that ISO is self-transformable [Sc81].

All NP-complete sets are commitable. For,

Proposition 10: If $A \leq_m^P B$, and $B \leq_m^P A$ and A is commitable, then so is B.

Proof: Let f reduce A to B and g reduce B to A. Let C_A be a commitment function for A. Clearly, for a witness that will see x in B, we can use a string which is a witness that sees g(x) in A. Therefore, the following C_B is a commitment function for B:
$C_B(x,y) = f(C_A(g(x),y))$. ∎

Corollary 11: All NP-complete sets are commitable.

Proof: Follows from Propositions 9 and 10 and the NP-completeness of SAT. ∎

It is interesting to note that with respect to d-self-reducibility or kernel constructibility, only a weaker statement is known to hold [Se86]: All **paddable** NP-complete sets are d-self-reducible (and hence kernel constructible). This is because in the proof p-isomorphism is invoked. Thus, sets which are complete but not known to be paddable, e.g., k-creative sets [JY85], are not known to be kernel constructible, though, from Corollary 11, we have that even such sets are commitable.

4. Some Connecting Results

Theorem 12: Every d-self-reducible set is commitable.

Proof: Let A be a d-self-reducible set and let M be an oracle Turing machine as per the definition of d-self-reducibility such that $A = L(M,A)$. We need the following definitions:

Definition 13: [Se86] The self-reducing tree for every x in Σ^* is defined as follows:

The root of the tree is x. For each node y in the tree, its children are those elements of Σ^* which are queried by M on input y. These children are ordered left-to-right in their canonical order.

We define the <u>address</u> of each node in such a tree as follows:

Definition 14: The address of the root in the self-reducibility tree is the empty string ε. For any other node y, if y is the smallest child of its parent, then the address of y is v0 where v is the address of the parent of y. Otherwise the address of y is u1 where u is the address of the sibling of y which is immediately smaller than y.

The following claims are easy consequences of these definitions:

1: The length of the address string of any node in the self-reducing tree of x is bounded above by $p(|x|)$, where $p(.)$ is some fixed polynomial.

2: Let u be the address of some node y in a self-reducing tree. The address of a node z has the prefix u0 iff z is a descendent of y in the tree.

We define eligible witnesses for the members of our d-self-reducible set A as follows (the corresponding eligible relation will be clear from the context):

Definition 15: A (binary) string u is said to be an eligible witness of x in A if u is the address of a <u>leaf node</u> v in the self-reducing tree for x, where v is a member of A.

The above clearly satisfies the requirements for an eligible witness, because given u we can verify in polynomial time that v is a descendent of x in the tree and v is in A, and because if x is not a leaf node then its witness must begin with a 0.

Finally we define a commitment function C_A for A. Let w be a fixed string not in A. We define:

$C_A(x,y)$ is w if y is not an address of any node in the self-reducing tree for x, otherwise $C_A(x,y)$ is that node in the tree whose address is y.

Note that we can check in polynomial time whether or not y is a valid address by constructing a portion of the tree, as specified by the successive prefixes of y, until we go off the tree or find the node whose address is y.

To see that $C_A(.,.)$ is indeed a commitment function, we argue as follows. Suppose y0 is a prefix of an eligible witness of x. Then there is a leaf node v which is in A and whose address has prefix y0. Then from claim 2 above, the node at address y is an ancestor of v. Hence this node is also in A. On the other hand, suppose there is no leaf node which is in A whose address has a prefix y0. Then from claim 2, no descendent of the node at address y is a leaf node which is in A, therefore the node at address y cannot be in A.

Thus the d-self-reducible set A is indeed commitable. This completes the proof of Theorem 12. ∎

Note: For an x in the d-self-reducible set A, what we are using as witness of x is a binary string that codes a sequence $y_1, y_2, \ldots y_k$, where $y_1 = x$, y_k is an element of A which the oracle Turing machine accepts without any queries to the oracle, and each y_{i+1} is a child of y_i in the self-reducing tree for x. One may wonder why we are not using this sequence itself as a witness and define a more direct commitment function C_A in the following manner: Given x and y, where $y = \langle y_1, y_2, \ldots y_j \rangle$, let $C_A(x,y)$ be y_j provided $y_1 = x$ and each y_{i+1} is a child of y_i in the self-reducing tree for x. The problem occurs when $y_1 = x$ and y_{i+1} is a child of y_i for $1 \leq i \leq j-2$, but y_j is not a child of y_{j-1}, though y_{j-1} has some m children each with y_j as a proper prefix. Then x is in A iff any of these m children is in A, but we do not have a unique string to which $C_A(x,y)$ may be mapped.

A way out is to stop using prefixes of arbitrary witnesses as such in the definition of C_A and look for witnesses in which we can introduce separator symbols after the prefix. Whatever is between this separator and the previous one can now be regarded as a full specification of a node in the self-reducing tree, and may not be a proper substring of one.

The proof above shows that a single bit can act in the role of a separator, and thus give us a commitment function of the kind we have defined for each d-self-reducible set.

It can now be appreciated why we chose not to define commitability directly as:

(*)   ($\forall x,y$) [$C_A(x,y) \in A$ iff y is a prefix of a witness of x].

To wit, we do not know how to prove Theorem 12 with this more direct definition of commitability. When a single bit is added to a partial witness, it may not always be possible to clearly specify what additional commitment is being made.

However, the function specified in (*) above exists in most natural cases and from such a function it is easy to construct a commitment function as per Definition 8.

With our commitment function, we are unable to extend Theorem 12 to kernel constructible sets as well. We need, it seems, at least two bits for a separator. If we weaken the commitment function to, say,

(**)   ($\forall x,y$) [$C_A(x,y) \in A$ iff either y is an eligible witness of x <u>or</u>

y00 is a prefix of an eligible witness of

x],

then it can be shown that every kernel constructible language has such a commitment function. However, it turns out that all sets in NP satisfy (**). Analogous notions do not seem to be interesting.

Theorem 16: If a set is paddable as well as commitable then it is also d-self-reducible.

Proof: Let A be paddable and commitable with a commitment function C_A. We show the d-self-reducibility of A by showing that it is p-isomorphic to a d-self-reducible set A_w.

Let # be a symbol not in Σ. We define A_w as

A_w = { x#y#z | $C_A(x,y) \in A$ }.

Let R_A be a polynomial time verifiable relation for A which sees A in NP with eligible witnesses and let $p_A(.)$ be a polynomial bound on the length of witnesses. Now, A $\leq^P_m A_w$, for given an $x \in \Sigma^*$, if ϵ is not a witness of x (we can check this easily, and if it is a witness, account for it separately):

$x \in A$ iff $x\#\# \in A_w$. Also, $A_w \leq_m^P A$, because $x\#y\#z \in A_w$ iff $C_A(x,y) \in A$. Further, A_w is clearly paddable. Thus, the two sets A and A_w are paddable and each polynomially reduces to the other. Therefore, from Theorem 3, we have that A and A_w are p-isomorphic with some suitable bijection $f: \Sigma^* \longrightarrow (\Sigma \cup \{\#\})^*$.

Next, we show that A_w is d-self-reducible.

Let $y <_w x$ iff $[(x = u\#v\#w) \wedge (y = u\#z\#w) \wedge$
$$(z = v0 \vee z = v1) \wedge$$
$$(|z| \leq p_A(|u|))].$$

Let $g_w(x) = \{\}$ iff $x = u\#v\#w \wedge |v| \geq p_A(|u|)$
$$= \{ y \mid y <_w x \} \text{ otherwise.}$$

Let an oracle Turing machine M_w with oracle A_w execute the following algorithm:

On input x:

if $x = u\#v\#w \wedge R_A(u,v)$ then accept x

else if $x = u\#v\#w \wedge [(|v| = p_A(|u|) \wedge \sim R_A(u,v)) \vee$
$$|v| > p_A(|u|)] \text{ then reject } x$$

else construct $g_w(x)$ and query the oracle for each element of $g_w(x)$, accepting x iff at least one element of $g_w(x)$ is accepted by the oracle for A_w.

It can be seen that M_w defines a d-self-reducibility for A_w. (Here, the partial order that is used is the reflexive, transitive closure of the relation $<_w$ defined above.) The d-self-reducibility of A follows from the p-isomorphism of A and A_w. ∎

Corollary 17: The class of commitable sets is the class obtained from the class of d-self-reducible sets with closure under $\equiv_m^P$.

Proof: Follows from Theorems 12 and 16 and the fact that paddable sets exist in each $\leq_m^P$-degree. ∎

Theorem 16 may be contrasted with the following one which shows that paddability on its own guarantees a kind of self-reducibility, viz. kernel constructibility.

Theorem 18: Every paddable set in NP is kernel constructible.

Proof: Let $A \in NP$ be paddable and let R_A be a polynomial time verifiable relation which sees A in NP; i.e.
$x \in A$ iff $(\exists y) [|y| \leq p(|x|) \wedge x R_A y]$,
where $p(.)$ is some fixed polynomial. Let S_A, D_A^1 and D_A^2 be a set of padding functions for A.

We demonstrate kernel constructibility of A by exhibiting K_A, a kernel and Q_A, a constructing relation for A. Define K_A as
$x \in K_A$ iff $D_A^1(x) R_A D_A^2(x)$.

The relation Q_A is defined as follows:

If $D_A^1(x)$ is undefined

then $S_A(x,0) Q_A x$ as well as $S_A(x,1) Q_A x$.

Otherwise, let $u = D_A^1(x)$ and $v = D_A^2(x)$.

If $|v| > p(|u|)$ or if $|v| = p(|u|)$ and $u R_A v$ does not hold,

then $S_A(x,0) Q_A x$ as well as $S_A(x,1) Q_A x$.

On the other hand, if $|v| < p(|u|)$, then we define

$S_A(u,v0) Q_A x$ as well as $S_A(u,v1) Q_A x$.

This completes the definition of Q_A.

It is clear that for every non-kernel member x of A, there exist $y_1, y_2, \ldots y_{n-1}, y_n$ such that
$y_1 \in K_A$, $y_1 Q_A y_2$, $y_2 Q_A y_3$, $\ldots$ $y_{n-1} Q_A y_n$ and $y_n Q_A x$,
where $n < 2 * p(|x|)$ and each y_i is bounded in length by some fixed polynomial in the length of x. This proves, therefore, that A is kernel constructible. ∎

5. Commitability captures an aspect of d-self-reducibility

Commitability incorporates in essence a structural feature of d-self-reducible sets which is the basis of certain important results on reductions of d-self-reducible sets or their complements to sparse sets [Be78, F79, M80]. The form this feature takes in commitable sets is the existence of what may be termed as the commitment tree.

Definition 19: Let A be a commitable set with C_A a commitment function for A in the context of an eligible defining relation R_A. We assume here, without loss of generality, that if x is in A, then every witness of x with respect to R_A is exactly of length $p(|x|)$, where $p(.)$ is a fixed polynomial. Then, for an x in Σ^*, the commitment tree T_x for x is as follows:

The root of T_x is labeled $C_A(x,\epsilon)$ and its address is ϵ. The label of a node with address y is $C_A(x,y)$. If the label of a node in the tree is $C_A(x,y)$ with $|y| < p(|x|)$, then the node is an internal node which will have r children labeled

$C_A(x,y0)$, $C_A(x,y01)$, $C_A(x,y011)$, . . . $C_A(x,y01^{r-1})$,

with addresses y0, y01, y011, . . . y01^{r-1} respectively, arranged left to right in that order, where $r = p(|x|) - |y|$.

The following claim can easily be seen to hold for a tree T_x as above:

Lemma 20: The depth of T_x is bounded by a polynomial in $|x|$. For every leaf node in T_x, one can verify in time polynomial in $|x|$ whether the label of the node belongs to A (given x and the address of the leaf node). The label of an internal node is in A iff at least one of its children has a label which is in A.

Because of the above Lemma, the tree search method of Berman [Be78] is applicable to commitable sets as well and we can use the method to prove the following result analogous to one by Fortune [F79]:

Theorem 21: If the complement of a commitable set A is $\leq_m^P$-reducible to a sparse set, then A is in P.

6. Concluding Remarks

It appears that commitable sets are, in some sense, close to self-

1-helper sets [Ko87] and sets in NP with self-computable witnesses [Ba87]. Balcazar proves [Ba87] that the latter two classes of sets are identical. Commitability, however, appears to be a stronger notion. For if A has self-computable witnesses, then for x in A, we can compute in polynomial time using A as oracle <u>a</u> witness for x, but if A is commitable, then for x in A, we can compute in time $n*p(|x|)$ using A as oracle <u>all</u> the witnesses for x, where p(.) is a polynomial and n is the number of witnesses for x.

Though all P and NP-complete sets are commitable, it is reasonable to believe that there are sets in NP-P which are not commitable. For, if E ≠ NE then there are p-selective sets in NP-P [Se79]; however, such a set cannot be commitable as one can easily show that if a set is p-selective as well as commitable then it is in P. Can we construct a non-commitable set under the weaker assumption P ≠ NP ?

<u>Acknowledgment</u>: We are grateful to the referees for their critical comments which helped us in removing a couple of errors and also in improving the presentation.

7. References

- [A87] - Arvind, V., On some structural properties of NP, Ph. D. thesis, I.I.T. Kanpur, 1987.
- [AB83] - Arvind, V. and Biswas, S., Kernel constructible languages, Proc. of the 3rd FST & TCS conference, 1983.
- [Ba87] - Balcázar, J. L., Self-reducibility, Proc. 4th STACS, Lect. Notes in Comp. Sc., Vol. 247, pp. 136 - 147, 1987.
- [Be78] - Berman, P., Relationships between density and deterministic complexity of NP-complete languages, Proc. 5th ICALP, Lect. Notes in Comp. Sc., vol. 62, pp. 63 - 71, 1978.
- [BH77] - Berman, L. and Hartmanis, J., On isomorphism and density of NP and other complete sets, SIAM Journal of Computing 6,

pp. 305 - 322, 1977.

- [F79] - Fortune, S., A note on sparse complete sets, SIAM Jl. Comput. vol. 8, pp. 431 - 433, 1979.

- [JY85] - Joseph, D. and Young, P., Some remarks on witness functions for nonpolynomial and noncomplete sets in NP, Theor. C. Sc., vol. 39, pp. 225 - 237, 1985.

- [Ko87] - Ko, Ker-I, On helping by robust oracle machines, Theor. Comp. Sc., vol. 52, pp. 15 - 36, 1987.

- [M80] - Mahaney, S., Sparse complete sets for NP: solution of a conjecture of Berman and Hartmanis, Proc. 21st IEEE Symp. on FOCS, pp. 54 - 60, 1980. Final version in Jl. of Comp. Syst. Sc., vol. 25, pp. 130 - 143, 1982.

- [MP79] - Meyer, A. R. and Paterson, M. S., With what frequency are apparently intractable problems difficult?, Tech. Report, MIT/LCS/TM-126, 1979.

- [MY85] - Mahaney, S. and Young, P., Orderings of polynomial isomorphism types, Theor. Comput. Sc., 39(2), pp. 207 - 224, 1985.

- [Sc81] - Schnorr, C.P., On self-transformable combinatorial problems, Math. Programming Study, Vol. 14, pp. 95 - 103, 1982.

- [Se79] - Selman, A., P-selective sets, tally languages, and the behavior of polynomial time reducibilities on NP, Math. Syst. Theory, 13, pp. 55 - 65, 1979.

- [Se86] - Selman, A., Natural self-reducible sets, preprint, 1986.

THE COMPLEXITY OF A
COUNTING FINITE-STATE AUTOMATON

Craig A. Rich
Computer Science Department
California State Polytechnic University, Pomona
Pomona, CA 91768-4034, USA

Giora Slutzki
Computer Science Department
Iowa State University
Ames, IA 50011, USA

Abstract. A counting finite-state automaton is a nondeterministic finite-state automaton which, on an input over its input alphabet, (magically) writes in binary the number of accepting computations on the input. We examine the complexity of computing the counting function of an NFA, and the complexity of recognizing its range as a set of binary strings. We also consider the pumping behavior of counting finite-state automata. The class of functions computed by counting NFA's
 (1) includes a class of functions computed by deterministic finite-state transducers;
 (2) is contained in the class of functions computed by polynomially time- and linearly space-bounded Turing transducers;
 (3) includes a function whose range is the composite numbers.

1. Introduction

The counting finite-state automaton—or counting NFA—is a finite-state analogue of the counting Turing Machine of Valiant [8]. It is known that the class #P of functions computed by polynomially time-bounded counting TMs includes the class FP of functions computed by polynomially time-bounded Turing transducers; however, it is not known if this inclusion is proper. Valiant [8,9] has shown several functions to be complete for #P, and these functions in #P are not computable in polynomial time if P ≠ NP. These results suggest that FP is properly included in #P.

We consider finite-state analogues of these questions. We show that the class #NFA of functions computed by counting NFAs includes a class #DFT of counting functions computed by deterministic finite-state transducers. Although it is not known whether FP ≠ #P, we show that #DFT is properly included in #NFA by exhibiting a counting NFA whose range as a set of binary strings is not context-free, whereas the ranges of deterministic finite-state transducers are regular [2]. While some functions in #P are apparently not computable in polynomial time, we show that functions in #NFA can be computed using time polynomial and space linear in the the length of the input.

Since functions in #DFT have ranges which are regular and functions in #NFA have ranges which are not necessarily context-free, it is natural to investigate the complexity of counting NFA ranges. Intuitively, one might expect the range of a counting NFA to be efficiently recognizable simply because it is a finite-state model, but that is apparently not the case. We establish an upper bound by showing that the range of a counting NFA is recognizable nondeterministically using space linear in the length of the input, i.e., a context-sensitive language. We suggest an intractable lower bound by showing that the composite numbers—which are not known to be in P—are the range of a counting NFA.

In §2, we give notational conventions and formally define the counting function of an NFA. In §3, we show that the counting functions computed by deterministic finite-state transducers are properly included among those computed by nondeterministic finite-state automata, and give a counting NFA whose range is not context-free. In §4, we examine the complexity of computing the counting function of an NFA, and the complexity of recognizing its range as a set of binary strings. In §5, we consider the pumping behavior of a counting finite-state automaton. For a fixed input string, we show that the number of accepting computations—considered as a function of the number of times a fixed substring is pumped—satisfies a homogeneous linear recurrence equation of finite degree having integer coefficients.

2. Preliminary Definitions

In this section, we present notational conventions and our notions of counting function computed by finite-state automata. A *string* x is a finite sequence of *symbols* from a finite *alphabet*. The *length* of x, denoted $|x|$, is the number of symbols composing x. The *empty string*, denoted ϵ, is the string having length 0. The *concatenation* of two strings x and y is the string consisting of the symbols of x followed by the symbols of y, denoted xy. A *language* L is a set of strings over an alphabet, and $\|L\|$ denotes the cardinality of L. The empty set is denoted by ϕ; the set of integers $\{\ldots, -1, 0, 1, \ldots\}$ is denoted by $\mathcal{Z}$; and the set of natural numbers $\{0, 1, 2, \ldots\}$ is denoted by $\mathcal{N}$.

In this work, we frequently consider natural numbers as binary strings and vice versa. Formally, these conversions are functions $s: \mathcal{N} \to \{0,1\}^*$ and $\#: \{0,1\}^* \to \mathcal{N}$ defined by

$s(k) = $ the binary representation of k without leading zeroes,

$\#(x) = $ the number represented in binary by x.

Note that $s(0) = \epsilon$. We extend s and $\#$ to sets of natural numbers and binary strings in the usual way by defining $s(K) = \{\, s(k) \mid k \in K \,\}$, and $\#(L) = \{\, \#(x) \mid x \in L \,\}$.

A *nondeterministic finite automaton (NFA)* is a 5-tuple $M = (Q, \Sigma, \delta, I, F)$, where Q is a finite set of *states*; Σ is a finite *input alphabet*; δ is a *transition function* from

$Q \times \Sigma^*$ to subsets of Q; $I \subseteq Q$ is a set of *initial states*; and $F \subseteq Q$ is a set of *final states*. The *counting function* $\#\delta: Q \times \Sigma^* \to \mathcal{N}$ is defined recursively by

$$\#\delta(q, \epsilon) = \begin{cases} 1, & \text{if } q \in F; \\ 0, & \text{if } q \notin F, \end{cases}$$

$$\#\delta(q, \sigma x) = \sum_{p \in \delta(q, \sigma)} \#\delta(p, x).$$

The *counting function* $\#M: \Sigma^* \to \mathcal{N}$ is defined by

$$\#M(x) = \sum_{q \in I} \#\delta(q, x).$$

Intuitively, the counting function $\#M(x)$ ($\#\delta(q, x)$) is the number of accepting computations of M on input x (starting from state q). We extend the counting functions to languages $L \subseteq \Sigma^*$ in the usual way by defining $\#\delta(q, L) = \{\#\delta(q, x) \mid x \in L\}$, and $\#M(L) = \{\#M(x) \mid x \in L\}$. We consider the range of a counting NFA M to be the set of binary strings $s(\#M(\Sigma^*))$. The class of counting functions of NFAs is defined by $\#\text{NFA} = \{\#M \mid M \text{ is an NFA}\}$, and the class of their ranges is defined by $\text{range}(\#\text{NFA}) = \{s(\#M(\Sigma^*)) \mid M \text{ is an NFA with input alphabet } \Sigma\}$.

We also want to consider a deterministic counterpart of the counting NFA which produces a binary string by transduction rather than counting accepting computations. Intuitively, our deterministic finite-state transducer is a special case of the deterministic Generalized Sequential Machine (GSM) [1] in which the output alphabet is fixed to be $\{0, 1\}$ and all states are considered final, so that its computation on any input produces a binary string.

Formally, a *deterministic finite-state transducer (DFT)* is a 5-tuple $D = (Q, \Sigma, \delta, \lambda, q_1)$, where Q is a finite set of *states*; Σ is a finite *input alphabet*; $\delta: Q \times \Sigma \to Q$ is a *transition function*; $\lambda: Q \times \Sigma \to \{0, 1\}^*$ is an *output function*; and $q_1 \in Q$ is the *initial state*. The transition function and output function are extended to $\delta: Q \times \Sigma^* \to Q$ and $\lambda: Q \times \Sigma^* \to \{0, 1\}^*$, defined recursively by

$$\delta(q, \epsilon) = q,$$
$$\delta(q, \sigma x) = \delta(\delta(q, \sigma), x);$$
$$\lambda(q, \epsilon) = \epsilon,$$
$$\lambda(q, \sigma x) = \lambda(q, \sigma) \lambda(\delta(q, \sigma), x).$$

The *output function* $D: \Sigma^* \to \{0, 1\}^*$ is defined by $D(x) = \lambda(q_1, x)$ and the *counting function* $\#D: \Sigma^* \to \mathcal{N}$ is defined by $\#D(x) = \#(D(x))$. Intuitively, the counting function $\#D(x)$ is the number represented by the binary string produced by the transduction of D on input x. We extend the output and counting functions to languages $L \subseteq \Sigma^*$ in the usual way. We consider the range of a DFT to be the set of binary strings $s(\#D(\Sigma^*))$. Note that it can be obtained from $D(\Sigma^*)$ by truncating the leading zeroes of each string. The class of counting functions of DFTs is defined by $\#\text{DFT} = \{\#D \mid D \text{ is a DFT}\}$, and the class of their ranges is defined by $\text{range}(\#\text{DFT}) = \{s(\#D(\Sigma^*)) \mid D \text{ is a DFT with input alphabet } \Sigma\}$.

3. Inclusions among Counting Functions and their Ranges

In this section, we show that the counting functions computed by deterministic finite-state transducers are properly included among those computed by nondeterministic finite-state automata, and give a counting NFA whose range is not context-free. We denote the class of regular and context-free languages by REG and CFL, respectively. Since the range of every deterministic Generalized Sequential Machine (DGSM) is regular [2], and a DFT is a special case of a DGSM, it follows that the range of a DFT (with leading zeroes truncated) is regular.

Theorem 3.1. range(#DFT) $\subseteq$ REG.

Theorem 3.2. #DFT $\subseteq$ #NFA.

Proof. Let $D = (Q, \Sigma, \delta, \lambda, q_1)$ be a DFT, and construct an NFA M with input alphabet Σ such that for $x \in \Sigma^*$, $\#M(x) = \#D(x)$. Suppose $Q = \{q_1, \ldots, q_s\}$, and let $l = \max\{|\lambda(q,\sigma)| \mid q \in Q \wedge \sigma \in \Sigma\}$. Let $M = (Q', \Sigma, \delta', \{q_1\}, F)$, where $Q' = Q \cup \{q_i^j \mid 1 \leq i \leq s \wedge 1 \leq j \leq 2^l\}$, $F = \{q_i^j \mid 1 \leq i \leq s \wedge 1 \leq j \leq 2^l\}$, and δ' is defined by

$$\delta'(q_i, \sigma) = \{\delta(q_i, \sigma)\} \cup \{\delta(q_i, \sigma)^j \mid 1 \leq j \leq \#(\lambda(q_i, \sigma))\},$$
$$\delta'(q_i^k, \sigma) = \{\delta(q_i, \sigma)^j \mid 1 \leq j \leq 2^{|\lambda(q_i, \sigma)|}\}.$$

First we prove, by induction on $|x|$, that $\#\delta'(q_i^k, x) = 2^{|\lambda(q_i, x)|}$. For the empty string ϵ,

$$\#\delta'(q_i^k, \epsilon) = \begin{cases} 1, & \text{if } q_i^k \in F; \\ 0, & \text{if } q_i^k \notin F \end{cases} = 1 = 2^{|\epsilon|} = 2^{|\lambda(q_i, \epsilon)|},$$

and for strings σx of length at least 1,

$$\#\delta'(q_i^k, \sigma x) = \sum_{p \in \delta'(q_i^k, \sigma)} \#\delta'(p, x)$$
$$= \sum_{1 \leq j \leq 2^{|\lambda(q_i, \sigma)|}} \#\delta'(\delta(q_i, \sigma)^j, x)$$
$$= 2^{|\lambda(q_i, \sigma)|} \cdot 2^{|\lambda(\delta(q_i, \sigma), x)|}$$
$$= 2^{|\lambda(q_i, \sigma)\lambda(\delta(q_i, \sigma), x)|}$$
$$= 2^{|\lambda(q_i, \sigma x)|}.$$

Next we prove, by induction on $|x|$, the claim (*) $\#\delta'(q_i, x) = \#(\lambda(q_i, x))$. For the empty string ϵ,

$$\#\delta'(q_i, \epsilon) = \begin{cases} 1, & \text{if } q_i \in F; \\ 0, & \text{if } q_i \notin F \end{cases} = 0 = \#(\epsilon) = \#(\lambda(q_i, \epsilon)),$$

and for strings σx of length at least 1,

$$\#\delta'(q_i, \sigma x) = \sum_{p \in \delta'(q_i,\sigma)} \#\delta'(p, x)$$

$$= \left(\sum_{1 \leq j \leq \#(\lambda(q_i,\sigma))} \#\delta'(\delta(q_i,\sigma)^j, x) \right) + \#\delta'(\delta(q_i,\sigma), x)$$

$$= \#(\lambda(q_i,\sigma)) \cdot 2^{|\lambda(\delta(q_i,\sigma),x)|} + \#(\lambda(\delta(q_i,\sigma), x))$$

$$= \#(\lambda(q_i,\sigma)\lambda(\delta(q_i,\sigma), x))$$

$$= \#(\lambda(q_i, \sigma x)).$$

If we take $i = 1$ in $(*)$, then

$$\#M(x) = \#\delta'(q_1, x) = \#(\lambda(q_1, x)) = \#(D(x)) = \#D(x). \blacksquare$$

Lemma 3.3. #NFA is closed under addition and multiplication.

Proof idea. (addition) Let $M' = (Q', \Sigma, \delta', I', F')$, $M'' = (Q'', \Sigma, \delta'', I'', F'')$ be NFAs, and construct an NFA M with input alphabet Σ such that for $x \in \Sigma^*$, $\#M(x) = \#M'(x) + \#M''(x)$. M is obtained by a disjoint union construction. The states, transitions, initial states, and final states of M are the disjoint unions of those in M' and M''.

(multiplication) Let $M' = (Q', \Sigma, \delta', I', F')$, $M'' = (Q'', \Sigma, \delta'', I'', F'')$ be NFAs, and construct an NFA M with input alphabet Σ such that for $x \in \Sigma^*$, $\#M(x) = \#M'(x) \cdot \#M''(x)$. M is obtained by a cartesian product construction. The states, transitions, initial states, and final states of M are the cartesian products of those in M' and M''. $\blacksquare$

In this research, we give two examples of counting NFAs whose ranges are not context-free. The first is presented here, and the second—whose range is the binary encodings of the composite numbers—is presented in §4.

Example. A counting NFA whose range is $L = \{1^n 0^n 1^n \mid n \in \mathcal{N}\}$.

We construct an NFA M with input alphabet $\{0\}$ such that $s(\#M(0^*)) = L$. For $k \in \mathcal{N}$, define an NFA $M_k = (Q, \{0\}, \delta, I, F)$, where $Q = \{q_1, \ldots, q_{2k}, p_1, \ldots, p_{2k+1}\}$, $I = \{q_1\}$, $F = \{p_1, \ldots, p_{2k+1}\}$, and δ is defined by

$$\delta(q_i, 0) = \{q_1, \ldots, q_{2k}, p_1, \ldots, p_{2k}\},$$
$$\delta(p_i, 0) = \{p_1, \ldots, p_{2k+1}\}.$$

First we prove, by induction on n, that $\#\delta(p_i, 0^n) = 2^{(k+1)n}$. For $n = 0$,

$$\#\delta(p_i, \epsilon) = \begin{cases} 1, & \text{if } p_i \in F; \\ 0, & \text{if } p_i \notin F \end{cases} = 1 = 2^{(k+1)0},$$

and for $n > 0$,

$$\#\delta(p_i, 0^n) = \sum_{p \in \delta(p_i, 0)} \#\delta(p, 0^{n-1})$$

$$= \sum_{1 \leq j \leq 2^{k+1}} \#\delta(p_j, 0^{n-1})$$

$$= 2^{k+1} \cdot 2^{(k+1)(n-1)} = 2^{(k+1)n}$$

Next we prove, by induction on n, the claim (∗) $\#\delta(q_i, 0^n) = 2^{(k+1)n} - 2^{kn}$. For $n = 0$,

$$\#\delta(q_i, \epsilon) = \begin{cases} 1, & \text{if } q_i \in F; \\ 0, & \text{if } q_i \notin F \end{cases} = 0 = 2^{(k+1)0} - 2^{k \cdot 0},$$

and for $n > 0$,

$$\#\delta(q_i, 0^n) = \sum_{p \in \delta(q_i, 0)} \#\delta(p, 0^{n-1})$$

$$= \left(\sum_{1 \leq j \leq 2^k} \#\delta(q_j, 0^{n-1}) \right) + \left(\sum_{1 \leq j \leq 2^k} \#\delta(p_j, 0^{n-1}) \right)$$

$$= 2^k \cdot (2^{(k+1)(n-1)} - 2^{k(n-1)}) + 2^k \cdot 2^{(k+1)(n-1)}$$

$$= 2^{(k+1)n} - 2^{kn}.$$

Using Lemma 3.3, construct an NFA M with input alphabet $\{0\}$ such that for $n \in \mathcal{N}$, $\#M(0^n) = \#M_2(0^n) + \#M_0(0^n)$. If we take $i = 1$ in (∗), then

$$s(\#M(0^*)) = \{ s(\#M(0^n)) \mid n \in \mathcal{N} \}$$
$$= \{ s(\#M_2(0^n) + \#M_0(0^n)) \mid n \in \mathcal{N} \}$$
$$= \{ s((2^{3n} - 2^{2n}) + (2^n - 2^0)) \mid n \in \mathcal{N} \}$$
$$= \{ s(8^n - 4^n + 2^n - 1) \mid n \in \mathcal{N} \}$$
$$= \{ 1^n 0^n 1^n \mid n \in \mathcal{N} \} = L. \blacksquare$$

Corollary 3.4. range(#NFA) $\not\subset$ CFL.

Corollary 3.5. range(#DFT) $\subset$ range(#NFA) (range(#DFT) is properly contained in range(#NFA)).

Proof. It follows from Theorems 3.1, 3.2, Corollary 3.4, and the fact that REG $\subset$ CFL. $\blacksquare$

4. The Complexity of Counting Functions and their Ranges

In this section, we examine the complexity of computing the counting function of an NFA, and the complexity of recognizing its range. The latter problem—deciding whether a given binary string represents the number of accepting computations on some input—is considered both for a fixed NFA and when the NFA is given as an additional parameter. We show that a fixed counting NFA's range is context-sensitive, and suggest an intractible lower bound by showing that the composite numbers—which are not known to be in P—are the range of a counting NFA. The second of these is called the range membership problem for counting NFAs and is shown to be PSPACE-complete.

An important tool which we use in solving these problems is a matrix algebraic characterization of the counting function of an NFA which allows us to compute it in polynomial time and linear space. Let $M = (Q, \Sigma, \delta, I, F)$ be an NFA with state set $Q = \{q_1, \ldots, q_s\}$, and let $x = \sigma_n \ldots \sigma_1 \in \Sigma^*$. For each $\sigma \in \Sigma$, let $\vec{e}$, A^σ, $\vec{f}$ be the $1 \times s$, $s \times s$, $s \times 1$ matrices defined by

$$\vec{e} = (e_1 \ e_2 \ \cdots \ e_s), \quad \text{where } e_j = \begin{cases} 1, & \text{if } q_j \in I; \\ 0, & \text{if } q_j \notin I, \end{cases}$$

$$A^\sigma = \begin{pmatrix} A^\sigma_{11} & A^\sigma_{12} & \cdots & A^\sigma_{1s} \\ A^\sigma_{21} & A^\sigma_{22} & \cdots & A^\sigma_{2s} \\ \vdots & \vdots & \ddots & \vdots \\ A^\sigma_{s1} & A^\sigma_{s2} & \cdots & A^\sigma_{ss} \end{pmatrix}, \quad \text{where } A^\sigma_{ij} = \begin{cases} 1, & \text{if } q_j \in \delta(q_i, \sigma); \\ 0, & \text{if } q_j \notin \delta(q_i, \sigma), \end{cases}$$

$$\vec{f} = \begin{pmatrix} f_1 \\ f_2 \\ \vdots \\ f_s \end{pmatrix}, \quad \text{where } f_i = \#\delta(q_i, \epsilon).$$

The symbol $*$ denotes the usual matrix multiplication. The following lemma and its proof are well-known, and can also be proved using formal power series, as in Salomaa and Soittola [4].

Lemma 4.1. $\vec{e} * A^{\sigma_n} * \cdots * A^{\sigma_1} * \vec{f} = \#M(x).$

Proof. We prove, by induction on n, the following claim for $1 \leq i \leq s$:

(*) $\qquad (A^{\sigma_n} * \cdots * A^{\sigma_1} * \vec{f})_i = \#\delta(q_i, \sigma_n \ldots \sigma_1).$

For $n = 0$, $(\vec{f})_i = f_i = \#\delta(q_i, \epsilon)$, and for $n > 0$,

$$(A^{\sigma_n} * \cdots * A^{\sigma_1} * \vec{f})_i = \sum_{j=1}^{s} A^{\sigma_n}_{ij} \cdot (A^{\sigma_{n-1}} * \cdots * A^{\sigma_1} * \vec{f})_j$$

$$= \sum_{j=1}^{s} A^{\sigma_n}_{ij} \cdot \#\delta(q_j, \sigma_{n-1} \ldots \sigma_1)$$

$$= \sum_{q_j \in \delta(q_i, \sigma_n)} \#\delta(q_j, \sigma_{n-1} \ldots \sigma_1)$$

$$= \#\delta(q_i, \sigma_n \ldots \sigma_1).$$

Applying (*), we have

$$\vec{e} * A^{\sigma_n} * \cdots * A^{\sigma_1} * \vec{f} = \sum_{j=1}^{s} \vec{e}_j \cdot (A^{\sigma_n} * \cdots * A^{\sigma_1} * \vec{f})_j$$

$$= \sum_{j=1}^{s} \vec{e}_j \cdot \#\delta(q_j, x)$$

$$= \sum_{q_j \in I} \#\delta(q_j, x)$$

$$= \#M(x). \quad \blacksquare$$

The algebraic characterization of Lemma 4.1 gives us the following algorithm for computing $\#M(x)$ which processes the symbols of x from right to left, producing an s-entry column vector after each of n matrix multiplications.

```
        input x;   {= σ_n ... σ_1 ∈ Σ*}
        v⃗ := f⃗;
        for i := 1 to n do
            v⃗ := A^{σ_i} * v⃗;
        output e⃗ * v⃗
```

After n multiplications, we obtain $A^{\sigma_n} * \cdots * A^{\sigma_1} * \vec{f}$, whose ith entry is $\#\delta(q_i, x)$. This computation can be done in time polynomial in n and, since $\#\delta(q_i, x) \leq s^n$, each entry can be represented in binary using space linear in n.

In the remainder of this section, we turn our attention to the ranges of counting NFAs. We apply the method of computing $\#M(x)$ given by the previous algorithm to show that the range $s(\#M(\Sigma^*))$ of a counting NFA M is context-sensitive, i.e., is in NSPACE(n).

Given a binary string y, how can we decide if $y \in s(\#M(\Sigma^*))$? That is, how can we decide if y represents the number of accepting computations of M on some input x? A first approach using Lemma 4.1 is to guess symbols $\sigma_1, \ldots, \sigma_n$ of x from right to left, computing after each guess a column vector $\vec{v}$ whose ith entry is $v_i = \#\delta(q_i, x)$, and accepting if and only if y is the binary representation of $\vec{e} * \vec{v} = \#M(x)$:

```
        input y;
        v⃗ := f⃗;
        while true do
            begin
                if s(e⃗ * v⃗) = y then accept;
                guess σ ∈ Σ;
                v⃗ := A^σ * v⃗
            end
```

Some computations of this nondeterministic algorithm may not halt and will require an unbounded amount of space in which to store the entries of $\vec{v}$. In the following development, we show how to impose a linear space bound on the computations of this algorithm by placing a cap on the size of the entries of $\vec{v}$.

Let $y \in \{0,1\}^*$. We define $\text{cap}_y : \mathcal{N} \to \mathcal{N}$ by $\text{cap}_y(m) = \min\{m, \#(y) + 1\}$. We extend cap_y to matrices of natural numbers by applying cap_y to each entry of the matrix. We will need the following properties of the cap function in order to impose a bound on the space required by the previous algorithm and maintain its correctness.

Lemma 4.2. Let $y \in \{0,1\}^*$; $m, l \in \mathcal{N}$; and A, B compatible matrices of natural numbers.

(1) $s(\text{cap}_y(m)) = y \iff s(m) = y$
(2) $\text{cap}_y(m + l) = \text{cap}_y(\text{cap}_y(m) + \text{cap}_y(l))$
(3) $\text{cap}_y(m \cdot l) = \text{cap}_y(m \cdot \text{cap}_y(l))$
(4) $\text{cap}_y(A * B) = \text{cap}_y(A * \text{cap}_y(B))$

Proof. (1) $s(\text{cap}_y(m)) = y \iff s(\min\{m, \#(y) + 1\}) = y \iff s(m) = y$.
(2) We consider two cases. If $m + l > \#(y)$, then $\text{cap}_y(m + l) = \text{cap}_y(\text{cap}_y(m) + \text{cap}_y(l)) = \#(y) + 1$. If $m + l \leq \#(y)$, then $\text{cap}_y(m+l) = \text{cap}_y(\text{cap}_y(m) + \text{cap}_y(l)) = m + l$.

(3) Proof is similar to (2).

(4)
$$\begin{aligned}
\operatorname{cap}_y(A * B)_{ik} &= \operatorname{cap}_y\left(\sum_j A_{ij} \cdot B_{jk}\right) \\
&= \operatorname{cap}_y\left(\sum_j \operatorname{cap}_y(A_{ij} \cdot B_{jk})\right), \quad \text{by (2);} \\
&= \operatorname{cap}_y\left(\sum_j \operatorname{cap}_y(A_{ij} \cdot \operatorname{cap}_y(B_{jk}))\right), \quad \text{by (3);} \\
&= \operatorname{cap}_y\left(\sum_j A_{ij} \cdot \operatorname{cap}_y(B_{jk})\right), \quad \text{by (2);} \\
&= \operatorname{cap}_y(A * \operatorname{cap}_y(B))_{ik}. \quad \blacksquare
\end{aligned}$$

Theorem 4.3. range(#NFA) $\subseteq$ CSL.

Proof. We show that for a fixed NFA M with input alphabet Σ, $s(\#M(\Sigma^*)) \in$ NSPACE(n). Consider the following modification of our previous algorithm which decides whether or not $y \in s(\#M(\Sigma^*))$:

> input y;
> $\vec{v} := \vec{f}$;
> **while** true **do**
>   **begin**
>   **if** $s(\operatorname{cap}_y(\vec{e} * \vec{v})) = y$ **then** accept;
>   **guess** $\sigma \in \Sigma$;
> $\vec{v} := \operatorname{cap}_y(A^\sigma * \vec{v})$
>   **end**

The matrices $\vec{e}$, A^σ, and $\vec{f}$ can be kept in finite control and the space required by $\vec{v}$ is $O(|y|)$, since its entries are at most $\#(y) + 1$; therefore, this algorithm can be implemented by a nondeterministic linear space-bounded Turing machine. To show correctness, let $\sigma_1, \ldots, \sigma_n$ be a sequence of guesses of the algorithm and $x = \sigma_n \ldots \sigma_1$. By Lemma 4.2(4), the value of $\vec{v}$ at the beginning of the while-loop after guessing x will be
$$\vec{v} = \operatorname{cap}_y(A^{\sigma_n} * \operatorname{cap}_y(A^{\sigma_{n-1}} * \cdots * \operatorname{cap}_y(A^{\sigma_1} * \vec{f}) \cdots))$$
$$= \operatorname{cap}_y(A^{\sigma_n} * \cdots * A^{\sigma_1} * \vec{f}).$$

By this observation, Lemma 4.1, and Lemma 4.2(1,4), we have
$$\begin{aligned}
s(\operatorname{cap}_y(\vec{e} * \vec{v})) = y &\iff s(\operatorname{cap}_y(\vec{e} * \operatorname{cap}_y(A^{\sigma_n} * \cdots * A^{\sigma_1} * \vec{f}))) = y \\
&\iff s(\operatorname{cap}_y(\vec{e} * A^{\sigma_n} * \cdots * A^{\sigma_1} * \vec{f})) = y \\
&\iff s(\operatorname{cap}_y(\#M(x))) = y \\
&\iff s(\#M(x)) = y,
\end{aligned}$$
so the algorithm accepts y if and only if $s(\#M(x)) = y$, for some $x \in \Sigma^*$. $\blacksquare$

It is interesting to consider whether the information in this algorithm can be further compressed into space which is logarithmic in $|y|$, giving us an NSPACE(log($|y|$))

algorithm for recognizing the range of a counting NFA. In the following example, we give evidence that, if possible, it will be difficult to achieve, by showing that the composite numbers—which are not known to be in P—are the range of a counting NFA.

Example. A counting NFA whose range is Composites $\cup \{0\}$.

We construct an NFA M with input alphabet Σ such that $\#M(\Sigma^*) =$ Composites$\cup\{0\}$. First, construct an NFA M' with input alphabet $\Sigma = \{0,1\}$ such that $\#M'(0^m 1 0^l) = m \cdot l$. Let M' be the NFA pictured in the transition graph of Figure 4.1.

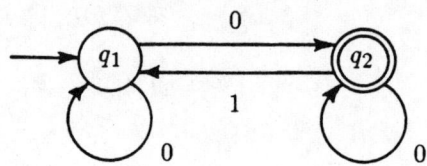

Figure 4.1. A counting NFA which multiplies unary numbers

We prove, by induction on l, the following claims:

$$\#\delta(q_1, 0^l) = l;$$
$$\#\delta(q_2, 0^l) = 1.$$

For $l = 0$,

$$\#\delta(q_1, \epsilon) = \begin{cases} 1, & \text{if } q_1 \in F; \\ 0, & \text{if } q_1 \notin F \end{cases} = 0;$$

$$\#\delta(q_2, \epsilon) = \begin{cases} 1, & \text{if } q_2 \in F; \\ 0, & \text{if } q_2 \notin F \end{cases} = 1,$$

and for $l > 0$,

$$\#\delta(q_1, 0^l) = \sum_{p \in \delta(q_1, 0)} \#\delta(p, 0^{l-1})$$
$$= \#\delta(q_1, 0^{l-1}) + \#\delta(q_2, 0^{l-1})$$
$$= (l-1) + 1 = l;$$
$$\#\delta(q_2, 0^l) = \sum_{p \in \delta(q_2, 0)} \#\delta(p, 0^{l-1})$$
$$= \#\delta(q_2, 0^{l-1}) = 1.$$

Next we prove, by induction on m, the following claims:

$$\#\delta(q_1, 0^m 1 0^l) = m \cdot l;$$
$$\#\delta(q_2, 0^m 1 0^l) = l.$$

For $m = 0$,

$$\#\delta(q_1, 10^l) = \sum_{p \in \delta(q_1, 1)} \#\delta(p, 0^l) = 0 = 0 \cdot l;$$

$$\#\delta(q_2, 10^l) = \sum_{p \in \delta(q_2, 1)} \#\delta(p, 0^l)$$

$$= \#\delta(q_1, 0^l) = l,$$

and for $m > 0$,

$$\#\delta(q_1, 0^m 10^l) = \sum_{p \in \delta(q_1, 0)} \#\delta(p, 0^{m-1} 10^l)$$

$$= \#\delta(q_1, 0^{m-1} 10^l) + \#\delta(q_2, 0^{m-1} 10^l)$$

$$= (m-1) \cdot l + l = m \cdot l;$$

$$\#\delta(q_2, 0^m 10^l) = \sum_{p \in \delta(q_2, 0)} \#\delta(p, 0^{m-1} 10^l)$$

$$= \#\delta(q_2, 0^{m-1} 10^l) = l.$$

Therefore, we have $\#M'(0^m 10^l) = \#\delta(q_1, 0^m 10^l) = m \cdot l$. Consider the regular language $R = \{0^m 10^l \mid m, l \geq 2\}$. Let M'' be a DFA which accepts R. Then

$$\#M''(0^m 10^l) = \begin{cases} 1, & \text{if } m, l \geq 2; \\ 0, & \text{otherwise.} \end{cases}$$

Using Lemma 3.3, construct an NFA M such that $\#M(x) = \#M'(x) \cdot \#M''(x)$.

$$\#M(0^m 10^l) = \#M'(0^m 10^l) \cdot \#M''(0^m 10^l)$$

$$= \begin{cases} m \cdot l, & \text{if } m, l \geq 2; \\ 0, & \text{otherwise,} \end{cases}$$

so $\#M(\Sigma^*) = \text{Composites} \cup \{0\}$. ∎

When the range membership problem is considered as a function of both a given NFA and binary string, we are able to pinpoint its complexity by giving a completeness result for PSPACE.

Range Membership
Instance: M, an NFA with input alphabet Σ; $y \in \{0,1\}^*$.
Question: $y \in s(\#M(\Sigma^*))$?

Theorem 4.4. Range Membership is PSPACE-complete.

Proof. We have shown in Theorem 4.3 that membership can be decided nondeterministically using space $O(\|Q\| \cdot |y|)$, where $\|Q\|$ is the number of states in M. By Savitch's Theorem, Range Membership $\in$ NSPACE(n^2) $\subseteq$ PSPACE. We show hardness by logspace reduction from the nonuniversality problem for NFAs, which was proved PSPACE-complete by Stockmeyer and Meyer [6,7]. Let M be an NFA with input alphabet Σ.

$$L(M) \neq \Sigma^* \iff \exists x \in \Sigma^*, x \notin L(M)$$
$$\iff \exists x \in \Sigma^*, \#M(x) = 0$$
$$\iff 0 \in \#M(\Sigma^*)$$
$$\iff \epsilon \in s(\#M(\Sigma^*)). \blacksquare$$

5. Pumping Behavior and Linear Recurrences

In this section, we consider the pumping behavior of a counting finite-state automaton. For a fixed input string, we show that the number of accepting computations—considered as a function of the number of times a fixed substring of the input is pumped—satisfies a homogeneous linear recurrence equation of finite degree having integer coefficients. We precede this result with some relevant definitions and facts from the theories of recurrence equations and matrices.

Let $g: \mathcal{N} \to \mathcal{N}$. g *satisfies a homogeneous linear recurrence equation of degree s having integer coefficients* if there exist $a_1, \ldots, a_s \in \mathcal{Z}$ such that for $n \in \mathcal{N}$,

$$g(n+s) = \sum_{k=1}^{s} a_k \cdot g(n+s-k).$$

Let A be an $s \times s$ matrix of integers, and I be the $s \times s$ identity matrix with 1's on the diagonal and 0's elsewhere. The *characteristic polynomial* of A is the polynomial p defined by $p(\lambda) = \det(A - \lambda \cdot I)$, where det is the determinant function. Note that the characteristic polynomial is of degree s and has integer coefficients, since A has integer entries. The *characteristic equation* of A is the equation $\det(A - \lambda \cdot I) = 0$. The characteristic polynomial is said to be *monic*, since the coefficient of λ^s is $(-1)^s = \pm 1$; therefore, the characteristic equation can be written as

$$\lambda^s = \sum_{k=1}^{s} a_k \cdot \lambda^{s-k},$$

where $a_1, \ldots, a_s \in \mathcal{Z}$. One of the most important results in matrix theory is the Cayley-Hamilton Theorem, which states that a matrix satisfies its own characteristic equation. We use it to analyze the pumping behavior of a counting finite-state automaton.

Theorem 5.1. Let $M = (Q, \Sigma, \delta, I, F)$ be an NFA with state set $Q = \{q_1, \ldots, q_s\}$, and let $w, x, z \in \Sigma^*$. There exist $a_1, \ldots, a_s \in \mathcal{Z}$ such that for every $n \in \mathcal{N}$,

$$\#M(wx^{n+s}z) = \sum_{k=1}^{s} a_k \cdot \#M(wx^{n+s-k}z).$$

Proof. Let $\vec{e}, A^\sigma, \vec{f}$ be defined as in section 4, and let $A^x = A^{\sigma_1} * \cdots * A^{\sigma_{|x|}}$, where $x = \sigma_1 \ldots \sigma_{|x|}$. We define A^w and A^z similarly. As discussed before, the characteristic equation of A^x can be written as

$$\lambda^s = \sum_{k=1}^{s} a_k \cdot \lambda^{s-k},$$

where $a_1, \ldots, a_s \in \mathcal{Z}$. By the Cayley-Hamilton Theorem,

$$A^{x^s} = \sum_{k=1}^{s} a_k \cdot A^{x^{s-k}}.$$

By this observation and Lemma 4.1, we have for $1 \leq i \leq s$ and $n \in \mathcal{N}$,

$$\begin{aligned}
\#\delta(q_i, wx^{n+s}z) &= (A^w * A^{x^{n+s}} * A^z * \vec{f})_i \\
&= (A^w * A^{x^n} * A^{x^s} * A^z * \vec{f})_i \\
&= \left(A^w * A^{x^n} * \left(\sum_{k=1}^{s} a_k \cdot A^{x^{s-k}}\right) * A^z * \vec{f}\right)_i \\
&= \left(\sum_{k=1}^{s} a_k \cdot \left(A^w * A^{x^n} * A^{x^{s-k}} * A^z * \vec{f}\right)\right)_i \\
&= \sum_{k=1}^{s} a_k \cdot (A^w * A^{x^{n+s-k}} * A^z * \vec{f})_i \\
&= \sum_{k=1}^{s} a_k \cdot \#\delta(q_i, wx^{n+s-k}z).
\end{aligned}$$

$$\begin{aligned}
\#M(wx^{n+s}z) &= \sum_{q_i \in I} \#\delta(q_i, wx^{n+s}z) \\
&= \sum_{q_i \in I} \left(\sum_{k=1}^{s} a_k \cdot \#\delta(q_i, wx^{n+s-k}z)\right) \\
&= \sum_{k=1}^{s} a_k \cdot \left(\sum_{q_i \in I} \#\delta(q_i, wx^{n+s-k}z)\right) \\
&= \sum_{k=1}^{s} a_k \cdot \#M(wx^{n+s-k}z). \blacksquare
\end{aligned}$$

Stearns and Hunt [5] showed that the number of accepting computations over all inputs of a given length—considered as a function of the length—satisfies a homogeneous linear recurrence equation of finite degree having rational coefficients. The technique of Theorem 5.1 can be used to strengthen and simplify the proof of their result, obtaining integer coefficients and a recurrence equation which is satisfied regardless of which state is considered to be the start state, by applying the Cayley-Hamilton Theorem with the matrix $A = \sum_{\sigma \in \Sigma} A^\sigma$.

6. Summary and Open Questions

We summarize some of the results contained heretofore, and ask open questions about improvements and extensions of our results.

In §3, we showed that range(#NFA) includes range(#DFT)—the ranges of deterministic finite-state transducers. It follows from the Generalized Sequential Machine results of Ginsburg and Greibach [2] that the latter is the class of all regular languages comprised of binary strings without leading zeroes. Is the class of all context-free languages comprised of binary strings without leading zeroes included in range(#NFA)?

In §4, we showed that the range $s(\#M(\Sigma^*))$ of a counting NFA is in NSPACE(n). How tight is this upper bound? Respecting the fact that the composite numbers are the range of a counting NFA, is there a subclass of NSPACE(n) which contains range(#NFA)? Are there ranges of counting NFAs which are complete for NSPACE(n)? NP? some other time- or space-bounded complexity class?

In §5, we showed that for a fixed input string, the number of accepting computations—considered as a function of the number of times a fixed substring of the input is pumped—satisfies a homogeneous linear recurrence equation of finite degree having integer coefficients. Does this lead to a simple pumping lemma which can be used to show that a function is not in #NFA or a language is not in range(#NFA)? Which arbitrary functions satisfying linear recurrences as in Theorem 5.1 are computed by counting NFAs? That is, can we precisely characterize #NFA as a class of functions satisfying a restricted class of recurrence equations?

References

[1] Ginsburg, S. "Examples of abstract machines," *IEEE Trans. on Electronic Computers* **11**: 2 (1962), 132–135.

[2] Ginsburg, S., and Greibach, S.A. "Abstract families of languages," *Studies in Abstract Families of Languages*, pp. 1–32, Memoir No. 87, American Mathematical Society, Providence, R.I., 1969.

[3] Hopcroft, J.E., and Ullman, J.D. "Introduction to automata theory, languages, and computation," Addison-Wesley, Reading, Mass., 1979.

[4] Salomaa, A., and Soittola, M. "Automata-Theoretic Aspects of Formal Power Series," Springer-Verlag, Berlin, 1978.

[5] Stearns, R.E., and Hunt, H.B. III. "On the equivalence and containment problems for unambiguous regular expressions, regular grammars, and finite automata," *SIAM J. Comput.* **14** (1985), 598–611.

[6] Stockmeyer, L.J., and Meyer, A.R. "Word problems requiring exponential time," *Proc. Fifth Annual ACM Symposium on the Theory of Computing* (1973), 1–9.

[7] Stockmeyer, L.J. "The Complexity of Decision Problems in Automata Theory and Logic," Doctoral Thesis, Dept. of Electrical Engineering, Massachusetts Institute of Technology, Cambridge, Mass., 1974.

[8] Valiant, L.G. "The complexity of computing the permanent," *Theor. Comput. Sci.* **8** (1979), 189–201.

[9] Valiant, L.G. "The complexity of enumeration and reliablity problems," *SIAM J. Comput.* **8**: 3 (1979), 410–421.

A HIERARCHY THEOREM FOR PRAM-BASED COMPLEXITY CLASSES

Walter W. Kirchherr
Department of Mathematics and Computer Science
San Jose State University, San Jose, California 95112

ABSTRACT: The main result in this paper is to show that $P^jT^i \subset P^{j+l}T^{i+k}$, that is, the PT-hierarchy is a proper hierarchy (i.e., it does not collapse). Here P^jT^i denotes the class of languages accepted by a PRAM using $O(n^j)$ processors and $O(\log^i n)$ parallel steps. It is also (implicitly) shown in this paper that $NC \subseteq PT(uniform)$ thus improving on Stockmeyer and Vishkin's result [6] that $NC \subseteq PT(non-uniform)$.

INTRODUCTION: A longstanding open question in theoretical computer science is $NC^i \subset? NC^{i+k}$ for some $k \in \mathbf{N}$. This question has analogues in other classes defined in terms of simultaneous resource bounds. For example, consider the Turing Machine (TM)-based class

$$TR^i = \{\, L \mid L \text{ is accepted by a deterministic TM which uses}$$
$$n^{O(1)} \text{ time steps and } O(\log^i n) \text{ reversals}\,\},$$

where n is the bit length of the input. Let $TR = \bigcup_{i \in \mathbf{N}} TR^i$. In 1979 Pippenger [4] demonstrated the importance of this class by proving that $TR = NC$. Implicit in this proof is the implication

$$\exists k \in \mathbf{N}\, \forall i \in \mathbf{N}\ TR^i \subset TR^{i+k} \Longrightarrow \exists l \in \mathbf{N}\, \forall i \in \mathbf{N}\ NC^i \subset NC^{i+l}.$$

Thus, the analogous question for the TR-hierarchy is $TR^i \subset? TR^{i+k}$.

Other classes are possible. Stockmeyer and Vishkin [6] studied the class we will call PT (for Processors, Time). This is defined in terms of Parallel Random Access Machines (PRAM's) as follows:

$$PT^i = \{\, L \mid L \text{ is accepted by a PRAM with } N^{O(1)} \text{ processors}$$
$$\text{and using } O(\log^i N) \text{ time steps}\,\},$$

where N is the number of *words* (not bits) input to the PRAM.

Let $PT = \bigcup_{i \in \mathbf{N}} PT^i$. Stockmeyer and Vishkin showed that $PT \subseteq NC$. (They also showed that $NC \subseteq PT(non-uniform)$. $PT(non-uniform)$ is defined in terms of non-uniform PRAM's., i.e., each processor is allowed to have a different program. Implicit in this paper is the fact that $PT = NC$, i.e., the non-uniformity in Stockmeyer and Vishkin's proof [6] can be dispensed with.) Thus, the analagous question in the PT-hierarchy is $PT^i \subset? PT^{i+k}$.

The resolution of the question $NC^i \subset? NC^{i+k}$ would be a major breakthrough in complexity theory. However, NC is really a "2-dimensional" class; that is, if we let

$$N^j C^i = \{ L \mid L \text{ is accepted by a circuit family } C$$

$$\text{of size } O(n^j) \text{ and depth } O(\log^i n) \},$$

the question $N^j C^i \subset? N^{j+l} C^{i+k}$ naturally arises. In this paper we address the analagous question for the PT-hierarchy, $P^j T^i \subset? P^{j+l} T^{i+k}$, and answer it in the affirmative. (l turns out to be a function of j.) Specifically, we show

$$\exists k, l \in \mathbf{N} \; \forall i, j \in \mathbf{N} \; (P^j T^i \subset P^{j+l} T^{i+k}).$$

To prove this, we adapt many of the ideas found in Pippenger's proof [4] that $TR = NC$. [4] is an extended abstract. A fully detailed proof of Pippenger's theorem, along with the fully detailed proofs of the theorems in this paper, can be found in [3].

DEFINITIONS: For our PRAM model we use essentially the same model studied in Stockmeyer and Vishkin [6]. A PRAM consists of individual processors, each with its own local memory. These processors share a series of common memory cells to which they may read or write. Any number of processors may read a common cell at a time. If more than one processor simultaneously attempts to write on a common cell, the processor with the lowest number succeeds. Every processor has the same program. (Thus we are using the uniform concurrent-read concurrent-write priority PRAM model.) Let S be the number of instructions in a program.

A processor receives its input in the first N common cells. Upon receiving its input, $O(P(N))$ processors start up. If the PRAM computes function $f(N)$, then $f(N)$ appears left-justified in common memory after $O(T(N))$ processor steps. If the PRAM is a language recognizer, a '1' ('0') appears in common cell 1 after $O(T(N))$ processor steps if it accepts (rejects).

The instructions which constitute a processor's program are from the following list.

1) $AC_i \leftarrow$ constant   (load a constant)
2) $AC_i \leftarrow P\#$ (load processor number)
3) $AC_i \leftarrow$ binary-op(AC_j, AC_k) (binary operation)
4) $AC_i \leftarrow$ unary-op(AC_j) (unary operation)
5) $AC_i \leftarrow [AC_j]_{local}$ (indirect read from local memory)
6) $AC_i \leftarrow [AC_j]_{common}$ (indirect read from common memory)
7) $[AC_i]_{local} \leftarrow AC_j$ (indirect write to local memory)
8) $[AC_i]_{common} \leftarrow AC_j$ (indirect write to common memory)
9) GOTO label
10) IF comp-op(AC_i, AC_j) THEN GOTO label
11) HALT

where:
AC_i indicates the ith accumulator;

$i, j, k \in \{1, 2, 3\}$; $i \neq j \neq k$ (there are three accumulators);
P# indicates the processor number;
$[AC_i]$ indicates the contents of AC_i (for indirect addressing);
binary-op $\in \{+, -, \wedge, \vee\}$;
unary-op $\in \{not, shift-1, rotate-1\}$;
comp-op $\in \{<, >, =\}$.

Let $l(N)$ be the length of an input word. Let $W(N)$ be the wordsize of the PRAM, that is, the number of bits required to store the longest number the PRAM will hold. Since the length of the result of an operation may not exceed the length of its longest operand by more than a constant, $W(N) = O(\max(l, N, S, \log P) + T)$.

This is based on the above restrictions and the following two facts:

(1) Each processor may use no more than T cells of its local memory (since it may address no more than one local cell per instruction); and

(2) At most $PT + N$ common memory cells will be used (the N cells containing the input and T others per processor).

Our proof will show that a Turing Machine can simulate a PRAM and vice-versa without "too large" an increase in TM resources (which are time and reversals) or PRAM resources (which are processors and time). For this we need the following definition: A function $F: N \to N$ is *2-tape time and log-reversal constructible* if there exists a 2-tape TM which on input unary(n) (i.e., n in unary) outputs unary($f(n)$) within $O(\max(n, f(n)))$ time and $O(\max(\log f(n), \log n))$ reversals.

FACT: Most common functions (in particular n^k and $\log^k n$) are 2-tape time and log-reversal constructible.

PROOF: Left to the reader.

Let L be a language. We define the following complexity classes:

$$P^j T^i = \{ L \mid L \text{ is accepted by a PRAM with } O(N^j) \text{ processors}$$
$$\text{and using } O(\log^i N) \text{ processor steps} \};$$

$$T^i R^i_k = \{ L \mid L \text{ is accepted by a deterministic } k-\text{tape TM which}$$
$$\text{uses } O(n^j) \text{ time steps and } O(\log^i n) \text{ reversals} \};$$

$$T^j R^i = \bigcup_{k \in N} T^j R^i_k \; ; \; TR^i = \bigcup_{j \in N} T^j R^i \; ; \; TR = \bigcup_{i \in N} TR^i \; .$$

Note that TR is a 3-dimensional hierarchy (time, reversals, and tapes). Note also that in the above definitions n refers to the bit length of an input (for TM's) and N refers to the number of words in an input (for PRAM's). We will observe this notational convention throughout this paper.

MAJOR PROOFS: Central to our argument is the following corollary to a theorem by Pippenger. In his 1979 paper [4] Pippenger showed that any language $L \in TR$ can be accepted by an oblivious TM which also makes polynomially many time steps and polylog many reversals. (An oblivious TM is one whose head positions are functions of time and input length only. In other words, they are independent of the actual input contents. For details about this concept see [5] and [2].) Letting OTR be the class analagous to TR but defined in terms of oblivious deterministic machines, Pippenger's theorem can be stated as:

THEOREM 1: $TR_k^i \subseteq OTR^{3+i}$.

Pippenger did not consider the number of tapes on the simulating oblivious machine. But a close look at the details of a proof of Pippenger's theorem (a sketch of the proof is found in [4]; a fully detailed proof is found in [3]) reveals that:

COROLLARY 2: $T^j R_k^i \subseteq OT^{3kj+1} R_2^{3+i}$.

In other words, if L is accepted by a k-tape TM which makes $O(n^j)$ time steps and $O(\log^i n)$ reversals, then L is accepted by a 2-tape oblivious TM which makes $O(n^{3kj+1})$ time steps and $O(\log^{3+i} n)$ reversals. The proof is based on the following three observations:

(1) A 2-tape TM can sort N items each of bit length l using $O(Nl \log N)$ time steps and $O(\log^2 N)$ reversals. This can be done through an implementation of the shuffle-exchange sort of Batcher [1] and Stone [7]. A sequential algorithm is found in [7].

(2) With repeated shuffling of the string $(01)^{k/2}$, the integers in binary from 0 to $k-1$ for some k can be generated by a 2-tape TM in time $= O(k \log k)$ and reversal $= O(\log k)$. Further, each number will occupy exactly $\lceil \log k \rceil$ bits.

(3) Let a *situation* of a k-tape machine M be a $(k+1)$-tuple giving positions for each of the k heads and a state of M. Then a 2-tape oblivious machine S can simulate M within the the above mentioned time and reversal bounds by sorting the possible situations of M (see [4]).

These observations lead naturally to the following corollary based on a diagonalization argument:

COROLLARY 3: $T^j R_k^i \subset T^{3kj+1} R_4^{4+i}$.

PROOF: $\subseteq$ follows immediately from corollary 2.
$\neq$: The proof is by diagonalization. We construct a 4-tape machine M of time bound $O(n^{3kj+1})$ and reversal bound $O(\log^{4+i} n)$ which diagonalizes over all k-tape machines of time bound $O(n^j)$ and reversal bound $O(\log^i n)$. Assume an encoding scheme of all TM's in which each TM has an arbitrarily long encoding. Then S on input $\bar{x}$ acts as follows:

(1) S constructs unary$(3kj+1)$ and unary$(\log^{4+i} n)$, the former on tape 3 and the latter on tape 4. (i, j and k are in S's finite control).

(2) S examines $\bar{x}$ to insure that $\bar{x}$ is the code for a k-tape machine, $M_{\bar{x}}$. If $\bar{x}$ is such a code, S determines the size of $M_{\bar{x}}$'s tape alphabet and the number of states of $M_{\bar{x}}$.

(3) S simulates $M_{\bar{x}}$ on $\bar{x}$ accepting *iff* $M_{\bar{x}}$ rejects $\bar{x}$ within the time and reversal bounds constructed in (1). M uses tapes 1 and 2 for the simulation and tapes 3 and 4 to count time and reversals. M halts if it ever exceeds the time and reversal bounds it constructed in (1).

The simulation proceeds exactly as the simulation described by Pippenger in [4] for the proof of Theorem 1, with the exception that instead of holding the transition function of M in its finite control, S uses the input to ascertain M's transition function. A standard diagonalization argument completes the proof.

□ □

We will sketch in this section how a 2-tape TM can simulate a PRAM, then how a PRAM can simulate a k-tape TM. We first show how these simulations yield the main result. The TM simulation of a PRAM gives the following:

LEMMA 4: $P^j T^i \subseteq T^{2j+2} R_2^{4+i}$

The PRAM simulation of a k-tape TM gives the following:

LEMMA 5: $T^j R_k^i \subseteq P^{2kj} T^{2+i}$

Combining these with Corollary 3, we arrive at our main result:

THEOREM 6: $P^j T^i \subset P^{96j+104} T^{8+i}$

(No attempt was made to minimize the exponents.)

Lemmas 4 and 5 also imply that $PT = TR$. Since $TR = NC$, we conclude that $PT = NC$. It remains to demonstrate Lemmas 4 and 5.

SKETCH OF THE PROOF OF LEMMA 4: The idea of the simulation is that the TM, M keeps on a track of tape 1 $PT + N$ blocks, each of bit-length W, to represent common memory of the PRAM it is simulating. On a track of tape 2 M keeps PT blocks, each of bit-length W, to represent local memories of the processors. Further, on another track of tape 1, M keeps a list of P "instruction pointers" (IP's), which indicate the next instructions to be executed by the P processors.

It is crucial to observe that although P instructions are executed at each step of the PRAM, only a constant number of *types* of instructions are executed at a given step. For example, the list of instructions given earlier consists of $91 + C$ different instruction types (considering that $i, j, k \in \{1, 2, 3\}$, $i \neq j \neq k$), where C represents the number of constants a processor may load. Then, by sorting, M can simulate each step of the PRAM.

Recall that the first three local memory cells of each processor serve as the accumulators. That is, the jth accumulator of the ith processor is the same as the jth local memory cell of the ith processor.

We now describe the simulation of a PRAM by a 2-tape TM, M.

M receives as input $N \cdot l$ bits representing the N common cells of the PRAM, each l bits long. First, M performs some pre-processing.

(a) On different tracks of tape 2, M creates unary(T), unary(P), unary$(\log P)$, unary(W) and unary$(PT + N)$.

(b) M then re-formats tape 1 to consist of $PT + N$ cells of W bits each, representing common memory. This gives:

$$\underbrace{|{<}{><}{>}\cdots{<}{>}|}_{N \text{ cells (initial input)}} \underbrace{{<}{><}{>}\cdots{<}{>}|}_{PT \text{ cells}}$$

(c) M numbers these cells 0 through $(PT + N - 1)$.

(d) On tape 2 M creates PT blocks, each of length W, to represent local memory.

(e) Let $L(i,j)$ ("local cell i,j") represent the jth cell of processor P_i. (In line with the previous remark, for $j \in \{1,2,3\}$, $L(i,j)$ refers to an accumulator.) Then M creates all pairs of numbers (i,j), $0 \le i \le P-1$ and $0 \le j \le T-1$. M sorts these numbers with j as the primary key and i as the secondary key. This gives on tape 2:

$$L(0,0), L(1,0), \ldots, L(P-1,0), L(0,1), L(1,1), \ldots, L(P-1,1), \ldots,$$
$$L(0,T-1), L(1,T-1), \ldots, L(P-1,T-1)$$

(f) On tape 1 M creates P instruction pointers (IP's). Recall that each program consists of S instructions. An instruction pointer, designated $IP(i,j)$, is a block of length $O(\log P + \log S)$ bits and indicates that the next instruction processor P_i is to execute is the jth instruction of the program. Initially, this list is

$$IP(0,1), IP(1,1), \ldots, IP(P-1,1)$$

indicating that each processor begins with its first instruction.

The resource bounds for the pre-processing are time $= O((PT+N)W + PTW\log^2(PT))$ and reversal $= O(\log^2(PT))$.

To simulate a single step of the PRAM, M does the following:

(a) To each instruction in the list of instruction pointers, M attaches the type number of the instruction. Thus M has a list of 3-tuples, $IP(i,j,k)$ where k is the type number of the jth instruction of processor P_i's program. Call this list the IP-list.

(b) M sorts this IP-list with the instruction type as the primary key and the processor number as the secondary key. This results in a list consisting of no more than a constant number of sub-lists, each sub-list consisting of IP's with the same type number:

$$\text{IP} - \text{LIST} \quad |\underbrace{{<}{><}{>}\cdots{<}{>}}_{\text{same type}}|\underbrace{{<}{><}{>}\cdots{<}{>}}_{\text{same type}}|\cdots|\underbrace{{<}{><}{>}\cdots{<}{>}}_{\text{same type}}|$$

(c) M simulates the execution of each instruction type (one type at a time) for those processors which are to execute an instruction of that type.

Thus, if M requires no more that K time steps and L reversals to simulate a single PRAM instruction, M can complete its simulation in time $= O(KT(N))$ and reversal $= O(LT(N))$.

In the interest of space we describe M's simulation of instructions $AC_1 \leftarrow AC_2 + AC_3$ and $[AC_1] \leftarrow [AC_2]_{common}$. These descriptions encompass the ideas needed for other instructions.

Let $\bar{P}$ be the number of IP's in some single sub-list of the IP-list sorted by instruction type. This means that $\bar{P}$ processors are all to execute the same type of instruction at a single time step. Call these the *active processors*.

To simulate $AC_1 \leftarrow AC_2 + AC_3$, M does the following:

(a) M flags the $\bar{P}$ IP's and sorts these in with the P tuples of $L(p,1)$, $0 \le p \le P-1$. Call this list L1. This list is sorted by processor number, that is, p of $L(p,j)$ and p of $IP(p,j,k)$.

(b) M sorts the $\bar{P}$ IP's (as flagged) in with the P tuples $L(p,2)$, $0 \le p \le P-1$. Call this list L2.

(c) M does the same for the $\bar{P}$ IP's and the P tuples of $L(p,3)$. Call this list L3. M now has (aligned on a single tape):

$$\text{L1}: <\ ><\ ><\ ><\ >\cdots <\ ><\ >\cdots <\ ><\ >$$
$$\text{L2}: <\ ><\ ><\ ><\ >\cdots <\ ><\ >\cdots <\ ><\ >$$
$$\text{L3}: <\ ><\ ><\ ><\ >\cdots <\ ><\ >\cdots <\ ><\ >$$

(d) M performs the binary operation of the instruction between the tuples immediately left of a *'d tuple of L2 and the tuple in the corresponding position of L3. The result is put into the corresponding tuple in L1. (Note that each binary operation can be performed in a single sweep of M's head.)

(e) L1 is compressed in the obvious way for a new copy of $L(p,1)$ $0 \le p \le P-1$.

To simulate $[AC_1] \leftarrow [AC_2]_{common}$ M does the following:

(a) M flags the $\bar{P}$ cells $L(p,2)$ representing the $\bar{P}$ "active" accumulators as described in (a) above (that is, the $\bar{P}$ AC_2's). M then attaches all AC_1's to this list giving (for example):

$$\text{L1}: < L(0,j) >< L(1,j) > \cdots < \overset{*}{L(p,j)} >< L(P-1,j) >$$
$$\phantom{\text{L1}:}< L(0,i) >< L(1,i) > \cdots < \overset{*}{L(p,i)} >< L(P-1,i) >$$

($\bar{P}$ *'s appear in L1.)

(b) M makes P copies of common memory and attached the numbers $0\ldots P-1$ to them, giving:

L2: $|<C(0,0)>\ldots<C(0,PT+N-1)>|\ldots$

$|<C(P-1,0)>\ldots<C(P-1,PT+N-1)>|$

where $C(i,j)$ represents the ith copy of common memory cell j, $0 \le i \le P-1, 0 \le j \le PT+N-1$.

(c) M sorts L1 and L2 together using :

primary key - L1: p of $L(p,j)$ (processor number of AC_j)
L2: i of $C(i,j)$
secondary key - L1: the contents of $L(p,j)$
L2: j of $C(i,j)$
ternary key - for both lists, the flag is used $(* > $ no $*)$

This gives:

L3: $|<L1><L1>\ldots<L1><\overset{*}{L2}>\ldots<L1>|\ldots$
$<L2>$

$|<L1><L1>\ldots<L1><\overset{*}{L2}>\ldots<L1>|\ldots$
$<L2>$

where $<L1>$ represents a tuple which is from L1 and

$<\overset{*}{L2}>$ represents a tuple which is from $L2$
$<L2>$

(d) For every tuple in L3 which is immediately left of a *'d tuple (which represents a common memory cell), M copies that portion of it which represents its contents to the lower tuple of the neighboring *'ed tuple (which represents the local accumulator which is to receive the data). The tuples to which the copying is done represent the new copy of $L(p,i)$ for the $\bar{P}$ active processors. (That is, they form the new list of AC_i's.)

The simulation of the instructions $[AC_i] \leftarrow [AC_j]_{common}$ and $[AC_i]_{common} \leftarrow [AC_j]$ are the most resource consuming. These can be done (by the observations menioned previously) in time $= O((P^2T + PN)W \log^2(P^2T + PN))$ and reversal $= O(T \log^2(P^2T + PN))$. Hence the entire simulation can be completed within time $= O(T(P^2T + PN)W \log^2(P^2T + PN))$ and reversal $= O(T \log^2(P^2T + PN))$. In the worst case, both W and N are $O(n)$ (n is the bit length of the input); hence, restricting our attention to $P(N) = O(N^j)$ and $T(N) = O(\log^i N)$, Lemma 4 follows.

□□

SKETCH OF THE PROOF OF LEMMA 5: A PRAM, A, to simulate a TM can be constructed by adapting the simulation of a TM by an oblivious TM as given in

Pippenger's proof of Theorem 1 [4], that is, by sorting the possible situations of M (see observation 3 of Corollary 2 above).

Let M be a k-tape TM with S states. Let M have time bound $T(n)$ and reversal bound $R(n)$. Recall that a *situation* of M is a $(k+1)$-tuple, $< S_i, pos(1), \ldots, pos(k) >$, of bit-length $O(\log T)$, where S_i is a state of M and $pos(j)$ is the position of the jth workhead. There are ST^k possible situations of M.

We construct a PRAM, A, to simulate M. A will have T^{2k} processors. Each processor will handle S situations of M.

Let **SIT** be the set of all possible situations of M. Let the 2^l-step situation-transition function, δ^{2^l}, be a map from **SIT** to **SIT**. $\delta^{2^l}(SIT(q,i))$ is defined to be the situation in which M is found after 2^l time steps of a single reversal phase when, given the tape contents of M at the outset of that phase, M starts the phase in situation $< q, i >$. Here, q is a state of M and i indicates k head positions.

Let situations $< 1, i >, \ldots, < S, i >$ constitute the ith *group of situations*. There are T processors assigned to each group, $P_i, P_{T+i}, P_{2T+i}, \ldots, P_{(T-1)T+i}$. These processors will calulate the 2^l-step transition functions out of $SIT(q,i)$ for $l \in \{0, 1, \ldots, \log T\}$ and $q \in \{1, 2, \ldots, S\}$.

For each reversal phase of M, A acts as follows:

(1) Processor P_{jT+i} reads the common cells indicated by its processor number in the following manner. If i is the k-tuple $< pos(1), \ldots, pos(k) >$ then P_{jT+i} reads common cells $pos(i), \ldots, pos(k)$.

(2) P_{jT+i} calculates $\delta^1(SIT(0,i))$ through $\delta^1(SIT(S,i))$. (Each processor has the usual transition function of M in its program.) Then for $q := 1$ to S, P_{0T+i} writes the k symbols written by M as it moves from $SIT(q,i)$ to $\delta^1(SIT(q,i))$ to common memory.

(3) For $l := 1$ to $\log T$, P_{jT+l} does the following. For each $q \in \{1, \ldots, S\}$, P_{jT+i} calculates the 2^l-step situation-transition function and writes the $O(2^l)$ symbols written by M as it moves from $SIT(q,i)$ to $\delta^{2^l}(SIT(q,i))$. To do this, it uses $\delta^{2^{l-1}}(SIT(q,i))$ calculated in the previous step.

The above steps can be accomplished by reduction to sorting.

No step in the above process requires more than $O(\log T(n))$ steps. Hence, the entire process for one phase can be completed in $O(\log^2 T(n))$ steps, and the complete simulation of M can be completed in $O(R(n) \log^2 T(n))$ steps. T^{2k} processors were used.

Recall that n is the bit-length of the input to M. Resource bounds of a PRAM are commonly expressed in terms of N, the number of input cells occupied. Since the n input bits occupy the first N input cells, $N = n$.

□ □

REFERENCES:

1. Batcher, K., Sorting Networks and Their Applications, 1968 Spring Joint Computer Conference, *AFIPS Proceedings*, Vol. 32, 1968, pp. 307-314.

2. Hopcroft, J. and Ullman, J., *Introduction to Automata Theory, Languages, and Computation*, Addison-Wesley, Reading, Massachusetts, 1979.

3. Kirchherr, W., *Reversal Bounded Turing Machines*, Ph.D. Thesis, Research Report in Computer Science No. 29, Department of Mathematics, Statistics and Computer Science, University of Illinois at Chicago, Febraury, 1988.

4. Pippenger, N., On Simultaneous Resource Bounds (Preliminary Version), 20*th Proceedings of IEEE Symposium on the Foundations of Computer Science*, 1979, pp. 307-311.

5. Pippenger, N. and Fischer, M., Relations Among Comlexity Measures, *Journal of the ACM*, Vol. 26, No. 2, April, 1979, pp. 361-381.

6. Stockmeyer, L. and Vishkin, U., Simulation of Parallel Random Access Machines by Circuits, *SIAM Journal of Computing*, Vol. 13, No. 2, May, 1984, pp. 409-422.

7. Stone, H., Parallel Processing with the Perfect Shuffle, *IEEE Transactions on Computers*, Vol. c-20, No. 2, February, 1971, pp. 153-161.

A Natural Deduction treatment of Operational Semantics

Rod Burstall[1] and Furio Honsell[2]
University of Edinburgh and University of Turin

Abstract
We show how Natural Deduction extended with a replacement operator can provide a framework for defining programming languages, a framework which is more expressive than the usual Operational Semantics presentation in that it allows hypothetical premises. This allows us to do without an explicit environment and store. Instead we use the hypothetical premises to make assumptions about the values of variables. We define the extended Natural Deduction logic using the Edinburgh Logical Framework.

1. Introduction

The Edinburgh Logical Framework (ELF) provides a formalism for defining Natural Deduction style logics (Harper et al, 1987). Natural Deduction is rather more powerful than the notation which is commonly used to define programming languages in "inference-style" Operational Semantics, following Plotkin [1981] and others (for example Kahn 1987). So one may ask
   "Can a Natural Deduction style be used with advantage to define programming languages?".
We show here that, with a slight extension, it can, and hence that the ELF can be used as a formal meta-language for defining programming languages. However ELF employs the "propositions as types" paradigm and takes the form of a higher order typed lambda calculus. We do not need all this power here, and in this paper we present a slight extension of Natural Deduction, simply typed, as a semantic notation for programming language definition. This extension can itself be defined in ELF.

The inspiration for using a meta-logic for Natural Deduction proofs comes from Martin-Löf. Our work benefited from that of Mason [1987] who did a proof system for Hoare logic in the ELF, encountering problems about the treatment of program variables. In particular he adopted the non-interference relation originally used by Reynolds [1978].

The main feature of Natural Deduction proofs, used in our semantics but not used in the usual style of Operational Semantics, is that the premises of a rule may be hypothetical: they may themselves be of the form "Q is derivable from P_1 and ... and P_n". We write a premise of this form thus

$$\frac{\begin{array}{c}(P_1, ..., P_n)\\ \vdots \\ Q\end{array}}{R}$$

Using these techniques we are able to give an operational semantics which dispenses with the traditional notions of environment and store. This makes our semantic definitions and our proofs of evaluations appreciably simpler than the traditional ones. Our proofs are the

---
[1] Dept of Computer Science, Edinburgh University, JCMB, King'sBdgs., Mayfield Rd., Edinburgh EH9 3JZ
[2] Dipartimento di Informatica, Universita di Torino, Corso Svizzeria 185, Torino, Italy

same shape as the traditional ones, but each formula is simpler; the environment and store do not appear repeatedly in formulas as they do in the traditional system. Instead of environment and store we use the notions of expression with an attached substitution and evaluation of an expression after a command (compare Dynamic Logic). Instead of evaluating an expression M with respect to an environment we consider its value given some assumptions about the values of the variables which occur in it.

The main technical difficulty is to define the substitution operation; this plays a crucial role in our semantics. We need substitution both for expressions and for commands. This is not a textual substitution; it depends on the binding operators in the language being defined. The meaning of [m/x]M (substitute value m for identifier x in expression M) is that when we come to evaluate M we assume the value of x to be m and ignore any previous assumptions about the value of x. To express this we use the hypothetical premises of Natural Deduction, with side conditions to ensure that we have a fresh variable. However we are not able to express substitution purely in a Natural Deduction logic. The difficulty can be reduced to substituting a (new) identifier for an (old) one. Thus we have to add a primitive operator for identifier replacement, just textual replacement, which we call α. (It is named from α conversion in lambda calculus.) We define this with a special rule schema.

In using an editor or a programming language you probably learn from a "Users' Manual" and then, having got some experience, look up the fine points in a "Reference Manual". For our style of doing operational semantics the "Reference Manual" is a formal description in ELF. We try to provide also a less formal "Users' Manual" which describes the form of the semantic rules and the criteria for proofs; this takes the form of "Alpha Logic". Alpha Logic will be described with about the degree of precision with which the rules of predicate logic might be defined in a text book. As usual we will give the Users' Manual first, asking the reader to suspend critical judgement while getting an intuitive feel for the style of semantics we propose.

We proceed on four steps.
- We define Alpha Logic: Natural Deduction extended with an operator α to replace variables.
- We specialise this to Evaluation Logic, by using Alpha Logic with evaluation predicates, =>, and substitution operators, [/], obeying suitable rules.
- We use Evaluation Logic to define the semantic rules for a sample programming language which features lambda expressions, commands, procedures and expressions with side effects.
- We give a formal definition of Alpha Logic in the Edinburgh Logical Framework.

This last step puts Alpha Logic on a firm foundation and shows the connection of our approach with the ELF treatment of logical languages.

Comparison with the Edinburgh Logical Framework
Our original aim was to use the ELF as a definition medium for Programming Languages. We achieve this in the last step above. Our semantic rules can be written in ELF notation by mere transliteration. However the rules do not use all the power of the ELF except in defining the substitution operations. It seemed to us better to present Evaluation Logic as a

simpler framework for semantics. It is not higher order and does not use dependent types, instead it makes use of the primitive operator α. The semantic rules do not even mention α, once we have defined substitution. In short

> ELF approach: If you understand lambda calculus with dependent types you can define many logics formally.

> Alpha Logic approach: If you understand Natural Deduction with variable replacement you can define many programming languages formally.

In alpha logic we lose the ELF advantage of a built-in type checker for dependent types, so that we have to write a separate static semantics (not treated in this paper). Even in ELF we may have to write a static semantics, for example to handle phenomena such as the polymorphism in ML.

Acknowledgements
We thank the UK Science and Engineering Research Council for support (RB and FH) and the Italian Ministry of Public Instruction for support (FH). Much of the work was carried out while FH was at Edinburgh University, and we thank our colleagues at the Laboratory for Foundations of Computer Science for stimulating interaction. RB thanks Butler Lampson of DECSRC for experience gained in their joint work on the semantics of the Pebble language, and he thanks the Conference Programme Committee for the invitation to present a paper.

2. Definition of a Framework for Operational Semantics

Alpha logic is about syntactic entities, namely identifiers and expressions. The required property of identifiers is that they have equality defined over them.

2.1. Alpha logic

Let Σ be a first order signature with two sorts, Id (identifiers) and Expr (expressions), some predicates P and some function symbols F. There is a distinguished function symbol α: Id * Id * Expr -> Expr, which denotes the replacement of an identifier in a term by another identifier. There are distinguished binary predicates = and $\neq$ over Id.

We define Terms and (atomic) Formulas over the signature and variables as usual and Rules as in Natural Deduction.

An alpha logic over a signature Σ has the sorts Id and Expr with the above distinguished operator and predicates together with a set of rules which must include the equivalence axioms for =, symmetry for $\neq$ and a set **R**, which we now define.

An element of **R** is a well formed instance of the following schema:

$$\frac{C[\,J\,],\ A_{x_1},\ ...,\ A_{x_n}}{C[\,\alpha_{j/i}\,I\,]}$$

where C[ ] is any context (formula with a hole) and where J is the term obtained from the term I by replacing all occurrences of identifiers x such that x = i with j
and where for each identifier x occurring in I there is a corresponding premise A_x of the form x = i or x ≠ i.

Thus to prove $\alpha_{y/x}(x+z) < 3$ we have to prove y+z < 3 and x ≠ z, or prove y+y < 3 and x = z.

A proof in alpha logic is a natural deduction proof (Prawitz 1966).

Later we will give a formal account of the notion of alpha proof in the Edinburgh Logical Framework. Actually the very definition of alpha logic was given keeping in mind its smooth definability in the Edinburgh Logical Framework.

More generally a "many sorted alpha logic" has sorts Id_{s_1}, ..., Id_{s_n} and $Expr_{t_1}$, ..., $Expr_{t_n}$ with function symbols α_{st}: Id_s * Id_s * $Expr_t$ -> $Expr_t$, predicates $=_s$ and $\neq_s$ and the corresponding rules.

2.2. Evaluation logic - 1

We now specialise the alpha logic to "evaluation logic". We consider first the case with two sorts Id (identifiers) and Expr (expressions). An evaluation logic is an alpha logic whose signature contains two distinguished predicates, a distinguished function and certain rules which they obey.

The distinguished predicates are evaluation and value
_ => _ over Expr * Expr
Value _ over Expr

The distinguished functions are expr (to convert Id to expr) and substitution
expr : Id -> Expr
[_ / _] : Expr * Id * Expr -> Expr

For ease of reading we will usually omit the conversion function expr hereafter, treating Id as a subsort of Expr.

We use the following symbols (possibly primed)
x, y, z for identifiers
M, N, m, n, p for expressions

The rules are

$$\frac{\begin{array}{c}(w_1 \neq x',..., w_k \neq x', \quad x' => n)\\ \vdots \\ \text{value } n, \qquad \alpha_{x'/x} M => \alpha_{x'/x} m\end{array}}{[n/x]\, M \;=>\; m} \quad x' \text{ is a new variable}$$

where $w_1,..., w_k$ are the list of identifiers occurring in x, M and m

By "x' is a new variable" we mean that is it does not occur in any assumption except the ones on the top line nor in n, x, M and m. (The assumptions on the top line are discharged by an application of this rule.)

This rule is really no more complex than the usual rule for, say, existential elimination.

$$\frac{\text{value } n}{n => n}$$

The rule for substitution is the key definition. It encapsulates the way we handle object language variables. One of the virtues of the Natural Deduction framework used in evaluation logic is that it provides uniformity in handling scopes of variables, avoiding side conditions on rules. This is important in practice because handling variables is a traditional pitfall in defining logics or programming languages. Our approach is to define substitution in terms of evaluation.

A naive version of the substitution rule might have been

$$\frac{\begin{array}{c}(x => n)\\ \vdots \\ \text{value } n, \qquad M => m\end{array}}{[n/x]\, M \;=>\; m}$$

but the evaluation of M in the hypothetical premise could make use not only of $x => n$, but also of any other statement about the value of x in the context in which the rule is used; we might be evaluating $[n/x]\, M$ in a context in which $x => n'$ and this should not affect the value. Thus we need to introduce a new variable x' local to the hypothetical premise. We have to replace x by x' in M and m.

Syntactic sugar
We will mostly use infix syntax for expressions, e.g.
let x = M in N   for   let(x, M, N)
When we introduce a syntax for a particular object language in what follows this is to be understood as syntactic sugar.

Example proof
We now give a proof in alpha-logic with the substitution rule above, constants 1,2,3, an operation + and three extra rules

$$\frac{M => 1, N => 2}{M+N => 3} \qquad \overline{\text{value 1}} \qquad \overline{\text{value 2}}$$

We will show that under the assumption $x \neq y$ we have
$[1/x][2/y]\ x+y => 3$

$$\cfrac{\text{value 1} \quad \cfrac{x \neq y \quad \cfrac{\text{value 2} \quad \cfrac{[y \neq x']_{(1)} \quad \cfrac{[x' => 1]_{(1)},\ [y' => 2]_{(2)}}{x'+y' => 3}}{\alpha_{y'/y}\ x'+y => \alpha_{y'/y}\ 3}}{[2/y]\ x'+y => 3}\ (2)\ y'}{\alpha_{x'/x}\ [2/y]\ x+y => \alpha_{x'/x}\ 3}}{[1/x][2/y]\ x+y => 3}\ (1)\ x'$$

The square brackets enclose hypotheses which are discharged at the level indicated by the subscript. The scope of a variable is shown by writing it at the end of the line below the scope.

We could write this proof more briefly omitting the applications of the α rules and the inequality statements for new variables. We may think of the α expression brought in by the substitution rule being immediately reduced. A proof editor could do this step automatically. We recommend this style of proof display. The α is a technical device for making the machinery of substitution explicit. It does not appear in the semantic rules once we have defined substitution, and it can well be omitted from the proofs.

$$\cfrac{\text{value 1} \quad x \neq y \quad \cfrac{\text{value 2} \quad \cfrac{[x' => 1]_{(1)},\ [y' => 2]_{(2)}}{x'+y' => 3}\ y'}{[2/y]\ x'+y => 3}\ (2)\ x'}{[1/x][2/y]\ x+y => 3}\ (1)$$

We have treated the case with one sort Id and one sort Expr, in a many sorted case these would be indexed families Id_s and $Expr_t$. The distinguished functions and predicates, when required, would be indexed accordingly.

2.3. Conventions for syntax

To extend the evaluation logic signature (Id, Expr, => value and [/]) we will use the usual conventions of syntax. These allow us to introduce function symbols together with the infix notation for them. We will use the names allocated to schematic variables for the syntax classes. For example using

x, y, z for identifiers
M, N, m, n, p for expressions
the syntax definition
$$M ::= K \mid \textbf{let } x = M \textbf{ in } N \mid \textbf{lambda } x . M$$
introduces the new function symbols
K: Expr
let: Id * Expr * Expr -> Expr
lambda: Id * Expr -> Expr

3. Example semantics

3.1. A basic functional language

In this section we will give the semantics for a simple functional language as a signature and a set of rules in evaluation logic.

Signature

We use a signature with sorts Id and Expr.
We use the following symbols (possibly primed)
x, y, z for identifiers
M, N, m, n, p, f, k for expressions
$M ::= K_1 \mid ... \mid K_k \mid M N \mid \textbf{let } x = M \textbf{ in } N \mid \textbf{lambda } x . M$
To be explicit, M N means apply(M, N).

We need a new unary predicate over expressions
closed M - (informally) M has no free variables, except ones assumed to be closed.

The evaluation of a **let** and the application of a **lambda** expression (assuming call by value) are easily formulated in terms of our substitution operation.

Since our language allows a lambda expression to appear as the result of evaluating an expression, we must ensure that it carries with it enough information about the values of its free variables to enable it to be applied in any context, so we use Landin's notion of "closure" (Landin [1964]). Our Natural Deduction technique really corresponds to stack discipline and we cannot expect it to handle function values without some further device. We do not have an explicit environment, instead we give rules which successively bind the variables appearing in the body until the body is "closed". We have to define closed, essentially by induction on the syntax. This means that for each syntactic constructor (let, lambda and so on) we need not only a rule for => but also a rule for closed. The predicate closed conveys the binding nature of the operators; it really belongs to the static semantics. An illustrative example follows the rules.

Evaluation rules

$$\frac{}{\text{value } K_i} \text{ for all } i$$

$$\frac{N => n, \quad [n/x]M => m}{\textbf{let } x = N \textbf{ in } M => m}$$

$$\frac{M => (\textbf{lambda } x.\ M'), \quad N => n, \quad [n/x]\ M' => m'}{M\ N => m'}$$

$$\frac{M => [p/y]\ f, \quad N => n, \quad [p/y]\ (f\ n) => m'}{M\ N => m'}$$

$$\frac{M => k\ (\text{or}\ M => k\ m'), N => n}{M\ N => ...} \quad \text{(delta rules for primitive functions)}$$

$$\frac{\begin{array}{c}(\text{closed } x)\\ \vdots \\ \text{closed } M\end{array}}{\textbf{lambda } x.\ M => (\textbf{lambda } x.\ M)}$$

$$\frac{y => p, \quad \begin{array}{c}(\text{closed } y)\\ \vdots \\ \textbf{lambda } x.\ M => m\end{array}}{\textbf{lambda } x.\ M => [p/y]\ m}$$

The reader might like to compare these with the usual treatment using an explicit environment, ρ. For example

$$\frac{\rho \vdash N => n, \quad \rho[n/x] \vdash M => m}{\rho \vdash \textbf{let } x = N \textbf{ in } M => m}$$

$$\frac{\rho \vdash M => k\ (\text{or}\ \rho \vdash M => k\ m'),\quad \rho \vdash N => n}{\rho \vdash M\ N => ...} \quad \text{(delta rules for primitive functions)}$$

In the latter rule the environment is not used; it is simply passed down. This is implicit in out Natural Deduction formulation. We only mention the environment when it is used.

Rules for closed

$$\frac{\text{closed n}, \quad \begin{array}{c}(\text{closed x})\\ \vdots\\ \text{closed M}\end{array}}{\text{closed}(\,[n/x]M)}$$

$$\frac{}{\text{closed K}}$$

$$\frac{\text{closed M}, \quad \text{closed N}}{\text{closed}(M\ N)}$$

$$\frac{\text{closed N}, \quad \begin{array}{c}(\text{closed x})\\ \vdots\\ \text{closed M}\end{array}}{\text{closed}(\,\textbf{let}\ x = N\ \textbf{in}\ M)}$$

$$\frac{\begin{array}{c}(\text{closed x})\\ \vdots\\ \text{closed M}\end{array}}{\text{closed}(\,\textbf{lambda}\ x.\ M)}$$

Rule for value

$$\frac{M => m}{\text{value m}}$$

Example of evaluation

As an example of proofs using these rules we assume y≠x and evaluate
(**let** y = 2 **in lambda** x.x+y) 1
We use two Lemmas, A and B, to simplify the layout. They are proved below.

Main evaluation proof

$$\cfrac{\cfrac{\cfrac{y \ne x}{A}}{2=>2,\quad [2/y](\textbf{lambda}\ \text{x.x+y}) => [2/y](\textbf{lambda}\ \text{x.x+y})}{\textbf{let}\ y=2\ \textbf{in lambda}\ \text{x.x+y} => [2/y](\textbf{lambda}\ \text{x.x+y}),\quad 1=>1,\quad \cfrac{\cfrac{[y'=>2]_{(2)}}{B}}{(\textbf{lambda}\ \text{x. x+y'})1 => 3,\quad y \ne x}}{[2/y]((\textbf{lambda}\ \text{.x.x+y})1)\ =>3}_{(2)}}}{(\textbf{let}\ y = 2\ \textbf{in lambda}\ \text{x.x+y})\ 1 => 3}$$

Lemma A
Assume y≠x and show [2/y](lambda x.x+y) => [2/y](lambda x.x+y)

$$\cfrac{\cfrac{\cfrac{[closed\ (y')]_{(4)},\ [closed(x)]_{(5)}}{closed\ (x+y')}}{[y' => 2]_{(6)},\ lambda\ x.x+y => lambda\ x.x+y}\ (5)}{\cfrac{[y' => 2]_{(6)},\ y≠x,\ \ lambda\ x.x+y => [2/y'](lambda\ x.x+y)}{[2/y](lambda\ x.x+y) => [2/y](lambda\ x.x+y)}\ (6)}\ (4)$$

Lemma B
Assume y'=> 2 and show **(lambda x. x+y')1 => 3**

$$\cfrac{\cfrac{\cfrac{\cfrac{y'=>2}{closed\ (y')},\ [closed(x)]_{(3)}}{closed\ (x+y')}}{lambda\ ...\ =>\ lambda\ ...,}\ (3)\quad 1 => 1,\quad \cfrac{\cfrac{[x' => 1]_{(1)},\ y'=>2}{x'+y' => 3}}{[1/x](x+y') => 3}\ (1)}{(lambda\ x.\ x+y')1 => 3,}$$

3.2. Complex declarations

We now consider allowing **let** to be followed by a complex declaration, formed with "**and**" (parallel declarations) and ";" (sequential declarations). Such declarations will form a new syntax class and will need to have as values just the environments which we have otherwise succeeded in eliminating. This seems unavoidable for languages, such as Standard ML, which permit such a declaration feature. However the "environments" only appear as values (declaration values).

Signature
We extend the previous signature as follows.
We introduce a new Expr-like sort Declaration with a new evaluation predicate =>.
We use the following symbols
R, S,r,s   for declarations
R::= x=M | R **and** S | R; S
We generalise the syntax class Expr, introducing a new **let** and { }:
M ::= **let** R **in** N| {r}M
Finally we introduce the new rules for => and closed.

Evaluation rules
$$\cfrac{M => m}{x = M => m/x}$$

$$\frac{R => r, S => s}{R \text{ and } S => r \text{ and } s}$$

$$\frac{R => r, \ \{r\}S => s}{R\ ;\ S => r \text{ and } s}$$

$$\frac{[n/x]M => m}{\{n/x\}M => m}$$

$$\frac{R => r, \ \{r\}M => m}{\text{let } R \text{ in } M => m}$$

$$\frac{\{r\}(\{s\}M) => m}{\{r \text{ and } s\}M => m}$$

Rules for closed

$$\frac{\text{closed}([n/x]M)}{\text{closed}(\{n/x\}M)}$$

$$\frac{R => r, \ \text{closed}(\{r\}M)}{\text{closed}(\text{let } R \text{ in } M)}$$

$$\frac{\text{closed }(\{r\}(\{s\}M))}{\text{closed }(\{r \text{ and } s\}M)}$$

3.3. An assignment language
Signature

We extend the previous signature as follows.
We introduce a new Expr-like sort Command.
We use the following symbols
C,D   for commands.
C ::= x:=M | C; D | if M do C | while M do C
We extend the syntax class M
M ::= [C] M
The intended meaning of this new kind of expression is " evaluate M after doing the command C". For example if $x \neq y$ then

[x:=1; y:=2] x+y

evaluates to 3. These expressions have no side effect.
The use of [ ] for commands should not be confused with the notation for substitution. However there is a suggestive analogy.

We introduce a new predicate over Commands closed$_{comm}$(C), which we will write simply as closed(C).
Finally we introduce the new rules for => and closed.

Evaluation rules

$$\frac{M => m, \quad [m/x] N => n}{[x:=M] N => n}$$

$$\frac{[C] ([D] M) => m}{[C; D] M => m}$$

$$\frac{N => true , [C]M => m}{[if N do C] \ M => m}$$

$$\frac{N => false, \quad M => m}{[if N do C] \ M => m}$$

$$\frac{[if N do (C; while N do C)] M => m}{[while N do C] M => m}$$

Rules for closed

$$\frac{closed\ C, \quad closed\ M}{closed\ [C]M}$$

$$\frac{closed\ M}{closed(\ x:=M\ )}$$

$$\frac{closed\ C, closed\ D}{closed(\ C; D)}$$

$$\frac{closed\ N, \quad closed\ C}{closed(if\ N\ do\ C)}$$

$$\frac{closed\ N, \quad closed\ C}{closed(while\ N\ do\ C)}$$

3.4. Expressions with side effects

How can we extend the system to deal with expressions which may have side effects? Here are some tentative thoughts. In the above C had a side effect but with the given semantics for the functional language [C]M had no side effects. Now let us change the semantics of the functional language to allow expressions, M, to have side effects. To accomplish this we adopt the following device: write [M]N to mean the value of N after evaluating the expression M. Now for example

[M+N] P has the same value as [M]([N] P)
M+N => m+n if M=>m and [M]N => n

The revised semantic rules might be as follows. We do not give them all, just enough to illustrate the idea.

$$\frac{N => n}{[x]N => n}$$

$$\frac{N=>n}{[K_i]N => n}$$

$$\frac{N=>n}{[\text{lambda } x. M] N => n}$$

The rules for evaluating an application become

$$\frac{M => \text{lambda } x. P, \ [M] N=>n, \ [n/x] P => p}{M N => p}$$

$$\frac{M => k \ (\text{or} => k \ m'), \ [M] N=>n}{M N => ...} \quad \text{(delta rules for primitive functions)}$$

$$\frac{[C]([M] N) => n}{[[C] M] N => n}$$

4. Framework for Operational Semantics - continued
4.1.Evaluation logic - 2

In a semantics we may have several sorts of identifiers and expressions and more than one substitution operation. For example we may have local variables in commands.

We may define an evaluation logic over a multi-sorted alpha logic with sorts Id_s and $Expr_t$ with more distinguished evaluation and value predicates and substitution functions. Thus we have

α_{ij} : $Id_i * Id_j * Expr_j \rightarrow Expr_j$
$expr_{ik}$: $Id_i \rightarrow Expr_k$
$=>_k$ over $Expr_k * Expr_k$
$Value_k$ over $Expr_k$
$[\_/\_]_{ikm}$: $Expr_k * Id_i * Expr_m \rightarrow Expr_m$

Corresponding to each substitution function an appropriate substitution rule schema is added, or even several rule schemas corresponding to different evaluation predicates. These schemas will always be of a similar pattern. (Since we do not specify such a pattern here the notion of evaluation logic is somewhat loose.)

Substitution rule
We consider as an example of a substitution rule the one needed for the language features introduced in the next section. We have
x, w for identifiers
N,m,n for expressions
C for commands (a second sort of expressions)

We want a rule for substituting expressions for identifiers in commands. The rule is (dropping subscripts)

$$(w_1 \neq x',..., w_k \neq x', \quad x' => m)$$
$$\vdots$$
$$\frac{[\alpha_{x'/x} C]N => \alpha_{x'/x} n}{[[m/x]C]N => n} \quad x' \text{ is a new variable}$$

where $w_1,..., w_k$ are the list of identifiers occurring in x, C and n,
and provided that x' is a new variable, that is it does not occur in any assumption except the ones on the top line nor in m, x, C, N and n.

5. Further example semantics

5.1. Local declarations and procedures with parameters

In this example we illustrate the semantics of a language with local variables in commands and with procedure declaration facilities. More precisely we discuss procedures with one parameter, passed by value, and possibly with local variables. We do not consider kinds of parameters other than value ones or procedures as parameters. We do not address the issue of recursive procedures here.

Signature
We extend the signature of the assignment language as follows.
A distinguished substitution function
[/] : Expr * Id * Command -> Expr
obeying the substitution rule introduced in the previous section. This will enable us to take care of local variables.
We introduce a new Expr-like sort Procedures and an Id-like sort Procedure_names, with a corresponding evaluation predicate ==>.
We use the following symbols

Q, h for Procedures
P   for Procedure_names
P ::= P_0 | ... | P_k
Q ::= **lambda** x. C

We generalise the syntax class Command to
C ::= **begin new** x = M **in** D **end** | **proc** P(x) = C **in** D | P(M)

We use the substitution [m/x]C defined in the previous section. We omit the definition of the other substitution which we need, [h/P]C. The definition will be similar to [m/x]C, and it will give us the mechanism for procedure call. We do not need to introduce procedure closures.

Finally we introduce the new rules for => and closed.

Evaluation rules

$$\frac{M => m, \quad [[m/x]C]\ N => n}{[\textbf{begin new } x = M\ ;\ C\ \textbf{end}]\ N => n}$$

$$\frac{[\ [\textbf{lambda } x.\ C/P]\ D\ ]\ N => n}{[\textbf{proc } P(x) = C\ \textbf{in}\ D]\ N => n}$$

$$\frac{P ==> \textbf{lambda } x.\ C, \quad M => m, \quad [[m/x]C]\ N => n}{[P(M)]\ N => n}$$

Rules for closed

$$\frac{\text{closed } n, \quad \begin{array}{c}\text{closed } x\\ \vdots\\ \text{closed } C\end{array}}{\text{closed}([n/x]\ C)}$$

$$\frac{\text{closed } M, \quad \begin{array}{c}\text{closed } x\\ \vdots\\ \text{closed } C\end{array}}{\text{closed}(\textbf{begin new } x = M\ ;\ C\ \textbf{end})}$$

$$\frac{\text{closed } [[\textbf{lambda } x.\ C/P]D]}{\text{closed } [\textbf{proc } P(x) = C\ \textbf{in}\ D]}$$

$$\frac{\text{closed } M, \quad \text{closed } N}{\text{closed } [P(M)]\ N}$$

$$\frac{closed(C), \quad closed([D]N)}{closed([[\textbf{lambda } x. C/P]D]N)} \quad \begin{array}{c} closed(x) \\ \vdots \\ \end{array}$$

6. Definition of Alpha Logic in the Edinburgh Logical Framework

In this section we outline a definition of the minimal signature of Alpha Logic in the Edinburgh Logical Framework. This is a signature with two sorts Id and Expr, one function symbol

α : Id -> Id -> Expr -> Expr

and no predicates except = and $\neq$.

In order to encode in ELF such an instance of Alpha Logic we proceed as follows. First of all we will introduce an ELF type corresponding to the collection of sorts and a type constructor, Term, defined on sorts.
Sorts : Type
Term : Sorts -> Type

We will introduce constants corresponding to Id and Expr and two new constants. The first $\supset$, is intended to denote the higher order sort constructor (written as an infix and bracketed to the right), while the second is intended to denote syntactic application
Id : Sorts
Expr : Sorts
$\supset$: Sorts -> Sorts -> Sorts
app : Π s,t : Sorts. Term(s$\supset$t) -> Term(s) -> Term(t) .

Corresponding to a function in the signature we declare a constant of type Term(s) for the appropriate s
α : Term(Id $\supset$ Id $\supset$ Expr $\supset$ Expr).
Corresponding to the class of formulae we introduce an ELF type
Form : Type.
Corresponding to a predicate in the signature we would introduce a constant over types Term(s) for appropriate sorts s. Here the only predicates are = and $\neq$.
= : Term(Id) -> Term(Id) -> Form
$\neq$: Term(Id) -> Term(Id) -> Form

Finally we introduce a judgement forming operator, asserting the truth of Alpha Logic formulas
True : Form -> Type.
The Alpha Logic rules about = and $\neq$ are simply translated by using True. For example reflexivity of = becomes

$$\frac{}{\text{True}(x = x)} \; x : \text{Term}_{Id}$$

We now encode the rules regulating the replacement operator α. This is the most elaborate part. We have to introduce in the ELF signature a number of new predicates, new constants, new formula forming operators, and new rules governing the provability of these new formulae. More precisely we define

$\in \; : \; \Pi s : \text{Sorts. Term(Id)} \rightarrow \text{Term(s)} \rightarrow \text{Type}$

$\notin \; : \; \Pi s : \text{Sorts. Term(Id)} \rightarrow \text{Term(s)} \rightarrow \text{Type}$

The judgement $x \in M$ says that the identifier x occurs in M, while $x \notin M$ says that it does not occur. To translate the rules of Alpha Logic we introduce constants of the types which follow. (For ease of reading we will write rules using a somewhat more suggestive notation than the ELF Π and ->. We will subscript arguments which are sorts)

$$\frac{x \in_s M}{x \in_t \text{apps}_{s\,t}\, N\, M} \quad \text{s,t: Sorts, x,y:Term}_{Id}, \; M: \text{Term}_s, \; N: \text{Term}_{s \supset t}$$

$$\frac{x \in_{s \supset t} N}{x \in_t \text{apps}_{s\,t}\, N\, M} \quad \text{s,t: Sorts x,y:Term}_{Id}, \; M: \text{Term}_s, \; N: \text{Term}_{s \supset t}$$

$$\frac{x \notin_s M, \; x \notin_{s \supset t} N}{x \notin_t \text{apps}_{s\,t}\, N\, M} \quad \text{s,t: Sorts x,y:Term}_{Id}, \; M: \text{Term}_s, \; N: \text{Term}_{s \supset t}$$

$$\frac{\text{True}(x = y)}{x \in_{Id} y} \; x,y : \text{Term}_{Id}$$

$$\frac{\text{True}(x \neq y)}{x \notin_{Id} y} \; x,y : \text{Term}_{Id}$$

$$\frac{}{x \notin_{Id \supset Id \supset Exp \supset Expr} \alpha} \; x : \text{Term}_{Id}$$

We are now ready to illustrate how to encode the set of rules about the α operator in ELF. We introduce a constant of the following LF type

$$\frac{x \notin_{Expr} F(y), \quad True(G(F(y)))}{Term_{Id}} \quad F:Term_{Id} \to Term_{Expr}, \quad G:Term_{Expr} \to Form, \quad x,y:$$
$$True(G(\alpha_{y/x} F(x)))$$

In the last rule we have omitted app before α for ease of reading.

Evaluation Logic in ELF

We will now consider a more elaborate example: translating the minimal signature of Evaluation Logic.

Besides the standard ELF types and constants we will introduce here a judgement forming operator corresponding to =>, one corresponding to value and constants for the expression constructors.

The first part of the ELF signature will then be as before:
Sorts : Type
Form : Type
Term : Sorts -> Type
True : Form -> Type
Id : Sorts
Expr : Sorts
$\supset$: Sorts -> Sorts ->Sorts
app : Π s,t : Sorts. Term(s$\supset$t) -> Term(s) -> Term(t)
α : Term(Id $\supset$ Id $\supset$ Expr $\supset$ Expr)
= : Term(Id) -> Term(Id) -> True
$\neq$: Term(Id) -> Term(Id) -> True
$\in$: Π s : Sorts.Term(Id) -> Term(s) -> Form
$\notin$: Π s : Sorts.Term(Id) -> Term(s) -> Form

with the addition of
expr : Term(Id $\supset$ Expr)
[/] : Term(Expr $\supset$ Id $\supset$ Expr $\supset$ Expr)
value: Term(Expr) -> Form
=> :Term(Expr) -> Term(Expr) -> Form

A few more rules specific to the particular Σ of Evaluation Logic have to be introduced in addition to the ones we had before. As before we we will limit ourselves to giving the type

$$\frac{}{x \notin_{Id \supset Expr \supset Expr \supset Expr} [/]} \quad x: Term_{Id}$$

$$\frac{ x: \text{Term}_{\text{Id}}}{Tx} \quad x \notin_{\text{Id} \supset \text{Expr}} \text{expr}$$

The translations of the rules specific to Evaluation Logic in ELF are straightforward:

$$\frac{\text{True}(\text{value}(n))}{\text{True}(n => n)} \quad n:\text{Term}_{\text{Expr}}$$

and

$$\frac{w \in_{\text{Id}} x}{w:\text{Term}_{\text{Id}}} \quad \frac{w \in_{\text{Expr}} M}{w:\text{Term}_{\text{Id}}} \quad \frac{w \in_{\text{Expr}} m}{w:\text{Term}_{\text{Id}}}$$

$$w \notin_{\text{Id}} x', \qquad w \notin_{\text{Id}} x', \qquad w \notin_{\text{Id}} x', \qquad \text{True}(x' => n)$$

$$\frac{\text{True}(\text{value}(n)) \qquad \text{True}(\alpha_{x'/x} M => \alpha_{x'/x} m)}{\text{True}([x/n]\ M => m)} \quad \begin{array}{l} x':\text{Term}_{\text{Id}} \\ x:\text{Term}_{\text{Id}},\ M,N,m,n:\text{Term}_{\text{Expr}} \end{array}$$

In the last rule for ease of reading we have omitted expr, also app before α and $[/]$.

The extension to Evaluation Logic for commands will be analogous.

Concluding remarks

We have shown how to define semantics of a simple but non-trivial language in our Natural Deduction style. We have not treated reference variables, exceptions or data types, nor have we defined the type discipline by a static semantics. These remain to be investigated. Another area for exploration would be the application of the technique to defining logics. We would also like to consider program verification and transformation in this formalism based on this style of semantics.

Although our system relies on the Edinburgh Logical Framework for a formal definition, it can be applied without explicit reference to ELF, basing it on Alpha Logic.

References

Avron, A. ,Honsell, F, Mason, I, (1987) Using Typed Lambda Calculus to Implement Formal Systems on a Machine, Report LFCS87-31, Comp. Sci Dept. Edinburgh Univ. UK

Kahn, G. (1987) Natural Semantics, Rapport de Recherche N. 601, INRIA, France

Harper, R. , Honsell, F., Plotkin, G. (1987) A Framework for Defining Logics, Proceedings of the Second Annual Conference on Logic in Computer Science, Cornell, USA

Landin, P.J. (1964) The Mechanical Evaluation of Expressions, Computer Journal, 6.

Mason, I. (1987) Hoare's Logic in the LF, Report LFCS-87-32, Comp. Science Dept. Edinburgh University, UK

Plotkin, G.(1981) A Structural Approach to Operational Semantics, DAIMI FN-19, Computer Science Department ,Aarhus University, Denmark

Prawitz, D. (1965) Natural Deduction: A Proof-Theoretic study, Almqvist & Wiksel, Stockholm

Reynolds J.C. (1978) Syntactic Control of Interference, 5th Annual Symp. on Principles Of Prog. Langs., Tucson, ACM

UNIFORMLY APPLICATIVE STRUCTURES, A THEORY OF COMPUTABILITY AND POLYADIC FUNCTIONS

Patrick BELLOT

*Centre Scientifique de Paris, Compagnie IBM-France,
3 et 5 Place Vendôme, 75021 Paris Cedex 01, France.*

Véronique JAY

*LITP - Paris 6, Université Pierre et Marie Curie,
2 Place Jussieu, 75251 Paris Cedex 05, France.*

Abstract : This article describes a Computability theory developed from the theory of URS described by E.G. Wagner and H.R. Strong and a Combinatory theory named TGE presented by the authors. Its main contribution is that the theory handles polyadicity as a primitive notion and allows a natural representation of functions with variable arity, that is functions which can be applied to sequences of arguments of any length. Aside from classical computability results, we prove a General Abstraction theorem which allows us to construct representations for a large class of functions with variable arity.

Keywords : computability, recursive function, algorithmic, abstraction, definability, representability, polyadicity.

1. Introduction and Justifications

The theory of Uniformly Applicative Structures (UAS) is intended to be a Computability theory. The presentation of the theory is axiomatic and very close to that of URS theory (12,15,16). The justification of the theory is as follows. If we look at theories (1,6,8,15) supporting functions and functional programming, we must remark that *polyadicity* is almost never a primitive concept. It is carried out through *curryfication* or *structuration*.

Curryfication transforms a single application of a function of n arguments into n repeated applications of a functional of one argument whereas structuration gives a structure, list or cartesian product, to the arguments of a function. Theories such as Recursive Function Theory (RFT) have polyadic functions but they need strong *artefacts* such as *coding* to handle functions which can be applied to a variable number of arguments such as *plus* defined as :
$$\forall n \geq 0, \forall x_0, x_1, ..., x_n \in \mathbb{N}, \text{plus}(x_0, x_1, ..., x_n) = x_0 + x_1 + ... + x_n$$

A function like *plus* above is called a Function with Variable Arity (Fva) in this article. A Fva ϕ can be viewed as an indexed family of functions $\{\phi_n : D^n \to D, n \geq 1\}$ where D is a domain. The intuitive idea behind Fva's is that such families of functions can be natural and coherent so that it seems fitting represent them by a single operator. That is to say that overloading of the operator is meaningful.

The proposed theory allows to handle *naturally* such functions, that is to say that they are representable without any artefact. Moreover, it is also a Computability theory because we prove that any UAS contains a model N of the non negative integers such that the restriction of UAS functions to N contains all the recursive functions. In this sense, UAS are similar to URS (15).

The main result is the proof of a *General Abstraction* theorem which allows to construct a large class of functions with variable arity which could be informally denoted as : $f(x_1, ..., x_n) = E$ where n remains *unspecified* and E is a special kind of term, called a *A-term*, which can contain subterms x_i, x_{n-j} and *unspecified* subsequences $x_i...x_{n-j}$ with i and j being natural numbers. This is a very general class of functions with variable arity. For instance, we can construct the function *plus* above in any UAS. The representation for this function does not require any of the artefacts needed with usual theories.

The need for UAS theory comes from the functional programming language GRAAL (3,4), acronym of General Recursive Applicative and Algorithmic Language, where polyadicity is primitive. In this language, a set of *functional forms* has been designed to handle a variable number of arguments. Languages such as Lisp handle variable number of arguments but arguments are structured into a list. It is the aim of UAS to provide a clear and simple formalization of polyadicity without the use of constructions over the basic theory (such as *tupling*).

Usefulness of UAS in Computer Science is characterized by the fact that it gives *efficient* models of programming languages. Thanks to *naturality*, there is no need to take into account intermediate computation steps generated by Curryfication, structures used by structuration or coding needed by Recursive Function Theory. Therefore, this formalization of polyadicity, beyond its *conceptual interest*, provides fast *reduction machines* such as that of the language GRAAL.

2. Axioms of UAS

Let U be an infinite set called a *domain*, we denote by U^∞ the union set

$$U^\infty = \bigcup_{k=1}^{\infty} U^k$$

of tuples of elements of U. We write $.(..): U \times U^\infty \to U$ to denote a function and $f(a_1, ..., a_n)$ the application of f in U to the tuple $(a_1, ..., a_n)$ in U^∞. The left associating parenthesis can be omitted. For instance, $f(a_1, ..., a_n)(b_1, ..., b_m)$ is the same as $(f(a_1, ..., a_n))(b_1, ..., b_m)$.

2.1. Definition

A Uniformly Applicative Structure is a structure $<U, *, K, S, T, L, D, E, .(..)>$ where U is a *domain*, $*, K, S, T, L, D$ and E are elements of U, $.(..): U \times U^\infty \to U$ a function called the *application* such that for all $f, a_1, ..., a_n, b_1, ..., b_m$ in $U - \{*\}$, we have axioms 1 to 8 :

1. $*(a_1, ..., a_n) = *$
    $f(a_1, ..., *, ..., a_n) = *$

2. $K(a_1, ..., a_n)(b_1, ..., b_m) = a_1$

3. $S(f) = *$
    $S(f, a_1, ..., a_n) \neq *$
    $S(f, a_1, ..., a_n)(b_1, ..., b_m) = f(b_1, ..., b_m)(a_1(b_1, ..., b_m), ..., a_n(b_1, ..., b_m))$

4. $T(a_1, ..., a_n)(b) = *$
    $T(a_1, ..., a_n) \neq *$
    $T(a_1, ..., a_n)(b_1, b_2, ..., b_m)(b_2, ..., b_m) = a_1(b_1, b_2, ..., b_m)(b_2, ..., b_m)$

5. $L(f) = *$
    $L(f, a_1, ..., a_n) \neq *$
    $L(f, a_1, ..., a_n)(b_1, ..., b_m) = f(b_1, ..., b_m)(a_1(b_1, ..., b_m), b_1, ..., b_m)$

6. $D(f) = *$
   $D(a_1, a_2, ..., a_n) \neq *$
   $D(a_1, a_2, ..., a_n)(b) = a_1(b)$
   $D(a_1, a_2, ..., a_n)(b_1, b_2, ..., b_m) = a_2(b_1, b_2, ..., b_m)$

7. $E(f) = *$
   $E(a_1, a_2, ..., a_n)(b_1, b_2, ..., b_m) = b_1$ if $a_1 = a_2$
   $E(a_1, a_2, ..., a_n)(b_1, b_2, ..., b_m) = b_2$ if $a_1 \neq a_2$

8. $S \neq K$

2.2. Convention

For sake of brevity, we will say "Let U be a UAS" instead of "Let $<U,*,K,S,T,L,D,E,.(..)>$ be a UAS". Names of constants will remain fixed through the article.

2.3. Examples of UAS

Thanks to structuration of multiple arguments, any URS is a UAS with the application $f(a_1, ..., a_n) = \{f\} . <a_1, ..., a_n>$ where $\{f\}$ is the Gödel number of f, $<a_1, ..., a_n>$ is a structure constructed in the URS (list for instance) and . is the binary application of the URS. In particular, Kleene's URS (1) is a UAS.

3. First Results in Computability Theory

This section proposes some theorems which are classical in Computability theory. These results are shown in order to prove that UAS is as powerful as any classical theory.

3.1. Definition of Terms and Sequences

Let U be a UAS and V be an enumerable set of variables, *terms* and *sequences* over U are inductively defined as follows :

- Every element of U is a term (a *constant*)
- Every element of V is a term (a *variable*)
- If t is a term, (t) is a sequence
- If t is a term and (s) is a sequence, (t,s) is a sequence
- If t is a term and (s) is a sequence, t(s) is a term (an *application*)
- Closure Rule

Remark : A sequence is the concatenation of several terms separated with commas and surrounded with parenthesis. For sake of clarity, sequences will be denoted as $(a_1, ..., a_n)$ where $a_1, ..., a_n$ are terms. With this syntactic remark, the definition of terms can be turned into :

- Every element of U is a term
- Every element of V is a term
- If $t, a_1, ..., a_n$ are terms, $t(a_1, ..., a_n)$ is a term

The second definition will be used because it is simpler.

3.2. Definition of Assignment and Valuation

Let U be a UAS and V be an enumerable set of variables, an *assignment* of V is a map $\beta: V \to U$. β can be uniquely extended to the set T of terms in a map, called a *valuation*, $\underline{\beta}: T \to U$ as follows :

- $\underline{\beta}[u] = u$ if $u \in U$, u is a *constant*
- $\underline{\beta}[v] = \beta[v]$ if $v \in V$, v is a *variable*
- $\underline{\beta}[t(a_1, ..., a_n)] = \underline{\beta}[t](\underline{\beta}[a_1], ..., \underline{\beta}[a_n])$

3.3. Identity and Selectors

Let U be a UAS and $I = S(K,K)$, then we have $I(a_1, ..., a_n) = a_1$ and there exists a family $(P_i)_{i \geq 1}$ in U such that :

$$P_i(a_1, ..., a_n) = a_i \text{ if } i \leq n$$
$$P_i(a_1, ..., a_n) = * \text{ otherwise}$$
Proof: We have $S(K, K)(a_1, ..., a_n) = K(a_1, ..., a_n)(K(a_1, ..., a_n)) = a_1$ and we choose $P_1 = I$ and $P_{k+1} = T(K(P_k))$.

3.4. Undefined Function

Let U be a UAS, there exists an element π in U-{*} such that :
$$\forall a_1, ..., a_n \in U, \pi(a_1, ..., a_n) = *$$
Proof: Let $\hat{\pi} = S(S(K(E), S(I, I), K(S)), K(K), K(S))$, we have the following :
$$\hat{\pi}(\hat{\pi}) = S \text{ if } \hat{\pi}(\hat{\pi}) \neq S$$
$$\hat{\pi}(\hat{\pi}) = K \text{ if } \hat{\pi}(\hat{\pi}) = S$$
$$\hat{\pi}(\hat{\pi}) = * \text{ if } \hat{\pi}(\hat{\pi}) = *$$
Thus, the only possibility is that we have $\hat{\pi}(\hat{\pi}) = *$ and we set $\pi = S(K(\hat{\pi}), K(\hat{\pi}))$, so that :
$$\pi(a_1, ..., a_n) = S(K(\hat{\pi}), K(\hat{\pi}))(a_1, ..., a_n) = K(\hat{\pi})(a_1, ..., a_n)(K(\hat{\pi})(a_1, ..., a_n)) = \hat{\pi}(\hat{\pi}) = *$$

3.5. Completeness Theorem

Let U be a UAS and V an enumerable set of variables, let $x_1, ..., x_n$ be variables, for each term t with at most $x_1, ..., x_n$ as variables, there exists a term $\underline{t} \in U-\{*\}$ called an *abstraction* and denoted $\lambda x_1, ..., x_n.t$ such that for every assignment β of V :
$$\beta[t] = \underline{t}(\beta[x_1], ..., \beta[x_n])$$
Proof: The term $\underline{t}$ is inductively constructed from t,
$$\text{If } t = *, \quad \underline{t} = \pi$$
$$\text{If } t \in U-\{*\}, \quad \underline{t} = K(t)$$
$$\text{If } t = x_i, \quad \underline{t} = P_i$$
$$\text{If } t = f(t_1, ..., t_n), \quad \underline{t} = S(\underline{f}, \underline{t_1}, ..., \underline{t_n})$$
Remark : As usual, this result can be generalized to multilevel abstraction such as $\lambda x_1, ..., x_n.(\lambda y_1, ..., y_m.t)$. It is just a little bit more cumbersome to express.

3.6. Fixed-Point Operators Family

Let U be a UAS and $n \geq 1$, there exists an element Y_n of U such that :
$$\forall t \in U-\{*\}, \forall x_1, ..., x_n \in U, \quad Y_n(t) \neq * \text{ and } Y_n(t)(x_1, ..., x_n) = t(Y_n(t))(x_1, ..., x_n)$$
Proof: $Y_n = \Omega_n(\Omega_n)$ with $\Omega_n = \lambda a.(\lambda t.(\lambda x_1, ..., x_n.(t(a(a)(t))(x_1, ..., x_n))))$

A more general fixed-point operator is constructible in any UAS. It allows to uniformly extract fixed-points. The terminology *uniform* is explicated in (15), it clearly applies to UAS.

3.7. Uniform Recursion Theorem

Let U be a UAS, there exists Y such that for all t in U-{*} we have :
1. $Y(t) \neq *$
2. $\forall x_1, ..., x_n \in U, Y(t)(x_1, ..., x_n) = t(Y(t))(x_1, ..., x_n)$

Proof: The proof of this theorem is more complicated than that of the previous theorem.
Lemma 1 : Let $\Gamma(f) = L(K(T(T(K(f)))), K(I))$, then we have :
$$\Gamma(f) \neq * \text{ if } f \neq *$$
$$\Gamma(f)(x_1, ..., x_n) = f(x_1, ..., x_n)(x_1, ..., x_n)$$
Proof : trivial.
Lemma 2 : Let $\Delta(f) = S(K(f), S(S(I, I), K(f)))$, then we have :
$$\Delta(f) \neq * \text{ if } f \neq *$$
$$\Delta(f)(a) = f(a(a)(f))$$
Proof : trivial.
Lemma 3 : Let x and y be variables, let t be a term with at most x and y as variables, then :
$$(\lambda x.(\lambda y.t))(n) \neq * \text{ if } n \neq *$$
Proof : The result of $(\lambda x.(\lambda y.t))(n)$ is $(\lambda(y).t)$ where all occurrences of x have been replaced by n. But such occurrences can only appear in subterms $K(x)$ giving $K(n)$ which is defined if n is.

Now, let us take $\Omega = \lambda a.(\lambda f.\Gamma(S(K(\Delta(f)), K(a))))$. We have :
$$\Omega \neq * \text{ because of the definition of } \lambda$$
$$\Omega(\Omega) \neq * \text{ because of Lemma 3 above}$$
$$\Omega(\Omega)(f) = \Gamma(S(K(\Delta(f)), K(\Omega))) \neq * \text{ if } f \neq *$$

And we choose $Y = \Omega(\Omega)$ since :
$$\Omega(\Omega)(f)(x_1, ..., x_n)$$
$$= \Gamma(S(K(\Delta(f)), K(\Omega)))(x_1, ..., x_n)$$
$$= S(K(\Delta(f)), K(\Omega))(x_1, ..., x_n)(x_1, ..., x_n)$$
$$= K(\Delta(f))(x_1, ..., x_n)(K(\Omega)(x_1, ..., x_n))(x_1, ..., x_n)$$
$$= \Delta(f)(\Omega)(x_1, ..., x_n)$$
$$= f(\Omega(\Omega)(f))(x_1, ..., x_n)$$

3.8. Iteration theorem

For all natural numbers $n \geq 1$ and $m \geq 1$, there exists an element $S_{m,n}$ of U such that :
$$S_{m,n}(x_0)(x_1, ..., x_m)(y_1, ..., y_n) = x_0(x_1, ..., x_m, y_1, ..., y_n)$$
Proof: $S_{m,n} = \lambda x_0.\lambda x_1, ..., x_m.\lambda y_1, ..., y_n.(x_0(x_1, ..., x_m)(y_1, ..., y_n))$ is given by the Completeness theorem.

3.9. Theorem

Every UAS is a URS.
Proof: We choose $a.b = a(b)$ as the binary application of the URS.

3.10. Conclusions

The preceding results show that UAS may be thought as a Computability theory without any restriction since theorems analogous to the basic theorems of classical Computability theory (7,11) are established.

A very important theorem is that of *Uniform Recursion* which allows to extract fixed-points of functionals independently of the arity of the associated function.

The last theorem is easily provable and emphasizes the computability character of the theory. This theorem proves that the large class of theorems proved in URS theory are still valid in UAS but they are done for the Curryfied application $a.b = a(b)$.

But the main advantage of this theory is that it gives a simple and natural formalization of polyadicity using the concepts of sequence and that of application of an element to a sequence of elements. It seems that UAS have carried the complexity of polyadicity on the syntax thanks to the use of uncurryfied combinators. Other theories have constructed polyadicity which is not a primitive notion.

4. Recursive Functions in an arbitrary UAS

Let U be a UAS, we will show that U contains a model N of natural numbers such that the functions of the UAS restricted to N contain the recursive functions. Moreover, if N is *computable*, then it also contains the *partial* recursive functions.

4.1. Notation

If f and x are elements of U and n is a natural number, $f^n(x)$ denotes an element of U defined as :
$f^0(x) = x$ and $f^{n+1}(x) = f(f^n(x))$.

4.2. Definition of a Splinter

A splinter (12) in a URS is an infinite subset of the URS representing natural numbers. An infinite subset N of a UAS U is a splinter (*successor set*) if there exists elements 0 (*zero*) and s (*successor function*) such that $N = \{s^n(0), n \geq 0\}$.

4.3. Definition of a Computable Splinter

A splinter N is computable if there exists an element Δ_N of U such that :
$$\Delta_N(x) = \begin{cases} K & \text{if } x \in N \\ S & \text{if } x \in U-N-\{*\} \\ * & \text{if } x = * \end{cases}$$

4.4. Theorem

Every UAS contains a splinter $N = \{[n], n \geq 0\}$
Proof: We choose the elements $[0] = P_2$ and $[s] = S(K(S), K(I), I)$. It is easy to show that the splinter defined with *zero* $[0]$ and *successor function* $[s]$ is infinite.

Remark: We will note $[n] = [s]^n([0])$. These numerals are called *Church's Iterators* because we can show that $[n](f, x) = f^n(x)$.

4.5. Definition of Natural Definability

A partial function f on natural numbers is said *naturally definable* (we just say *definable*) on a splinter N if there exists an element $[f]$ of U such that for all natural numbers $n_1, ..., n_k, r$ we have :

$$f(n_1, ..., n_k) = r \Leftrightarrow [f]([n_1], ..., [n_k]) = [r]$$
$$f(n_1, ..., n_k) \text{ is undefined} \Leftrightarrow [f]([n_1], ..., [n_k]) = *$$

4.6. Definition of Basic Functions

Basic functions of Recursive Function Theory are naturally definable. They are functions Zero, Succ, U_n^i, $i, n \in \mathbb{N}$ such that for all $x, x_1, ..., x_n \in \mathbb{N}$ we have :

$Zero(x) = 0$ zero function
$Succ(x) = x + 1$ successor function
$U_n^i(x_1, ..., x_n) = x_i$, $1 \leq i \leq n$ projection

Proof: $[Zero] = K([0])$, $[Succ] = [s]$, $[U_n^i] = P_i$

4.7. Substitution Closure

Let $g, h_1, ..., h_k$ be elements of U, there exists an element f of U such that :

$$\forall x_1, ..., x_n \in U, \ f(x_1, ..., x_n) = g(h_1(x_1, ..., x_n), ..., h_k(x_1, ..., x_n))$$

Proof: $f = S(K(g), h_1, ..., h_k)$

4.8. Primitive Recursion Closure

Let $N = \{[n], n \geq 0\}$ be a splinter, let $g, h \in U$ and $n \geq 1$, there exists f in U such that :

$$\forall x_1, ..., x_n \in U, \ \forall k \geq 0, \ \begin{cases} f(x_1, ..., x_n, [0]) = g(x_1, ..., x_n) \\ f(x_1, ..., x_n, [k+1]) = h(x_1, ..., x_n, k, f(x_1, ..., x_n, [k])) \end{cases}$$

Proof: using theorem 3.6, it is similar to the proof of the same result in URS (15).

4.9. Minimalisation Closure

Let $N = \{[n], n \geq 0\}$ be a splinter, let $g \in U$ and $n \geq 1$ such that for all elements $y, x_1, ..., x_n$ of N we have $g(y, x_1, ..., x_n) \neq *$ and there exists an element u of N such that $g(u, x_1, ..., x_n) = [0]$. Then, there exists an element f of U such that for all $x_1, ..., x_n$ in U, $f(x_1, ..., x_n) = [k]$ where k is the least $z \in \mathbb{N}$ such that $g([z], x_1, ..., x_n) = 0$. In other words :

$$f(x_1, ..., x_n) = [\mu_{z \geq 0}(g([z], x_1, ..., x_n) = [0])]$$

Proof: very long but easy, it is similar to the proof of the same result in URS (15).

4.10. μ-recursive Natural Definability

Recursive Functions are naturally definable in any UAS.
Proof: Previous theorems show that recursive functions are naturally definable on any splinter and that any UAS contains a splinter.

Now, we show that *Partial* Recursive Functions are naturally definable in a UAS provided that it contains a *computable* splinter.

4.11. Extended Minimalisation Closure

Let $N = \{[n], n \geq 0\}$ be a computable splinter, let $g \in U$ and $n \geq 1$, there exists $f \in U$ such that :

$$\forall x_1, ..., x_n \in \mathbb{N}, \ f(x_1, ..., x_n) = \begin{cases} [k] & \text{if } k \in N \text{ exists such that } g([k], x_1, ..., x_n) = [0] \\ & \text{and for all } y \in [0, k[, \text{ we have } g([y], x_1, ..., x_n) \notin \{[0], *\} \\ * & \text{if no such } k \text{ exists} \end{cases}$$

Proof: It is deduced from Minimalisation Closure using the decidability of the splinter membership. See (1) for a similar proof in URS theory.

4.12. Partial Recursive Natural Definability

Partial Recursive Functions are naturally definable in any UAS containing a computable splinter.
Proof: It is a consequence of previous theorems.

Remark : There exists a UAS which cannot contain a computable splinter. In (1), it is given a very abstract example of URS which does not contain a computable splinter. According to 2.3, this URS is also a UAS.

4.13. Conclusions

Till now, the main benefit of UAS theory with respect to classical theories is the fact that polyadicity is primitive. This feature has some interesting consequences at the theoretical level: proofs are simpler. But the result of the next section seems more interesting.

5. General Abstraction in a UAS Structure

This section establishes that UAS theory is able to give a *natural* representation (that is to say *without artefact*) to functions which handle a variable number of arguments. We call them *Functions with Variable Arity* (Fva for short). Such functions are programmable in most of functional languages thanks to different artefacts. The language GRAAL (3,4) has natural programs for Fva but it is very close to UAS. Most programming languages use *structuration*. That is the case for Lisp languages which assume that all arguments are given in a list.

Nevertheless, classical theories are unable to give a simple formalization of this feature of functional languages. In Curryfied theories, a variable arity requires strong artefacts. For instance, we can set a special marker always following the last argument of a function or we can, as it seems more usable, give a structure to arguments. Recursive Function Theory deals with polyadic functions but it has no primitive construction which allows to treat a variable number of arguments. Thus, functions with variable arity are handled with the coding of N^∞.

This section shows that UAS are well adapted to the formalization of polyadicity and more precisely to the representation of functions with variable arity. We give an algorithm (the *General Abstraction Algorithm*) which allows to find representations for a very large class of FVA.

Note: For the rest of this section, we assume implicitly a given UAS named U.

5.1. Definition of a Function with Variable Arity

A function with variable arity (Fva) is a map $f:U^\infty \to U$. This is a function which can be applied to any number of arguments.

Example: B such that $B(f, g_1, ..., g_n) = S(K(f), g_1, ..., g_n)$ is a function with variable arity.

5.2. Definition of Natural Representability of Fva

A partial function with variable arity $f:U^\infty \to U$ is *naturally* representable if there exists an element $[f]$ of U called the *representation* of f such that :

$$\forall n \geq 1, \forall x_1, ..., x_n, y \in U, \quad \begin{cases} f(x_1, ..., x_n) = y \\ f(x_1, ..., x_n) \text{ is undefined} \end{cases} \Leftrightarrow \begin{matrix} [f](x_1, ..., x_n) = y \\ [f](x_1, ..., x_n) = * \end{matrix}$$

5.3. Example of Representation

It can be checked that $[B] = T(S(K(L), K(K(S)), S(K(K), S(K(K), I))))$ is a valid representation for the function with variable arity B given above.

5.4. Setting the problem

We want to find algorithmically *natural* representations for a large class of functions with variable arity. The first thing is to specify this class. A function with variable arity belongs to the class if it can be given by a formula

$$f(x_1, ..., x_n) = E$$

where the number of arguments n remains *entirely unspecified* (we just know that $n \geq 1$) and where the right hand side is a *special* term which can contain subterms like $x_i, i \geq 1$, $x_{n-j}, j \geq 0$ and subsequences like $x_i, ..., x_{n-j}, i \geq 1, j \geq 0$ where n is the *unspecified* number of arguments. In other words, we must note that i and j are metavariables standing for integer constants whereas n is not. Because the argument sequence $x_1, ..., x_n$ is unspecified (it has no definite length), this equation defines the result of applying f to any number of arguments : it defines a Fva. We will give a formal description of this class of functions with variable arity.

5.5. Convention concerning Variables Names

In the rest of this section, the name x is devoted to the notation of the unspecified argument sequences whereas n is reserved for the notation of the indefinite length.

5.6. Minimal Arity of a Function with Variable Arity

When we are looking at the class of functions with variable arity informally defined above, we may remark that the number of arguments of the functions has a minimal bound. For instance, if a term contains x_4 then there must be at least four arguments. If it contains x_{n-2}, then there must exist at least three arguments. This minimal arity is included in the formal definition of our class of functions with variable arity.

Example: The function defined as $f(x_1, ..., x_n) = S(K(x_1), K(x_2), x_2, ..., x_{n-1})$ must have at least three arguments.

5.7. Definition of A_k-terms and A_k-sequences

An A_k-term is a term which can occur in the right hand side of the definition of a Fva with minimal arity k. Thus the index is called the *minimal arity*. These new terms and sequences are defined inductively :

- Every constant (element of U) is a A_1-term
- If $i \geq 1$, x_i is a A_i-term
- If $j \geq 0$, x_{n-j} is a A_{j+1}-term
- If $i \geq 1$ and $j \geq 0$, $(x_i, ..., x_{n-j})$ is a A_{i+j}-sequence
- If t is a A_k-term, (t) is a A_k-sequence
- If $i \geq 1, j \geq 0$ and (s) is a A_k-sequence, $(s, x_i, ..., x_{n-j})$ is a $A_{\max(i+j,k)}$-sequence
- If t is a A_i-term and (s) is a A_j-sequence, (s, t) is a $A_{\max(i,j)}$-sequence
- If t is a A_i-term and (s) is a A_j-sequence, $t(s)$ is a $A_{\max(i,j)}$-term
- Closure Rule

Example: $K(x_1, x_2)(x_3, x_5, ..., x_{n-4}, x_3)$ is a A_9-term.

Remark : Ordinary sequences in previous sections were defined from right to left whereas A_k-sequences are defined in the reverse order. This has no consequence on the nature of sequence but it reveals itself much more practical for the construction and the proof of the algorithm.

5.8. Definition of an A_k-assignment

Let $k \geq 1$ be a natural number, an A_k-assignment is a sequence $(X_1, ..., X_N)$ with a definite length $N \geq k$ and $X_1, ..., X_N \in U$.

5.9. Definition of a A_k-valuation

Let $k \geq 1$ be a natural number and $(X_1, ..., X_N)$ be an A_k-assignment, it defines a A_k-valuation $\beta(X_1, ..., X_N)$ which maps A_k-terms on U and A_k-sequences on finite sequences over U. $\beta(X_1, ..., X_N)$ is defined inductively as :

- $\beta(X_1, ..., X_N)[u] = u$ if $u \in U$
- $\beta(X_1, ..., X_N)[x_i] = X_i$, $i \geq 1$
- $\beta(X_1, ..., X_N)[x_{n-j}] = X_{N-j}$, $j \geq 0$
- $\beta(X_1, ..., X_N)[(x_i, ..., x_{n-j})] = (X_i, ..., X_{N-j})$, $i \geq 1$, $j \geq 0$
- $\beta(X_1, ..., X_N)[(t)] = (\beta(X_1, ..., X_N)[t])$
- $\beta(X_1, ..., X_N)[(s, t)] = (\beta(X_1, ..., X_N)[s], \beta(X_1, ..., X_N)[t])$
- $\beta(X_1, ..., X_N)[(s, x_i, ..., x_{n-j})] = (\beta(X_1, ..., X_N)[s], X_i, ..., X_{N-j})$
- $\beta(X_1, ..., X_N)[t(s)] = \beta(X_1, ..., X_N)[t](\beta(X_1, ..., X_N)[s])$

Example: $\beta(a, b, c)[S(K(x_1), x_2, ..., x_n)] = S(K(a), b, c)$

5.10. A_k-equations

An A_k-equation is an equation
$$f(x_1, ..., x_n) = E$$
where E is a A_k-term.

5.11. Definition of a Function with Variable Arity

A function with variable arity f is defined by an A_k-equation
$$f(x_1, ..., x_n) = E$$
This equation defines f as follows :

$$\forall X_1, ..., X_N \in U\text{-}\{*\}, \quad \begin{cases} f(X_1, ..., X_N) = \beta(X_1, ..., X_N)[E] & \text{if } N \geq k \\ f(X_1, ..., X_N) = * & \text{if } N < k \end{cases}$$

and: $f(X_1, ..., X_N) = *$ if one of the X_i is $*$.

As we can remark, the class of functions with variable arity covered by this definition is very general. The functions that we are unable to represent directly as A_k-equations have complex specifications.

5.12. Example of Definition

The A_3-equation $f(x_1, ..., x_n) = T(x_1, x_2)(x_3, .., x_n)$ defines the function with variable arity f such that $f(a) = *$, $f(a, b) = *$, $f(a, b, c) = T(a, b)(c)$, $f(a, b, c, d) = T(a, b)(c, d)$, and so on.

5.13. General Abstraction Theorem

This theorem is the main theorem of the article because it establishes that UAS theory is able to handle functions with variable arity in a natural way.

MAIN THEOREM: Every function with variable arity defined by an A-equation is naturally representable in any Uniformly Applicative Structure.

6. Proof and algorithm for the Natural Representation Theorem

The proof is rather long because it requires several existence lemmas. It is constructive in the sense that it gives the algorithm for finding a natural representation for functions with variable arity defined using A-equations. The proof is given in this section which begins with several lemmas. Proofs are rather technical and repetitive and the reader may jump directly to the main proof.

In all these lemmas, the fact that an expression is different from $*$ is done by construction using the rules given in the axioms or that an abstraction or a uniform fixed-point is always defined following lemma 3 of 3.7.. These proofs will not be explicited in the following lemmas.

6.1. Lemma Alpha

There exists an element α of U such that :

$$\forall n \geq 1, \forall f \in U\text{-}\{*\}, \forall a_1, ..., a_n \in U, \quad \begin{cases} \alpha(f) \neq * \\ \alpha(f)(a_1, ..., a_n) = f(a_1, ..., a_n)(a_1, ..., a_n) \end{cases}$$

Proof : α is the Γ of the Lemma 1 in 3.7.

6.2. Lemma Theta 1

There exists an element θ_1 of U such that :

$$\forall n \geq 2, \forall f \in U\text{-}\{*\}, \forall a_1, ..., a_n \in U, \quad \begin{cases} \theta_1(f) \neq * \\ \theta_1(f)(a_1)(a_2, ..., a_n) = f(a_1, a_2, ..., a_n) \end{cases}$$

Proof : Let us compute,
$$f(a_1, a_2, ..., a_n)$$
$$= K(f)(a_2, ..., a_n)(K(a_1)(a_2, ..., a_n), a_2, ..., a_n)$$
$$= L(K(f), K(a_1))(a_2, ..., a_n)$$
Thus, we choose $\theta_1 = \lambda f.(\lambda a_1.(L(K(f), K(a_1))))$

6.3. Lemma Theta 2

There exists an element θ_2 of U such that :

$$\forall n \geq 2, \forall f \in U\text{-}\{*\}, \forall a_1, ..., a_n \in U, \quad \begin{cases} \theta_2(f) \neq * \\ \theta_2(f)(a_1, ..., a_n) = f(a_1)(a_2, ..., a_n) \end{cases}$$

Proof : Let us compute,
$$f(a_1)(a_2, ..., a_n)$$
$$= f(I(a_1, ..., a_n))(a_2, ..., a_n)$$
$$= B(f, I)(a_1, ..., a_n)(a_2, ..., a_n) \quad \text{B is given in 5.1 and 5.3}$$
$$= T(B(f, I))(a_1, ..., a_n)$$

Thus, we choose $\theta_2 = \lambda f.(T(B(f, I)))$

6.4. Lemma Eta

There exists an element η of U such that :

$$\forall n \geq 1, \forall f, m \in U\text{-}\{*\}, \forall a_1, ..., a_n \in U, \quad \begin{cases} \eta(f, m) \neq * \\ \eta(f, m)(a_1, ..., a_n) = f(a_1, ..., a_n, m) \end{cases}$$

Proof : We distinghish the cases $n = 1$ and $n > 1$ in order to use D,

$n = 1 \quad \eta(f, m)(a_1)$
$\quad = f(a_1, m)$
$\quad = f(I(a_1), K(m)(a_1))$
$\quad = B(f, I, K(m))(a_1)$

$n > 1 \quad \eta(f, m)(a_1, a_2, ..., a_n)$
$\quad = f(a_1, a_2, ..., a_n, m)$
$\quad = \theta_1(f)(a_1)(a_2, ..., a_n, m)$
$\quad = \eta(\theta_1(f)(a_1), m)(a_2, ..., a_n) \quad \eta \text{ used at level n-1}$
$\quad = \eta(\theta_1(f)(a_1), K(m)(a_1))(a_2, ..., a_n)$
$\quad = B(\eta, \theta_1(f), K(m))(a_1)(a_2, ..., a_n)$
$\quad = \theta_2(B(\eta, \theta_1(f), K(m)))(a_1, a_2, ..., a_n)$

Thus, it suffices to have :
$$\eta(f, m) = D(B(f, I, K(m)), \theta_2(B(\eta, \theta_1(f), K(m))))$$

We just have to extract the uniform fixed-point using 3.5 and 3.7 :
$$\eta = Y(\lambda n.(\lambda f, m.(D(B(f, I, K(m)), \theta_2(B(n, \theta_1(f), K(m))))))$$

6.5. Lemma Delta

There exists an element δ of U such that :

$$\forall n \geq 1, \forall f, g \in U\text{-}\{*\}, \forall a_1, ..., a_n \in U, \quad \begin{cases} \delta(f, g) \neq * \\ \delta(f, g)(a_1, ..., a_n) = f \text{ if } n = 1 \\ \delta(f, g)(a_1, ..., a_n) = g \text{ if } n > 1 \end{cases}$$

Proof : Let us take $\delta = S(K(D), S(K(K), P_1), S(K(K), P_2))$,
then we have : $\delta(f, g)(a_1, ..., a_n) = D(K(f), K(g))(a_1, ..., a_n)$

6.6. Lemma Epsilon

There exists an element ε of U such that :

$$\forall n \geq 2, \forall f \in U\text{-}\{*\}, \forall a_1, ..., a_n \in U, \quad \begin{cases} \varepsilon(f) \neq * \\ \varepsilon(f)(a_1, ..., a_n) = f(a_1, ..., a_{n-1}) \end{cases}$$

Proof : The proof is similar to that of Lemma Eta, it distinghishes the cases $n = 2$ and $n > 2$ in order to use D. The reader may check that :
$$\varepsilon(f)(a_1, a_2) = f(a_1) = B(f, I)(a_1, a_2)$$
$$\varepsilon(f)(a_1, a_2, ..., a_n) = f(a_1, ..., a_{n-1}) = \theta_2(B(\varepsilon, \theta_1(f)))(a_1, ..., a_n) \quad \text{if } n > 2$$

Therefore, the function which must be applied to $a_1, ..., a_n$ is :
$$\delta(B(f, I), \theta_2(B(\varepsilon, \theta_1(f))))(a_2, ..., a_n)$$

And the result is :

$$\delta(B(f, I), \theta_2(B(\varepsilon, \theta_1(f))))(a_2, ..., a_n)(a_1, ..., a_n)$$
$$= K(\delta(B(f, I), \theta_2(B(\varepsilon, \theta_1(f))))(a_1, ..., a_n)(a_2, ..., a_n)(a_1, ..., a_n)$$
$$= T(K(\delta(B(f, I), \theta_2(B(\varepsilon, \theta_1(f))))(a_1, ..., a_n)(a_1, ..., a_n)$$
$$= \alpha(T(K(\delta(B(f, I), \theta_2(B(\varepsilon, \theta_1(f)))))))(a_1, ..., a_n)$$

Then, we just have to extract the uniform fix-point :
$$\varepsilon = Y(\lambda e.(\lambda f.\alpha(T(K(\delta(B(f, I), \theta_2(B(e, \theta_1(f)))))))))$$

6.7. Lemma Chi

There exists a family $(\chi_p)_{p \geq 0}$ of elements of U such that :
$$\forall p \geq 0, \ n \geq p+1, \ \forall a_1, ..., a_n \in U, \quad \chi_p(a_1, ..., a_n) = a_{n-p}$$

Proof : Let us compute the number of arguments,
$$[I](a_1) = [1] = K([1])(a_1)$$
$$[I](a_1, a_2, ..., a_n) = [s]([I](a_2, ..., a_n)) = B([s], [I])(a_2, ..., a_n) = T(K(B([s], [I])))(a_1, ..., a_n)$$

Thus : $[I] = D(K([1]), T(K(B([s], [I]))))$
And : $[I] = Y(\lambda I.(D(K([1]), T(K(B([s], I))))))$
Now :

$$
\begin{aligned}
a_{n-p} &= I(a_{n-p}, ..., a_n) \\
&= B(T, K)(I)(a_{n-p-1}, ..., a_n) \\
&= B(T, K)(B(T, K)(I))(a_{n-p-2}, ..., a_n) \\
&= ... \\
&= [n - (p-1)](B(T, K), I)(a_1, ..., a_n) \quad \text{see remark in 4.4} \\
&= [-]([n], [p-1])(B(T, K), I)(a_1, ..., a_n) \quad [-] \text{ is substraction} \\
&= [-]([I](a_1, ..., a_n), K([p-1])(a_1, ..., a_n))(B(T, K), I)(a_1, ..., a_n) \\
&= B([-], [I], K([p-1]))(a_1, ..., a_n)(B(T, K), I)(a_1, ..., a_n) \\
&= S(B([-], [I], K([p-1])), K(B(T, K)), K(I))(a_1, ..., a_n)(a_1, ..., a_n) \\
&= \alpha(S(B([-], [I], K([p-1])), K(B(T, K)), K(I)))(a_1, ..., a_n)
\end{aligned}
$$

Thus :
$$\chi_p = \alpha(S(B([-], [I], K([p-1])), K(B(T, K)), K(I)))$$

6.8. Lemma Kappa

There exists a family $(\kappa_q)_{q \geq 0}$ of elements of U such that :

$$\forall q \geq 1, \ n > q, \ \forall f \in U\text{-}\{*\}, \ \forall a_1, ..., a_n \in U, \quad \begin{cases} \kappa_q(f) \neq * \\ \kappa_q(f)(a_1, ..., a_n) = f(a_1, ..., a_{n-q}) \end{cases}$$

Proof : We distinguish the cases where $q = n-1$ and $q < n-1$.
If q = n-1, $\kappa_q(f)(a_1, ..., a_n) = f(a_1) = f(I(a_1, ..., a_n)) = B(f, I)(a_1, ..., a_n)$
If $q < n-1$, $\kappa_q(f)(a_1, ..., a_n) = f(a_1, ..., a_{n-q}) = \theta_2(B(\kappa_q, \theta_1(f)))(a_1, ..., a_n)$

In order to choose the good function using D, we remark that the sequence $a_2, ..., a_{n-(q-1)}$ has length 1 whenever $q = n-1$. Thus the function to apply is :
$$\delta(B(f, I), \theta_2(B(\kappa_q, \theta_1(f))))(a_2, ..., a_{n-(q-1)})$$
and the result is :
$$
\begin{aligned}
&\delta(B(f, I), \theta_2(B(\kappa_q, \theta_1(f))))(a_2, ..., a_{n-(q-1)})(a_1, ..., a_n) \\
&= T(K(\delta(B(f, I), \theta_2(B(\kappa_q, \theta_1(f))))))(a_1, ..., a_{n-(q-1)})(a_1, ..., a_n) \\
&= \kappa_{q-1}(T(K(\delta(B(f, I), \theta_2(B(\kappa_q, \theta_1(f))))))(a_1, ..., a_n)(a_1, ..., a_n) \\
&= \alpha(\kappa_{q-1}(T(K(\delta(B(f, I), \theta_2(B(\kappa_q, \theta_1(f)))))))))(a_1, ..., a_n)
\end{aligned}
$$

Thus : $\kappa_q(f) = \alpha(\kappa_{q-1}(T(K(\delta(B(f, I), \theta_2(B(\kappa_q, \theta_1(f))))))))$
So that :
$$\begin{cases} \kappa_q(f) = Y(\lambda k.(\lambda f.(\alpha(\kappa_{q-1}(T(K(\delta(B(f, I), \theta_2(B(k, \theta_1(f)))))))))))) \\ \kappa_1 = \varepsilon \end{cases}$$

6.9. Lemma Tau

There exists a family $(\tau_p^q)_{p\geq 1, q\geq 0}$ of elements of U such that :

$\forall p \geq 1,\ q \geq 0,\ n \geq p+q,\ \forall f \in U\text{-}\{*\},\ \forall a_1, ..., a_n \in U,\ \begin{cases} \tau_p^q(f) \neq * \\ \tau_p^q(f)(a_1, ..., a_n) = f(a_p, ..., a_{n-q}) \end{cases}$

Proof : Let us compute with $p > 1$, thus $n > 1$,

$$f(a_p, ..., a_{n-q}) = \tau_{p-1}^q(f)(a_2, ..., a_n) = T(K(\tau_{p-1}^q(f)))(a_1, ..., a_n)$$

Therefore :

$\begin{cases} \tau_1^q = \kappa_q \\ \tau_p^q = \lambda f.(T(K(\tau_{p-1}^q(f)))) \end{cases}$

6.10. Lemma Nu

There exists a family $(v_p^q)_{p\geq 1, q\geq 0}$ of elements of U such that :

$\forall p \geq 1,\ q \geq 0,\ n \geq 1,\ m \geq p+q,\ \forall f, a_1, ..., a_n \in U\text{-}\{*\},\ \forall b_1, ..., b_m \in U,$

$\begin{cases} v_p^q(f) \neq * \\ v_p^q(f)(a_1, ..., a_n) \neq * \\ v_p^q(f)(a_1, ..., a_n)(b_1, ..., b_m) = f(a_1, ..., a_n, b_p, ..., b_{m-q}) \end{cases}$

Proof : We distinguish cases $n = 1$ and $n > 1$ in order to use D,

$n = 1$
$\begin{aligned} & f(a_1, b_p, ..., b_{m-q}) \\ =\ & \theta_1(f)(a_1)(b_p, ..., b_{m-q}) \\ =\ & \tau_p^q(\theta_1(f)(a_1))(b_1, ..., b_m) \\ =\ & B(\tau_p^q, (\theta_1(f)))(a_1)(b_1, ..., b_m) \end{aligned}$

$n > 1$
$\begin{aligned} & f(a_1, ..., a_n, y_p, ..., y_{m-q}) \\ =\ & \theta_1(f)(a_1)(a_2, ..., a_n, b_p, ..., b_{m-q}) \\ =\ & v_p^q(\theta_1(f)(a_1))(a_2, ..., a_n)(b_1, ..., b_m) \qquad v_p^q \text{ used at level } n-1 \\ =\ & B(v_p^q, \theta_1(f))(a_1)(a_2, ..., a_n)(b_1, ..., b_m) \\ =\ & \theta_2(B(v_p^q, \theta_1(f)))(a_1, ..., a_n)(b_1, ..., b_m) \end{aligned}$

Therefore, it suffices to have :

$$v_p^q(f) = D(B(\tau_p^q, \theta_1(f)), \theta_2(B(v_p^q, (\theta_1(f)))))$$

And as usual :

$$v_p^q = Y(\lambda n.(\lambda f.(D(B(\tau_p^q, \theta_1(f)), \theta_2(B(n, (\theta_1(f))))))))$$

6.11. The main proof

Now we enter the main proof. Let $f(x_1, ..., x_n) = M$ be the definition of a function with variable arity. We construct a term $\Lambda(M) \in U$ which is the natural representation of the function f. We construct the element $\Lambda(M)$ inductively on the structure of M. We must take into account the cases where M is a constant, a variable x_i or x_{n-j} and the cases where M is an application f(s). In this last case, we make an induction on the sequence s. We give the proof that the constructed $\Lambda(M)$ is such that $\Lambda(M)(X_1, ..., X_N) = \beta(X_1, ..., X_N)[M]$ whenever N is greater than the minimal arity of M. When N is less than this minimal arity or if one of the X_i is *, it is easy to check that $\Lambda(M)(X_1, ..., X_N) = *$. As usual, the symbol $\equiv$ is to be read as ... is identical to ... .

6.11.1. M is an constant

If $M \equiv u$ and $u \in U$, then $\Lambda(M) = K(u)$ since we have :

$\begin{aligned} & \Lambda(M)(X_1, ..., X_N) \\ =\ & K(u)(X_1, ..., X_N) \\ =\ & u \\ =\ & \beta(X_1, ..., X_N)[u] \\ =\ & \beta(X_1, ..., X_N)[M] \end{aligned}$

6.11.2. M is a variable x_i

If $M \equiv x_i, i \geq 1$, then $\Lambda(M) = P_i$ since we have:
$$\Lambda(M)(X_1, ..., X_N)$$
$$= P_i(X_1, ..., X_N)$$
$$= X_i$$
$$= \beta(X_1, ..., X_N)[x_i]$$
$$= \beta(X_1, ..., X_N)[M]$$

6.11.3. M is a variable x_{n-j}

If $M \equiv x_{n-j}, j \geq 0$, then $\Lambda(M) = \chi_j$ since we have:
$$\Lambda(M)(X_1, ..., X_N)$$
$$= \chi_j(X_1, ..., X_N)$$
$$= X_{N-j}$$
$$= \beta(X_1, ..., X_N)[x_{n-j}]$$
$$= \beta(X_1, ..., X_N)[M]$$

6.11.4. M is an application $f(x_i, .., x_{n-j})$

If $M \equiv f(x_i, .., x_{n-j}), i \geq 1, j \geq 0$, then $\Lambda(M) = \alpha(\Lambda(\tau_i^j(f)))$ since we have:
$$\Lambda(M)(X_1, ..., X_N)$$
$$= \alpha(\Lambda(\tau_i^j(f)))(X_1, ..., X_N)$$
$$= \Lambda(\tau_i^j(f))(X_1, ..., X_N)(X_1, ..., X_N)$$
$$= \beta(X_1, ..., X_N)[\tau_i^j(f)](X_1, ..., X_N)$$
$$= \tau_i^j(\beta(X_1, ..., X_N)[f])(X_1, ..., X_N)$$
$$= \beta(X_1, ..., X_N)[f](X_i, .., X_{N-j})$$
$$= \beta(X_1, ..., X_N)[f(x_i, .., x_{n-j})]$$
$$= \beta(X_1, ..., X_N)[M]$$

6.11.5. M is an application $f(a_1, ..., a_k)$

If $M \equiv f(a_1, ..., a_k), k \geq 1$, then $\Lambda(M) = S(\Lambda(f), \Lambda(a_1), .., \Lambda(a_k))$ since we have:
$$\Lambda(M)(X_1, ..., X_N)$$
$$= S(\Lambda(f), \Lambda(a_1), .., \Lambda(a_k))(X_1, ..., X_N)$$
$$= \Lambda(f)(X_1, ..., X_N)(\Lambda(a_1)(X_1, ..., X_N), .., \Lambda(a_k)(X_1, ..., X_N))$$
$$= \beta(X_1, ..., X_N)[f](\beta(X_1, ..., X_N)[a_1], .., \beta(X_1, ..., X_N)[a_k])$$
$$= \beta(X_1, ..., X_N)[f(a_1, ..., a_k)]$$
$$= \beta(X_1, ..., X_N)[M]$$

6.11.6. M is an application $f(s,t)$

If $M \equiv f(s, t)$ where s is a A_k-sequence and t is a term, then $\Lambda(M) = \Lambda(\eta(f, t)(s))$ since we have:
$$\Lambda(M)(X_1, ..., X_N)$$
$$= \Lambda(\eta(f, t)(s))(X_1, ..., X_N)$$
$$= \beta(X_1, ..., X_N)[\eta(f, t)(s)]$$
$$= \beta(X_1, ..., X_N)[\eta](\beta(X_1, ..., X_N)[f], \beta(X_1, ..., X_N)[t])(\beta(X_1, ..., X_N)[s])$$
$$= \eta(\beta(X_1, ..., X_N)[f], \beta(X_1, ..., X_N)[t])(\beta(X_1, ..., X_N)[s])$$
$$= \beta(X_1, ..., X_N)[f](\beta(X_1, ..., X_N)[s], \beta(X_1, ..., X_N)[t])$$
$$= \beta(X_1, ..., X_N)[f](\beta(X_1, ..., X_N)[s, t])$$
$$= \beta(X_1, ..., X_N)[f(s, t)]$$
$$= \beta(X_1, ..., X_N)[M]$$

6.11.7. M is an application $f(s, x_i, .., x_{n-j})$

If $M \equiv f(s, x_i, .., x_{n-j})$, s being a A_k-sequence and $i \geq 1, j \geq 0$, then $\Lambda(M) = \alpha(\Lambda(v_i^j(f)(s)))$ since we have :

$$\begin{aligned}
&\Lambda(M)(X_1, ..., X_N) \\
&= \alpha(\Lambda(v_i^j(f)(s)))(X_1, ..., X_N) \\
&= \Lambda(v_i^j(f)(s))(X_1, ..., X_N)(X_1, ..., X_N) \\
&= \beta(X_1, ..., X_N)[v_i^j(f)(s)](X_1, ..., X_N) \\
&= \beta(X_1, ..., X_N)[v_i^j](\beta(X_1, ..., X_N)[f])(\beta(X_1, ..., X_N)[s])(X_1, ..., X_N) \\
&= v_i^j(\beta(X_1, ..., X_N)[f])(\beta(X_1, ..., X_N)[s])(X_1, ..., X_N) \\
&= \beta(X_1, ..., X_N)[f](\beta(X_1, ..., X_N)[s], X_i, .., X_{N-j}) \\
&= \beta(X_1, ..., X_N)[f]\beta(X_1, ..., X_N)[(s, x_i, .., x_{n-j})] \\
&= \beta(X_1, ..., X_N)[f(s, x_i, .., x_{n-j})] \\
&= \beta(X_1, ..., X_N)[M]
\end{aligned}$$

As presented in this abstract, the proof is not complete. The definition of $\Lambda(M)$ follows the inductive definition of A_k-terms and A_k-sequences. It contains the sketch of the proof which can be formally done by a recurrence on $\zeta(M) = \zeta_1(M) + \zeta_2(M)$ where $\zeta_1(M)$ is the number of subsequences $x_i, .., x_{n-j}$ occuring in M and $\zeta_2(M)$ is the maximal length of a A_k-sequence containing some indexed x at first level in M.

6.12. Optimizations

As usual, an abstraction algorithm is first given in a simple form which allows simple proofs of its behaviour and there exists always a better version of it. A usual and very useful optimization is the rule :

$$\Lambda(M) = K(M) \quad \text{if M does not contain any } x_i, x_{n-j} \text{ or } x_i, .., x_{n-j}.$$

which is used in most of the Abstraction algorithms (6). This rule allows to shorten the representations of Fva. Some other rules are possible, they come mainly from the works on abstraction in Combinatory calculi.

6.13. Example

Let us find the representation of a rotation functional defined as :

$$rotl(f)(x_1, ..., x_n) = f(x_2, .., x_n, x_1)$$

We have that :

$$rotl = \lambda f.\Lambda(f(x_2, .., x_n, x_1))$$

Let us compute :

$$\begin{aligned}
&\Lambda(f(x_2, .., x_n, x_1)) \\
&= \Lambda(\eta(f, x_1)(x_2, ..., x_n)) \\
&= \alpha(\Lambda(\tau_2^0(\eta(f, x_1)))) \\
&= \alpha(S(\Lambda(\tau_2^0), \Lambda(\eta(f, x_1)))) \\
&= \alpha(S(K(\tau_2^0), S(\Lambda(\eta), \Lambda(f), \Lambda(x_1)))) \\
&= \alpha(S(K(\tau_2^0), S(K(\eta), K(f), P_1)))
\end{aligned}$$

Thus, we have :

$$rotl = \lambda f.\alpha(S(K(\tau_2^0), S(K(\eta), K(f), P_1)))$$

which is a classical computation using the λ-algorithm given in section 3.5.

6.14. Example

Let us search the representation of a function *plus* such that :

$$plus(x_1, ..., x_n) = x_1 + ... + x_n$$

This definition is not in the form of an Λ-equation. We must translate it as :

$$plus(x_1, ..., x_n) = \begin{cases} x_1 & \text{if } n = 1 \\ +(x_1, plus(x_2, .., x_n)) & \text{if } n > 1 \end{cases}$$

Thus we can use the element D of the URS and write :

$$plus = D(\Lambda(x_1), \Lambda(+(x_1, plus(x_2, .., x_n))))$$

Then, we can extract a fixed-point with the element Y of *Uniform Recursion* theorem :

$$plus = Y(\lambda p.D(\Lambda(x_1), \Lambda(+(x_1, p(x_2, .., x_n)))))$$

Thus, we have constructed an addition function with variable arity (*plus*) from a binary addition (+).

6.15. Example

A paradigmatic example which shows the interest of this uncurryfied theory is the function f such that :
$$f(x_1, ..., x_n) = x_n$$
Its translation is $\Lambda(x_n) = \chi_0$. This function has no counterpart in Curryfied theories.

7. Conclusions

Uniformly Applicative Structures inherit the philosophy of URS but it is more than just another Computability theory. UAS proposes particular features which can be recovered under the informal concept of *naturality*, that is the ability to describe computable functions without extending the *toolbox* of the theory with special constructs. This abstract notion of naturality is essential for a practical use in Computer Science.

As it has been mentioned, the UAS theory has been benefitly used in the design of the programming language GRAAL which has a very fast reduction machine based on the principles presented in this article. The authors claim that naturality is the main reason for this efficiency because the design of application is free from any construction and any constraint.

The main result presented in this article is the *General Abstraction* theorem. It gives natural representations for functions with variable arity starting from the very general form called A-equation. As we have seen in previous examples, it allows to define functions which would be very difficult to define in other theories (such as *rotl*). But it is sometimes needed to translate primitive definitions into A-equations. This is obviously a research area. Another one is the use of several different *unspecified* sequences at the same time in the definition of a function in order to handle definitions such as :
$$f(x_1, ..., x_n)(y_1, ..., y_m) = E$$

Moreover, the example 6.14 above shows that some functions whose specification seems complex can be turned into A_k-definitions. It is not known at the present time if we can generalize this scheme.

It seems that the *General Abstraction* theorem has no equivalent in other known theories. Natural representation of functions with variable arity has no sense in a Curryfied theory since Curryfication cannot handle a variable number of arguments. Even generalized to polyadic functions, the λ-notation seems to have no way to describe functions with variable arity unless the theory is extended with A-terms and A-substitution as a primitive. Other theories need the coding of U^∞ or explicit use of structures (a special way of coding). Therefore, the natural and algorithmic representation of functions with variable arity is a particular property of Uniformly Applicative Structures.

Ackowledgments : The authors are thankfull to the Commitee members, to Remi LEGRAND to Eric PEROTTET to Djamil SARNI for helpful discussions and comments.

Bibliography

[1] H.P. Barendregt, *Normed Uniformly Reflexive Structures*, in Notes on Logic and Computer Science (LOCOS) **24** (1975).
[2] H.P. Barendregt, *The λ-calculus, its Syntax and Semantics*, Studies in Logic and Foundations of Mathematics, North Holland **103** (Amsterdam, 1981).
[3] P. Bellot, *A Functional Programming system with Uncurryfied Combinators and its Reduction Machine*, in First European Symposium on Programming (ESOP86), Lecture Notes in Computer Science **213** (Saarbrücken, 1986) pp. 82-98.
[4] P.Bellot, *Sur les sentiers du GRAAL, Etude, Conception et Réalisation d'un Système de Programmation sans Variable*, Thèse d'Etat, Université Pierre et Marie Curie (Paris 6), Rapport LITP **86-62** (Paris, 1986).
[5] P. Bellot, V. Jay, *A theory for Natural Modelisation and Implementation of Functions with Variable Arity*, in Third International Conference on Functional Programming Languages and Computer Architecture (FPLCA87), Lecture Notes in Computer Science **274** (Portland, 1987) pp. 212-233.
[6] H.B. Curry, R. Feys, *Combinatory Logic, Vol. I*, North Holland (Amsterdam, 1958).
[7] N.J. Cutland, *Computability, an Introduction to Recursive Function Theory*, Cambridge University Press (1980).
[8] S. Eilenberg, C.C. Elgot, *Recursiveness*, Academic Press (New-York, 1970).
[9] S.C. Kleene, *Introduction to Metamathematics*, Van Nostrand (1952).

[10] G. Kreisel, J. Krivine, *Elements of Mathematical Logic*, North Holland (Amsterdam, 1967).
[11] H. Rogers, *Theory of Recursive Functions and Effective Computability*, Mc Graw Hill (New-York, 1967).
[12] H.R. Strong, *Algebraically Generalized Function Theory*, in IBM Journal for Research and Development (New-York, 1968) pp. 465-475.
[13] H.R. Strong, *An Algebraically Approach through URS to General Recursive Function Theory*, Doctoral Dissertation, University of Washington (Washington, 1967).
[14] H.R. Strong, *Construction for Models of Algebraically Generalized Function Theory*, in Journal of Symbolic Logic **35** (1970) pp. 401-435.
[15] E.G. Wagner, *Uniformly Reflexive Structures : An axiomatic approach to Computability*, RADC-HAC join Symposium on Logic, Computability and Automata (New-York, 1965).
[16] E.G. Wagner, *Constructible and Highly Constructible URS*, (1974).
[17] E.G. Wagner, *Functorial Hierarchies of Functional Languages*, in Formal Description of Programming Concepts, D. Bjorner ed. (North-Holland, 1983).
[18] E.G. Wagner, *Uniformly Reflexive Structure : On the Nature of Godelization and Relative Computability*, in Trans ΛMS **144** (1969) pp. 1-41.

A PROOF TECHNIQUE FOR REGISTER ATOMICITY
(Preliminary Version)

Baruch Awerbuch [1]
Lefteris M. Kirousis [2]
Evangelos Kranakis [3]
Paul M. B. Vitányi [3,4]

ABSTRACT

An implementation of a concurrent data object is wait-free if any process can complete any operation in a bounded number of steps, independently of the execution speeds of the programs. Much recent work has been done on concurrent access of shared variables by asynchronous processes. That work shows that implementing such shared variables does not require synchronization (by e.g. mutual exclusion), but can be solved in a wait-free manner. A fruitful paradigm in this context is the notion of a shared register satisfying a niceness condition called atomicity. Recent proposed solutions have led to the realization that: (1) neither the problem to be solved nor the model required were rigorously defined, (2) there was no clear insight in what constitutes a good proof of correctness in the area, and (3) the proposed protocols are so complicated that although correctness may be possible in a "platonic fashion", verifiability seems impossible to attain by human beings. A lot of controversy and allegations about constructions and proofs have arisen. Consequently, we have spent great effort to put the area on a rigorous basis. The thrust of this paper is to provide a new proof technique, and demonstrate its applicability by a nontrivial example. In other words, a new model is rigorously presented for the first time, and then a new method is given for proving register atomicity. It is then used to give a simple proof of the atomicity of the first and only direct construction of a multireader multiwriter register from atomic 1-reader 1-writer registers. (This construction was given in [8], by two of the present authors, with a completely different proof.)

---

(1) Department of Mathematics and Laboratory for Computer Science, MIT, Cambridge MA 02139, USA
(2) University of Patras, Department of Mathematics, Patras, Greece
(3) Centrum voor Wiskunde en Informatica, P.O. Box 4079, 1009 AB Amsterdam, The Netherlands
(4) Faculteit Wiskunde en Informatica, Universiteit van Amsterdam, The Netherlands

1. Introduction

Concurrency control of asynchronous processes is often realized by actively serializing concurrent actions, using synchronization primitives like mutual exclusion, semaphores, and locking. Thus, although it *seems* that the actions are executed concurrently, in the system they are *actually* executed serially in some order. It has been pointed out in [3] that to implement such primitives we first need interprocess communication through a shared memory unit, which we shall call a *register*, even if the processors communicate by message passing. This suggests that the problem of simultaneous memory access needs to be solved without recourse to synchronisation primitives. It is desired that such a solution involves *no waiting* by one operator for another one. Thus we kill two birds with one stone, since it is the waiting involved in synchronization methods to control the communication between asynchronous participants, which may make such solutions unacceptable. Note, that asynchrony need not be due solely to hardware, but can also be caused by multiple users on the various machines. The problem of providing general wait-free asynchronous communication interfaces becomes more acute, as more and more hardware from different technologies, scale and speed continue to be connected in computer networks and other complexes. The purpose of the present investigation is to examine the feasibility of such general interfaces. In particular, we analyse the problem of how to implement a shared register which can be read by different asynchronous processors (the readers) and be written by different asynchronous processors (the writers) in a truly concurrent fashion. That is, without any restrictions to prevent simultaneous access and making no assumptions, either about the relative durations of the reads and writes, or about the actual timing of the lower level constituent operation executions.

More precisely, we are given some registers with certain restrictions on their mode of operation, e.g. that only a certain number of operators are allowed to access each one of them. We are asked to construct a more powerful (*compound*) register without some of the original restrictions, while retaining some of the positive characteristics of the subregisters, e.g. their serializable mode of operation (otherwise called *atomicity*). These compound registers will comprise a set of registers (i.e. *subregisters*) and an operation execution on the compound register will consist of a sequence of operation executions on the subregisters that follow a given *protocol*. All we require from the constructed protocol is that it guarantees the *existence* of some total (i.e., linear) order in which the operation executions on the compound register could have taken place (external consistency). This order, in some sense, represents the succession these operations *seemingly* follow. Of course, for such a total order to be meaningful, it must satisfy certain additional requirements. For example, there should be no second write placed by this order between a read and the write it reads (internal consistency). If we assume that there is a global (i.e. referring to all registers) time-reference system (otherwise, *a global clock*), and if all subactions of an operation execution on the compound register precede in time all the subactions of a second operation execution on the compound register, then this order must place the second operation execution after the first one. In general, we have a relation on the operation executions which is naturally imposed by the problem (e.g., an acyclic relation that tells if an operation execution can have an influence on another), and we desire the existence of a total order that extends this relation, but without violating the above restrictions. If this is possible for each scenario of operation executions of a proposed register, then the register is atomic.

In the next section we present the model rigourously, and give two general atomicity criteria that are suitable for proving register atomicity (the second criterion is a simple variation of the first, but is more suitable for 1-writer registers). Our work is in the spirit of the general 'causality' model proposed by Lamport [3], and we have no need to assume the existence of a global clock. It considerably extends Lamport's work, notably so by treating multiwriter registers in an order setting for the first time. Lamport avoids this issue, and is explicit that his framework only covers single writer registers. Moreover, we focus sharper on concurrent register access, as opposed to concurrent operation executions in general. We also investigate how the assumption of global time affects these criteria, by proving a rather general shrinking function theorem. In Section 3 we prove the atomicity of a multiwriter, multireader compound register directly constructed from atomic 1-writer, 1-reader subregisters. This is the first atomic multiwriter register, and was introduced by two of us in [8]. Using unbounded tags, it incorporates the essence of the problem area in a simple and comprehensible algorithm. At this time of writing, it still is the only published direct implementation from atomic 1-reader 1-writer registers. The atomicity proof given here is based solely on causality considerations.

Previous work in this area is due to Bloom, Lamport, Peterson, and Vitányi and Awerbuch (see [1], [3], [6], [8]). More recent work can be found in PODC87 and FOCS87.(*) Generally, the algorithms and proofs, especially of the ambitious bounded tag algorithms in [8] and in the related papers in PODC87 and FOCS87, defy comprehension even by other workers in the field. Reference [8] contains the fairly simple unbounded tag algorithm we present here, and a complicated bounded tag algorithm for a subcase of the general question, together with a proof method. The bounded tag algorithm contains an error (see Errata, FOCS87). A 'patched up' version of this algorithm was presented by Peterson and Burns in FOCS87 [7], but was recently found to be erroneous as well by Russell Schaefer. The reader, when consulting these references, will find that inventing the 'right' formalism and level of rigour is of major importance in this complicated area. In this paper we have succeeded developing *simple* formal criteria and proof methods, and demonstrate their usefulness by proving a major but simple protocol correct in a *convincing* manner.

2. The Model

A **proto-register** is an abstract data type, capable of holding **values** out of a given **domain** of values. Initially the proto-register is empty. The operations that can be performed on the proto-register are writes and reads. A *write* of a value puts that value in the proto-register. A *read* reports a value from the domain.

(*) PODC87 stands for "Proceeding of 6th ACM Symposium on Principles of Distributed Computing" held in Vancouver, Canaca, 1987, and FOCS87 stands for "28th Annual IEEE Symposium on Foundations of Computer Scince" held in New York, USA, 1987.

We assume that such values have an identity apart from a value. That is, values written by different write operation executions may have the same value, e.g. 0, but they are not identical. The **identity** $id(v)$ of a value v written by a write w is defined by $id(v)=w$. (Thus, $v=v'$ and $id(v){\neq}id(v')$ may be both true.) If a read operation execution reports a value v, then either $id(v)=w$ for a particular write w or else $id(v)$ is undefined. If a read r reports v with $id(v)=w$ for some write w, then we say that r reports the value written by w. The proto-register can be implemented by a **multiset** over a given domain. That is, an unordered list of elements, where the same element can occur more than once. A proto-register has associated with it a finite set of processors called the **writers** and a finite set of processors called the **readers**. A processor can be both a reader and a writer. A write can only be performed by a writer, while a read can only be performed by a reader.

A **sequential** register is a proto-register where all operations are executed in sequence, and an execution of a read operation reports the value written by the execution of the last write operation that precedes it. A sequential register can be implemented by a **linear list**. Originally, the list is empty. A write adds an element to the end of the list, and a read reports the element at the end of the list.

We address the problems arising from true concurrency, where we allow simultaneous operation executions by different processors. However, simultaneous operation executions by the same processor are excluded. Informally, we aim at a specification of a general **concurrent** register, register for short, which corresponds as closely as possible to that of the sequential register. In the atomic register defined below, the operations may be **actually** executed concurrently, yet it will **seem** as if they were executed in sequence. For read operations to report a value which was written by a write operation to the register, there must be causal relations between the operations. We define an 'apparent' precedence relation ($\rightarrow$) on the set of operation executions, which captures the crucial aspect of the causal relations between operation executions to the same register.

Remark. Lamport [3] defines two precedence relations $\rightarrow$ and $--\rightarrow$, the semantics of which are intended to be problem independent. If a "precedes" relation on the subactions of a,b is defined, then $a --\rightarrow b$ means "some subaction of a precedes some subaction of b", and $a \rightarrow b$ means "each subaction of a precedes each subaction of b." In the context of shared register access there is always an intended way for the actions to interact, which ensures correctness of the algorithm. Therefore, it is advantageous to reflect this essential causal relation between the actions of a particular algorithm by a single made-to-measure precedence relation. This relation is our $\rightarrow$, not to be confused with Lamport's $\rightarrow$, and will have an algorithm dependent semantics.

To define various degrees of niceness conditions on a register with simultaneous operation executions, we need some formal definitions first. We use 'action' as synonym for 'operation execution'.

A **run** $\rho = (A, \rightarrow, \pi)$ consists of the following:

(R1) A finite or countably infinite set A of **read** and **write** actions. If R is the set of read actions and W is the set of write actions, which were actually performed during the course of the run, then $A = W \cup R$ and $W \cap R = \emptyset$.

(R2) A **reading mapping** which is a partial function $\pi : R \to W$.

(R3) An irreflexive partial order $\to$ on the set A of actions. We call $\to$ a **precedence relation**. If $a \to b$ then we say a **precedes** b. To initialize the run, there is an **initial** write that precedes all other actions. We moreover require that, for each $a \in A$, there are only finitely many $b \in A$ such that $\neg(a \to b)$. Informally, this means that a run begins at some point in time, rather than extending in the infinite past [3], and that an action cannot be infinitely long or infinitely small in duration.

Intuitively, $a \to b$ will imply that, in the aspect we deem important, a may influence b, but b cannot influence a. Two actions a, b are called **concurrent** if $\neg(a \to b$ or $b \to a)$. I.e., if they are incomparable in the relation $\to$. If w is a write and r is a read, then w **directly precedes** r, **if** $w \to r$ **and there is no write** w'**, such that** $w \to w' \to r$.

Irreflexive orders.

All **orders** in this paper are irreflexive. For convenience, "total order" and "partial order" will henceforth mean "irreflexive total order" and "irreflexive partial order," respectively.

A run $\rho = (A, \to, \pi)$ can now be classified into the following categories according to how well it behaves under concurrent operations. The definitions below closely follow the presentation of Lamport [3]. The 'normal' run is a new category we found advantageous to introduce.

1. **(safe)** For each read r, that has no concurrent writes, $\pi(r)$ is defined, and directly precedes r.

2. **(normal)** For each read r, $\pi(r)$ is defined, and $\pi(r)$ either precedes r or is concurrent with r.

3. **(regular)** For each read r, $\pi(r)$ is defined, and $\pi(r)$ directly precedes r or is concurrent with r. (Hence a regular run is both safe and normal.)

4. **(atomic)** A run is atomic if it is normal and there is a total order $\Rightarrow$, which we call an **atomic precedence** relation, on the set A of actions, as follows.

    (i) if $a \to b$ then $a \Rightarrow b$ (**external consistency**), and

    (ii) for each read r, $\pi(r)$ is the write directly $\Rightarrow$-preceding r (**internal consistency**).

We say that $\Rightarrow$ **atomically extends** the precedence relation $\to$.

Without proof we state the hierarchy involved. Every atomic run is regular, but not every regular run is atomic. By definition, regular runs are exactly the ones which are both safe and normal. There are runs which are safe but not normal, and there are runs which are normal but not safe.

A run is a possible set of operation executions by a register, a possible 'history'. We now tie up the notion of a register and the notion of a run. Intuitively, a register is a deterministic 'black box' that reports a value in response to a read query. We can view the function of this black box as associating a reading mapping with a given pair $(A,\rightarrow)$. Since $(A,\rightarrow)$ is a high-level description, it is actually an equivalence class of different finer grained descriptions. These differences may give rise to different responses to the same read query. Therefore, the register associates a *set* of reading mappings with each $(A,\rightarrow)$. Let Π be the set of all its possible reading mappings. Formally, a **register mapping** $REG: \{(A,\rightarrow)\} \rightarrow 2^\Pi$ is a total mapping, that associates a nonempty set of reading mappings π with each pair $(A,\rightarrow)$ satisfying (R1), (R2) and (R3). With each register we associate a register mapping. We assume that each processor actually executes operations to the register serially. This assumption is embodied in requirement (R4) below. If K is a register and REG_K is its associated register mapping, then a run $\rho=(A,\rightarrow,\pi)$ of K satisfies

(R4) if a and b are different actions by the same processor then either $a \rightarrow b$ or $b \rightarrow a$, and this total $\rightarrow$-order on the actions by the same processor is identical with the serial order in which a processor executes its actions in A;

(R5) $\pi \in REG_K(A,\rightarrow)$; and

(R6) if a read r returns a value v and $id(v)=w$, then $\pi(r)=w$.

A register is **atomic** (respectively **regular, normal, safe**) if each of its runs is atomic (respectively regular, normal, safe). Obviously, the atomic register is the ideal register; the operations may be concurrent, yet they seem to be executed in a serial fashion, extending the given precedence relation (external consistency) and consistent with the reading function (internal consistency).(*) Given a particular implementation of a data structure, and having selected the particular precedence relation $\rightarrow$ we wish to employ, it is often simple to check whether it is a safe, a normal, a regular register or none of these. However, proving atomicity using the given definition, or its 'shrinking' variant which we will meet below, turns out to be a difficult matter. Therefore, in the next section we propose simple criteria which are necessary and sufficient for atomicity. In a later section we show how to use these atomicity criteria for verifying that a proposed construction implements an atomic register.

2.1. Atomicity Criteria

For a proposed data structure K to be an atomic register, it suffices to prove that each of its runs, as defined in (R1) through (R6), is atomic. Let $\rho = (A,\rightarrow,\pi)$ be a normal run of K, so π is total. We divide the set of actions A into equivalence classes induced by π. Each such equivalence class, called a clan, is associated with a write. The **clan** associated with a write w is the set $[w] = \{w\} \cup \{r \in R : \pi(r) = w\}$. For any two writes w, w'

(*) The notion of register atomicity is closely related to what is called '(strict) serializability' in conventional concurrency control, in particular in the context of databases with concurrent 'transactions'. See e.g. [5]. Concurrent transactions are usually called atomic if they are both serializable and **recoverable**. Recoverability means that each transaction appears all-or-nothing: either it executes to completion (in which case we say that it **commits**) or it cannot influence other transactions (in which case we say that it **aborts**). Recoverability is a problem only in the presence of failures. We assume that registers are failure-free, so we do not consider recoverability.

define $[w] \to^\pi [w']$ if and only if $w \neq w'$ and there exist actions $a \in [w]$ and $a' \in [w']$ such that $a \to a'$. Note that $\to^\pi$ is not necessarily acyclic. The following theorem is basic for proving the atomicity of runs.

Theorem 2.1. (Atomicity Criterion)

Let $\rho = (A, \to, \pi)$ be a run. The following statements are equivalent:
(1) ρ is atomic.
(2) ρ is normal and $\to^\pi$ is acyclic.

Proof.

(1) implies (2). Let ρ be atomic. By definition, atomicity implies normality, which shows the first part of (2). To show the second part of (2), let $\Rightarrow$ be a total order that atomically extends $\to$. I.e., for each read r, we have

(i) $\pi(r) \Rightarrow r$, and

(ii) there is no write w with $\pi(r) \Rightarrow w \Rightarrow r$.

We prove that $\to^\pi$ is extendible to a total order, which implies acyclicity of $\to^\pi$. It is enough to show that for any two writes w, w', if $[w] \to^\pi [w']$ then $w \Rightarrow w'$.

Since $\Rightarrow$ is a total order, the negation of $w \Rightarrow w'$ is equivalent to $w' \Rightarrow w$. Therefore, we only need to show that for any two writes w, w', if $w' \Rightarrow w$ then $\neg([w] \to^\pi [w'])$. Thus, suppose $w' \Rightarrow w$. Exhaustive analysis of all cases shows that then the combination of (i) and (ii) implies $w' \Rightarrow r' \Rightarrow w \Rightarrow r$, for all reads $r \in [w]$ and $r' \in [w']$. Hence, there are no $a \in [w]$ and $a' \in [w']$ such that $a \to a'$. Therefore, $\neg([w] \to^\pi [w'])$.

(2) implies (1). Assume (2) holds. It is clear that the transitive closure of $\to^\pi$ is a partial order, which in turn can be extended to a total order $\Rightarrow^\pi$. Since ρ is normal, for each read $r \in [w]$, we have $\neg(r \to w)$. Hence, there is a total order $\Rightarrow_{[w]}$ on each $[w]$ atomically extending $\to$ and such that $w \Rightarrow_{[w]} r$, for each read $r \in [w]$. Define a unique relation $\Rightarrow$ on the set A as follows. For all $a, a' \in A$, $a \Rightarrow a'$ if and only if either

(i) $a, a' \in [w]$ and $a \Rightarrow_{[w]} a'$, or

(ii) $a \in [w]$, $a' \in [w']$, and $[w] \Rightarrow^\pi [w']$.

Clearly, $\Rightarrow$ is a total order atomically extending $\to$. It follows that ρ is atomic. ●

The second atomicity theorem refers to registers with only one writer. In this case, for each pair of different writes $w, w' \in A$, either $w \to w'$ or $w' \to w$, by (R4). The theorem is similar to a corresponding theorem in Lamport [3].

Theorem 2.2. (1-writer Atomicity Criterion)

Assume that K is a register with only one writer. Then for each run $\rho = (A, \to, \pi)$ of K the following statements are equivalent:
(1) ρ is atomic.
(2) ρ is regular and π is weakly monotonic (i.e., if $r \to r'$, then either $\pi(r) \to \pi(r')$ or $\pi(r) = \pi(r')$).

Proof.

(1) implies (2). Let ρ be atomic. Atomicity implies regularity. Therefore we only need to prove weak monotonicity of π.

Let $r, r' \in A$ be different reads with $r \to r'$. Since there is only one writer, we have by (R4) that either $\pi(r) \to \pi(r')$ or $\pi(r) = \pi(r')$ or $\pi(r') \to \pi(r)$. Atomically extend $\to$ to a total order $\Rightarrow$, as in the definition of an atomic run. Exhaustive case analysis shows that, by the properties of $\Rightarrow$, either $\pi(r) \Rightarrow r \Rightarrow \pi(r') \Rightarrow r'$, or $\pi(r) = \pi(r')$.

(2) implies (1). Let ρ be regular and π be weakly monotonic. By Theorem 2.1, if we prove that $\to^\pi$ is acyclic, then we are done. Assume to the contrary, there is a cycle

$$[w] \to^\pi [w'] \to^\pi \cdots \to^\pi [w].$$

Since $[w] \to^\pi [w']$, there are $a \in [w]$ and $a' \in [w']$, $w \neq w'$, such that $a \to a'$. If both a and a' are writes then $w \to w'$. If a, a' are both reads, then by weak monotonicity of π, we have $w \to w'$. If a is a read and $a' = w'$, then $a \to w' \to w$ ($=\pi(a)$) contradicts normality of ρ. Therefore $w \to w'$ by (R4). If $a = w$ and a' is a read, then $w' \to w \to a'$ ($\pi(a') = w'$) contradicts safety of ρ, and therefore $w \to w'$ by (R4) again. Hence, $[w] \to^\pi [w']$ implies $w \to w'$. Since this argument holds for all pairs of adjacent clans in the cycle, we obtain a cycle $w \to w' \to \cdots \to w$. This contradicts that $\to$ is a partial order. •

2.2. Compound Register

The most obvious approach to constructing a register is to build it from simpler ones. The existence of such a simpler register is either postulated, or it is constructed from still simpler registers. More precisely, a **compound register** consists of a finite number of registers, called **subregisters**. The set of readers and writers of the compound register is the union of the set of readers and writers of the subregisters. The subregisters are allowed to hold a value out of a given domain. We can distinguish essentially two cases. In one case the subregisters are simpler than the compound register in that their domain of values is smaller than the value domain of the compound register. Then the construction for the compound register **distributes** the value to be stored piecemeal over the subregisters. E.g., a positive integer n can be distributed in $\log n$ bits over $\log n$ boolean subregisters. In the other case the set of readers and writers associated with the compound register is larger than the set of readers and writers associated with each subregister. Then the construction for the compound register **replicates** the value to be stored as versions in several subregisters. A reader has to determine the 'latest' version among the versions it obtains from different subregisters. To make this possible, extra information such as a 'timestamp' is attached to each version. As a result, the value domain of each subregister has to be larger than the value domain of the compound register. The construction of a compound register in this paper is of the latter type. To express their complexity we use the following cost measures. Let V be the value domain of the compound register, $v = |V|$, and let there be n readers and m writers associated with the compound register. Let $S, T: V \times N \times N \to N$ be total cost functions, with N the set of nonnegative integers. Let the value domain of each subregister of the compound register be (isomorphically) contained in $TAG \times V$, with $|TAG| = S(v, n, m)$, the number of elements in TAG. Then the **space** complexity of the compound register is $\log S(v, n, m)$. The processors execute read or write actions on the compound register, independently of each other but following a protocol. Let each read or write action by a given processor on the compound register consist of at most $T(v,n,m)$ read and/or write actions on the subregisters. Then the **time** complexity of the compound register is $T(v,n,m)$. An action on the compound register is considered to be a higher-level operation execution of the same nature as its subactions. Thus, with each run of the compound register is associated a run of each subregister which constitutes the compound register. This means that we associate with each subregister a set of subactions related by a precedence relation. Sets of subactions associated with different subregisters are disjoint. We assume that a processor actually executes all its subactions in serial order. The disjoint precedence relations of the subactions on respective subregisters are related by the order in which each processor executes its subactions. For the compound register we define a transitive precedence relation ($-\gg$) on the set of all subactions involved, as follows.

Let K be a compound register comprising subregisters $K_1, \ldots, K_n$. Let $\rho = (A, \rightarrow, \pi)$ be a run of K and let $\rho_i = (A_i, \rightarrow_i, \pi_i)$ be the associated run of subregister K_i, $1 \leq i \leq n$. The **precedence** relation $-\gg$ on the set $\bigcup_{i=1}^{n} A_i$, is defined as the minimal transitive relation that extends all precedence relations $\rightarrow_i$, $1 \leq i \leq n$, such that

(R7) if α and β are different subactions by the same processor, then either $\alpha -\gg \beta$ or $\beta -\gg \alpha$, but not both, and this total $-\gg$-order on the subactions by the same processor is identical with the actual serial order in which the processor executes these subactions; and

(R8) if $a, b \in A$ and for each subaction α of a and each subaction β of b holds $\alpha -\gg \beta$, then $a \rightarrow b$.

Lemma 2.3.

$-\gg$ *is a partial order.*

Proof.

Clearly, (R7) precludes $-\gg$-cycles containing two subactions by the same processor. Therefore, since the sets of subactions on the same subregisters are disjoint, any $-\gg$-cycle contains only subactions on the same subregister. But these subactions are partially ordered, which contradicts such a $-\gg$-cycle. •

Finally, we need to express the 'registerhood' of the compound by suitably restricting the choice of $\rightarrow$. That this is necessary can be seen from the following example. Let K be a compound register consisting of subregisters K_1, K_2. Let p be a writer associated with subregister K_1, and let q be a reader associated with subregister K_2, $p \neq q$. Then there is no way that q can read what p has written. Yet runs of K can satisfy (R1) through (R8) and even be atomic. For example, atomicity of K_1, K_2 implies atomicity of K. Such anomalies are due to the fact that we have not yet required the existence of causal relations between actions by different processors. There must be some causal relation between a write and a read, since otherwise a reader cannot report what a writer wrote. There must be some causal relation between two writes, because otherwise a writer cannot replace the value in the register by the value it wants to write. However, it is not necessary to have a causal relation between two reads; this is because neither do reads have to change the value contained by the register, nor do they need to report what the another read wrote. The following condition expresses these requirements on the compound register in terms of subregisters. Assuming the general setting above:

(R9) if $a,b \in A$ are not both reads, then there are subactions α of a and β of b, α,β are not both subreads, and some i ($1 \leq i \leq n$), such that $\alpha, \beta \in A_i$. (α and β act on the same subregister K_i.)

It follows that a choice of $\rightarrow$ satisfying (R9) is 'proper' if the choices of the $\rightarrow_i$'s are 'proper.' This can be argued as follows. Assume that the ultimate subsub..subregister is atomic. If a,b are not both reads, then there are subactions α of a and β of b, not both reads, which act on the same subregister, and so on. At the atomic subsub..subregister level the subsub..subactions involved have an apparent total order. Choose this as the precedence relation. For convenience, let the K_i's be the basic atomic subregisters, so the $\rightarrow_i$'s are total orders. Then either $\alpha \rightarrow_i \beta$ or $\beta \rightarrow_i \alpha$, but not both, by (R7). Suppose $\alpha \rightarrow_i \beta$. If $c,d \in A$, $c \rightarrow a$ and $b \rightarrow d$, then by (R8) we have $c \rightarrow d$. Suppose $\beta \rightarrow_i \alpha$. If $c,d \in A$, $a \rightarrow c$ and $d \rightarrow b$, then by (R8) we have $d \rightarrow c$. Using the precedence relations at the previous level, we induce in this fashion a 'coarse' precedence relation at each next higher level compound register. Our choice of $\rightarrow$ is constrained to be an extension of this coarse precedence relation. That is, (R7) through (R9) restrict the freedom of our choice of $\rightarrow$ appropriately, by ultimately reducing the constraints on our choice of precedence $\rightarrow$ to precedence at the elemental level.

2.3. Naming of Registers

Unfortunately, the naming conventions for types of registers are inconsistent. For a 1-writer register, the operator who writes can simply remember the value it wrote last. Therefore, the name '1-writer, 1-reader' register is used for a register that can be read by both writer and reader [3]. By analogy, we use '1-writer, $(n-1)$-reader' register for a register that can be written by one writer and read by $n-1$ readers that cannot write. The writer can always read as above. However, in an m-writer register, with $m > 1$, while a writer can remember what it wrote last, this value can have been overwritten by a later write of another writer. Hence, here we might as well have writers that cannot read (in addition to readers that cannot write). We will, however, only consider registers where the writers can also read. For us, an 'm-writer, n-reader' register, $m > 1$, designates a register that can be written by m processors, and read by n processors including the m writers ($n \geq m$).

2.4. New Proof Technique

In the present paper we propose a new proof technique for proving the atomicity of compound registers. In summary, our approach consists of the following method:

1. Find an appropriate partial order $\rightarrow$ between the high level reads and writes defined in terms of the assumed partial order between the lower level reads and writes. Induce the $\rightarrow^\pi$ relation on the set of clans defined by the reading mapping.

2. Find a way to totally order the writes, using the intuition which makes you believe the protocol works correctly. Use this total order to prove that $\rightarrow^\pi$ is acyclic.

3. Example: Multiwriter Register

The matrix register is a compound n-writer, n-reader register constructed as a matrix of atomic 1-writer, 1-reader subregisters. The domain of values of the subregisters is the cartesian product of the domain of values of the compound register with the nonnegative integers. This is the first atomic multiwriter register [8], and at the time of writing still is the only direct construction from atomic 1-reader 1-writer subregisters. It may well be a register of practical importance, because of its simplicity, elegance and low complexity (cf. below). We prove correctness by application of the atomicity Theorem (Theorem 2.1).

Architecture.

Let $p_1,...,p_n$ be n processors and let K be an $n \times n$ matrix register consisting of n^2 atomic, 1-reader, 1-writer registers $K_{i,j}$, $i,j = 1,...,n$. Each p_i is a writer of (i.e., is connected to the write terminal of) each $K_{i,j}$. Each p_i is also a reader (i.e., is connected to the read terminal) of each $K_{j,i}$. Let V be the domain of values of the compound register. Then $\mathbf{N} \times \{1, ..., n\} \times V$, with $\mathbf{N}$ the nonnegative integers, is the domain of values of each subregister. A **tag** is a pair (k,i), where k is a nonnegative integer and $i \in \{1,...,n\}$. We say that each subregister can hold a tag, next to a value from the domain V of the compound register. All subregisters are initialized with tag $(0,1)$ and value 0. Moreover, each run of the compound register starts with a write action, which precedes all other actions, as required by (R3). The architecture is depicted in Figure 1.

Protocol.

The register K obeys the following protocol.

p_i **writes the value** v:

1. for all $j = 1,...,n$ read $K_{j,i}$ (i.e., read the ith column);
2. determine the lexicographically largest tag (k_{max}, m);
3. set own tag to $(k_{max}+1, i)$;
4. for all $j = 1,...,n$ write on $K_{i,j}$ (i.e., write to the ith row) the new tag, as well as the value v.

p_i **reads**:

1. for all $j = 1,...,n$ read $K_{j,i}$ (i.e., read the ith column);
2. determine the lexicographically largest tag (k_{max}, m) and let v_m be the value contained in a register with such a tag;
3. set own tag to (k_{max}, m);
4. for all $j = 1,...,n$ write to $K_{i,j}$ (i.e., write to the ith row) the new tag, as well as the value v_m, which was determined in 2. (Also, report v_m.)

Each action a by processor p_i consists of a set of subreads $R(a,1,i), ..., R(a,n,i)$ followed by a set of subwrites $W(a,i,1), ..., W(a,i,n)$, where the last two indices i,j

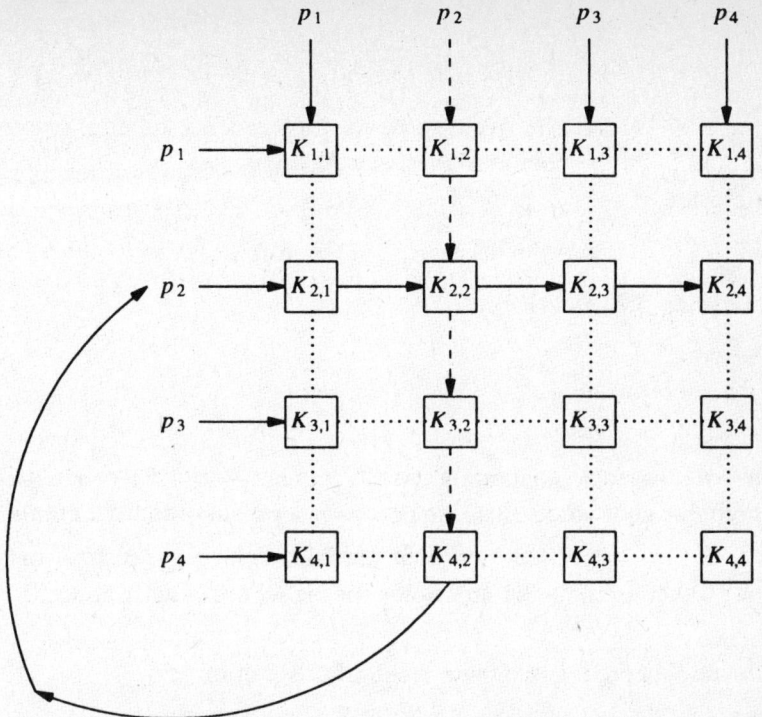

Figure 1: An action by processor p_2 in the 4-reader, 4-writer, matrix register.

indicate the subregister $K_{i,j}$ on which the subaction took place. The order in which these subreads and subwrites take place is arbitrary, but for the fact that each subread precedes each subwrite. Each subregister $K_{i,j}$ ($1 \leq i,j \leq n$) of K is atomic. Let $\rho = (A, \to, \pi)$ be a run of K. Let A^i be the subset of actions in A that are executed by p_i ($1 \leq i \leq n$). Define, for all $1 \leq i,j \leq n$, $\rho_{i,j} = (A_{i,j}, \to_{i,j}, \pi_{i,j})$, the run of $K_{i,j}$ associated with ρ, where

$$A_{i,j} = R_{i,j} \cup W_{i,j},$$

$$R_{i,j} = \{R(a,i,j): a \in A^j\},$$

$$W_{i,j} = \{W(a,i,j): a \in A^i\};$$

$R_{i,j}$ is the set of subreads, and $W_{i,j}$ is the set of subwrites on subregister $K_{i,j}$. Since $K_{i,j}$ is atomic, there is an atomic extension $\Rightarrow_{i,j}$ of $\to_{i,j}$, for all $1 \leq i,j \leq n$. This atomic extension is a total order on the subactions executed on the subregister concerned. Moreover, if a subread reads a subwrite (on a subregister), then there is no other subwrite placed between them by this order. The orders on the disjoint sets of subactions associated with each subregister are related by the orders on the disjoint sets of subactions by each processor. Let $-\gg$ be the minimal transitive relation on the subactions in $\bigcup_{i,j=1}^{n} A_{i,j}$ extending the $\Rightarrow_{i,j}$'s and satisfying (R7). By (R7), the subactions by the same processor p are totally ordered by $-\gg$. This order is the serial execution order of the subactions by

p. In particular, $\twoheadrightarrow$ must satisfy:

$$R(a,i,j) \twoheadrightarrow W(a,j,k), \tag{3.1}$$

for all $a \in A^j$ and all $1 \le i,j,k \le n$. We now define a precedence relation $\to$ on A. For any two actions a and b on the compound register K, by p_i and p_j, respectively, let $\to$ be the transitive closure of $\to'$:

$$a \to' b \text{ iff } W(a,i,j) \twoheadrightarrow R(b,i,j). \tag{3.2}$$

Clearly, this satisfies (R8) and (R9).

Lemma 3.1.

$\to$ *is a partial order on* A.

Proof.

Existence of a $\to$-cycle containing $a \in A^j$, implies $W(a,j,k) \twoheadrightarrow R(a,i,j)$, for some k,i ($1 \le k,i \le n$). This contradicts (3.1), since $\twoheadrightarrow$ is a partial order by Lemma 2.3. •

Remark. If $\twoheadrightarrow$ extends the original partial orders $\to_{i,j}$, instead of the apparent total orders $\Rightarrow_{i,j}$, then Lemma 3.1 still holds for the $\to$ resulting from (3.2). This will be useful in the proof of Theorem 3.5.

The following theorem is the main result of this section.

Theorem 3.2.

The matrix register K is an atomic, n-writer, n-reader compound register, which is implemented with n^2 atomic, 1-writer, 1-reader registers.

Proof.

Let $\rho = (A, \to, \pi)$ be a run of K. Examine the write protocol. For a write $w \in A$, let $v(w)$ be the value written by w to the compound register, and, if $t(w)$ denotes the tag determined in step 3 of w, let $(t(w), v(w))$ be the value written to the subregisters in step 4 of w's execution. For a read $r \in A$, let $v(r)$ be the value reported by r from the compound register, and, if $t(r)$ is the tag associated with $v(r)$, let $(t(r), v(r))$ be the value written to the subregisters in step 4 of its execution. The pair $(t(r), v(r))$ is selected in step 3 of the read protocol.

Claim. For each read r, there is a write w, such that

$$t(r) = t(w) \ \& \ id(v(r)) = id(v(w)) \ (=w). \tag{3.3}$$

If $id(v(r)) = w$ then $\pi(r) = w$. Hence, π is total.

Proof of Claim. The subregisters are initialized with tag $(0,1)$, and there is a write preceding all other actions, by (R3). Hence, there is an $a \in A$, such that $(t(r), v(r)) = (t(a), v(a))$. If a is a write then we are done, else a is a read and we repeat the argument. If $r \to a$, then, by (3.2) and atomicity of the subregisters, r can not read the value written by a to the subregister involved. There are only finitely many a, such that $\neg(r \to a)$, $\to$ is a partial order, and there is an initial write preceding all other actions, by (R3). Hence, we need only finitely many repetititions of the argument before we find a write w such that (3.3) holds. If $id(v(r)) = w$ then $\pi(r) = w$ by (R6). Since this holds for each read r, π is total. This proves the Claim.

Let $<_{lx}$ be the irreflexive **lexicographic** order on pairs of integers. If $a,b \in A$ such that $a \to b$ (therefore $a \neq b$), then it follows by (3.2) and the choosing of the new tag in step 3 of the write and read protocols, that:

$$t(a) \leq_{lx} t(b) \quad (t(a) <_{lx} t(b) \text{ if } b \in W). \tag{3.4}$$

The prove atomicity, by Theorem 2.1, we only need to prove that ρ is normal and that there is a total order extending the $\to^\pi$ relation among the clans. Intuitively, we proceed by *first* choosing a plausible total order on the set of writes, and *next* showing that the corresponding total order on the set of clans extends $\to^\pi$. In the matrix register, the obvious total order on the set of writes is the lexicographical order of the associated tags. Proceeding this way, the conclusion of the theorem follows from Theorem 2.1 and by the following lemma.

Lemma 3.3.

(1) ρ is normal, and

(2) if $[w] \to^\pi [w']$, then $t(w) <_{lx} t(w')$. In particular, $\to^\pi$ is acyclic.

Proof.

(1). By the Claim above, π is a total function. Let $\pi(r)=w$ (i.e., $r \in [w]$). Then, by (3.3), $t(r) = t(w)$. However, if $r \to w$, then by (3.4) we have $t(w) >_{lx} t(r)$, which is a contradiction. Hence, $\neg(r \to w)$, i.e., ρ is normal.

(2). Let $[w] \to^\pi [w']$. By definition of $\to^\pi$, there exist actions $a \in [w]$ and $b \in [w']$ such that $a \to b$.

Suppose $b = w'$. Then by (3.3) and (3.4) it follows that $t(w') >_{lx} t(w)$, which is as claimed.

Suppose that $a = w$ and b is a read. By (3.3) and (3.4), $t(w) \leq_{lx} t(b) = t(w')$. If w, w' are writes by different processors, then their tags have different processor numbers; if they are writes by the same processor then, since $w \neq w'$, one of them $\to$-precedes the other. Therefore, by (3.4), they must have different tags. In both cases, $t(w) \neq t(w')$, which is as claimed.

Suppose both a, b are reads. Then $t(a) = t(w) \leq_{lx} t(b) = t(w')$, by (3.3) and (3.4). The proof of $t(w) \neq t(w')$ is now exactly as before. This proves the lemma. Hence the proof of theorem 3.2 is complete. ●

3.1. Complexity and Optimality

The time complexity of the matrix register is $2n$ (or rather $2n-2$, as follows from Theorem 3.4 below) which seems to be as low as it can possibly be. The space complexity of the matrix register is unbounded. In theory this is pretty bad. In practice, however, this solution uses far less space than many solutions which theoretically do better. For instance, in [8] a solution has been proposed where the space complexity of the compound register is $5n^2 \log n$. However, we can assume that a system executes only a limited number of actions on the compound register in its total lifetime. If we set a generous bound of at most 2^{50} such actions, the matrix solution is superior in terms of space complexity, with respect to the mentioned bounded space solution, for any number $n \geq 3$ of associated processors. Thus the matrix register has effectively a lower space complexity than comparable solutions with bounded space complexity, even for solutions which solve only subproblems of the one addressed by the matrix solution. An exception is the Bloom register in [1] (with only two writers), which both effectively and theoretically cannot be improved in space and time complexity.

Another complexity criterion is the number of subregisters of a certain type used in the compound register. Leaving out the subregisters on the main diagonal, which are redundant, the matrix solution is optimal in the number of 1-writer, 1-reader subregisters used.

Theorem 3.4. (Optimality)

The implementation of a compound safe n-writer, n-reader register from 1-writer, 1-reader subregisters, requires at least $n(n-1)$ such subregisters (atomic or not). Register K, minus the subregisters on the main diagonal, is such an optimal implementation.

Proof.

Suppose we have implemented a safe compound n-writer, n-reader register R, with associated processors $p_1, \ldots, p_n$, from 1-writer, 1-reader subregisters. For each ordered pair of processors (p_i, p_j), $1 \leq i, j \leq n$ and $i \neq j$, we can consider a run $(\{w, r\}, \rightarrow, \pi)$ of R, consisting solely of two nonoverlapping operation executions: a write w by p_i, followed by a read r by p_j. Since R is safe, $\pi(r) = w$. Since $i \neq j$, there must be a subregister $R_{i,j}$, such that p_i is the associated writer and p_j is the associated reader. There are $n(n-1)$ different ordered pairs (p_i, p_j), $i \neq j$. In each such ordered pair the first element is a writer and the second element is a reader. No subregister $R_{i,j}$ can be associated with more than one such (writer, reader) pair, since the subregisters have only one associated writer and one associated reader other than the writer. Hence, there must also be $n(n-1)$ different subregisters $R_{i,j}$ in the compound register R. This is exactly achieved by the presented matrix register K, noting that the subregisters on the main diagonal are superfluous. I.e., p_i can remember what it wrote last in $K_{i,i}$. •

4. Global Time, Intervals and Shrinking

In [1], [6], [7], [8], atomicity is related to the assumption of a global time reference frame (also called global clock). We show that the theory as developed here is more general. In particular, a register is atomic in global time if and only if it is atomic for a particular choice of the $\rightarrow$ precedence relation. This precedence relation turns out to be the interval order induced by the time intervals representing the actions.

An important aspect of atomic runs is the following property. Although their actions have a duration on a global time scale, and such durations may overlap, each action may be considered to take place instantaneously, i.e., as if it happened completely at a particular time instant. If all of these time instants are distinct, then the apparent time instants of the actions orders the actions totally. This relates the order approach to atomicity with the global time approach.

Time is represented by the set of real numbers **R**, ordered as usual. Assume that every action a is **represented** by an open time interval $(s(a), f(a))$, $s(a)<f(a)$, within the bounds of which the action is supposed to have taken place. $s(a)$ (respectively, $f(a)$) is a real number called the **starting** (respectively, **finishing**) time of the action a.

Remark. To exclude some technical difficulties, there is usually an assumption that $s(a)\neq s(b)$, $s(a)\neq f(b)$ and $f(a)\neq f(b)$, for any two distinct actions $a,b \in A$, and $s(a)\neq f(a)$ for each action $a \in A$. The fact that we should be allowed to assume that no two starting or finishing times are equal, is justified by appeal to the sensibility of natural law [3]. "No physical meaningful result could depend on upon completely accurate knowledge of these times. (It makes no physical sense to specify starting and finishing times of an operation execution down to the fraction of a micropicosecond.)" By excluding the starting and finishing times from the duration associated with action a, to obtain the desired effect in the mathematical framework, we may come closer to the spirit of physics. Thus, we choose to represent durations of actions as open intervals.

Define the precedence relation $\rightarrow$, as the natural relation $a \rightarrow b$ iff $f(a) \leq s(b)$. A relation which is so induced by a set of intervals of the real line **R**, satisfies the axioms of a special type of partial order called interval order. Formally, an **interval order** on a set A is an irreflexive relation $\rightarrow$ that satisfies

$$a \rightarrow b \ \& \ c \rightarrow d \text{ implies } a \rightarrow d \text{ or } c \rightarrow b, \text{ for all } a,b,c,d \in A \text{ (see [2])}. \quad (4.1)$$

Every interval order is a partial order, and hence the previously developed theory applies. Since not every (irreflexive) partial order is an interval order, the global time approach requires more from the precedence relation ($\rightarrow$) than the general approach in (R3). We now proceed with the definitions of this more conventional global time approach to atomicity. The relation between the two approaches is analysed in Theorem 4.1.

A **shrinking function** on the set of actions of a run $\rho=(A,\rightarrow,\pi)$, with $\rightarrow$ the interval order induced by the set of intervals $\{(s(a),f(a)) \subseteq \mathbf{R}: a \in A\}$, is a one-to-one function σ that associates with each action a of the run a time instant (i.e., a real number) $\sigma(a)$ such that:

(S1) $\sigma(a)$ belongs to the interval $(s(a),f(a))$ of a.

A shrinking function gives a possible serialization of the actions. Condition (S1) enforces external consistency of the serialization. In the order approach, external consistency follows from the fact that the serialisation extends $\rightarrow$. Define the precedence relation $\rightarrow_\sigma$, induced by σ, as $a \rightarrow_\sigma b$ iff $\sigma(a)<\sigma(b)$. Obviously, $\rightarrow_\sigma$ is a total order on A. Then (S1) implies that $\rightarrow_\sigma$ extends $\rightarrow$. A shrinking function σ is consistent with the reading mapping π if

(S2) $(A,\rightarrow_\sigma,\pi)$ is atomic.

A run ρ is **shrinking** atomic if there is a shrinking function σ such that (S1) and (S2) are satisfied.

Theorem 4.1. (Shrinking Function Theorem)

Let $\rho=(A,\rightarrow,\pi)$ be a run, and let $\rightarrow$ be the interval order induced by a representation of open (time) intervals of the actions in A. The following statements are equivalent:
(1) ρ is atomic, and
(2) ρ is shrinking atomic.

Proof.

(1) implies (2). Suppose (1) holds. Let $\Rightarrow$ be a total order which atomically extends $\rightarrow$. Define $Q(a)=\{b: \neg(a\rightarrow b)\ \&\ \neg(b\Rightarrow a)\}$. Note that, by (R3), $Q(a)$ is finite, and that $Q(a)$ is nonempty since $a\in Q(a)$. Define, by induction on a, $\sigma(a)$ to be a real number such that:

(i) if $b\Rightarrow a$ then $\sigma(a)>\sigma(b)$,

(ii) $\sigma(a)>s(a)$, and

(iii) $\sigma(a)<\mu$, with $\mu=\min\{f(b): b\in Q(a)\}$.

Note that (ii) and (iii) imply (S1), and (i) implies (S2). Induction is possible if:

(a) if $b\rightarrow a$ then $\sigma(b)<\mu$, and

(b) $s(a)<\mu$.

Let $b_{\min}\in Q(a)$ be an action such that $\mu=f(b_{\min})$.

Ad (a). Assume $b\Rightarrow a$. If $b\rightarrow b_{\min}$ then $\sigma(b)<f(b)\leq s(b_{\min})<f(b_{\min})=\mu$. If $\neg(b\rightarrow b_{\min})\ \&\ \neg(b_{\min}\rightarrow b)$ then, since $b\Rightarrow a$, we have $\neg(b_{\min}\Rightarrow b)$. Therefore, $b_{\min}\in Q(b)$. Then, $\sigma(b)<\min\{f(c): c\in Q(b)\}\leq f(b_{\min})=\mu$. If $b_{\min}\rightarrow b$ then $b_{\min}\rightarrow b\Rightarrow a$, contradicting $b_{\min}\in Q(a)$.

Ad (b). Since $\neg(a\rightarrow b_{\min})\ \&\ \neg(b_{\min}\Rightarrow a)$ we have $s(a)<f(b_{\min})=\mu$.

(2) implies (1). Assume (2). Since $\rightarrow_\sigma$ is a total order extending $\rightarrow$ and satisfying (S2), atomicity of ρ is immediate. ●

Corollary.

The matrix register is shrinking atomic.

Proof sketch.

The argument goes as follows. Assume global time. The interval representations of the subactions induce the $\rightarrow_{i,j}$ precedence relations on the subregisters. Each such relation is therefore an interval order. The intervals associated with the subactions of each processor are linearly ordered (do not overlap) by definition. Since each subregister $K_{i,j}$ is atomic, each run $\rho_{i,j}=(A_{i,j},\rightarrow_{i,j},\pi_{i,j})$ has a shrinking function $\sigma_{i,j}$ such that $(A_{i,j},\rightarrow_{\sigma_{i,j}},\pi_{i,j})$ is shrinking atomic, by Theorem 4.1. Since the associated intervals are open, we can always choose the $\sigma_{i,j}$'s such that $\sigma'=\bigcup_{i,j=1}^{n}\sigma_{i,j}$ is one-to-one. Define $-\!\gg$ as the total order of the real images of the subactions under σ', i.e., $-\!\gg$ agrees with the usual total order $<$ on the reals. Then $-\!\gg$ satisfies (R7) and (3.1). Define $a\rightarrow''b$ iff $\sigma'(\alpha)<\sigma'(\beta)$ for all subactions α of a and β of b. Then $\rightarrow''$ is an interval order. This satisfies (R8) and (R9), and $\rightarrow$ is a refinement of $\rightarrow''$. The proof of Theorem 3.2 goes through exactly as before, with interval order $\rightarrow''$ instead of $\rightarrow$, which implies that register K is shrinking atomic by the Shrinking Function theorem (Theorem 4.1). •

5. Conclusion

To recapitulate the main result of this paper we propose a method of proving atomicity of shared registers in an order setting. It seems to us that it can be applied in many cases where we have to prove atomicity (e.g. we have used the methods presented in the present paper to prove the atomicity of the 2-writer register given in [1]). In outline:

1. Find an appropriate partial order $\rightarrow$ between the high level reads and writes defined in terms of the assumed partial order between the lower level reads and writes. Induce the $\rightarrow^\pi$ relation on the set of clans defined by the reading mapping.
2. Find a way to totally order the writes, using the intuition which makes you believe the protocol works correctly. Use this total order to prove that $\rightarrow^\pi$ is acyclic.

Acknowledgement

Conversations with Bard Bloom, Leslie Lamport, Arjen Lenstra and Nancy Lynch are gratefully acknowledged. Lambert Meertens' comments had a profound influence on this paper.

References

[1] Bloom, B., *Constructing Two-writer Atomic Registers*, Proceedings of the 6th Annual ACM Symposium on Principles of Distributed Computing, Vancouver, Canada, 1987.

[2] Fishburn, P.C., *Interval Orders and Interval Graphs*, Wiley, 1985.

[3] Lamport, L., *On Interprocess Communication, Part I: Basic Formalism, Part II: Algorithms*, Distributed Computing, vol. 1, pp. 77-101, 1986.

[4] Lamport, L., *The mutual exclusion problem, part I - A theory of interprocess communication*, Journal ACM, vol. 33, pp.313-326, 1986.

[5] Papadimitriou, C., *The serializability of concurrent database updates*, Journal ACM, vol. 26, pp. 631-653, 1979.

[6] Peterson, G. L., *Concurrent Reading While Writing*, ACM Transactions on Programming Languages and Systems, Vol. 5, No. 1, Jan. 1983, pp. 46-55.

[7] Peterson, G.L. and J.E. Burns, *Concurrent Reading While Writing II, the Multi-writer Case*, Proceedings 28th IEEE Symposium on Foundations of Computer Science, New York, USA, 1987.

[8] Vitanyi, P. M. B., and Awerbuch, B., *Atomic Shared Register Access by Asynchronous Hardware*, Proceedings 27th IEEE Symposium on Foundations of Computer Science, 1986, 233-243. (Errata, in Proceedings 28th IEEE Symposium on Foundations of Computer Science, New York, USA, 1987.)

RELATION LEVEL SEMANTICS

Jules Desharnais
Nazim H. Madhavji

School of Computer Science, McGill University,
3480 University Street, Montréal, Québec, CANADA H3A 2A7

ABSTRACT

It is common to consider a program as a relation on the set of its possible states. The relational equations describing the behavior of programs can be object level, i.e., they refer to states and values of variables, or they can be relation level, i.e., the constants and variables in the equations range over relations. Relation level work using binary relations has been mostly limited to the study of statements. This is partly because the calculus of binary relations has no operator for accessing the cartesian components of the space of the program, so that it is difficult to discuss expressions and declarations. This paper introduces an algebra that combines features of Codd's relational algebra and of the algebra of binary relations. Using this hybrid algebra, we give a relation level semantics of a language with types, procedures, and variable declarations.

CR Categories: D.1.4 [**Programming Techniques**] Sequential Programming; D.3.1 [**Programming Languages**] Formal Definitions and Theory: *Semantics*; F.3.1 [**Logics and Meanings of Programs**] Specifying and Verifying and Reasoning about programs: *Relations*; F.3.2 [**Logics and Meanings of Programs**] Semantics of Programming Languages: *Algebraic approaches to semantics, Denotational Semantics*; F.3.3 [**Logics and Meanings of Programs**] Studies of Program Constructs: *Control Structures, Procedures, Expressions*;

1. INTRODUCTION

According to Backus [Backus 85], one of the reasons for the lack of useful theorems about programs is the *object level* orientation of the programming activity. That is, a program is synthesized from various objects that are not programs. Conventional programs are object level: They are built from expressions, statements, control constructs, they are concerned with low level details, etc. In order to overcome this problem, Backus proposes *function level* programming, i.e., programming by applying operations (combining forms, functionals, and program-forming operations) to existing programs. If these operations have attractive algebraic properties, then it becomes possible to state and prove general theorems about programs.

Though conventional programs are object level, reasoning about them need not be object level, as is examplified by Hoare et al. in "Laws of programming" [Hoare 87], which presents many algebraic laws that conventional programs should obey. These laws describe the meaning of a complex program in terms of the meanings of the simpler programs that compose it. The mathematical model underlying these laws is that of binary relations on the space (the set of possible states) of the program. But the notation used by Hoare in formulating these laws is object-free, in the style of the calculus of relations of Tarski [Tarski 41]. The constants and variables in the equations expressing the laws range over programs (relations); for example, P;(Q;R) = (P;Q);R expresses the associativity of the sequential composition of programs. We term this approach a *relation level* approach, in analogy with the term *function level* introduced by Backus. Other papers using such a calculus of relations include: [Berghammer 86, Blikle 77, Hoare 86, Mili 83, Mili 87, and Schmidt 81].

The laws obtained by modelling programs using binary relations largely concern statements. One reason is that it is difficult (within the calculus of binary relations) to access the components of the space, or to modify the number of its components. As a consequence, expressions and declarations, though important components of conventional languages, have not been studied with relation level methods.

Specifications of programs can also be considered as binary relations [Hoare 86, Hoare 87, Mili 83, Mili 87]. In [Mili 87], some relation level strategies are given for the derivation of a program from a specification. But concrete specifications, and derivations from concrete specifications, are carried out at object level. For example, a typical relational specification is:

$$Sp = \{(s,s') \mid x(s') = x(s) + y(s)\}$$

Here the *value* of variable x in the final *state* s', denoted x(s'), is to be equal to the initial value of x, x(s), added to the initial value of y, y(s). In order to express Sp in an object-free notation, we need relational axioms describing the domains of x and y, and the properties of the addition operator. Also we need to separate the x and y components of the space of the specification.

This paper presents a relational calculus which permits operations on the cartesian components of the program space. The basic idea is to consider that programs can be represented by tables. For example, let P(x:integer, y:integer) be a procedure that, given x, returns in variable y the square of x and leaves x unchanged. P can be represented by the following table:

x	y
<1,1>	<0,1>
<1,1>	<1,1>
<1,1>	<2,1>
...	...
<2,2>	<0,4>
<2,2>	<1,4>
<2,2>	<2,4>
...	...
<3,3>	<0,9>
<3,3>	<1,9>
...	...

In this table, the first line, for example, corresponds to the case where the initial and final values of x are 1, the initial value of y is 0 and its final value is 1. Since the initial value of y is not specified, all the possible cases are included in the table.

By using Codd's relational algebra [Codd 70], such a table can be manipulated. Codd's calculus includes operators to access individual components or group of components (e.g., projection, join, and renaming). But it has no composition operator similar to the relative product operator in the algebra of binary relations. Such an operator is necessary, because it is used to model sequential composition of programs. By allowing entries in a table to be ordered pairs, we are able to define such a relative product operator.

We report in this paper some preliminary results that we have obtained. Part 2 presents a relational algebra; it is a mixture of a variant of Codd's algebra and of the algebra of binary relations. In part 3, we use this algebra to give a relation level denotational semantics of while programs with types, procedures and variable declarations. Showing that a substantial portion of a conventional language can be modeled by this hybrid algebra is a first step towards the goal of relation level derivation of programs from relational specifications. Part 4 discusses some applications of this semantic definition, and finally, we conclude in part 5 with prospects for further research.

2. A RELATIONAL ALGEBRA

2.1. Relations as tables

This subsection defines relations, and presents operations on relations that are similar to those in the relational algebra of Codd [Codd 70, Maier 83]. There are, however, some differences which are pointed out in subsection 2.4.

NOTATION 2.1. Let X and Y be sets. Then, {} and $P(X)$ denote the empty set and the power set of X, respectively. Also, **Pfn**(X→Y) denotes the set of partial functions from X to Y, and **Tfn**(X→Y) denotes the set of total functions from X to Y.

Let f be a function. Then, dom(f) is the *domain* of f. Also, f↾X denotes the *restriction* of f to X. That is,
$$f \upharpoonright X \equiv \{(x,y) | (x,y) \in f \wedge x \in X\}$$
Note that this definition is valid even if X⊄dom(f). In particular, if X and dom(f) are disjoint, then f↾X={} (the function that is undefined everywhere). □

DEFINITION 2.2. Let S and A be sets, where A is countable. A *relation* on the set of *component names* A and the set of *values* S is a subset of **Pfn**(A→S). □

An element of A will also be called an *attribute*, as is usual in database terminology. An element of a relation is a function from A into S. Such an element will also be called a *tuple*. In what follows, the symbols f, g, h, p, q, r will stand for functions in **Pfn**(A→S); P, Q, R for relations; and C, D for sets of attributes.

We will denote the set of relations on A and S by **Rel**, i.e. **Rel** ≡ $P(\mathbf{Pfn}(A{\to}S))$. The usual set-theoretical operations: union (∪), intersection (∩), difference (−) and complement (¬), are defined on **Rel**. **Rel** is a complete lattice under (∪, ∩, ⊆). Some particular relations of interest are:

(a) The empty relation: $\emptyset$. It is the empty set, but we use a different symbol, in order to prevent possible confusion.

(b) The universal relation $U \equiv \mathbf{Pfn}(A \rightarrow S)$. The complement operation is taken relative to this relation U.

(c) The relation that contains only the empty tuple: $I \equiv \{\{\}\}$.

Relations can be pictured as tables, possibly with undefined entries. For example, let A={a,b,c,d,e} and S={1,2,3,4}. Then the relations Q={{(a,1),(b,2),(c,3)}, {}, {(a,2),(c,1)}} and R={{(b,1)}, {(b,2)}} are best seen as the following tables (where "-" stands for an undefined entry):

$$Q = \begin{array}{ccc} a & b & c \\ 1 & 2 & 3 \\ - & - & - \\ 2 & - & 1 \end{array} \qquad R = \begin{array}{c} b \\ 1 \\ 2 \end{array}$$

DEFINITION 2.3. The *scheme* of a relation R is $\text{sch}(R) \equiv \bigcup_{r \in R} \text{dom}(r)$ □

For example, $\text{sch}(U) = A$, $\text{sch}(\emptyset) = \{\}$, and $\text{sch}(I) = \{\}$.

We now define the operations of projection, join and renaming. Each definition is followed by an example using the sets A={a,b,c,d,e} and S={1,2,3,4}.

DEFINITION 2.4. Let R be a relation. The *projection* of R on C, where C⊆A, is

$$R[C] \equiv \{q \mid \exists r \in R, q = r \wedge C\} \qquad □$$

EXAMPLE 2.5

$$R = \begin{array}{cccc} a & b & c & d \\ 1 & 2 & - & - \\ 1 & 2 & 3 & 4 \\ 4 & 1 & 1 & 1 \end{array} \qquad R[\{a,b\}] = \begin{array}{cc} a & b \\ 1 & 2 \\ 4 & 1 \end{array} \qquad R[\{e\}] = I \qquad R[A-\{b,c,d\}] = \begin{array}{c} a \\ 1 \\ 4 \end{array}$$

Note that R[A−{b,c,d}] acts as a projection that eliminates the b, c, d components (complementary projection).   □

PROPOSITION 2.6. The following properties of projection can be derived directly from the definition.

$$I[C] = I \qquad\qquad Q[C] = \emptyset \Leftrightarrow Q = \emptyset$$
$$R \neq \emptyset \Leftrightarrow R[\{\}] = I \qquad\qquad R[B][C] = R[C][B] = R[B \cap C] \qquad □$$

DEFINITION 2.7. The *join* of relations Q and R is

$$Q \bowtie R \equiv \{p \mid p \in \mathbf{Pfn}(A \to S) \land (\exists q \in Q, \exists r \in R, p = q \cup r)\} \quad \square$$

That is, the join is formed by taking the pairwise union of tuples in Q and R and keeping only those that define a function.

EXAMPLE 2.8

	b	c	d				d	e			b	c	d	e
Q =	1	2	-		R =	3	4		Q⋈R =	1	2	3	4
	-	3	4				-	1			1	2	-	1
							4	3			1	2	4	3
											-	3	4	1
											-	3	4	3	□

PROPOSITION 2.9. Some properties of join are:

$Q \bowtie R = R \bowtie Q$ commutativity
$P \bowtie I = P$ I identity for $\bowtie$
$P \bowtie \emptyset = \emptyset$ $\emptyset$ zero for $\bowtie$
$P \bowtie (Q \bowtie R) = (P \bowtie Q) \bowtie R$ associativity
$R \subseteq R \bowtie R$

It is possible to have $R \neq R \bowtie R$. Take, for instance, $A = \{a,b\}$, $S = \{1\}$ and $R = \{\{(a,1)\},\{(b,1)\}\}$. Then, $R \bowtie R = \{\{(a,1)\},\{(b,1)\},\{(a,1),(b,1)\}\}$. □

DEFINITION 2.10. Let R be a relation and $v: A \to A$ be a bijective mapping. We define the *renaming* operation

$$R \ll v \gg \equiv \{q \mid \exists r \in R, \forall a \in A, q \upharpoonright \{v(a)\} = r \upharpoonright \{a\}\} \quad \square$$

In that definition, $q \upharpoonright \{v(a)\} = r \upharpoonright \{a\}$ could have been written $q(v(a)) = r(a)$ with the convention that equality holds if both sides are undefined, and does not hold if only one side is defined.

Let $a_k, b_k \in A$, $1 \leq k \leq n$. We will usually denote a renaming operation by

$$R \ll a_1 \to b_1, \ldots, a_n \to b_n \gg$$

The meaning of such an expression is that of $R \ll v \gg$, where v is defined by the following clauses:

(a) $v(a_k) = b_k$ $k = 1, \ldots, n$

(b) $v(a)=a$ for $a \in \text{sch}(R)$ and $a \neq a_k$, $k=1,\ldots,n$

(c) $v(a)$, for $a \notin \text{sch}(R)$, is an extension to v such that v is bijective, if such an extension exists; otherwise, the expression is not defined.

EXAMPLE 2.11

$$R = \begin{array}{cc} a & b \\ \hline 1 & 2 \\ 2 & 3 \end{array} \qquad R \ll a \to b, b \to c, c \to d, d \to a \gg = \begin{array}{cc} b & c \\ \hline 1 & 2 \\ 2 & 3 \end{array} \qquad R \ll a \to d \gg = \begin{array}{cc} b & d \\ \hline 2 & 1 \\ 3 & 2 \end{array}$$

$R \ll a \to d, a \to e \gg$, $R \ll a \to d, b \to d \gg$, $R \ll a \to b \gg$ are not defined. □

PROPOSITION 2.12. The renaming operator satisfies the following identities.

$\emptyset \ll v \gg = \emptyset$

$I \ll v \gg = I$

$R \ll a \to b \gg$ is defined iff $b \notin (\text{sch}(R) - \{a\})$ □

NOTATION 2.13. We now present one abbreviation and a particular relation that will be used in section 3.

For $a \in A$ and $T \subseteq S$, let $T(a) \equiv \{\{(a,t)\} \mid t \in T\}$. $T(a)$ is the "one-column table" with attribute a, whose entries are values from T.

For each $a, b \in A$, let $EQUAL(a,b) \equiv \{f \mid f \in \mathbf{Tfn}(\{a,b\} \to S) \wedge f(a) = f(b)\}$. □

EXAMPLE 2.14. With $A = \{a,b,c\}$, $S = \{1,2,3\}$ and $T = \{1,2\}$, we have

$$T(a) = \begin{array}{c} a \\ \hline 1 \\ 2 \end{array} \qquad EQUAL(b,c) = \begin{array}{cc} b & c \\ \hline 1 & 1 \\ 2 & 2 \\ 3 & 3 \end{array} \quad \square$$

2.2. Pairs

This subsection introduces one primitive operation, namely the relative product, and one derived operation, the transitive closure.

We assume that the elements of S are ordered pairs. More precisely, let $S = B^2$ for some set B, where $B^2 = B \times B$ is the cartesian product of B by itself. As usual, $<x,y>$ denotes the ordered pair of objects x, y. Also, if $s = <x,y>$, then $s_1 \equiv x$ and $s_2 \equiv y$.

DEFINITION 2.15. Let Q, R be relations. Then, the *relative product* of Q and R is
$Q \circ R \equiv \{f |\ \exists q \in Q,\ \exists r \in R,\ \text{dom}(f) = \text{dom}(q) \cup \text{dom}(r)$
$\wedge\ (\forall a \in \text{dom}(f),\ a \in \text{dom}(q) \wedge a \notin \text{dom}(r) \wedge f(a) = q(a)$
$\vee\ a \notin \text{dom}(q) \wedge a \in \text{dom}(r) \wedge f(a) = r(a)$
$\vee\ a \in \text{dom}(q) \wedge a \in \text{dom}(r) \wedge q(a)_2 = r(a)_1$
$\wedge\ f(a) = <q(a)_1, r(a)_2>)\}$ □

Composition (by the relative product) on a component basis is similar to the composition of binary relations, except for the treatment of undefined values. Also, the relationship between two components of Q∘R is not arbitrary, but is determined by their relationship in Q and R. One can verify that, because of the definition of S as B^2 for some B, Q∘R belongs to Rel. That would not be the case if we could have $<x,y> \in S$, $<y,z> \in S$, and $<x,z> \notin S$.

EXAMPLE 2.16

	a	b		b	c		a	b	c
Q =	-	<1,2>	R =	-	<3,4>	Q∘R =	-	<1,2>	<3,4>
	<5,6>	<7,1>		<1,2>	<8,9>		<5,6>	<7,1>	<3,4>
							<5,6>	<7,2>	<8,9> □

PROPOSITION 2.17. The relative product satisfies the following identities:

$P \circ (Q \circ R) = (P \circ Q) \circ R$ associativity

$R \circ I = I \circ R = R$ I is the identity for ∘

$R \circ \emptyset = \emptyset \circ R = \emptyset$ ∅ is a zero for ∘

$R \circ U = U\ \vee\ U \circ \neg R = U$

The last one can be verified easily by noting that if $\{\} \in R$, then, $R \circ U = U$; otherwise, $\{\} \in \neg R$, and then $U \circ \neg R = U$. □

DEFINITION 2.18. The *reflexive transitive closure* of a relation R is
$$R^* \equiv I \cup R \cup R \circ R \cup R \circ R \circ R \cup \ldots$$ □

This definition of the transitive closure is the usual one.

EXAMPLE 2.19.

$$R = \begin{array}{cc} a & b \\ \hline \langle 1,2\rangle & \langle 3,4\rangle \\ \langle 2,3\rangle & \langle 4,6\rangle \\ \langle 2,5\rangle & \langle 7,8\rangle \end{array} \qquad R^* = \begin{array}{cc} a & b \\ \hline - & - \\ \langle 1,2\rangle & \langle 3,4\rangle \\ \langle 2,3\rangle & \langle 4,6\rangle \\ \langle 2,5\rangle & \langle 7,8\rangle \\ \langle 1,3\rangle & \langle 3,6\rangle \end{array} \qquad \square$$

We close this subsection with some useful properties of the transitive closure.

PROPOSITION 2.20.

$$R^* = I \cup R \circ R^* \qquad R^* = (R^*)^* \qquad R \circ R^* = R^* \circ R \qquad \square$$

2.3. Distributivity and continuity properties

To limit the number of parentheses in expressions, we give the following precedence to the operators, starting from the highest: (a) unary operators $\neg$, $[\ ]$, $\ll \gg$, $*$; (b) $\cap$, $\circ$, $\bowtie$; and (c) $-$, $\cup$. With the exception of $\neg$, the unary operators are left associative, e.g. $R[C][D] = (R[C])[D]$.

The operators that we have introduced satisfy many distributive laws. The following proposition presents some of them.

PROPOSITION 2.21

$$(Q \cup R)[C] = Q[C] \cup R[C] \qquad (Q \cup R) \bowtie P = Q \bowtie P \cup R \bowtie P$$
$$(Q \cup R) \circ P = Q \circ P \cup R \circ P \qquad (Q \cup R) \ll v \gg = Q \ll v \gg \cup R \ll v \gg$$
$$P \circ (Q \cup R) = P \circ Q \cup P \circ R \qquad \square$$

The operators $\cup$, $\cap$, $\bowtie$, $*$, $\circ$, $[C]$ (for a fixed C), and $\ll v \gg$ (for a fixed v), are continuous (and hence monotonic). Since **Rel** is a complete lattice, a consequence of monotonicity is that there is always a least solution to the equation $R=f(R)$, where $f(R)$ is a relational expression in R involving only the aforementioned operators [Tarski 55]. Furthermore, because of continuity, there is an explicit formula giving that solution, (e.g., see [Stoy 77]), namely:

$$R = \bigcup_{k \in N} f^k(\emptyset)$$

where N is the set of natural numbers, $f^0(\emptyset) = \emptyset$, and $f^{k+1}(Q) = f(f^k(Q))$. As an example, one can see that R^* is the least fixed point of the operator $g(X) = I \cup R \circ X$.

2.4. Comparison with the standard algebras

In this subsection, we will first compare the algebra to the Codd's relational algebra [Codd 70, Maier 83], and then to the calculus of binary relations [Tarsky 41].

The set of relations normally considered in database theory is the following set:
$$\mathbf{EqDom} \equiv \{R \subseteq \mathbf{Tfn}(C \rightarrow S) | C \subseteq A\}$$
All tuples of a relation in **EqDom** have the same domain. Given $C \subseteq A$, the set of relations $R \subseteq \mathbf{Tfn}(C \rightarrow S)$ is a lattice under $(\cup, \cap, \subseteq)$, but **EqDom** itself is not, because it is not closed under union and intersection. This is why, in Codd's algebra, union and intersection are defined only for two relations with the same scheme. Some laws can be strengthened, when the argument relations belong to **EqDom**.

PROPOSITION 2.22. Let $Q, R \in \mathbf{EqDom}$. Then

$R = R \bowtie R$ idempotence (compare with proposition 2.9)

$\operatorname{sch}(Q) = \operatorname{sch}(R) \Rightarrow Q \bowtie R = Q \cap R$ □

Undefined values (called *nulls*) are sometimes incorporated in Codd's algebra. However, their use has not been standardized yet, and the literature describes many types of nulls. For a discussion of these matters, we refer to [Maier 83], chapter 12.

The operations $[\ ]$, $\bowtie$, and $\ll\gg$, as we have defined them, behave exactly like the standard ones [Maier 83] when they are applied in the same conditions.

We have not defined selection, which is an operation in Codd's algebra. But it can be verified that if $R \in \mathbf{EqDom}$, and if $a, b \in \operatorname{sch}(R)$, then $R \bowtie \operatorname{EQUAL}(a,b)$ gives the same result as the selection for equality of attributes a and b. In what follows, the EQUAL relation will mostly be used to make a "copy" of a component. For example, let A={a,b,c}, S={1,2,3}. Then,

a b			a b		b c		a b c
1 1	$\bowtie$	EQUAL(b,c) =	1 1	$\bowtie$	1 1	=	1 1 1
1 2			1 2		2 2		1 2 2
3 2			3 2		3 3		3 2 2

makes a copy of component b into component c.

The operations ∪, ∩, ∘ and ¬, together with the relations ∅, U and I, satisfy all the axioms of the calculus of relations [Tarski 41] that concern them. An operator that we have not defined, but that is heavily used in the context of binary relations is the *converse* operator. It is a simple matter to define it as an operator that reverses all pairs in a relation, i.e. <a,b> becomes <b,a>; with that definition, however, the converse operator does not verify all the axioms of Tarski's calculus.

3. RELATIONAL SEMANTICS

Using the algebra developed in section 2, we will define the semantics of a small language that includes basic types, procedures, and variable declarations. The procedures can have variable parameters. We will assume some primitive relations that define the basic types and the operators of the language; a program can then be seen as a query on a "database" of primitive relations.

Section 3.1 presents the syntax of the language. In section 3.2, we will define the semantics of the primitive syntactic categories. This is where we define, among others, the sets A and S from which all relations will be built. Finally, in section 3.3, we treat the composite syntactic categories.

3.1. Syntax

The syntactic categories of our language are the following.

$K \in $ Con   (constants) $D \in $ Dec   (declarations)
$X \in $ Ide   (identifiers) $E \in $ Exp   (expressions)
$Z \in $ Typ   (types) $C \in $ Com   (commands)
$O \in $ Ope   (operators) $P \in $ Pro   (procedure declarations)

The syntax is:
1 K ::= true | false | ...
2 Z ::= t_1 | t_2 | ... | t_n
3 O ::= < | ... | + | ...
4 D ::= dummy | var X:Z | $D_1;D_2$

5 $E ::= K \mid X \mid E_1 \text{ O } E_2 \mid ...$
6 $C ::= \text{skip} \mid X:=E \mid \text{if } E \text{ then } C_1 \text{ else } C_2 \mid \text{while } E \text{ do } C \mid$
   $C_1;C_2 \mid X(X_{11} \to X_{12}, ..., X_{n1} \to X_{n2})$
7 $P ::= \text{procedure } X(D_1); D_2; C$

For simplicity, we will study only binary operators; the description of operators with different arities would be similar. The command $X(X_{11} \to X_{12}, ..., X_{n1} \to X_{n2})$ is a call to procedure X, with the X_{k1}'s being the formal parameters, and the X_{k2}'s the actual ones. In the procedure declaration P, D_1 is the declaration of the parameters and D_2 is the declaration of the local variables of the procedure. Note that the syntax does not define what a program is. The highest level construct is the procedure. We will assume that there exists a collection of procedures, such that a procedure can call any other. The reason for this approach will be discussed in section 4.1.

EXAMPLE 3.1. Here is a simple program that will be used all along to help understand the semantic definitions. We take as types $t_1=$"bool", $t_2=$"int".

procedure P(var x:bool);
    var y:int;
    y:=2;
    if y<3 then x:=true else y:=1   □

3.2. Semantics of primitive syntactic categories

We will look here at the basic syntactic categories, that is, the identifiers, the constants, the types and the operators of the language.

We choose
$$A = \text{Ide} \cup \{\&t, \&op1, \&op2\}$$
as the set of attribute names. We assume that Ide is disjoint from the set $\{\&t, \&op1, \&op2\}$; attributes in this set will be used to denote components holding "temporary" results.

The semantic function mapping the language identifiers to the attribute names is simply

$\xi: \text{Ide} \to A$
$\xi[\![X]\!] \equiv X$

Because it is the identity on Ide, we will omit ξ from the definitions that follow, i.e.

we will write X instead of $\xi[\![X]\!]$.

Let $B_1,...,B_n$ be *disjoint* sets with $B_1 \equiv \{F,T\}$; the set of *basic values* is $B \equiv \bigcup_k B_k$. The semantic function κ will map a constant of the language to its value.

κ: Con$\to$B

$\kappa[\![\text{true}]\!] \equiv T$

$\kappa[\![\text{false}]\!] \equiv F$

EXAMPLE 3.2. To continue with the same example, assume that the only possible constants of the language are "true", "false", "1", "2", and "3". We will use the primitive sets $B_1=\{F,T\}$ and $B_2=\{1,2,3\}$. The mapping for the new constants is $\kappa[\![1]\!]=1$, $\kappa[\![2]\!]=2$, $\kappa[\![3]\!]=3$. □

From the primitive sets, we derive the following ones.

$S \equiv B^2$

$\mathbf{Rel} \equiv P(\mathbf{Pfn}(A \to S))$

$I_B \equiv \{<s,s> \mid s \in B\}$

I_B, as a binary relation, is the identity on B; it will be used in subsection 3.3.

The next semantic function is ς; it associates to the type t_k of a variable a set of pairs:

ς: Typ $\to \{B_1^2, ..., B_n^2\}$

$\varsigma[\![t_k]\!] \equiv B_k^2$

EXAMPLE 3.3

$\varsigma[\![\text{bool}]\!] = \{F,T\}^2 = \{<F,F>,<F,T>,<T,F>,<T,T>\}$

$\varsigma[\![\text{int}]\!] = \{1,2,3\}^2$ □

The semantic function ρ maps various syntactic categories into the set of relations **Rel**:

ρ: (Ope $\cup$ Dec $\cup$ Exp $\cup$ Com $\cup$ Pro) $\to$ **Rel**

In this subsection, we study the application of ρ to Ope. The only operator that we treat here is "<". Suppose that for some k's a binary predicate $<_k$ is defined on B_k. Let $D \equiv \{k \mid <_k \text{ is defined}\}$. Then

$\rho[\![<]\!] \equiv \bigcup_{k \in D} \{\{(\&\text{op1},<s,s>), (\&\text{op2},<t,t>), (\&t,<u,u>)\} \mid$
$s<_k t \wedge u=T \vee \sim s<_k t \wedge u=F\}$

We have decided that comparisons would be made only between elements that belong to the same B_k. Depending on the language, comparisons could be made between elements of B_k and B_j, $k \neq j$; e.g., some languages allow comparisons between integers and reals. Because of the definition of $\rho[\![<]\!]$, $<$ is potentially polymorphic. The definitions for other operators (NOT, +, −, ...) would be done in a similar fashion.

EXAMPLE 3.4. For our example language, we decide that $F<_{bool}T$, $1<_{int}2<_{int}3$. Hence,

$$\rho[\![<]\!] = \begin{array}{c|ccc} & \&op1 & \&op2 & \&t \\ \hline & <F,F> & <F,F> & <F,F> \\ & <F,F> & <T,T> & <T,T> \\ & <T,T> & <F,F> & <F,F> \\ & <T,T> & <T,T> & <F,F> \\ & <1,1> & <1,1> & <F,F> \\ & <1,1> & <2,2> & <T,T> \\ & <1,1> & <3,3> & <T,T> \\ & <2,2> & <1,1> & <F,F> \\ & <2,2> & <2,2> & <F,F> \\ & <2,2> & <3,3> & <T,T> \\ & <3,3> & <1,1> & <F,F> \\ & <3,3> & <2,2> & <F,F> \\ & <3,3> & <3,3> & <F,F> \end{array}$$ □

3.3. Composite syntactic categories

We will complete the description of the remaining syntactic categories, i.e. Dec, Exp, Com and Pro. In order to do so, we will need two other semantic functions:

λ: Dec $\rightarrow P(A)$

γ: (Exp $\cup$ Com $\cup$ Pro) $\rightarrow P(A)$

The function λ associates to a declaration the set of identifiers that are declared; hence these identifiers are local to the block containing the declaration. The function γ associates to an expression or a command the set of identifiers that are used in the expression or command; it associates to a procedure declaration the set of variables that are global to the procedure.

In the relational expressions that follow, the application of semantic functions has a higher priority than that of the relational operators.

3.3.1. Declarations

(a) dummy

$$\rho[\![dummy]\!] \equiv \{\{\}\} = I$$
$$\lambda[\![dummy]\!] \equiv \{\}$$

(b) Variable declaration. Recall the convention introduced by notation 2.13; T(a) denotes a relation with scheme a, and values in set T.

$$\rho[\![var\ X{:}t_k]\!] \equiv \varsigma[\![t_k]\!](X) \bowtie I_B(X) = B_k^2(X) \bowtie I_B(X)$$
$$\lambda[\![var\ X{:}t_k]\!] \equiv \{X\}$$

The denotation of a variable is a pair. The first component of that pair keeps track of the initial value of the variable, and the second one, of the final value. ρ indicates that the initial and the final values are the same, since a declaration does not change the value of a variable. Because the variable is not initialized by the declaration, all the initial values that are compatible with the type are contained in the table of the relation ρ.

EXAMPLE 3.5

$$\rho[\![var\ x{:}bool]\!] = \begin{array}{c} x \\ \hline <F,F> \\ <T,T> \end{array} \qquad \rho[\![var\ y{:}int]\!] = \begin{array}{c} y \\ \hline <1,1> \\ <2,2> \\ <3,3> \end{array}$$

$$\lambda[\![var\ x{:}bool]\!] = \{x\} \qquad \lambda[\![var\ y{:}int]\!] = \{y\} \qquad \square$$

(c) Declaration sequence

$$\rho[\![D_1;D_2]\!] \equiv \rho[\![D_1]\!] \bowtie \rho[\![D_2]\!]$$
$$\lambda[\![D_1;D_2]\!] \equiv \lambda[\![D_1]\!] \cup \lambda[\![D_2]\!]$$

Because $\bowtie$ is commutative, the order of declarations does not matter. Also, the same name can be redeclared; if both declarations are identical, the result is the same as with a unique declaration; otherwise, the result is $\emptyset$ because the B_k's are disjoint.

3.3.2. Expressions

The evaluation of an expression E generates a relation with attribute &t that contains the result of the evaluation of E. The expressions considered here involve no side effects. We will study the various forms of expression.

(a) E is a constant K

$\rho[\![K]\!] \equiv \{ \{(\&t, <\kappa[\![K]\!], \kappa[\![K]\!]>)\} \}$

$\gamma[\![K]\!] \equiv \{\}$

(b) E is X, a variable

$\rho[\![X]\!] \equiv I_B(X) \bowtie EQUAL(X, \&t)$

$\gamma[\![X]\!] \equiv \{X\}$

(c) E is E_1 O E_2

$\rho[\![E_1 \ O \ E_2]\!] \equiv (\rho[\![E_1]\!] \ll \&t \rightarrow \&op1 \gg \bowtie \rho[\![E_2]\!] \ll \&t \rightarrow \&op2 \gg \bowtie \rho[\![O]\!])$

$[A - \{\&op1, \&op2\}]$

$\gamma[\![E_1 \ O \ E_2]\!] \equiv \gamma[\![E_1]\!] \cup \gamma[\![E_2]\!]$

EXAMPLE 3.6. We calculate $\rho[\![y<3]\!]$, using the value of $\rho[\![<]\!]$ from example 3.4.

$\rho[\![y]\!] = \begin{array}{cc} y & \&t \\ <F,F> & <F,F> \\ <T,T> & <T,T> \\ <1,1> & <1,1> \\ <2,2> & <2,2> \\ <3,3> & <3,3> \end{array}$
$\quad \rho[\![3]\!] = \begin{array}{c} \&t \\ <3,3> \end{array}$
$\quad \rho[\![y<3]\!] = \begin{array}{cc} y & \&t \\ <1,1> & <T,T> \\ <2,2> & <T,T> \\ <3,3> & <F,F> \end{array}$

$\gamma[\![y<3]\!] = \{y\}$ □

REMARK 3.7. All entries in the table of the relation $\rho[\![E]\!]$ associated to an expression E have the form $<s,s>$ (there are no side effects). Also, $\rho[\![E]\!]$ belongs to **EqDom**. It is clear (partly by proposition 2.22) that any relations Q and R having these properties satisfy $R \circ R = R \bowtie R = R$ and $Q \circ R = Q \bowtie R$ □

3.3.3. Statements

(a) skip

$\rho[\![skip]\!] \equiv I$

$\gamma[\![skip]\!] \equiv \{\}$

(b) Assignment

$\rho[\![X:=E]\!] \equiv (\rho[\![E]\!] \circ (\bigcup_k B_k^2(X)) \circ (EQUAL(X, \&t) \bowtie I_B(\&t)))$ $[A-\{\&t\}]$

$\gamma[\![X:=E]\!] \equiv \gamma[\![E]\!] \cup \{X\}$

EXAMPLE 3.8

$\rho[\![y:=2]\!] = (\rho[\![2]\!] \circ (\bigcup_k B_k^2(y)) \circ (EQUAL(y,\&t) \bowtie I_B(\&t)))\ [A-\{\&t\}]$

$$= (\ \begin{array}{c}\&t\\ \hline <2,2>\end{array}\ \circ\ \begin{array}{c}y\\ \hline <F,F>\\ <F,T>\\ <T,F>\\ <T,T>\\ <1,1>\\ <1,2>\\ <1,3>\\ <2,1>\\ <2,2>\\ <2,3>\\ <3,1>\\ <3,2>\\ <3,3>\end{array}\ \circ\ \begin{array}{cc}\&t & y\\ \hline <F,F> & <F,F>\\ <T,T> & <T,T>\\ <1,1> & <1,1>\\ <2,2> & <2,2>\\ <3,3> & <3,3>\end{array}\ )\ [A-\{\&t\}]$$

$$= (\ \begin{array}{cc}\&t & y\\ \hline <2,2> & <1,2>\\ <2,2> & <2,2>\\ <2,2> & <3,2>\end{array}\ )[A-\{\&t\}] \ =\ \begin{array}{c}y\\ \hline <1,2>\\ <2,2>\\ <3,2>\end{array}\quad \square$$

(c) Conditional. For readability purposes, we introduce the abbreviations

$\rho[\![E]\!]_T \equiv (\rho[\![E]\!] \bowtie \{\{(\&t,<T,T>)\}\})\ [A-\{\&t\}]$

$\rho[\![E]\!]_F \equiv (\rho[\![E]\!] \bowtie \{\{(\&t,<F,F>)\}\})\ [A-\{\&t\}]$

Then,

$\rho[\![\text{if } E \text{ then } C_1 \text{ else } C_2]\!] \equiv \rho[\![E]\!]_T \circ \rho[\![C_1]\!] \cup \rho[\![E]\!]_F \circ \rho[\![C_2]\!]$

$\gamma[\![\text{if } E \text{ then } C_1 \text{ else } C_2]\!] \equiv \gamma[\![E]\!] \cup \gamma[\![C_1]\!] \cup \gamma[\![C_2]\!]$

Note that if the evaluation of E had side effects, these side effects would be propagated by the use of $\circ$.

EXAMPLE 3.9. We use the relation $\rho[\![y<3]\!]$ from example 3.6.

$\gamma[\![\text{if } y<3 \text{ then } x:=\text{true else } y:=1]\!] = \{x,y\}$

$\rho[\![\text{if } y<3 \text{ then } x:=\text{true else } y:=1]\!]$

$$=\ \begin{array}{c}y\\ \hline <1,1>\\ <2,2>\end{array}\ \circ\ \begin{array}{c}x\\ \hline <F,T>\\ <T,T>\end{array}\ \cup\ \begin{array}{c}y\\ \hline <3,3>\end{array}\ \circ\ \begin{array}{c}y\\ \hline <1,1>\\ <2,1>\\ <3,1>\end{array}\ =\ \begin{array}{cc}x & y\\ \hline <F,T> & <1,1>\\ <F,T> & <2,2>\\ <T,T> & <1,1>\\ <T,T> & <2,2>\\ - & <3,1>\end{array}\quad \square$$

(d) Iteration. We use the same abbreviation as above for $\rho[\![E]\!]_T$ and $\rho[\![E]\!]_F$.

$$\rho[\![\text{while } E \text{ do } C]\!] \equiv (\rho[\![E]\!]_T \circ \rho[\![C]\!])^* \circ \rho[\![E]\!]_F$$
$$\gamma[\![\text{while } E \text{ do } C]\!] \equiv \gamma[\![E]\!] \cup \gamma[\![C]\!]$$

(e) Statement sequence

$$\rho[\![C_1;C_2]\!] \equiv \rho[\![C_1]\!] \circ \rho[\![C_2]\!]$$
$$\gamma[\![C_1;C_2]\!] \equiv \gamma[\![C_1]\!] \cup \gamma[\![C_2]\!]$$

EXAMPLE 3.10. We use the results of examples 3.8 and 3.9.

	x	y
$\rho[\![y:=2; \text{ if } y<3 \text{ then } x:=\text{true else } y:=1]\!] \quad =$	$<F,T>$	$<1,2>$
	$<F,T>$	$<2,2>$
	$<F,T>$	$<3,2>$
	$<T,T>$	$<1,2>$
	$<T,T>$	$<2,2>$
	$<T,T>$	$<3,2>$

□

We remark here that the semantic definitions of the conditional, iteration and sequence have a form similar to the definitions given using binary relations: see e.g., [Blikle 77].

(f) Procedure call. Let $P \equiv [\![\text{procedure } X(D_1); D_2; C]\!]$ (see 3.3.4 for the semantic definition of procedure declarations). We define the predicate

$$OK \equiv \{X_{11}, ..., X_{n1}\} = \lambda[\![D_1]\!]$$
$$\wedge \gamma(P) \cap \{X_{12}, ..., X_{n2}\} = \emptyset$$
$$\wedge (\forall j,k, 1 \leq j,k \leq n \wedge j \neq k \Rightarrow X_{j1} \neq X_{k1} \wedge X_{j2} \neq X_{k2})$$

that is, (a) the identifiers used to refer to the formal parameters in the procedure call are exactly those that are declared in the procedure declaration, (b) no name global to procedure X can be an actual parameter (no aliasing between global identifiers and formal parameters), and (c) the formal parameters in the procedure call are distinct, and so are the actual parameters (one consequence is that there can be no aliasing between two formal parameters, i.e. they cannot refer to the same actual parameter).

$$\rho[\![X(X_{11} \to X_{12}, ..., X_{n1} \to X_{n2})]\!]$$
$$\equiv \rho(P) \ll X_{11} \to X_{12}, ..., X_{n1} \to X_{n2} \gg \quad \text{if } OK$$
$$\equiv \emptyset \quad \text{otherwise}$$

$$\gamma[\![X(X_{11} \to X_{12}, ..., X_{n1} \to X_{n2})]\!]$$
$$\equiv \gamma(P) \cup \{X_{12}, ..., X_{n2}\} \quad \text{if OK}$$
$$\equiv \{\} \quad \text{otherwise}$$

This definition implies that we use dynamic scope rules; in effect, the global components of procedure X will compose with the components having the same name in the environment of the caller. One way to get static semantics is by appropriately renaming the global variables of the procedure. The above definition will be discussed further in section 4.1.

3.3.4. Procedure declaration

Let the predicate OK be OK $\equiv \lambda[\![D_1]\!] \cap \lambda[\![D_2]\!] = \{\}$, i.e., no formal parameter name can also be declared locally in the procedure.

$$\rho[\![\text{procedure } X(D_1); D_2; C]\!]$$
$$\equiv ((\rho[\![D_1]\!] \bowtie \rho[\![D_2]\!]) \circ \rho[\![C]\!]) \, [A - \lambda[\![D_2]\!]] \quad \text{if OK}$$
$$\equiv \emptyset \quad \text{otherwise}$$

$$\gamma[\![\text{procedure } X(D_1); D_2; C]\!]$$
$$\equiv \gamma[\![C]\!] - (\lambda[\![D_1]\!] \cup \lambda[\![D_2]\!]) \quad \text{if OK (the global variables of X)}$$
$$\equiv \{\} \quad \text{otherwise}$$

EXAMPLE 3.11. It is easy to see that OK is true for our example program. Using the results of examples 3.5 and 3.10, we obtain

$$\rho[\![\text{procedure P(var x:bool);} \atop \text{var y:int;} \atop \text{y:=2;} \atop \text{if y<3 then x:=true else y:=1}]\!] = \begin{array}{c} x \\ \hline <F,T> \\ <T,T> \end{array} \quad \square$$

4. DISCUSSION

4.1. On the semantic definitions

The relation $\rho[\![P]\!]$ assigned to a program fragment P does not depend on the "environment" of P. Rather, the environment is built bottom-up; every identifier corresponding to a variable appearing in P gets its component in $\rho[\![P]\!]$. And all possible valuations of that component are assumed at once. The result is that P is considered as a polymorphic fragment, because a component may consist of values of many different types. When program fragments are merged, contradictory assumptions are eliminated by the join or relative product operation. The use of operators that cannot be applied to a certain type of values also eliminates the values of that type.

A consequence of the fact that a variable assumes all its possible values is that uninitialized variables can receive a natural treatment. There is no need to give them a special value that indicates that they are not initialized (though of course it is possible to do so). The use of such an uninitialized variable propagates multiple values, and the results of the program are unpredictable. This is what happens in many conventional languages.

Procedure calls have been treated differently: when fragment P calls procedure Q, then no Q component containing all possible procedure values is created in $\rho[\![P]\!]$. This would require operators for nesting (or unnesting) relations within relations, and these have not been introduced here. Rather, we assume that $\rho[\![Q]\!]$ has been calculated and can be substituted in the relational expression representing the call to Q. If a procedure P calls itself, then $\rho[\![P]\!]=E(\rho[\![P]\!])$ for some relational expression E; by section 2, this equation has a least fixpoint, which can be taken as the semantics of P.

We are currently investigating ways to provide a more consistent treatment of procedure values. Here, we briefly describe (informally) a possible solution for the simpler case of procedures without parameters. Let $P \equiv [\![\text{procedure X; D; C}]\!]$ be the declaration of a parameterless procedure. The relation that we associate to this declaration P is $\{\{(X, <\rho(P),\rho(P)>)\}\}$, where $\rho(P)$ is as in subsection 3.3.4. We make two remarks about that definition. Firstly, it obviously requires some operator for nesting relations within relations. We are presently studying the properties of such an operator. Secondly, note that the entry in the table of the resulting relation is a pair of procedure values. Non pairs could be allowed, provided that the definition of the relative product operator is changed.

We can now discuss the procedure call, which has the simple form $[\![X]\!]$, since X has no parameters. Assume that we have defined a set PROC $\subseteq$ **Rel** such that if the program fragment P is a procedure declaration then $\rho(P) \in PROC$. To the call $[\![X]\!]$ we associate the relation

$$CALL_X \equiv \{f | \exists R \in PROC, f(X) = <R,R> \land f \upharpoonright (A-\{X\}) \in R\}$$

When this relation $CALL_X$ is composed with relations corresponding to other program fragments, then one of two things can happen. Either X is declared, and the irrelevant procedure values are eliminated, or X is not declared, and the identifier X is global to the program resulting from the composition of the fragments. Whether this is legal or not depends on the context and on the language.

4.2. Laws of programming

It is an interesting exercise to examine laws of programming in the light of the above relational semantics. Some identities that can be easily derived are:

(a) $\rho[\![\text{if true then P else Q}]\!] = \rho[\![P]\!]$

(b) $\rho[\![\text{if false then P else Q}]\!] = \rho[\![Q]\!]$

(c) $\rho[\![\text{var x:t; var x:t}]\!] = \rho[\![\text{var x:t}]\!]$

(d) $\rho[\![\text{var x:t1; var y:t2}]\!] = \rho[\![\text{var y:t2; var x:t1}]\!]$

(e) $\rho[\![\text{skip; P}]\!] = [\![\text{P; skip}]\!] = \rho[\![P]\!]$

(f) $\rho[\![P;(Q;R)]\!] = \rho[\![(P;Q);R]\!]$

In these equations, P, Q, and R stand for the appropriate program fragments. Equation (f) holds when P, Q, R are all declarations or all commands. We have not defined $\rho[\![D;C]\!]$ above; a suitable definition would be $\rho[\![D;C]\!] = \rho[\![D]\!] \circ \rho[\![C]\!]$. Equations (e) and (f) would then be valid for mixed declarations and commands.

Some laws that are valid when a fixed program space is assumed are not true when the above semantics is used. For example, using axiomatic definitions [Hoare 69], one has $\{p\}[\![x:=x]\!]\{p\}$ and $\{p\}[\![skip]\!]\{p\}$ for any assertion p on the space (which is assumed to have a x component), so that $[\![x:=x]\!]$ and $[\![skip]\!]$ are considered equivalent. But $\rho[\![x:=x]\!] \neq \rho[\![skip]\!]$, because $\rho[\![x:=x]\!]$ introduces a x component, and $\rho[\![skip]\!]$ does not. On the other hand $\rho[\![\text{var x:t; x:=x}]\!] = \rho[\![\text{var x:t}]\!]$ holds. Now, assume a fixed program space SP. Is it possible to have $\rho(P) = \rho(Q)$ and $\{p\}P\{q\} \neq \{p\}Q\{q\}$ for some programs P, Q on SP and assertions p, q about states in SP? A simple argument shows that the answer is no. The relation $\rho(P)$ corresponding to a fragment P has a component for every variable that is mentioned in P; variables not mentioned cannot change. Hence, $\rho(P)$ gives all the information about the possible state transitions induced by P.

Finally, let us look at the two programs $[\![$if b then P else if b then Q else R$]\!]$ and $[\![$if b then P else R$]\!]$.

$\rho[\![$if b then P else if b then Q else R$]\!]$
$= \rho[\![b]\!]_T \circ \rho[\![P]\!] \cup \rho[\![b]\!]_F \circ \rho[\![$if b then Q else R$]\!]$
$= \rho[\![b]\!]_T \circ \rho[\![P]\!] \cup \rho[\![b]\!]_F \circ (\rho[\![b]\!]_T \circ \rho[\![Q]\!] \cup \rho[\![b]\!]_F \circ \rho[\![R]\!])$

By proposition 2.21 and remark 3.7 we have
$= \rho[\![b]\!]_T \circ \rho[\![P]\!] \cup \rho[\![b]\!]_F \circ \rho[\![b]\!]_T \circ \rho[\![Q]\!] \cup \rho[\![b]\!]_F \circ \rho[\![R]\!]$

Now, $\rho[\![$if b then P else R$]\!] = \rho[\![b]\!]_T \circ \rho[\![P]\!] \cup \rho[\![b]\!]_F \circ \rho[\![R]\!]$. Since Q can be any relation, the two programs will be equivalent iff $\rho[\![b]\!]_F \circ \rho[\![b]\!]_T = \emptyset$. But

$\rho[\![b]\!]_F \circ \rho[\![b]\!]_T = \rho[\![b]\!]_F \bowtie \rho[\![b]\!]_T$ by remark 3.7
$= \rho[\![b]\!]_F \cap \rho[\![b]\!]_T$ by proposition 2.22

Hence the two programs will behave the same provided that the evaluation of b in a given state always yields T, or always F. For our language, this will be the case if the primitive operators are deterministic, which is a reasonable assumption. But if the language is non deterministic and allows user-defined functions as operators in expressions, then the two program fragments may behave differently.

4.3. Application: new operations

Considering a program as a relation (table) suggests new ways of combining programs.

Let R=$\rho[\![$procedure X ...$]\!]$. Consider the relation R[C], where C$\subset$sch(R). This corresponds to a procedure Y, similar to X, but with a reduced number of parameters or global identifiers; that is, R[C]=$\rho[\![$procedure Y ...$]\!]$ for some Y. What are the restrictions on C such that Y is meaningful? This problem can be studied with the help of a notion that has received a lot of attention in database theory [Maier 83]: that of dependencies. As an example, take X to be

procedure X (var x:int; var y:int; var z:bool) ...

and assume that X has no global variables. Suppose that the following dependencies

hold:
$$x \to y, x \to z$$
that is, y and z are uniquely determined by x. Then obviously, suppressing the x component of X should not be done; but removing z still allows y to be computed. Hence a definition of a procedure Y could have the form
$$\text{procedure } Y = X[x,y]$$
Given the dependencies, a syntactical transformation could be done on X, with result Y.

As another operation that might promote software reuse, we mention the following. Let X and Y be procedure declarations. Define procedure Z by
$$\rho[\![Z]\!] = \rho[\![X]\!] \bowtie \rho[\![Y]\!]$$
i.e., Z is the "join" of X and Y. For example, suppose that $X(x,r,\theta)$ computes the x coordinate of a point (r,θ) given in polar coordinates, and that $Y(y,r,\theta)$ computes the y coordinate. Then, $Z(x,y,r,\theta)$ computes the point (x,y).

5. CONCLUSION

In this paper, we have given a *relation level* denotational semantics of a programming language that includes procedures, basic types, and variable declarations. The algebra that we have used is a variant of Codd's relational algebra [Codd 70] augmented by a *relative product* operation and a *transitive closure* operation. The level of the semantic definitions is that of axiomatic definitions [Hoare 69] rather than that of traditional denotational semantics [Scott 76, Stoy 77]; for example, locations are not considered. This level of description is suitable for the study of correctness of programs with respect to specifications.

Programming in the language that we have defined is object level programming, because programs are built from variables, expressions, declarations, etc. But in an ideal situation, a specification would be given by a relational expression, and a program correct with respect to the specification would be generated by a sequence of relation level transformations, followed by a mapping of the last relational expression to a program. This derivation process is similar to the function level transformations of Backus [Backus 85], which start from a high level functional program and end with a low level efficient one.

Other control constructs could possibly be described by extending the relational framework that we have presented. However, our present interests are different, and our research efforts are proceeding in the following two main directions. First, we are examining ways to produce relation level specifications. For this, we describe the primitive domains and the primitive relations by relational axioms, instead of giving object level definitions like the ones we have given for the operator "<" and the relation EQUAL [Desharnais 88]. We also refer to [De Bakker 73, Berghammer 86] for examples of (binary) relation level specifications of the domain of integers.

We are also investigating the addition of nesting and unnesting operators to our algebra. These permit the nesting of relations within relations, so that components of a relation could be complex types, procedures, modules, etc. Similar operators, but in the context of databases, have recently been studied by, e.g., Fischer and Thomas [Fischer 83]. Our aim is to find laws of programming (in the style of those of [Hoare 87]) that can be applied to constructs that are higher level than the control constructs of conventional while programs.

ACKNOWLEDGEMENTS

The authors are thankful to the referees for making helpful and interesting comments that have improved this paper. This work is supported in part by NSERC (Canada) and l'Université Laval (Québec).

6. REFERENCES

[Backus 85] J. Backus. From function level semantics to program transformation and optimization. *Mathematical Foundations of Software Development*. Proc. Int. Joint Conf. on Theory and Practice of Software Development (TAPSOFT), Berlin, March 1985, Vol. 1, Lecture Notes in Comp. Sci. 185, Springer-Verlag 1985, 60-91.

[De Bakker 73] J. W. De Bakker and W. P. De Roever. A calculus for recursive program schemes. *Automata, languages and programming*. Proc. symp. organized by IRIA, Rocquencourt, France, July 1972, (M. Nivat, ed.), North-Holland 1973, 167-196.

[Berghammer 86] R. Berghammer and H. Zierer. Relational algebraic semantics of deterministic and nondeterministic programs. *Theor. Comput. Sci.* 43, 1986, 123-147.

[Blikle 77] A. Blikle. A comparative review of some program verification methods. *Proc. 6th Symp. Math. Found. Comput. Sci.*, (J. Gruska, ed.), Lecture Notes in Comp. Sci. 53, Springer-Verlag 1977, 17-33.

[Codd 70] E.F. Codd. A relational model for large shared data banks. *Commun. ACM* 13, 6, June 1970, 377-387.

[Desharnais 88] J. Desharnais and N. Madhavji. Object-free relational specification and program derivation. Internal technical report, available from the authors.

[Fischer 83] P.C. Fischer and S.J. Thomas. Operators for non-first-normal-form relations. *Proc. 7th Int. Computer Software & Applications Conference (COMPSAC 83)*, Chicago, IL, IEEE Comp. Soc. Press 1983, 464-475.

[Hoare 69] C. A. R. Hoare. An axiomatic basis for computer programming. *Commun. ACM* 12, 10, October 1969, 576-581.

[Hoare 86] C. A. R. Hoare and He Jifeng. The weakest prespecification. *Fundam. Inform.* IX, 1986, Part I: 51-84, Part II: 217-252.

[Hoare 87] C.A.R. Hoare, I.J. Hayes, He Jifeng, C.C. Morgan, A.W. Roscoe, J.W. Sanders, I.H. Sorensen, J.M. Spivey and B.A. Sufrin. Laws of Programming. *Commun. ACM* 30, 8, August 87, pp. 672-686. Plus Corrigenda: *Commun. ACM* 30, 9, September 87, p. 770.

[Maier 83] D. Maier. *The theory of relational databases.* Computer Science Press, Inc., Rockville, MD, 1983.

[Mili 83] A. Mili. A relational approach to the design of deterministic programs. *Acta Inform.* 20, 1983, 315-328.

[Mili 87] A. Mili, J. Desharnais and F. Mili. Relational heuristics for the design of deterministic programs. *Acta Inform.* 24, 1987, 239-276.

[Schmidt 81] G. Schmidt. Programs as partial graphs I: Flow equivalence and correctness. *Theor. Comput. Sci.* 15, 1981, 1-25.

[Scott 76] D. Scott. Data types as lattices. *SIAM J. Comput.* 5, 3, September 1976, 522-587.

[Stoy 77] J. E. Stoy. *Denotational semantics: The Scott-Strachey approach to programming language theory.* The MIT Press, Cambridge, MA, 1977.

[Tarski 41] A. Tarski. On the calculus of relations. *J. Symb. Log.* 6, 3, September 1941, 73-89.

[Tarski 55] A. Tarski. A lattice-theoretical fixpoint theorem and its applications. *Pacific J. Math.* 5, 1955, 285-309.

A CONSTRUCTIVE SET THEORY FOR PROGRAM DEVELOPMENT
Martin C. Henson & Raymond Turner
Department of Computer Science,
University of Essex, Wivenhoe Park, Colchester, Essex,
ENGLAND

ABSTRACT

We present a constructive theory of types and kinds (called TK5) designed with program development as the major desideratum. We motivate its definition with respect to existing research in the area of program logics (in particular Martin-Lof's theory of types) and establish suitable infrastructure for program extraction from proofs of specifications.

1 INTRODUCTION

In recent years there has been a great deal of interest in the development of programs within some constructive framework. The most popular theory seems to be Martin Lof's constructive theory of types. This theory has been used more or less directly (for example in [Khamiss 86] and [Abbas 87]) and forms the essential basis for the most well-developed and well-known program logic, NuPRL [Constable 86]. Other paradigms have also been studied, for example, the Theory of Constructions [Mohring 85], Feferman's theory T_0 [Beeson 86] [Hayashi 87], and variants of Intuitionistic Zermelo-Fraenkel set theory which incorporate primitive notions of 'rules' [Beeson 88]. In this paper we propose an alternative theory of constructive sets based on elementary comprehension and a programming notation based on Miranda [Turner 85].

Research in program development using Martin-Lof's type theory, in particular, has highlighted a number of interesting problems. These arise as a consequence of certain demands which the task of program development imposes upon the theory. We shall examine several of these problem areas in this introduction as a way of motivating the constructive theory of sets, TK5, which we introduce in section 2. In section 3 we introduce and develop some notions of realizabilty which are designed to recover the computational content of proofs in a natural fashion and we also elaborate some meta-mathematical results of interest. For reasons of space we have not been able to provide full details of the proofs of the theorems stated in section 3, nor yet the proof of the consistency of the theory we are proposing. These we intend to incorporate in a somewhat more extended treatment of this material elsewhere.

1.1 Subtypes

Martin-Lof's type theory (MLTT) is based on a notion of *completely presented set*. That is to say, every member of a type carries its own proof that it is, indeed, a member of that type. For example, an element of the set of even natural numbers is an even number, n, (in the informal sense) together with witnessing evidence of its 'evenness' (a natural number, m, and the 'proof' 2.m = n). This principle of complete presentation makes the theory very rigidly typed. Quite early in the computational investigation of MLTT it was found necessary to introduce the notion of a sub-type. [Petersson 84] provides one approach but there are a number of other possibilities, for example that utilised in NuPRL. The sub-type construction was to be used to supress certain witnessing information (of the kind we have just illustrated) which is not to occur in, or is not to be manipulated by (at least conventional) programs. One might wonder, then, why some form of 'separation type' was not included in MLTT in the first instance. However, a completely presented form of separation already exists in the guise of the general sum type. Subtyping in the sense it has been included in MLTT is, because it does

not respect the principle of complete presentation, an incoherent extension. This
is not just a philosophical point: many researchers [Nordstrom 87] have commented
that supressing information at one point in a derivation may irrecoverably lead to
problems at a later stage.

We were drawn from this evidence to design a constructive set theory which is much
more flexibly typed; one in which sub-types, that is a principle of separation (in
fact, in TK5 we allow elementary comprehension) is seen as a major desideratum. In
this respect it resembles Feferman's theories more closely than Martin Lof's.

1.2 General recursion

Another problem of MLTT is the absence of general recursion. This is not a
mathematical limitation because general recursions on some base type can be
realized as primitive recursions at a higher type. For example, in [Smith 83]
the Ackermann function is derived as a primitive recursive functional. From a
computational perspective, which is concerned amongst other things with intensions
as well as extensions, this seems awkward. Moreover, although the general type
constructor for inductive types in MLTT, known as the W-type constructor, is, as
expected, consistent with the principle of complete presentation, it is somewhat
unnatural from a computational viewpoint, since we do not expect our programs to
manipulate information regarding their termination properties explicitly. Finally,
it has also been noted [Saaman 87] that the W-types interface rather badly with the
sub-type construction, for the reasons outlined at the end of 1.1.

These three areas of concern have led to a further addition to MLTT, namely, the
acc-type [Nordstrom 87]. If we consider the issue of complete presentation once
again it seems that acc-types stand in relation to the W-type rather as the
sub-types do to the general sum types. This new type construction has been used to
overcome the problem areas outlined above, but one is left with the feeling that
there is something much more systematically inappropriate with the underlying
theory which these additions serve to highlight, but which they do not solve
satisfactorily. In particular, it seems curious that there should be two notions
of sub-type and two notions of inductive type in the theory.

It is clear that we must include some way of introducing inductive sets in TK5.
This must be done in a natural way so that it subsumes the roles that both the
W-type and the acc-type play in the extended versions of MLTT.

1.3 Expressivity

MLTT is also based on the 'propositions as types' idea. Newcomers to the theory
are often suprised at the 'logic free' nature of the judgement forms and think
Martin-Lof excessively parsimonious in identifying complex assertions with types.
Viewed naively it seems that the assertion structure of the system has been pared
down to the atomic assertions (regarding membership and equality) and that the more
complex formulae are re-embedded into the type structure. Philosophically there is
rather more to this issue for Martin-Lof makes a crucial distinction between
propositions on the one hand and judgements on the other, but this is not the place
to elaborate these ideas further. In order to express some of the rules (those for
sub-types for example) it has been found necessary to extend MLTT, once again, by
recovering the logical force of types by including a new judgement form: 'A true'
which is to be read as: 'there is a member of the type A'. For computer scientists
types are most naturally thought of as collections of data structures (which we
take to include functions, polymorphic functions and data abstractions) and this
pun seems at first sight rather arcane. We take, the introduction of the new
judgement form: 'A true' as evidence to support the conceptually distinct roles for
data types and for assertions.

With this in mind we are drawn to a theory in which types are essentially the
expected collections of data structures and which supports a conventional language

of assertions. A corollary of this is that it is possible to unpack what it is for
something to be a type in TK5 by a simple context free grammar (rather than by
proof theoretic means like those adopted by Martin-Lof and Feferman). The
correspondence between propositions and types is still available within TK5 via an
internal interpretation of assertions as types, but we do not force the complete
identification which exists in MLTT (see section 3.4).

So much for logical expressivity. We are also concerned that the term structure of
the theory should support a suitably expressive programming language. Initially we
felt that the term language of the theory should itself be such a language. This
seems to follow the advice of Beeson [Beeson 86] and certainly [Hayashi 87] in
which LISP is such a choice. We now believe that the system should support a
design philosophy rather than a language, that is to say, the passage from the
language to the term structures should be natural (in some sense). These issues
extend beyond the design of the term structure of the theory and impinge on the
type structures and program extraction techniques too. In order to find the
correct balance between mathematical tractability and practical utility we have
found it appropriate to allow the higher level programming notation to appear in
the combinatorial operations which correspond (via a realizability interpretation)
to the logical rules of the theory. TK5 has been designed with programming
languages like Miranda [Turner 85] in mind. We will see later (particularly in
1.6, 3.1 and 3.3.2) how the nature of such languages have guided our design.

1.4 Extracting programs from proofs

One of the fundamental reasons for considering *constructive* theories is the
computational content of proofs. The most widely known technique for making this
explicit are the techniques of realizability, a concept originally due to Kleene
[Kleene 45], and MLTT is, in some sense, a theory of abstract realizability. A
crucial idea behind 'propositions as types' is that if an assertion is derivable
then the type of its realizers (the collection of 'programs' which make a
constructive proof computationally explicit) is inhabited.

Let us look at this a little more carefully. Consider the assertion x∈A in some
constructive theory of sets. What is a realizer for this? That is, what makes the
content of a proof of this explicit? Presumably something like: evidence that x
meets the defining conditions of A. This idea has a long heritage and has been
formalised [Kreisel 70] by:

   $e \rho x \in A$ is $<x,e> \in A*$

In this we are to read: "$e \rho \Phi$" as "e realizes Φ" and $A*$ is some completely
presented version of A which can be defined by cases over the forms which A can
take. For example, and most importantly, let $A = \{z | \Phi(z)\}$ then:
$A* = \{<e,x> | e \rho \Phi(x)\}$. This technique can be used to internalise realizability by
the device of completely presented sets. Indeed, providing the notion of
realizability is sound, we may drop all reference to the incompletely presented
sets.

Since we have argued in 1.1 that completely presented sets are rather unwieldy we
have designed TK5 so that program extraction (by some notion of realizability) is
separated from the logical derivation of specifications. Moreover, this separation
allows for a good deal of flexibility in establishing techniques for extracting
programs from proofs (as we shall see in 1.6 and section 3).

1.5 Higher order types

The theory ML_0 is certainly insufficient for program development. In order to
define even the most trivial inductive types it is necessary to use the first
universe (that is the theory ML_1). This also follows if we wish to formalise
polymorphism and data abstraction. TK5 is, therefore, like MLTT a stratified

theory (employing a 'kind' hierarchy) with each additional level containing the universe of its predecessor. However, there is a major design decision, highlighted by the various versions of MLTT which Martin-Lof has considered, which we have to take. In MLTT-75 [Martin-Lof 75] and MLTT-79 [Martin-Lof 79] the types of one level are members of the universe introduced at the next. This is captured by a rule that states that from 'A∈U' we may conclude 'A type'. In MLTT-80 [Martin-Lof 82] it is the names of types which are members of the corresponding universe. An operation T is employed to obtain the types from the names. Thus the inference rule above is recast: from 'a∈U' we may conclude that 'T(a) type'.

In TK5 we also have a choice along these lines. We must ask whether kinds are to classify types or terms. If we adopt the former we should conclude that (for example) a pair of types, which belongs to a suitable cartesian product kind, is a type. But this seems inconsistent with the idea of types as collections (constructive sets). If we take the latter approach we see a pair of types as a special sort of term which happens to belong to a certain kind. Under this interpretation kinds of various levels all classify terms, and since every kind at one level may be construed as a kind at the next, we see the kind hierarchcy as a sequence of term classification systems, each a refinement of its predecessor. Since, as we indicated in 1.3, terms and types (and indeed kinds of arbitrary level) are to be given in TK5 by a context free grammar we have no need for an operation analogous to T, for the inclusion of types in terms is controlled by the grammar of terms and the axioms which govern membership in kinds.

1.6 Polymorphism

The notion of type polymorphism is now unquestionably of profound importance in language design and in programming. Leivant [Leivant 83] describes two kinds of polymorphism which, while mathematically equivalent, represent different approaches to polymorphic programming. The *type abstraction* approach leads to programming notations similar in spirit to second order lambda calculus whereas the *type quantificational* notion is consonant with languages like Miranda. There are three ways of considering polymorphism within MLTT. The first is to see that the rules of the system are in some sense polymophic with respect to the types which they mention. For example, in a premise of the form "A type" A is an arbitrary placeholder for a type. From this observation we see that proof objects may be constructed from derivations which are 'polymorphic' over such genericity in the rules. Such polymorphism is rather weak, since it relies on meta notions; we cannot actually express this polymorphism within the theory. The second approach is to utilise the general product rules of the first universe for this allows the construction of higher order types which quantify over types of a lower order. Since the rules for products in MLTT correspond to the type abstraction notion of polymorphism we are forced to accept this as our interpretation of polymorphism. The third approach (which is detailed in [Malcolm 88], though they attribute the technique to Nordstrom) is to include a new type constructor into MLTT, roughly an 'intersection type'. This allows for the type quantification approach to polymorphism within the theory, although at the expense of yet another extension to the theory; this time 'ghosting' the general product types, much as the subtypes and acc-types ghost the general sum and W-types respectively.

Since we are attempting to design a theory which follows the philosophy of languages like Miranda we prefer to adopt a different interpretation of higher order products so that we obtain a regime of polymorphism of the type quantificational kind. However, we ensure that this approach to polymorphism is taken as a basic desideratum of the theory; we do not wish to have to adopt some ad-hoc modification of the theory. The issue is described in detail in 3.1.

1.7 Intensionality

Should the sets of a constructive set theory for program development be extensional or intensional? There are two versions of MLTT (which we have already mentioned) one of which [Martin-Lof 75] is intensional and one extensional [Martin-Lof 79]. Work within the MLTT framework has proceeded within the more recent extensional version but there does not seem to be much in the way of a debate as to whether this is for historical reasons or for reasons concerned with program development philosophy.

We are convinced that intensional theories are appropriate for our application. Firstly, we note that programming concerns itself with both extensional and intensional properties of programs. When we view collections of programs (functions) as data types in an extensional theory we lose their intensional structure. Secondly, it is impossible to link the intensional structure of a program with the intensional structure of its domain of definition in an extensional theory of types. Thirdly, we wish the *object* theory to support the intensional distinctions which we regard as important. In general, mathematical formalisations of computing objects underwrite extensional equivalence (for example, sanctioning the individual steps in a program transformation exercise) and it is left to the *meta* theory to articulate these intensional distinctions (for example, to conclude that the result of a program transformation exercise yields a more efficient program).

These brief remarks hardly do justice to the issue. It is rather difficult in this introduction to do more than just raise the question. In fact, we feel that the subject of intensionality has been more or less overlooked so far and deserves much more attention. It seems to the authors that the logical structure of the theory (which, of course, is constructive) is in some sense a philosophical consequence of the underlying intensionality of the set theory. This area requires more research but suggests that intensionality is the most fundamental property of a theory of program development. Unfortunately we shall not be able to pursue this topic further in the current paper for it is best studied in connection with the practice of the theory. We refer the reader to [Henson 88] for further details.

1.8 Partiality

MLTT considers only total mappings. Whilst it is certain that the task of designing programs which are what has been called 'totally correct' is of fundamental importance we are not yet sure that we are ready to abandon the possible role for partial functions. On this issue, then, we follow at least the spirit of the NuPRL approach.

2 THE CONSTRUCTIVE SET THEORY TK5

2.1 Terms

The term structure of TK5 is the untyped lambda calculus extended by the addition of some arbitrary constants, kind abstractions, kind expressions (of arbitrary level) and formulae:

$$t \to x \mid c \mid \lambda x.t \mid \lambda x^n.t \mid (t\ t) \mid K^n \mid \Phi$$

We will use, without further elaboration, standard syntactic sugarings for pairing and selectors, conditional, boolean constants and so on. Although it might be better to include these as basic, for well known reasons, it does little to improve the presentation in the present context.

Other sugarings are more sophisticated and in a sense constitute a formal compilation process: we write, in particular, function definitions using pattern directed recursion equations. These are unpacked via a collection of combinators

(which are of course lambda definable) due to Turner [Turner 79] (but see also
[Henson 87] and [Peyton-Jones 87] for example). We shall see terms of this kind
just a little in this paper (in sections 3.1 and 3.3); there are many more examples
in the companion paper [Henson 88].

We have adopted an untyped calculus for two reasons. Firstly, it supports the
programming notation we have just discussed and secondly, it corresponds to a
principle of comprehension which forms the basis of the type structure we are about
to expound. In other investigations we have introduced a type theory TK3 based on
a typed calculus. This corresponds to a principle of separation for types and to a
programming language similar syntactically to the second order lambda calculus.

Finally, a word about 'formulae as terms'. This has been chosen for meta-
mathematical convenience only; although in the future it may be justified when we
consider operations on specifications. We could have omitted formulae as terms but
this would complicate the analysis of 3.4 by requiring some explicit Gödel
coding in that context.

2.2   Types and Kinds

The type structure of TK5 is hierarchical. The base level consists of a language
of *types* (or 'kinds of level zero') written: K^0. Thereafter we iterate
through *kinds* (K^1) to a hierarchy of higher order kinds: K^n.

At each level we inherit kinds of the preceeding level, and introduce variables,
restricted comprehension and induction. As we shall see, comprehension allows for
the definition of the expected type constructors (products, function spaces, data
abstractions, polymorphisms and so on) while the inductive generation provides us
with a mechasnism for satisfying certain recursive type specifications (natural
numbers, lists, trees and so on). In fact there are a number of subtly different
forms of general inductive generation which we can consider; other possibilities
(in particular a principle of monotone induction) will be reported on in due
course.

$$K^0 \rightarrow x^0 \mid \{x \mid \Phi^0\} \mid \Xi(\Phi^0(x), K^0)$$
$$K^n \rightarrow x^n \mid \{x \mid \Phi^n\} \mid \Xi(\Phi^n(x^{n-1}), K^n) \mid K^{n-1}$$

Note that, in line with our discussion in section 1.5, the comprehension terms at
each level collect objects (denotations of terms) and not kinds of the previous
level. The variable x in the comprehension terms is considered to be bound. The
situation for inductive kinds is a little more involved. In $\Xi(\Phi^n(x^{n-1}), K^n)$, x^{n-1} is a tuple of variables (of kind index not exceeding
n-1) free in Φ^n. These become bound in the inductive kind expression
$\Xi(\Phi^n(x^{n-1}), K^n)$. It will usually be quite clear which variables
free in Φ^n remain free in the inductive kind, and apart from here, where it is
important to be precise, we will avoid excessive pedantry over this issue.

2.3   Formulae

TK5 is a theory over the *logic of partial terms* [Beeson 85]. Atomic assertions
correspond to membership in kinds, equality of terms, definedness and absurdity:

$$\alpha \rightarrow t \in K^n \mid t = t \mid t\downarrow \mid \perp$$

Well-formed formulae of the theory are constructed in the expected way, but include
quantification at all levels of the kind hierarchy:

$$\Phi \rightarrow \alpha \mid \Phi \wedge \Phi \mid \Phi \vee \Phi \mid \Phi \rightarrow \Phi \mid (\forall x)\Phi \mid (\forall x^n)\Phi \mid (\exists x)\Phi \mid (\exists x^n)\Phi$$

In 2.2 the reader will notice that formulae in some contexts are subscripted. This
restricts the formation of comprehension and inductive kinds at each level. We

take Φ^n to be that class of formulae involving bound variables with indices strictly less then n (for this purpose we treat object variables as having a negative index). Note that since terms appear within formulae by virtue of the atomic assertions we can have variables bound by lambda abstraction, by comprehension and by inductive generation (as well as by the usual quantifiers).

2.4 Axioms

The axiom system of TK5 falls into three categories. First we have the theory of the partial lambda calculus. This is based on the logic of partial terms which we turn to first.

The logic of partial terms is a version of predicate calculus which allows the formation of terms which may not denote. Term and formulae formation remain as usual but atomic formulae are extended to include the assertion $t\downarrow$ which is to be read "t denotes". The only changes to the inference rules concern the rules for universal elimination, existential introduction and equality. The former are recast in such a way as to remove the possibility of infering something of a non-denoting term.

$$\frac{(\forall x)\Phi \quad t\downarrow}{\Phi(t)} \qquad \frac{\Phi(t) \quad t\downarrow}{(\exists x)\Phi}$$

We assume a standard rule system for the rest of the logic but will not list them here. For equality we introduce the shorthand $t \simeq t'$ for $t\downarrow \vee t'\downarrow \to t = t'$. The axioms for equality and denotation are then:

E1 $t = t \wedge (t_1 = t_2 \to t_2 = t_1)$
E2 $t_1 \simeq t_2 \wedge \Phi(t_1) \to \Phi(t_2)$
D1 $(t_1 = t_2) \to t_1\downarrow \wedge t_2\downarrow$
D2 $(t_1 t_2)\downarrow \to t_1\downarrow \wedge t_2\downarrow$
D3 $t \in K^n \to t\downarrow$
D4 $x\downarrow \wedge c\downarrow \wedge K^n\downarrow \wedge \Phi\downarrow$

Beeson shows [Beeson 81] that the logic of partial terms is only a convenient expression for standard (classical or intuitionistic) predicate calculus.

The axioms for the partial lambda calculus are now expressed as follows:

(alpha) $\lambda x.t = \lambda y.t[x \leftarrow y]$ (y not free in t)
(beta) $(\lambda x.t)y \simeq t[x \leftarrow y]$
(beta-n) $(\lambda x^n.t)y^n \simeq t[x^n \leftarrow y^n]$

Where $t[x \leftarrow y]$ is our notation for the term t in which free occurences of x are replaced by y (the definition is as expected). The other expected rules for the lambda calculus now follow as elementary consequences of axiom E2.

We can now turn to the second category, the axioms governing membership in kinds:

COMP^n $z \in \{x \mid \Phi^n\} \leftrightarrow \Phi^n(z)$

CLO1^n $z \in K^n \to z \in \Xi(\Phi^n, K^n)$

CLO2^n $(\forall x)(\Phi^n(z,x) \to x \in \Xi(\Phi^n, K^n)) \to z \in \Xi(\Phi^n, K^n)$

The first is an axiom of comprehension, the second and third are closure axioms for the inductive kinds.

The third category consists of just one axiom scheme; the induction principle of TK5:

$\text{IND}^n \quad (\forall z)(z \in \Xi(\Phi^n, K^n) \rightarrow$
$\qquad\qquad (\forall x)(\Phi^n(z,x) \rightarrow \psi(x)) \rightarrow \psi(z)) \rightarrow (\forall z)(z \in \Xi(\Phi^n, K^n) \rightarrow \psi(z))$

We will find it convenient to adopt a modified axiom for closure, in the form of a single biconditional:

$\text{CLOS}^n \quad z \in \Xi(\Phi^n, K^n) \leftrightarrow$
$\qquad\qquad z \in K^n \vee ((\forall x)(\Phi^n(z,x) \rightarrow x \in \Xi(\Phi^n, K^n))) \rightarrow z \in \Xi(\Phi^n, K^n)$

Proposition 2.4.1

CLOS^n is equivalent to $\text{CLO1}^n + \text{CLO2}^n$

proof
($\leftarrow$) trivial. ($\rightarrow$) by $\Xi(\Phi^n, K^n)$-induction
∎

2.5 Infrastructure for program development

TK5 as it stands lacks the infrastructure necessary for program development, but this is easily rectified. In 2.1 we indicated how the term structure is designed to support a programming notation like that of Miranda by means of a formal compilation strategy. In this section we turn our attention to types.

2.5.1 Basic type constructions

Elementary comprehension supports the definition of expected data types, like products, sums and functions. Although we may define them at arbitrary levels in the kind hierarchy we present what follows in the first two kind levels. For clarity of presentation we shall use capital letters to represent variables of index 0, that is, variables which range over the types (kinds of level 0).

$$
\begin{array}{lcl}
X \otimes Y & = & \{z \mid (\text{fst } z) \in X \wedge (\text{snd } z) \in Y\} \\
X \oplus Y & = & \{z \mid (\text{fst } z) \rightarrow (\text{snd } z) \in X, (\text{snd } z) \in Y\} \\
X \cup Y & = & \{z \mid z \in X \vee z \in Y\} \\
X \rightarrow_p Y & = & \{z \mid (\forall x \in X)((z\ x)\!\downarrow \rightarrow (z\ x) \in Y)\} \\
X \rightarrow_T Y & = & \{z \mid (\forall x \in X)((z\ x)\!\downarrow \wedge (z\ x) \in Y)\} \\
\{x1, \ldots, xn\} & = & \{z \mid z = x1 \vee \ldots \vee z = xn\} \\
\text{Bool} & = & \{\text{true, false}\} \\
X \subseteq Y & \leftrightarrow & (\forall x \in X)(x \in Y) \\
X \equiv Y & \leftrightarrow & X \subseteq Y \wedge Y \subseteq X
\end{array}
$$

In the above we have utilised two extensions to the assertion language. Bounded quantification is defined as expected: $(\forall x \in X)\Phi \leftrightarrow (\forall x)(x \in X \rightarrow \Phi)$. The *conditional assertion* used in the elaboration of disjoint union types is less familiar. An assertion similar (though not equivalent) to this was first adopted in [Hayashi 87]. There are two (equivalent) interpretations of these assertions:

$$
\begin{array}{lcl}
t \rightarrow \Phi, \psi & \leftrightarrow & (t = \text{true} \wedge \Phi) \vee (t = \text{false} \wedge \psi) \\
t \rightarrow \Phi, \psi & \leftrightarrow & t \in \text{Bool} \wedge (t = \text{true} \rightarrow \Phi) \wedge (t = \text{false} \rightarrow \psi)
\end{array}
$$

In section 3.3 we explain why such sugaring of assertions is crucial and why, in particular, we adopt two formulations for conditional assertions.

Above and beyond these elementary constructions we can introduce polymorphisms and data abstractions.

$$
\begin{array}{lcl}
\pi(X,Y) & = & \{z \mid (\forall X)(z \in Y)\} \\
\sigma(X,Y) & = & \{z \mid (\exists X)(z \in Y)\}
\end{array}
$$

π(X,Y) is a collection of objects which have the property of belonging to all instantiations of some type scheme (Y, in interesting cases, is instantiated with an expression with X free) it therefore contains what are usually understood as polymorphic objects. σ(X,Y), on the other hand, contain elements which belong to some instantiation of the type scheme Y. σ(X,Y) is a data abstraction every member of which belongs to a type formed from Y with respect to an implementing type X. Note that both of these are definitions of constructions in K^1 (because each comprehension term utilize bound variables over types (K^0)) and that X is bound in both π(X,Y) and σ(X,Y).

2.5.2 Recursive types

We now illustrate the inductive type construction by introducing a number of useful recursive types. We begin by defining the following assertions:

$$\Phi(x,y) \Leftrightarrow x = (\text{succ } y)$$
$$\psi(x,y) \Leftrightarrow (\exists a \in A)(x = \langle a,y \rangle)$$
$$\beta(x,y,z) \Leftrightarrow x = \langle y,z \rangle$$

and use these as the basis for the following inductive types:

$$\text{Nat} = \Xi(\Phi,\{0\})$$
$$\text{List} = \Xi(\psi,\{[\,]\})$$
$$\text{Sexp} = \Xi(\beta,A)$$

These are natural numbers, lists (of elements of A) and s-expressions (over the set A). The tokens succ, 0 and [] are just arbitrary constants of the term language.

In fact it might be more natural to define lists and s-expressions as operations which yield types given some base type:

$$\text{List} = \lambda X.\Xi(\psi,\{[\,]\}) \quad \text{where:} \quad \psi(X,x,y) \Leftrightarrow (\exists z \in X)(x = \langle z,y \rangle)$$
$$\text{Sexp} = \lambda X.\Xi(\beta,X)$$

It is now possible to prove the following:

Proposition 2.5.2.1

(i)   Nat   ≡ {0} ∪ {succ} ⊗ Nat
(ii) List(X) ≡ {[]} ∪ X ⊗ List(X)
(iii) Sexp(X) ≡ X ∪ Sexp(X) ⊗ Sexp(X)

proof
(→) by Ξ-induction. (←) by closure.
∎

In each case we obtain from the axiom scheme IND the expected induction principles for Nat, List(A) and Sexp(A). It is worth mentioning that the 'official' syntax for the inductive kind, List, is $\lambda X.\Xi(\psi(x,y),\{[\,]\})$, that is to say, X remains free in List.

The types we have introduced are those one might expect to come across in a modern functional programming language (like Miranda in particular). We have omitted one or two important type constructions (which appear in MLTT for example) but these will be considered in their proper context; that is when we turn to our interpretation of the slogan 'propositions as types' in section 3.4.

3 REALIZABILITY, PROGRAM EXTRACTION AND PROPOSITIONS AS TYPES

In this section we introduce a notion of realizability for TK5 and show how it can be used to internalise a mechanism for obtaining programs (in the sugared term language) from proofs of specifications (articulated in the assertion language).

3.1 DESIGNING A REALIZABILTY INTERPRETATION FOR TK5

The technique of realizability was originally introduced [Kleene 45] to capture formally the constructive meaning of the logical operations. To each formula, Φ, we associate another, written "$e \, \rho \, \Phi$", which is to be read "e realizes Φ" or more suggestively: "e is a program which meets the specification Φ". The idea is that the translation makes the constructive character of assertions explicit.

Realizability interpretations are very useful for proving meta-theorems for a wide variety of constructive theories. For this purpose the fact that an assertion is realizable is sufficient; the realizing terms are rarely of much interest. Indeed, for certain meta-mathematical applications, versions of realizability exist (notably those based on Kleene 'slash' realizability) for which there are no realizing terms. From the perspective of program development this attitude to the realizing terms will not do. We will pay careful attention to the structure of terms in our interpretation as these are the backbone of programs we extract from proofs. This attitude explains the title of the current section and explains why the majority of it is devoted to a careful discussion of options which are open to us.

Before we move on, we need to make a few technical remarks. The free variables of $e \, \rho \, \Phi$ are those of Φ in addition to e (which is not free in Φ). We shall take it that ρ binds more tightly in expressions than the binary logical connectives but less tightly than quantifiers and membership (note, however, that expressions of the form $e \, \rho \, \Phi$ are meta-notation). The standard definition of abstract realizability, for first order predicate logic, runs as follows:

$e \, \rho \, \Phi$ is Φ (atomic Φ)
$e \, \rho \, (\Phi \wedge \psi)$ is (fst e) $\rho \, \Phi \wedge$ (snd e) $\rho \, \psi$
$e \, \rho \, (\Phi \vee \psi)$ is (fst e) $\to$ (snd e) $\rho \, \Phi$, (snd e) $\rho \, \psi$
$e \, \rho \, (\Phi \to \psi)$ is $(\forall x)(x \, \rho \, \Phi \to (e\,x){\downarrow} \wedge (e\,x) \, \rho \, \psi)$
$e \, \rho \, \forall x \Phi$ is $(\forall x)((e\,x){\downarrow} \wedge (e\,x) \, \rho \, \Phi)$
$e \, \rho \, \exists x \Phi$ is (snd e) $\rho \, \Phi((\text{fst } e))$

For a reason connected with the extraction of programs from proofs (which we elaborate in section 3.2) we need to make one other change to the clauses for disjunction and existential quantification:

$e \, \rho \, (\Phi \vee \psi)$ is (fst e) $\to \Phi \wedge$ (snd e) $\rho \, \Phi$, $\psi \wedge$ (snd e) $\rho \, \psi$
$e \, \rho \, \exists x \Phi$ is $\Phi((\text{fst } e)) \wedge$ (snd e) $\rho \, \Phi((\text{fst } e))$

For a technical reason these two changes force a third:

$e \, \rho \, (\Phi \to \psi)$ is $(\forall x)(\Phi \wedge (x \, \rho \, \Phi \to (e\,x){\downarrow} \wedge (e\,x) \, \rho \, \psi))$

This formulation, still restricted to first order predicate logic, is known as Q-realizability and forms the heart of the approach to program extraction.

There are two possible approaches to extend realizability to the other quantifiers. These correspond to the two notions of polymorphism which have been referred to [Leivant 83] as the *type abstraction* approach [Reynolds 74] and the *type quantification* approach [McQueen 82] which we briefly touched on in 1.6.

For type abstraction we mirror, exactly, quantification at the object level. We refer to this as the *Kleene approach*:

$\quad$ e ρ ∀x^n Φ $\quad$ is $\quad$ (∀x^n)((e x^n)↓ ∧ (e x^n) ρ Φ)

Let us consider the intuitive meaning of such assertions. The universal assertion is claiming that e is a program which satisfies Φ for all types (taking n=0, for example). e is thus a polymorphic object. Note that under this interpretation e must take a type as an argument and then meet the specification Φ. So we are introducing terms which resemble those of the second order lambda calculus: For example a polymorphic specification of the form: ∀X∀xΦ has realizers of the form: λX.λx.e (where (e X x) ρ Φ(X,x)).

The type quantification approach to polymorphism is that adopted in languages like Miranda. Terms are no longer uniquely typed for we supress the explicit type abstraction at the object level. This suggests:

$\quad$ e ρ ∀x^n Φ $\quad$ is $\quad$ (∀x^n)(e ρ Φ)

Note how the type information remains in the assertion and, in this case, does not appear in the realizer e. We call this the *Kreisel–Troelstra approach* [Kreisel 70].

It is the Kreisel–Troelstra approach to realizability which we adopt, since our intention is to build a system which is in some sense congruent to the programming notation and polymorphic types of Miranda.

There are similar options open to us for the realization of the higher order existential formulae. The first (the Kleene approach) is to mirror the clause for object level existentials:

$\quad$ e ρ ∃x^n Φ $\quad$ is $\quad$ (snd e) ρ Φ((fst e))

Note that this mimics the unmodified object level existential and not the Q-realizability formulation. The reason for this concerns program extraction techniques which we introduce later.

The second (the Kreisel–Troelstra approach) is to take:

$\quad$ e ρ ∃x^n Φ $\quad$ is $\quad$ ∃x^n(e ρ Φ)

Now an existential assertion of the form ∃XΦ, for example, is to correspond to the specification of an abstract data type [Mitchell 85]. A realizer of such a specification should be a realizer of the specification Φ(Y) for some implementing type Y. This is captured by the Troelstra–Kreisel definition above. The Kleene approach would make e a pair of the form <Y, e'> where e' ρ Φ(Y). There seem to be arguments for both approaches and we are as yet uncomitted. We have adopted the Kreisel–Troelstra definition for the time being.

We now turn to the atomic assertions of TK5. We have to be more proscriptive about those involving membership in types. We are led to define:

$\quad$ e ρ ⊥ $\qquad\qquad$ is $\quad$ ⊥
$\quad$ e ρ t↓ $\qquad\qquad$ is $\quad$ t↓
$\quad$ e ρ t = t $\qquad\quad$ is $\quad$ t = t
$\quad$ e ρ t∈Ξ(Φ^n, K^n) $\;$ is $\quad$ t∈Ξ(Φ^n, K^n)
$\quad$ e ρ t∈{x | Φ^n} $\;\;$ is $\quad$ e ρ Φ^n(t)

We call Φ^n(t) the *characteristic formula* of the set abstract. Note how realizability passes through set abstractions. For other atomic formulae the definition is consonant with the definition for predicate logic.

We can now present our complete realizability interpretation for TK5.

Definition 3.1.2

$$\begin{array}{lll}
e\ \rho\ \bot & \text{is} & \bot \\
e\ \rho\ t\!\downarrow & \text{is} & t\!\downarrow \\
e\ \rho\ t = t & \text{is} & t = t \\
e\ \rho\ t \in \Xi(\Phi^n, K^n) & \text{is} & t \in \Xi(\Phi^n, K^n) \\
e\ \rho\ t \in \{x \mid \Phi^n\} & \text{is} & e\ \rho\ \Phi^n(t) \\
e\ \rho\ (\Phi \wedge \psi) & \text{is} & (\text{fst}\ e)\ \rho\ \Phi \wedge (\text{snd}\ e)\ \rho\ \psi \\
e\ \rho\ (\Phi \vee \psi) & \text{is} & (\text{fst}\ e) \to \Phi \wedge (\text{snd}\ e)\ \rho\ \Phi,\ \psi \wedge (\text{snd}\ e)\ \rho\ \psi \\
e\ \rho\ (\Phi \to \psi) & \text{is} & (\forall x)(x\ \rho\ \Phi \to (e\ x)\!\downarrow \wedge (e\ x)\ \rho\ \psi) \\
e\ \rho\ \forall x \Phi & \text{is} & (\forall x)((e\ x)\!\downarrow \wedge (e\ x)\ \rho\ \Phi) \\
e\ \rho\ \exists x \Phi & \text{is} & \Phi((\text{fst}\ e)) \wedge (\text{snd}\ e)\ \rho\ \Phi((\text{fst}\ e)) \\
e\ \rho\ \forall x^n \Phi & \text{is} & (\forall x^n)(e\ \rho\ \Phi) \\
e\ \rho\ \exists x^n \Phi & \text{is} & (\exists x^n)(e\ \rho\ \Phi)
\end{array}$$

■

Proposition 3.1.3

TK5 ⊢ $(e\ \rho\ \Phi)[x \leftarrow t] \leftrightarrow e\ \rho\ (\Phi[x \leftarrow t])$

■

It will turn out, for reasons that are not to be examined until section 3.3, that our realizability interpretation for TK5 is a little more involved than definition 3.1.2 but before we turn to these subtleties we investigate what we have above in more detail.

3.2 BASIC PROGRAM EXTRACTION

We wish to view realizability as expressing the meaning of the logical apparatus. Thus we can think of realizability as defining a model in the following sense: if Φ can be proved then there is a t such that $t\ \rho\ \Phi$ (can be proved). More exactly we have the following proposition which lies at the heart of the process of program extraction.

Proposition 3.2.1 (soundness of realizability)

If TK5 ⊢ Φ then there is a term t such that TK5 ⊢ $t\ \rho\ \Phi$

proof
(by induction on the length of the derivation ⊢ Φ)
Many of the cases are quite standard and so we just examine the case for elimination of inductive sets which is the induction principle. In fact we attack a *rule* for induction, which is equivalent to the axiom IND.

$$\frac{(\forall z)(z \in K^n \to \psi(z)) \qquad (\forall z)((\forall x)(\Phi^n(z,x) \to \psi(x)) \to \psi(z))}{(\forall z)(z \in \Xi(\Phi^n, K^n) \to \psi(z))}$$

In the official term language we should require:

irec = $Y(\lambda \xi.\lambda wxyz.(\text{fst}\ z) \to (w\ y\ (\text{snd}\ z)),\ (x\ y\ (\lambda uv.(\xi\ w\ x\ u\ ((\text{snd}\ z)\ u\ v))))$

but using the compilation rules alluded to in section 2.1 we may write the much more attractive:

irec x y z <true, w> ≃ x z w
irec x y z <false, w> ≃ y z (λuv.irec x y u (w u v))

which is equivalent to the fixpoint expression above via the compilation process.

Instances of irec for particular inductive types (like those examples in 2.5.2)
are even more attractive but there is an issue regarding typing which is handled in
a rather odd way in this presentation (indeed it is not congruent to the Miranda
typing regime) which we will pick up in section 3.3 and develop further. Moreover,
it is an easy proposition to establish that the partial equality can be replaced by
equality in the equations above. When we look later at instances of irec we
will incorporate this observation.
∎

We do not base our program extraction from proofs directly on realizability but via
a rule corresponding to the *negative axiom of choice* AC_{neg}. In order to
explain this we need to begin with a number of simple concepts.

Definition 3.2.2

Φ is a *negative formula* if it is constructed from atomic formulae
mentioning membership only in *negative kinds* by conjunction,
disjunction, implication and universal quantification.

K^n is a *negative kind* if it is an inductive kind or if it is
a comprehension kind whose characteristic formula is negative.
∎

Definition 3.2.3

A formula Φ is *self-realizing* if $TK5 \vdash \Phi \Leftrightarrow (\exists x)(x \, \rho \, \Phi)$.
∎

Proposition 3.2.4

If Φ is negative then Φ is self-realizing.
∎

This much is standard, except for a technical change to the ordinary definition of
negative formula. We can now prove the rule corresponding to AC_{neg}:

Proposition 3.2.5   Program Extraction

If $TK5 \vdash (\forall x)(\Phi(x) \rightarrow (\exists y)(\psi(x,y)))$ where $\Phi(x)$ is negative, then for some
closed term t, $TK5 \vdash (\forall x)(\Phi(x) \rightarrow (t\,x)\downarrow \wedge \psi(x, (t\,x)))$.
∎

The proof of this, in TK5, is not substantially different from the proof that the
rule corresponding to AC_{neg} is supported by a number of theories (see for EON
[Beeson 85] and (more significantly for program extraction) for FT [Beeson 86]).

Further discussion of the issues surrounding program extraction, particularly in
connection with MLTT, can be found in [Henson 88].

3.3   EXTENSIONS TO REALIZABILITY

Realizability interpretations are highly intensional: there may be many
possibilities open to us all of which are sound. Since our choice influences the
nature of programs extracted from proofs we see the examination of these choices as
extremely important. In particular there may be certain kinds of assertion which
play a special role in program specification and these could be isolated and given
realizability interpretations independently from those they would inherit by virtue
of the standard interpretation of their logical structure. In this section we
shall be specific about two classes of common formulae: bounded quantification and
the conditional assertion, which we turn to first.

3.3.1 Conditional Assertions

In 2.5.1 we introduced the conditional assertion and provided two equivalent
unpackings, one of which is negative. It is when we turn to modifications of
realizability that this device carries force, after all, we have nothing but a
little syntactic sugar so far. How should we realize such formulae? Two
possibilites are immediate consequences of the unpackings given earlier, but there
is a third, much more satisfactory solution.

$$e \; \rho \; t \rightarrow \Phi, \psi \quad \text{is} \quad t \rightarrow e \; \rho \; \Phi, e \; \rho \; \psi$$

Proposition 3.3.1.1

∎   Proposition 3.2.1 may be extended to include conditional assertions.

The proof of this proposition (omitted) shows that conditional expressions of the
form $t \rightarrow t'$, t'' can be extracted from proofs utilising the elimination rule for
conditional assertions. One can think of conditional assertions as intermediate
stages between specifications and programs as they combine term and assertion
components. The interpretation above reflects an intuitive notion of
specification refinement in which the overall structure (a conditional form) is
maintained.

3.3.2 Bounded quantification

Another very common style of assertion are bounded quantifications. These are
unpacked in the obvious way (see 2.5.1). Again we could take the realizability of
these assertions via the syntactic unpacking, but there is a better, and indeed
crucial, alternative (we call this the 'non-standard' interpretation):

$$e \; \rho \; (\forall x \in K^n)\Phi \quad \text{is} \quad (\forall x \in K^n)((e \; x) \; \rho \; \Phi)$$

Note that whilst the typing remains in the assertion structure in this definition
the standard interpretation would lead to:

$$e \; \rho \; (\forall x \in K^n)\Phi \quad \text{is}$$
$$e \; \rho \; (\forall x)(x \in K^n \rightarrow \Phi) \quad \text{is}$$
$$(\forall x)((e \; x) \; \rho \; (x \in K^n \rightarrow \Phi)) \quad \text{is}$$
$$(\forall x)((\forall z)(z \; \rho \; (x \in K^n) \rightarrow (e \; x \; z) \; \rho \; \Phi))$$

Note that the realizing function e is supplied with a pair consisting of an
arbitrary object together with information as to its' type (in K^n). In
programming terms the standard interpretation corresponds to a run-time typed
programming language in which each value comes equipped with its type. This might
be appropriate if we wished to design a constructive set theory for, say, an object
oriented language but we have based the current work around the principles of
Miranda. In this circumstance the non-standard approach is appropriate for it
corresponds directly to a language which is compile time typed. We have to be a
little careful here because the kind expression in the bounded quantifier can be
arbitrary. We may wish to restrict the situation further and allow the non-
standard interpretation only for certain 'simple' kinds. This would be important
if for example we needed the compile time typechecker to be decidable. This is the
case for Miranda but not for, say, PEBBLE [Burstall 84].

We examine the implications of adopting the non-standard interpretation in
connection with the combinator associated with the induction princple IND^n. Let
us present the induction rule with bounded quantification:

$$\frac{(\forall z \in K^n)\psi(z) \quad (\forall z \in \Xi(\Phi^n, K^n))((\forall x \in \Xi(\Phi^n, K^n))(\Phi^n(z,x) \Rightarrow \psi(x)) \Rightarrow \psi(z))}{(\forall z \in \Xi(\Phi^n, K^n))\psi(z)}$$

or even:

$$\frac{(\forall z \in K^n)\psi(z) \quad (\forall z \in \Xi(\Phi^n, K^n))((\forall x \in \{v \in \Xi(\Phi^n, K^n) \mid (\Phi^n(z,v)\}) \psi(x)) \Rightarrow \psi(z))}{(\forall z \in \Xi(\Phi^n, K^n))\psi(z)}$$

If we now rework the soundness of realizability using this rule for induction we obtain the following definition of irec:

```
irec x y z  ≃  x z              (when z ∈ Kⁿ)
irec x y z  ≃  y z (λw∈{v∈Ξ(Φⁿ, Kⁿ)|(Φⁿ(z,v)}.irec x y w)
```

In many cases of interest the set abstract is finite so the lambda abstraction (from a finite domain) can be replaced by a finite sequence. If we follow up the examples of 2.5.2 we obtain the following derived rules of induction and recursion combinators:

$$\frac{\psi(0) \quad (\forall x \in \text{Nat})(\psi(x) \Rightarrow \psi(\text{succ } x))}{(\forall x \in \text{Nat})(\psi(x))} \qquad \frac{\psi([\,]) \quad (\forall x \in \text{List})(\forall a \in A)(\psi(x) \Rightarrow \psi(<a, x>))}{(\forall x \in \text{List})(\psi(x))}$$

```
nrec x y 0        = x
nrec x y (succ n) = y (succ n) (nrec x y n)

lrec x y []       = x
lrec x y <a,l>    = y <a,l> (lrec x y l)
```

$$\frac{(\forall x \in A)(\psi(x)) \quad (\forall x,y \in \text{Sexp})(\psi(x) \wedge \psi(y) \Rightarrow \psi(<x, y>))}{(\forall x \in \text{Sexp})(\psi(x))}$$

```
srec x y a        = x a
srec x y <s₁,s₂>  = y <s₁,s₂> (srec x y s₁) (srec x y s₂)
```

3.4 PROPOSITIONS AS TYPES versus REALIZABILITY

It is the notion of 'propositions as types' which allows for the extraction of programs from proofs in theories like MLTT. In TK5 program extraction is based on realizability. It is well known that these two concepts are very closely related. In this section we show why this is the case in the theory TK5 and we rephrase our formulation of program extraction in terms of the propositions as types identification.

We begin by seeing that we can use comprehension to collect together all the realizers of an assertion (programs which meet a specification) by setting:

$$\tau(\Phi) = \{e \mid e \rho \Phi\}$$

Proposition 3.4.1

$$e \in \tau(\Phi) \Leftrightarrow e \rho \Phi$$

∎

This, of course, is trivial by COMP. It is also possible to demonstrate certain closure conditions on the family of sets $\tau(\Phi)$. To do this we must introduce some new type constructors which collect realisers for certain classes of formulae. In some cases (for example conjunctions, where realizers are pairs and so belong to a product space) we already have appropriate type operations, but in others, notably the object level quantifiers, we do not. For the purposes of universal (object level) quantification we define:

$$\Pi(x,X) = \{z \mid (\forall y)(z(y) \in X[x \leftarrow y])\}$$

and for object level existential quantification we set:

$$\Sigma(x,X) = \{z \mid (\text{snd } z) \in X[x \leftarrow (\text{fst } z)]\}$$

It is also necessary to extend the operations for polymorphism and data abstraction which we introduced in 2.5.1 over the entire kind hierarchy:

$$\pi^n(x^{n-1},x^n) = \{z \mid (\forall x^{n-1})(z \in x^n)\}$$
$$\sigma^n(x^{n-1},x^n) = \{z \mid (\exists x^{n-1})(z \in x^n)\}$$

$\pi^n(x^{n-1},x^n)$ and $\sigma^n(x^{n-1},x^n)$ belong to K^n. These definitions do not just generalise the definitions of π and σ to arbitrary kind indicies because $\pi^1(\sigma^1)$ is not equal to $\pi(\sigma)$. π^1 is in itself more general than π for it allows entities of K^1 in its second argument. In 2.5 we were at pains to avoid generalising beyond what is actually required for the explication of the programming notation but here we are trying to investigate the type structure of propositions. We wish to maintain the distinction between the operators $\pi^1(\sigma^1)$ and $\pi(\sigma)$.

For reasons which emerge shortly we find it useful to make three further set definitions:

$$\nabla = \{z \mid z = z\}$$
$$\Delta = \{z \mid z \neq z\}$$
$$U^n = \{z \mid (\exists x^n)(z = x^n)\}$$

The first two are, respectively, the type of everything and the type of nothing. Notice that the formulae used to form these sets involve only object level variables. Consequently these are available at every level of the kind hierarchy. The third definition establishes universes of kinds (of all levels). Since the set abstract for U^n contains a bound variable of level n we see that U^n is a kind of level n+1. We find it convenient to use the following terminology: 'z lives in K^n' is taken to mean that there is an $x^n \in U^n$ such that $z \in x^n$. Of course if z lives in K^n then it will live in K^m for all $m > n$.

Proposition 3.4.2

(i) $\tau(\Phi \wedge \psi) = \tau(\Phi) \otimes \tau(\psi)$
(ii) $\tau(\Phi \vee \psi) = \{z \in \tau(\Phi) \mid \Phi\} \oplus \{z \in \tau(\psi) \mid \psi\}$
(iii) $\tau(\Phi \to \psi) = \tau(\Phi) \to \tau(\psi)$
(iv) $\tau(\forall x \Phi) = \Pi(x, \tau(\Phi))$
(v) $\tau(\exists x \Phi) = \{z \in \Sigma(x, \tau(\Phi)) \mid \Phi\}$
(vi) $\tau(\forall x^n \Phi) = \pi^n(x^n, \tau(\Phi))$
(vii) $\tau(\exists x^n \Phi) = \sigma^n(x^n, \tau(\Phi))$

■

This formulation defines the 'tau-types' in terms of realizability. We prefer a different approach in which tau is introduced as a recursive mapping satisfying the closure conditions above. We then have to show that we can still establish the proposition analogous to proposition 3.4.1.

Definition 3.4.3

Let Y be any fixpoint combinator. For every n we define a mapping τ^n as follows:

$\tau^n = Y(\lambda\xi.\lambda z.(z=\Phi^n \wedge \psi^n) \to \xi(\Phi^n) \otimes \xi(\psi^n),$
$\qquad (z=\Phi^n \vee \psi^n) \to \{z \in \xi(\Phi^n) \mid \Phi^n\} \oplus \{z \in \xi(\psi^n) \mid \psi^n\},$
$\qquad (z=\Phi^n \to \psi^n) \to \xi(\Phi^n) \to_T \xi(\psi^n),$
$\qquad (z=\forall x\Phi^n) \to \Pi(x,\xi(\Phi^n)),$
$\qquad (z=\exists x\Phi^n) \to \{z \in \Sigma(x,\xi(\Phi^n)) \mid \Phi^n \},$
$\qquad (z=\forall x^{n-1}\Phi^n) \to \pi^n(x^{n-1},\xi(\Phi^n)),$
$\qquad (z=\exists x^{n-1}\Phi^n) \to \sigma^n(x^{n-1},\xi(\Phi^n)),$
$\qquad (z=t\downarrow) \to \{z \mid t\downarrow\},$
$\qquad (z=(t_1 = t_2)) \to \{z \mid t_1 = t_2\},$
$\qquad (z=\bot) \to \{z \mid \bot\},$
$\qquad (z=(x \in K^{n-1})) \to \xi(\Phi^{Kn-1}), \Delta)$

■

Proposition 3.4.4

for every n;
(i) $\quad \tau^n(\Phi^n \wedge \psi^n) = \tau^n(\Phi^n) \otimes \tau^n(\psi^n)$
(ii) $\quad \tau^n(\Phi^n \vee \psi^n) = \{z \in \tau^n(\Phi^n) \mid \Phi^n\} \oplus \{z \in \tau^n(\psi^n) \mid \psi^n\}$
(iii) $\quad \tau^n(\Phi^n \to \psi^n) = \tau^n(\Phi^n) \to_T \tau^n(\psi^n)$
(iv) $\quad \tau^n(\forall x \Phi^n) = \Pi(x, \tau^n(\Phi^n))$
(v) $\quad \tau^n(\exists x \Phi^n) = \{z \in \Sigma(x, \tau^n(\Phi^n)) \mid \Phi^n \}$
(vi) $\quad \tau^n(\forall x^{n-1}\Phi^n) = \pi^n(x^{n-1}, \tau^n(\Phi^n))$
(vii) $\quad \tau^n(\exists x^{n-1}\Phi^n) = \sigma^n(x^{1-1}, \tau^n(\Phi^n))$

■

In order to investigate the family τ^n further we introduce a family of inductive kinds Ψ^n which we can use to establish codomain kinds for the τ^n.

Definition 3.4.5

for every n we define an inductive kind $\Psi^n = \Xi(\theta, \{\nabla, \Delta\})$ where:
$\theta(x^n, y^n, z^n) \leftrightarrow (x^n = y^n \otimes z^n) \vee (x^n = y^n \oplus z^n) \vee (x^n = y^n \to_T z^n) \vee$
$(x^n = \Pi(v, y^n)) \vee (x^n = \Sigma(v, y^n)) \vee (x^n = \pi^n(v^{n-1}, y^n)) \vee (x^n = \sigma^n(v^{n-1}, y^n))$

Proposition 3.4.6

for every n; $\quad \tau^n \in \nabla \to_T \Psi^n$

■

Corollary 3.4.7

τ^n lives in K^{n+1}

■

Proposition 3.4.8

for every n;
$e \in \tau^n(\Phi^n) \leftrightarrow e \rho \Phi^n$

■

Corollary 3.4.9

There exists an n;
$e \in \tau^n(\Phi) \Leftrightarrow e \in \tau(\Phi)$

∎

Proposition 3.4.10

If TK5 ⊢ Φ then there is an n and a term t such that TK5 ⊢ t ∈ $\tau^n(\Phi)$

∎

These last results ensure that the family τ^n contains everything captured by the mapping τ. τ^n is an internal mapping for every n so our techniques for program extraction are internal to the theory. In practical examples (see especially [Henson 88]) we seem to work within a programming development paradigm requiring only the first two levels of the kind hierarchy K^0 and K^1. Thus we require the mapping τ^1 which lives in K^2 by virtue of proposition 3.4.7. The first three levels, then, seem to suffice for the theory of program development and program extraction as it stands at present.

4 CONCLUSIONS AND FUTURE WORK

We have presented a constructive set theory designed to support program development. In section 1 we outlined a number of critisisms of work in this area which utilise Martin-Lof's Theory of Types. In this paper we hope to have demonstrated that TK5 is a more suitable vehicle for such work. In particular the more flexible typing, the separation of the notions of data type and propositional type, the flexibility in designing realizability interpretations and the overall simplicity of the theory go some way, we hope, to support our claims. In spirit, our work most closely follows that of Hayashi who began the idea that a theory of program development should be based around a high level programming notation. His choice was to place this explicitly as the term language of the theory. The results we believe are mixed; in particular the ramifications on the assertion structures are rather obscure. Our tactic is a little different. We retain the simplicity of the term language and allow the high level notation to appear (via a complex syntactic sugaring) as the language of program extraction. That is, such expressions are attached to the logical rules in the proof of soundness for realizability. There are a number of points which we have not addressed here, mainly those concerned with practical program development. For example we have not demonstrated the power of the inductive types and the role which intensionality plays in supporting general recursion, type simulations (for transfromational programming) or even mutually inductive types and mutually recursive programs. For these we refer the reader to [Henson 88].

5 REFERENCES

[Abbas 87] Abbas, A., **Programming with types and rules in Martin Lof's theory of types** PhD thesis, London Univeristy, 1987
[Beeson 81] Beeson, M., **Formalising constructive mathematics: why and how?** Constructive mathematics: proceedings, New Mexico, 1980, Lecture Notes in Mathematics, Vol 873, pp 146-90, Springer, 1981
[Beeson 85] Beeson, M., **Foundations of constructive mathematics** Springer-Verlag, 1985
[Beeson 86] Beeson, M., **Proving programs and programming proofs** Logic, Methodology and Philosophy of Science VII, Elsevier, pp 51-82, 1986
[Beeson 88] Beeson M., **Towards a computation system based on set theory,** Tech. Report. Dept. Maths and Computer Science, San Jose State University
[Burstall 84] Burstall, R. and Lampson, B., **A kernel language for abstract data types and modules** Symp. on semantics of data types, Lecture notes in computer science, Vol. 173, pp 1-50, Springer, 1984

[Constable 86] Constable, R., et.al., **Implementing Mathematics with the NuPRL proof development system**, Prentice Hall, 1986
[Feferman 75] Feferman, S., **A language and axioms for explicit mathematics** Algebra and Logic, Lecture notes in mathematics, Vol. 450, pp 87-139, North Holland, Amsterdam, 1975
[Hayashi 87] Hayashi, S., **The PX system - a computational logic** University of Tokyo, tech rep. 1987
[Henson 87] Henson, M. C., **Elements of functional languages**, Blackwells, 1987
[Henson 88] Henson, M. C., **Program development in the constructive set theory TK5** submitted for publication and University of Essex, tech rep. No. 110, 1988
[Hindley 86] Hindley, J. R. and Seldin, J. P., **Introduction to combinators and lambda calculus** London Math. Soc. students texts, Vol. 1, Cambridge, 1986
[Khamiss 86] Khamiss, A. **Algorithm development in Martin-Lof's theory of types** PhD thesis, University of Essex, 1986
[Kleene 45] Kleene, S., **On the interpretation of intuitionistic number theory** J. Symb. logic, Vol. 10, pp 109-24, 1945
[Kreisel 70] Kreisel, G. and Troelstra, A., **Formal systems for some branches of intuitionistic analysis** Annals of Math. logic, Vol. 1, pp 229-387, 1979
[Leivant 83] Leivant, D., **Polymorphic type inference** Proc. 10th ACM symp. on principles of programming languages, 1983
[McQueen 82] McQueen D. and Sethi, R., **A semantic model of types for applicative languages** Proc. ACM conf. on LISP and functional programming, pp 243-52, 1982
[Malcolm 88] Malcolm, G. and Chisholm, P., **Polymorphism in Martin-Lof's type theory**, Private Communication, Unpublished notes, Rijksuniversiteit Groningen, 1988
[Martin-Lof 75] Martin-Lof, P., **An intuitionistic theory of types: predicative part** Logic Coll. 73, North-Holland, Amsterdam, 1975
[Martin-Lof 79] Martin-Lof, P., **Preprint of [Martin-Lof 82]**, Report No. 11 University of Stockholm, 1979
[Martin-Lof 82] Martin-Lof, P., **Constructive Mathematics and Computer Programming** Logic, Methodology and Philosophy of Science VI, pp 153-179, North Holland, Amsterdam, 1982
[Mitchell 85] Mitchell, J. and Plotkin, G., **Abstract types have existential type** Proc. 12th ACM conf. on principles of programming languages, pp 37-51, 1985
[Mohring 85] Mohring, C., **Algorithm development in the calculus of constructions** Proc. IEEE symp. on logic in computer science, 1986
[Nordstrom 87] Nordstrom, B., **Terminating general recursion** Tech rep., University of Goteborg, Programming Methodology Group, 1987
[Peyton-Jones 87] Peyton-Jones, S., **The implementation of functional programming languages** Prentice Hall, 1987
[Reynolds 74] Reynolds, J. C., **Towards a theory of type structures** Proc. Programming symposium, Lecture notes in computer science, Vol. 19, Springer, 1974
[Turner 79] Turner, D., **A new implementation technique for applicative languages** Software, Practice and Experience, Vol. 9, pp 31-49, 1979
[Turner 85] Turner, D., **Miranda: a non strict functional language with polymorphic types** Proc. Conf. on functional programming and computer architecture, Lecture notes in computer science, Vol. 201, Springer, 1985
[Turner 87] Turner, R., **A theory of properties** J. Symb. logic, Vol. 52, No. 2, pp 445-472, 1987
[Turner 88] Turner, R., **Combinatory logic and type theory via stable truth** submitted for publication and University of Essex, tech rep. 109, 1988

McCarthy's Amb Cannot Implement Fair Merge

Prakash Panangaden
Vasant Shanbhogue
Computer Science Department, Cornell University

Abstract

In this paper we establish that **fair merge** is a powerful non-determinate primitive that cannot be implemented in terms of other well-known primitives. It is well known that fair merge embodies countable non-determinacy. It has also been known that McCarthy's **amb** embodies countable non-determinacy. It had not been known, however, whether **amb** could implement a **fair merge**. We show that **amb** cannot implement fair merge even in dynamic dataflow networks. This settles a question posed by Abramsky over four years ago. Earlier work had suggested this result by showing that for *static* dataflow networks, one cannot implement **fair merge** using angelic merge.

1 Introduction

We examine the relative expressive power of non-determinate primitives in the context of dynamic dataflow networks. Our main result is that it is impossible to implement a **fair merge** using McCarthy's **amb**, so called "angelic non-determinacy." The key point of the result is that one cannot implement **fair merge** without some sort of time sensitivity built into the primitives.

The results described in the present paper were suggested by earlier results [13,14] that applied to static networks, i.e. to networks whose structure is fixed throughout execution. We use a denotational model suggested by [3].

Apt and Plotkin [2] observe that one can program fairness using countable non-determinacy. In the case of parallel dataflow programs, however, the situation is complicated by the fact that a fair merge not only has to choose fairly, but has to avoid waiting forever for data on an empty channel. In this situation, fairness is not the same as countable non-determinacy as is shown in [13]. In the present paper we show that countable non-determinacy, the ability to detect and avoid nonterminating computation, and the ability to define dynamically expanding networks, *even combined*, do not suffice to implement a fair merge.

By countable non-determinacy or unbounded non-determinacy, we mean the dataflow analogue of the "random" assignment statement $x :=?$. We prefer not to use the word "random" because of its associations with probabilistic computing. The countable non-determinacy (CN) process has one input channel and one output channel, and for each value sent out onto the input channel, the value gets read and some positive integer gets output.

McCarthy's **amb** may be represented by a process with two input channels and one output channel. The output sequence is one of the two input sequences, whichever is non-empty, if any.

A **fair merge** primitive, as well as an **angelic merge** primitive, has a pair of input channels and a single output channel. Tokens from different channels appear interleaved in the output sequence in an unpredictable fashion, but the relative order of tokens from a single input channel are preserved. The two primitives differ in the sense that, for a **fair merge** primitive, every token that appears at an input channel appears on the output channel eventually, but for an **angelic merge** primitive, all that is guaranteed is that the output sequence is infinite if at least one of the input sequences are infinite. Note that the **angelic merge** primitive is fair, if both its input sequences are finite.

We can consider a primitive that has the "opposite" property, i.e. a merge primitive that is fair if both its input sequences are *infinite*. Such a merge is called an "infinity-fair" merge by Park [15]. If either input sequence is finite, then the output sequence is finite, consisting of an interleaving of a finite input sequence and a prefix of the other input sequence. This kind of merge can be implemented by a CN process by simply using the sequence of integers generated by the CN process as an "oracle" to a process that reads the integers and uses them to determine how many tokens to consume from an input channel before switching to the other input channel. The rather surprising result proved in [13] says that even the combination of angelic merge and infinity-fair merge cannot implement a fair merge.

The method of proof used in [13] to establish this result involves the idea of residuals, from the lambda calculus. Certain maximal computations are identified with respect to an appropriate preorder and it is shown that completed computations coincide with the maximal ones. This is then used to show that a particular monotonicity property holds in networks built out of determinate processes, angelic merge and CN processes. The monotonicity property does not hold for fair merge, thus establishing the non-implementability result. The method used in [14] is based on showing that a monotonicity property is preserved by network composition, using structural induction. This is then used to show that any network composed of determinate processes, angelic merge and CN processes satisfies the monotonicity property. The major problem left unsolved by these approaches was how to apply these arguments to infinite networks such as potentially arise in the dynamic case.

2 The Network Scenario Model

In this section, we introduce the scenario formalism, that we use. We first recall the basic model of static dataflow computing due to Gilles Kahn [6], and then introduce dynamic networks. A *static dataflow network* is a directed graph. The vertices represent autonomous computing agents, each one executing a sequential, determinate program. These are called determinate Kahn processes. The arcs represent communication channels between the computing agents. We assume that the channels are unidirectional, unbounded queues. The computing agents communicate with each other, and, in general, with the environment, by passing data values, called "tokens," along the channels. The computing agents interact with the channels by **read** and **write** commands. Unlike CSP or CCS, communication is entirely asynchronous. A **write** is executed unconditionally and a **read** causes a computing agent to suspend until data becomes available.

Under these circumstances, one can define the semantics of a network in a simple way. One associates with each channel a stream, i.e. a potentially infinite sequence of tokens, and with each computing agent, a function from streams to streams. The collection of streams forms a Scott domain under the prefix ordering. One can show that the functions associated with the computing agents are all continuous. The relationship between the streams associated with different channels are expressed equationally. The network may contain feedback loops and, thus, the equations between the streams may be mutually recursive. Using standard fixed-point theory, the least fixed-point solution is the meaning of the network. It can be shown that this agrees with an operational semantics for these so called "Kahn" networks.

The presence of non-determinacy complicates the above picture. The behaviour of a computing agent can no longer be expressed as a function. Several semantic theories have been proposed. Sets of possible streams cannot be used to represent the meanings of non-determinate networks, because causal anomalies arise, as observed by Keller [7] and by Brock and Ackerman [3]. The solution is to use the computational events in the network as the building blocks of the semantic theory. Such an approach was proposed by Keller [7] and Brock and Ackerman [3] and Pratt [17] and also developed by Keller and Panangaden [8]. Recently, very interesting work has been done by Joost Kok [9,10] in developing a fully abstract semantics for such nets.

The semantic model that we use is based on a formalism that encodes the relation of causal precedence between computational events. In an earlier investigation, we used a trace semantics to prove expressiveness results of static dataflow networks [14], but for the dynamic case it is advantageous to use a model in which event sequences are not interleaved. The formalism we use is essentially that of Brock and Ackerman [3].

We define an asynchronous dataflow network to be a finite set of autonomous computing agents, called *nodes*, connected by directed arcs, called *channels*. The directed arcs coming into a node are called input channels and those leaving a node are called output channels. The interconnection structure is fixed throughout execution. Communication between nodes is effected by the transmission of messages along the channels. The channels are unbounded queues where the sending of a message and the receipt of the message are distinct activities. There is no synchronization on message passing such as in CSP [5] or CCS [11].

Definition 1. A *network* is a finite set of nodes connected by directed arcs. Each arc is labeled by a distinct identifier. There are some arcs entering the network that are not output arcs to any node in the network. These are called *input arcs*; similarly there are *output arcs* that are not input arcs to any node in the network.

Definition 2. An **event** is a triple consisting of a channel name, a value and a tag which is either + or −.

An event of the form $(\mathbf{a}, +, v)$ is interpreted as the appearance of a value v on the channel $\mathbf{a}$. An event of the form $(\mathbf{a}, -, v)$ is interpreted as the consumption of a value v from the channel $\mathbf{a}$.

A particular computation sequence may contain several instances of an event, for example, two identical tokens might arrive on a channel. Each instance of an event is called an **event occurrence**. In what follows, "event" refers to its event occurrence.

A sequence of +-events on channel c is called a *+-c-stream*, and a sequence of −-events on channel c is called a *−-c-stream*.

Definition 3. A **scenario** of a network consists of a well-founded, partial ordering on the individual event occurrences on the input and output channels of the network, such that

(i) +-events on a single channel are totally ordered,

(ii) −-events on a single channel are totally ordered,

(iii) there is an edge from a +-event on an input channel to the corresponding −-event on the same channel, and,

(iv) the only edges into +-events on input channels are those arising from (i).

Well-foundedness is intuitively motivated by the requirement that every event can have only finitely many causes. Winskel [19] observes that this is connected with Scott's thesis that computable functions are continuous.

A scenario may be drawn graphically as follows : For each input channel, draw a sequence of +-events and a sequence of −-events, and draw an arrow from each event to the next in both these sequences, and also draw an arrow from every +-event to the corresponding −-event. For each output channel, draw a sequence of +-events

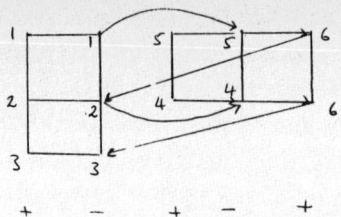

Figure 1: A scenario for **adder**

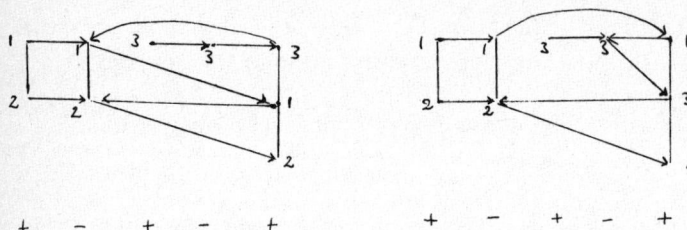

Figure 2: Scenarios for **fair merge**

and arrows from each event to the next. Also draw arrows between −-events on input channels and +-events on output channels, as required by causal precedence.

Example : Define a process **adder** with two input channels and one output channel. The process reads an integer from each input channel, outputs their sum, and keeps repeating these actions. When the input streams are $(1 \cdot 2 \cdot 3, 5 \cdot 4)$, the scenario representing the computation is shown in Figure 1.

For another example, consider a **fair merge** process with two input channels and one output channel. The process outputs some interleaving of the two input streams. When the input streams are $(1 \cdot 2, 3)$, some of the possible scenarios are shown in Figure 2.

Definition 4. The denotation of a network is the set of possible scenarios of that network. We write $\mathcal{S}(N)$ to stand for the set of scenarios of network N.

We now describe how composition of networks is expressed in terms of operations on scenario sets. This discussion for the static case provides the key intuition in getting the scenario set for an infinite network from the scenario sets of its component subnetworks. It may be justified using an operational semantics.

We assume that networks may be composed in three ways. These are aggregation, loop formation and restriction.

Definition 5. If M and N are networks, we define a new network, called the **aggregation** of M and N. The input channels are all the input channels of M and N.

In aggregation, two networks are viewed as a single network, but no new channels are constructed.

In loop formation, a new network is obtained from an old network by connecting an output channel of the old network to an input channel of the old network.

Definition 6. Given a network N we define the **loop composition** of N with b and c to be the network obtained from network N by connecting the output channel b to the input channel c.

A new network may also be formed from an old one by hiding some input channels of the old network.

Definition 7. Given a network N, we define the **restriction** of N with respect to the channel a as the network obtained by hiding the channel.

No new channels are constructed by restriction.

Definition 8. Suppose that S_1 and S_2 are scenarios with disjoint sets of events. Their **union** is the scenario obtained by forming the union of the underlying sets of events, and the partial order is the union of the partial orders of S_1 and S_2.

If N_1 and N_2 are two networks, and a new network N_3 is formed by the aggregation of N_1 and N_2, then $\mathcal{S}(N_3)$ is the set of unions of all pairs (S_1, S_2), where $S_1 \in \mathcal{S}(N_1)$ and $S_2 \in \mathcal{S}(N_2)$.

If N is a network, and a new network N' is formed by loop composition, say the output channel x of network N is connected to the input channel y of network N, then we obtain the scenario set of N' as follows. Discard all scenarios of N in which the $+$-y-stream, the stream on channel y, is not equal to the $+$-x-stream. For each remaining scenario, identify together the $+$-y-stream and the $+$-x-stream, that is, identify corresponding events in the $+$-x-stream and the $+$-y-stream. Discard all the scenarios that produce a directed cycle, because these cannot possibly represent a computation of the network N'. Now, for each remaining scenario, remove the events corresponding to the identified streams (since they do not appear externally for network N'), preserving the partial order. The resulting set characterizes the new network N'.

Example: Define a process **double-adder** with two input channels i_1 and i_2, and two output channels o_1 and o_2. The process first outputs a 0 on o_2, then repeats the following action : read an integer from i_1, then from i_2, and then output their sum on both the output channels. A possible scenario is shown in Figure 3. Now connect o_2 and i_2 together to form an internal channel. We show how to get a scenario for the new network in Figure 3.

The remaining operation on networks is restriction. If N is a network, and $o_1, \ldots o_n$ are output channels to be hidden, then the scenarios for the new network are

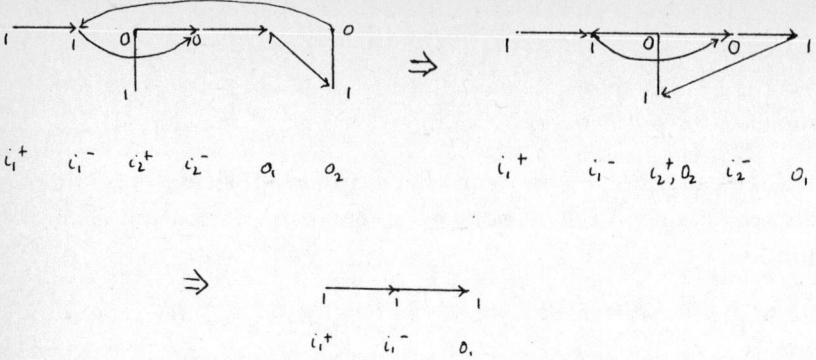

Figure 3: Loop composition of scenarios

all the partial orders S' such that there exists $S \in \mathcal{S}(N)$, and S' is obtained from S by removing the streams corresponding to $o_1, \ldots o_n$ but preserving the partial order, i.e. if u, v are events in S', then

$$\langle u, v \rangle \in S' \Leftrightarrow \langle u, v \rangle \in S$$

If N is a network, and $i_1, \ldots i_m$ are input channels to be hidden, then the scenarios for the new network are all the scenarios S' such that there exists $S \in \mathcal{S}(N)$, with the streams corresponding to $i_1, \ldots i_m$ all null, and S' is the scenario with these null streams removed.

The final issue to be discussed in this section is the notion of implementation. We wish to use a weak notion of implementability. This will make our proofs of non-implementability strong. Of course, if our interest is in implementability results, then we would need a strong notion of implementability.

Definition 9. Given a network N with C as its set of input and output channels and $\mathcal{S}(N)$ as its scenario set, we define the **IO-relation** of N as the set of all C-indexed tuples of streams such that for each tuple there is a scenario in $\mathcal{S}(N)$ that has exactly these streams corresponding to the $+-$ event streams on the channels.

Example : Define a process **plus1** with one input channel and one output channel. It reads integers and outputs them after incrementing them by 1. The IO-relation of such a process consists of all pairs of streams of integers $\langle a_1 a_2 \ldots, b_1 b_2 \ldots \rangle$ and all pairs of streams $\langle a_1 a_2 \ldots a_k, b_1 b_2 \ldots b_k \rangle$ for all $k \geq 0$, such that $b_i = a_i + 1$, for all $i > 0$. A pair $\langle 1 \cdot 2, 2 \cdot 3 \rangle$ corresponds to the scenario in Figure 4.

This captures the directly observable aspects of a network behavior. The discussion of Brock and Ackerman[3] shows that different networks with the same IO-relation may produce networks with different IO-relations when they are connected

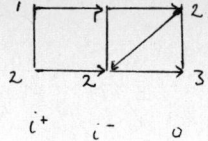

Figure 4: A scenario for **plus1**

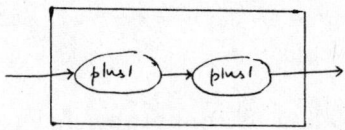

Figure 5: an implementation using **plus1**

to other identical networks. Thus IO-equality is not a congruence with respect to network composition.

Definition 10. A set M of processes is said to **implement** a relation R if there is a finite network, built out of copies of the processes in M, having R as its IO-relation.

Example : Let M consist of the process **plus1**, and let the relation R consist of all pairs of streams of integers $\langle a_1 a_2 \ldots, b_1 b_2 \ldots \rangle$ and all pairs of streams $\langle a_1 a_2 \ldots a_k, b_1 b_2 \ldots b_k \rangle$ for all $k \geq 0$, such that $b_i = a_i + 2$, for all $i > 0$. Then M can implement R, as illustrated by the network in Figure 5.

We shall say that a network N implements network M if they have the same IO-relation, upto renaming of channels. By this definition, we do not care if the two networks have different internal configurations. But they must present the same interface to the external world.

We need some notation here.

Definition 11. A **vertex** of a partial order $(A, \rightarrow)$ is any element of A. A is called the **vertex-set**.

Definition 12. $a_1, a_2, \ldots a_n$ is said to be a **path** from a_1 to a_n in the partial order $(A, \rightarrow)$, if $a_1, \ldots a_n \in A$ and for all i from 1 to $n - 1$, $\langle a_i, a_{i+1} \rangle \in (A, \rightarrow)$.

We now define an ordering on scenarios, and use this ordering to define monotonicity and continuity. Monotonicity will turn out to be the key idea in establishing our expressiveness theorem. The ordering captures the idea of "extending" a computation.

Definition 13. For a given network, if S_1 and S_2 are scenarios, then $S_1 \sqsubseteq S_2$ iff

(a) for all channels c, the $+$-c-stream in S_1 is a prefix of the $+$-c-stream in S_2, and the $-$-c-stream in S_1 is a prefix of the $-$-c-stream in S_2,

(b) there does not exist $\langle u,v \rangle \in S_2$, such that $\langle u,v \rangle \notin S_1$ and $v \in \text{vertex-set}(S_1)$, and

(c) for any two vertices u and v in vertex-set(S_1), the pair $\langle u,v \rangle \in S_1$ iff $\langle u,v \rangle \in S_2$.

The second condition says that there are no new "causal" paths into old events. The third condition states that all the old causal paths persist in the extended scenario.

Definition 14. A network is said to be **monotone** if, for any scenario S_1 of the network, if the input $+$-streams are extended, then there exists a scenario S_2 with the extended streams, such that $S_1 \sqsubseteq S_2$.

Definition 15. A network is said to be **continuous** if whenever $S_1 \sqsubseteq S_2 \sqsubseteq \ldots$ is a sequence of scenarios of the network, $\sqcup S_i$ is also a scenario of the network, where vertex-set$(\sqcup S_i) = \cup_i \text{vertex-set}(S_i)$, and

$$\sqcup S_i = \cup S_i.$$

In the above definition, we are viewing a scenario as a poset and thus as a set of ordered pairs. When we say union of relations, we mean union of the sets of ordered pairs that are in the relation. Note that the union of a chain of partial orders is automatically a partial order, so the above definition makes sense.

We wish to show that **amb** cannot implement **fair merge**, but we prove a stronger result: we allow other primitives also, and show that no network of **amb** processes and these extra primitives can implement **fair merge**. These extra processes that we allow are those with determinate, monotone and continuous scenario sets.

Definition 16. A network is said to be **determinate** if for every tuple of input streams to the network, there is a unique tuple of output streams.

Processes, as described by Gilles Kahn [6], are determinate in this sense, and also have a monotone and continuous scenario set.

We have not formalized the notion of *sequential* process as it is not essential to our proofs. Our results thus apply even if we had non-sequential processes like "parallel or" as described by Plotkin [16].

We now clarify what we mean by "recursion." A network X with m input channels and n output channels may be defined as a specific network of processes and also of "black boxes" marked X, with m input channels and n output channels. The idea is that X may expand to the network represented by it, and this network may contain more copies of X. In this way, by suitably defining X, we may generate multiple, even unboundedly many but countably many, copies of any processes of interest.

X is called a **recursively defined process**. If M is a set of processes, then a **recursively defined M-process** X is defined as a network of copies of processes in M and recursively defined M-processes, possibly including X.

Now, we define the notion of *implementation with recursion*, similar to the earlier definition of implementation.

Definition 17. A set of processes M is said to **implement** process B **with recursion** if there is a recursively defined M-process with the same IO-relation as B.

With each recursively defined process, we associate the maximal "limiting" network to which it may evolve.

Definition 18. A **completely expanded network** is a network in which no recursive definition is left unexpanded.

This network is potentially infinite. Of course, at any finite stage of the execution, the actual dynamic network is finite. We started with a finitely described network, so the resulting completely expanded network has finitely many input and output channels. We now need a way of describing the scenario set of a network in terms of the scenario sets of the countably many components of the network.

Let N be a network built up from countably many component networks $N_1, N_2, \ldots$. Let $S_1, S_2, \ldots$ be scenarios, with $S_i \in \mathcal{S}(N_i)$ for all i, satisfying the following condition: for every internal channel connecting output port y in N_i to input port x in N_j, N_i not necessarily distinct from N_j, the $+$-y-stream in S_i is equal to the $+$-x-stream in S_j. The preorder S', obtained by merging together the corresponding $+$-streams for internal channels, is not a scenario since it contains events on channels that are internal to the network. Then the **scenario set of the network** N consists of all the S'' such that there is a well-founded S', and S'' is S' with the streams corresponding to any internal channels removed, and for any u, v not events on any internal channel,

$$\langle u, v \rangle \in S'' \Leftrightarrow \langle u, v \rangle \in S'$$

This may be justified using an operational semantics. In the next section, we show that if M is the set of processes consisting of **amb** and all processes with determinate, monotone and continuous scenario sets, then **fair merge** cannot be implemented by **amb** with recursion.

3 The Non-Implementation Theorem

In the presence of recursive definition we can implement both angelic merge and unbounded nondeterminacy using **amb**. **amb** selects one of its two arguments. If one of them is a divergent expression then the other one gets selected so **amb** will not wait for a divergent computation if there is a data value available to it. Now consider the function f defined as follows

$$f(n) = \mathbf{amb}(n, f(n+1))$$

If we evaluate this on 0 we get any integer as a result without the possibility of divergence. Thus **amb** implements unbounded nondeterminacy. It is easy to write an implementation of angelic merge with **amb**. The unsolved question posed by Abramsky [1] was whether **amb** could implement fair merge. Clearly one can get iteration for free if one has the ability to make recursive definitions. Thus many of the simple arguments that suffice for the static case do not apply here.

We now prove the main theorem in this paper, i.e. that a network composed, using aggregation and loop composition, of countably many monotone and continuous components is monotone. In other words, we need to show that if we start with a network scenario and we extend the inputs, then we obtain an extended scenario. What follows is a description of how to construct the extended scenario.

Let S be a scenario of the network. Then there exist scenarios S_i for each component such that when we combine them we get the network scenario. Let this be called *Stage 0* in the construction.

Stage 1: Extend the input +-streams of the network. This causes some of the input +-streams of the components to get extended. By monotonicity of the components we can extend their scenarios, thus extending their output +-streams.

Stage 2: The extension of the outputs of some of the components causes the input +-streams to other components to get extended. We use monotonicity to extend the affected component scenarios again.

We continue this process to get a possibly infinite increasing sequence of scenarios for each component. Using continuity of the components, we get a least upper bound (lub) scenario for each component. By construction, all the lub scenarios match up in their channel streams. It now remains to be shown that these lub scenarios for the components can be combined to form a network scenario.

We identify together the appropriate internal +-streams of the network. If this fails to give a network scenario, then there is an infinite descending chain in the graph representing the resulting poset. We show that this is not possible.

We need the following definition to represent the partial stage in the construction of the final network scenario.

Definition 19. At stage n, for every channel connecting output port x to input port y, we know that +-x-stream $\sqsupseteq$ +-y-stream by construction. Combine the scenarios of all the components by merging together the +-y-stream with the prefix of the +-x-stream equal to the +-y-stream. Do this for all the internal channels of the network. This preorder is defined to be the **graph at stage** n.

We will follow the convention that if an event added at stage n is merged with an event added at stage $n+1$, then the resulting event corresponds to stage n.

Lemma 1. For every stage, there is no path in the graph at that stage from an event added at that stage to an event added at an earlier stage.

Proof: This is proved by induction on the stage number. At stage 0, there are no earlier stages, so the statement trivially holds.

Suppose the statement is true upto stage n; consider the graph at stage $n+1$. Consider any event a added at stage $n+1$. If this is an output +-event, then the only paths from it will be to input --events and output +-events added at stage $n+1$, by the way scenarios get extended, and the way the graph at stage $n+1$ is constructed. If a is an input +-event, then the only paths from it will be to input +-events and input --events added at that stage, from which there are no paths to events added at an earlier stage. ∎

Lemma 2. For every stage n, the graph at stage n is well-founded, that is, there is no infinite descending chain.

Proof: This is proved by induction on the stage number. At stage 0, the graph is well-founded, because the component scenarios can be combined to obtain a network scenario. Suppose the graphs at all the stages upto n are well-founded. Consider the graph at stage $n+1$.

Suppose there is an infinite descending chain of events $e_0 \leftarrow e_1 \leftarrow e_2 \leftarrow \ldots$. If e_0 was added at an earlier stage, say stage m, then using lemma 1, the entire chain is in the graph at stage m, which gives a contradiction by using the inductive hypothesis. So e_0 was added at stage $n+1$ and the entire chain is in the graph at stage $n+1$. Now all the events on the chain must have been added at stage $n+1$, because if any e_i was added at an earlier stage, then the infinite descending chain $e_i \leftarrow \ldots$ would have been in the graph at an earlier stage, contradicting the inductive hypothesis. e_0 cannot be an input +-event, because by the convention adopted, every merged +-event is considered to be an event at an earlier stage, and by the definition of scenario, every +-event at an input channel of the network has only finitely many predecessors. So e_0 is either an input --event or an output +-event of some component N_i of the network. Moreover, if e_j is an input --event or an output +-event in the scenario for N_i, then for e_{j+1} to be an event in the scenario for some other $N_{i'}$, it must be a merged +-event of N_i, and by the convention adopted, every merged +-event is considered to be an event at an earlier stage. Therefore the entire chain is in the scenario for N_i, violating the well-foundedness of the scenario.

Thus there is no infinite descending chain of events in the graph at any stage. ∎

Lemma 3. There is no infinite descending chain in the constructed preorder.

Proof: Suppose there is an infinite descending chain $e_0 \leftarrow e_1 \leftarrow \ldots$ in the final preorder. e_0 was added at some finite stage n. Using lemma 1, the entire chain must be in the graph at stage n, contradicting lemma 2. ∎

Theorem 1. A network composed, using aggregation and loop composition, of at most countably many monotone and continuous components is monotone.

Proof: By the described construction and the above lemmas, we can extend a scenario S to get another scenario S'. We must now show that $S \sqsubseteq S'$. In other words, we must check that the three conditions in definition 13 are satisfied.

That every channel stream gets extended is clear. If there is a path from u to v in the constructed preorder and v is an event at stage 0, then, by lemma 1, the whole path must be in the graph at stage 0, since the construction does not add any new edges between old events. This proves the second condition in definition 13. Moreover, any path in the graph at stage 0 persists in the constructed preorder. This proves the third condition in definition 13 too. ∎

This theorem by itself is not quite enough since the definition of implementation is stated in terms of the input-output relation. We need to know that restricting a channel does not destroy monotonicity, and that the IO-relation is monotone.

Lemma 4. If N is a monotone network, and a new network N' is obtained from N by hiding some input channels and some output channels of N, then N' is monotone.

Proof: Suppose S_1' is a scenario for N', and suppose that S_1 is the scenario for N from which S_1' was obtained. We extend the input streams in S_1', thus extending the input streams in S_1. By monotonicity of N, we get a scenario S_2 with the extended input streams, such that $S_1 \sqsubseteq S_2$. Let S_2' be the corresponding scenario for N'. We need to show that $S_1' \sqsubseteq S_2'$.

First, for every input or output channel of N', the streams in S_1' are the same as in S_1. Since $S_1 \sqsubseteq S_2$, the streams in S_1 are prefixes of those in S_2, and for every input or output channel of N', these are equal to the streams in S_2'. Hence, for every input or output channel of N', the streams in S_1' are prefixes of those in S_2'.

Next, we need to show that there does not exist $\langle u, v \rangle \in S_2'$, such that $\langle u, v \rangle \notin S_1'$, and $v \in$ vertex-set(S_1'). Suppose $\langle u, v \rangle \in S_2'$ and $\langle u, v \rangle \notin S_1'$ and $v \in$ vertex-set$(S_1') \subseteq$ vertex-set(S_1). Then $\langle u, v \rangle \in S_2$, and this implies that $\langle u, v \rangle \in S_1$, because $S_1 \sqsubseteq S_2$ and $v \in$ vertex-set(S_1). Since $\langle u, v \rangle \in S_2'$, neither u nor v corresponds to a hidden channel. Hence $\langle u, v \rangle \in S_1'$, which contradicts the assumption.

Next, we need to show that for any two vertices u and v in vertex-set(S_1'), the pair $\langle u, v \rangle \in S_1'$ iff $\langle u, v \rangle \in S_2'$. This is clear by using this fact for S_1 and S_2, since $S_1 \sqsubseteq S_2$. ∎

Corollary 1. Any network built up from monotone and continuous networks is monotone, and hence has a monotone IO-relation.

Proof: Any network built up from monotone and continuous networks is obtained by composing the networks using aggregation and loop composition, and then hiding some input and output channels. As proved earlier, any network obtained by composing, using aggregation and loop composition, monotone and continuous components is monotone. By the earlier lemma, hiding some input and output channels preserves monotonicity. Now, for any tuple of input streams and output streams in the IO-relation of the network, there is a corresponding scenario. Extending the input streams extends this scenario, by the monotonicity of the scenario set. The tuple of streams corresponding to this extended scenario is in the IO-relation, and extends the original tuple. Hence the IO-relation is monotone. ∎

Lemma 5. The IO-relation of **fair merge** is not monotone.

Proof: Let the input channels of the **fair merge** be a and b and the output channel be c. Consider a computation where the input on channel a is the single token 1 and the input on b is the stream 2^∞. The possible outputs on c are of the form $2^i \cdot 1 \cdot 2^\infty$. Now consider a computation where we extend the input on a to $1 \cdot 1$. The possible outputs in this case are of the form $2^i \cdot 1 \cdot 2^j \cdot 1 \cdot 2^\infty$. None of these are extensions of any of the former output streams. Thus the IO-relation of **fair merge** is not monotone. ∎

Corollary 2. A **fair merge** cannot be implemented by any finite network of recursively defined M-processes and copies of processes in M, where M is the set consisting of **amb** and all processes with determinate, monotone and continuous sets.

Proof: Suppose N is any finite network of recursively defined M-processes and copies of processes in M, where M is as described. By a straightforward examination of their possible scenarios, **amb** and CN are monotone and continuous. So, by corollary 1, the completely expanded network for N is monotone. Hence N is monotone, because N and its completely expanded form have the same scenario sets. So N has a monotone IO-relation, but fair merge does not, by an earlier lemma. So no such network N can implement fair merge. ∎

4 Conclusions

The results in this paper establish that fair merge is a powerful primitive that does more than merely cause countable non-determinacy. Past investigations have focussed on differentiating countable non-determinacy from finite non-determinacy. There are a whole class of such results. Other investigations that we have carried out show that signaling adds to the expressive power of dataflow networks. Thus there are more levels of expressiveness then had been suspected before. It is also an interesting question to investigate how these expressiveness properties relate in the presence of richer languages, for example, those with λ-abstraction or higher-order functions.

It is necessary to describe an operational semantics corresponding to the denotational model presented here to formally justify the reasonableness of the model. We have not presented an operational semantics here, but the work of Stark [18] shows that satisfactory operational semantics can be defined.

A related area of investigation into expressiveness is the finite delay operators of Milner's Calculus for Communicating Systems (CCS) [11]. One finds in the literature on CCS two different primitives for expressing finite delay, one due to Milner [12] and one due to Hennessy [4]. Milner's delay operator will always produce finite delay sequences whereas Hennessy's will produce an infinite delay sequence if there is nothing it can synchronize with but only finite delay if there is something for it to synchronize with. We suspect that these are provably inequivalent.

5 Acknowledgements

We would like to thank Radhakrishnan Jagadeesan for extremely useful discussions, and Abha Moitra for reading an earlier draft of this paper. We have also benefited from discussions with Joost Kok, Gene Stark and Samson Abramsky. This research was supported by NSF grant DCR-8602072 to Cornell University.

References

[1] Samson Abramsky. Private communication, 1984.

[2] K. R. Apt and Gordon Plotkin. Countable nondeterminism and random assignment. *Journal Of The ACM*, 33(4):724–767, 1986.

[3] J. Dean Brock and William B. Ackerman. Scenarios: A model of nondeterminate computation. In *Formalization of Programming Concepts*, pages 252–259, 1981. LNCS 107.

[4] Mathew Hennessy. Axiomatizing finite delay operators. *Acta. Inform.*, pages 61–88, 1984.

[5] C. A. R. Hoare. *Communicating Sequential Processes*. Series in Computer Science. Prentice-Hall International, London, 1985.

[6] Gilles Kahn. The semantics of a simple language for parallel programming. In *Information Processing 74*, pages 993–998. North-Holland, 1977.

[7] Robert M. Keller. Denotational models for parallel programs with indeterminate operators. In *Formal Description of Programming Concepts*, pages 337–366. North-Holland, 1978.

[8] Robert M. Keller and Prakash Panangaden. Semantics of digital networks containing indeterminate operators. *Distributed Computing*, 1(4):235–245, 1986.

[9] Joost Kok. Denotational semantics of nets with nondeterminism. In *Proceedings of the 1986 European Symposium on Programming*, pages 237–249, 1986.

[10] Joost Kok. A fully abstract semantics for dataflow nets. In *Proceedings of Parallel Architectures And Languages Europe 1987*, pages 351–368, Berlin, 1987. Springer-Verlag.

[11] Robin Milner. *A Calculus for Communicating Systems*, volume 92 of *Lecture Notes in Computer Science*. Springer-Verlag, 1980.

[12] Robin Milner. A finite-delay operator in synchronous ccs. Technical Report CSR-116-82, University of Edinburgh, 1982.

[13] P. Panangaden and E. W. Stark. Computations, residuals and the power of indeterminacy. In Timo Lepisto and Arto Salomaa, editors, *Proceedings of the Fifteenth ICALP*, pages 439–454. Springer-Verlag, 1988. Lecture Notes in Computer Science 317.

[14] Prakash Panangaden and Vasant Shanbhogue. On the expressive power of indeterminate primitives. Technical Report 87-891, Cornell University, Computer Science Department, November 1987.

[15] David Park. The "fairness problem" and non-deterministic computing networks. In *Proceedings of the Fourth Advanced Course on Theoretical Computer Science, Mathematisch Centrum*, pages 133–161, 1982.

[16] Gordon Plotkin. Lcf considered a programming language. *Theoretical Computer Science*, 5(3):223–256, 1977.

[17] Vaughn Pratt. Modeling concurrency with partial orders. *International Journal Of Parallel Programming*, 15(1):33–71, 1986.

[18] Eugene W. Stark. Concurrent transition system semantics of process networks. In *Proceedings Of The Fourteenth Annual ACM Symposium On Principles Of Programming Languages*, pages 199–210, 1987.

[19] Glynn Winskel. Event structures. Technical Report 95, University of Cambridge, Computer Laboratory, 1986.

GHC — A Language for a New Age of Parallel Programming

Koichi Furukawa and Kazunori Ueda

Institute for New Generation Computer Technology
4-28, Mita 1-Chome, Minato-ku, Tokyo 108, Japan

Abstract

A parallel logic programming language GHC, proposed by Ueda (1985), is now playing a very important role in the Fifth Generation Computer Project. It is a successor of Relational Language (Clark and Gregory 1981), Concurrent Prolog (Shapiro 1983) and Parlog (Clark and Gregory 1984). Since GHC is totally based on parallelism, it provides a genuine tool for parallel programming. It encourages programmers to write parallel algorithms and therefore gives a foundation of parallel programming. We have also developed a program transformation technique for GHC programs which preserves the external behaviour of the original programs. To show the validity of the transformation technique, we have developed a formal semantics of possibly non-terminating GHC programs. The highly parallel prototype hardware of our project is now being developed to support the efficient execution of GHC programs.

1. Introduction

The Fifth Generation Computer Project started in 1982 to develop an entirely new computer system for knowledge processing. There are two significant technical characteristics of the project: the adoption of logic programming as the central concept of the system and the pursuit of highly parallel computer architecture for the very fast execution of logic programs. At the beginning, we provisionally chose Prolog as the project's kernel language, since there were no other realistic logic programming languages. We appreciated the potential ability of Prolog as a very high level user language for developing knowledge processing application programs. However, we noticed a major defect of the language in its expressiveness for parallel situations: It is very hard to write an operating system in Prolog because it has no concurrency concept.

In 1981, an entirely new logic programming language, called Relational Language, was proposed by Clark and Gregory (1981). It is a logic programming language with the concept of concurrency, but without the concept of backtracking. To introduce concurrency, they adopted the notion of "guarded commands" proposed by Dijkstra (1975). Each clause has a guard which must be satisfied in order to be selected as the subsequent computation branch. They also introduced the notion of suspension for synchronisation.

After that, there appeared two successors of the language: Concurrent Prolog by Shapiro (1983) and Parlog by Clark and Gregory (1984). We selected these two languages as candidates for the kernel language of our project, and started very careful studies on both of these languages from various viewpoints including expressive power, semantics and ease of implementation. As a result, Ueda (1985) developed another parallel logic language, called Guarded Horn Clauses (GHC). GHC turned to be a good compromise of Concurrent Prolog and Parlog. For ordinary programs, it is as expressive as Concurrent Prolog and as efficient as Parlog. Moreover, GHC is both syntactically and semantically the simplest of them.

Flat GHC (FGHC), which is a simplified version of GHC, has been selected as the core of the FGCS kernel language, KL1, which interfaces parallel software and the highly parallel prototype hardware, the Parallel Inference Machine (PIM).

2. GHC — A Brief Introduction

GHC is a general-purpose parallel language for programming with communicating processes.

Although both Prolog and GHC are based on input resolution and unification, the purposes of the languages are quite different. Prolog is a (restricted) theorem prover for Horn-clause logic, while GHC is not directly aimed at theorem proving that involves searching. The primary design goal of GHC is to provide a simple way to describe a process that may interact with other processes and the outside world. This has been achieved by regarding a goal as a process.

A process is defined in terms of other processes. Interprocess communication is realised by the information transfer caused by unification. The result of a GHC computation is the history of its interaction (i.e., the observation and the generation of substitutions) with the outside world, while the result of a Prolog computation is an answer substitution returned upon success.

A GHC program is a set of *guarded Horn clauses* (also called *(program) clauses*) of the form
$$h \;\text{:-}\; G \mid B$$
where h is an atomic formula called the *head* and G and B are multisets of atomic formulae. Each element of the multisets is called a *goal*. A non-empty multiset with n atomic formulae is written as $g_1, g_2, \ldots, g_n$, and an empty multiset is written as true.

The *commitment operator* '|' divides the clause into two parts: the left-hand side is called the *guard* and the right-hand side is called the *body*. The head h is part of the guard. Roughly speaking, each clause describes a conditional rewrite (or reduction) rule for goals. The head is the template of a goal to be rewritten; the rest of the guard specifies the additional conditions for rewriting; and the body specifies the multiset of new goals that replaces the old goal.

The execution of a program begins with the initial multiset of goals specified by a goal clause of the following form:
$$\text{:-}\; B$$

Each goal (say g) in B rewrites itself using one of the program clauses unless it is a predefined unification goal of the form $t_1 = t_2$. A unification goal $t_1 = t_2$ unifies t_1 and t_2, and the generated substitution, if any, is applied to all the goals running. Goals run in parallel.

The clause used for rewriting a goal g is determined by executing the guards of the program clauses in parallel. For g to execute the guard h :- G of a program clause C means to execute $g = h$ and G in parallel. The important rule is that *the execution of $g = h$ and G cannot instantiate g*. The fragment of computation that would instantiate g is suspended. The suspended fragment of computation can be resumed when g gets more instantiated by other goals running in parallel with g. This rule is called *the rule of synchronisation*, because it is used for the synchronisation of goals running in parallel.

If the goal g succeeds in solving the guard of C, it can *commit to C* and replace itself by the body goals of C. When g can commit to two or more program clauses, g selects one of them and commits to it. This rule is called the *rule of commitment* and the mechanism is called *committed-choice nondeterminism*. A goal g is said to *succeed* if it becomes an empty multiset of goals by repeated rewriting.

Let us consider a ticket reservation counter with two windows. Two queues will be formed, one for each window. We assume that the requests from the two queues should be serialised behind the counter to gain access to a single shared resource. The serialiser can be defined in GHC as a process merge(Xs, Ys, Zs) which merges two queues Xs and Ys into a single queue Zs:

M_1: merge([X|Xs],Ys,Zs) :- true | Zs=[X|Us], merge(Xs,Ys,Us).
M_2: merge(Xs,[Y|Ys],Zs) :- true | Zs=[Y|Us], merge(Xs,Ys,Us).
M_3: merge([],Ys,Zs) :- true | Zs=Ys.
M_4: merge(Xs,[],Zs) :- true | Zs=Xs.

The first argument of M_1, [X|Xs], means that M_1 is waiting for a request from the first window. Similarly, M_2 is waiting for a request from the second window. M_3 and M_4 handle the cases where no more requests will arrive at the first and the second windows, respectively.

The following is a simple example using the merge program:

:- queue1(As), queue2(Bs), merge(As,Bs,Cs), serve(Cs).

The goals queue1(As) and queue2(Bs) create two queues As and Bs, which are merged into Cs and served by serve(Cs).

Suppose neither queue1(As) nor queue2(Bs) has generated a queue of requests, or, both As and Bs are uninstantiated. The process merge(As,Bs,Cs) will attempt to unify As with the first argument [X|Xs] of M_1, but this attempt is suspended because it would instantiate As. Suppose now queue1(As) has instantiated As to [john|Rest]. Then the suspended unification becomes [john|Rest]=[X|Xs], which can now succeed without instantiating As. Thus, the guard of M_1 will succeed, and merge(As,Bs,Cs) can commit to it. After commitment, the goal Zs=[X|Us], which has now become Cs=[john|Us], will run and the first element of Cs will be determined. The remaining body goal of M_1, merge(Rest,Ys,Us), merges the rest of the first queue and the second queue.

If merge(As,Bs,Cs) finds that both As and Bs have been instantiated to non-empty queues, it will commit either to M_1 or to M_2, but not to both.

3. Programming in GHC

Processes play a very important role in GHC programs. "Process" is a synonym of "goal" in GHC. A process, defined using subprocesses, reduces itself into the subprocesses and terminates when all the subprocesses terminate.

For example, four processes, queue1, queue2, merge and serve, are created at the beginning of the execution of the last example:

```
:- queue1(As), queue2(Bs), merge(As,Bs,Cs), serve(Cs).
```

The merge process uses either M_1 or M_2 for each reduction while neither the rest of As nor the rest of Bs is known to be empty. A merge subprocess is created in each reduction, and thus the original merge process will continue to be alive. The original merge process will terminate and be deleted when either M_3 or M_4 is selected.

Using the process creation and deletion capability, it is possible to realise a flexible assembly line which dynamically changes its structure during the execution of the program. We explain a list compaction program which removes duplications as an example showing such behaviour. Let compact(Xs, Ys) be a process which eliminates duplications from the list Xs and returns the result through Ys. The compact process is defined in GHC as follows:

C_1:   compact([],Ys) :- true | Ys=[].
C_2:   compact([X|Xs],Ys) :- true |
        Ys=[X|Ys1], remove(X,Xs,Xs1), compact(Xs1,Ys1).

R_1:   remove(X,[],Us) :- true | Us=[].
R_2:   remove(X,[X|Xs],Us) :- true | remove(X,Xs,Us).
R_3:   remove(X,[X1|Xs],Us) :- X=\=X1 | Us=[X1|Vs], remove(X,Xs,Vs).

The execution of a goal clause

```
:- compact([1,3,2,1,3,1,4,2],Ys).
```

first creates a single compact process. Since this process successfully solves the guard of C_2, C_2 is selected and the three processes appearing in the body of C_2 are created. Since the remove process is defined recursively, it will continue to be alive as long as the second argument is not empty. Each time the compact process is reduced using C_2, a new remove process is created, resulting in process proliferation as shown in Fig. 1. Ease of process creation is very important for parallel programs, because processes are

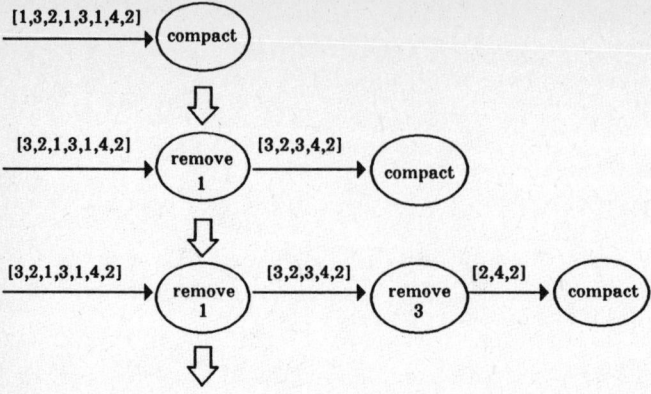

Fig. 1 Process proliferation in the compact program

```
search((Key,Value),nt_node(Key,Value,Left,Right)) :- !.
search((Key,Value),nt_node(Key1,Value1,Left,Right)) :-
        Key<Key1, !, search((Key,Value),Left).
search((Key,Value),nt_node(Key1,Value1,Left,Right)) :-
        Key>Key1, !, search((Key,Value),Right).
search((Key,Value),t_node) :- Value=undefined.

update((Key,Value),nt_node(Key,Value1,Left,Right),
        nt_node(Key,Value,Left,Right)) :- !.
update((Key,Value),nt_node(Key1,Value1,Left,Right),
        nt_node(Key1,Value1,Left1,Right)) :-
        Key<Key1, !, update((Key,Value),Left,Left1).
update((Key,Value),nt_node(Key1,Value1,Left,Right),
        nt_node(Key1,Value1,Left,Right1)) :-
        Key>Key1, !, update((Key,Value),Right,Right1).
update((Key,Value),t_node,nt_node(Key,Value,t_node,t_node)).
```

Fig. 2 Ordered binary tree search program in Prolog

the units of parallel execution and easy process creation facilitates the extraction of parallelism that may vary in the course of computation.

The role of processes in parallel programs corresponds to that of data in sequential programs and process structures to data structures (Shapiro 1984). Let us consider binary tree search programs to compare Prolog and GHC. Fig. 2 shows a Prolog program for searching and updating an ordered binary tree. In the program, ordered binary trees are represented as terms that are passed through the second and third arguments of search and update. Each tree is either a constant t_node representing an empty tree or of the form nt_node(*Key, Value, Left, Right*), a structure representing a non-empty tree whose root has a pair of *Key* and *Value* and two subtrees, *Left* and *Right*.

In the GHC program shown in Fig. 3, on the other hand, each node of an ordered binary tree is represented by a process and each link is represented by a variable shared

```
nt_node([],_,_,Left,Right) :- true | Left=[], Right=[].
nt_node([search(Key,Value)|Cs],Key,Value1,Left,Right) :-
      true | Value=Value1,nt_node(Cs,Key,Value1,Left,Right).
nt_node([search(Key,Value)|Cs],Key1,Value1,Left,Right) :-
      Key<Key1 | Left=[search(Key,Value)|Left1],
      nt_node(Cs,Key1,Value1,Left1,Right).
nt_node([search(Key,Value)|Cs],Key1,Value1,Left,Right) :-
      Key>Key1 | Right=[search(Key,Value)|Right1],
      nt_node(Cs,Key1,Value1,Left,Right1).
nt_node([update(Key,Value)|Cs],Key,Value1,Left,Right) :-
      true | nt_node(Cs,Key,Value,Left,Right).
nt_node([update(Key,Value)|Cs],Key1,Value1,Left,Right) :-
      Key<Key1 | Left=[update(Key,Value)|Left1],
      nt_node(Cs,Key1,Value1,Left1,Right).
nt_node([update(Key,Value)|Cs],Key1,Value1,Left,Right) :-
      Key>Key1 | Right=[update(Key,Value)|Right1],
      nt_node(Cs,Key1,Value1,Left,Right1).
t_node([]) :- true | true.
t_node([search(Key,Value)|Cs]) :- true |
      Value=undefined, t_node(Cs).
t_node([update(Key,Value)|Cs]) :- true |
      nt_node(Cs,Key,Value,Left,Right),
      t_node(Left), t_node(Right).
```

Fig. 3 Ordered binary tree search program in GHC

by two node processes. Instead of the data structure nt_node(*Key, Value, Left, Right*) appearing in the Prolog program, the GHC program defines a process of the form nt_node(*Cs, Key, Value, Left, Right*), where *Cs* is the communication variable through which messages come from the parent process, *Key* and *Value* are the internal states of the process, and *Left* and *Right* are the communication variables leading to their son processes. While *Left* and *Right* in the Prolog program are considered as data structures representing subtrees, *Left* and *Right* in the GHC program can be thought of as communication channels for passing commands such as search(*Key, Value*) and update(*Key, Value*).

The most significant difference between these two programs lies in their ways of updating. In the Prolog program, each node on the path from the root down to the updated node is copied because destructive assignment is not allowed. The GHC program, on the other hand, does not copy any data structures. Instead, it passes an update message along a tree branch to the target process and finally updates the value by changing the internal state of the process.

As explained above, operations on an ordered binary tree in the GHC program are designated by a sequence of commands given to the first arguments of nt_node processes and t_node processes. Thus, this program is considered to follow the object-oriented programming style.

4. Program Transformation in GHC

It is widely recognised that the program transformation technique provides a powerful, systematic tool for improving programs. Having a set of transformation rules for GHC programs will be useful for deriving efficient parallel programs from straightforward ones. Since GHC inherits many aspects of pure logic programming, one may be tempted to define the set of rules by adapting the unfold/fold rules developed for logic programs (Tamaki and Sato 1984). However, this is not a simple task because logic programming and GHC are quite different in their frameworks. We want to use GHC as a process description language. This means that our rules should preserve the *behaviour* of the processes defined by a program, whereas Tamaki's and Sato's rules were designed so as to preserve the least model semantics. Furthermore, we must be able to handle non-terminating but useful programs.

We have developed a set of transformation rules for Flat GHC programs (Ueda and Furukawa 1988). The set is based on unfolding and folding, and considers the control aspect of the language defined by the rule of synchronisation. It consists of four rules: normalisation, immediate execution, case-splitting, and folding. *Normalisation* executes the unification goals in the guard and the body of a clause as far as possible. The result is a clause with no unification goals in the guard and normalised unification goals in the body. *Immediate execution* unfolds a non-unification body goal g, replacing it by the body goals of a clause to which g can commit. A new clause is created for each clause to which g can commit. Immediate execution is applied only when the set of clauses to which g can commit is known statically; it is not applied if there is a clause to which g cannot immediately commit but some instance $g\theta$ of g can. *Case-splitting* also unfolds a non-unification body goal g, but it can promote the guards of the clauses used for unfolding to the guard of the clause being unfolded. This rule is the most complicated of the four and will be illustrated in the example below. *Folding* is very similar to the folding rule for pure logic programs.

We leave the formal definition of the rules to (Ueda and Furukawa 1988), and illustrate them using an example of process fusion (Furukawa and Ueda 1985). We consider a simple program that computes the sequence of the partial sums of an integer sequence.

F_1: `integerSums(I,N,Sums) :- true | integers(I,N,Is), sums(Is,Sums).`

F_2: `integers(I,N,Is) :- I=<N |`
`        Is=[I|Is1], I1:=I+1, integers(I1,N,Is1).`

F_3: `integers(I,N,Is) :- I >N | Is=[].`

F_4: `sums(Is,Sums) :- true | sums1(Is,0,Sums).`

F_5: `sums1([],     _,Sums) :- true | Sums=[].`

F_6: `sums1([I|Is1],S,Sums) :- true |`
`        S1:=I+S, Sums=[S1|Sums1], sums1(Is1,S1,Sums1).`

The above program uses two tail-recursive processes, `integers` and `sums1`, to compute Sums. Our objective is to obtain an equivalent program with a single tail-recursive process. We first execute the second body goal of F_1 so that it has two tail-recursive goals:

F_1
$\downarrow$ *Immediate Execution*
F_7:   `integerSums(I,N,Sums) :- true | integers(I,N,Is), sums1(Is,0,Sums).`

Then we introduce a new clause for the final single process by parameterising the second argument of `sums1` in F_7 and leaving `Is` local. The resulting clause is:

F_8:   `fused_integerSums(I,N,S,Sums) :- true |`
        `integers(I,N,Is), sums1(Is,S,Sums).`

The second argument of `sums1` has been generalised to a variable `S`, and it is included in the clause head. Now we try to obtain a tail-recursive definition of `fused_integerSums` using case-splitting and folding. First, we split F_8 by case-splitting:

F_8
$\downarrow$ *Case-splitting*
F_9:   `fused_integerSums(I,N,S,Sums) :- I=<N |`
        `Is=[I|Is1], I1:=I+1, integers(I1,N,Is1), sums1(Is,S,Sums).`
F_{10}: `fused_integerSums(I,N,S,Sums) :- I >N | Is=[], sums1(Is,S,Sums).`

Case-splitting enumerates all the possible ways in which one of the body goals of F_8 commits first. In the case of F_8, it is impossible for `sums1(Is,S,Sums)` to commit before `integers(I,N,Is)`, because `sums1(Is,S,Sums)` requires the value of `Is`, which never comes through the arguments of `fused_integerSums`. Therefore, F_9 and F_{10}, obtained by unfolding using F_2 and F_3, are the only cases we must consider.

For the time being we leave F_{10} and work on F_9. F_9 can be transformed further, starting from the execution of the unification goal `Is=[I|Is1]`:

F_9
$\downarrow$ *Normalisation*
F_{11}: `fused_integerSums(I,N,S,Sums) :- I=<N |`
        `I1:=I+1, integers(I1,N,Is1), sums1([I|Is1],S,Sums).`

$\downarrow$ *Immediate execution*
F_{12}: `fused_integerSums(I,N,S,Sums) :- I=<N |`
        `I1:=I+1, integers(I1,N,Is1),`
        `S1:=I+S, Sums=[S1|Sums1], sums1(Is1,S1,Sums1).`

Now we can fold `integers(I1,N,Is1)` and `sums1(Is1,S1,Sums1)` using F_8:

F_{12}
$\downarrow$ *Folding by F_8*
F_{13}: `fused_integerSums(I,N,S,Sums) :- I=<N |`
        `I1:=I+1, S1:=I+S, Sums=[S1|Sums1],`
        `fused_integerSums(I1,N,S1,Sums1).`

F_{10} can be simplified also:

F_{10}
$\downarrow$ *Normalisation and Immediate execution*
F_{14}: `fused_integerSums(I,N,S,Sums) :- I >N | Sums=[].`

The remaining task is to express the original predicate `integerSums` in terms of the newly introduced predicate `fused_integerSums`:

F_7
$\downarrow$ *Folding by F_8*
F_{15}: `integerSums(I,N,Sums) :- true | fused_integerSums(I,N,0,Sums).`

The resulting clauses, F_{13}, F_{14} and F_{15}, give a new definition of the `integerSums` program. This program has eliminated the intermediate stream `Is` and the operations on it.

5. Formal Semantics

There have been several proposals of the formal semantics of parallel logic programming languages (Saraswat 1987) (Gerth et al. 1988) (Murakami 1988). Here, we briefly introduce a simple semantics of Flat GHC designed for justifying the transformation rules described in Section 4. A complete description of the semantics will be found in (Ueda and Furukawa 1988).

The design criteria of our semantics are as follows:

(1) *Modelling behaviour:* A multiset of GHC goals can be regarded as a process that communicates with the outside world by observing and generating substitutions. The semantics should model this behavioral aspect.

(2) *Abstractness:* The semantics should concentrate on communication. It should abstract internal affairs of a process such as the number of (sub)goals and the number of commitments made. It should also abstract *how* unification is specified in the source text.

(3) *Modelling non-terminating programs:* It must be possible to define the semantics of programs that do not terminate but are still useful.

(4) *Modelling anomalous behaviour:* Anomalous behaviour such as the failure of a unification goal in a clause body, the irreducibility of a non-unification goal and infinite computation without observable substitution must be modelled, because we have to prove that such behaviour is not introduced by program transformation.

(5) *Simplicity and generality:* The semantics should be as simple and general as possible to be widely used. We decided to use standard tools like *finite* terms, substitutions defined over them, and least fixpoints. We decided *not* to use mode systems. We also decided *not* to handle discontinuous concepts like fairness.

(6) *Usefulness:* It should not be just a description; it should be a useful tool at least for proving the correctness of the transformation rules.

The semantics of a multiset B_0 of goals under a program $\mathcal{P}$, denoted $[\![B_0]\!]_\mathcal{P}$, is modelled as the set of all possible finite sequences of transactions with it. A *(normal) transaction*, denoted $\langle \alpha, \beta \rangle$, is an act of providing a multiset of goals with a possibly empty *input substitution* α and obtaining an observable (see below) *output substitution* β. An output substitution is also called a *partial answer substitution*.

The first transaction $\langle \alpha_1, \beta_1 \rangle$ must be made through the variables in B_0. The above observability condition for β_1 can be written as $B_0 \alpha_1 \beta_1 \not\equiv B_0 \alpha_1$. As a result of the first transaction, B_0 will be reduced to a multiset B_1 of goals, which represents the rest of the computation. Then the second transaction $\langle \alpha_2, \beta_2 \rangle$ must be made through the variables in $B_0 \alpha_1 \beta_1$.

The size of a transaction depends on how the outside world observes an output substitution. Suppose B_0 returns a complex data structure t in response to an input α_1. What should β_1 be, or what should the outside world see in one transaction? The answer is that the outside world can observe any *finite* template of t (i.e., a term of which t is an instance). In our model, the result of one unification goal may be observed using two or more transactions, and the result of two or more unification goals may be observed in one transaction. A transaction is of a finite nature; it is realised by a finite number of reductions and can return only a finite data structure.

The outside world may not communicate with B_0 at all. This is modelled by always including ϵ (empty sequence) in $[\![B_0]\!]_\mathcal{P}$. The empty sequence is used as a base case in defining the model of B_0 inductively.

An input α_1 to B_0 may not necessarily cause a normal transaction as defined above. First, it may cause failure of a unification goal in a clause body. This is modelled by letting $[\![B_0]\!]_\mathcal{P} \ni \langle \alpha_1, \mathsf{T} \rangle$, where T means failure. Second, B_0 may succeed (i.e., be reduced out) with no observable output. Third, B_0 may deadlock (i.e., be reduced to a multiset of goals that does not allow further reduction) with no observable output. Fourth, B_0 may fall into infinite computation that generates no observable output. The last three cases mean the *inactivity* of B_0 and cannot be distinguished from outside; so they are all modeled by letting $[\![B_0]\!]_\mathcal{P} \ni \langle \alpha_1, \bot \rangle$, where $\bot$ stands for 'no output'. However, if necessary, these cases could be distinguished in the model by using $\bot_{success}$, $\bot_{deadlock}$ and $\bot_{divergence}$ instead of $\bot$. Failure and inactivity are called *special transactions* and are used as base cases in defining the model of B_0.

Consider a single clause program

$\mathcal{P}$: p(X) :- true | X=f(Y), p(Y).

and autonomous (i.e., empty input) transactions with $\mathcal{P}$. Then $[\![p(X)]\!]_\mathcal{P}$ has

$\epsilon,$
$\langle \emptyset, \{X \leftarrow f(X1)\} \rangle,$
$\langle \emptyset, \{X \leftarrow f(X1)\} \rangle \langle \emptyset, \{X1 \leftarrow f(X2)\} \rangle,$
$\langle \emptyset, \{X \leftarrow f(X1)\} \rangle \langle \emptyset, \{X1 \leftarrow f(X2)\} \rangle \langle \emptyset, \{X2 \leftarrow f(X3)\} \rangle,$
$\ldots$

and also

$\langle \emptyset, \{X \leftarrow f(f(X2))\} \rangle,$
$\langle \emptyset, \{X \leftarrow f(f(f(X3)))\} \rangle,$
$\ldots.$

$[\![p(X)]\!]_{\mathcal{P}}$ has $\langle \emptyset, \bot \rangle$ also, because the semantics allows unfair execution in favour of the recursive goal $p(Y)$.

Our model successfully circumvents the Brock-Ackerman anomaly (Brock and Ackerman 1981). Let $\mathcal{BA}$ be:

```
d([A|_],O) :- true | O=[A,A].

merge([A|X1],Y,Z) :- true | Z=[A|Z1], merge(X1,Y,Z1).
merge(X,[A|Y1],Z) :- true | Z=[A|Z1], merge(X,Y1,Z1).
merge([],Y,Z) :- true | Z=Y.
merge(X,[],Z) :- true | Z=X.

p1([A|Z1],O) :- true | O=[A|O1],p11(Z1,O1).
p11([B|_],O1) :- true | O1=[B].

p2([A,B|_],O) :- true | O=[A,B].

g1(I,J,O) :- true | d(I,X), d(J,Y), merge(X,Y,Z), p1(Z,O).
g2(I,J,O) :- true | d(I,X), d(J,Y), merge(X,Y,Z), p2(Z,O).
```

Then, the computation

$\langle \{I \leftarrow [5|\_]\}, \{O \leftarrow [5|O']\} \rangle$

belongs both to $[\![g1(I,J,O)]\!]_{\mathcal{BA}}$ and to $[\![g2(I,J,O)]\!]_{\mathcal{BA}}$ (O' being a fresh variable), but

$\langle \{I \leftarrow [5|\_]\}, \{O \leftarrow [5|O']\} \rangle \langle \{J \leftarrow [6|\_]\}, \{O' \leftarrow [6]\} \rangle$

belongs only to $[\![g1(I,J,O)]\!]_{\mathcal{BA}}$ and not to $[\![g2(I,J,O)]\!]_{\mathcal{BA}}$.

6. Conclusion

This paper presented a parallel logic programming language GHC. It showed that GHC is a genuine parallel programming language and hence encourages programmers to write parallel programs. The paper also described transformation rules for GHC programs which will help to optimise them. To prove the correctness of the transformation rules, we introduced a simple formal semantics of Flat GHC programs which allows non-terminating computations.

In the Fifth Generation Computer Project, we are developing experimental parallel hardware for FGHC. We are developing two systems in parallel. One is a multi-processor system, called the Multi-PSI, composed of 64 Personal Sequential Inference machines (PSIs). Each PSI enables fast execution of FGHC programs (around 100 KLIPS) by firmware support of WAM-like instructions for FGHC. The main purpose of the system is to provide software researchers with a stable tool for developing software systems, including the operating system for the Multi-PSI itself. Currently, the hardware of the system is completed and its system software is under development. It is planned to be completed by the end of this fiscal year.

The other system is a VLSI-based parallel processor called the Parallel Inference Machine (PIM) which is expected to be our final target. We are planning to connect about 1000 processing elements (PEs) in the final stage. Before jumping to such a large scale, we are now developing a smaller scale prototype consisting of around 100 PEs. It has a hybrid architecture of shared memory and distributed memory. About ten PEs are connected tightly to compose a cluster of a shared memory architecture. These clusters are then connected together via a network, resulting in a distributed memory architecture. Currently, we are concentrating on the development of a single cluster. The prototype will be completed by 1989.

Much research is required to make our parallel computers truly useful. First, we need to enhance the expressive power of GHC. There have been several significant achievements in increasing the expressive power of Prolog. The introduction of constraints in Prolog and efficient algorithms for searching recursive databases are the most important. To realise the same extended functionalities in GHC has turned out to be quite difficult due to the lack of a backtracking capability. We need to realise Prolog variables in terms of GHC data structures. However, this method is expected to cause a slowdown of one order of magnitude, which we want to avoid.

Second, we need to develop parallel programming technologies for extracting maximum parallelism. There are several research subjects. The first is to develop new programming paradigms appropriate for formulating various application problems. The second is to solve the load balancing problem in the execution of programs on an actual parallel computer. The third is to develop a computation model reflecting the characteristics of real parallel processors such as the non-homogeneous distances among PEs, and to develop a useful measure of the complexity of parallel algorithms.

Acknowledgments

We wish to express our thanks to Kazuhiro Fuchi, Director of ICOT Research Center, who provided us with the opportunity to pursue this research. We would also like to thank Ryuzo Hasegawa, Chief of ICOT First Research Laboratory, and its members who contributed a lot to the research reported here.

References

Brock, J. D. and Ackerman, W. B. (1981) Scenarios: A Model of Non-determinate Computation. In *Formalization of Programming Concepts*, LNCS 107, Springer-Verlag, pp. 252–259.

Clark, K. L. and Gregory, S. (1981) A Relational Language for Parallel Programming. In *Proc. ACM Conf. on Functional Programming Languages and Computer Architecture*, ACM, pp. 171–178.

Clark, K. L. and Gregory, S. (1984) *PARLOG: Parallel Programming in Logic*. Research Report DOC 84/4, Dept. of Computing, Imperial College of Science and Technology, London. Also in *ACM. Trans. Prog. Lang. Syst.*, Vol. 8, No. 1 (1986), pp. 1–49.

Dijkstra, E. W. (1975) Guarded Commands, Nondeterminacy and Formal Derivation of Programs. *Comm. ACM*, Vol. 18, No. 8, pp. 453–457.

Furukawa, K. and Ueda, K. (1985) GHC Process Fusion by Program Transformation. In *Second Conf. Proc. Japan Soc. Softw. Sc. Tech.*, pp. 89–92.

Gerth, R., Codish, M., Lichtenstein, Y. and Shapiro, E. (1988) Fully Abstract Denotational Semantics for Flat Concurrent Prolog. In *Proc. Third Annual Symp. on Logic in Computer Science*. IEEE Computer Society Press, pp. 320–335.

Murakami, M. (1988) A Declarative Semantics of Parallel Logic Programs with Perpetual Processes. To be presented at the Int. Conf. on Fifth Generation Computer Systems 1988, Tokyo.

Saraswat, V. J. (1987) GHC: Operational Semantics, Problems and Relationship with $CP(\downarrow,|)$. In *Proc. 1987 Symposium on Logic Programming*. IEEE Computer Society Press, pp. 347–358.

Shapiro, E. Y. (1983) *A Subset of Concurrent Prolog and Its Interpreter*. Tech. Report TR-003, Institute for New Generation Computer Technology, Tokyo.

Shapiro, E. Y. (1984) Systolic Programming: A Paradigm of Parallel Processing. In *Proc. Int. Conf. on Fifth Generation Computer Systems 1984*, ICOT, Tokyo, pp. 458–470.

Tamaki, H. and Sato, T. (1984) Unfold/Fold Transformation of Logic Programs. In *Proc. Second Int. Logic Programming Conf.*, Uppsala Univ., Sweden, pp. 127–138.

Ueda, K. (1985) Guarded Horn Clauses. ICOT Tech. Report TR-103, ICOT, Tokyo (revised in 1986). Revised version in *Proc. Logic Programming '85*, Wada, E. (ed.), LNCS 221, Springer-Verlag, 1986, pp. 168–179.

Ueda, K. and Furukawa, K. (1988) Transformation Rules for GHC Programs. To be presented at the Int. Conf. on Fifth Generation Computer Systems 1988, Tokyo.

Accumulators: New Logic Variable Abstractions for Functional Languages

Keshav Pingali[†]
Computer Science Department
Cornell University
Ithaca, N.Y.

Kattamuri Ekanadham
IBM Research
T.J.Watson Research Center
Hawthorne, N.Y.

Abstract

Much attention has been focused by the declarative languages community on combining the functional and logic programming paradigms. In particular, there are many efforts to incorporate logic variables into functional languages. We propose a generalization of logic variables called *accumulators* which are eminently suited for incorporation into functional languages. We demonstrate the utility of accumulators by presenting examples which show that accumulators can be used profitably in many scientific applications to enhance storage efficiency and parallelism.

CR Classification Numbers: D.1.1, D.3.2, D.3.3, D.3.4, D.1.3

---

[0][†]Supported by NSF grant CCR-8702668 and an IBM Faculty Development Award.

1 Introduction

Declarative languages, such as functional and logic programming languages, have received much attention lately as appropriate vehicles for programming parallel machines. Conventional imperative languages such as FORTRAN or PASCAL have sequential operational semantics based on commands that cause side-effects in a global store. These languages can be adapted for parallel machines by extending them with annotations, using which the programmer can request parallel execution in chosen parts of his program. Unfortunately, imperative languages with parallel annotations can exhibit unintended non-deterministic behavior because of races between updating and reading of storage locations. A more satisfactory alternative is to make the compiler responsible for finding parallelism. Parallelism in imperative language programs is severely limited by reuse of storage locations and parallelizing compilers enhance parallelism by eliminating such reuse of storage through transformations such as renaming, scalar expansion *etc.* [9]. Evidently, the imperative programming model encourages the programmer to reuse storage only to have the compiler eliminate the reuse! This seems rather pointless - why not begin with a programming model in which storage reuse cannot arise?

Declarative languages provide precisely such a model to the programmer. In contrast to imperative languages, declarative languages can be given an operational semantics which is naturally parallel since it is based on rewrite rules rather than on updating of a global store. The entire program is considered to be an expression that is rewritten to the answer by successively simplifying sub-expressions. Sub-expressions of the program can be rewritten in parallel and a variety of parallel rewriting strategies such as parallel innermost, parallel outermost, dataflow rule etc., have been studied extensively. Moreover, parallelism comes with a guarantee of determinacy - there are a variety of theorems such as the Church-Rosser theorem that guarantee that the final result of the rewriting is independent of the order in which sub-expressions are rewritten. Much of the current interest in declarative languages stems from this unique combination of natural parallelism and guaranteed determinacy.

One active area of research in declarative languages is combining the functional and logic paradigms[5,6]. Logic languages provide a number of computational features like logic variables and backtracking which are not present in functional languages. Of particular interest to us is the introduction of logic variables into functional languages. In a functional language, an identifier obtains its value as the result of evaluation of a single applicative expression. In contrast, a *logic variable* in logic programming languages obtains its value incrementally by the intersection of successively applied constraints. The incorporation of logic variables into an otherwise functional language provides the programmer with a powerful tool for writing elegant and efficient programs for problems such as the construction of large arrays in scientific programming [4], owner-coupled sets in database programming [11], and the coding of constraint-based algorithms such as Milner's polymorphic type deduction algorithm.

The research reported in this paper arose from our efforts to use logic variables to alleviate the so-called 'copying problem' of purely functional data structures[4]. In a pure functional language, a data structure is a value (just like an integer or floating point number) which is produced as the result of evaluating a single applicative expression. This is satisfactory when the data structure is built bottom-up (as lists are): first, the components of the data structure can be constructed, and then these components can be assembled together to produce the desired data structure. However, this does not work for 'flat' data structures, such as arrays and matrices. Constructing large arrays and matrices functionally is difficult because usually, there is no uniform rule for computing matrix elements; for example, the computation of boundary elements may be quite different from the computation of interior elements. In such situations, writing a single applicative expression for defining the entire matrix can be inefficient and the resulting program may be quite obscure[4]. An alternative is to compute the desired matrix as the limit of a sequence of matrices which differ incrementally from each other. Unfortunately, the absence of an update operation in functional languages means that each matrix in this sequence is a different value, and the construction of a matrix of size $n \times n$ may involve making n^2 copies of the matrix! Logic variables provide an elegant solution to this problem because they allow the programmer to define an array incrementally without making intermediate copies. To construct a large matrix, the programmer first allocates a matrix of the desired size, in which each element is an uninitialized logic variable. These logic variables can be bound incrementally in the program, without having to copy the entire data structure; for example, the array can be passed to two procedures, one of which instantiates variables on the boundary while the other instatiates variables in the interior. In this way, large data structures can be constructed without the copy overhead of functional data structures. This use of logic variables is similar to the use of 'difference-lists' in pure logic programming.

In Section 2 we examine the notion of logic variables and observe that the means through which they acquire values is unnecessarily limited to term unification and propose a generalization to other user defined functions. We argue that logic variables should be generalized to enable the programmer to specify any commutative and associative function (such as +, *, max, min, set insertion etc.) in place of unification for giving values to logic variables. These generalized logic variables have the flavor of objects in object-oriented languages. As with any new language construct, there are two questions that must be answered. First, is the extension useful? Second, can it be easily implemented? We believe that both questions can be answered affirmatively for generalized logic variables. They can be used to lower the storage requirements of declarative language programs without any loss of parallelism; in fact, in many problems, their use enhances parallelism. Section 3 provides many examples to illustrate that logic variables are very useful for writing standard scientific programs. Section 4 presents a formal operational semantics for a functional language with logic variables and Section 5 briefly discusses some implementation considerations. Section 6 presents our conclusions and suggestions for future work.

2 Logic Variables

In functional languages, the notion of a 'variable' is absent - one only has identifiers that are synonyms for values. An identifier is introduced through a *binding* that associates it with an expression; the identifier is a synonym for the value of that expression. The programming model does not support manipulation of identifiers. As an example, consider the following definition of a function. The curly braces denote a *let-rec* style block which is a set of local bindings followed by a return expression. When the function pq is invoked with an argument value for N, an applicative interpreter first evaluates the expression $p(N)$. The identifier X is then bound to the resulting value, after which the function q is invoked. Thus, an identifier never participates in any operation until it is replaced by a value.

$$pq(N) = \{ \quad X = p(N)$$
$$Y = q(N, X)$$
$$Z = Y + X$$
$$\textbf{\textit{return}} \ Z \ \}$$

This is true even under normal order evaluation. A normal order evaluator delays the evaluation of expressions until they are needed to produce the output of the program. In the program shown above, the computation of the values of X and Y would be 'delayed' until an attempt was made to evaluate $Y+X$. At that point, the expressions for Y and X would be evaluated, and the identifiers bound to their values. Under normal-order evaluation, the transformation from a name to a value involves two steps: first the name X is replaced by some sort of a descriptor that points to the computation of $p(N)$ and later the descriptor is replaced by a computed value. The intermediate form is transparent to the program, because the program can never check whether the value of X has been computed at any point - the interpreter checks this internally and prevents the intermediate form to participate in any operations, except in argument passing.

Logic languages extend this behavior even further by introducing variables as 'first-class citizens'. A variable in a logic programming language represents a place holder; therefore, it can be introduced in the program without necessarily binding it to a value. Variables are bound to values by unification performed during pattern matching of arguments in a function call. This permits textual separation of the creation of a variable from the specification of a value for it. For example, the following logic program is intended to specify the same function pq.

$$pq(N, Z) \ :- \ p(N, X), q(N, X, Y), add(Y, X, Z).$$

Invoking a goal like $pq(5,Z)$, binds N to the value 5 and instantiates two new variables X and Y, which are initially undefined. By including appropriate definitions for the functions p and q it is possible to achieve the expected sequence of events, viz. computing $p(5,X)$ binds X to some value and computing $q(N,X,Y)$ binds Y to some value and so on.

However, logic programs offer a lot more flexibility than is apparent in the above definition of pq. For instance, we can define the functions p and q very differently to create effects that are not possible to reproduce in a functional language. Consider the clauses

$$p(N, X).$$
$$q(N, 0, 0).$$

Invoking $p(5,X)$ returns the unbound variable X and invoking $q(5,X,Y)$ binds both X and Y to 0. This program illustrates the fact that the behavior of a variable in logic languages is fundamentally different from anything found in functional languages: the direction of flow of information is not determined a priori and the variable can participate in unification any number of times. Note that the values bound by each unification must be consistent. For example, if a variable is bound to 5, an attempt to unify it with 6 will cause a failure of unification. This ensures that the program output is determinate, even under parallel evaluation.

Operationally, a variable is associated with some storage which undergoes state transitions as depicted in Figure 1. The initial state corresponds to the variable being unbound and the final state corresponds to the variable being *grounded* or completely defined. Actually we should imagine several final states, one for each different constant value that the variable can assume. Figure 1 shows only a prototypical part of the state diagram. A transition is caused by unification. As long as the variable is unified with other unbound variables, the state remains the same. Once it is unified with a constant value, it reaches the final state and its value cannot be changed any more. Further unifications can only reinforce that its value is what was defined. An attempt to unify it with some other value results in failure (that is, an error state) which is denoted by the symbol ⊥.

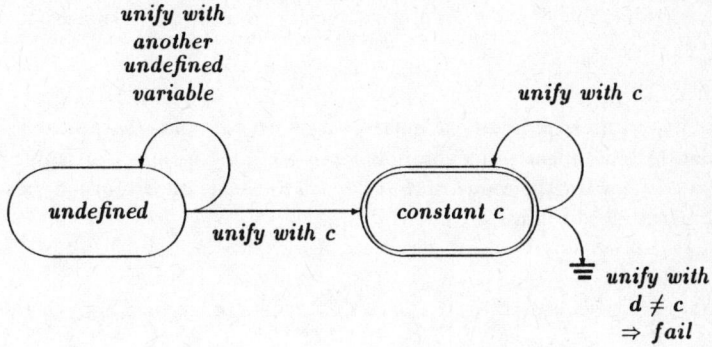

Figure 1: Prototypical state diagram of a scalar variable

How can we introduce logic variables into a functional language? In logic languages, unification is done during pattern matching of arguments in a function instantiation. Since unification may cause a 'side-effect' on the state of the variable, we prefer that the side-effect take place through an explicit command rather than implicitly during function calling. Therefore, we use the syntax

$$A = variable()$$

to introduce a logic variable and name it A, while the command

$$A \leftarrow x$$

indicates that the value x is to be unified with the variable A. These commands can occur wherever a binding can occur in the base functional language. Furthermore, this also fixes the directionality of information flow, by requiring that unification is always between a variable and a constant value. We do not consider unifying a variable with another variable.

In the next subsection, we generalize the notion of unification and its role in binding values to variables. This generalization is very different from other attempts in the literature to generalize the notion of logic variables. For instance, in constraint logic programming [10], the value of a variable is viewed as the solution to a set of constraints. Each equation is an additional constraint that potentially narrows the domain of values for the variable. This not only permits the more general notion of having constraints as values, (e.g., $4 \leq X \leq 5$), but also facilitates inferencing (e.g., $4 \leq X \leq 5$, $X \leq 4 \Rightarrow X = 4$). We do not deal with this kind of generality in this paper. Other examples of extreme generality are imperative programs, which provide explicit control over the storage of a variable, thus making the value of a variable as a function of time as well as the order of evaluation. The problems with imperative variables were discussed in the introduction.

2.1 Generalization

To generalize the notion of logic variables, we make a number of changes to the conventional logic variables shown in Figure 1. First, we permit a logic variable to undergo several state changes, rather than just 2 changes as with conventional term unification depicted in Figure 1. Second, we associate a state transition function, Φ_A, with each logic variable, A, which maps a state and an input to a new state. For conventional logic variables, this function is unification. In our generalization, the transition function can be any general function defined in the program, subject to certain constraints which we will describe shortly. A variable is created by the equation:

$$A = \textbf{\textit{variable}}(s, f)$$

This defines A to be a variable, whose initial state is set to s and whose state transition function Φ_A is the function f. Subsequently the command $A \leftarrow x$ has the effect of replacing the current state, s, of the variable A with the value of $\Phi_A(s, x)$. The state transition diagram for the generalized variable is illustrated in Figure 2.

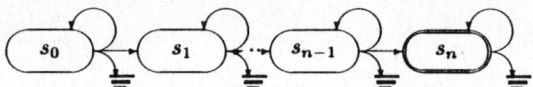

Figure 2: Generalized state diagram of a scalar variable

In order to preserve determinacy, we can use only certain functions as proper state transition functions for logic variables. As is the rule in functional languages, we will assume that the only sequencing constraints between computations are data dependencies. This means that the state transitions of a logic variable may take place in any order. To guarantee determinacy, we require that a transition function be commutative and associative as shown below.

$$\Phi(\Phi(s, x), y) = \Phi(\Phi(s, y), x), \quad \forall \; s, x, y \qquad (1)$$

That is, for any state s, the transitions for any two inputs x and y can be made in any order and the result will be the same. Functions like *add, multiply, min, max* are examples that have this property. For conventional logic variables, the state transition function is unification, which is also commutative and associative.

The value of the final state (if and when it is reached) replaces the variable throughout the program. Thus, we need to establish criteria to determine when a state is final. To achieve this, we keep a counter with each variable. This counter is initialized to some positive integer when the variable is created, and is decremented on each state transition. A state is *final* when the counter is 0; any attempt to make a state transition on a variable whose counter is zero is an error. In the rest of the paper, we will include the counter in the state of the variable, and write (u, v) to denote a variable whose value is v and whose counter has the integer u.

The machine implementation of a command $A \leftarrow x$ can be summarized as the following sequence of steps:

- Let (u, v) be the current state of a variable.
- Evaluate $(u', v') = \Phi_A((u, v), x)$
- If $u = 0$ and $(u, v) \neq (u', v')$ then the program fails
  Else (u', v') replaces the state of the variable.
- If $u' = 0$ then the value v' replaces the variable A throughout the program.

Note that the above steps are executed atomically, in the sense that while (u', v') is being computed, the state is not available for any other command. Later we elaborate how this can be implemented in practice.

From Figure 2, it is clear that each intermediate state is used only by the next transition that takes place. This implies that the state change can be done in the same storage without any problems. The specification of a transition function can take advantage of this and specify only the necessary changes to the state. For example if the state consists of an array and only one element of the array is changed, it should suffice to specify only that change. To facilitate this we introduce the notation of a shadow state. A shadow state, $s!$, is an uninitialized variable, identical in structure to the state s. Bindings can be made to the components of $s!$ as if it were a normal structure. When the execution of the transition function terminates, uninitialized components of the shadow are filled with copies of the state s. The following example illustrates this.

$$countup((n, A), i) = \{\ A![i] = A[i] + 1$$
$$return\ (n - 1, A!)\ \}$$

The function specifies the change of state from (n, A) to $(n - 1, A!)$ where the array $A!$ is identical to A except that the ith element is incremented by one.

We will call these generalized logic variables *accumulators*.

3 Examples

3.1 Example 1: Write-once Variables

Our first example is a *write-once* variable whose state transitions follow the pattern depicted in Figure 1. Its initial state is $(1, 0)$ and its final state is $(0, c)$ where c is any constant to which it can be assigned. The state transition function and the usage of the variable are illustrated by the following program segment:

$$assign((u, v), x) = (0, x)$$
$$A = variable((1, 0), assign)$$
$$A \leftarrow 67$$
$$b = A + 5$$

The *assign* function satisfies the commutative property of equation (1), because for any $x \neq y$ the commands $A \leftarrow x$ and $A \leftarrow y$ result in error in whichever order they are executed. Notice that the evaluation of the expression $A + 5$ is automatically delayed until the command $A \leftarrow 67$ takes effect.

I-structures[4] are simply arrays whose elements are the logic variables described above. For example, we can construct an aggregate, A, of n variables, where each $A[i] = variable((1, 0), assign)$, $\forall\ i = 1, n$. Individual array elements can be assigned values using commands of the form $A[i] \leftarrow c$.

The expressive power of these arrays can be illustrated by the inverse-permutation example: Given an array B of length n containing a permutation of integers $1..n$, compute the array A such that $A[B[i]] = i$. The following program accomplishes this. We use the informal array notation to indicate the allocation of contiguous storage, initializing each element with the specified value. For clarity, we also use the obvious iterative construct in place of tail recursion.

$$\begin{aligned}
inverse\text{-}permute(B, n) \ = \ & \{A = \textbf{\textit{array}}(n) \ \textbf{\textit{of}} \ \textbf{\textit{variable}}((1, 0), assign); \\
& \{\textbf{\textit{for}} \ i \ \textbf{\textit{from}} \ 1 \ \textbf{\textit{to}} \ n \ \textbf{\textit{do}} \\
& \qquad A[B[i]] \leftarrow i \ \}; \\
& \textbf{\textit{return}} \ A \ \}
\end{aligned}$$

Building inverse permutations in a purely functional language incurs severe copying penalty, as each iteration must produce a new array by appending the new element to the old array. I-structures take advantage of the fact that each element is written only once and permit the assignments to take place anywhere in the program. Non-strictness permits A to be returned even before the elements have been computed, thus providing opportunity for some additional parallelism. One can also build open lists using these arrays. A conventional *cons* cell can be viewed as an array of 2 elements. Empty cons cells can be created and used in lists and their contents can be filled later.

3.2 Example 2: Accumulation

Consider the following definition of a tail recursive function:

$$sum(s, n) = \textbf{\textit{if}} \ n = 0 \ \textbf{\textit{then}} \ s \ \textbf{\textit{else}} \ sum(s + f(n), n - 1)$$

Assuming f is some known function, the application $sum(0, n)$ computes the summation $\sum_{x=1}^{n} f(x)$. In a conventional evaluation scheme, the partial sums $f(n), f(n) + f(n-1), ..$ are computed and passed along the chain of recursive calls. A parallel evaluator, such as a dataflow machine, might concurrently evaluate several $f(x)$, but performs the summation sequentially. Storage for each intermediate sum is allocated dynamically and is reclaimed when its value has been consumed by the recursive call.

In contrast, we can perform the above summation using generalized logic variables as follows. The initial state of the variable is $(n, 0)$ indicating n more summations have to be done starting with zero as the initial sum. The final state is $(0, final\text{-}sum)$.

$$\begin{aligned}
addup((u, v), x) \ = \ & (u - 1, v + x); \\
sum(n) \ = \ & \{A = \textbf{\textit{variable}}((n, 0), addup); \\
& \{\textbf{\textit{for}} \ i \ \textbf{\textit{from}} \ 1 \ \textbf{\textit{to}} \ n \ \textbf{\textit{do}} \\
& \qquad A \leftarrow f(i) \ \}; \\
& \textbf{\textit{return}} \ A \ \}
\end{aligned}$$

All $f(i)$ can be computed concurrently and the additions in the summation are performed in arbitrary order as and when the element values arrive. The partial sums are not circulated, but are *updated in place*, much like in imperative programs. Determinacy is guaranteed as the function *addup* satisfies the constraint of equation (1).

3.3 Example 3: Histograms

The usefulness of logic variables is greatly enhanced when the state of a variable is large, so that there is potential for concurrent operations on different parts of the state. The histogram problem illustrates this. Given a list of n numbers, each of which can be classified into one of k classes, the problem is to find the frequency of each class. An imperative program for this problem keeps the frequencies in an array, which is initialized to all zeroes. It sequentially computes the class for each number and increments the corresponding element of the frequency array. This takes advantage of the sequential nature of computation and economizes storage by performing updates in place. A functional program to solve this problem will be forced to produce a new frequency array for each number in the list, since the concept of updating is not supported. The new frequency array will be identical to the old array except for one element, which would be incremented by one. This copying overhead results in extreme inefficiency. It is possible to improve on this situation by making the compiler detect that copying is unnecessary because the updates are done in sequence[8]. However, techniques for doing this analysis are not very general, and even then, the resulting solution exhibits no parallelism. The following solution using logic variables explicitly indicates that updating can take place in the same storage.

We first observe that the frequency array cannot be modeled as an array of accumulators, where each element is like the accumulator of Section 3.2. This is because we know only the total number of accumulations for the entire frequency array and the number of accumulations for each class is not known apriori. Hence we use one accumulator whose state includes the entire frequency array. The functions *zero-array* and *classof* have meanings obvious from the context. The transition function *countup*, specifies that the ith element of the frequency array A is to be incremented. The notation of $A!$ is as explained in Section 2.1.

$$countup((n, A), i) = \{ A![i] = A[i] + 1$$
$$return\ (n - 1, A!) \};$$
$$histogram(n, k, classof) = \{H = variable((n, zero\text{-}array(k)), countup);$$
$$\{for\ i\ from\ 1\ to\ n\ do$$
$$H \leftarrow classof(i) \};$$
$$return\ H \}$$

Some functional programmers [14] have argued that the histogram problem can be solved by introducing a new array primitive *functional-accumulate* that takes a combining function and an index list (*i.e.*, a list whose elements are pairs (i,v) where i is an integer index) as arguments, and returns an array in which the ith element is the result of applying the combining function to all values v whose index is i. In contrast to our solution, which uses a very natural generalization of logic variables, this solution seems somewhat *ad hoc*. Moreover, in many problems that we have looked at, building the index list explicitly introduces a lot of overhead in time and storage. We will demonstrate this using the particle-in-cell problem discussed next.

3.4 Example 4: Convex Hull

Jarvis' March for constructing the convex hull in a plane illustrates another situation where logic variables naturally fit in. Given a set of points in a plane, the algorithm successively finds the hull vertices as if it were gift wrapping the set of points. A basic step in this algorithm is to take a set of points and an origin and determine which of those points has minimal polar angle relative to the origin. Figure 3 illustrates this. If *H1* and *H2* are two consecutive vertices in the hull, the next vertex *H3* on the hull is obtained by scanning the set of points for minimal polar angle relative to *H2*. This is done as follows: Given the cartesian coordinates of 3 points, *p0,p1,p2*, there is a simple algorithm to determine whether *p1* or *p2* has minimal polar angle relative to *p0*. That is, there is a function *min-polar(p0,p1,p2)* that returns either *p1* or *p2* accordingly. Thus, a sequential algorithm to find *H3* in Figure 3 would be

$$a1 = \textit{min-polar}(H2, H1, p);\ a2 = \textit{min-polar}(H2, a1, q);\ a3 = \textit{min-polar}(H2, a2, r);\ ...$$

That is, starting from the extreme vertex *H1* as the current *min-polar* point, successively compare with each point *p,q,r,...* in the set, each time keeping track of the current minimum. The final point will be the hull vertex *H3*. Given two consecutive hull vertices, *H1* and *H2* and an array of points, *POINTS*, the following program uses logic variables to find the next hull vertex, *H3*:

$$\begin{aligned}
scan((n, p1), p2) &= (n-1, \textit{min-polar}(H2, p1, p2));\\
H3 &= \{A = \textit{\textbf{variable}}((n, H1), scan);\\
&\quad \{\textit{\textbf{for}}\ i\ \textit{\textbf{from}}\ 1\ \textit{\textbf{to}}\ n\ \textit{\textbf{do}}\\
&\quad\quad A \leftarrow POINTS[i]\ \};\\
&\quad \textit{\textbf{return}}\ A\ \}
\end{aligned}$$

This example illustrates the flexibility of the logic variable abstraction. The state transformation function is not a simple *min* function, but computes a relation (*viz. minimal polar angle*) between the old state and the new state. Ofcourse, proving that the function *scan* satisfies the constraint of equation (1) gets more complicated. But in this case, it is clear from the application.

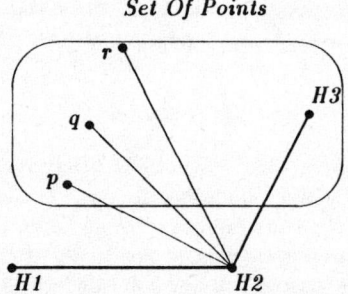

Figure 3: Computing Convex Hull in a Plane

3.5 Example 5: Particle in Cell

The particle in cell, popularly known as PIC [12], is a compute intensive problem in high energy physics that illustrates the usefulness of logic variables. The relevant parts of the problem can be abstracted as follows: A number of particles are randomly distributed over a rectangular grid of cells in a plane. Each particle is associated with a number of properties like velocity, acceleration, position within the cell *etc.* Each cell is associated with the list of particles in it, a notion of neighboring cells, charge accumulated at the cell *etc.* The presence of a particle p in cell c contributes certain amount of charge to each neighboring cell c' of c. The actual amount of charge is a function of the attributes of the particle p and the position of p relative to the target cell c'. We use the following nomenclature:

cells   = list of all cells
plist(c)   = list of particles in the cell c
neighbors(c)   = list of cells which are neighbors of cell c
contribution(p,c) = amount of charge contributed by particle p to the cell c
CHARGE   = array, so that CHARGE[c] = the charge collected at cell c

Each cell has exactly 4 neighbors, which are adjacent to it in 4 specified directions. If p is a particle in cell c then $contribution(p, c') = 0$ if c' is not a neighbor of c. Given an initial distribution of the particles, the first step in the PIC problem is to find the charge accumulated at each cell by all the particles. An imperative program might compute the charge matrix as follows:

$$\forall \quad c \in cells \qquad CHARGE[c] = 0, \; initially,$$

$$\forall \left\{ \begin{array}{l} c \in cells), \\ p \in plist(c), \\ c' \in neighbors(c) \end{array} \right\} \quad CHARGE[c'] := CHARGE[c'] + contribution(p, c')$$

Obviously a functional program cannot perform the assignment in place. Hence it would try to specify the accumulation of charge at each cell as a single expression. For instance, one approach would be to use the inverse of the *neighbors* function. That is $c' \in neighbors^{-1}(c)$ if and only if $c \in neighbors(c')$. The idea is that all particles in cells $neighbors^{-1}(c)$ would contribute to the charge at cell c. The inverse function is simple to compute. It is the set of the 4 neighboring cells that can influence the given cell. A functional program for this problem would create a functional array, $CHARGE$, in which each element $CHARGE[c]$ is given by the function:

$$charge(c) = \forall \left\{ \begin{array}{l} c' \in neighbors^{-1}(c), \\ p \in plist(c') \end{array} \right\} \sum contribution(p, c')$$

where $\sum$ denotes the summation over the ranges specified. Although this solution performs the same number of charge computations as the imperative solution presented above, it incurs more control overhead because in this scheme each particle will be traversed 4 times, whereas the imperative solution traverses each particle only once. The solution using logic variables is presented below. Here the charge matrix is a logic variable and is updated in place using the same control structure as the imperative program, without the complication of the inverse for the *neighbors* relation. It uses the knowledge that there are altogether n particles in the system and each particle makes contributions to 4 neighboring cells. Hence the charge matrix can be bound to its value after $4n^2$ accumulations are done. The *chargeup* function performs the state change. Given the current state, a cell identifier c and a charge value q, the function increments the cth element of the charge matrix by the amount q.

$$chargeup((u, H), (c, q)) = \{ \; H![c] = H[c] + q$$
$$\mathbf{return} \; (u - 1, H!) \; \}$$

$$CHARGE = variable((4n^2, zero\text{-}matrix), chargeup)$$

$$\forall \left\{ \begin{array}{l} c \in cells), \\ p \in plist(c), \\ c' \in neighbors(c) \end{array} \right\} \quad CHARGE \leftarrow (c', contribution(p, c'))$$

Using the charge at each cell, certain equations are solved to determine the electric field and using this, the new positions of the particles are computed. Particles can move only to the neighboring cells in each step. Thus, we must construct a new *plist*. This can also be done using logic variables to update the linked list of particles in each cell. We omit the details.

3.6 Example 6: Zero of a Polynomial

Finally we illustrate another application of a logic variable in which the successive state transitions take place autonomously without any external input, until certain condition holds true. Consider the computation of the zero of a polynomial, $f(x)$, using Newton's method of approximation. Starting with an initial guess of x_0 we must compute successive refinements for the solution using the relation

$$x_{n+1} = x_n - f(x_n)/f'(x_n)$$

where f' is the first derivative of f. This must be repeated until x_n is smaller than some epsilon. Hence the successive iterations need no further input. We accomplish this by the special primitive, *autovariable*(s_0, f), which creates a variable with the initial state s_0 and computes the sequence of states $s_1, s_2, ...$, where each $s_{i+1} = f(s_i)$. The sequence terminates when the state is final. In the following program, the variable X takes a final value when either the difference between two successive states is less than epsilon or when the number of iterations exceeds n. Notice that this effect cannot be achieved by the use of the *variable* abstraction, as there is no provision to execute the transition commands based on the current value of the state.

$$\begin{aligned}
newton(n, x) &= \{ \ y = x - f(x)/f'(x); \\
&\qquad m = \textbf{if} \ \ y > epsilon \ \ \textbf{then} \ \ n - 1 \ \ \textbf{else} \ \ 0; \\
&\qquad \textbf{return} \ \ (m, y) \ \} \\
X &= \textit{autovariable}((n, x_0), newton);
\end{aligned}$$

4 Operational Semantics

In this section, we formalize the semantics of a functional language extended with accumulators. First, we introduce a simple functional language and give a rewrite rule semantics for it. This functional language has no syntactic sugaring, so as to keep the rewrite rules simple. We then extend this language with accumulators, and extend the rewrite rules appropriately.

4.1 Syntax of a Base Functional Language

The syntax of a primitive functional language is shown in Figure 4. A program is a set of function definitions, followed by a query expression. For notational convenience, we distinguish the names of the functions from other variable names. A function expects a single argument. Multiple values can be composed into a single aggregate argument. A function body is enclosed in braces and consists of a set of equations followed by a return expression. Each equation binds a name to an expression. An expression can be a constant, a name, a conditional or the result of a binary operator applied to two expressions, in the usual manner. We omit the details of the definitions of constants, names and operators and appeal to the intuition of the reader. A function application is denoted by the function name followed by an argument enclosed in paratheses. Three other forms of expressions are given to deal with aggregate values. An aggregate is a sequence of values enclosed in angular brackets. The values in the sequence are separated by commas. A component value is selected from it using the usual subscript notation. Thus, $\langle a_1, a_2, .., a_n \rangle [i]$ gives the component a_i. The last production is a convenient abbreviation for producing aggregates. For instance, $[1 .. n]\langle f, x \rangle$ gives the aggregate $\langle f(x,1), f(x,2), .. f(x,n) \rangle$. Thus, it is equivalent to an array a of n elements, which is constructed in an imperative language using a loop of the form: *for* $i := 1$ *to* n *do* $a[i] = f(x,i)$.

$$
\begin{aligned}
program &::= definition; \ldots definition; functionname(constant) \\
definition &::= functionname(name) = \{equation; \ldots equation \\
&\qquad\qquad\qquad\qquad\qquad\qquad \textbf{return } expression\} \\
equation &::= name = expression \\
expression &::= constant \mid name \mid expression \ op \ expression \mid \\
&\quad \textbf{\textit{if}} \ expression \ \textbf{\textit{then}} \ expression \ \textbf{\textit{else}} \ expression \mid \\
&\quad functionname(expression) \mid \\
&\quad \langle expression, \ldots expression \rangle \mid \\
&\quad name[expression] \mid \\
&\quad [expression .. expression] expression
\end{aligned}
$$

Figure 4: Syntax of a basic functional language

4.2 Rewrite Rule Semantics for Base Functional Language

Operational semantics can be provided for the above language using rewrite rules. Rewrite rules describe an abstract machine that maintains a state and transforms it into a final state, by repeated application of a given set of rules. Each rewrite rule specifies a set of pre-conditions and a set of actions. Whenever the pre-conditions are satisfied, the state can be transformed by executing the specified actions. Rules can be repeatedly selected and applied in arbitrary order, until no further rules can be applied. The final state is defined to be the result of the computation. Usually the rewrite rules possess certain properties which guarantee that the result is the same for all possible orders in which rules are applied. Concurrency in the application of several rules directly relates to parallel execution by a machine. Thus, rewrite rule semantics are suggestive of the potential parallelism in a program and at the same time guarantee deterministic results. Ofcourse care is needed for selecting only non-interfering rules for concurrent execution. That is, the preconditions for the rules and the effects caused by the rules must operate on disjoint parts of the state.

We now describe the state of an abstract machine. We have the usual notion of constants which are numbers, string and boolean constants, aggregates all of whose components are constants etc. *Error* is a special constant and when an expression evaluates to it, the whole computation terminates. Similarly names are identifiers defined appropriately, distinguishing variable names from function names used in the program. The state of the machine has 3 components: (1)a set of equations giving the current bindings in effect, (2)a result expression and (3)a countably infinite set of new names, that can be used during rewriting. For notational purposes, we treat a command like $A \leftarrow c$, also as an equation. The set of new names can be represented by a distinct name α and a counter. Initially, the counter is zero and each time a new name is needed, the counter is incremented and the name $\alpha_{counter}$ is used. A rewrite rule has the following form:

$$
\begin{array}{ll}
\ldots \textit{pattern} \ldots & \ldots \textit{new-pattern} \ldots \\
\textit{List of preconditions like} & \textit{List of changes like} \\
eqn: \quad x = c & new\text{-}eqn: \quad \hat{x} = d \\
const: \quad c \quad \Longrightarrow & delete\text{-}eqn: \quad y \leftarrow d \\
fdefn: \quad f & mod\text{-}eqn: \quad x = c' \\
& abbrev: \quad c' = c + 1
\end{array}
$$

This means that if *pattern* is found *anywhere in the result expression or on the right-hand side of any equation, but not within the arms of a conditional*, and all the stated preconditions are satisfied, then *pattern* is replaced by *new-pattern* and other stated changes are made to the state. The illustrated preconditions state that the equation $x = c$ is present in the machine state, c is a constant and f is a function name for which a definition is known. Similarly the actions state a new equation $\hat{x} = d$ must be added to the machine state, equation $y \leftarrow d$ must be deleted from the state, the equation for x in the state must be modified as $x = c'$, where c' is used as an abbreviation for $c + 1$ etc.

Figure 5 gives the rewrite rules for the base functional language described in Figure 4. Rule 1 simply says that if we find a pattern of two constants around a binary operator, they can be replaced by the result obtained in accordance with the rules of the operator. For example, $2 + 3$ is replaced by 5 whereas $\langle 1, 2 \rangle + 5$ might be replaced by error, which halts the rest of the execution. Similarly, Rules 2 and 3 specify how an arm of a conditional is selected. Note that the expressions in either arm of a conditional are not touched until the condition evaluates to a boolean constant. Rule 4 gives the usual substitution rule for a name. We insist that a name cannot be substituted for, until its value reduces to a constant. This avoids recomputation of the same expression in many places. Finally rule 5 says that multiple bindings to the same name result in error.

The rule for function application is somewhat complicated. We must prepare a copy of the body of the function by replacing all the names with new unique names, so that we do not get confused by naming conflicts between various instantiations of the functions. Rule 6 obtains a new name $\hat{x}$ for each name x that appears in the function definition, using the α counter described earlier. We use the notation, $|text|_{x,y,z \to \hat{x},\hat{y},\hat{z}}$ to denote the result of replacing all occurrences of the names x, y, z in *text* by $\hat{x}, \hat{y}, \hat{z}$ respectively. New equations are added to the state by renaming the equations in the function definition as shown in Rule 6 and the function application is replaced by the renamed return expression of the function.

Aggregate selection and construction are intuitive. Component selection is performed only after the index and the corresponding element reduce to constants. Similarly, an aggregate is constructed after the bounds reduce to constants.

Rules for Substitution

$$\ldots m \ op \ n \ldots \quad \Longrightarrow \quad \ldots r \ldots \qquad (1)$$
$$consts: \quad m, n \qquad\qquad abbrev: \quad r = m \ op \ n$$

$$\ldots if \ \text{true} \ then \ \text{e1} \ else \ \text{e2} \ldots \quad \Longrightarrow \quad \ldots \text{e1} \ldots \qquad (2)$$
$$\ldots if \ \text{false} \ then \ \text{e1} \ else \ \text{e2} \ldots \quad \Longrightarrow \quad \ldots \text{e2} \ldots \qquad (3)$$

$$\ldots x \ldots \quad \Longrightarrow \quad \ldots c \ldots \qquad (4)$$
$$eqn: \quad x = c$$
$$const: \quad c$$

$$eqn: \quad x = e1 \quad \Longrightarrow \quad error \qquad (5)$$
$$eqn: \quad x = e2$$

Rule for Function Application

$$\ldots f(e_0) \ldots \quad \Longrightarrow \quad \ldots \hat{e}_{n+1} \ldots \qquad (6)$$
$$fdefn: \ f(x_0) = \qquad\qquad new\text{-}eqn: \quad \hat{x}_0 = e_0,$$
$$\{x_1 = e_1; \ldots x_n = e_n; \qquad new\text{-}eqns: \quad \hat{x}_1 = \hat{e}_1, \ldots \hat{x}_n = \hat{e}_n$$
$$\quad \textbf{return} \ e_{n+1}\} \qquad\qquad new\text{-}names: \quad \hat{x}_i$$
$$\qquad\qquad\qquad\qquad\qquad abbrev: \quad \hat{e}_i = |e_i|_{x_0,x_1,..x_n \to \hat{x}_0,\hat{x}_1,..\hat{x}_n}$$

Rules for Aggregate construction and selection

$$\ldots \langle c_1, c_2, ..c_n \rangle [i] \ldots \quad \Longrightarrow \quad \ldots c_i \ldots \qquad (7)$$
$$int: \quad 1 \leq i \leq n$$
$$const: \quad c_i$$

$$\ldots [i \ .. \ j]\langle f, x \rangle \ldots \quad \Longrightarrow \quad \ldots \langle \hat{x}_i, \hat{x}_{i+1}, .., \hat{x}_j \rangle \ldots \qquad (8)$$
$$int: \quad i \leq j \qquad\qquad new\text{-}eqn: \quad \hat{x} = x$$
$$fdefn: \ f \qquad\qquad new\text{-}eqns: \quad \hat{x}_k = f(\langle \hat{x}, k \rangle), _{i \leq k \leq j}$$
$$\qquad\qquad\qquad new\text{-}names: \quad all \ \hat{x}$$

Figure 5: Rewrite Rules giving the Operational Semantics for a Base Functional Language

4.3 Syntax and Semantics for Logic Variables

Figure 6 shows additional productions used to introduce logic variables into the base functional language of Figure 4. A variable expression creates a logic variable with the specified initial state and transition function. The autovariable expression does the same, except that the state transitions take place autonomously. The equation using the left arrow symbol effects a state transition on the logic variable given on the left, supplying the expression as an argument. We permit logic variables to be components of aggregates and a selector expression could be used on the left-hand side of the arrow, to specify the transitions for the selected variable. Finally, binding to a name appended by the exclamation mark indicates delayed binding within a state transition function. The rules we give later show how this is used to achieve safe updates in place.

$$
\begin{aligned}
expression &::= \ \textbf{\textit{variable}}(expression, functionname) \mid \\
&\quad \ \textbf{\textit{autovariable}}(expression, functionname) \\
equation &::= \ name \leftarrow expression \mid \\
&\quad \ name[expression] \leftarrow expression \\
name &::= \ identifier \mid identifier!
\end{aligned}
$$

Figure 6: Additional Syntax to add Logic Variables

We now specify the semantics for these constructs. The essential difference between ordinary variables and logic variables is that a logic variable cannot be substituted by its value until it reaches a final state. But at the same time, its name must be available for other operations such as parameter passing, aggregate construction, selection from aggregates *etc*. We accomplish this by introducing a new class of names called β-names which are used only by the machine internally. Intuitively, a β-name corresponds to the address of the storage in which the state of a logic variable is maintained. The state of the machine is augmented with another counter and the β-names are generated from it in the same manner as the α-names we described earlier. We assume the β-names are distinguishable from other names.

The rules concerning β-names are described in Figure 7. Rule 9 specifies how a variable is created. New storage is allocated and it is referred by a new β-name β. The storage is initialized with the state value s_0 and the transition function f. β-names play a dual role. They are like address constants and can be substituted just like any other constants as specified by rule 10. Names occurring on the left-hand side of a transition command can also be replaced by a β-name as shown by rule 11. Intuitively this means that the address is passed for performing transitions on the state of a variable. The second role played by a β-name is that of a regular name, except that its value cannot be substituted until the variable reaches a final state. Rule 12 specifies that a β-name can be replaced when the variable reaches a final state.

State transitions can be performed one at a time using the address β, until a final state is reached. Rule 13 prohibits further transitions from a final state. Rule 14 gives the effect of a simple transition. The transition command $\beta \leftarrow c$ causes the state $\langle n, s \rangle$ of the variable to be replaced by the value of $f(\langle n, s \rangle, c)$ in an atomic manner. The command is deleted (from the machine state),

Logic Variable Creation

$$\ldots variable(s_0, f) \ldots \implies \ldots \beta \ldots \qquad (9)$$

$const: \; s_0 \qquad\qquad\qquad new\text{-}eqn: \quad \beta = \langle s_0, f \rangle$
$fdefn: \; f \qquad\qquad\qquad new\text{-}\beta\text{-}name: \; \beta$

Address Substitution for a Logic Variable

$$\ldots x \ldots \implies \ldots \beta \ldots \qquad (10)$$

$eqn: \quad x = \beta$

Address Substitution on the left-hand side of a transition command

$$eqn: \quad x \leftarrow e \implies mod\text{-}eqn: \quad \beta \leftarrow e \qquad (11)$$
$eqn: \quad x = \beta$

Value Substitution for a Logic Variable

$$\ldots \beta \ldots \implies \ldots c \ldots \qquad (12)$$

$eqn: \quad \beta = \langle \langle 0, c \rangle, f \rangle$
$const: \; c$

No Transitions from Final State

$$eqn: \quad \beta \leftarrow c \implies error \qquad (13)$$
$eqn: \quad \beta = \langle \langle 0, e \rangle, f \rangle$

Simple State Transition for a Logic Variable

$$eqn: \quad \beta \leftarrow c \implies delete\text{-}eqn: \quad \beta \leftarrow c \qquad (14)$$
$eqn: \quad \beta = \langle \langle n, s \rangle, f \rangle \qquad\qquad mod\text{-}eqn: \quad \beta = \langle f(\langle \langle n, s \rangle, c \rangle), f \rangle$
$consts: \quad c, s, n \neq 0$

Figure 7: Rewrite Rules giving the Operational Semantics for Logic Variables

to avoid repeated application of the same command. If the transition function f is simple (like add, multiply etc.), then this replacement can be done atomically and we do not need any further rules. More general functions are dealt with in the next section.

4.4 Semantics for Complex State Transition Functions

Conceptually, rule 14 of Figure 7 works for any function f, as long as the computation of $f(\langle\langle n, s\rangle, c\rangle)$ and the replacement take place atomically. But if the computation of f takes a long time, then we must not tie up other computations. While the computation of f proceeds, care must be taken (1) not to initiate another state transition for this variable and (2) to replace the state by the result of f, only after all concurrent computations within f terminate. We can express these constraints through rewrite rules given in Figure 9, which use a new class of names called γ-names. Intuitively, a γ-name is just like a β-name and both stand for the address of the storage where the state of a variable is stored. However, the type of access to the storage is different for β-names and γ-names. A β-name provides access to the variable only to specify transitions and to obtain its final value. A γ-name provides exclusive access to the state of a variable for changing its value in place. Using γ-names, the above two requirements are satisfied as illustrated below.

Figure 8 shows how a state transition takes place. Let β be the address of a variable, which is currently in state s. A transition command $\beta \leftarrow x$ obtains a new name γ to refer to the current state and initiates the function f passing γ as an argument. The transition function expands into a bunch of equations, replacing the parameter name by γ. The result expression of the transition function is the shadow name $\gamma!$, which represents the new state obtained by performing the specified changes. In Figure 8, we illustrate a few changes like the first component of the state is incremented, the second component is multiplied by some thing etc. The shadow name $\gamma!$ replaces the function application in the equation for β. The bindings for the shadow variables are rewritten as bindings to the corresponding $\gamma!$-selectors. The value s of γ is substituted for evaluating any expressions on the right-hand sides of the equations. Finally when no more substitution for γ is possible, the updates specified by the shadow bindings can take place in the same storage, yielding a new state value s'. Until this is done, no other transition can take place for β, as the value $\gamma!$ is not considered as a constant.

$$\begin{pmatrix} \beta = \langle s, f \rangle \\ \beta \leftarrow x \end{pmatrix} \Rightarrow \begin{pmatrix} \beta = \langle f(\langle \gamma, x \rangle), f \rangle \\ \gamma = s \end{pmatrix} \Rightarrow \begin{pmatrix} \beta = \langle \gamma!, f \rangle \\ \gamma = s \\ n = \gamma[1] \\ n! = n + 1 \\ w = \gamma[2] \\ w! = w * \ldots \end{pmatrix}$$

$$\begin{pmatrix} \beta = \langle \gamma!, f \rangle \\ \gamma = s \\ \gamma![1] = \gamma[1] + 1 \\ \gamma![2] = \gamma[2] * \ldots \end{pmatrix} \Rightarrow \begin{pmatrix} \beta = \langle \gamma!, f \rangle \\ \gamma = s \\ \gamma![1] = s[1] + 1 \\ \gamma![2] = s[2] * \ldots \end{pmatrix} \Rightarrow \beta = \langle s', f \rangle$$

Figure 8: Execution of a Complex State Transition Function

Rule 15 specifies that the storage must be replaced by the instantiation of the transition function,

General State Transition for a Logic Variable

$eqn:$	$\beta \leftarrow c$	$\Longrightarrow$	$delete\text{-}eqn:$	$\beta \leftarrow c$		(15)
$eqn:$	$\beta = \langle\langle n,s\rangle, f\rangle$		$mod\text{-}eqn:$	$\beta = \langle f(\langle\gamma,c\rangle), f\rangle$		
$consts:$	$c, s, n \neq 0$		$new\text{-}eqn:$	$\gamma = \langle n, s\rangle$		
$fdefn:$	f		$new\text{-}\gamma\text{-}name:$	γ		

Abbreviation: $x[..c..] \equiv x[c1][c2]..[cn]$, where c is a list of constants $c1, c2, .., cn$.

Substitution of unevaluated γ-selector expressions

$$... x ... \Longrightarrow ... \gamma[..c..] ... \qquad (16)$$
$$eqn: \quad x = \gamma[..c..]$$

γ-selector substitution on left-hand side of an equation

$$eqn: \quad x![..c1..] = e \Longrightarrow mod\text{-}eqn: \quad \gamma![..c2, c1..] = e \qquad (17)$$
$$eqn: \quad x = \gamma[..c2..]$$

Value Substitution only for arithmetic and logical operations

$$... \gamma[..c..]\ op\ e ... \Longrightarrow ... a[..c..]\ op\ e ... \qquad (18)$$
$$eqn: \quad \gamma = a$$
$$const: \quad a$$

$$... if\ \gamma[..c..] ... \Longrightarrow ... if\ a[..c..] ... \qquad (19)$$
$$eqn: \quad \gamma = a$$
$$const: \quad a$$

Rules to Perform Update in place

$eqn:$	$\gamma![..c..] = d$	$\Longrightarrow$	$delete\text{-}eqn:$	$\gamma![..c..] = d$	(20)
$eqn:$	$\gamma = a$		$mod\text{-}eqn:$	$\gamma = a'$	
$consts:$	a, d		$abbrev:$	$a' \equiv a$, except the	
$check:$	no other occurrence of γ			component $a[..c..]$	
				is replaced by d	

Release New state for next Transition

$eqn:$	$\beta = \langle\gamma!, f\rangle$	$\Longrightarrow$	$mod\text{-}eqn:$	$\beta = \langle a, f\rangle$	(21)
$eqn:$	$\gamma = a$				
$const:$	a				
$check:$	no other occurrence of $\gamma!$				

Figure 9: Rewrite Rules for updating in place

while the old state is made available through the new γ-name γ. Rules 16 and 17 specify that the γ-selectors are treated as constants and can be substituted in place of names to which they are bound. Even γ!-selector names on the left-hand side of equations can be replaced. Rules 18 and 19 specify that the values for γ-selectors (*i.e.*, old state values) are substituted only when an arithmetic or logical operation must be performed using them. Indiscriminate substitution of values for γ can result in non-determinacy. For instance, suppose we have the two equations: $x = \gamma[2]$ and $x! = 5$ and we permitted the substitution of γ-selectors any where. Applying the rules in one order will give the update $\gamma![2] = 5$ and another order will leave the second equation irreducible.

Finally, rules 20 and 21 specify the updating of the components of the state and making the state available for the next transition. These two rules have the peculiar condition to check that the γ-names are not present anywhere else in the machine state (other than their bindings). We comment on this later.

5 Implementation Considerations

The rewrite rules presented in the preceding section provide a simple graph reduction implementation. However, literal graph reduction is not particularly efficient and alternative implementations can be more efficient if some architectural aids are available. We outline some of them here. We assume that data structures are implemented in a separate memory and the structure accesses are asynchronous as is the case with a dataflow machine [3]. That is, memory and processor operate asynchronously. Read and store requests are sent as messages to the memory and the processor continues with further processing. Later, when the requests are satisfied, the memory unit sends responses as messages to the processor. There must be appropriate support to tag the messages so that a processor can relate the messages to the state of its computation. Such features – *viz.* some form of asynchronous interfaces with memory and limited arithmetic/logical operations at the memory – are becoming common with many modern multi-processors, such as CEDAR, RP3 *etc.*

5.1 Simple Transition Functions

Logic variables with simple transition functions such as *add*, *multiply etc.* can be implemented using a tagged memory that can perform these simple functions as part of the memory controller. For example, consider the accumulation function of Section 3.2. The storage for this variable stores the count and the partial sum. A tag bit associated with this storage indicates whether the accumulator is closed or not. The execution of a transition command results in sending a request to the memory, which examines the contents of this storage. The memory controller must increment the count, update the sum and set the tag if the count becomes zero. Use of the variable in an expression results in sending a read request to the memory. The request is satisfied if the tag indicates that the accumulator is closed. Otherwise the request is delayed by entering it in a queue associated with this storage. When an accumulator is closed, the memory controller must check to see if there are pending read requests for the accumulator and release all of them. Thus, use of a memory controller guarantees atomicity for the update operation. Depending on the transition functions, the memory controllers can get significantly complex. Tagged memory is a principal component of the MIT Tagged-Token dataflow machine [3] for implementing the I-structures. Accumulators for simple functions have been implemented in a simulator for the tagged-token dataflow machine [2].

Serialization of accumulation at the memory cells may result in some loss of parallelism. If this is a serious concern, a combining network of the kind proposed for the NYU ultracomputer [7] or RP3 can be used to perform some combing of the operations in the network itself. In fact, the accumulator construct can be seen as a way of exposing the capabilities of such a combining network to the programmer.

5.2 Complex Transition Functions

Implementing arbitrary transition functions require different support. First we observe that the rewrite rules do not render straightforward implementations. For example, rules 20 and 21 involve a global check to see that all occurrences of a given name have been replaced by its value. Checking this at run time is equivalent to the garbage collection problem and can get very hairy. Compiler analysis can help this situation greatly. Transition functions can be regulated using special syntax and the use of the old state can be tracked by the compiler. A number of schemes can be adopted to determine when it is no longer needed by the function. One can use reference counts or introduce artificial dependences to trigger certain operations when their pre-conditions are met. Or one may translate these functions into sequential threads. Alternatively, architectural support can be provided by associating a key with each memory element. Memory accesses must be accompanied by appropriate keys such as, read-final, read-intermediate, update-intermediate, update-final *etc.*

Given these complications, we are skeptical of the utility of using complex transition functions. We have included them in our discussion to demonstrate the scope of accumulators.

6 Conclusion

We have described a complete (operational) semantic framework to encapsulate the notion of incremental definition of values. Conventional functional languages insist that a value be completely specified as the result of a single expression. Logic languages provide the notion of an undefined variable and permit repeated binding of values to it, as long as they are consistent. The consistency is usually restricted to successful term unification. Consequently, once a value is defined, it remains a constant. Computing the nth value in a recurrence forces us to produce all the intermediate values, as if they were needed by other computations as well. They consume memory resources and are reclaimed only as part of a general garbage collection mechanism. Imperative languages, on the other hand, perform extremely well in these situations taking advantage of the fact that the order of execution is predetermined and that a compiler can determine that the intermediate values are unnecessary and hence can be replaced by the new values of the recurrence. The logic variable notion introduced in this paper captures precisely this notion and presents a model to achieve similar implementation efficiencies when the operations involved are commutative and associative. One can look at this new notion of accumulators from three aspects: expressiveness, parallelism and efficiency.

As illustrated by the examples in the paper, accumulators arise very naturally in a variety of problems. In many problems, the use of accumulators is more natural than the use of functional primitives like *functional-accumulate* discussed in Section 3.3. However, it does open up the question of determinacy for arbitrary transition functions. A reasonable compromise may be to restrict the transition function to primitives like $+, *,$ *unify* etc. which are known to the compiler as being commutative and associative.

On the parallelism aspect, accumulators improve the opportunities for parallelism. The new construct provides for combining the values in arbitrary order, if they can be generated independently. Conventional and dataflow models for parallel execution must sequentialize the combining operations. Often this sequencing requires passing feedback values from one iteration to the other in a loop and the overhead for this can be substantial [1]. Accumulators eliminate the need to circulate the values around a loop in this situation and thereby save some overhead. By delegating the arithmetic/logical operations involved in a transition function to the memory unit, the processor is freed up to do other computation to that extent.

The final aspect of efficiency is more important. The major advantage of this approach that we see is that when the accumulation is to be performed upon the elements of a structure, accumulators provide an update mechanism, which is as efficient as in an imperative program, and yet preserves the determinacy of the computation. Functional programs to solve the same problem incur either substantial copying overheads or substantial restructuring of a program to get around the problem. This is illustrated by the examples of histograms and particle in cell.

Above all, we feel that the concept of logic variables as presented in this paper bears strong resemblance to object oriented programming. The logic variables are objects, and state transitions are the methods that operate on them. The abstraction hides the representational details and provides a higher level view of the object to the rest of the program. One can confine to the analysis of the transition functions, in order to establish the validity of the operations on the object. The implementation of an accumulator naturally embodies the notions of mutual exclusion and sequentialization of certain portions of code. One can use accumulators to express these constraints at a programming level. Commutative and associative transition functions are very useful as they guarantee deterministic results. Even otherwise, these abstractions are useful for modeling non-deterministic portions of computation, such as a resource scheduler that receives requests in arbitrary order and performs state changes. We have not examined this aspect and whether logic variables provide a natural framework for solving these problems or not, is a subject for future study.

Acknowledgements: We have received useful feedback about this paper from Arvind and Nikhil at M.I.T. Accumulators were implemented in Id Nouveau by Bhaskar Guharoy. We have benefited from discussions with Alex Nicolau and John Solworth at Cornell University.

References

[1] Arvind, D.E.Culler and K.Ekanadham, The Price of Asynchronous Parallelism: An Analysis of Dataflow Architectures, To appear in: *Proceedings of CONPAR 88, at University of Manchester, UK. (September 1988)*.

[2] Arvind, B.Guharoy and R.S.Nikhil, MIT Laboratory for Computer Science, Cambridge, MA (August 1987), *private communication*

[3] Arvind and R.S.Nikhil, Executing a Program On the MIT Tagged-Token Dataflow Architecture, in: *Proceedings of the PARLE Conference, Eindhoven, The Netherlands. Springer-verlag LNCS 259 (June 1987)*.

[4] Arvind, R.S.Nikhil and K.K.Pingali, I-structures: Data Structures for Parallel Computing, in: *Proceedings of Workshop on Graph Reduction, Santa Fe, NM. Springer-verlag LNCS 279 (September 1986)*.

[5] Bellia,M. and G.Levi, The Relation Between Logic and Functional Languages: A Survey, in: *The Journal of Logic Programming, 3:217-236 (1986)*.

[6] DeGroot,D. and G.Lindstrom, Logic Programming: Functions, Relations and Equations, *Prentice-Hall, Englewood Cliffs, NJ (1986)*.

[7] Gottlieb, A. *et al*, The NYU Ultracomputer - designing an MIMD shared memory parallel computer, in: *IEEE Transactions on Computers, C-32, 175-189, February 1983*.

[8] Hudak, P., A Semantic Model of Reference Counting and its Abstraction, in: *Proceedings of the 1986 ACM Conference on Lisp and Functional Programming*.

[9] Kuck,D.J. *et al*, Dependence Graphs and Compiler Optimizations, in: *Proceedings of the 8th ACM Symposium on Principles of Programming Languages, 1981*.

[10] Lassez, J-L and J.Jaffar, Constraint Logic Programming, in: *Proceedings of 14th ACM POPL conference, Munich, W.Germany. (January 1987)*.

[11] Lindstrom,G., Functional Programming and the logical Variable, in: *Proceedings of the 12th ACM Symposium on Principles of Programming Languages, 1985*.

[12] Lubeck,O.M., Los Alamos National Laboratory, Los Alamos, CA (August 1987), *private communication*

[13] Martelli,A. and U.Montanari, An efficient unification algorithm, in: *ACM Transaction on Programming Languages and Systems, vol 4, No 2:258-282 (1982)*.

[14] Turner, D., *private communication*

A RESOLUTION RULE FOR WELL-FORMED FORMULAE

K.S.H.S.R.Bhatta
Harish Karnick
Department of Computer Science & Engineering
Indian Institute of Technology, Kanpur
U.P. 208 016 India.

Abstract

A resolution proof procedure that operates on well-formed formulae with *all* quantifiers in place is presented. Extension of the unification algorithm to *Q-unification* (i.e. with quantifiers in place) is also discussed. The procedure involves a single inference rule called *WFF-resolution* which is proved to be sound and complete.

1. Introduction

Interactive theorem proving through resolution becomes more tractable if we can retain the original form of the formula which will make it easier for humans to guide the theorem prover.

NC-resolution (for non-clausal resolution) proposed by Murray [Mur 82] requires the wffs to be quantifier free. Although this addresses the disadvantages of Robinson's clausal resolution [Rob 65], both these resolution principles still have the following inherent disadvantages:

(1) The intuition behind selecting appropriate quantifiers in expressing the problem is lost in the conversion.

(2) The sentence becomes too complex when quantifiers are removed, in particular those within the scope of (nested) equivalences.

Manna & Waldinger [MaW 82] have dealt with a non-clausal deductive system applied to sentences that may have *some* of their quantifiers intact.

Usually, Skolem functions (or constants) are substituted for existentially quantified variables after the quantifiers have been pulled out. In our method we dispense with Skolem functions and instead use the dependencies (defined later) of an existential variable.

1.1 Definitions

Terms are defined recursively as follows:

(i) A constant is a term.

(ii) A universal variable is a term.

(iii) An existential variable is a term whenever its dependencies (defined later) are terms.

(iv) If f is an n-place function symbol, and $t_1,\ldots,t_n$ are terms, then $f(t_1,\ldots,t_n)$ is a term.

(v) All terms are generated by applying the above rules.

We are taking into account *constants* and *functions* since we may have explicit occurrences of constants and functions different from Skolem constants and Skolem functions.

The definitions of an atom, a literal and a wff are the same as given in [Rob 65]. The concepts of positive and negative as applied to atoms in clausal resolution can be generalized to define polarity. The polarity of a sub-wff in a wff is the parity of the explicit and implicit negations within the scope of which the sub-wff appears in the wff. The formal definitions can be found in [Mur 82]. We extend the definition of polarity to quantifiers as follows:

Let Q be a quantifier, S_1 and S_2 be wffs.

(∅) Q is positive in QS_1.

(1) If Q is positive (negative) in S_1, then it is negative (positive) in $\sim S_1$ and $(S_1 \longrightarrow S_2)$,

(2) If Q is positive (negative) in S_1, then it is positive (negative) in $(S_1 \& S_2)$, $(S_1 \lor S_2)$ and $(S_2 \longrightarrow S_1)$,

(3) If Q occurs in S_1, then it is both positive and negative in $(S_1 \longleftrightarrow S_2)$.

An existential variable in a wff is a *dependent existential variable*, if at least one universal quantifier precedes it. The *dependency information (or dependencies)* of such a dependent variable, analogous to the arguments of Skolem functions, is a list of all universally quantified variables preceding it.

For example, in the wff $(\forall x) [P(x) \longrightarrow (\exists y) Q(x, y)]$, y is a dependent existential variable and its dependency information is (x).

An existential variable in a wff is an *independent existential variable*, if it is not dependent.

For example, in the wff $(\exists x) (\forall y) (P(x) \& Q(x, y))$, x is an independent existential variable.

We shall introduce the notion of a dual quantifier which is different from the already existing notion of quantification [Qui 61].

A quantifier Q that is both positive and negative in a wff is a *dual quantifier*. In other words, a quantifier Q that occurs within the scope of an equivalence is a *dual quantifier*.

For example, in $[(Qx) P(x) \longleftrightarrow R]$ where Q is a quantifier, Q is dual. It can act as both universal and existential depending on the polarity chosen. The variable x is said to be *dually quantified*. When Q is positive, it is Q, and when it is negative, it is Q^c, the complement of Q.

Since resolution can be done on sub-wffs we need to know when two wffs are resolvable. Basically, they can be resolved if they are structurally equivalent and are complementary (i.e. have opposite polarity). For formal definitions of structural equivalence and complementarity see [Bha 88].

This paper describes an algorithm for obtaining dependency information of an existential variable in a wff without paraphrasing the wff in any manner and with quantifiers in place. This also introduces the concept of unification in the context of quantified variables, termed *Q-unification,* and describes how to perform WFF-resolution which is proved to be sound and complete by showing that it is equivalent to quantifier free NC-resolution.

2. Obtaining Dependencies

Intuitively, to obtain the dependencies of an existential instance of a variable in a wff, our algorithm scans the wff from left-to-right and prepares a list of universally quantified variables occurring in it. For any existential variable, the dependencies are the list of universal variables so far obtained.

We assume that any variable in the given set of wffs is uniquely named, and that each wff is properly parenthesized. The processing is recursive in nature; if the connective is binary, then each sub-wff is processed separately and the dependencies are modified accordingly; if the connective is unary (i.e. ~), then the only sub-wff is processed by interchanging the notions of universal and existential quantifications.

The algorithm in Pascal like notation is given below:

INPUT:
```
    f - well-formed formula in prefix notation i.e.
        ({(Q1 x1) (Q2 x2) ... } (<opr> <sub-wff1> <sub-wff2>))
        if <opr> is binary,
        else ({(Q1 x1) (Q2 x2) ...} (<opr> <sub-wff1>))
```

flag1 - polarity flag. TRUE if f is positive in the main
        wff, and FALSE otherwise.
flag2 - dual flag. TRUE if f is dual (both positive and
        negative) in the main wff, and FALSE otherwise.

OUTPUT:

dlists - a list of two sub-lists. Is of the form
         (<uvarlist> <evarlist>) where
         <uvarlist> is a list of all universally quantified
         variables in f, and
         <evarlist> is a list of all existentially
         quantified variables in f.
deps - all dependencies are maintained globally, which are
       initialised to null lists and modified as and when
       necessary.

All the functions used are self-explanatory.

```
function dependencies(f flag1 flag2)
  begin
    if is-atf(f) then return(make-dlists(() ()));
    {make a dlist whose uvarlist and evarlist both are ().}
    if (is-quantifier(first(f)) and flag2)
        then begin
                var <-- get-var(first(f));
                dlists <-- dependencies(rest(f) flag1 flag2);
                modify-deps(var evarlist(dlists));
                if is-universal-quantifier(first(f) TRUE)
                    then return(add-to-uvarlist(var dlists))
                    else return(add-to-evarlist(var dlists));
             end;
    if is-quantifier(first(f))
        then begin
                var <-- get-var(first(f));
                dlists <-- dependencies(rest(f) flag1 flag2);
                if is-universal-quantifier(first(f) flag1)
                    then begin
                            modify-deps(var evarlist(dlists));
                            return(add-to-uvarlist(var dlists));
                         end
                    else return(add-to-evarlist(var dlists));
             end;
    if is-negation(opr(f))
        then return(dependencies(remove-neg(f) toggle(flag1)
                                                  flag2));
    if (is-disjunction(opr(f)) or is-conjunction(opr(f)))
        then begin
                dl1 <-- dependencies(sub-wff1(f) flag1 flag2);
                dl2 <-- dependencies(sub-wff2(f) flag1 flag2);
                modify-deps(uvarlist(dl1) evarlist(dl2));
                return(merge(dl1 dl2));
             end;
    if is-implication(opr(f))
        then begin
                dl1 <-- dependencies(sub-wff1(f) toggle(flag1)
                                                   flag2);
                dl2 <-- dependencies(sub-wff2(f) flag1 flag2);
                modify-deps(uvarlist(dl1) evarlist(dl2));
                return(merge(dl1 dl2));
             end;
```

```
      if is-equivalence(opr(f))
         then begin
                  dl1 <-- dependencies(sub-wff1(f) flag1 TRUE);
                  dl2 <-- dependencies(sub-wff2(f) flag1 TRUE);
                  modify-deps(uvarlist(dl1) uvarlist(dl2));
                  modify-deps(evarlist(dl1) evarlist(dl2));
                  dl <-- merge(dl1 dl2);
                  l <-- set-union(uvarlist(dl) evarlist(dl));
                  return(make-dlists(l l));
              end;
      if (length(f) = 1)
         then return(dependencies(first(f) flag1 flag2))
         {if more than one pair of parentheses enclose f
           remove the extra pair of parentheses and obtain
           the dependencies.}
         else ERROR; {error in input format}
   end.
```

Our algorithm ignores inter-dependencies which arise when equivalences are paraphrased into implications and we justify it by observing that in NC-resolution [Mur 82] we use only one part of the two implications that an equivalence gives rise to during resolution. Henceforth the two implications which make up an equivalence will be called *implicants* for stylistic reasons. From this we can assert that in a refutation we use only one instance, either universal or existential, of a dual variable. But, a dual variable can have more than one existential or universal instance, the number depending on the number of equivalences within whose scope it occurs. In our method since we do not paraphrase equivalences two existential variables could be treated as the same variable and it may appear that we could have two resolution sequences involving that formula which derive *complementary literals (or wffs)*, say $P(x)$, $\sim P(x)$ and so we are able to derive *FALSE* in a satisfiable set. This would not be possible if the formulae were in quantifier free form; because then $P(x)$, $\sim P(x)$ would be $P(f(s_1,...,s_n))$, $\sim P(g(t_1,...,t_m))$ and they cannot be resolved. In other words, our system would be unsound. However, the following lemmas show the soundness of the method.

Lemma 2.1

If f, g are any two Skolem functions substituted for two existential instances of a dually quantified variable in a set of wffs U, and if U is satisfiable, then two wffs $P(\ldots,f(s_1,\ldots,s_n),\ldots)$ and $\sim P(\ldots,g(t_1,\ldots,t_m),\ldots)$ or $\sim P(\ldots,f(s_1,\ldots,s_n),\ldots)$ and $P(\ldots,g(t_1,\ldots,t_m),\ldots)$ can not be deduced by NC-resolution.

Proof: Refer to [Bha 88].

Analogous to the above lemma, which is valid for NC-resolution, we have the following lemma for our method.

Lemma 2.2

If a wff in a set of wffs U contains a dually quantified variable x that occurs within the scope of at least two equivalences, and if U is satisfiable, then two wffs of the form $(\exists x)\ P(x)$ and $(\exists x)\ \sim P(x)$ can not be deduced by our method.

Or, in other words, WFF-resolution together with our algorithm to obtain dependencies of an existential variable is sound.

Proof: The proof is analogous to that of Lemma 2.1.

We note here that normally $(\exists x)\ P(x)$ and $(\exists x)\ \sim P(x)$ are not contradictory. Here since existentially quantified variables must be uniquely and consistently tagged $(\exists x)\ P(x)$ and $(\exists x)\ \sim P(x)$ would be the equivalent of $P(a)$ and $\sim P(a)$ (where a is a Skolem constant) in the quantifier free case and would be contradictory.

Thus, we are justified in treating all existential instances of a dually quantified variable to be same. But, in such a case, all the existential instances are made to depend on the same universal variables, even though some are actually not dependent.

3. Substitution and Q-Unification

All the definitions, such as substitution, instantiation, standardization (essentially renaming of variables), and composition of substitution, of [Rob 65] carry over to our method, with an understanding that a variable in those definitions means universally quantified variable. For the purpose of matching or unification, an existential variable v_i with dependencies $(t_1,\ldots,t_n)$ is treated and written as an n-place function symbol $v_i(t_1,\ldots,t_n)$. To distinguish between a universal variable v_i and an independent existential variable v_i, the latter is written as $v_i()$.

In order to unify two sub-wffs, we need to get the sequences of terms in those sub-wffs. The *sequence of terms* in a sub-wff F is obtained as below:

(a) If $F = P(t_1,\ldots,t_n)$ where P is an n-place predicate symbol, then it is $((Q_1 t_1),\ldots,(Q_n t_n))$, where Q_i is the quantification of a term t_i, taking polarity of Q_i into account.

(b) If $F = \sim F_1$, then it is the sequence of terms in F_1, with the notions of universal and existential quantifications of terms interchanged.

(c) If $F = F_1 \, b \, F_2$ for some binary connective b ($b \neq \langle\text{-->}\rangle$ if there are quantifiers in F_1 or F_2; we will explain this a little later), then it is the sequence of terms in F_1 appended to the sequence of terms in F_2; the sequence of terms obtained taking polarity into account.

(d) If $F = (Qx) \, F_1$ where Q is some quantifier, and x is some variable in F_1, then it is the sequence of terms in F_1 such that x is written as $(Q_1 x)$ where Q_1 is either Q or its complement, determined by the polarity.

As an example, the sequence of terms in

$(\forall x)[P(x) \lor ((\forall y) \; Q(x, y) \longrightarrow (\exists z) \; \{R(x, z) \; \& \; (\forall u) \; S(z, u)\})]$

is $((\forall x), (\exists y((\forall x))), (\exists z((\forall x))), (\forall u))$, which when transformed into the notation as described earlier in this section would be $(x, y(x), z(x), u)$.

It is not necessary to define sequence of terms for $F_1 \longleftrightarrow F_2$ if there are quantifiers in F_1 or F_2. If a quantifier is within the scope of $\longleftrightarrow$, we cannot resolve two sub-wffs, $(F_1 \longleftrightarrow F_2)$ and $\sim(F_1 \longleftrightarrow F_2)$ directly. Since each quantifier is dual, we cannot determine the substitutions. We will have to resolve only by parts (i.e. F_1, F_2 separately).

So from the polarity of the wff being resolved we can determine the sequence of terms because each quantifier will then have a single polarity. For example, in a wff $[(\forall x) \; A \longleftrightarrow B]$, if we decide to take the polarity of $(\forall x) \; A$ to be negative, then x is only existentially quantified.

Two sub-wffs are *unifiable*, if the sequence of terms in one, and the sequence of terms in the S-equivalent form of the other are unifiable. Since the terms to be unified contain quantifiers, we call our unification *Q-unification*. However, the basic unification algorithm of [Rob 65] extends to our method.

For unifying two existential variables, we check for their origin and if it is the same, then only do we proceed to unify their dependencies, just as in the case of unifying two Skolem functions. Since the existential variables do not change in syntactic form during resolution, by *same origin of existential variables* we mean *their syntactic equivalence*. For instance, the terms $x(y, z)$ and $x(u(), v)$ unify with $\{u()/y, v/z\}$, where as the terms $x(y, z)$ and $w(u(), v)$ do not because x, w are not syntactically same.

4. WFF-resolution

This is basically NC-resolution, but with quantifiers in place. We define a WFF-resolvent as follows:

For any wffs S_1, S_2, F and G, if F occurs positively in S_1 $(S_1\langle F\rangle)$ and G occurs negatively in S_2 $(S_2\langle G\rangle)$, and θ is the mgu of F and G under Q-unification, such that $F\theta = G\theta = H$, then the result of simplifying

$$S_1\theta\{FALSE/H\} \lor S_2\theta\{TRUE/H\}$$

is the *WFF-resolvent* of S_1 and S_2.

The simplification may involve dropping, adding or merging quantifiers. For example, let us consider the wffs

$$U_1: (\forall x)\ (A(x) \longrightarrow B(x))$$
$$U_2: (\exists y())\ (C(y) \longrightarrow A(y))$$

in which the atom with A is complementary. We can resolve these two wffs on A with the mgu $\{y()/x\}$ and the resolvent is

$$R_1: (\exists y())\ [B(y) \lor \sim C(y)].$$

Thus, we drop the quantifiers $(\forall x)$, $(\exists y())$ respectively from U_1, U_2 and add a quantifier $(\exists y())$ as prefix to the resolvent because the existential variable y substitutes for the universal variable x.

When we *instantiate* a universal variable (i.e. substitute an existential variable for a universal variable), we drop the universal quantification of that variable and add existential quantification of the variable being substituted in the resolvent. Such dropping and addition respectively of universal and existential quantifiers can be viewed as analogous to the *Universal Instantiation* and *Existential Generalization* in *Quantification Theory* [Qui 61].

As for *renaming* variables in a resolvent, we do so only for universally quantified variables, but not for any existentially quantified variable. Essentially, an existential variable *retains* its syntactic form obtained from the origin wff of the variable through out the refutation.

We illustrate WFF-resolution when there are equivalences in the set of wffs and quantifiers within their scope by considering a problem from [Pel 86] concerning set equality (Q).

Two sets are equal when they have exactly the same members. We have to prove that equality is symmetric. Predicate F stands for *"is an element of"*. The wffs are

U_1: $(\forall x) (\forall y) [Q(x, y) <--> (\forall z) (F(z, x) <--> F(z, y))]$
U_2: $(\forall u) (\forall v) (Q(u, v) <--> Q(v, u))$

The wffs with negated theorem (U_2) and with functional dependencies substituted are

U_1: $(\forall x) (\forall y) [Q(x, y) <--> (\forall z(x, y)) (F(z, x) <--> F(z, y))]$
U_2: $\sim(\forall u()) (\forall v()) [Q(u, v) <--> Q(v, u)]$

Since the variable z is dual it will be dependent on x, y only when it acts as existential variable.

The refutation sequence and the substitutions therein are as given below:

$U_1 + U_2 ---> R_1$:
  $(\exists u()) (\exists v()) [\sim(\forall z(u, v)) (F(z, u) <--> F(z, v)) \lor \sim Q(v, u)]$
      ;{$(\exists u())/(\forall x)$, $(\exists v())/(\forall y)$}

$U_1 + R_1 ---> R_2$: $(\exists u()) (\exists v()) [\sim(\forall z(u, v)) (F(z, u) <--> F(z, v))$
$\lor \sim(\forall z(v, u)) (F(z, v) <--> F(z, u))]$;{$(\exists v())/(\forall x)$, $(\exists u())/(\forall y)$}

$U_1 + R_2 ---> R_3$:
  $(\exists u()) (\exists v()) [\sim Q(u, v) \lor \sim(\forall z(v, u)) (F(z, v) <--> F(z, u))]$
      ;{$(\exists u())/(\forall x)$, $(\exists v())/(\forall y)$, $(\exists z(u, v))/(\forall z_1)$}

$U_1 + R_3 \longrightarrow R_4$: $(\exists u()) \; (\exists v()) \; \sim Q(u, v)$

;{$(\exists u())/(\forall x)$, $(\exists v())/(\forall y)$, $(\exists z(v, u))/(\forall z_1)$}

and merging into $\sim Q(u, v)$.

$U_2 + R_4 \longrightarrow R_5$: $\sim [(\forall u()) \; (\forall v()) \; \sim Q(v, u)]$;{}

$U_1 + R_5 \longrightarrow R_6$: $(\exists u()) \; (\exists v()) \; (\forall z) \; (F(z, v) \longleftrightarrow F(z, u))$

;{$(\exists v())/(\forall x)$, $(\exists u())/(\forall y)$}

$R_2 + R_6 \longrightarrow R_7$: $(\exists u()) \; (\exists v()) \; [\sim(\forall z(u, v)) \; (F(z, u) \longleftrightarrow F(z, v))]$

;{$(\exists z(v, u))/(\forall z_1)$}

$R_6 + R_7 \longrightarrow R_8$: FALSE ;{$(\exists z(u, v))/(\forall z_1)$}

5. Soundness and Completeness of WFF-resolution

We now prove the soundness and completeness of WFF-resolution by showing that it is equivalent to quantifier free NC-resolution, which is known to be sound and complete [Mur 82].

For these proofs, we shall induce on the total number of equivalences in the set of wffs U taking the base step to be the case when there are no equivalences. For this base step we first state two lemmas before going to the main proof.

Lemma 5.1

If U is a set of wffs without equivalences, and QF is its quantifier free version, then for every wff U_i from U there exists an equivalent wff QF_j in QF and vice-versa.

Proof: Refer to [Bha 88].

Lemma 5.2

If two wffs U_1, U_2 can be resolved to give R_1 by WFF-resolution and two quantifier free wffs QF_1, QF_2 can also be resolved to give QFR_1, and $U_1 \equiv QF_1$, $U_2 \equiv QF_2$, then the resolvents, if the resolutions are performed on similar sub-wffs, satisfy $R_1 \equiv QFR_1$. (The wffs are assumed to be free of equivalences).

Proof: Refer to [Bha 88].

Based on these results, we now prove that WFF-resolution *(WR)* and quantifier free NC-resolution *(QFR)* are equivalent when there are no equivalences in the given set of wffs on which these resolutions are performed.

Theorem 5.1

If U is an unsatisfiable set of wffs without equivalences, and QF is its quantifier free version, then *FALSE* can be deduced from U by *WR* iff *FALSE* can be deduced from QF by *QFR*.

Proof:

To prove the theorem both ways, it suffices to show that the resolution sequences with equivalent wffs in *WR* and *QFR* are equivalent.

Let $QFR_1, \ldots, QFR_n$ be the sequence of resolution steps in *QFR* and the resolvent in QFR_i be QR_i. Let $WR_1, \ldots, WR_k$ be the resolution sequence in *WR* and the resolvent in WR_i be R_i.

By Lemma 5.1, we have, for every wff in U there is a corresponding and equivalent wff in QF and *vice-versa*. If any two wffs QF_i, QF_j are resolved in QFR_1, then the equivalent resolution step in *WR*, say WR_1, must consist of wffs U_i, U_j, such that $QF_i \equiv U_i$ and $QF_j \equiv U_j$, and resolution must be on equivalent sub-wffs. Then, by Lemma 5.2, the resolvents QR_1 and R_1 satisfy $QR_1 \equiv R_1$. Hence, the derivation of an equivalent wff must be equally long in both *QFR* and *WR*. Hence, $k = n$.

We shall prove the equivalence of the two resolution sequences by inducing on the number of resolution steps. We show that every QFR_i can be transformed into a valid, equivalent WR_i.

Base step: First resolution steps QFR_1, WR_1.

If wffs QF_i, QF_j are resolved in QFR_1, then these wffs must be from the initial set QF. By Lemma 5.1, we can choose two wffs U_i, U_j from U, such that $QF_i \equiv U_i$ and $QF_j \equiv U_j$, for resolution step WR_1. Then, by Lemma 5.2, the resolvents QR_1, R_1 satisfy $QR_1 \equiv R_1$. Thus, we have an equivalent resolution step in WR for the one in QFR.

Hypothesis: For resolution steps $< m$, we have, for every resolution step in QFR, an equivalent step in WR.

Inductive step: Consider the mth resolution step QFR_m. We have 3 different cases here.

Case (i): When both the wffs in QFR_m are from QF.

As explained for base step, we can find an equivalent WR_m for QFR_m.

Case (ii): When one wff is from QF and the other from the set of resolvents $\{QR_1,\ldots,QR_{m-1}\}$.

From Lemma 5.1, we can choose an equivalent wff U_i for the one from QF. From the hypothesis, we can always choose a wff from the resolvent set of WR, $\{R_1,\ldots,R_{m-1}\}$, such that it is equivalent to the one from $\{QR_1,\ldots,QR_{m-1}\}$. By Lemma 5.2, the resolvent of these two wffs in WR is equivalent to QR_m. Hence, we have an equivalent WR_m for QFR_m.

Case (iii): When both the wffs are from the resolvent set of QFR, $\{QR_1,\ldots,QR_{m-1}\}$.

From the hypothesis, we can always find two wffs in $\{R_1,\ldots,R_{m-1}\}$, such that they are equivalent to the wffs in QFR_m.

Hence, by Lemma 5.2, we have a resolvent R_m in WR, such that $R_m \equiv QR_m$. Thus, we have an equivalent WR_m for QFR_m.

Hence, in all possible cases, we have shown that there exists a WR_m, which is equivalent to QFR_m.

Now, by induction, for every resolution sequence in QFR, we have an equivalent sequence of resolutions in WR.

Hence, $FALSE$ can be deduced from U in WR iff $FALSE$ can be deduced from QF in QFR.

We shall now look at the proof to show that WFF-resolution is sound and complete, when equivalences are present.

Theorem 5.2

If U is an unsatisfiable set of wffs, and QF is its quantifier free version, then $FALSE$ can be deduced by WR iff $FALSE$ can be deduced by QFR.

Proof:

To prove the theorem both ways, it suffices to show the equivalence of WR and QFR.

We prove this by inducing on n, the total number of equivalences in the set of wffs U.

If $n = \emptyset$, then we have by Theorem 5.1, that WR and QFR are equivalent.

Suppose that the Theorem is true for $n < m$. Consider, now, a set of wffs with m equivalences. Let us assume that a wff U_1 contains an equivalence. If we show that there exists an equivalent (equivalence of functional dependencies also) wff in QF for this U_1, then the proof for the equivalence of WR and QFR goes in the same lines as in the proof of Theorem 5.1.

Now, we have 3 different cases here.

Case (i): When there are no quantifiers within the scope of this equivalence, this equivalence does not affect the equivalence of WR and QFR. Hence, we are through.

Case (ii): When there is only one quantifier within the scope of equivalence, then also we are through, because we can always assume that the implicant containing the existential instance of the variable, precedes the other one.

Case (iii): When there is more than one quantifier within the scope of equivalence.

Let a sub-wff containing this equivalence have the form

$$(Q_{11}x_1)\ldots(Q_{1k}x_k)\ F_1 \longleftrightarrow (Q_{21}y_1)\ldots(Q_{2l}y_l)\ F_2$$

For any existential variable that follows this sub-wff containing equivalence, we have exactly $k+l$ universal variables, k from the first sub-wff of this equivalence and l from the second, coming out of this sub-wff as dependency, because every variable is both universally quantified and existentially quantified. This would be the case in QF also. Hence, for any functional dependency of an existential variable that follows this equivalence, there is no difference between U and QF.

This will have the following two implicants:

(1) $(Q_{11}x_1)\ldots(Q_{1k}x_k)\ F_1 \longrightarrow (Q_{21}y_1)\ldots(Q_{2l}y_l)\ F_2$
(2) $(Q_{21}y_1)\ldots(Q_{2l}y_l)\ F_2 \longrightarrow (Q_{11}x_1)\ldots(Q_{1k}x_k)\ F_1$

The functional dependencies, generated from one implicant, for an existential variable in the other part, are being ignored by our algorithm of section 2, which otherwise would have been taken into account in the set QF. But, as explained in section 2, we use only one implicant of any equivalence in a resolution. So, irrespective of what substitutions could have been made in the functional dependencies of an existential variable in one part, when the other part is reduced to *FALSE*, the whole sub-wff gets reduced to *FALSE*, making such existential variables disappear. Hence, such dependencies need not be considered.

Hence, depending on the chosen polarity of a sub-wff in this equivalence, we will be using only one of the dual quantifications of a variable quantified as $(Q_{ij} v_j)$ in a resolution step. We can always assume that the implicant that participates in resolution precedes the other part.

The resolvent in *WR* when one implicant is eliminated completely, will be equivalent to the resolvent in *QFR* when the corresponding implicant is also eliminated completely.

Thus, we have shown that there exists an equivalent wff in *QF* for U_i, and also that the descendants of both these wffs are also equivalent, though not after a single resolution step, but after some resolution steps in which the implicants participating in resolution have been erased completely.

Thus, by induction, we have for every sub-wff containing an equivalence in a wff U_i of *U*, there is an equivalent wff in *QF* containing equivalent sub-wff in terms of implications.

Now, going along the same lines as in the proof of Theorem 5.1, we will have the equivalence of *WR* and *QFR*. By this and also by Lemma 2.2 which establishes soundness of *WR*, we have, *FALSE* can be deduced in *WR* from a set *U* iff *FALSE* can be deduced in *QFR* from *QF*, the quantifier free version of *U*.

Thus, WFF-resolution has been proved to be sound and complete.

6. Conclusion

In this paper we have described a resolution proof rule for well-formed formulae with quantifiers in place and proved its soundness and completeness.

For proving theorems in real life domains the standard resolution methods turn out to be intractable. It is also difficult to use them interactively since the original formulae are broken up and the intuitive content of the formulae is thus completely lost. WFF-resolution by retaining the formulae intact will, hopefully, obviate this problem. At the same time the advantages of resolution methods (e.g. large number of strategies available) can always be made use of.

Acknowledgements

We would like to thank Drs. S.Biswas, R.Sangal and an anonymous referee for useful suggestions which improved the presentation. We also thank Mr. Vijayan Rajan without whose expertise this report would not have been in its present form.

References

[Bha 88]   Bhatta, K.S.H.S.R. *Many-Sorted Resolution for Well-Formed Formulae with Equality,* M.Tech. Dissertation, I.I.T. Kanpur, 1988.

[ChL 73]   Chang, C.L., and Lee, R.C. *Symbolic Logic and Mechanical Theorem Proving,* Academic Press, Orlando, Fla., 1973.

[MaW 82]   Manna, Z., and Waldinger, R. *Special Relations in Program-Synthetic Deduction,* Tech. Report, Comp. Sci. Dept., Stanford Univ., Stanford, California, and Artificial Intelligence Center, SRI International, Menlo Park, California, March 1982.

[Mur 82] Murray, N.V. "Completely Non-Clausal Theorem Proving", *AI* **18(1)**, 1982, pp.67-85.

[Pel 86] Pelletier, F.J. "Seventy-Five Problems for testing Automatic Theorem Provers", *J. of Automated Reasoning* 2, 1986, pp. 191-216.

[Qui 61] Quine, W.V. *Methods of Logic,* Holt, Rinehart and Winston Inc., New York, 1961.

[Rob 65] Robinson, J.A. "A Machine-oriented Logic Based on Resolution Principle", *JACM* **12(1)**, 1965, pp.23-41.

ALGEBRAIC AND OPERATIONAL SEMANTICS

OF POSITIVE / NEGATIVE

CONDITIONAL ALGEBRAIC SPECIFICATIONS

Stéphane Kaplan[1,2,3]

Abstract :
This paper introduces positive/negative conditional term rewriting systems, with rules of the generic form :
$$u = v \wedge u' \neq v' \implies \lambda \to \rho,$$
as they often appear in algebraic specifications. We consider the algebraic semantics of such systems (viewed as sets of axioms). They do not in general have initial models ; however, we show that they admit *quasi-initial models*, that are in some sense extremal within the class of all models. We then introduce the subclass of *reducing* rewrite systems, constrained by the condition : $\lambda > \rho, u, v, u', v'$ (for some reduction ordering >). For such systems, we show that an optimal *rewrite relation* $\to$ may be defined, and constructed as a "limit". We prove the total validity of an interpreter that computes the normal forms of terms for $\to$. It is then shown that when $\to$ is confluent, the algebra of normal forms is a quasi-initial model. We state a general result about the converse. Lastly, we present a complete critical-pair criterion à la Knuth-Bendix to check for the confluence of reducing systems.

1. Introduction : positive/negative conditional TRS

The field of term rewriting systems has seen important developments during the last decade. One crucial aspect of rewriting is that it provides a natural, operational interpretation of algebraic specifications. Strong connections are known to exist between the two domains – from the algebraic, operational and logical points of view.

Originally, term rewriting systems were limited to *equational* rules, i.e. formulae of the form : $\lambda \to \rho$. These rules are not, however, expressive enough to simulate the algebraic specifications one tends to write naturally. More recently, attention has been devoted to *positive conditional* rules, of the generic form : $u = v \implies \lambda \to \rho$. In this paper, we further generalize the class of rules under consideration, introducing *positive/negative conditional* rules of the form :
$$u = v \wedge \overline{u} \neq \overline{v} \implies \lambda \to \rho.$$
These correspond exactly to the axioms used, naturally, when writing algebraic specifications. In spite of their obvious importance, this class of rules has not been studied so far, perhaps for the following reasons :
- They do not exhibit a straightforward algebraic behaviour. This is to be contrasted with the cases of equational and positive conditional systems, which have initial algebra semantics. In the positive/negative case, as shown below, the specifications do not admit, in general, an initial model.

---
[1] Computer Science Department, Hebrew University, Givat Ram, Jerusalem (Israel) - *kaplan@humus.bitnet*
[2] L.R.I., Bât. 490, Université des Sciences, F-91405 Orsay Cedex (France) - *kaplan@lri.lri.fr*
[3] Computer Science Department, Bar-Ilan University, Ramat-Gan (Israel) - *kaplan@bimacs.bitnet*

However, we show that they admit what we call *quasi-initial* models, having interesting algebraic properties ; among them, that there exists a privileged model that precisely captures the intuition of the specifier. Moreover, under favourable circumstances, this model may be described by rewriting.

• *positive/negative* systems are at least as complicated as positive ones, about which not much was known until recently. However, we feel that recent results about positive systems have implications for positive/negative ones. In particular, we systematically use in this paper the notion of *reducing* systems, satisfying the condition :

$$\lambda > \rho, \; u, v, \overline{u}, \overline{v}.$$

(for some reduction ordering >). Intuitively, this means that the complexity of a computation decreases monotonically along the rewrite sequences, as well as along the "recursive calls" to evaluate u, v, $\overline{u}$ and $\overline{v}$. Reducing systems are shown to have various interesting properties. In particular, they may be assigned a minimal semantics (which is not necessarily the case for non-reducing systems), closely connected to the algebraic notion of quasi-initial models.

Note that an inequation "$\overline{u} \neq \overline{v}$" cannot be replaced by an expression such as "$\neg Eq(\overline{u},\overline{v})$" or even "notEq($\overline{u},\overline{v}$)", for defined predicates (or boolean functions) 'Eq' or 'notEq'. This is because definitions by predicate generate semi-decidable specifications (cf. e.g. [BBTW 81], [Kaplan 82]), whereas inequations allow to define co-semi-decidable specifications.

The paper is organized as follows :
- Section 1 introduces general definitions.
- Section 2 deals with the algebraic aspects of positive/negative systems ; it is shown that such specifications do not admit in general an initial model. Quasi-initial models are introduced as a natural extension of the notion of initial model, and general results about the existence and completeness of quasi-initial models are presented.
- Section 3 considers positive/negative rewriting. It is proved that in the case of reducing systems, there exists a minimal rewrite relation. This relation may be constructed as a (non-monotonic) limit, and is decidable. We show the total correctness of a universal interpreter to compute it. When the relation is known to be confluent, the normal form algebra is a quasi-initial model. A converse result is also stated, establishing a strong link between the algebraic and the operational aspects of such systems.
- Lastly, section 4 considers the confluence of reducing systems. A general critical pair theorem à la Knuth-Bendix is proved.

In sections 2 to 4, only the most interesting proofs are presented. The remaining proofs are to be found in the appendices.

We assume that the reader has basic knowledge about term rewriting systems and algebraic specifications. We refer to the papers [HO 80], [Klop 87], and to [ADJ 78], [EM 85], as general introductions to the former and to the latter fields, respectively.

Throughout this paper, a signature Σ is given, together with a set of variables X. T_Σ stands for the set of ground terms on Σ, and $T_\Sigma(X)$ for the set of terms with variables on Σ and X.

> **Definition 1.1:**
> - a *positive/negative conditional term rewriting system* (P/N CTRS) is a finite set of formulae of the form :
> $$r : (\wedge_{i=1}^{n} u_i = v_i) \wedge (\wedge_{j=1}^{m} \overline{u}_j \neq \overline{v}_j) \Rightarrow \lambda \to \rho,$$
> where λ, ρ, the u_i, the v_i, the $\overline{u}_j$ and the $\overline{v}_j$ are in $T_\Sigma(X)$ and satisfy :
> $$\text{Var}(\lambda) \supseteq \text{Var}(\rho), \text{Var}(u_i), \text{Var}(v_i), \text{Var}(\overline{u}_j), \text{Var}(\overline{v}_j).$$
> - a *reducing* P/N CTRS is a P/N CTRS such that there exists a reduction ordering '>' that satisfies, for any ground substitution σ :
> $$\lambda\sigma > \rho\sigma, u_i\sigma, v_i\sigma, \overline{u}_j\sigma, \overline{v}_j\sigma.$$

Thus, a P/N CTRS is simply a collection of equational clauses with a distinguished, oriented positive literal.

We recall that a reduction ordering is a partial ordering on the set of ground terms, that is *well-founded* and satisfies the following *monotonicity* property :
$$\text{if } t > t', \text{ then } f(\ldots, t, \ldots) > f(\ldots, t', \ldots)$$

The case $n = m = 0$ corresponds to classical, unconditional term rewriting systems (TRS) [HO 80], [Klop 87], while the case $m = 0$ and $n > 0$ corresponds to classical *positive* conditional term rewriting systems (or simply "conditional TRS" - CTRS) [Kaplan 84a], [RZ 84,85], [Ganzinger 86].

The condition on the variables is in order to avoid rules with more variables in the premise than in the left-hand side ; equation solving is needed in order to apply such rules. Thus, they fall outside the scope of rewriting, which should be a "direct" process.

The condition '$\lambda > \rho$' is often assumed for classical TRS to ensure termination. The condition '$\lambda > u_i, v_i$', has been introduced in [Kaplan 84b] and further developed in [JW 86], [Ganziger 86]. This proved to be very fruitful for classical CTRS, for reasons that are recalled hereafter. We will demonstrate that for our generalization to P/N CTRS, is even more useful (even "necessary" for defining the semantics of the rewriting).

Examples :
- Algebraic specifications are often written in the following way :
$$p(x) = 0 \Rightarrow f(x) \to e_1(x)$$
$$p(x) \neq 0 \Rightarrow f(x) \to e_2(x),$$
which is more natural than the version :
$$\text{zerop?}(x) = \text{True} \Rightarrow f(x) \to e_1(x)$$
$$\text{zerop?}(x) = \text{False} \Rightarrow f(x) \to e_2(x),$$
that one needs to use when restricted to strictly positive CTRS.

- The following system, inspired by the work of [BBK 87] on *priority rewrite rules* :
$$EQ(x,x) \to \text{True}$$
$$x \neq y \Rightarrow EQ(x,y) \to \text{False},$$
specifies in an elegant and generic way an equality predicate above any (canonical) specification. Note

that many interesting case of priority rewrite rules may be modelized by P/N CTRS.

We are now going to consider the algebraic, and then the operational semantics, of P/N systems.

2. Algebraic semantics

In this chapter, we address the question of the *algebraic* semantics of P/N systems, i.e. the class of their models. Rigorously, we have to consider P/N conditional *axioms*, that are like non-oriented P/N conditional rules (each '→' sign being replaced by an '=' sign). The satisfiability of a P/N axiom is defined as for positive conditional axioms.

A crucial difficulty is that, as opposed to the case of equations or strictly positive conditional axioms, *P/N axioms do not necessarily admit an initial model*. For instance, the system :
$$\{ \ a \neq b \ \Rightarrow \ a = c \ \}$$
(which *algebraically* equivalent to : a=b∨a=c, but not *operationally* - cf. hereafter), admits as finitely generated models :

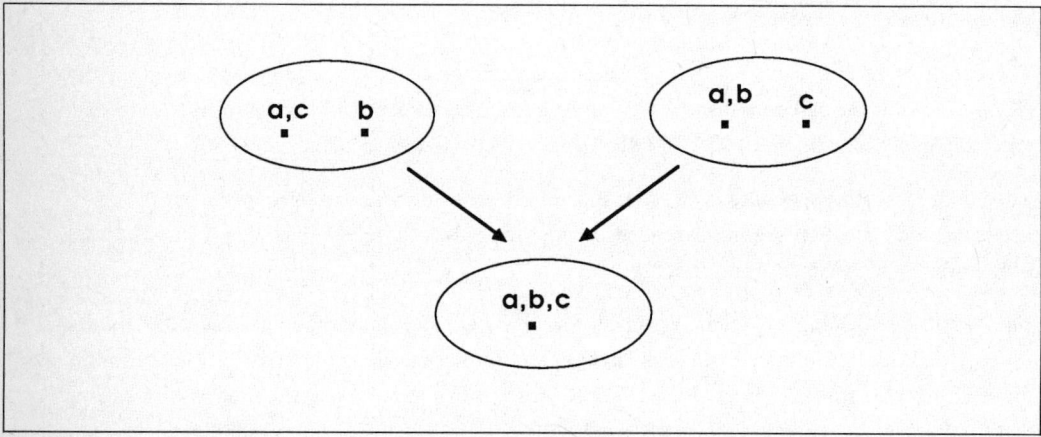

and thus no initial model. In this case, what is the algebraic semantics of a P/N system ?

To answer this question, let E be a given P/N system. Consider the following classical ordering between the models (up to an isomorphism) of E :
$$M \leq M' \quad \textit{iff} \quad \text{there exists a unique morphism } \phi \text{ from M into M'}.$$
We say that a model is *quasi-initial* if it is minimal for '≤'.

Theorem 2.1 :
(1) The models of E admit a non-empty class of quasi-initial models.
(2) The quasi-initial models are finitely generated.
(3) For any E-model M, there exists a quasi-initial model Q such that $Q \leq M$.

Proof of theorem 2.1 : cf. Appendix 1

Pictorially :

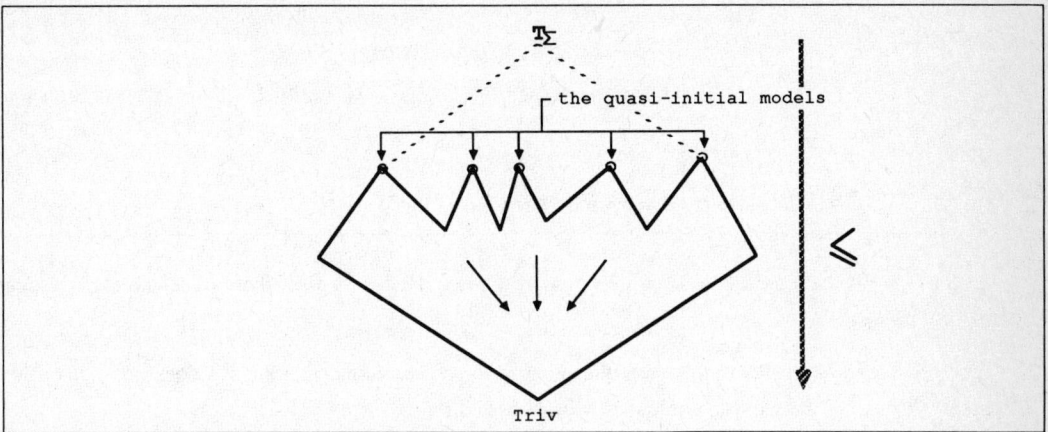

The quasi-initial models are the peaks of the class of the E-models.

We shall consider the semantics of a P/N system to be precisely the class of its quasi-initial models. We show in section 3 that, under favourable circumstances, the quasi-initial models are obtained as the normal-form algebra of the system, interpreted as a CTRS in "every possible fashion". In the case of the above example, there are two quasi-initial models, corresponding to the two (*reducing*) systems :

$$a \neq b \Rightarrow a \rightarrow c \quad \text{and} \quad a \neq c \Rightarrow a \rightarrow b.$$

A converse result may also be stated.

3. Operational semantics

In this section, we consider how P/N *rewrite rules* work, i.e. the operational semantics of P/N systems. As before, one difficulty with P/N systems stems from the fact that there is no smallest precongruence ("rewrite *relation*") satisfying the rules. For instance, for the system :

$$S_1 : \{ \ a \neq b \ \Rightarrow \ a \rightarrow c \ \},$$

the two relations :

$$R_1 : \{ a \rightarrow c \} \quad \text{and} \quad R_2 : \{ a \rightarrow b \}$$

are minimal, "satisfy" S_1, but are incomparable.

We draw the attention of the reader to the following point. A system such as S_1 is equivalent, from an algebraic point of view, to $\{a=b \lor a=c \}$, and thus to $\{a \neq c \Rightarrow a \rightarrow b\}$. However, when a specifier writes S_1, he adds an information, from the operational point of view, that does not exist under the form $\{a=b \lor a=c\}$. For instance, a definition such as $\{p(x) \neq 0 \Rightarrow f(x) \rightarrow exp\}$ should certainly not be operationally understood as $\{p(x)=0 \lor f(x)=exp\}$, nor as $\{f(x)=exp \Rightarrow p(x) \rightarrow 0\}$! Our treatment of positive/negative systems therefore has to take into account this additive information.

We now have the following result :

> **Definition and property 3.1**
> Given a reducing P/N system, there exists a well-defined, unique precongruence $\to_R$ on T_Σ such that :
>
> $\quad t \to_R t'$ *iff*
> $\quad\quad$ there exists a context $K[X]$, a substitution σ,
> $\quad\quad\quad$ a rule $r : (\wedge_{i=1}^{n} u_i = v_i) \wedge (\wedge_{j=1}^{m} \overline{u}_j \neq \overline{v}_j) \Rightarrow \lambda \to \rho$ of R
> $\quad\quad$ such that :
> $\quad\quad\quad t = K[\lambda\sigma], \ t' = K[\rho\sigma]$
> $\quad\quad\quad \forall i \in [1..n], \ u_i\sigma \downarrow_R v_i\sigma \ \text{and} \ \forall j \in [1..m], \ \overline{u}_j\sigma \downarrow_R \overline{v}_j\sigma$

As usual, $p\downarrow_R p'$ iff there exists a q such that $p\to_R^* q$, $p'\to_R^* q$, and $p\not\downarrow_R p'$ iff there exists no such q such that $p\to_R^* q$, $p'\to_R^* q$.

With the previous system $R = S_1$, $\to_R$ is the relation R_1. The second relation R_2 does not satisfy the statement : "$t \to t'$ *iff* there exists a rule r ..." with $t = a$ and $t' = b$.

Note :
The rewrite relation is defined on ground terms. It is easily extended to terms with variables, by having the variables play the role of constants. However, the resulting relation is *not* closed under substitution, i.e. $t\to_R t'$ does not imply $t\sigma\to_R t'\sigma$ (as opposed to the case of equational, or positive conditional rules). This justifies our consideration of rewriting on T_Σ mainly.

Proof of property 3.1
In order to prove property 3.1, we provide an explicit construction for $\to_R$. To this effect, we define the following sequence of binary relations :
- $\to_0 \ = \ \emptyset$
- $\to_{k+1} \ = \ \{(t,t') \mid$ there exists a context $K[X]$, a substitution σ and a rule r
  $\quad\quad$ that satisfy : $t = K[\lambda\sigma], \ t' = K[\rho\sigma]$
  $\quad\quad\quad \forall i \in [1..n], \ NF_{\to_k}(u_i\sigma) \cap NF_{\to_k}(v_i\sigma) \neq \emptyset$
  $\quad\quad\quad \forall j \in [1..m], \ NF_{\to_k}(\overline{u}_j\sigma) \cap NF_{\to_k}(\overline{v}_j\sigma) = \emptyset \ \}$

Here, '$NF_{\to_k}(t)$' stands for the set of the normal forms of t for $\to_k$. The next lemma ensures that this is meaningful :

> **Lemma 3.2**
> Given a reducing P/N CTRS R, for any term t, for any $k \geq 0$, each set $NF_{\to_k}(t)$ is well-defined, finite and computable.

Proof of lemma 3.2
- This is obvious for $k = 0$.
- We assume that the property holds for a given k and prove it for k+1. Let us define the ordering :
  $\quad\quad t >^{st} t'$ *iff* $t > t'$ or t' is a strict subterm of t.

$>^{st}$ is well-founded [JK 84]. We establish the desired property by $>^{st}$-induction [Huet 77], as most of the proofs in this paper. To this effect, consider the predicate :

$P(t)$: $NF_{\rightarrow_{k+1}}$ is well-defined, finite and computable.

We assume that, for a given t,

$$\forall \tau,\ t >^{st} \tau \Rightarrow P(\tau),$$

and we prove that $P(t)$. This will show that $P(t)$ holds for *any* t.

Given t as above, and a "matching triple" (K,σ,r), the sets $NF_{\rightarrow_k}(u_i\sigma)$, $NF_{\rightarrow_k}(v_i\sigma)$, $NF_{\rightarrow_k}(\overline{u}_j\sigma)$, $NF_{\rightarrow_k}(\overline{v}_j\sigma)$ are well-defined, finite and computable, by the hypothesis *on k*. Thus one may decide whether $t \rightarrow_{k+1} t'$ or not. If this is the case, due to the fact that $t >^{st} t'$, we have that $NF_{\rightarrow_{k+1}}(t')$ is well-defined, finite and computable ; this is then also the case for $NF_{\rightarrow_{k+1}}(t)$. □ lemma 3.2

This establishes that each relation $\rightarrow_k$ is well-defined.

We then have the next lemma :

Lemma 3.3 :

Given a reducing P/N CTRS R, for any t, there exists an integer $\psi(t)$ such that :

for any t',

either $\forall k \geq \psi(t),\ t \rightarrow_k t'$

or $\forall k \geq \psi(t),\ t \not\rightarrow_k t'$

Example :

Consider the system : $S_2 = \{\ a(0) \rightarrow \alpha,\ \text{even?}(n) = T \wedge a(n) \neq \alpha \Rightarrow a(s(n)) \rightarrow \alpha,$

$\text{even?}(n) = T \wedge a(n) = \alpha \Rightarrow a(s(s(n))) \rightarrow \alpha\ \}$

'even' is a built-in predicate, defined by : $\{\text{even}(0) \rightarrow T,\ \text{even}(s(0)) \rightarrow F,\ \text{even}(s(s(x))) \rightarrow \text{even}(x)\ \}$. We have :

$\rightarrow_k\ =\ \{\ a(0) \rightarrow \alpha,\ a(2) \rightarrow \alpha,\ ...,\ a(2k-2) \rightarrow \alpha,$

$a(2k-1) \rightarrow \alpha,\ a(2k+1) \rightarrow \alpha,\ a(2k+3) \rightarrow \alpha,\ ...\ \}$.

We can thus adopt : $\psi(a(n)) = n/2 + 1$.

Proof of lemma 3.3 :

As before, we proceed by $>^{st}$-induction. Consider the predicate :

$P(t)$ *iff* $\exists \psi(t),\ \forall t',\ $ either $\forall k \geq \psi(t), t \rightarrow_k t'$

or $\forall k \geq \psi(t), t \not\rightarrow_k t'$

(i.e. : the redexes of t are "stable" after some index $\psi(t)$). Suppose that, for a given t, $t >^{st} \tau$ implies that $P(\tau)$ holds. If (K,σ,r) is a matching triple for t, we have :

$$t >^{st} u_i\sigma,\ v_i\sigma,\ \overline{u}_j\sigma,\ \overline{v}_j\sigma.$$

Thus : $P(u_i\sigma)$, $P(v_i\sigma)$, $P(\overline{u}_j\sigma)$ and $P(\overline{v}_j\sigma)$. Let :

$$\psi\ =\ \text{Sup}_{K,\sigma,r}\ \text{Sup}_{i,j}\{\ \psi(u_i\sigma),\ \psi(v_i\sigma),\ \psi(\overline{u}_j\sigma),\ \psi(\overline{v}_j\sigma)\ \}$$

ψ is well-defined since $\text{Sup}_{K,\sigma,r}$ and $\text{Sup}_{i,j}$ range over finite sets of indices. Then $\psi(t) = \psi$ shows that $P(t)$. Thus, $P(t)$ holds for *any* t. □ lemma 3.3

We finally define '$\to_R$' by :

$$t \to_R t' \quad \textit{iff} \quad t \to_k t' \text{ for } k \geq \psi(t).$$

It is left to the reader to check that $\to_R$ satisfies definition 3.1.

Example :
With the previous system S_2, we have as "limit" :
$$\to_R = \{ a(0) \to \alpha, a(2) \to \alpha, \dots, a(2n) \to \alpha, \dots \}.$$

Lastly, the uniqueness of a relation satisfying the property of 3.1 is proved by $>^{st}$-induction, using the predicate :
$$P(t): \forall \tau (t s \tau \Leftrightarrow t \to_R \tau)$$
for another possible relation 's' ■ property 3.1

Note :
For strictly *positive* CTRS, as shown in [Kaplan 84a], the functional ∂ that associates to a finitely terminating and finitely branching precongruence $\to = \to_k$ the precongruence $\to_{k+1}$ as above, is shown to be continuous on the lattice of the precongruences ordered by inclusion. The least fixpoint of ∂ is the rewrite relation $\to_R$. It is constructed as l.u.b. of the $(\to_k)_{k \geq 0}$, starting with *any* $\to_0$. However, even for *reducing* positive/negative systems, the sequence $(\to_k)_{k \geq 0}$ is in general non-monotonic, as shown by the system S_2 above. However, lemma 3.3 ensures the existence of a "limit" $\to_R$. The choice of $\to_0$ matters for $\to_R$; for instance, with the reducing system S_1,
- starting with $\to_0 = \varnothing$ gives as a limit : $\{ a \to c \}$
- starting with $\to_0 = \{ a \to b \}$ gives as a limit : $\{ a \to b \}$ (which is not satisfactory).

For non-reducing systems, there may even be no "limit" to the sequence, as shown by the next example :

Let $S_3 = \{ a \neq b \Rightarrow c \to d, c \neq d \Rightarrow a \to b \}$
Then :
$$\to_0 = \varnothing, \quad \to_1 = \{ c \to d, a \to b \},$$
$$\to_2 = \varnothing, \quad \to_3 = \{ c \to d, a \to b \}, \quad \dots$$

All these points demonstrate the utility of *reducing* systems. This is even more striking for P/N systems than for strictly positive systems, since in the latter case $\to_R$ is always definable while this is not so in the former. On the other hand, this does not seem to be too drastic a restriction : the systems that one would write naturally are reducing in general. Lastly, notice that reducing systems are *finitely terminating*.

Consider now the following nondeterministic procedure :

```
function F(t)
    choose a rule r : (∧ⁿᵢ₌₁ uᵢ=vᵢ)∧(∧ᵐⱼ₌₁ ūⱼ≠v̄ⱼ) ⇒ λ → ρ in R
    such that t = K[λσ] and
             ∀i∈[1..n], F(uᵢσ) ∩ F(vᵢσ) ≠ ∅ ,
             ∀j∈[1..m], F(ūⱼσ) ∩ F(v̄ⱼσ) = ∅
    then return( F(K[ρσ]) )
    when-no-other-choice return( t )
end function
```

Here, computing the intersection of $F(u_i\sigma)$ and $F(v_i\sigma)$ (resp. $F(\bar{u}_j\sigma)$ and $F(\bar{v}_j\sigma)$) means that, after finding a possible match σ, one recursively performs *all* the non-deterministic computations of the F's ; this produces *sets* of results that are compared two by two. Note that this may be improved when $\to_R$ is known to be confluent (cf. theorem 3.4). We then have the following correctness result :

Theorem 3.4
(1) For a reducing P/N system R, the function 'F' computes in a totally correct fashion the normal forms of t for $\to_R$.
(2) Let R a reducing P/N system such that $\to_R$ is confluent. Then 'F' is still totally correct if instead of comparing the *sets* $F(u_i\sigma)$ and $F(v_i\sigma)$ (resp. $F(\bar{u}_j\sigma)$ and $F(\bar{v}_j\sigma)$), one checks whether :
$$F(u_i\sigma) = F(v_i\sigma) \text{ and } F(\bar{u}_j\sigma) \neq F(\bar{v}_j\sigma)) \quad (\forall i,j)$$
for *any* execution of the recursive calls.

Total correctness means that all parallel branches eventually terminate, and that the set of results computed this way is the set of the normal forms of t.

Proof :
(1) Consider the predicate :
    $P(t)$: $F(t)$ computes the set $NF_R(t)$ in a totally correct fashion.
Let t such that $t >^{st} \tau \Rightarrow P(\tau)$. Let (K,σ,r) be a matching triple for t ; we have :
$$t >^{st} u_i\sigma, v_i\sigma, \bar{u}_j\sigma, \bar{v}_j\sigma,$$
and F computes correctly the set of the normal form of these terms. Let :
$$\psi = \text{Sup} (\psi(t), \text{Sup}_{K,\sigma,r} \text{Sup}_{i,j} \{\psi(u_i\sigma), \psi(v_i\sigma), \psi(\bar{u}_j\sigma), \psi(\bar{v}_j\sigma) \})$$
Then the normal forms $\to_R$ and for $\to_\psi$ coincide on t and the $u_i\sigma, v_i\sigma, \bar{u}_j\sigma, \bar{v}_j\sigma$. This implies the (total) correctness of F on t, i.e. $P(t)$. □
(2) The second point follows from the fact that when $\to_R$ is confluent, each *set* $F(u_i\sigma)$, etc... is actually a singleton. ■

We then have the fundamental result :

Theorem 3.5

Given a *reducing* P/N CTRS R such that $\to_R$ is confluent, the algebra Q_R of the normal forms for $\to_R$ of the terms of T_Σ is a quasi-initial model of R.

Proof : cf. Appendix 2

This result states the connection between the algebraic and the operational aspects of P/N systems : the algebra of normal forms, which may be computed by the above procedure, provides one *peak* in the class of the models of R (considered canonically as a set of P/N axioms).

Having shown that rewriting determines quasi-initial models, we now examine the converse. To this effect, we associate to any P/N axiom in *premise form* :

$$(\wedge_{i=1}^n u_i = v_i) \wedge (\wedge_{j=1}^m \overline{u}_j \neq \overline{v}_j) \;\Rightarrow\; \lambda = \rho$$

its *disjunctive form* :

$$(\wedge_{i=1}^n u_i = v_i) \;\Rightarrow\; \lambda = \rho \;\vee\; (\vee_{j=1}^m \overline{u}_j = \overline{v}_j).$$

Conversely, to any disjunctive form : $\wedge_{i=1}^n u_i = v_i \Rightarrow \vee_{k=1}^p a_k = b_k$, one may associate *2p* distinct P/N axioms in premise form (factor '2' coming from the fact that one is a priori free to chose the orientation of the conclusion).

Similarly, to a finite family of P/N axioms, we can associate a family of disjunctive form axioms, to which we can in turn associate a family of P/N *premise form* rewriting systems (choosing the orientation in the premises). For instance :

$$\{\, a \neq b \;\Rightarrow\; c \to d \,\} \quad\text{-->}\quad \{\, a = b \vee c = d \,\} \quad\text{-->}\quad \begin{array}{l} \{\, a \neq b \;\Rightarrow\; c \to d \,\} \\ \{\, c \neq d \;\Rightarrow\; a \to b \,\} \end{array}$$

$\longleftarrow$-- P/N CTRS --$\longrightarrow$ $\qquad\qquad$ $\longleftarrow$-- disjunctive form --$\longrightarrow$ $\qquad\qquad$ $\longleftarrow$-- family of P/N CTRS --$\longrightarrow$

For axioms having variables, we take as disjunctive normal form the family of all the ground instances of the disjunctive form of the axiom, and then only consider the possible P/N CTRS. For instance, with the system :

$$S_5 \;=\; \{\, a(x) \neq b(x) \;\Rightarrow\; c(x) \to d(x) \,\}$$

one possible association is :

$$\begin{array}{rcl}
a(0) \neq b(0) & \Rightarrow & c(0) \to d(0) \\
c(s(0)) \neq d(s(0)) & \Rightarrow & a(s(0)) \to b(s(0)) \\
a(s(s(0))) \neq b(s(s(0))) & \Rightarrow & c(s(s(0))) \to d(s(s(0))) \\
c(s(s(s(0)))) \neq d(s(s(s(0)))) & \Rightarrow & a(s(s(s(0)))) \to b(s(s(s(0)))) \\
& \cdots &
\end{array}$$

> **Theorem 3.6**
> Given a family of P/N axioms E in disjunctive form, such that for any premise form rewriting system R of it, R is reducing and $\to_R$ is confluent. Then the family of the Q_R obtained this way coincides with the family of quasi-initial models.

Proof : cf. Appendix 3

Intuitively, this states that all the quasi-initial models may be obtained by rewriting (provided that the premise form systems are all reducing and confluent). The theorem is mainly interesting as a converse of theorem 3.5. Notice that its hypothesis is fulfilled for instance by the above systems S_1 and S_5.

For example, as announced before, the quasi-initial models of $\{a = b \lor c = d\}$ are obtained as normal form algebras of $\{a \neq b \Rightarrow c \to d\}$ and $\{c \neq d \Rightarrow a \to b\}$.

4. Confluence results

In this section, we address the question of the *confluence* of *reducing* P/N systems, by providing a criterion *à la* Knuth-Bendix.

To introduce our results, consider the following example :
$$\text{even?}(x) = T \Rightarrow \text{odd?}(x) \to F,$$
$$\text{even?}(x) \neq T \Rightarrow \text{odd?}(x) \to T,$$
(the predicate 'even?' having been defined previously). We notice that, with the traditional approach, $<T,F>$ is a critical pair [deduced from the term 'odd?(x)']. However, this critical pair may be obtained only under the condition even?(x)=T∧even?(x)≠T, which is never realized; we say that even?(x)=T∧even?(x)≠T $\Rightarrow$ $<T,F>$ is a *contextual critical pair*, the context of which 'even?(x)=T∧even?(x)=F' is not "satisfiable". Such pairs need not of course be considered when checking for confluence.

> **Definition 4.1**
> • Given a reducing system R and two rules in R :
> $$r_1 : (\wedge_{i=1}^{n_1} u_{1,i} = v_{1,i}) \wedge (\wedge_{j=1}^{m_1} \overline{u}_{1,j} \neq \overline{v}_{1,j}) \Rightarrow \lambda_1 \to \rho_1$$
> and
> $$r_2 : (\wedge_{i=1}^{n_2} u_{2,i} = v_{2,i}) \wedge (\wedge_{j=1}^{m_2} \overline{u}_{2,j} \neq \overline{v}_{2,j}) \Rightarrow \lambda_2 \to \rho_2$$
> such that $\lambda_{1|\omega}$ and λ_2 are unifiable, ω being a non variable occurrence of λ_1. Let μ be their most general unifier. The formula :
> $$((\wedge_{i=1}^{m_1} u_{1,i} = v_{1,i}) \wedge (\wedge_{i=1}^{m_2} u_{2,i} = v_{2,i}) \wedge (\wedge_{j=1}^{m_1} \overline{u}_{1,j} \neq \overline{v}_{1,j}) \wedge (\wedge_{j=1}^{m_2} \overline{u}_{2,j} \neq \overline{v}_{2,j}))\mu$$
> $$\Rightarrow <\lambda_1\mu[\omega \leftarrow \rho_2\mu], \rho_1\mu>$$
> is called a *contextual critical pair* [abbreviated CCP] with associated *critical context*:
> $$((\wedge_{i=1}^{m_1} u_{1,i} = v_{1,i}) \wedge (\wedge_{i=1}^{m_2} u_{2,i} = v_{2,i}) \wedge (\wedge_{j=1}^{m_1} \overline{u}_{1,j} \neq \overline{v}_{1,j}) \wedge (\wedge_{j=1}^{m_2} \overline{u}_{2,j} \neq \overline{v}_{2,j}))\mu$$

From now on, we abbreviate the premises of r_1 and r_2 by P_1 and P_2 when no confusion arises. The critical context is then $P_1\mu \wedge P_2\mu$.

For a positive/negative clause C : $(\wedge_{i=1}^{n} a_i = b_i) \wedge (\wedge_{j=1}^{m} \overline{a}_j \neq \overline{b}_j)$, we write $(C)\downarrow_R$ whenever : $a_i \downarrow_R b_i$ and $\overline{a}_j \downarrow_R \overline{b}_j$ ($\forall i,j$).

We then have the result :

Theorem 4.2
[Knuth-Bendix theorem for reducing positive/negative conditional TRS]
Given a reducing system R,
$\rightarrow_R$ is locally confluent (and thus confluent) on T_Σ *iff*
for any contextual critical pair $C \Rightarrow <t,t'>$, for any substitution $\zeta : X \rightarrow T_\Sigma$,
if $(C\zeta)\downarrow_R$, then $t\zeta \downarrow_R t'\zeta$.

Proof : cf. Appendix 4

This result extends the classical Knuth-Bendix criterion for equational systems (cf. [Huet 77]) and for conditional systems (cf. [Kaplan 84b], [JW 86], [Ganziger 86]), to the framework of positive/negative systems.

CONCLUSION

We defined in this paper a rigorous basis for the treatment of positive/negative conditional rules. Our approach manages to preserve the coherence between the algebraic and the operational aspects of such systems, in spite of the non-existence of *one* "optimal" model. We assign precise semantics to the information contained in a formula such as $a \neq b \Rightarrow c \rightarrow d$, which is certainly relevant to a specifier but disappears in the algebraic formulation $a=b \vee c=d$.

For these purposes, the notion of reducing systems appears essential. It allows one to define proper semantics for such systems, which is not possible for certain non-reducing systems. The correctness of a universal interpreter was proved. For confluent reducing systems, normal form algebras are quasi-initial models and conversely, under favorable circumstances, the quasi-initial models are obtained by normal form algebras. Lastly, a critical pair criterion is obtained, to check for the confluence of these systems.

On the whole, positive/negative conditional reducing systems do not appear, within our approach, to be more intractable *in practice* than the positive systems studied for instance in [Kaplan 84b,87], [JW 86], [RZ 84,85], [Ganziger 86], etc. (though their mathematical semantics are more complex).

As a direction for future research, the connection between negative conditional rewriting and logic programming with failure ([BH 86], [ABW 87], [Lifshitz 86]) should be examined. The previous works have been extended by [Przymusinski 86], which relies on the notions of locally stratified programs and perfect models; these concepts bear close resemblance respectively to our reducing systems and to our quasi-initial models. Przymusinski's systems are constrained to conditions interpretable into $\lambda\sigma > \overline{u}_j\sigma, \overline{v}_j\sigma$ (though not necessarily $\lambda\sigma > u_i\sigma, v_i\sigma$). However, they manipulate boolean predicates (instead of equations between terms in our case), and via outermost reduction strategies.

As already mentioned, we make use the partial information stated by a specifier, when writing a formula $a \neq b \Rightarrow c \rightarrow d$ instead of $a=b \vee c=d$. It might also be interesting to examine the latter form, which concerns properties that hold in *all* the quasi-initial models. However, we believe that the first approach, which is the one developed in this paper, is more natural as a specification method and as a high-level programming paradigm.

ACKNOWLEDGEMENTS :

I thank Nachum Dershowitz, Krzysztof Apt and Jan-Willem Klop for fruitful discussion and comments.

The research reported on here has been partially supported by the METEOR Esprit Contract.

REFERENCES

[ABW 87] K. Apt, H. Blair, A. Walker, *Towards a theory of declarative knowledge*, I.B.M. T.J. Watson Research Center Report, submitted for publication (1987)

[ADJ 78] J.A. Goguen, J.W. Thatcher, E.G. Wagner, *An Initial Algebra Approach to the Specification, Correctness, and Implementation of Abstract Data Types*, Current Trends in Programming Methodology, Vol. 4, Ed. Yeh R., Prentice-Hall, pp. 80-149 (1978)

[BBK 87] J. Baeten, J. Bergstra, J.W. Klop, *Term rewriting systems with priority*, Proc. of the RTA'87 Conf., LNCS 256, Springer Verlag (1987)

[BBWT 81] J. Bergstra, M. Broy, M. Wirsing, J. Tucker, *On the power of algebraic specifications*, Proc. of the MFCS'81 Conference, LNCS 118 (1981)

[BH 86] N. Bidoit, R. Hull, *Positivism vs. Minimalism in Deductive Data Bases*, Proc. of the ACM SIGACT-SIGMOD Symposium on Principle of Data Base Systems, Cambridge (1986)

[Dershowitz 85] N. Dershowitz, *Termination*, Proc. of the 1st Conf. on Rewriting Techniques and Applications, LNCS 202, Dijon - France (1985)

[EM 85] H. Ehrig, B. Mahr, *Fundamentals of algebraic specifications. I : Equations and initial semantics*, EATCS monographs on Theoretical Computer Science, Springer Verlag (1985)

[Ganziger 86] H. Ganziger, *Ground term confluence in parametric conditional equational specifications*, Proc. of the STACS'87 Conf., LNCS 252, Springer Verlag (1987)

[Huet 77] G. Huet, *Confluent reductions : abstract properties and applications to term rewriting systems*, Proc. of the 18th FOCS Conf., Providence (1978)

[HO 80] G. Huet, D.C. Oppen, *Equations and rewrite rules : a survey*, Formal languages : Perspective and open problems, R. Book Ed., Academic Press (1980)

[JK 84] J.-P. Jouannaud, C. Kirchner, *Completion of a set of rules modulo a set of equations*, Proc. of the 11th POPL Conf. (1984)

[JW 86] J.-P. Jouannaud, B. Waldmann, *Reductive conditional term rewriting systems*, Proc. of the 3rd TC2 Working Conf. on the formal Description of Programming Concepts, North-Holland Pub. Company (1986)

[Kaplan 82] S. Kaplan,

Specifications of abstract data types: the power of several classes of axioms with semi-decidable congruence, Proc. of the AFCET Mathematics for Computer Science Conf., Paris (1982)

[Kaplan 84a]   S. Kaplan, *Conditional rewrite rules*, TCS 33 (1984)

[Kaplan 84b]   S. Kaplan, *Fair conditional term rewrite systems*, Report 194, University of Paris-South (1984)

[Kaplan 87]   S. Kaplan, *Simplifying conditional term rewriting systems,* to appear in the Journal of Symbolic Computation (1987)

[Klop 87]   J.W. Klop, *Term rewriting systems : a tutorial*, Bulletin of the EATCS, 32, pp. 143-183 (1987)

[Lifschitz 86]   V. Lifschitz, *On the declarative semantics of logic programs with negation*, Workshop on the Foundations of Deductive Data Bases and Logic Programming, Washington D.C. (1986)

[Przymusinski 86]   T.C. Przymusinski, *On the semantics of stratified deductive databases*, Workshop on the Foundations of Deductive Data Bases and Logic Programming, Washington D.C. (1986)

[RZ 84]   J.L. Rémy, H. Zhang, *REVEUR4 : a system for validating conditional algebraic specifications of abstract data types,* Proc. of the 6th ECAI Conf. (1984)

[RZ 85]   J.L. Rémy, H. Zhang, *Contextual rewriting*, Proc. of the 1st RTA Conf., LNCS 202, Springer Verlag (1985)

Appendix 1 : Proof of theorem 2.1

(1) We show that the class of the E-models is inductive. Let $(M_i)_{i \in I}$ be an decreasing chain for '$\leq$'. Let M_∞ be the "limit" defined as the set of chains $(t_i)_{i \in I}$ with :
- $t_i \in M_i$
- $t_{i+1} = \phi_i(t_i)$, where f_i is the unique morphism from M_i to M_{i+1}.

Let $\overline{M_\infty}$ be the finitely generated part of M_∞. Then $\overline{M_\infty}$ is an inf of $(M_i)_{i \in I}$: $inj \circ \pi_i$ (where 'inj' is the canonical injection $\overline{M_\infty} \to M_\infty$, and '$\pi_i$' is the projection $M_\infty \to M_i$) is a morphism from $\overline{M_\infty}$ into M_i, and it is unique.

Via Zorn's lemma, the class of the E-models admits a minimal element, which is quasi-initial by construction. □

(2) This comes from the fact that for any model M, there exists a unique morphism from its finitely generated part Gen(M) into M. □

(3) For a given E-model M, let Gen_M be the class of the E-models N such that $Gen(M) \leq N$. Then, similarly, Gen_M is inductive ; any minimal element Q of Gen_M is quasi-initial, and satisfies $Q \leq M$. ■

Appendix 2 : Proof of theorem 3.5

Firstly, Q_R is considered as an algebra by letting :
$$f^{Q_R}[NF_{\to_R}(t_1),...,NF_{\to_R}(t_n)] =_{def} NF_{\to_R}[f(t_1,...,t_n)].$$
The confluence of $\to_R$ ensures the well-definedness of each f^{Q_R}.

Since Q_R is known to be a R-model, we simply have to prove its minimality. By *reductio ad absurdum*, we suppose that there exists an R-model M and a morphism $\phi : M \to Q_R$. We may suppose that M is finitely generated. If ϕ is not an isomorphism, there exist τ and τ' in M such that $\tau \neq \tau$' and $\phi(\tau) = \phi(\tau')$. We have :
$$\tau = t^M \quad \text{and} \quad \tau = t'^M,$$
for two terms t and t'. Since there is a unique morphism from T_Σ into Q_R, it coincides with $\phi \circ (\ )^M$. Thus : $t\downarrow_R = t'\downarrow_R = \alpha$. One shows by $>^{st}$-induction that if $u \to_R v$, then $u^M = v^M$. Thus, $t^M = \alpha^M = t'^M$, which contradicts $\tau \neq \tau$'. ■

Appendix 3 : Proof of theorem 3.6

It is sufficient to show that any (finitely generated) quasi-initial model M is isomorphic to some Q_R. So, for any ground instance of the disjunctive form of an axiom of E :
$$\wedge_{i=1}^n u_i \sigma = v_i \sigma \Rightarrow \lambda = \rho \vee (\vee_{j=1}^m \overline{u}_j \sigma = \overline{v}_j \sigma),$$
one chooses one of the literals of the disjunction that is valid in M, say : $\overline{u}_{j_0} \sigma = \overline{v}_{j_0} \sigma$. Then one considers the rule :
$$\wedge_{i=1}^n u_i \sigma = v_i \sigma \wedge \lambda \neq \rho \wedge (\wedge_{j \neq j_0} \overline{u}_j \sigma \neq \overline{v}_j \sigma) \Rightarrow \overline{u}_{j_0} \sigma \to \overline{v}_{j_0} \sigma$$
(up to the orientation). We assume, as in the theorem, that the orientations may be globally chosen such that the resulting system R is reducing and confluent. Consider the reduction ordering > associated to R. We show by $>^{st}$-induction that for any term t, $M \vDash t^M = NF_{\to_R}(t)$.

Assume that this holds for any τ such that $t >^{st} \tau$. If t is irreducible for $\to_R$, there is nothing to prove. Otherwise, we suppose that $t \to_R t' \to_R^* NF_{\to_R}(t)$. Then, since $t >^{st} t'$, $M \models t'^M = NF_{\to_R}(t') = NF_{\to_R}(t)$. Now, by construction of the rules of R, $M \models t = t'$.

Then, the application ϕ from Q_I into M defined by : $\phi(NF_{\to_R}(t)) = t^M$ is well-defined. It is a morphism, and is unique since Q_I is finitely generated. So, it is an isomorphism. ∎

Appendix 4 : Proof of theorem 4.2

We prove by $>^{st}$-induction that, under the assumptions of the theorem, for any term τ such that $\tau \to_R^* \tau_1, \tau_2$, then $\tau_1 \downarrow_R \tau_2$. We assume that this holds for any τ such that $t >^{st} \tau$, and prove that this is also true for t. We suppose that $t \to_{r_1} \bar{t}_1 \to_R^* t_1$ and $t \to_{r_2} \bar{t}_2 \to_R^* t_2$. Since $t >^{st} \bar{t}_1, \bar{t}_2$, it is sufficient to prove that $\bar{t}_1 \downarrow_R \bar{t}_2$. Let us denote by ω_1 and ω_2 the occurrences of the term t where the rules r_1 and r_2 apply, and σ_1 and σ_2 the respective matching substitutions. As usual, there are three cases to consider.

(1) ω_1 and ω_2 are *orthogonal* (i.e. no one is on the path from the root of t to the other). Then :
$$\bar{t}_1 \to_{r_2} t[\omega_1 \leftarrow \rho\sigma_1, \omega_2 \leftarrow \rho\sigma_2] \text{ and } \bar{t}_2 \to_{r_1} t[\omega_1 \leftarrow \rho\sigma_1, \omega_2 \leftarrow \rho\sigma_2].$$

(2) ω_1 is between the root of t and ω_2, so that ω_2 is a *not* the occurrence of a variable of $\lambda\sigma_1$. Then $\sigma = \sigma_1 \cup \sigma_2$ is a unifier of $\lambda_{1|\omega}$ and λ_2 (with $\omega = \omega_1 - \omega_2$). Thus, we have : $\sigma = \mu\zeta$ for a certain substitution ζ. Now, since $(P_1\sigma_1)\downarrow_R$ and $(P_2\sigma_2)\downarrow_R$, this implies that $((P_1 \wedge P_2)\mu\zeta)\downarrow_R$. The hypothesis of the theorem yields : $\bar{t}1 \downarrow_R \bar{t}2$.

(3) ω_1 is between the root of t and ω_2, so that ω_2 is the occurrence of a variable x of $\lambda\sigma_1$. Then $t_{|\omega_1} \to_{r_2} \lambda_1\sigma_1[\omega \leftarrow \rho_2\sigma_2] \to_{r_2}^* \lambda_1\sigma_1[x \leftarrow \rho_2\sigma_2]$. Let $\sigma'_1 = \sigma \cup \{x \leftarrow \rho_2\sigma_2\}$. We are going to show that $(P_1\sigma'_1)\downarrow_R$. Then, it will be possible to apply r_1 to $\lambda_1\sigma'_1$, yielding $t_{2|\omega_1} \to_R^* \rho_1\sigma'_1 = t'$. On the other hand, it is clear that $t_{1|\omega_1} \to_R^* t'$, which terminates the proof.

Proof that $(P_1\sigma'_1) \downarrow_R$:

Let $P_1 = (\wedge_i a_i = b_i) \wedge (\wedge_j \bar{a}_j \neq \bar{b}_j)$. Then :

• For any i, we have : $a_i\sigma'_1 \stackrel{*}{\leftarrow}_R a_i\sigma_1 \to_R^* b_i\sigma_1 \to^* b_i\sigma'_1$. Now, one may apply the $>^{st}$-induction hypothesis, since $t >^{st} a_i\sigma_1$, $b_i\sigma_1$. This gives : $a_i\sigma'_1 \downarrow_R b_i\sigma'_1$.

• For any j, we have : $\bar{a}_j\sigma_1 \to_R^* \bar{a}_j\sigma'_1$, $\bar{b}_j\sigma_1 \to_R^* \bar{b}_j\sigma'_1$. We derive that : $\bar{a}_j\sigma'_1 \not\downarrow_R \bar{b}_j\sigma'_1$, since otherwise, one would have : $\bar{a}_j\sigma_1 \downarrow_R \bar{b}_j\sigma_1$.

This terminates the proof of theorem 4.2 ∎

Semi-Unification*

Deepak Kapur
State University of New York at Albany
Computer Science Department
Albany, NY 12222

David Musser
Rensselaer Polytechnic Institute
Computer Science Department
Troy, NY 12181

Paliath Narendran
General Electric Company
Corporate Research and Development
Schenectady, NY 12345

Jonathan Stillman
State University of New York at Albany
Computer Science Department
Albany, NY 12222

Abstract

Semi-unification is a generalization of both matching and ordinary unification: for a given pair of terms s and t, two substitutions ρ and σ are sought such that $\rho(\sigma(s)) = \sigma(t)$. Semi-unifiability can be used as a check for non-termination of a rewrite rule, but constructing a correct semi-unification algorithm has been an elusive goal; for example, an algorithm given by Purdom in his RTA-87 paper was incorrect. This paper presents a decision procedure for semi-unification based on techniques similar to those used in the Knuth-Bendix completion procedure. When its inputs are semi-unifiable, the procedure yields a canonical term-rewriting system from which substitutions ρ and σ are easily extracted. Though exponential in its computing time, the decision procedure can be improved to a polynomial time algorithm, as will be shown.

1 Introduction

Term rewriting systems have many uses, including formula simplification, deciding equations, program transformation, program verification, and checking consistency and completeness of abstract data type specifications. In these and many other applications, it is necessary that a set of rewrite rules have the property of *uniform termination*; i.e., every sequence of rewrites using the rules is finite (ends with a term to which no rule applies). Although uniform termination is undecidable in general [6], a number of sufficient conditions have been proposed in the literature [3] and checks for these conditions have been implemented in theorem proving systems such as RRL [9]. Here we consider the dual problem, i.e., that of exhibiting a

---

*Some of the results reported here are a partial fulfillment of the Ph.D. requirements of the last author, and will be part of his dissertation.

sufficient condition for *nontermination*. One condition that has been proposed [12] is based on *left-unification*, a generalization of matching and unification. This is a local condition on a single rule and is useful as a first check on rules proposed to be included in a term rewriting system as they may be generated, for example, by the Knuth-Bendix procedure [10,7] for completing a given set of rules into a decision procedure for an equational theory. A rule that satisfies the condition is nonterminating by itself; thus, there is no point in attempting to prove uniform termination of a term rewriting system that includes it. A typical situation in a rewrite rule based theorem prover such as RRL is that if a newly generated equation cannot be oriented under a termination ordering used to orient previously considered equations, then an extension to the ordering is attempted under which the new equation can be oriented. In case such an extension cannot be guessed easily, it might be useful to perform the check for left-unification of both the orientations of the new equation before the user has to backtrack to a previous decision point where the ordering was last extended and try a different extension.

The purpose of this paper is to present a left-unification algorithm, outline a proof of its correctness (an algorithm previously given by Purdom [15] was incorrect, as we will show), and to improve the efficiency of the algorithm from exponential to polynomial time. First, we return to the motivation for generalizing unification.

There are some obvious conditions on a rule that are sufficient for it to be nonterminating. For example, if the left-hand side of a proposed rule *matches* a nonvariable subterm of the right-hand side, as in

$$f(x) \to g(x, a, f(h(x)))$$

then the rule is nonterminating (in these examples, a, b, c are constants and x, y, z are variables). Another sufficient condition for nontermination is that the left-hand side *unifies* with a nonvariable subterm, as in

$$f(a, x) \to g(f(x, a)),$$

where the substitution $\theta = \{x \leftarrow a\}$ unifies the left side with the subterm $f(x, a)$ of the right side.

However, in an example like

$$f(g(x), a, y) \to f(g(g(x)), y, a) \tag{1}$$

the left-hand side neither matches nor unifies with any subterm of the right-hand side, but the rule is nonterminating: e.g.,

$$f(g(x), a, a) \to f(g(g(x)), a, a) \to f(g(g(g(x))), a, a) \to \ldots.$$

A more comprehensive sufficient condition for nontermination is based on the following:

Definition 1 *Given an ordered pair of terms s and t, we say s* left-unifies *with t if there is a pair of substitutions ρ and σ such that*

$$\rho(\sigma(s)) = \sigma(t).$$

For example, with the rule (1), the left-hand side left-unifies with the right-hand side, with $\sigma = \{y \leftarrow a\}$ and $\rho = \{x \leftarrow g(x)\}$.

Left-unification properly generalizes both matching (the case when σ is the identity substitution) and ordinary unification (when ρ is the identity substitution). Of course, one could define a corresponding notion of *right-unification*; we use the term *semi-unification* to signify either left- or right-unification. It is obvious that two terms may be semi-unifiable despite their being not unifiable; the pair of terms x and $f(x)$ is a simple example.

We have the following simple theorem, which says that left-unification can be used as a basis of a sufficient condition for nontermination.

Theorem 1 *If the left-hand side of a rewrite rule left-unifies with a nonvariable subterm of the right-hand side, the rule is nonterminating.*

Proof: Suppose $L \to R$ is the rule and $\rho(\sigma(L)) = \sigma(R')$ for some nonvariable subterm R' of R. Then
$$\rho(\sigma(L)) \to \rho(\sigma(R))$$
and within $\rho(\sigma(R))$ the subterm $\rho(\sigma(R'))$ occurs, which is equal to $\rho(\rho(\sigma(L)))$ and therefore can be rewritten to $\rho(\rho(\sigma(R))$, and so on. □

The condition of Theorem 1 is not necessary for nontermination; a simple example (given in [3]) is
$$f(g(x)) \to g(g(f(f(x))))$$
which is nonterminating (consider the term $f(f(g(a)))$, for example) even though the $f(g(x))$ fails to left-unify with any nonvariable subterm of $g(g(f(f(x))))$. Nevertheless, many nonterminating rules found in practice do satisfy the condition.

Musser and Lankford defined the notion of left-unification and discussed its use as a sufficient condition for nontermination based on the above theorem in a privately circulated 1978 memo [12]. Attempts were made to use the test in the Affirm program verification system [16] as part of an implementation of the Knuth-Bendix completion procedure, but a fully correct left-unification algorithm was not known at the time. Dershowitz cited [12] and discussed the problem as part of his comprehensive survey of rewrite-rule termination and nontermination in [3]. Purdom [15] studied the problem, presented a left-unification algorithm and a generalization of Theorem 1, and reported extensive positive experience with its use in testing for nontermination of rules in the Knuth-Bendix completion procedure. Unfortunately, however, Purdom's algorithm was not correct; a counter-example is the pair of terms $s = f(h(y), x)$ and $t = f(x, h(h(y)))$, which will be discussed later.

Another practical application of left-unification which has been suggested recently arises in the area of *type inference* in extensions of the Milner Calculus (the typed λ-calculus which underlies the programming languages ML, Miranda, and several other strongly typed polymorphic functional languages). This is discussed more fully in [4], where it is shown that one can reduce the polymorphic type inference problem for an extension of the Milner Calculus to a generalized left-unification problem.

In this paper we present two algorithms for left-unification and outline proofs of their correctness. (Obviously a left-unification algorithm can also be used as a right-unification algorithm merely by reversing the order of the pair of input terms s and t.) The first algorithm is presented mainly for expository purposes, as it takes exponential computing time in the worst case; we show that the second, more complex algorithm has a polynomial time bound.

The first algorithm is presented in two parts: a decision procedure for semi-unifiability, and an algorithm for extracting the semi-unifying substitutions from information computed by the decision procedure. Note that the application to testing for nontermination of a rewrite rule only requires the result of the decision procedure.

2 A Decision Procedure

We show how to construct, given an instance of semi-unification, an equational algebra such that semi-unifiability of the original problem is equivalent to a certain syntactic condition on the algebra. The equational algebra can be said to "model" the semi-unification problem. The construction of this equational algebra is outlined below.

Let s and t be the input terms and ρ and σ be the substitutions that we are looking for, such that $\rho(\sigma(s)) = \sigma(t)$. Let V stand for the set of variables occurring in s and t and F stand for the set of function symbols in s and t. For each variable x in V, we have a constant symbol s_x which represents $\sigma(x)$. Let θ be the substitution that maps every x in V to the corresponding s_x; i.e.,

$$\theta = \{x \leftarrow s_x \mid x \in V\}.$$

Note that since θ is a bijection, θ^{-1} is also a bijection.

The equational algebra $E(s,t)$ consists of the equation

$$\rho(\theta(s)) = \theta(t),$$

along with the following equations which expresses the fact that ρ "distributes" over the function symbols; thus for each f in F, we have

$$\rho(f(x_1,\ldots,x_n)) = f(\rho(x_1),\ldots,\rho(x_n))$$

where $x_1, \ldots, x_n$ are variables and n is the arity of f.

We also have some meta-rules expressing the cancellativity of functions in F. That is,

$$f(x_1,\ldots,x_n) = f(y_1,\ldots,y_n) \text{ implies } x_1 = y_1, \ldots, x_n = y_n$$

for every function f in F, where $n = \text{arity}(f)$. These meta-rules are obtained from the fact that in order to unify (or match) two terms with the same outermost function symbol, their respective arguments must be unified (matched).

It can be seen easily that this equational theory is essentially a collection of properties that ρ and σ have to satisfy in order for them to semi-unify s and t. For instance, the "distribution" equations express the fact that the substitutions are applied only to variables.

Let $=_E$ stand for the congruence generated by $E(s,t)$.

We can now give an algorithm for the semi-unification problem, which we divide into two parts:

Algorithm A-1: This algorithm decides whether two given terms can be semi-unified or not, and produces a canonical rewriting system [7] if the given terms are semi-unifiable.

Algorithm A-2: This algorithm extracts the matching substitution ρ and the unifying substitution σ from the rewriting system produced by Algorithm A-1.

This algorithm is simple at the cost of being exponential in the size of the input terms. In the next section, a modification of Algorithm A-1 is discussed which is shown to run in a number of steps polynomial in the size of the input terms.

Algorithm A-1 (For deciding semi-unifiability):

Step 1. Start with the equation

$$\rho(\sigma(s)) = \sigma(t).$$

Step 2. Apply the distributivity equations and the meta-rules of cancellativity discussed above to obtain equations such that at least one side of every equation is either of the form s_x or $\rho^i(s_x)$, where x is a variable in V. In this process, if either of the following two conditions arises, then we stop and report failure.

1. *Root conflict*, i.e., an equation $f(s_1, \ldots, s_n) = g(t_1, \ldots, t_m)$ is encountered where f and g are distinct function symbols.

2. An equation $\rho^i s_x = f(\ldots \rho^{i+j} s_x \ldots)$ is encountered, where by $f(\ldots \rho^{i+j} s_x \ldots)$ we mean a term with f as the top-level symbol and $\rho^{i+j} s_x$ as a subterm. This situation is similar to the "occurs check" in ordinary unification.

It is shown later that the above two conditions are necessary and sufficient for terms s and t to be not semi-unifiable.

Step 3. The equations derived in Step 2 are oriented into rewrite rules as follows:

1. A total ordering $\succ$ is defined on the set $S = \{ s_x \mid x \in V \}$.

2. A term containing symbols from F is always considered *lower* than one that does not.

3. Terms containing ρ and symbols from S are considered as strings and compared lexicographically from right to left using $\succ$.

It is shown below that terms s and t are semi-unifiable if and only if there are no root conflicts in obtaining equations from $\rho(\sigma(s))$ and $\sigma(t)$ and the rewrite rules obtained from them are always terminating.

Step 4. For each rule, reduce each side (if reducible) by a single step of rewriting by other rules. Replace the rule by the new equation thus obtained and go to Step 2. If no rule can be rewritten any further, report semi-unifiability and return the rewriting system $R(s,t)$. □

Note that this procedure has some resemblance to a procedure described by Plaisted in [14] in the way nontermination of rewrite rules is detected.

It can be shown that Algorithm A-1 will always terminate either reporting failure or semi-unifiability; in the latter case, the rewrite system $R(s,t)$ is generated which is a reduced canonical rewriting system (modulo cancellativity) and every rule in it is of the form
$$\rho^i s_x \to t$$
where $i \geq 0$ and t is a ground term.

Algorithm A-2 below is a method for determining ρ and σ from $R(s,t)$ in the case Algorithm A-1 decides that s and t are semi-unifiable. Before discussing Algorithm A-2, we illustrate Algorithm A-1 on several examples.

Example 1: Consider the terms $s = g(f(x,y), f(y,z))$ and $t = g(z,x)$. After distributing ρ over function symbols in equations obtained from s and t and applying cancellativity (Step 2), we have
$$f(\rho(s_x), \rho(s_y)) = s_z$$
$$f(\rho(s_y), \rho(s_z)) = s_x.$$

From these equations, we obtain the following rewrite rules (Step 3):
$$s_z \to f(\rho(s_x), \rho(s_y))$$
$$s_x \to f(\rho(s_y), \rho(s_z)).$$

After the first rule is used to rewrite the second rule (Step 4) and after "pushing ρ's down" using distributivity of ρ, we obtain the equation:
$$s_x = f(\rho(s_y), f(\rho^2(s_x), \rho^2(s_y))).$$
which implies that s and t are not semi-unifiable (condition 2 in Step 2). □

The following example illustrates non-semi-unifiability due to a root conflict.

Example 2: Consider the terms $i(f(x), f(f(y)), g(x,v), g(h(y), f(w)))$ and $i(v,v,z,z)$. After distributing ρ over function symbols in equations obtained from these terms and applying cancellativity (Step 2), we have
$$f(\rho(s_x)) = s_v$$
$$f(f(\rho(s_y))) = s_v$$
$$g(\rho(s_x), \rho(s_v)) = s_z$$
$$g(h(\rho(s_y)), f(\rho(s_w))) = s_z.$$

In Step 3, the above equations are oriented as rewrite rules as follows:
$$s_v \to f(\rho(s_x))$$
$$s_v \to f(f(\rho(s_y)))$$
$$s_z \to g(\rho(s_x), \rho(s_v))$$
$$s_z \to g(h(\rho(s_y)), f(\rho(s_w))).$$

In Step 4, the first rule is used to rewrite the second rule and the third rule is used to rewrite the fourth rule, which give the following equations replacing the second and fourth rules:

$$f(\rho(s_x)) = f(f(\rho(s_y)))$$
$$g(\rho(s_x), \rho(s_v)) = g(h(\rho(s_y)), f(\rho(s_w))).$$

In Step 2, using cancellativity, we get new equations:

$$\rho(s_x) = f(\rho(s_y))$$
$$\rho(s_x) = h(\rho(s_y))$$
$$\rho(s_v) = f(\rho(s_w)).$$

From these equations, we get new rules in Step 3:

$$\rho(s_x) \to f(\rho(s_y))$$
$$\rho(s_x) \to h(\rho(s_y))$$
$$\rho(s_v) \to f(\rho(s_w)).$$

The second rule above is rewritten using the first rule to give the following equation in Step 4:

$$f(\rho(s_y)) = h(\rho(s_y)).$$

Then, in Step 2, the root conflict is detected and non-semi-unifiability is declared. □

The following example illustrates the algorithm for the case when the given terms are semi-unifiable.

Example 3: Consider the terms $g(f(x), f(z))$ and $g(y, x)$. After distributing ρ over function symbols in equations obtained from s and t and applying cancellativity in Step 2, we have:

$$f(\rho(s_x)) = s_y$$
$$f(\rho(s_z)) = s_x.$$

In Step 3, we get the following rewrite rules:

$$s_x \to f(\rho(s_z))$$
$$s_y \to f(\rho(s_x)).$$

After the first rule is used to rewrite the second rule in Step 4, we obtain a new equation which, after distributing ρ in Step 2, is

$$s_y = f(f(\rho^2(s_z)))$$

In Step 3, this equation gives a new rule, replacing the second rule. We thus have:

$$s_x \to f(\rho(s_z))$$
$$s_y \to f(f(\rho^2(s_z))).$$

These rewrite rules cannot be further rewritten, thus giving a reduced canonical system. Algorithm A-1 reports that the given terms are semi-unifiable. □

3 Substitution extraction algorithm

We now discuss how to generate ρ and σ from a reduced canonical system $R(s,t)$ when Algorithm A-1 reports semi-unifiability of terms s and t.

The left-hand side of every rule in $R(s,t)$ is of the form $\rho^i(s_x)$, where x is a variable in V and $i \geq 0$. We introduce new variables, and thereby new symbols of the form s_u, to get rid of the ρ's. For example, if $\rho(s_x)$ occurs in a rule we will uniformly replace it with some new symbol s_u, where u is a new variable not in V. Clearly there cannot be a rule with s_x as its left-hand side, for otherwise ρs_x would have been reduced further. We take $\sigma(x) = x$ and $\rho(x) = \sigma(u)$, after $\sigma(u)$ is computed by repeating the process. On the other hand, if s_x does appear as a left-hand side for some variable x, and the right-hand side does not contain ρ's, then applying θ^{-1} to the right-hand side gives us $\sigma(x)$. It can be seen that this process will terminate giving us the semi-unifiers.

Algorithm A-2 (For extracting ρ and σ from $R(s,t)$):

Step 1. Initialize:
$$\rho = \emptyset;\ \sigma = \emptyset;\ \mathcal{V} = V.$$

Step 2. Process the right-hand sides:

> For all variables x in $\mathcal{V}$ do
>> if ρs_x appears in an rhs,
>>> replace ρs_x everywhere with s_u where u is a new variable;
>>> $\rho := \rho \cup \{x \leftarrow u\}$;
>>> $\mathcal{V} := \mathcal{V} \cup \{u\}$.

Repeat this until there are no ρ's on the right-hand side of any rule.

Step 3. Compute σ:

> For every rule in which ρ does not occur do
>> For all variables x in $\mathcal{V}$ do
>>> if s_x occurs in the rhs
>>> then $\sigma(x) = x$
>>> else $\sigma(x) = \theta^{-1}(r)$ where r is the rhs.

Recall that θ^{-1} merely replaces s_y by y.

Step 4. Compute the remaining part of ρ:

> For all rules of the form $\rho^i s_x \rightarrow t$ do
>> Introduce new variables $u_1, \ldots, u_{i-1}$ and make
>> $\rho(x) = u_1$,
>> $\rho(u_1) = u_2$,
>> $\vdots$

$$\rho(u_{j-1}) = u_j,$$
$$\vdots$$
$$\rho(u_{i-1}) = \theta^{-1}(t). \quad \Box$$

After these steps, we have obtained ρ and σ. Note that the above algorithm may introduce unnecessary new variables. In particular, if no function symbol in F is used in a $R(s,t)$, then we do not need to introduce any new variable to get the semi-unifiers.

Let us illustrate Algorithm A-2 first on the result of Algorithm A-1 on Example 3 above.

Example 3 continued: The rewrite system obtained as the result of Algorithm A-1 on Example 3 is:

$$s_x \to f(\rho(s_z))$$
$$s_y \to f(f(\rho^2(s_z))).$$

In Step 2 above, we replace $\rho(s_z)$ by s_{u_1} and $\rho(s_{u_1}) = \rho^2(s_z)$ by s_{u_2}. This makes $\rho = \{z \leftarrow u_1, u_1 \leftarrow u_2\}$. In Step 3, we obtain $\sigma = \{x \leftarrow f(u_1), y \leftarrow f(f(u_2))\}$. $\Box$

The following example illustrates both parts of the algorithm. This is also a counter-example to Purdom's algorithm.

Example 4: Consider the terms $s = f(h(y), x)$ and $t = f(x, h(h(y)))$. In Step 2 of Algorithm A-1, after pushing ρ down and applying cancellativity, we have

$$h(\rho(s_y)) = s_x$$
$$\rho(s_x) = h(h(s_y))$$

From these equations, we get the rewrite rules in Step 3,

$$s_x \to h(\rho(s_y))$$
$$\rho(s_x) \to h(h(s_y))$$

Since the former reduces the latter (Step 4), we replace the second rule by the new equation

$$h(\rho(\rho(s_y))) = h(h(s_y)),$$

and, in Step 2, after cancelling h, we get the rewrite rule in Step 3,

$$\rho(\rho(s_y)) \to h(s_y).$$

Both of these rules are already reduced thus giving a reduced canonical rewrite system:

$$s_x \to h(\rho(s_y))$$
$$\rho(\rho(s_y)) \to h(s_y).$$

Using Algorithm A-2, we can extract the solution as follows. In Step 2, we replace $\rho(s_y)$ in the right-hand side of the first rule by s_u, and make $\rho = \{y \leftarrow u\}$. In Step 3, we get $\sigma = \{x \leftarrow h(u)\}$. In Step 4, ρ is extended to include $u \leftarrow h(y)$. The following are the semi-unifiers.

$$\sigma = \{\, x \leftarrow h(u) \,\} \text{ and } \rho = \{\, y \leftarrow u, u \leftarrow h(y) \,\}.$$

Purdom's algorithm [15] fails on this example, since it first adds $\{\, x \leftarrow h(y) \,\}$ to σ. This would result in terms $f(h(y), h(y))$ and $f(h(y), h(h(y)))$ which are not semi-unifiable. □

The reader can easily observe that in the worst case, this algorithm may take exponentially many steps to obtain a reduced canonical rewriting system in Algorithm A-1. In addition, the number of occurrences of ρ may increase exponentially. Consider, for example, the case where one of the terms is "right-heavy", and the other is "left-heavy" (e.g., let $s = f(x_1, f(x_2, \ldots, f(x_{n-1}, x_n) \cdots))$, and $t = f(f(f(\cdots f(x_{n-1}, x_n) \cdots), x_2), x_1))$. Here the number of occurrences of ρ in the canonical system generated by Algorithm A-1 is exponential in the original presentation. In a later section, we discuss a modification of Algorithm A-1 which can decide semi-unifiability in polynomial time. In the following section we give the necessary and sufficient conditions for semi-unifiability which serve as the basis of correctness of the algorithm discussed above.

4 Underlying theory

The equational congruence $E(s, t)$ is said to have a *root conflict* if and only if there exist distinct functions f and g in F such that $f(t_1, \ldots, t_m)$ is congruent modulo E to $g(r_1, \ldots, r_n)$, where $t_1, \ldots, t_m, r_1, \ldots, r_n$ are terms and m and n are the arities of f and g respectively.

Theorem 2 *Two terms s and t are not semi-unifiable if and only if $=_E$, the congruence generated by $E(s, t)$, satisfies either of the following properties:*

(1) *$E(s, t)$ has a root conflict.*

(2) *There exists a variable x in V, a function f in F, and non-negative integers i, j such that*
$$\rho^i s_x =_E f(\ldots \rho^{i+j} s_x \ldots).$$

Proof: The 'if' case is straightforward, since (a) no substitution on the variables can change the top-level symbol of a term, and (b) no substitution can "shrink" a term. We prove the 'only if' part by construction, i.e., by showing how ρ and σ can be obtained if conditions (1) and (2) are not satisfied. The basic idea is this: if (1) and (2) are not satisfied, we can construct a reduced canonical term rewriting system equivalent to $E(s, t)$ using Algorithm A-1 discussed above and from which ρ and σ can be "extracted" from Algorithm A-2 above.

The theorem follows from the following two lemmas.

Define the *weight* of a term r, denoted by $w(r)$, as the number of function symbols from F in it. It can be shown that the second condition specified in the statement of the above theorem is equivalent to that of having two terms of different weights that are congruent modulo $E(s, t)$ such that one is *homeomorphically embedded* in the other, provided the first condition does not hold (i.e., there are no root conflicts).

A term s is *homeomorphically embedded* in a term t, written $s \trianglelefteq t$, if

1. s and t are identical, or

2. t is $g(t_1, \ldots, t_n)$ and $s \trianglelefteq t_i$ for some i, or

3. s is $f(s_1, \ldots, s_m)$ and t is $f(t_1, \ldots, t_n)$ and $\bar{s} = (s_1, \ldots, s_m) \trianglelefteq \bar{t} = (t_1, \ldots, t_n)$

where $\bar{s} = (s_1, \ldots, s_m) \trianglelefteq \bar{t} = (t_1, \ldots, t_n)$ iff (length($\bar{s}$) $\leq$ length($\bar{t}$)) and

4. $\bar{s} = ()$, the empty list, or

5. $s_1 \trianglelefteq t_1$ and $(s_2, \ldots, s_m) \trianglelefteq (t_2, \ldots, t_n)$, or

6. $\bar{s} \trianglelefteq (t_2, \ldots, t_n)$.

Lemma 1 *Let s, t be two terms and $E(s,t)$ be as defined above. Further, assume that $E(s,t)$ has no root conflicts. Then the following two conditions are equivalent:*

(a) *There exists a variable x in V, a function f in F, and non-negative integers i, j such that*
$$\rho^i s_x =_E f(\ldots \rho^{i+j} s_x \ldots).$$

(b) *There exist terms t_1 and t_2 such that $w(t_1) < w(t_2)$, $t_1 =_E t_2$, and t_1 is homeomorphically embedded in t_2.*

Proof: Condition (b) can be easily seen to be implied by (a). Going the other way requires use of cancellativity. □

Lemma 2 *Let s, t be two terms and $E(s,t)$ be as defined above. Further, assume that $E(s,t)$ has no root conflicts. Then $E(s,t)$ has an infinite congruence class if and only if either of the following two conditions hold:*

(a) *There exist non-negative integers i,j such that $\rho^i s_x$ is congruent to $\rho^{i+j} s_x$ for some $x \in V$.*

(b) *There exist terms t_1 and t_2 such that $w(t_1) < w(t_2)$, t_1 is congruent to t_2, and t_1 is homeomorphically embedded in t_2.*

The proofs are straightforward and thus omitted.

Towards a Polynomial-time Algorithm

One of the major problems with the algorithm given in the previous section is the proliferation of ρ's in the suggested completion procedure. (There are other problems as well, such as expansion in size while getting a *reduced* canonical system. This is similar to the situation in standard unification.) Our way around this is to establish a notion of cancellativity for ρ as well, so that whenever we get an equation of the form
$$\rho t_1 = \rho t_2,$$
we can immediately cancel the ρ's and get $t_1 = t_2$.

We thus augment the equational theory $E(s,t)$ with a meta-rule for the cancellativity of ρ:
$$\rho t_1 = \rho t_2 \text{ implies } t_1 = t_2.$$

We refer to this modified equational theory by $E'(s,t)$ and abbreviate the congruence it generates by $=_{E'}$.

The following key theorem justifies our making ρ cancellative as far as checking for semi-unifiability is concerned:

Theorem 3 *For all s, t, t_1 and t_2, t_1 and t_2 are congruent modulo $E'(s,t)$ if and only if there exists a non-negative integer i such that $\rho^i t_1$ and $\rho^i t_2$ are congruent modulo $E(s,t)$.*

Proof: The 'if' part is trivial. The 'only if' part is proved by induction on the number of proof steps involved in showing that t_1 and t_2 are congruent modulo $E'(s,t)$, where a proof step is either (i) a cancellation step, or (ii) a replacement using an equation proved earlier. □

5 A Polynomial Algorithm for Semi-Unifiability

In this section we describe a polynomial algorithm for deciding semi-unifiability. We begin with a brief discussion of several key issues.

First, the data structure we use is a graph representation of the rewriting system described previously. We construct a *reduced directed acyclic graph*[1] (common subexpressions occur uniquely) corresponding to the two terms under consideration. (The algorithm we describe is closely related to the unification algorithm described by Paterson and Wegman in [13], the main difference being that we must deal with the ρ function. As a result of this, our arcs describing equivalences have arguments and a simple check for acyclicity is insufficient as a test for semi-unifiability. To see the similarity between the algorithm to be presented and the Paterson-Wegman unification algorithm, one may consider the special case of our algorithm when the initial call has the cost field of the arc set equal to 0.) Initially, these will be the only arcs in the graph, but the arcs that are added by the procedures below will be considered to be of a different type: the initial arcs simply denote the paths from a function symbol to its arguments; the second type is more critical to the algorithm, and will be denoted as tuples (tnode, hnode, cost, dir), where tnode and hnode represent the labels associated with the corresponding nodes, cost is a natural number and dir (for direction) is either $\rightarrow$ or $\leftarrow$, and the arc is from tnode to hnode. Thus the arc (tnode, hnode, i, $\rightarrow$) corresponds to the rule ρ^itnode $\rightarrow$ hnode, and the arc (tnode, hnode, i, $\leftarrow$) corresponds to the rule tnode $\rightarrow \rho^i$hnode.

Next, we must avoid the exponential number of occurrences of ρ that may occur as the computation progresses. This is easily addressed by storing a bit vector representing the number of occurrences of ρ at a given term. Thus, although the number of ρs may become exponential we can always store this information using a small number of bits.

Finally, we must show that the algorithm does not allow an exponential number of distinct rules to be introduced. This is done by showing that after a polynomial number of iterations (at each of which the costs on arcs may as much as double)

---

[1]It should be noted that as the algorithm proceeds, the graph may lose its acyclicity. This is not critical to the algorithm; the main advantage to starting with a reduced directed acyclic graph is that variables (actually the constants s_x representing them) occur uniquely.

the introduction of each new arc between two nodes in the graph will have its cost being at most half of any previously introduced arc between the same two nodes. Thus the number of bits needed to represent the new cost is at least one less than needed previously. Since the number of bits needed can be bounded from above by a polynomial, the algorithm is guaranteed to terminate in polynomial time. This is discussed in more detail after the algorithm is presented.

In the following we assume that $\mathcal{V}$ represents the set of constants introduced corresponding to the variables occurring in the original terms.

5.1 Algorithm B

We describe the algorithm below: (for left-unification, the initial call is to Propagate with the arc (root(t1), root(t2), 1, $\rightarrow$); the call for right-unification is to Propagate with the arc (root(t1), root(t2), 1, $\leftarrow$)). Once the procedure below terminates (when there are no more calls to propagate an arc, assuming no function-symbol conflicts were detected), it is a straightforward matter to compute whether there is an s_x such that

$$\rho^i s_x =_E f(\ldots \rho^{i+j} s_x \ldots)$$

(see Theorem 2 for details) by checking for a non-trivial (passing through at least one non-constant function symbol), positive-weight cycle starting from a variable node in the final graph, where the weights are determined by adding the cost of an arc traversed if dir $= \leftarrow$, and subtracting if dir $= \rightarrow$. (Arcs joining a function symbol with its arguments can be traversed, but have no effect on the cost.)

procedure Propagate (tnode, hnode, cost, dir);
begin
  if {tnode,hnode} $\cap \mathcal{V} \neq \phi$ then
    Add-arc (tnode, hnode, cost, dir)
  else
    if tnode $\neq$ hnode then **fail**
              Failure occurs since there is disagreement between two non-variable
              function symbols (i.e, a root-conflict occurs).
    else
      for j := 1 to n do
        Propagate (jth child of tnode, jth child of hnode, cost , dir);
end (* procedure Propagate *);

procedure Add-arc (tnode, hnode, cost, dir);
begin
  if tnode $\in \mathcal{V}$ and dir $= \rightarrow$ then
    add the arc (tnode, hnode, cost, dir) to the graph
  else if hnode $\in \mathcal{V}$ then
      add the arc (hnode, tnode, cost, dir) to the graph
    else
              tnode $\in \mathcal{V}$ and hnode isn't

```
        add the arc (tnode, hnode, cost, dir) to the graph;
    if adding an arc introduces multiple arcs from a tnode then
        if there is another arc from tnode to hnode (even marked for deletion) then
            call the procedure Multi-edge2 (tnode);
        else
                    the hnodes of the multiple arcs are distinct
            call Multi-edge1 (tnode);
end (* procedure Add-arc *)
```

```
procedure Multi-edge1 (tnode);
begin
                Note that tnode must be a variable; assume that the
                two arcs emanating from tnode are
                (tnode, h1, c1, dir1) and (tnode, h2, c2, dir2).
                (The two arcs under consideration are the one just added and the one
                that is not marked for deletion (there will be exactly one).)
                Assume wlg that c1 ≥ c2.
                While the algorithm runs we may want to simply mark certain
                edges as deleted rather than actually deleting them, as
                it may be useful to have access to it later, when duplicate
                arcs are added between two nodes.
    CASE 1: dir1 = dir2 = →
        mark for deletion the first arc
                Congruence will be preserved by the new edge(s) added.
        call Propagate (h2, h1, c1 - c2, →);
    CASE 2: dir1 = dir2 = ←
        mark for deletion the first arc;
                Congruence will be preserved by the new edge(s) added.
        call Propagate (h1, h2, c1 - c2, →);
                This case uses cancellativity of ρ cited in Theorem 3.
    CASE 3: dir1 ≠ dir2
        mark for deletion the first arc;
                Congruence will be preserved by the new edge(s) added.
        call Propagate (h2, h1, c1 + c2, →);
                Note that doubling of cost may occur with each call that matches
                CASE 3. Thus the cost can be exponential even if the number of
                calls is not. In the next section we show that this will not
                affect the running time of the algorithm adversely.
end (* Multi-edge1 *)
```

```
procedure Multi-edge2 (tnode);
begin
                Note that, as above, tnode must be a variable; assume that the
                two arcs emanating from tnode are
                (tnode, h1, c1, dir1) and (tnode, h1, c2, dir2).
```

> Actually, there may be three arcs between the two nodes under
> consideration (the new one, one undeleted, and one marked for
> deletion), but no more than two with the same dir field,
> and these are the two to be considered in the following should
> this occur. Assume wlg that c1 ≥ c2, and that the original
> arc may have been marked as deleted (see above).

if h1 = tnode, then
  if gcd(c1, c2) ≠ c2, then
    delete both arcs from the graph,
    replacing them with a new arc by calling Add-arc (tnode, tnode, gcd(c1, c2));
> Justification for using gcd(c1, c2) can be seen by examining the
> simplification procedure of the two corresponding rules by one another,
> which exactly follows the Euclidean greatest common divisor algorithm.

  else gcd(c1, c2) = c2, delete the arc with cost c1 from the graph;

else
> Assume tnode ≠ h1.

  CASE 1: dir1 = dir2 = →
    call Propagate (h1, h1, c1 - c2, →);
    call Propagate (tnode, tnode, c1 - c2, →);
    delete the arc with cost c1;
> Furthermore, note that
> using the fact that $\rho^{(c1-c2)}$ tnode = tnode, we have that
> if $c1 = (c1 - c2) + (c1 - c2) + \cdots + (c1 - c2) + r$, and that
> if $c2 \geq \frac{c1}{2}$ then we can delete the arc with cost c2
> and add the arc corresponding to ρ^r tnode = h1
> by calling Propagate (tnode, h1, r, →).
> Thus we have

    if $c2 \geq \frac{c1}{2}$ then
      delete the arc with cost c2
      and call Propagate (tnode, h1, r, →);
> Note that if a new arc is added it has cost
> strictly less than $\frac{c2}{2}$, thus the maximum number of times that
> this can occur is bounded by $\log_2$ maximum-cost
> This is discussed more fully in the next section.

  CASE 2: dir1 = dir2 = ←
> This case is symmetric to CASE 1 above

  CASE 3: dir1 ≠ dir2
> We will only consider this case when there is no other arc from tnode
> (even *marked* for deletion) which can match with CASE 1 or CASE 2
> above. Thus there will be exactly two edges between tnode and h1,
> and their dir values will disagree.

    call Propagate (h1, h1, c1 + c2, →);
    call Propagate (tnode, tnode, c1 + c2, →);
    mark the arc with cost *i* for deletion;
> Note that although the cost of calls to Propagate increases here,

it can only happen once for each (tnode, h1) pair. Any subsequent calls on this pair of nodes will match with CASE 1 or CASE 2 above.
end (* Multi-edge2 *)

5.2 A Polynomial Bound

We provide a sketch of why Algorithm B is guaranteed to run in time polynomial in the size (call it n) of the terms.

The initial call to Propagate directly results in no more calls to Add-arc than there are occurrences of variables in the original terms. It is only when multiple arcs are added to the graph emanating from a single variable node that problems (a potentially exponential number of calls to Propagate) can occur. Note that costs on arcs increase in calls to Multi-edge1 whenever the dir arguments disagree (in fact, they may double when this occurs). This also happens when a self-loop is added in the third case of Multi-edge2. Despite the increase in cost mentioned above, we note that we can only add $O(n^2)$ arcs to this graph before we begin to add duplicate arcs (with the same dir arguments) between nodes, thus guaranteeing that after a 'short' time, calls are made to Multi-edge2, each of which either match with the "self-loop" case or with the cited CASE 1 or CASE 2. The key points are:

1. When there are multiple arcs emanating from a variable we can eliminate all but one (and possibly a self-loop on the variable node) by adding new arcs through calls to Propagate, without changing the congruence (this makes the final check for a non-trivial cycle considerably easier); one can easily check this claim by examining the rules that correspond to such arcs, and

2. When an attempt is made to introduce a new arc between two nodes (not necessarily distinct) where some arc already exists, the cost either does not change (no call to Propagate results), or the cost argument to the new arc introduced between the two nodes is less than half the smaller of the costs of the two original arcs. (The key point here is that before this duplication of arcs happens the cost may become exponential but no larger. If this cost is cut in half each time a new arc is introduced, the algorithm must stabilize (terminate) in polynomial time.)

To understand why the second claim above holds, we examine what happens in CASE 1 of the procedure Multi-edge2 (the other cases are similar): Let the two arcs be (tnode, h1, i, dir1) and (tnode, h1, j, dir2). We assume without loss of generality that $i > j$. As mentioned in the comments to the procedure Multi-edge2, using the facts that $\rho^{(i-j)}$ tnode = tnode, $i = (i-j)k + r$, and $j = (i-j)(k-1) + r$, with $k \geq 1$, and r (the *remainder*) strictly less than $(i-j)$, we have the following:

- If $j < i/2$, then $r = j$ and no change occurs between the two nodes, since the arc to be added, (tnode, h1, j, dir) is already in the graph.

- If $j \geq i/2$ then we can delete the arc with cost i, mark for deletion the arc with cost j and add the arc corresponding to ρ^r tnode = h1. We maintain that the cost r on the new arc is strictly less than $j/2$. This is true for the following reason:

- If $j \geq i/2$, then $(i-j) < i/2$, and $j = (i-j)k + r$, with $k \geq 1$. As a result, if $r \geq j/2$, since $k \geq 1$, $(i-j) < j/2$, thus $j = (i-j)k+(i-j)+r'$, contradicting the assumption that $r < (i-j)$.

Since the introduction of new arcs is (after a polynomial number of iterations at each of which the costs on arcs may as much as double) effectively limited by the number of bits needed to represent the largest cost, it is a straightforward conclusion that the procedure runs in polynomial time.

5.3 An Example

We give an example below, illustrating failure of semi-unifiability and its detection using the method outlined above (in the interest of clarity we have included arcs between non-variable terms although these would not actually be added by the algorithm):

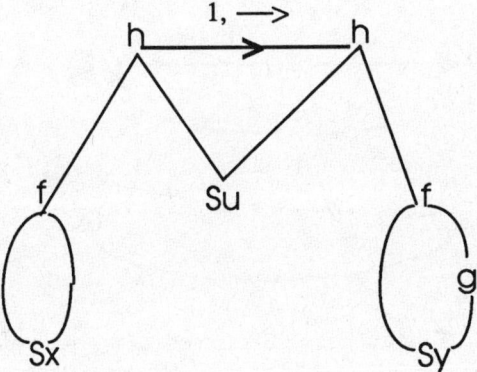

Figure 1: The graph of the initial call on terms $h(f(s_x, s_x), s_u), h(s_u, f(s_y, g(s_y)))$

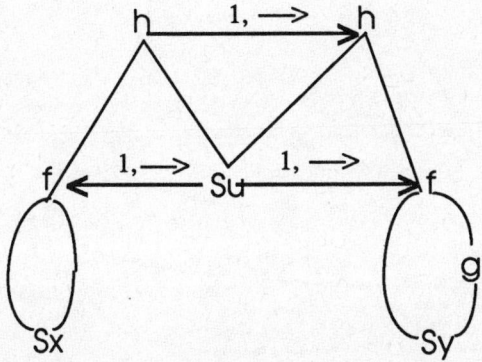

Figure 2: After propagating the initial call.

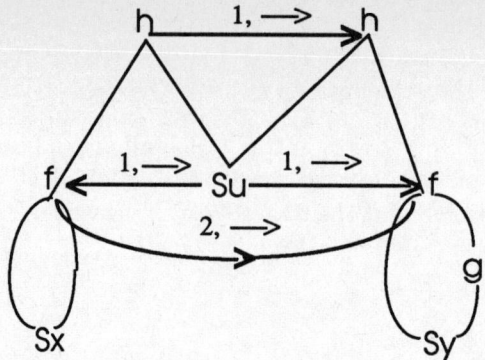

Figure 3: Multiple arcs from s_u are resolved.

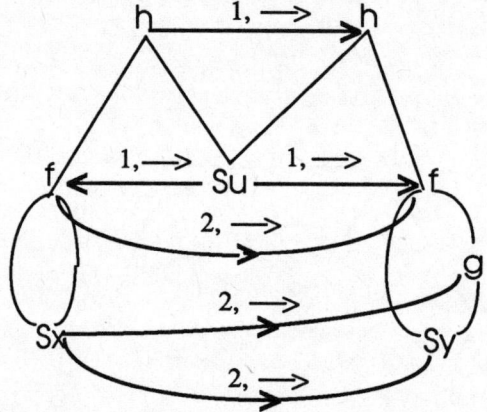

Figure 4: Again multiple arcs are introduced as a result of propagation.

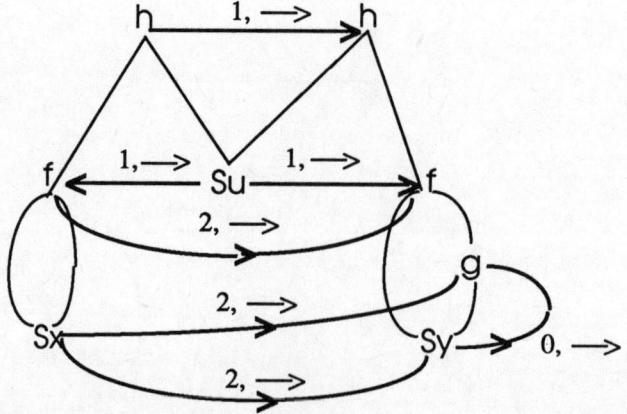

Figure 5: Finally, the graph stabilizes, with failure detected because of the non-negative cost cycle from s_y to itself through g.

References

[1] De Champeaux, D., "About the Paterson-Wegman Linear Unification Algorithm," in *J. of Computer and System Sciences* 32, 1986, pp. 79-90.

[2] Dershowitz, N., "Orderings for term-rewriting systems," in *Theoretical Computer Science* 17, 1982, pp. 279-301.

[3] Dershowitz, N., "Termination," in *Rewriting Techniques and Applications*, Jean-Pierre Jouannaud, ed., Springer Verlag, Berlin, 1985, pp. 180-224.

[4] Henglein, F., "Type Inference and Semi-Unification," in *Proceedings, ACM Conference on LISP and Functional Programming*, ACM, ACM Press, June 1988.

[5] Hsiang, J., and Dershowitz, N., "Rewrite methods for clausal and non-clausal theorem proving," in *Proc. 10th EATCS Intl. Colloq. on Automata, Languages, and Programming*, Barcelona, Spain, 1983.

[6] Huet, G., and Lankford, D.S., "On the Uniform Halting Problem for Term Rewriting Systems," Rapport Laboria 283, INRIA, Paris, 1978.

[7] Huet, G., and Oppen, D., "Equations and rewrite rules: a survey," in *Formal Languages: Perspectives and Open Problems* (R. Book, ed.), Academic Press, New York, 1980.

[8] Kapur, D., and Narendran, P., "An equational approach to theorem proving in first-order predicate calculus," in *9th Intl. Joint Conference on Artificial Intelligence*, Los Angeles, California, 1985.

[9] Kapur, D., Sivakumar, G., and Zhang, H., "RRL: a rewrite rule laboratory," in *Proceedings of the 8th Intl. Conference on Automated Deduction*, Oxford, U.K., 1986, LNCS 230, Springer-Verlag.

[10] Knuth, D.E., and Bendix, P.B., "Simple word problems in universal algebras," in *Computational Problems in Abstract Algebra* (J. Leech, ed.), Pergamon Press, Oxford, 1970, pp. 263-297.

[11] Kruskal, J.B., "Well-quasi-ordering, the Tree Theorem, and Vazsonyi's conjecture," in *Transactions of the American Mathematical Society* 95, 1960, pp. 210-225.

[12] Lankford, D.S., and Musser, D.R. "A finite termination criterion," Unpublished Draft, USC Information Sciences Institute, Marina Del Rey, California, 1978.

[13] Paterson, M.S., and Wegman, M.N., "Linear Unification," in *J. of Computer and System Sciences* 16, 1978, pp. 158-167. (see also [1]).

[14] Plaisted, D.A., "A simple non-termination test for the Knuth-Bendix method," in *Proceedings of the 8th Intl. Conf. on Automated Deduction*, Oxford, U.K., 1986, LNCS 230, Springer Verlag, NY, 79-88.

[15] Purdom, P.W., Jr., "Detecting Looping Simplifications," in *Proc. 2nd Conference on Rewrite Rule Theory and Applications (RTA)*, Bordeaux, France, May 1987, LNCS 250, Springer-Verlag, 54-62.

[16] Thompson, D.H., and Erickson, R.W. (eds.), *AFFIRM Reference Manual*, USC Information Sciences Institute, Marina Del Rey, California, 1981.

A METHOD TO CHECK KNOWLEDGE BASE CONSISTENCY

Alain Beauvieux
I.B.M. Paris Scientific Center
3 et 5 Place Vendôme
75021 PARIS CEDEX 01 - FRANCE

Abstract : *When developing expert systems, checking knowledge base consistency becomes more and more necessary. As it has been done in a Data Base Management System (DBMS), we propose to define along with the deductive rules, new relations to specify what is permitted and what is forbidden. A definition of knowledge base consistency, integrating these new relations, is presented, based on classical logic. We expose a method to prove this property, constructing new structures which model the knowledge base. A theorem is demonstrated which shows that proving the knowledge base consistency is equivalent to proving the consistency of our structures, which is easier to do. Finally, a method which allows an incremental construction of the knowledge base is presented.*

Keywords : *Knowledge base, consistency, integrity constraint, knowledge base model, incremental construction.*

Introduction

An expert system consists of two main components:

1. a knowledge base, generally composed of:
   a. a set of deductive rules,
   b. a set of facts, given by the user or deduced by the system,
2. an inference engine to interpret this knowledge.

When developing an expert system, one of the most important difficulties is precisely the building of the knowledge base. In fact, even if the rules are independent of each other, they fire from the same set of facts. So, their application can cause logical inconsistencies, and can make the system unusable.

Up to now, this kind of difficulty was bypassed by the knowledge engineer who eliminated these situations implicitly. But recent developments of expert systems, and their applications in many areas forbid this empiricism. Most of the new systems are shell systems where the builder of the knowledge base will not necessarily maintain it himself. Nothing can warrant that few years later, somebody will not add rules which can threaten the *balance* of the knowledge base.

Surprisingly enough, little work has been reported on this topic, and it shows the ambition of this project and the difficulty to obtain usable results. As in DBMS [ULL80,BRY86], logical consistency is necessary but not sufficient. In fact, it would be very useful to be able to point out what is permitted and what is forbidden. This is the reason why we propose to add a new set of rules, named *integrity constraints*, to the knowledge base which will define the consistency of this base [ROU86,ROU87]. A new definition of knowledge base consistency will be given, integrating these new rules.

Our system which is being developed at the IBM Paris Scientific Center, allows the knowledge engineer to define both integrity constraints and deductive rules, and to check their mutual interactions. Thus an incremental construction is made, and four main operations are defined on the knowledge base, which are: add a deductive rule or an integrity constraint or retract them. The problem is to find a method that allows us to know whether having performed one of these operations, the resulting set is consistent, without doing the complete proof again. Our work has been: firstly, to look for a criterion which allows to test the base quickly by constructing new structures called *base models* and testing them; secondly, to propose a method to build these models incrementally. From this point of view, our approach can be related to recent work done on the logic of theory change [MAK85].

Studied knowledge bases

Studied knowledge bases will be composed of production rules written in the propositional logic formalism, i.e. expressions of the form:

R : IF (PREMISES) THEN (CONCLUSIONS)

where (PREMISES) and (CONCLUSIONS) are two conjunctions of propositional variables, named *facts* . Negation, denoted ~, is permitted and we assume that the open world assumption holds, i.e. that the fact ~A is true if and only if it can be proved.

In this paper, *Prem(R)* and *Concl(R)* will respectively refer to the set of facts which appears in the left hand member and the right hand member of the rule R. The union of these two sets is called *vocabulary of the rule R*, denoted Voc(R). Finally, since no rule can retract facts which have been already deduced, studied knowledge bases are monotonic.

Previous works

The first software developed in order to check the construction of a knowledge base was TEIREISAS, which assumed that MYCIN's set of rules was complete, and helped the expert to specify the recorded rules. This was not really consistency checking.

A first direction of research has been to control the consistency of each rule taken separately. We can mention on this subject the work of P. Le Beux and D. Fontaine [LEB86] at Compiegne University or M. Ayel [AYE86] at Universite de Savoie.

A second direction is what is done with the ONCOCIN system [SUW82], and more recently the CHECK system [NGU85,NGU87], built for the Lockheed Expert System. CHECK identifies inconsistencies in a knowledge base by looking for redundant rules, subsumed rules, unnecessary IF conditions, circular rule chains and conflicting rules. If we except the first four cases which are not really inconsistencies, the only definition that is possible is one of conflicting rules, i.e.:

> **Two rules are conflicting if they succeed in the same situation but with conflicting conclusions.**

For example,   *IF (P) THEN (Q)*   and   *IF (P) THEN (~Q)* are conflicting rules.

This definition seems to be insufficient, and does not allow to take into account problems such as the following: consider the knowledge base built to characterize boats, and composed notably of these two rules:

> R_1 : IF (Sailing_boat & ~Keel) THEN (Portable & Sailing_dinghy)
> R_2 : IF (Sailing_boat & Habitable) THEN (~Portable & Cruise_boat)

The first rule means that a sailing boat without a keel is a sailing dinghy and can be carried, the second that an habitable sailing boat is generally used for cruises and is not portable.

If the initial facts set is {*Sailing_boat, Habitable, ~Keel*}, which is realistic, the contradictory facts *Portable* and *~Portable* can be deduced. In fact, the conflicting rules test cannot detect this mistake although the knowledge engineer should have been informed of this problem.

The last approach is what is done by M.C. Rousset [ROU86,ROU87] at LRI in France, who proposes a definition of rule base consistency which is based on classical logic.

What is the right definition ?

Specify consistency notion ...

In classical logic, one way to define consistency of a set of formulas is:

> **Let Δ be a set of formulas, Δ is consistent if and only if**
> $\not\exists$ **Y formula, $\Delta \mapsto Y$ and $\Delta \mapsto \sim Y$**

Although this condition is necessary to prove knowledge base consistency, we think it is not sufficient. On one hand, it is not applicable to systems which do not permit the use of negation, and on the other hand, it cannot take into account more general problems e.g. to detect {*tall,small*} as being inconsistent.

This is the reason why we propose to define, along with deductive rules, relations of exclusion between facts, named **integrity constraint**. These relations take the form:

IF (PREMISES) THEN $\bot$

where PREMISES is a conjunction of facts, and $\bot$ represents falsity, which means that the set of facts PREMISES is inconsistent. Note that such a relation is equivalent to ~(PREMISES).

For instance, in the propositional calculus formalism, the rule:

IF (Keel_boat & Sailing_dinghy) THEN $\bot$

indicates exclusion between these two kind of sailing boats.
Also, in an (Attribute Operator Value) framework, we will have rules of the form:

IF ((ATT > a) & (ATT < a)) THEN $\bot$

to show that the same attribute cannot be greater and less than a same value.

It is necessary to distinguish between what is expressed above and what is generally done in DBMS, to control input and output operations on the database [ULL80], as for example, inserting a new tuple. On the other hand, integrity constraints can be seen as the *ATMS nogood sets* [KLE86].

So we will obtain an integrity constraints set, that will be added to the set of deductive rules to constitute the knowledge base.

... and use classical logic as a basis

We propose the following definition of knowledge base consistency, where BR and IC respectively represent the whole set of deductive rules and of integrity constraints which are components of the same knowledge base KB.

Definitions :

A set of facts BF is consistent   if and only if
1. There exists no pair {A,~A} in BF
2. {BF,IC} $\not\vdash \bot$

A set of rules BR is consistent   if and only if $\forall$ BF consistent $\subset$ Voc(KB)
1. $\forall Y$, {BF,BR} $\not\vdash$ ~Y and Y
2. {BF,IC,BR} $\not\vdash \bot$

where Voc(KB) is the union of vocabulary of each rule or constraint of KB.

Note that the previous proposition is equivalent to [ROU86]:

A set of rules BR is consistent if and only if ∀ BF consistent, BR x BF is consistent

where BR x BF is the set of all facts deductible by applying BR rules.[1]

Remark: Rules in expert systems are not used with full logical deduction, i.e. they are not put in clause form to be used with the resolution rule. Rules respect a non logic semantic distinction between premises and conclusions, and are assumed to be applied in forward chaining. So, whereas in logical deduction one can conclude ~A, from the rule *IF A THEN B* and the fact ~B, nothing is deduced. Thus, ↦ in the definition must be understood as the deduction scheme $\frac{Prem(R), R}{Concl(R)}$ for R ∈ BR ∪ IC.

Consequence of this definition on the choice of a method

Let us assume that an initial consistent facts base BF exists but BRxBF is inconsistent. Two actions are possible:

- Remove the rules of BR or IC which generate this inconsistency.
- State that BF is inconsistent, i.e. record a new integrity constraint.

Reconsidering the above knowledge base, the expert might either declare the whole set {*Sailing_boat, Habitable, ~Keel*} (or one of its subsets) as inconsistent or change one of the two rules that are involved.

This duality of possible solutions leads to the implementation of a method allowing the user to easily modify the two sets of constraints and of deductive rules. Thus it will be possible at the end of each new recording of one of these relations to measure its effect on the consistency of the whole. This flexibility will guarantee better appreciation of interactions between rules and constraints by the expert conceiving the base.

These reasons lead us to reject the method with which we would have to calculate all the consistent sets of initial facts and then to saturate them up with BR rules in order to check if the resulting sets are consistent. Such a method seems too clumsy and would cause the whole proof to be recalculated after each modification of integrity constraints or rules. On the contrary, we have oriented our work along two principal axes:

- The search for a criterion which would be more operational than that of the above-mentioned definition and which would avoid saturating the facts bases by rules.
- The definition of a method allowing an incremental construction of the set of integrity constraints and the set of deductive rules to guarantee better interactivity.

Let us examine the way to meet these two goals.

---

[1] This operation is called saturation of BF by BR

Looking for an operational criterion

In this section, we consider a set of deductive rules BR, of integrity constraints IC, which are the two components of the same knowledge base KB. We suppose that each rule R is itself consistent (i.e. Voc(R) is consistent).

Maximal consistent base of facts

- We will call **base of facts** any subset BF of Voc(KB).

This base of facts will be said to be:

- *consistent* if it agrees with the conditions fixed by the above-mentioned definition.
- *consistent and maximal in Voc(KB)* if it is consistent and every proper superset of BF is inconsistent.[2]

In classical logic, the following lemma has been proved : [GAL86]
  Every consistent set Γ is a subset of some maximal consistent set Δ.

So, using this property and the monotonicity of the deduction rule, the previous definition can be reformulated as follows:
  BR *is consistent* $\Leftrightarrow$ $\forall$ BF **maximal** *consistent*, BR x BF *is consistent*

As BR x BF contains BF, we obtain:

Lemma : $\quad$ $\forall$ BF maximal consistent, BR x BF *is consistent* $\Leftrightarrow$ BR x BF = BF

i.e. **BF is a fixed point of saturation by BR.**

We will show that it is sufficient to prove the stability of BF for an appropriate subset of BR.

Set of compatible rules

- We will call **set of compatible rules** any set CR of rules where:

$$\text{Prem(CR)} = (\bigcup_{R \in CR} \text{Prem}(R)) \text{ is consistent}$$

- A set E of rules will be said to be **associated with** a set of facts **BF** if and only if
  $\quad$ Prem(E) $\subset$ BF

  Such a set is a set of compatible rules as soon as BF is consistent.

---

[2] By the sake of clarity, we will say *maximal consistent* for *consistent and maximal in Voc(KB)*.

- We will call maximal set of compatible rules associated with BF, a set CR where:

  - Prem(CR) is consistent,
  - Prem(CR) ⊂ BF,
  - $\forall R \in \overline{CR}$, with Prem(R) ⊂ BF, Prem(CR ∪ {R}) is inconsistent.[3]

Remark: For each consistent base of facts, there exists exactly one maximal set CR of compatible rules associated with BF: it is the biggest set of rules associated with BF. (Note that CR can be an empty set).

Knowledge base model

Let BF be a maximal consistent base of facts. The **base model associated with BF** is the set M defined by:

$$M = CR \times BF = BF \cup Concl(CR)$$

where CR is the maximal set of compatible rules associated with BF.

So, for any knowledge base KB (deductive rules + integrity constraints), it is possible to associate the **collection of base models**, which corresponds to all different maximal consistent bases of facts. This collection will be denoted $\zeta(KB)$.

Example

Consider a knowledge base on boats, which is composed of:

R_1 : IF (Sail & ~Keel) THEN (Sailing_dinghy)
R_2 : IF (Sailing_boat & Keel) THEN (Keel_boat)
R_3 : IF (Sailing_dinghy) THEN (One_mast)
R_4 : IF (Keel_boat) THEN (Habitable)

We obtain:

- two maximal consistent facts bases:

  BF_1 = {Sail,~Keel,Sailing_dinghy, Keel_boat,Sailing_boat, One_mast,Habitable }
  BF_2 = {Sail,Keel,Sailing_dinghy,Keel_boat,Sailing_boat, One_mast,Habitable }

- two associated maximal subsets of compatible rules:
  CR_1 = { R_1,R_3,R_4 } and CR_2 = { R_2,R_3,R_4 }

- and finally, two models: $M_1 = BF_1$ and $M_2 = BF_2$.

---

[3] $\overline{CR}$ is the complement of CR in BR

Consistency conditions

Let BF be a maximal consistent base of facts, and CR the maximal set of compatible rules associated with BF.

Lemma : $\qquad$ (BR x BF = BF) $\Leftrightarrow$ (CR x BF = BF)

Proof: The implication $\Rightarrow$ is obvious as BF $\subset$ CR x BF $\subset$ BR x BF.

Conversely, if $\overline{CR}$ is the complement of CR in BR, we obtain :
$$BR \times BF = \overline{CR} \times (CR \times BF)$$
because every rule of CR is fireable from BF.
Thus, if CR x BF = BF, we obtain BR x BF = $\overline{CR}$ x BF = BF because by definition of CR, there is no rule of $\overline{CR}$ which is fireable from BF. $\square$

Let M be the model defined by M = CR x BF = BF $\cup$ Concl(CR).

Lemma : $\qquad$ (CR x BF = BF) $\Leftrightarrow$ (Concl(CR) $\subset$ BF)

Proof: By definition of CR, Prem(CR) $\subset$ BF. So we can deduce
$\qquad$ (Concl(CR) $\subset$ BF) from (CR x BF = BF).

Conversely, each rule of CR being fireable from BF,
$\qquad$ (Concl(CR) $\subset$ BF) implies (CR x BF = BF). $\square$

It follows from these lemmas and the above-mentioned definitions :

Theorem 1 :

$\qquad$ Let M be a model defined by M = BF $\cup$ Concl(CR)
$\qquad$ M is consistent $\Leftrightarrow$ M = BF

The collection of base models will be said consistent if all its constituting models are consistent. Thus, we have this new theorem:

Theorem 2 :

$\qquad$ A knowledge base is consistent if and only if the
$\qquad$ collection of models associated with it, is consistent.

Building the associated collection

We are looking for a method which would allow us to construct gradually deductive rules and integrity constraints sets. Thus, we have to define as elementary operations: adding or retracting an element to each of these two sets. The problem is that we do not want to compute the whole proof again after each of these operations. So, we have studied how to minimize the set of operations to do when modifying the knowledge base. For the sake of clarity, our method is presented when adding a new deductive rule, and it will be seen afterwards that adding a new constraint can be done in the same way.

Presentation of the method

Let KB be composed of a set of rules BR and of a set of integrity constraints IC, and R a new rule to be added to BR. We suppose KB is consistent, so each model M of the associated collection is consistent, i.e. M = BF where BF is a maximal consistent base of facts.

Let $BR' = BR \cup \{R\}$, $KB' = \{BR', IC\}$ and $NF = \{F \in Voc(R) \text{ and } F \notin Voc(KB)\}$.

The collection $\zeta(KB')$ can be built directly from $\zeta(KB)$, in three steps.

Step 1 : *Calculate maximal consistent bases of facts of Voc(KB')*

Let BF' be one of these bases and $BFI = BF' \cap Voc(KB)$. We obtain $BF' \subset BFI \cup NF$. BFI is a consistent base of facts in Voc(KB) because it is included in Voc(KB). Thus, there exists some model M of collection associated with KB, as $BFI \subset M$, whence $BF' \subset M \cup NF$, i.e. BF' is a maximal consistent subset of $M \cup NF$.

> **To calculate all the maximal consistent bases of facts of Voc(KB'), it is sufficient to compute for each model M_i of the collection associated with KB, all the maximal consistent subsets BF_{ij} of $M_i \cup NF$.**

When this calculation is completed, computed bases of facts are not necessarily maximal in Voc(KB'). So, only the maximal sets will be kept.

Step 2 : *Calculate the set CR_{ij} of compatible rules associated with BF_{ij}*

It follows from the definition that:
$$M_{ij} = CR_{ij} \times BF_{ij} = BF_{ij} \cup Concl(CR_{ij}) \quad \text{with} \quad CR_{ij} = \{R \in BR' / Prem(R) \subset BF_{ij}\},$$

which is maximal in the set of compatible rules associated with BF_{ij}. Let us calculate CR_{ij}.

We have shown that $BF_{ij} \subset M_i \cup NF$, where $M_i = BF_i \cup Concl(CR_i)$.

Let $CR' = \{R \in BR' / Prem(R) \subset M_i \cup NF\}$, we obtain $CR_{ij} \subset CR'$.

If $R \in BR$, $(Prem(R) \subset M_i \cup NF) \Leftrightarrow (Prem(R) \subset M_i)$ because $Prem(R) \subset Voc(KB)$.

Consequently, the set $\{R \in BR \,/\, \text{Prem}(R) \subset M_i \cup NF\}$ is equal to CR_i, where CR_i is the maximal set of compatible rules associated with BF_i, a set which has been already constructed.

Thus, we obtain: $CR_{ij} \subset CR' \subset CR_i \cup \{R\}$.

> To calculate the maximal set CR_{ij} of compatible rules associated with BF_{ij}, it is sufficient to consider only the rules from $CR_i \cup \{R\}$.

We know that rules associated with BF_{ij} are compatible as soon as BF_{ij} is consistent. So, CR_{ij} is the set of rules $R_l \in CR_i \cup \{R\}$ as $\text{Prem}(R_l) \subset BF_{ij}$.

Step 3 : *Build the collection*

The models M_{ij} are built by calculating $BF_{ij} \cup \text{Concl}(CR_{ij})$. The knowledge base is consistent if and only if all the models are consistent.

Main Algorithms

We present in this section algorithms used in the previous computing.

Calculate maximal consistent bases of facts

Input: A set of facts BF and the list LC the elements NC of which are all subsets of BF of the form $\{A, \sim A\}$ or Prem(C) where C is a constraint.
Output: The list L_BF of all maximal consistent subsets EF of BF.

Algorithm:
- L_BF ← (BF)
- FOR ALL the elements NC of LC DO
  * FOR ALL the elements EF of L_BF DO
    - Calculate list L of all possible splittings of EF according to NC
    - Replace EF by L
  * Keep only the maximal sets of L_BF
- END

Calculate list L of all possible splittings of EF according to NC

- L ← empty list
- IF NC is not included in EF THEN
  * L = (EF)
- ELSE
  * FOR EACH element α of NC DO
    - Construct the set EF' = EF - α
    - Add EF' to L
- END

Keeping only the maximal sets of L_BF is a classical operation, for which several algorithms exist [KLE86].

Example

Consider the previous knowledge base KB on boats, which is composed of:

R_1 : IF (Sail & ~Keel) THEN (Sailing_dinghy)
R_2 : IF (Sailing_boat & Keel) THEN (Keel_boat)
R_3 : IF (Sailing_dinghy) THEN (One_mast)
R_4 : IF (Keel_boat) THEN (Habitable)

The associated collection ζ(KB) is composed of:

M_1 = { Sail,~Keel,Sailing_dinghy,Keel_boat,Sailing_boat,One_mast,Habitable }
M_2 = { Sail,Keel,Sailing_dinghy,Keel_boat,Sailing_boat,One_mast,Habitable }

The following rule is required to be added:

R_5 : IF (Engine & ~Sailing_boat) THEN (Speed_boat)

Note that NF is equal to { Engine, Speed_boat, ~Sailing_boat }.

Step 1 : Sets $M_1 \cup$ NF and $M_2 \cup$ NF are composed, respectively, of:

- {Sail,~Keel,Sailing_dinghy,Keel_boat,Sailing_boat,One_mast,Habitable,Engine,Speed_boat,~Sailing_boat}
- {Sail,Keel,Sailing_dinghy,Keel_boat,Sailing_boat,One_mast,Habitable,Engine,Speed_boat,~Sailing_boat}

These sets are inconsistent, because including {Sailing_boat,~Sailing_boat}. Thus, we obtain four consistent facts bases:

BF_{11} = {Sail,~Keel,Sailing_dinghy,Keel_boat,Sailing_boat, One_mast,Habitable,Engine,Speed_boat}
BF_{12} = {Sail,~Keel,Sailing_dinghy,Keel_boat,~Sailing_boat, One_mast,Habitable,Engine,Speed_boat}
BF_{21} = {Sail,Keel,Sailing_dinghy,Keel_boat,Sailing_boat, One_mast,Habitable,Engine,Speed_boat}
BF_{22} = {Sail,Keel,Sailing_dinghy,Keel_boat,~Sailing_boat, One_mast,Habitable,Engine,Speed_boat}

which are maximal in Voc({R_1,R_2,R_3,R_4,R_5}).

Step 2 : We obtain four sets of compatible rules CR_{11}, CR_{12}, CR_{21}, CR_{22} associated respectively with BF_{11}, BF_{12}, BF_{21}, BF_{22} :

- CR_{11} = { R_1,R_3,R_4 } and CR_{12} = { R_1,R_3,R_4,R_5 }
- CR_{21} = { R_2,R_3,R_4 } and CR_{22} = { R_3,R_4,R_5 }

Step 3 : Four models are created, which are maximal:

- $M_{11} = BF_{11} \cup Concl(CR_{11}) = BF_{11}$ and $M_{12} = BF_{12} \cup Concl(CR_{12}) = BF_{12}$
- $M_{21} = BF_{21} \cup Concl(CR_{21}) = BF_{21}$ and $M_{22} = BF_{22} \cup Concl(CR_{22}) = BF_{22}$

Thus, resulting collection is consistent. Recording R_5 is finished.

Other operations

Adding a new constraint: Constructing models has been considered in terms of adding a new rule. The same method can be used when recording a new constraint. In fact, in this case, we have to:

1. For each model M_i belonging to the collection $\zeta(KB)$, calculate maximal sets as described above, taking into account the new facts of the constraint.
2. Control that the resulting collection is still consistent.

Retracting a rule: Retracting a deductive rule from a knowledge base can not make it inconsistent. Consequently, this operation is always possible: any fact which only appears in the vocabulary of this rule will be suppressed from each model. Finally, collection will be simplified, rejecting non maximal models.

Retracting an integrity constraint: On the other hand, retracting an integrity constraint can modify the knowledge base consistency. We have studied a method to perform this operation, which is described in [BEA88].

Complexity of algorithms

When adding a new rule or a new constraint, we have seen that it is possible to construct collection $\zeta(KB')$ from collection $\zeta(KB)$, model by model.
Let $M = BF_i \cup Concl(CR_i)$ be such a model of the collection associated with KB.
We recall that set NF is defined by { $F \in Voc(Rel)$ and $F \notin Voc(KB)$ }, where Rel is either the rule or the constraint to be added.

When Rel is a rule, no constraints of IC can be applied to $BF_i \cup NF$, otherwise it would mean that a such constraint C could be applied to BF_i, which contradicts the assumption BF_i is consistent. Thus, to check that $BF_i \cup NF$ is consistent, when adding a new rule, it is sufficient to check that for each F member of NF, the negation $\sim F$ does not belong to BF_i.

When Rel is a constraint, the only constraint which can be applied to $BF_i \cup NF$ is Rel itself (for the same reason as above). Thus, we have to control if $Prem(Rel)$ is included in $BF_i \cup NF$. Moreover, it will be necessary to check that for each F member of NF, the negation $\sim F$ does not belong to BF_i.

Consequently, if we consider test of membership to a set as an elementary operation, **checking $BF_i \cup NF$ consistency is a linear calculation.**

Now, let us study the complexity of the above algorithm to **calculate consistent subsets**. We know that no more than one constraint C (the new one) can be applied to set $BF_i \cup NF$. So, if we consider the worst case, i.e. for every $F \in NF$, $\sim F \in BF_i$, the maximum number of subsets which are constructed from $BF_i \cup NF$ is proven to be equal to:

$2^{Card(NL)}$ when adding a rule,
$2^{Card(NL)} + Card(Prem(C)) - 1$ when adding a constraint C,

where $NL = \{F \in Voc(Rel) \:/\: F \notin Voc(KB)$ and $\sim F \in Voc(KB)\}$. This gives the time complexity, if we consider that removing an element from a set is an elementary operation.

Remark : If NL is empty, when *Rel* is a rule $\zeta(KB')$ is simply the collection of sets $BF_i \cup NF$ and when *Rel* is a constraint C those sets may be split by C.

When constructing the set CR_{ij} of compatible rules associated with facts base BF_{ij}, we have seen that this calculation can be done from the set CR_i plus the new rule if one is added. A set of rules associated with a consistent set is necessarily a set of *compatible* rules. Thus, CR_{ij} is the set of rules R from CR_i, as $Prem(R) \subset BF_{ij}$. Let n be the cardinal of $CR_i + 1$, m the maximal cardinal of all sets $Voc(R)$. **The time complexity of the algorithm to construct the set of compatible rules and to check consistency of the resulting model is equal to $O(n^*m)$.**

Conclusion

The different algorithms which are presented in this paper have been implemented in IBM VM/Prolog, and results confirm our assumptions on the flexibility of our system.

Several points seem important in our approach:

- The whole set of deductions of the rules are taken into account by our consistency definition. From this point of view, our definition is complete.

- A new criterion to check knowledge base consistency which avoids saturating facts bases by rules, is defined. Thus, this checking is reduced to constructing maximal consistent sets. Note that complexity of algorithms leads to reasonable computation time.

- This saving of time complexity allows an incremental construction of the knowledge base, and improves the interactivity of the system.

We extend this method to a knowledge base written in an (Attribute Operator Value) framework. The definition of knowledge base consistency is modified to take into account every operator. Thus, along with constraints which are given by the expert, new relations, written in the predicate logic formalism, are defined to specify consistency for each of the operators[BEA88].

Acknowledgements

The author wishes to thank Philippe Dague for invaluable assistance in this research and comments on this presentation.

Bibliography

[AYE86] : M. Ayel , E. Pipart, M.C. Rousset
Le contrôle de cohérence dans les bases de connaissances
PRC-GRECO - September 1986

[BEA88] : A. Beauvieux, P. Dague
Interactive checking of knowledge base consistency
Australian Joint Artificial Intelligence Conference, Adelaide, November 1988

[BRY86] : F. Bry , R. Manthey
Sur la validité des schémas de bases de données
Actes des deuxièmes journées "Bases de Données avancées" de Giens. April 1986

[GAL86] : J. Gallier
Logic for computer science - Foundations of automatic theorem proving
Harper & Row Publishers, 1986

[KLE86] : J. de Kleer
An Assumption-based TMS
Artificial Intelligence n°28 - March 1986

[LEB86] : P. Le Beux , D. Fontaine
Un système d'acquisition des connaissances pour systèmes experts
Technique et Science Informatiques (AFCET publications) Vol 5.1 1986

[MAK85] : D. Makinson
How to give it up: a survey of some formal aspects of logic of theory of change
Synthese 62. Published by Reidel Publishing Company 1985

[NGU85] : T.A. Nguyen,W.A. Perkins, T.J. Laffrey and D. Pecora
Checking an expert system knowledge base for consistency and completeness
Proceedings of IJCAI 85 p 375 - 378

[NGU87] : T.A. Nguyen,W.A. Perkins, T.J. Laffrey and D. Pecora
Knowledge Base Verification
A.I. Magazine Summer 1987.

[ROU86] : M.C. Rousset
Sur la cohérence et la validité des bases de connaissances
CIIAM 86 Marseille

[ROU87] : M.C. Rousset
Sur la validité des bases de connaissances : le système COVADIS
Septièmes journées Systèmes experts et applications Avignon 1987

[SUW82] : M. Suwa, A. Scott, H. Shortliffe
An approach to verifying completeness and consistency in RBS
A.I. Magazine, Fall 1982

[ULL80] : J.D. Ullman
Principles of Database Systems
Computer Science Press 1980

KNOWLEDGEBASES AS STRUCTURED THEORIES

José Fiadeiro, Amílcar Sernadas and Cristina Sernadas

INESC/IST
Rua Alves Redol, 9, 3º Esq, 1000 Lisboa, Portugal
uucp: mcvax!inesc!llf

Abstract - According to the structural paradigm of knowledge representation, knowledgebases are built by organizing facts along the semantic primitives of a conceptual modelling approach. Previous work of the authors has shown how these organizational principles can be brought into the logical view of knowledge representation by defining mechanisms for developing knowledgebases as structured theories. Herein, a formalization is proposed for such organizational principles and for the structure of the resulting knowledgebases. Conceptual modelling approaches are seen to define criteria for "well formed theories" in a π-institution. Such theories are accorded an explicit structure from which it is possible to have access to its components. The way is thus prepared to support the definition of higher level inference mechanisms able to manipulate the structure of knowledgebases.

1. Introduction

Recent developments in the area of conceptual modelling and knowledge representation [eg, Sernadas and Sernadas 86,88] have pointed out the necessity of integrating mechanisms for structuring theories in the logical approach to knowledge representation. The motivation for this kind of approach is (or should be) already well known: while listing vocabulary symbols and axioms is possible for defining a "small" knowledgebase as a theory in some logic, the development of and the access to a more or less complex knowledgebase cannot be supported by that unsophisticated approach. Essentially, it must be recognized that knowledge cannot be manipulated at the level of the formula but, instead, at the level of the theory. That is to say, a knowledgebase considered to be a theory in a certain logic should not be considered to be a collection of formulae but instead a structure of small, local theories which are related between themselves. Put yet in other words, we should shift from the formula to the theory as the adequate granularity for manipulating knowledge.

It is in this sense that logic has been accused to lack "structure" because logic does not support by itself mechanisms for structuring and manipulating theories. Of course, formulae of a logic are objects that have a certain structure and that is why logic has been used in a procedural way: the structure of the formulae (or terms) permits a procedural manipulation based on the underlying proof rules. However, what is being argued is that this is not the kind of "structure" that is of interest for manipulating knowledge at a higher level: a theorem prover should be used in the inference engine of a knowledge-based system only at the lowest level of the reasoning process, exactly for manipulating the formulae that have been selected by higher level reasoning mechanisms. The latter should be able to have access to the structure of theories just as an ordinary theorem prover has access to the structure of formulae in order to identify its components. Briefly, a more "semantical" reasoning is needed that abstracts from the syntax of formulae and uses instead the structure of theories.

But, how to define such structuring mechanisms? And, what criteria for choosing them?

First of all, a framework where the "syntax" of theories can be discussed is needed. That is to say, a framework is necessary where theories may be established, composed, derived, etc, as objects per se. Such a framework can be based on the notion of institution proposed by Goguen and Burstall [Goguen and Burstall 85], in particular on a version developed by the authors, π-institutions [Fiadeiro and Sernadas 88b]. Indeed, both concepts aim at the formalization of the notion of logical system, institutions centering this formalization around the satisfaction of a formula in a model, and π-institutions centering around the concept of a consequence relation between (sets of) formulae. Both provide an adequate level of abstraction for dealing with the manipulation of theories in an arbitrary logic (π-institutions further allowing to abstract from the model theory associated to the logic) as recent work [eg, Sannella and Tarlecki 84] on the semantics of specification languages has shown.

This successful work on the theory of specification led to the proposal of the institutional framework for establishing a general theory of conceptual modelling [Sernadas and Sernadas 86,88]. According to that approach, the desired tools for building knowledgebases as theories in the chosen institution are defined along a Conceptual Modelling Approach (CMA) (or *Knowledge Representation Approach* - both terms have been used in the literature and it is not within the spirit of the paper to argue about this terminology). A CMA, such as Chen's Entity Relationship Approach [Ng 80], provides semantic primitives (abstractions) that can be used for organizing the facts in the knowledgebase. These organizational principles can be brought into the logical view of knowledge representation by defining a collection of parameterized theories in the chosen institution that can be used to build theories from previous theories just as the semantic primitives are used to organize the knowledge in the knowledgebase. Along this approach, research has focused on the definition of the parameterized clausal theories associated to several CMAs [Sernadas and Sernadas 85a,85b], including abstractions for structuring behavioural knowledge [Fiadeiro and Sernadas 88a], and on the architecture of an extensible knowledgebase management system [Carapuça and Fiadeiro 86].

Herein, a deeper and formal account of the notion of structure of a theory built according to a CMA is given based on π-institutions. As each logic defines structural criteria for its well formed formulae (syntax), each CMA is seen to define criteria for the structure of its well formed theories: in the proposed formalization, theories will be composed under a CMA as objects per se according to their binding to the semantic primitives of the CMA. The resulting knowledgebases are structures of small, local theories related to each other in a diagram (in the categorial sense). Briefly, what this paper proposes is a formalization of such organizational principles along any given CMA and of the structure of the resulting knowledgebases. Research on the definition of inference mechanisms over such theories within a CMA is under way and will not be discussed herein.

Having these goals in mind, the paper proceeds as follows. In Section 2, basic concepts about π-institutions and theories in π-institutions are recalled from [Fiadeiro and Sernadas 88b]. The categorial constructs that are used in this Section and throughout the paper are quite standard (see [Arbib and Manes 75] or the tutorials in [Pitt et al 86]). In Section 3, a categorial formalization of the semantic primitives of a CMA is provided. The process of building a knowledgebase under such a CMA is then analysed. Finally, the structure of the resulting theory is formalized. In Section 4, envisaged directions of future research are outlined.

2. ∏-Institutions and Theories

Institutions were proposed by Goguen and Burstall as a reaction to the "population explosion among the logical systems being used in computer science" [Goguen and Burstall 85]. Having recognized that much of the formalization effort in computer science can be achieved independently of the logical system in which it happens to be carried out, they have proposed a precise generalization of the informal notion of a logical system through the concept of institution. In simple terms, an institution defines a logical system by describing the allowed signatures and, for each signature, a set of formulae, a collection of models and a satisfaction relation between models and formulae. A very abstract level for dealing with logics is thus obtained, allowing to do things once and for all in an arbitrary institution, to facilitate the transfer of results from one logical system to another and to permit the combination of different logical systems where required.

An alternative framework for manipulating theories in an arbitrary logic was presented in [Fiadeiro and Sernadas 88b] that is centered around the concept of a consequence relation between formulae instead of the satisfaction relation between models and formulae imposed in institutions. In such π-institutions it becomes possible to discuss logic issues independently of any model theory and to formalize things only on top of a primitive consequence relation. Taking into account that the main goal of this paper is to discuss the structuring of theories of a certain logic, it seems more adequate to place the discussion above model-theoretic issues and choose π-institutions instead of institutions as the underlying framework.

The definition of π-institution proposed below is taken from [Fiadeiro and Sernadas 88b] except for the fact that monotonicity has replaced compactness in RQ3. Briefly, the notion of π-institution generalizes the notion of *deductive system* in the sense of Tarski [Tarski 30]. It relativizes his primitive concepts of *proposition* and *consequence* subject to a given signature and defines the behaviour of these concepts subject to signature changes:

2.1   **Definition**: a π-institution is a triple (Sign, Φ, $\{Cn_\Sigma\}_{\Sigma: \text{Sign}}$) consisting of
1. a category **Sign** (of signatures);

2. a functor Φ: **Sign** -> **Set** (giving the set of formulae over each signature);
3. for each object Σ of **Sign**, a *consequence operator* $\mathbf{Cn}_\Sigma$ defined in the power set of $\Phi(\Sigma)$ satisfying for each A, B $\subseteq \Phi(\Sigma)$ and $\mu: \Sigma \to \Sigma'$:
   (RQ1) $A \subseteq \mathbf{Cn}_\Sigma(A)$ *(Extensiveness)*
   (RQ2) $\mathbf{Cn}_\Sigma(\mathbf{Cn}_\Sigma(A)) = \mathbf{Cn}_\Sigma(A)$ *(Idempotence)*
   (RQ3) if $A \subseteq B$ then $\mathbf{Cn}_\Sigma(A) \subseteq \mathbf{Cn}_\Sigma(B)$ *(Monotonicity)*
   (RQ4) $\Phi(\mu)(\mathbf{Cn}_\Sigma(A)) \subseteq \mathbf{Cn}_{\Sigma'}(\Phi(\mu)(A))$ *(Structurality)*   ◊

The category **Sign** provides the vocabularies that are used for building formulae together with the morphisms that say how vocabularies can be related to each other. The functor Φ gives the set of formulae built over each vocabulary (thus capturing the notion of a grammar) and says how formulae change when the vocabularies change. Notice that, from the point of view of knowledge representation, it is essential to support these signature changes because knowledgebases can evolve both through modifications operated over their axioms and over their language.

The consequence operator over a signature says which formulae are consequence of each set of formulae. The first three requirements express the usual properties of consequence operators: extensiveness, idempotence and monotonicity. It can be argued that these requirements can be too strong in certain contexts but it is not in the spirit of the paper to discuss these matters. Requirement RQ4 says that when signatures change the consequence relation is preserved.

It is now possible to define theories in a π-institution. A π-institution $\boldsymbol{\pi} = (\mathbf{Sign}, \Phi, \{\mathbf{Cn}_\Sigma\}_{\Sigma:\mathbf{Sign}})$ is assumed to be fixed for the rest of the paper.

2.2 Definition: The category **The** of <u>theories</u> is defined as follows: its objects are the pairs (Σ, A), where Σ is a signature and A is a set of Σ-formulae such that $\mathbf{Cn}_\Sigma(A) = A$ (such sets of formulae are said to be closed). Its arrows <u>(theory morphisms)</u> $\mu: (\Sigma, A) \to (\Sigma', A')$ are signature morphisms $\mu: \Sigma \to \Sigma'$ satisfying $\Phi(\mu)(\mathbf{Cn}_\Sigma(A)) \subseteq \mathbf{Cn}_{\Sigma'}(A')$.   ◊

This definition of theory morphism essentially requires that the properties introduced over the signature Σ through the set of formulae A be preserved when passing from the theory (Σ, A) to another one.

One of the most important concepts of this framework to the semantics of knowledge representation is that of interpretation of theories. Intuitively, this provides a mechanism for saying how a knowledgebase given by a theory in a π-institution "fits" a certain semantic primitive of a CMA given by another theory of the same π-institution:

2.3 Definition: Given a theory T in **The**, a <u>T-interpretation</u> (or an interpretation of T) is a theory T' together with a theory morphism $\sigma: T \to T'$, called the <u>interpreter</u>, that establishes how the theory T is being interpreted in T'. Naturally, many interpretations of T in T' may exist each of them characterized by its interpreter. Two interpretations (σ_1, T_1) and (σ_2, T_2) of a theory T are related to each other by the theory morphisms μ between T_1 and T_2 that make the diagram having T, T_1 and T_2 by vertices commute.

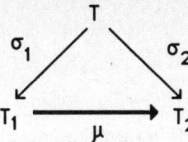

The category $\iota(T)$ of T-interpretations is thus defined. This category has a well known structure in Category Theory: it is the *comma category* (T↓The). ◊

Another essential mechanism is the *parameterized theory*. A parameterized theory establishes how, given a morphism between two theories, interpretations for the target theory can be "freely generated" from the interpretations of the argument theory. This notion is based on a well known categorial construction: pushouts.

Intuitively, pushouts give a way to construct a new theory from two given theories by combining them in a "free" way while identifying certain parts of them. The construction of pushouts in The from pushouts in Sign is well known [eg, Goguen and Burstall 85] and is recalled below:

2.4 Proposition: Assume that Sign admits pushouts. Let $\mu:(\Sigma,A)\to(\Sigma',A')$ and $\sigma:(\Sigma,A)\to(\Sigma'',A'')$ be theory morphisms. Let $(\Sigma^\$, \mu^\$, \sigma^\$)$ be the pushout of (Σ,μ,σ) in Sign and $A^\$$ be the set $Cn_{\Sigma^\$}(\mu^\$(A'')\cup\sigma^\$(A'))$. Then, $((\Sigma^\$,A^\$), \mu^\$,\sigma^\$)$ is a pushout in The. ◊

This construction generalizes trivially to colimits as shown in [Goguen and Burstall 85]. It is from now on assumed that the category Sign of the underlying π-institution is finitely co-complete.

2.5 Definition: For each theory morphism $\mu: T\to T'$, the <u>parameterized theory</u> associated to μ is the functor $\tau(\mu): \iota(T)\to\iota(T')$ defined by
- $\tau(\mu)(\sigma_1,T_1)$ is $(\sigma_1^\$,T_1^\$)$ given by $(T_1^\$,\mu_1^\$,\sigma_1^\$)$, the pushout of (T,μ,σ_1).
- $\tau(\mu)(\phi)$, where $\phi: (\sigma_1,T_1)\to(\sigma_2,T_2)$, is the unique morphism φ in $\iota(T')$ sending $\tau(\mu)(\sigma_1,T_1)$ to $\tau(\mu)(\sigma_2,T_2)$ and satisfying $\mu_1^\$; \varphi = \phi; \mu_2^\$$ (existence and unicity result from the definition of pushout).

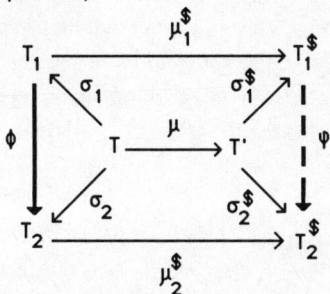

◊

This construction can be generalized to multiple arguments as follows:

2.6 **Definition**: Given theories $AT_1,...,AT_n$ define the category $\iota(AT_1,...,AT_n)$ whose objects are n-uples of interpretations (σ_i, T) of $AT_1,...,AT_n$. That is to say, each object is a <u>multiple interpretation</u> of the theories $AT_1,...,AT_n$ (notice that the theory part is the same for all interpretations). Arrows are n-uples of interpretation morphisms. Then, given a theory TT and a n-uple $(\mu_1,...,\mu_n)$ of theory morphisms $\mu_i: AT_i \to TT$, the <u>parameterized theory</u> associated to $(\mu_1,...,\mu_n)$ is the functor $\tau(\mu_1,...,\mu_n): \iota(AT_1,...,AT_n) \to \iota(TT)$ that generalizes the construction in 2.5 to colimits:

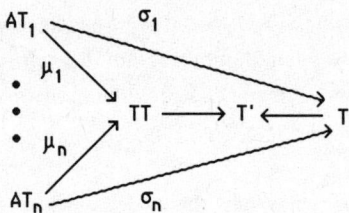

◊

2.7 **Remark**: Other mechanisms acting on interpretations such as restricting the interpretations of a theory to those that "preserve" some fragment of the theory (enforcement of data constraints in the sense of [Goguen and Burstall 80]) can be defined in this setting by introducing the notion of canonical interpretation of a theory [Fiadeiro and Sernadas 88b]. This and other constructions - renaming, enrichment, etc - are relevant to the definition of the parameterized theories associated to the semantic primitives of a CMA, ie to establishing the morphisms $\mu: T \to T'$ that give rise to parameterized theories. Indeed, the definition of the theories and theory morphisms relevant to a CMA requires a specification language such as Knowlog introduced in [Sernadas and Sernadas 88] along Clear [Goguen and Burstall 80]. These constructions - data constraints, renaming, enrichment - are used to define the semantics of such languages. Herein, the problem of defining these theories and theory morphisms using such a specification language is not adressed. This problem has been the object of the previous work related in [Sernadas and Sernadas 85a,85b]. This paper concentrates on the formalization of the notion of the structure of a knowledgebase as a theory that results from the application of the CMA parameterized theories.

However, it should be said that this formalization requires that those specification languages be given a semantics at most at the theory level in the sense of [Sannella and Tarlecki 84]. This implies that data constraints must be dealt with at the level of formulae of an extended π-institution or institution as proposed in [Goguen and Burstall 85]. ◊

3. Semantics of Conceptual Modelling

A Conceptual Modelling Approach (CMA) such as Infolog [Sernadas and Sernadas 85b] or Chen's Entity-Relationship Approach (ER) [Ng 80], can be considered as a set of *semantic primitives* (abstractions) that can be used to organize knowledge in a knowledgebase. The integration of the structural paradigm with the logical approach to knowledge representation, as recently proposed in [Sernadas and Sernadas 88], advocates the identification of the semantic primitives of a CMA with a collection of parameterized theories in a certain institution. A knowledgebase, considered as a theory in the chosen institution, is built through the successive application of those parameterized theories, following strictly the organization of the knowledge in the knowledgebase on the semantic primitives of the CMA.

The main goal of this section is, precisely, the formalization of these notions within the π-institutional framework. In particular, it will be shown how any CMA adds structuring mechanisms on the theories of the underlying logic, allowing the reference to and the use of the *structure* of any knowledgebase built according to that CMA.

Conceptual modelling approaches in π-institutions

Two different layers of knowledge can be distinguished on a knowledgebase [Sernadas and Sernadas 88, Fiadeiro and Sernadas 88a]: the object layer that contains factual knowledge, ie the current beliefs maintained about the world being modelled, and the schema layer or <u>conceptual schema</u> of the knowledgebase that maintains knowledge about the structure and dynamics of facts. For instance, assuming a stock management application, typical factual, state-dependent knowledge could be

    $\rightarrow$ price(bananas,15)
    between(X,9,12) $\rightarrow$ open(dep(12),X)

expressing that it is currently believed that "the price of bananas is 15" and that "depot number 12 is open from 9 to 12". Typical knowledge in the conceptual schema could be

    integer(X) $\rightarrow$ depot(dep(X))
    $\rightarrow$ number(dep(X),X)
    depot(X), number(X,Y), odd(Y) $\rightarrow$ location(X,south)
    integer(X) $\rightarrow$ product(pro(X))
    $\rightarrow$ code(pro(X),X)

expressing knowledge about the application domain that is state-independent, namely that depots and products are identified by integers and that depots identified by odd integers are located in the south.

Following [Sernadas and Sernadas 88], it is possible to distinguish between the theory mappings that operate on the conceptual schema of a knowledgebase and those that operate on its object level, ie, that manipulate its factual knowledge. Herein, and for the sake of simplicity, only the semantics of the construction of the conceptual schema will be analysed.

Following the structural approach to knowledge representation, the conceptual schema of a knowledgebase is built using the semantic primitives of a CMA. For instance, in the stock management example and adopting the ER modelling approach, the *entity type* DEPOT would be introduced for organizing knowledge about depots. Similarly, the entity type PRODUCT could be introduced for organizing knowledge about products and the *relationship type* STOCK of PRODUCT and DEPOT could be introduced for organizing knowledge about stocks.

Such semantic primitives of a CMA (like entity type and relationship type of ER) can be seen to define theories in the chosen π-institution. For instance, the theory ENTITY associated to entity types can be seen to be the enrichment of a theory DATA with the predicate symbols *domain*(1-ary) identifying the new domain introduced, *key-att* (2-ary) giving the identification of each element of the new domain, the function symbol *key-map* (1-ary) identifying each element of the domain and the axioms

$\quad$ data(X) $\rightarrow$ domain(key-map(X))
$\quad \rightarrow$ key-att(key-map(X),X)

stating precisely what was said about the identification mechanisms. The predicate symbol *data* (1-ary) is assumed to be part of the vocabulary of DATA. The theory DATA provides the data type over which the entity type is defined. The theory ENTITY can actually be much richer (see [Sernadas and Sernadas 85a]) but the purpose here is not to give full definitions of CMAs but only to formalize the approach for which simpler cases provide examples that are more intuitive and easier to grasp.

Notice that by mapping *data* to *integer*, *domain* to *depot*, *key-att* to *number* and *key-map* to *dep* the theory having axioms

$\quad$ integer(X) $\rightarrow$ depot(dep(X))
$\quad \rightarrow$ number(dep(X),X)
$\quad$ depot(X), number(X,Y), odd(Y) $\rightarrow$ location(X,south)
$\quad$ integer(X) $\rightarrow$ product(pro(X))
$\quad \rightarrow$ code(pro(X),X)

provides an interpretation of ENTITY. Moreover, by mapping *data* to *integer*, *domain* to *product*, *key-att* to *code* and *key-map* to *pro* the same theory yields another interpretation of ENTITY. Each of the interpretations of ENTITY consists in recognizing in the theory an occurrence of an entity type, respectively the entity types DEPOT and PRODUCT. Hence, a knowledgebase defined through this theory is much more than a vocabulary and a set of axioms: it consists of two interpretations of ENTITY. This constitutes an added semantical value in the sense that there is a higher level structure of the theory that consists of two interpretations of ENTITY both linked to the same interpretation of DATA.

The presence of the axiom

depot(X), number(X,Y), odd(Y) → location(X,south)

which is not a direct translation of ENTITY means that the conceptual schema contains more knowledge than what can be obtained by modelling depots as an entity type. Indeed, the theory ENTITY contains only knowledge that is common to every entity type, namely the existence of an identification mechanism. Hence, the interpretations of this theory will usually add knowledge that is proper to the domain of application.

This approach is now formalized within the chosen π-institution:

3.1 Definition: A CMA C consists of:
- a category $Prim(C)$ of theories admitting an initial theory $KER(C)$ called its <u>kernel</u>;
- a collection $Map(C)$ of <u>theory mappings</u> each of which is a tuple $(\mu_1,...,\mu_n)$ of theory morphisms in $Prim(C)$ with a common target, i.e., $\mu_i : AT_i \to TT$, $i=1,...,n$. ◊

The kernel theory defines the minimal knowledgebase that can be built according to that CMA. Each object in $Prim(C)$ corresponds to a semantic primitive of the CMA and each morphism in $Prim(C)$ establishes a relationship between two semantic primitives. For instance, there is an obvious (inclusion) morphism from DATA to ENTITY because ENTITY was defined as an enrichment of DATA. On the other hand, there are two distinct morphisms from ENTITY to RELATIONSHIP (the theory associated to relationship types) for a relationship type is defined over two entity types. The initiality of the kernel means that it is a "subtheory" of every theory in $Prim(C)$.

Recall (2.6) that each theory mapping defines a parameterized theory which when applied to a multiple interpretation of the argument theories returns an interpretation of the target theory. The theory mappings define the criteria for recognizing theories that are built according to C. This is done by defining a derivability relation in $|The|$ (the collection of theories of the underlying π-institution):

3.2 Definition: Given a CMA C, a derivability relation $\Rightarrow_c$ can be defined in $|The|$ as follows:
$T \Rightarrow_c T'$ iff there are
- $<\mu_i: AT_i \to TT>_{i\leq 1\leq n} \in Map(C)$;
- $<\phi_i: AT_i \to T>_{i\leq 1\leq n}$;
- $\delta: TT \to T'$;
- $\sigma: T \to T'$

such that $\mu_i;\delta = \phi_i;\sigma$ for every $i=1,...,n$. A triple $\lambda=(<\mu_i>,<\phi_i>,\delta)$ as above is said to be associated to the derivation $T \Rightarrow_c T'$. ◊

That is to say, T' is derivable from T if there is a morphism $\sigma: T \to T'$ and a theory mapping $<\mu_i : AT_i \to TT>_{i\leq 1\leq n}$ such that T can provide a multiple interpretation of the argument theories and T' can provide an interpretation of the target theory that "agree", ie such that $\mu_i;\delta = \phi_i;\sigma$. This condition basically says that there is a unique morphism that relates T' to the free extension of T along the theory mapping (application of the parameterized theory associated to $<\mu_i : AT_i \to TT>_{i\leq 1\leq n}$):

3.3 Proposition: Let C be a CMA and $<\mu_i: AT_i \to TT>_{i \leq 1 \leq n} \in \text{Map}(C)$. If $<\phi_i: AT_i \to T>_{i \leq 1 \leq n}$ are interpreters (fitting morphisms), and $\tau(\mu_1,...,\mu_n)((\phi_1,T),...,(\phi_n,T))=(\delta,T')$, then $T \Rightarrow_c T'$ with $(<\mu_i>,<\phi_i>,\delta)$ associated. Moreover, if $T \Rightarrow_c T''$ with $(<\mu_i>,<\phi_i>,\delta')$ associated, then there is a unique interpretation morphism from $\tau(\mu_1,...,\mu_n)((\phi_1,T),...,(\phi_n,T))$ to (δ',T''). ◊

A conceptual schema over a CMA is just a theory for which there is a derivation sequence from the kernel theory:

3.4 Definition: Let C be a CMA. A *C-conceptual schema* is a theory T for which there is a sequence $T_1,...,T_m$ of theories such that $T_1 = \text{KER}(C)$, $T_m = T$ and, for every $1 \leq j < m$, $T_j \Rightarrow_c T_{j+1}$. If λ_j is the triple associated to the jth derivation, the sequence $\lambda_1,...,\lambda_{m-1}$ is called a *construction sequence* of T. ◊

Proposition 3.3 puts in evidence the process of building conceptual schemata: conceptual schemata are obtained by applying parameterized theories to previously built conceptual schemata. In fact, enrichment with specific axioms usually complements the application of a parameterized theory in order to introduce additional knowledge that is not captured by the semantic primitives alone. Hence the interpretation morphism that is obtained between the result of the application of the parameterized theory and the new conceptual schema.

For instance, in the case of the ER modelling approach, the inclusion morphism between DATA and ENTITY, hereafter named **ins-ent**, belongs to Map(ER). The application of the associated parameterized theory to a conceptual schema that interprets DATA extends it with an interpretation of ENTITY. Notice that the result of the application of a parameterized theory is defined only up to isomorphism. This means that the enrichment of a conceptual schema with knowledge about products and depots (both entity types) by applying the parameterized theory **ins-ent** to a conceptual schema that interprets DATA through integers can be seen to provide different vocabulary symbols for the two extensions. In order to instantiate to the desired vocabulary symbols, it is necessary to (isomorphically) rename the theories. Moreover, in order to include knowledge that is not obtained through the application of the parameterized theory such as

   depot(X), number(X,Y), odd(Y) $\to$ location(X,south)

it is necessary to enrich the resulting theory with the specific axioms.

Other theory mappings besides **ins-ent** are relevant for formalizing the ER modelling approach, namely the one given through the pair <**ins-rel-1,ins-rel-2**> of theory morphisms in Prim(ER) that relate entity types to relationship types (notice that there are two such morphisms, each corresponding to one of the entity types in the relationship). This theory mapping allows the enrichment of a conceptual schema with a relationship type defined over two already existing entity types. That is to say, it allows the extension of a conceptual schema providing two interpretations of the theory ENTITY to an interpretation of the theory RELATIONSHIP. Another relevant theory mapping would allow enriching a conceptual schema with an attribute defined over an already existing entity type (for the domain of the attribute) and a data type (for the codomain of the attribute). The latter mapping corresponds to the pair <ins-att-ent,ins-att-dt> where **ins-att-ent**: ENTITY→ATTRIBUTE and **ins-att-dt**: DATA→ATTRIBUTE.

These mappings were defined in [Sernadas and Sernadas 85a] using Knowlog. Such a language provides adequate tools for defining the theories and theory morphisms in Prim(C) for any CMA C [Sernadas and Sernadas 88]. As argued in 2.7, these definitions should use only operations that have a semantics at the theory level, so that they may denote theories of the underlying π-institution. This implies that the underlying π-institution should have been extended with data-constraints as formulae, as suggested in [Goguen and Burstall 85]. Conceptual schemata then act as interpretations of such theories so that they constitute models of them in the π-institutional sense [Fiadeiro and Sernadas 88b]. The semantics of such specification languages is thus much more natural in π-institutions because knowledgebases are regarded as theories in the underlying π-institution and not as models.

The structure of conceptual schemata

Returning to the process of building conceptual schemata, by associating to each conceptual schema the sequence $\delta_1,...,\delta_{m-1}$ of the interpreters of the target theories in the construction sequence, the fitting of the conceptual schema to the argument theories of another theory mapping consists only in picking up the relevant interpreters among the sequence $\delta_1,...,\delta_{m-1}$. That is to say, it is not necessary to try to fit a (more or less huge) collection of axioms to the argument theories of a theory mapping *because the conceptual schema is structured*. In fact, the sequence $\delta_1,...,\delta_{m-1}$ of interpreters allows to look at the conceptual schema from the point of view of the different semantic primitives to which it has been fitted. In a way, this sequence works as a *prism* that refracts the structure of the theory against the semantic primitives of the underlying CMA.

It is this process of building a conceptual schema that makes it *structured*. In a way, a CMA can be seen to define a *grammar* on the theories of a π-institution in the sense that it defines the theories that are "well formed". Indeed, under a CMA, *theories can be composed as objects per se according to their binding to the semantic primitives of the CMA*. The conceptual schemata are thus theories that exhibit a certain structure ("syntax") as given through the sequence of interpreters obtained during construction. However, this sequence provides only a poor image of the "small" units (conceptual schemata) that compose a conceptual schema. This is due to the fact that the conceptual schema evolves as a *global* theory, although using the sequence of interpreters to avoid global fitting.

This shows that only certain fragments of the conceptual schema are necessary for the fitting to the argument parameters of the theory mappings. When the explicit identification of these relevant subschemata is possible, the evolution of the conceptual schema can be given in terms of the transformations operated on these fragments (ie, on its internal structure). Thus, it seems better to consider the conceptual schema as explicitly composed of small, local units to which the parameterized theories have access in order to put them together. This would allow a structured access to the conceptual schema allowing its structure to be *effectively* used by isolating pieces that have a semantical meaning from the point of view of the CMA.

Consequently, it seems that a better denotation for a conceptual schema is given in terms of diagrams in The:

3.5 Definition [Arbib and Manes 75]: A *directed graph* is an arbitrary class of *vertices* together with an assignement, to each ordered pair (i,j) of vertices, of a class of *edges from i to j*. A *diagram* in a category C is a directed graph whose vertices are labelled by objects of C and whose edges from i to j are labelled by morphisms in C(A,B) such that A is the label of i and B is the label of j.   ◊

A direct generalization of the definitions above is therefore given as follows:

3.6 Definition: Given a CMA C, if D and D' are diagrams in The, $D \Rightarrow_c D'$ iff
- there are vertices $V_1,...,V_n$ of D labelled $T_1,...,T_n$ and a theory T such that there are
  - $<\mu_i : AS_i \rightarrow TS>_{i \le 1 \le n} \in Map(C);$
  - $<\phi_i : AS_i \rightarrow T_i>_{i \le 1 \le n};$
  - $\delta: TS \rightarrow T;$
  - $<\sigma_i : T_i \rightarrow T>_{i \le 1 \le n}$
  satisfying $\mu_i; \delta = \phi_i; \sigma_i$ for every i=1,...,n.
- D' is obtained from D by adding a vertice labelled T and by linking it to the vertices $V_1,...,V_n$ through edges labelled by the morphisms $\sigma_i : T_i \rightarrow T$, i≤1≤n.
- For every vertice V for which there is a path to V_j and a path to V_k, the subdiagram linking V to the new vertice labelled T through the two paths extended with the edges labelled σ_j and σ_k, commutes.   ◊

Basically, this last condition on the commutativity of the diagrams induced by the extension means that the already existing structure is shared. That is to say, taking the colimits of the diagram consisting of the theories $T_1,...,T_n$ together with the fitting and the theory mapping is not correct in the sense that the subtheories shared by the theories $T_1,...,T_n$ as expressed by paths coming from a same vertice must also be shared by the resulting theory. Hence, the new theory must be computed by taking the colimit of the extension of that diagram to all the nodes that are ancestors of $V_1,...,V_n$. Notice that the colimit is not taken over the entire diagram D unless every node in D is an ancestor of one of $V_1,...,V_n$. Otherwise, taking the colimit over D would reduce to the previous approach by looking at the diagram as a global theory (its colimit).

This problem of taking care of shared subtheories has an elegant solution that uses the notion of *based object* proposed in [Burstall and Goguen 80] using the notion of *co-cone* of a diagram. Basically, a based object carries with it the relations of the object to the other objects (given through morphism from its base, a diagram, to its apex) thus allowing to deal explicitly with the problem of shared structures. The definitions above are easily extended to based-theories. This extension is omitted herein because, although very elegant, it is rather sophisticated.

A conceptual schema is then defined as follows:

3.7   Definition: Let C be a CMA. A *C-conceptual schema* is a diagram D for which there is a sequence $D_1,...,D_m$ of diagrams such that $D_1 = KER(C)$, $D_m = D$ and, for every $1 \leq j < m$, $D_j \Rightarrow_c D_{j+1}$. ◊

(Using based theories, conceptual schemata are then obtained as *environments* in the sense of [Burstall and Goguen 80].)

This definition differs from the preceding one (3.4) in that the conceptual schema is manipulated by letting the theory mappings operate in the subschemata that compose it. A more explicit denotation of the resulting structure of the conceptual schema is thus obtained. Notice that these diagrams provide a much more closer connection to the popular representation of conceptual schemata through directed graphs as illustrated in the example below.

3.8   Remark: The notion of conceptual schema is more "semantical" than the notion of environment or of structured theory used in [Sannella and Burstall 83] in the sense that it depends on the CMA that is being used. That is to say, besides enclosing knowledge on how the theory was syntactically built from other theories, a structured theory in a CMA has additional knowledge given through its "links" (interpreters) to the semantic primitives of the CMA. It is not yet clear how this knowledge can be used for guiding proofs and extending the tactics in [Sannella and Burstall 83], but this seems to be a most promising direction for future work.   ◊

3.9   Example: Returning to the example of stock management using the ER approach, assume that KER denotes its kernel heory. Given the diagram

$$KER \longrightarrow int$$

and assuming that **int** was introduced as a data type, that is to say, assuming that it was obtained from KER through the application of a theory mapping with codomain in DATA, there is a morphism from DATA to **int** that results from the derivation (its interpreter). This relationship is depicted in the diagram through a dotted edge as shown below:

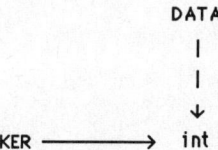

This morphism provides the necessary fitting for the application of the theory mapping **ins-ent** (including possible renamings and enrichments of the pushout) allowing the previous diagram to be extended as follows:

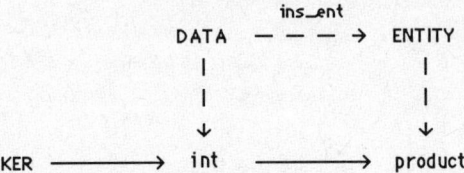

Notice the binding of the new vertex to the semantic primitive ENTITY. Using the previous binding, this diagram can also be extended through the aplication of the same theory mapping (with different renamings and enrichments):

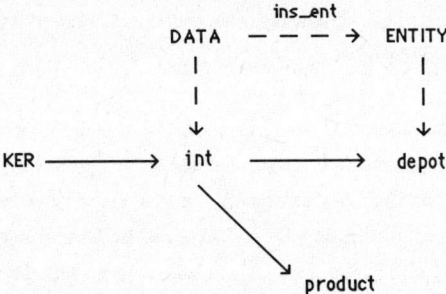

Notice that the nodes labelled **product** and **depot** are not linked to each other. The two edges departing from **int** suggest that the two applications of the theory mapping could have been done in any order. Also note that the dotted edge linking **product** to ENTITY was omitted for simplifying the diagram. The same will be done in the diagrams below: only the relevant fittings will be displayed.

The two bindings to ENTITY allow the application of the theory mapping associated to relationship types, extending the diagram as follows:

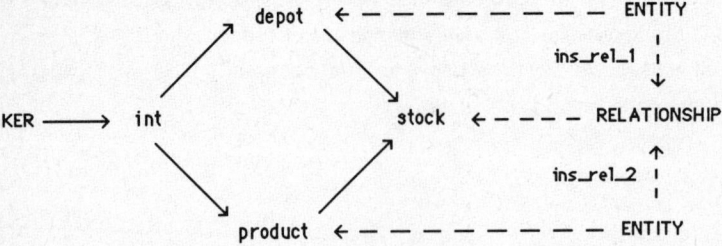

The morphisms in Prim(ER) also play an important role in the fitting of schemata to the argument theories of theory mappings. For instance, suppose that there was another semantic primitive,

SPECIALIZATION, linked to ENTITY through a morphism **is-a**: ENTITY→SPECIALIZATION (the arrow means that every interpretation of SPECIALIZATION is an interpretation of ENTITY). Suppose now that the specialization **frozen** of **product** had been added to the previous diagram, yielding

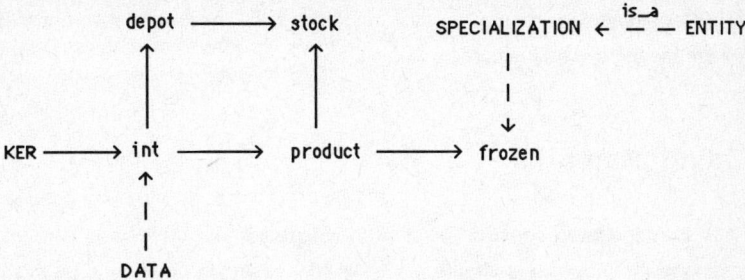

Apparently, it is impossible to add the attribute **temperature** to **frozen** because the theory mapping <**ins-att-ent,ins-att-dt**> requires a fitting to an entity type. However, the connection between ENTITY and SPECIALIZATION permits this fitting and, hence, the application of this theory mapping, yielding

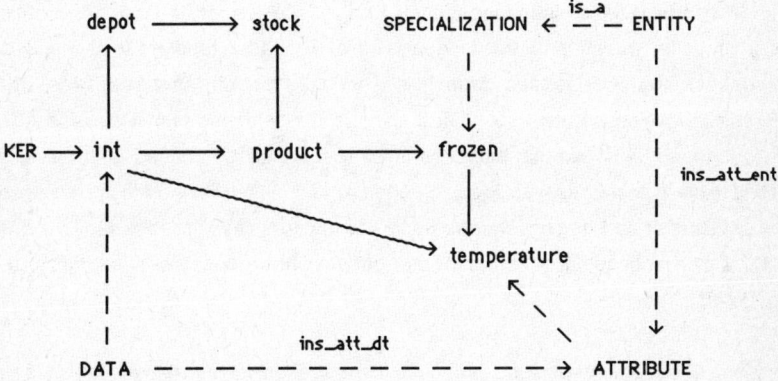

Notice that the previous diagram is extended independently of the sub-diagram concerning depots and stocks. This means that the colimit is taken over the subdiagram

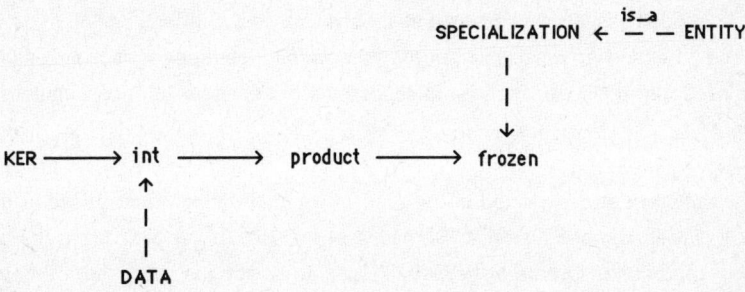

and, hence, there are no edges linking **temperature** to **depot** or **stock**. Naturally, it is possible to reason about the temperature of frozen products in stock for a certain depot by computing the colimit of the diagram. That is to say, the conceptual schema can be seen as a structure of modules that can be put together when desired. For instance, mechanisms are envisaged for, given a query to the knowledgebase, determining the fragment of the underlying theory that is relevant to answer the query. Here relevant means minimal according to the CMA.

4 Concluding Remarks

A formalization for the structured construction of knowledgebases as theories in a π-institution was proposed. According to the proposed semantics, a knowledgebase can be seen to be more then a raw collection of formulae: it can be seen as a structure of small, local theories that present a binding to the semantic primitives of a conceptual modelling approach (CMA). This structure was highlighted by defining conceptual schemata as diagrams in the category of the theories of the underlying π-institution. These diagrams evolve by application of parameterized theories, similarly to the organization of the knowledge in a knowledgebase using the semantic primitives of a CMA.

In a sense, CMA can be seen to introduce criteria for the "well formed theories" of a π-institution, in the same way that the grammar of the language of a logic (the functor Φ in the definition of a π-institution) defines the well formed formulae. This means that, under a CMA, theories are composed as objects per se according to their binding to the semantic primitives of the CMA. Taking the comparison further, it is hoped that inference mechanisms may be defined at the level of the CMA for manipulating such theories just as Modus Ponens manipulates formulae by recognizing in any implication its antecedent and its consequent. Such inference mechanisms would allow a higher level reaoning process over conceptual schemata. Later on it might be possible to recognize a CMA as a π-institution itself.

Another important achievement with the proposed formalization is that the semantics of conceptual schemata is placed in the very general and abstract setting of π-institutions. Therefore, it becomes possible to apply the wide body of tools that are being developed in the institutional framework in terms of relating and combining different formalisms, for instance to the refinement of conceptual schemata to their final stages in particular data models. Work in the direction of the transformation to the relational model has already been done [Sernadas and Sernadas 85c]. It would also be interesting to see how far the formalization of the network and hierarchical data models in categorial logic proposed in [Cartmell 86] can be used to support the implementation of conceptual schemata as defined herein.

Relevant side results are also expected in the area of communicating agents, able to maintain and exchange more or less complex theories [Sernadas et al 87b,87c], as well as in the semantics of object oriented approaches [Sernadas et al 87a,88]: it is not yet clear how these structuring principles can be combined with the concept of object.

References

[Arbib and Manes 75] M. Arbib and E. Manes, <u>Arrows, Structures, and Functors</u>, Academic Press 1975

[Burstall and Goguen 80] R. Burstall and J. Goguen, "The Semantics of Clear, a Specification Language", in LNCS 86, Proc. <u>1979 Copenhagen Winter School on Abstract Software Specification</u>, Springer-Verlag 1980, 292-332

[Carapuça and Fiadeiro 86] R. Carapuça and J. Fiadeiro, "Varying Representation Schemata vs Fact Updating in Knowledge Base Management", in <u>Knowledge and Data</u>, R. Meersman and A. Sernadas (eds), (to be published by North-Holland)

[Cartmell 86] J. Cartmell, "Formalizing the Network and Hierarchical Data Models - an Application of Categorical Logic", in [Pitt et al 86]

[Fiadeiro and Sernadas 88a] J. Fiadeiro and A. Sernadas, "Behavioural Aspects of Intelligent Knowledge Based Information Systems", in <u>Temporal Aspects in Information Systems</u>, C. Rolland, M. Léonard and F. Bodart (eds), North-Holland 1988, 77-92

[Fiadeiro and Sernadas 88b] J. Fiadeiro and A. Sernadas, "Structuring Theories on Consequence", in <u>Recent Trends in Data Type Specification: 5th Workshop on Specification of Abstract Data Types - Selected Papers</u>, D. Sannella and A. Tarlecki (eds), Springer-Verlag (to be published)

[Goguen and Burstall 85] J. Goguen and R. Burstall, "Institutions: Abstract Model Theory for Computer Science", CSLI - 85-30, Stanford University, 1985 (preliminary version in LNCS 164, Proc. <u>Logics of Programming Workshop</u>, E. Clarke and D. Kozen (eds), Springer-Verlag 1984, 221-256)

[Goguen and Burstall 86] J. Goguen and R. Burstall, "A Study in the Foundations of Programming Methodology: Specifications, Institutions, Charters and Parchments", in [Pitt et al 86], 313-333

[Ng 80] P. Ng, "A Formal Definition of Entity-Relationship Models", in <u>Entity-Relationship Approach to Systems Analysis and Design</u>, P. Chen (ed), North-Holland 1980

[Pitt et al 86] D. Pitt, S. Abramski, A. Poigné and D. Rydeheard, <u>Category Theory and Computer Programming</u>, LNCS 240, Springer-Verlag 1986

[Sannella and Burstall 83] D. Sannella and R. Burstall, "Structured Theories in LCF", in LNCS 159 <u>CAAP'83: 8th Colloquium on Trees in Algebra and Programming</u>, G. Ausiello and M. Protasi (eds), Springer-Verlag 1983, 377-391

[Sannella and Tarlecki 84] D. Sannella and A. Tarlecki, "Specifications in an Arbitrary Institution", in LNCS 173, <u>Proc. Int. Symposium on Semantics of Data Types</u>, Springer-Verlag 1984, 337-356

[Sernadas and Sernadas 85a] A. Sernadas and C. Sernadas, "The Use of E-R Abstractions for Knowledge Representation", in <u>Entity-Relationship Approach: The Use of ER Concept in Knowledge Representation.</u> P. Chen (ed), North-Holland and IEEE 1985, 224-231

[Sernadas and Sernadas 85b] C. Sernadas and A. Sernadas, "Conceptual Schema Abstraction Mechanisms for Knowledge Representation", in <u>Information Modelling and Data Base Management</u>, H. Kangassalo (ed), Proc. Workshop, Tampere, 1985 (to be published by Springer-Verlag)

[Sernadas and Sernadas 85c] C. Sernadas and A. Sernadas, "The Institutional Approach to Conceptual Schema Transformations", Infolog RR 41, 1985

[Sernadas and Sernadas 86] C. Sernadas and A. Sernadas, "Conceptual Modeling Abstraction Mechanisms as Parameterized Theories in Institutions", in <u>Database Semantics (DS-1)</u>, R. Meersman and T. Steel (eds), North-Holland 1986, 121-140

[Sernadas and Sernadas 88] A. Sernadas and C. Sernadas, "Abstraction and Inference Mechanisms for Knowledge Representation", in <u>Foundations of Knowledge Base Management</u>, J. Schmidt and C. Thanos (eds), Springer-Verlag 1988 (in print)

[Sernadas et al 87a] A. Sernadas, C. Sernadas and H.-D. Ehrich, "Object-Oriented Specification of Databases: an Algebraic Approach", <u>Proc. 13th VLDB</u>, P. Hammersley (ed), VLDB 1987, 107-116

[Sernadas et al 87b] C. Sernadas, H. Coelho and G. Gaspar, "Communicating Knowledge Systems: Part I - Big Talk among Small Systems", <u>Applied Artificial Intelligence</u> 1(3), 1987, 233-260

[Sernadas et al 87c] C. Sernadas, H. Coelho and G. Gaspar, "Communicating Knowledge Systems: Part II - Big Talk among Small Systems", <u>Applied Artificial Intelligence</u> 1(4), 1987, 315-335

[Sernadas et al 88] A. Sernadas, J. Fiadeiro, C. Sernadas and H.-D. Ehrich, "Abstract Object Types: A Temporal Perspective", in <u>Colloquium on Temporal Logic and Specification</u>, A. Pnueli, H. Barringer and B. Banieqbal (eds), 1988 (to be published by Springer-Verlag)

[Tarski 30] A. Tarski, "Fundamentale Begriffe der Methodologie der Deduktiven Wissenschaften", french translation in <u>Logique, Sémantique, Métamathématique</u>, vol 1, Armand Colin 1972, 67-116

ON FUNCTIONAL INDEPENDENCIES

Jürgen M. Janas
Universität der Bundeswehr München
Werner-Heisenberg-Weg 39, D-8014 Neubiberg
Federal Republic of Germany

1. <u>Introduction</u>

Logical design of relational databases on the basis of data dependencies - such as functional dependencies (cf. [CODD 70]) or multivalued dependencies (cf. [FAGIN 77] and [ZANIOLO 76]) - has a purely mathematical foundation which is still embodied in the design process: Given as input a set of data dependencies, which have to be satisfied by the relations of some database, the decomposition and synthesis algorithms (cf. [ULLMAN 82] for an introduction) produce a set of relation schemes all of which are in fourth normal form (cf. [FAGIN 77]), Boyce-Codd normal form (cf. [CODD 74]) or at least third normal form (cf. [CODD 72]), such that the decomposition is lossless (cf. [AHO et al. 79]) and preserves the given data dependencies (cf. [BEERI & HONEYMAN 81]). Thus, the adequacy of the resulting relation schemes solely depends on whether the given data dependencies are correct with respect to the real world. This may be satisfactory from a mathematical point of view, however, it is not from a pragmatical point of view, since specification of those data dependencies has to be done by humans who are subject to imperfection.

Three kinds of imperfection may be observed when comparing the set of data dependencies which are to be satisfied by the relations of some database with that facet of reality that is to be represented by that database: Firstly, the set of data dependencies may be redundant, i.e. a proper subset of it implies all the data dependencies in the set. Redundancy is not a big problem, since it does not affect adequacy of the resulting relation schemes, but only increases the run-time of the respective algorithms; besides, for functional and multivalued dependencies, there are efficient algorithms by means of which a non-redundant (cf. [BEERI 80] and [GALIL 82]) or even minimal (cf. [MAIER 80]) set of data dependencies which is equivalent to a given set of data dependencies may be computed.

The other two kinds of imperfection that may be detected are more severe: Secondly, the specified set of data dependencies may contain elements which do not have a counterpart in reality and, thirdly, there may be data dependencies which are missing in the specified set, although that part of reality that is to be represented by the database is subject to corresponding restrictions. In either case, such an incorrectly specified set of data dependencies may have detrimentral - if not disastrous - effects on the relation schemes that result from a decomposition algorithm. As an example, let T be a set of functional dependencies, $f \in T$, and g an additional functional dependency, such that $g \notin T$; it is obvious that a decomposition need not preserve $T \cup \{g\}$, if it preserves T, and it is easy to verify that a decomposition need not be lossless with regard to $T \setminus \{f\}$, if it is lossless with regard to T.

In view of this situation, it is amazing that the problem, how a database designer might be supported in the process of identifying the data dependencies, which have to be satisfied by the relations of some database, has hardly ever been attacked. As a matter of fact, we are only aware of the work of Silva and Melkanoff (cf. [SILVA & MELKANOFF 81], who proposed to synthesize an Armstrong relation (cf. [BEERI et al. 80]) from the functional and multivalued dependencies specified by the database designer and to display this Armstrong relation to the database designer for review. The main problem with this approach is that the cardinality - even of a minimal Armstrong relation - may be exponential in the number of dependencies, even if only functional dependencies are considered (cf. [BEERI et al. 80]).

In this paper, we shall present the theoretical foundations of an alternative way of supporting the database designer in the task of identifying the set of data dependencies, which are to be satisfied by the relations of the respective database. The idea is that this set of data dependencies is determined in an interactive, system-guided process during which the database designer is repeatedly asked, whether or not some data dependency has always to be satisfied by the relations of the database. Such a procedure enables the system to control at any time whether the specification of the database designer is contradictory and to what extent it is incomplete. Although our approach may be applied also to other classes of data dependencies, we shall restrict ourselves in this paper to the case where all of the data dependencies taken into consideration are functional dependencies.

Starting point for our considerations are the following observations: From the fact that a certain functional dependency is not satisfied by a relation, we may conclude that some other functional dependencies are not satisfied either by that relation. As an example, consider a functional dependency $AB \rightarrow C$; it is easy to see that if $AB \rightarrow C$ is not satisfied by some relation r, then $A \rightarrow C$ and $B \rightarrow C$ are not satisfied either by r. Moreover, the fact that a functional dependency is satisfied by a relation and that some other functional dependency is not satisfied by that relation, may imply that certain other functional dependencies are not satisfied by that relation. As an example, consider a relation r which satisfies $D \rightarrow AB$, but does not satisfy $D \rightarrow C$; again it is easy to verify that r does not satisfy $AB \rightarrow C$.

In order to gain a better understanding of these implications, it is desirable to find a formal system of inference rules which enables us to derive all functional dependencies which are not satisfied by a relation. In order to be able to find such a formal system, the fact that a functional dependency is not satisfied by a relation needs to be formalized; we shall do that in section 2 by introducing the concept "functional independency". Moreover, the second example given above seems to suggest that there is little use in considering functional independencies by themselves; rather we shall present a formal system which enables us to derive all functional dependencies and all functional independencies that are implied by a given set of both functional dependencies and functional independencies. We shall prove in section 3 that this formal system is both sound and complete.

The well-known formal systems for the derivation of functional dependencies [ARMSTRONG 74] or multivalued dependencies [BEERI et al. 77] illustrate that the mere existence of a formal system does not provide efficient algorithms for the fundamental computational problems related to the respective class of dependencies. In section 4, three basic computational problems related to functional independencies are investigated. The *contradiction problem* problem is genuine to functional independencies: Given a set of functional dependencies and a set of functional independencies, are there relations which satisfy both the functional dependencies and the functional independencies? The *implication problem* is well-known from all kinds of data dependencies: Given a set Γ of functional dependencies, a set Σ of functional independencies and an individual functional (in)dependency f, is f logically implied by Γ and Σ? The *equivalence problem* also applies to all kinds of data dependencies and is closely related to the implication problem: The equivalence problem is to tell whether two sets consisting of both functional dependencies and functional independencies are equivalent, i.e. whether they imply the same set of functional dependencies and independencies. For each of these problems we shall present an algorithm, prove its correctness, and briefly analyze its time complexity.

2. Functional Dependencies and Functional Independencies

A *relation scheme* R is a finite set of symbols which are called *attributes*, such that each attribute is associated with a *domain*, which is the set of all possible *values* for the respective attribute. We shall use the letters A, B and C in order to refer to individual attributes and the letters U, V, W, X, Y and Z in order to refer to sets of attributes. Usually we shall not distinguish between an attribute A and the set {A}; the union of U and V shall be denoted by UV. The entirety of the attributes of some relation scheme R will be referred to by atts(R) and dom(A) will denote the domain the attribute A is associated with.

A *relation* (also called *instance*) on a relation scheme R with atts(R) = $\{A_1,\ldots,A_n\}$ is a subset of the Cartesian product $dom(A_1) \times \ldots \times dom(A_n)$; relations will be denoted by $r, r_0, r_1, \ldots$. The elements of a relation are called *tuples*; tuples will be designated by $t, t_1, t_2, \ldots$. Finally, if t is a tuple of a relation on relation scheme R, A $\in$ atts(R) and X $\subseteq$ atts(R), then t[A] will denote the value of t with regard to A and t[X] is a tuple of a relation on some relation scheme R' with atts(R') = X; consequently, we shall not distinguish between the value t[A] and the tuple t[{A}] .

Throughout the remainder of this paper, we shall tacitly assume some arbitrary, but fixed relation scheme R to be given. Thus, whenever we talk about some relation r or some set of attributes X, it is assumed that r is a relation on R or that X is a subset of atts(R), respectively, even if this is not mentioned explicitly.

A *functional dependency* is a statement that describes a

semantic constraint on data (cf. [CODD 72]). Formally, a functional dependency is an expression of the form $X \rightarrow Y$, where X and Y are sets of attributes; a functional dependency $X \rightarrow Y$ is *satisfied* by a relation r, iff

$$\forall\, t_1, t_2 \in r \quad t_1[X] = t_2[X] \Rightarrow t_1[Y] = t_2[Y].$$

Each set T of functional dependencies the attributes of which are taken from some set $atts(R)$ determines a unique set of relations on R, namely the set of all those relations which satisfy all of the functional dependencies in T; this set is designated by $sat(T)$. A simple cardinality argument shows that there are sets ρ of relations for which there is no set T, such that $\rho = sat(T)$.

At first sight this seems to suggest that functional dependencies are of little use for specifying the set of admissible states of a database; however, the results reported in [GINSBURG & ZAIDDAN 82] imply that any set of relations may be "approximated" by a set of functional dependencies in a best and (except for equivalence) uniquely determined way. Therefore, sets of functional dependencies may be used as part of a *relation schema* to specify the set of all admissible relations on some relation scheme.

A *functional independency* is an expression of the form $X \nrightarrow Y$, where X and Y are sets of attributes. As a functional independency is meant as a statement that the corresponding functional dependency is not satisfied by a relation, it seems reasonable to define that a functional independency $X \nrightarrow Y$ is satisfied by a relation r, iff

$$\exists\, t_1, t_2 \in r \quad t_1[X] = t_2[X] \land t_1[Y] \neq t_2[Y].$$

A functional independency is not a data dependency in the sense that it describes a semantic constraint on data. This is indicated already by the observation that both the empty relation and any one-tuple relation will not satisfy a functional independency whatsoever.

Moreover, if we consider sets T of functional dependencies and sets Σ of functional independencies in combination in order to describe a set of admissible relations, then $sat(T \cup \Sigma)$ - if defined after the model of the definition of $sat(T)$ - would contain all relations which satisfy all of the functional dependencies in T and all of the functional independencies in Σ. On the other hand, our intuitive understanding of a functional independency as part of a relation schema suggests that there exists an admissible relation which satisfies that functional independency (i.e. does not satisfy the corresponding functional dependency) rather than that all admissible relations have to satisfy that functional independency (i.e. do not satisfy the corresponding functional dependency); therefore, an evident way to characterize $sat(T \cup \Sigma)$ would be to say that each relation in $sat(T \cup \Sigma)$ satisfies all of the functional dependencies in T and that for each functional independency in Σ there is at least one relation r in $sat(T \cup \Sigma)$, such that r satisfies that functional independency. Unfortunately, this characterization does not uniquely determine a set $sat(T \cup \Sigma)$ and, particularly, $sat(T)$ is a set which satisfies this characterization of $sat(T \cup \Sigma)$, provided that $sat(T \cup \Sigma) \neq \emptyset$.

As a consequence, we can say that functional independencies do not contribute anything new to the specification capabilities of functional dependencies.

Finally, our claim that functional independencies are no data dependencies is also supported by a purely formal argument: According to [BEERI & VARDI 81], a *dependency* is a first-order sentence

$$\forall t_1 \ldots \forall t_m \exists t_{m+1} \exists t_{m+n} (A_1 \wedge \ldots \wedge A_p \Rightarrow B_1 \wedge \ldots \wedge B_q)$$

where the A_i and B_j are atomic formulas, $m, p, q \geq 1$ and $n \geq 0$. Dependencies were introduced as a generalization of the known classes of data dependencies; it is obvious from the definitions that functional independencies are no dependencies.

In the following section, we shall present a formal system for the derivation of functional dependencies and independencies and prove completeness of that formal system. The idea of the proof is similar to the proof of completeness of the formal system for functional dependencies only; there, a relation r is constructed from a set X of attributes and a set Γ of functional dependencies, such that r satisfies all functional dependencies $X \rightarrow Y$ which are implied by Γ, but no other functional dependencies with left-hand side X. If a set Γ of functional dependencies and a set Σ of functional independencies are considered in combination, then the following problem arises: If X and Y are attribute sets, such that neither $X \rightarrow Y$ nor $X \not\rightarrow Y$ is implied by $\Gamma \cup \Sigma$, then there can be no relation r, such that neither $X \rightarrow Y$ nor $X \not\rightarrow Y$ is satisfied by r.

In order to overcome this problem, we introduce a special value "$\perp$" which is an element of all domains. Though precise semantics of "$\perp$" are not actually required in this paper, it is convenient to think of "$\perp$" as a kind of null value, the meaning of which is that the actual value is unknown. What is required, however, is a revision of the definitions of functional dependency and functional independency in the presence of "$\perp$".

Definition 2.1
Let $X, Y \subseteq atts(R)$; the functional dependency $X \rightarrow Y$ is satisfied by a relation r, iff

$$\forall t_1, t_2 \in r \ (\forall A \in X \ (t_1[A] \neq \perp \wedge t_1[A] = t_2[A])$$
$$\Rightarrow \forall B \in Y \ (t_1[B] \neq \perp \wedge t_1[B] = t_2[B])) \quad \square$$

Definition 2.2
Let $X, Y \subseteq atts(R)$; the functional independency $X \not\to Y$ is satisfied by a relation r, iff

$$\exists t_1, t_2 \in r \ (\forall A \in X \ (t_1[A] \neq \perp \land t_1[A] = t_2[A])$$
$$\land \ \exists B \in Y \ (t_1[B] \neq \perp \land t_2[B] \neq \perp \land t_1[B] \neq t_2[B])) \qquad \square$$

It is easy to see that according to these definitions there are relations r, such that neither $X \to Y$ nor $X \not\to Y$ is satisfied by r. Starting from Definition 2.1, the fundamental concepts and propositions of design theory for relational databases may be developed in exactly the same way as with the traditional definition of functional dependencies. In particular, we may define T^+ as the closure of a set T of functional dependencies, i.e. the set of all functional dependencies which are implied by T. Moreover, Armstrong's axioms (cf. [ARMSTRONG 74]) may be used without any modification in order to derive new functional dependencies $X \to Y$ from a given set T of functional dependencies (abbreviation: $T \vdash X \to Y$), and it can be shown that $X \to Y \in T^+$, iff $T \vdash X \to Y$, i.e. Armstrong's axioms are sound and complete with respect to Definition 2.1, too. Another concept we shall need is the closure X_T^+ of a set X of attributes with regard to some set T of functional dependencies, i.e. the set of all attributes A, such that $T \vdash X \to A$, and the fact that $T \vdash X \to Y$, iff $Y \subseteq X_T^+$.

The concept of the closure of a set of functional dependencies is now extended to sets of both functional dependencies and functional independencies.

Definition 2.3
Let $T \cup \Sigma$ be a set of functional dependencies and functional independencies.
(1) $T \cup \Sigma$ implies a functional dependency $X \to Y$, (or functional independency $X \not\to Y$, respectively), iff every relation which satisfies each functional dependency

from Γ and each functional independency from Σ also satisfies $X \rightarrow Y$ (or $X \not\rightarrow Y$, respectively).

(2) By $(\Gamma \cup \Sigma)^+$ we designate the closure of $\Gamma \cup \Sigma$, i.e. the set of all functional dependencies and functional independencies that are implied by $\Gamma \cup \Sigma$. □

Not every combination of a set Γ of functional dependencies and a set Σ of functional independencies is reasonable. If, e.g., $X \rightarrow Y \in \Gamma$ and $X \not\rightarrow Y \in \Sigma$, then there will be no relation which satisfies $\Gamma \cup \Sigma$. This observation gives rise to the following definition.

Definition 2.4
Let $\Gamma \cup \Sigma$ be a set of functional dependencies and functional independencies. $\Gamma \cup \Sigma$ is *free of contradictions* (f.o.c.), iff

$$\forall\ X,\ Y \subseteq atts(R)$$
$$X \rightarrow Y \notin (\Gamma \cup \Sigma)^+ \quad \vee \quad X \not\rightarrow Y \notin (\Gamma \cup \Sigma)^+ \qquad □$$

The question how to decide whether a set $\Gamma \cup \Sigma$ is f. o. c. or not will be answered in section 4.

3. A Formal System for the Derivation of Functional Dependencies and Independencies

So far we have no procedure to compute the closure of a set of functional dependencies and independencies. The basis of such a procedure may be a formal system, i.e. a set of inference rules which allow the derivation of new functional dependencies and independencies from a set of given ones. Such a formal system is said to be *sound*, iff any functional (in)dependency that may be derived from some $\Gamma \cup \Sigma$ by means of the formal system is an element of $(\Gamma \cup \Sigma)^+$. Such a formal system is said to be *complete*, iff any element of $(\Gamma \cup \Sigma)^+$ may be derived from $\Gamma \cup \Sigma$ by means of the formal system.

There is no general guideline how to find the inference rules for a sound and complete formal system; therefore it may be helpful, if one knows that certain classes of inference rules need not be considered at all. The following lemma will provide us with such knowledge.

Lemma 3.1
Let $\Gamma \cup \Sigma$ be a set of functional dependencies and independencies which is f. o. c.; then

$$X \rightarrow Y \in (\Gamma \cup \Sigma)^+ \Rightarrow X \rightarrow Y \in \Gamma^+$$

Proof: cf. [JANAS 85] □

Lemma 3.1 particularly implies that a formal system for the derivation of functional dependencies and functional independencies must not comprise inference rules which allow the derivation of functional dependencies and have functional independencies among their premises. Therefore, the desired formal system will contain Armstrong's axioms as a subset and additional inference rules which allow the derivation of functional independencies only.

Definition 3.2
(1) Let X, Y, $Z \subseteq$ atts (R).
  - (FD1) If $Y \subseteq X$, then $X \rightarrow Y$ may be derived.
  - (FD2) If $X \rightarrow Y$ may be derived, then $XZ \rightarrow YZ$ may be derived.
  - (FD3) If $X \rightarrow Y$ and $Y \rightarrow Z$ may be derived, then $X \rightarrow Z$ may be derived.
  - (FI1) If $X \nrightarrow Y$ may be derived, then $X \nrightarrow YZ$ may be derived.
  - (FI2) If $XZ \nrightarrow YZ$ may be derived, then $XZ \nrightarrow Y$ may be derived.
  - (FD-FI) If $X \rightarrow Y$ and $X \nrightarrow Z$ may be derived, then $Y \nrightarrow Z$ may be derived.

(2) Let $T \cup \Sigma$ be a set of functional dependencies and independencies.
   (a) A functional dependency $X \rightarrow Y$ may be derived from $T \cup \Sigma$ (notation: $T \cup \Sigma \vdash X \rightarrow Y$), iff $X \rightarrow Y \in T$ or $X \rightarrow Y$ may be obtained from T by a finite number of applications of the inference rules (FD1), (FD2) and (FD3).
   (b) A functional independency $X \not\rightarrow Y$ may be derived from $T \cup \Sigma$ (notation: $T \cup \Sigma \vdash X \not\rightarrow Y$), iff $X \not\rightarrow Y \in \Sigma$ or $X \not\rightarrow Y$ may be obtained from $T \cup \Sigma$ by a finite number of applications of the inference rules (FD1), (FD2), (FD3), (FI1), (FI2) and (FD-FI). □

Theorem 3.3 (Soundness)
Let $T \cup \Sigma$ be a set of functional dependencies and independencies; then
(1) $T \cup \Sigma \vdash X \rightarrow Y \Rightarrow X \rightarrow Y \in (T \cup \Sigma)^+$
(2) $T \cup \Sigma \vdash X \not\rightarrow Y \Rightarrow X \not\rightarrow Y \in (T \cup \Sigma)^+$

Proof:
(1) follows immediately from the soundness of Armstrong's axioms. In order to prove (2), soundness of (FI1), (FI2) and (FD-FI) has to be shown by means of definitions 2.1 and 2.2; we shall do so for (FD-FI): Let r be an arbitrary relation, such that $X \rightarrow Y$ and $X \not\rightarrow Z$ are satisfied by r; that means

$$\forall t_1, t_2 \in r \; (\forall A \in X \; (t_1[A] \neq \bot \land t_1[A] = t_2[A])$$
$$\Rightarrow \forall B \in Y \; (t_1[B] \neq \bot \land t_1[B] = t_2[B]))$$
$$\land \; \exists t_3, t_4 \in r \; (\forall A \in X \; (t_3[A] \neq \bot \land t_3[A] = t_4[A])$$
$$\land \; \exists C \in Z \; (t_3[C] \neq \bot \land t_4[C] \neq \bot \land t_3[C] \neq t_4[C])) \; .$$

As the first part of this sentence particularly applies to t_3 and t_4, we obtain

$$\exists t_3, t_4 \in r \; (\forall A \in X \; (t_3[A] \neq \bot \land t_3[A] = t_4[A])$$
$$\land \; \forall B \in Y \; (t_3[B] \neq \bot \land t_3[B] = t_4[B])$$
$$\land \; \exists C \in Z \; (t_3[C] \neq \bot \land t_4[C] \neq \bot \land t_3[C] \neq t_4[C]))$$

Dropping that part of the sentence, that refers to X results in

$$\exists\, t_3, t_4 \in r\ (\forall\, B \in Y\ (t_3[B] \neq \perp \land t_3[B] = t_4[B]$$
$$\land\ \exists\, C \in Z\ (t_3[C] \neq \perp \land t_4[C] \neq \perp \land t_3[C] \neq t_4[C])).$$

which means that $Y \not\to Z$ is satisfied by r. For (FI1) and (FI2) the proof is similar. □

The formal system given in Definition 3.2 does not contain a minimal set of inference rules; in fact (FI1), (FI2) and (FD-FI) may be replaced by a single inference rule, namely: If $X \to Y$ and $X \not\to Z$ may be derived, then $Y \not\to (Z \setminus Y) \cup V$ may be derived where $V \subseteq$ atts (R) is an arbitrary attribute set. The proof of this equivalence is left to the reader.

Theorem 3.4 (Completeness)
Let $\Gamma \cup \Sigma$ be a set of functional dependencies and independencies which is f. o. c.; then
(1) $X \to Y \in (\Gamma \cup \Sigma)^+ \Rightarrow \Gamma \cup \Sigma \vdash X \to Y$
(2) $X \not\to Y \in (\Gamma \cup \Sigma)^+ \Rightarrow \Gamma \cup \Sigma \vdash X \not\to Y$.

Proof:
(1) follows immediately from the completeness of Armstrong's axioms together with Lemma 3.1. In order to prove (2), let $X \not\to Y \in (\Gamma \cup \Sigma)^+$; in the following steps (a) through (g), we shall define a set R of relations and show how some subset of R may be used to construct a derivation for $X \not\to Y$.

(a) Let $\Sigma = \{V_i \not\to W_i \mid 1 \leq i \leq n\}$ and for each $V_i \not\to W_i$ in Σ let $W_i \setminus (V_i)^+_\Gamma = \{A_{i,1}, \ldots, A_{i,m_i}\}$;
we define two-tuple relations $r_{i,j} := \{t_{i,j}, t'_{i,j}\}$ where $1 \leq i \leq n$ and $1 \leq j \leq m_i$ in the following way:

$$t_{i,j}[A] := \begin{cases} a_i & \text{if } A \in \{A_{i,j}\} \cup (V_i)^+_\Gamma \\ \perp & \text{otherwise} \end{cases}$$

$$t'_{i,j}[A] := \begin{cases} a_i & \text{if } A \in (V_i)^+_T \\ a'_i & \text{if } A = A_{i,j} \\ \perp & \text{otherwise} \end{cases}$$

It is assumed that $a_i \neq a'_i$, $a_i \neq a_k$, $a_i \neq a'_k$ and $a'_i \neq a'_k$ whenever $1 \leq i < k \leq n$.

(b) First we show that for each $V_i \not\to W_i \in \Sigma$ there exists at least one relation $r_{i,j}$ as defined in (a). Suppose that $W_i \setminus (V_i)^+_T = \emptyset$ for some $V_i \not\to W_i \in \Sigma$; then W_i is a subset of $(V_i)^+_T$. This in turn implies that $V_i \to W_i \in \Gamma^+ \subseteq (\Gamma \cup \Sigma)^+$ and hence $\Gamma \cup \Sigma$ would not be f.o.c.. Thus, there is at least one $r_{i,j}$ for each $V_i \not\to W_i \in \Sigma$. Moreover, it is easy to see from the construction of $r_{i,j}$ that the functional independency $V_i \not\to W_i$ ($1 \leq i \leq n$) is satisfied by all relations $r_{i,j}$ with $1 \leq j \leq m_i$.

(c) Suppose now that there is a functional dependency $Z \to U \in \Gamma$ which is not satisfied by some of the relations $r_{i,j}$ ($1 \leq i \leq n$ and $1 \leq j \leq m_i$); then, by construction of $r_{i,j}$, Z would have to be a subset of $(V_i)^+_T$ and therefore $V_i \to Z \in \Gamma^+$ and - using (FD3) from Definition 3.2 - $V_i \to U \in \Gamma^+$. On the other hand, also by assumption and by construction of $r_{i,j}$, U is not a subset of $(V_i)^+_T$ and therefore $V_i \to U \notin \Gamma^+$ which is a contradiction. Thus, all the functional dependencies from Γ are satisfied by each of the relations $r_{i,j}$ ($1 \leq i \leq n$ and $1 \leq j \leq m_i$).

(d) Let $R := \{\bigcup_{i=1}^{n} r_{i,j_i} \mid 1 \leq j_i \leq m_i\}$; Γ is satisfied by each $r \in R$, because Γ is satisfied in each $r_{i,j}$ according to (c) and because different relations $r_{i,j}$ do not have common values (apart from $\perp$). Moreover, Σ is satisfied by each $r \in R$, because - according to (b) - each $V_i \not\to W_i \in \Sigma$ is satisfied by the subrelation r_{i,j_i}

of r already. As $T \cup \Sigma$ implies $X \not\to Y$ by assumption, we may conclude that $X \not\to Y$ is also satisfied by each relation $r \in R$.

(e) Suppose, for each i $(1 \leq i \leq n)$ there is some j_i $(1 \leq j_i \leq m_i)$, such that $X \not\to Y$ is not satisfied by r_{i,j_i}; then $X \not\to Y$ would not be satisfied by $r_0 := \overset{n}{\underset{i=1}{\cup}} r_{i,j_i}$ either, and this would be contradictory to (d), since $r_0 \in R$. So there is some i_0 $(1 \leq i_0 \leq n)$, such that $X \not\to Y$ is satisfied by $r_{i_0,j}$ for each j $(1 \leq j \leq m_{i_0})$.

(f) Let i_0 be as specified under (e); then X has to be a subset of $(V_{i_0})_T^+$. Furthermore, for each j $(1 \leq j \leq m_{i_0})$, there has to be an attribute in Y, such that the two tuples of $r_{i_0,j}$ have different values with regard to that attribute. By construction of $r_{i_0,j}$, the attribute in question can only be $A_{i_0,j}$ as defined under (a), i.e. in particular $A_{i_0,j} \in Y$. Using (e) and the fact that $\{A_{i,1},\ldots,A_{i,m_i}\} = W_i \setminus (V_i)_T^+$, we obtain $W_{i_0} \setminus (V_{i_0})_T^+ \subseteq Y$.

(g) Now we are ready to construct a derivation for $X \not\to Y$. From $V_{i_0} \not\to W_{i_0} \in \Sigma$ and the obvious functional dependency $V_{i_0} \to (V_{i_0})_T^+$ we derive $(V_{i_0})_T^+ \not\to W_{i_0}$ by means of (FD-FI). Applying (FI2), we obtain $(V_{i_0})_T^+ \not\to W_{i_0} \setminus (V_{i_0})_T^+$; using (f) and (FI1), we derive $(V_{i_0})_T^+ \not\to Y$. As the functional dependency $(V_{i_0})_T^+ \to X$ is obvious from (f), a final application of (FD-FI) yields $X \not\to Y$, and this completes the proof. □

4. Computational Problems Related to Functional Independencies

Lemma 3.1 and Theorem 3.4 require that $T \cup \Sigma$ is f. o. c. . Whereas Definition 2.4, which says under which circumstances

$T \cup \Sigma$ is f. o. c., is a statement about all pairs of attribute sets, the following theorem will show that not all of these pairs have actually to be considered in order to decide whether $T \cup \Sigma$ is f. o. c. .

Theorem 4.1
Let $T \cup \Sigma$ be a set of functional dependencies and independencies. $T \cup \Sigma$ is f. o. c., iff

$$\forall\; X \not\to Y \in \Sigma \quad X \to Y \notin T^+$$

Proof: cf. [JANAS 86] □

As an immediate consequence of Theorem 4.1 we obtain the following algorithm which, given a set T of functional dependencies and a set Σ of functional independencies as input parameters, returns the value TRUE, if $T \cup \Sigma$ is f. o. c. and the value FALSE otherwise.

Algorithm 4.2
function FOC(T, Σ) **return** BOOLEAN **is**
begin
    for each $X \not\to Y$ **in** Σ **loop**
        X_T^+ := CLOSURE(X, T) ;
        if $Y \subseteq X_T^+$
        then return FALSE;
    end loop;
    return TRUE;
end FOC; □

Algorithm 4.2 makes use of a function CLOSURE, which computes the closure X_T^+ of an attribute set X with regard to some set T of functional dependencies. It is known from [BEERI & BERNSTEIN 79] that such a function may be implemented to run in linear time depending on the cardinality of T; therefore, Algorithm 4.2 may be implemented in such a way that it requires $O(|T|*|\Sigma|)$ time.

The most central problem in dependency theory is the implication problem (also called membership problem) which may be stated in our context as follows: Given a set $T \cup \Sigma$ of functional dependencies and independencies and an individual functional (in)dependency f, is $f \in (T \cup \Sigma)^+$? If f is a functional dependency, then the problem may be reduced to the implication problem for functional dependencies only (because of Lemma 3.1) and therefore may be solved in $O(|T|)$ time (cf. [BEERI & BERNSTEIN 79]).

The following theorem shows that there is an efficient algorithm for the implication problem also in the case where f is a function independency.

Theorem 4.3
Let $T \cup \Sigma$ be a set of functional dependencies and independencies which is f. o. c.; then

$$X \not\to Y \in (T \cup \Sigma)^+$$
$$\iff \exists V \not\to W \in \Sigma \quad X \subseteq V_T^+ \land W \setminus V_T^+ \subseteq Y$$

Proof: cf. [JANAS 86]   □

From this theorem, we obtain immediately the following algorithm which, given a set T of functional dependencies, a set Σ of functional independencies and an additional functional independency $X \not\to Y$ as input parameters, returns the value TRUE, if $X \not\to Y \in (T \cup \Sigma)^+$ and the value FALSE otherwise.

Algorithm 4.4

```
function MEMBER(Γ, Σ, X ↛ Y) return BOOLEAN is
begin
      for each V ↛ W in Σ loop
          V⁺_Γ := CLOSURE(V, Γ) ;
          if  X ⊆ V⁺_Γ  and  W \ V⁺_Γ ⊆ Y
          then return  TRUE;
      end loop;
      return FALSE;
end MEMBER;
```
                                                                    □

Again it is easy to see that Algorithm 4.4 may be implemented in such a way that it runs in $O(|\Gamma| * |\Sigma|)$ time.

Given two sets $\Gamma_1 \cup \Sigma_1$ and $\Gamma_2 \cup \Sigma_2$ of functional dependencies and independencies, the equivalence problem is to tell whether $(\Gamma_1 \cup \Sigma_1)^+ = (\Gamma_2 \cup \Sigma_2)^+$. Obviously, the equivalence problem can be solved by means of Algorithm 4.4, because $\Gamma_1 \cup \Sigma_1$ and $\Gamma_2 \cup \Sigma_2$ are equivalent, iff $f \in (\Gamma_2 \cup \Sigma_2)^+$ for each $f \in \Gamma_1 \cup \Sigma_1$ and $f \in (\Gamma_1 \cup \Sigma_1)^+$ for each $f \in \Gamma_2 \cup \Sigma_2$; thus the equivalence problem is solvable in cubic time at least.

In fact, the equivalence problem may even be solved in quadratic time; this is achieved by not making use of Algorithm 4.4 directly, but rather compute $V^+_{\Gamma_2}$ only once for each $V \nrightarrow W \in \Sigma_2$, and then compare $V^+_{\Gamma_2}$ and $W \setminus V^+_{\Gamma_2}$ with all functional independencies from Σ_1. The following algorithm requires two sets Γ_1 and Γ_2 of functional dependencies and two sets Σ_1 and Σ_2 of functional independencies as input parameters and returns the value TRUE, if $\Gamma_1 \cup \Sigma_1$ and $\Gamma_2 \cup \Sigma_2$ are equivalent and the value FALSE otherwise.

Algorithm 4.5

```
function EQUI(Γ₁, Σ₁, Γ₂, Σ₂) return BOOLEAN is
begin
    return (INCL(Γ₁, Σ₁, Γ₂, Σ₂) and INCL(Γ₂, Σ₂, Γ₁, Σ₁)) ;
end EQUI;

function INCL(Γ₁, Σ₁, Γ₂, Σ₂) return BOOLEAN is
begin
    for each X → Y in Γ₁ loop
        if Y ⊄ CLOSURE(X, Γ₂) ;
        then return FALSE ;
    end loop ;
    Σ₃ := Σ₁ ;
    for each V ↛ W in Σ₂ loop
        if Σ₃ = ∅
        then return TRUE ;
        V⁺_{Γ₂} := CLOSURE(V, Γ₂) ;
        for each U ↛ Z in Σ₃ loop
            if U ⊆ V⁺_{Γ₂} and W \ V⁺_{Γ₂} ⊆ Z
            then Σ₃ := Σ₃ \ {U ↛ Z} ;
        end loop ;
    end loop ;
    return (Σ₃ = ∅);
end INCL ;
```
                                                                   □

Summarizing we can say that the contradiction problem, the implication problem and the equivalence problem all can be solved efficiently. The respective algorithms require moderately more time than the corresponding algorithms for functional dependencies only, but one cannot reasonably expect that complexity of the problems decreases when functional dependencies are combined with another class of restrictions, such as functional independencies. Thus, the results reported in this paper definitely encourage our approach to determine the relevant functional dependencies as described in the introduction.

References

[AHO et al. 79]
   Aho, A.V., Beeri, C., Ullman, J.D.
   The theory of joins in relational databases.
   ACM TODS, vol. 4 (1979), pp 279-314

[ARMSTRONG 74]
   Armstrong, W.W.
   Dependency structures of data base relationships.
   Proc. 1974 IFIP Congress, North Holland, Amsterdam (1974),
   pp 580-583

[BEERI 80]
   Beeri, C.
   On the membership problem for functional and multivalued
   dependencies in relational databases.
   ACM TODS, vol. 5 (1980), pp 241-259

[BEERI & BERNSTEIN 79]
   Beeri, C., Bernstein, P.A.
   Computational problems related to the design of normal form
   relational schemas.
   ACM TODS, vol. 4 (1979), pp 30-59

[BEERI & HONEYMAN 81]
   Beeri, C., Honeyman, P.
   Preserving functional dependencies.
   SIAM J. Computing, vol. 10 (1981), pp 647-656

[BEERI & VARDI 81]
   Beeri, C., Vardi, M.Y.
   The implication problem for data dependencies.
   Proc. ICALP 81, Springer LNCS 115 (1981), pp 73-85

[BEERI et al. 77]
   Beeri, C., Fagin, R., Howard, J.H.
   A complete axiomatization for functional and multivalued
   dependencies in database relations.
   Proc. ACM-SIGMOD 1977 Int. Conf. on Management of Data,
   Toronto (1977), pp 47-61

[BEERI et al. 80]
   Beeri, C., Dowd, M., Fagin, R., Statman, R.
   On the structure of Armstrong relations for functional
   dependencies.
   IBM Research Report RJ2901, San Jose (1980)

[CODD 70]
   Codd, E.F.
   A relational model for large shared data banks.
   Comm. ACM, vol. 13 (1970), pp 377-387

[CODD 72]
   Codd, E.F.
   Further normalization of the data base relational model.
   In: Data Base Systems (R. Rustin, ed.), Prentice Hall,
   Englewood Cliffs (1972), pp 33-64

[CODD 74]
   Codd, E.F.
   Recent investigations in relational data base systems.
   Proc. 1974 IFIP Congress, North Holland, Amsterdam (1974),
   pp 1017-1021

[FAGIN 77]
   Fagin, R.
   Multivalued dependencies and a new normal form for relational databases.
   ACM TODS, vol. 2 (1977), pp 262-278

[GALIL 82]
   Galil, Z.
   An almost linear-time algorithm for computing a dependency basis in a relational database.
   J. ACM, vol. 29 (1982), pp 96-102

[GINSBURG & ZAIDDAN 82]
   Ginsburg, S., Zaiddan, S.M.
   Properties of functional-dependency families.
   J. ACM, vol. 29 (1982), pp 678-698

[JANAS 85]
   Janas, J.M.
   A combined axiomatization for functional dependencies and functional independencies.
   Bericht 8503, Fakultät für Informatik, Universität der Bundeswehr München (1985)

[JANAS 86]
   Janas, J.M.
   Computational problems related to functional independencies.
   Bericht 8609, Fakultät für Informatik, Universität der Bundeswehr München (1986)

[MAIER 80]
   Maier, D.
   Minimum covers in the relational database model.
   J. ACM, vol. 27 (1980) pp 664-674

[SILVA & MELKANOFF 81]
   Silva, A.M., Melkanoff, M.A.
   A method for helping discover the dependencies of a relation.
   In: H. Gallaire, J. Minker, J.-M. Nicolas (eds.): Advances in Data Base Theory - vol. 1. New York: Plenum Press (1981), pp 115-133

[ULLMANN 82]
   Ullmann, J.D.
   Principles of database systems. 2nd ed.
   Rockville: Computer Science Press (1982)

[ZANIOLO 76]
   Zaniolo, C.
   Analysis and design of relational schemata for database systems.
   Tech. Rep. UCLA-ENG-7669, Dept. of Computer Science, University of California, Los Angeles (1976)

A Generic Algorithm for Transaction Processing During Network Partitioning

Bharat Bhargava and Shirley Browne
Department of Computer Sciences
Purdue University
West Lafayette, IN 47907

Abstract. This research presents an algorithm that allows transaction processing to proceed during site failures and network partitioning while ensuring the consistency of replicated data. Our algorithm can be used together with various voting schemes which provide varying degrees of data availability. Different voting schemes may be used simultaneously for different groups of data. Our algorithm contains as special cases: the site quorum method in which there is a single distinguished partition, and the virtual partition method in which a (possibly different) distinguished partition is determined for each logical data item. By grouping data items in various ways, our algorithm can be tuned to yield methods which lie between these two extremes.

1 Introduction

In a distributed database system (DDBS), data may be partially or fully replicated to improve the performance of the system and to increase availability. Performance is improved by enabling transactions to read local copies. Availability is enhanced during failures since replication increases the likelihood that at least one copy of a data item will be available. When failures occur, however, problems arise in maintaining the consistency of the replicated copies. Consistency requires that the concurrent execution of a sequence of transactions on the replicated database have the same effect as a serial execution of the same transactions on a single-copy database. Each transaction should also have a consistent view of the database state. These notions of correctness are formalized by the definitions of logical-serializability in [12] and of one-serializability in [3].

The algorithm for transaction processing described in this paper is fault-tolerant in that it can handle fail-stop types of failures of sites and communication links which may lead to network partitioning. Our algorithm is correct in that it ensures the logical-serializability of user transactions. We assume that the communication subsystem handles lost or delayed messages and link failures which do not lead to network partitioning by means of retransmission and rerouting, respectively. We assume that the DDBS runs a correct concurrency control algorithm which ensures conflict-serializable execution of transactions.

We use the notion of a distinguished partition to ensure consistency of the database state during network partitioning. Network partitioning occurs when site and/or link failures cause the network to be broken up into two or more connected subgraphs which cannot communicate with each other, each of which is called a partition. If site failures occur but the remaining sites can all communicate with each other, the operational sites compose a single partition. In any case, access to a particular domain of data items is allowed to proceed in at most one partition, which is called the distinguished partition (DP) for that domain.

We assume an algorithm is given that allows a site to determine whether or not its partition is the DP for a particular domain, based on local information and on information obtainable from the sites with which it can communicate. One possible algorithm is the lexicographic voting method described in [10]. Copies which have missed updates, either due to a site failure or network partitioning, are marked as unreadable when network reconfiguration causes these copies to again become part of a DP.

Each site maintains information concerning which other sites it can communicate with. This information is updated by means of special control transactions which are serialized with user transactions. Thus, a user transaction running in a partition has a consistent view of that partition since a reconfiguration must occur logically either before or after the user transaction.

The organization of the paper is as follows: In section 2, we discuss related research. Section 3 describes the distributed system model, as well as the necessary terminology and notation. In section 4 we describe our algorithm, and in section 5 we give a proof of its correctness in terms of logical-serializability. Conclusions and ideas for future work are given in section 6.

2   Related Work

Much previous research has been focused on the topic of transaction processing in non-partitioned networks in which site failures may occur. Algorithms for managing replicated data in this case are given in [2] and [5]. The general approach is to consider the occurrence of failures and recoveries to coincide with the execution of the corresponding control transactions. For example, the failure of a copy or a site is considered to occur at the same time that the transaction that announces that failure is executed. Use of a correct concurrency control algorithm then yields an execution history which is logical-serializable, provided a read-one/write-all-available (ROWAA) strategy is used for processing user transactions. This approach is not directly applicable when network partitioning can occur, since allowing a ROWAA strategy to be used simultaneously in different partitions can lead to the inconsistency of replicated data.

A survey of transaction processing methods in partitioned networks is given in [6]. This survey discusses both pessimistic and optimistic strategies and both syntactic and semantic approaches. In this paper, we restrict ourselves to pessimistic syntactic methods – that is, we use logical-serializability as the correctness criterion and we require that global inconsistencies between partitions not be allowed to occur.

Static and dynamic voting methods for partition processing are discussed in [14,7] and [9,10,4]. These methods require a transaction to access some threshold number of votes for a data item, called a quorum, before executing an operation on that item. In a partitioned network, these thresholds guarantee that conflicting operations cannot occur in different partitions. This guarantee is not without a cost, however, since accessing a quorum makes read operations expensive. The virtual partition approach in [1] requires a quorum of copies of a particular data item to be present in a given partition for access to that data item to be allowed to occur. Although a transaction does not need to access a quorum before performing an operation, it needs to know which sites are considered to be in its current partition. This knowledge is provided by identifying changes in the configuration of the network with the control transactions that announce those changes. Correctness is ensured by relying on the underlying concurrency control method to produce a logical-serializable execution history. The virtual partition method has the disadvantage that whenever a control transaction is executed within some partition, a read quorum must be accessed for each data item which has a read quorum in that partition.

Quorum-based commit and termination protocols that attempt to maximize data availability by taking into account the voting strategy used are described in [8]. Theoretical results in [13] and [11] show that, in general, nonblocking commit protocols for the case of network partitioning are impossible.

We have extended the ideas presented in [5] for managing site failures to the case of network partitioning. We propose a generic method which can incorporate various pessimistic, syntactic strategies for partition processing in an efficient manner. This flexibility allows use of the strategy which is most suitable for a particular domain.

3 Model and Terminology

As in the model of the DDBS described in [5], the users' view of an object is called a *logical data item*, or *data item*, denoted X. A data item is stored as a set of *physical copies* or *copies*. The copy of X stored at site k is denoted x_k, and the fact that X has a copy at site k is denoted $x_k \epsilon X$. We assume that the information regarding where the copies of data item X are located is available at least at the resident sites of X. In general, we use upper-case for notation pertaining to logical data and lower case for physical data.

The set of logical data items is grouped into (not necessarily disjoint) subsets called *domains*. At one extreme all data items are members of a single domain, while at the other extreme, each data item is a member of a separate domain. Data items may be grouped into domains according to different criteria. For example, data items that are replicated at the same subset of sites may compose a domain. Alternately, data items that are frequently accessed within the same transaction may be grouped into the same domain.

Users manipulate the database via *transactions*. A transaction is a program that accesses the database by issuing *logical operations READ* and *WRITE* on logical data items. Each transaction has a *coordinating* or *home* site and possibly some other *participating* or *slave* sites. We assume that a transaction's home site is the one at which the transaction is initiated.

There are two major functional modules running at each site. The *transaction manager* (TM) supervises the execution of transactions that are initiated at its site and interprets logical operations into requests for *physical operations*. The *data manager* (DM) carries out the physical operations on the copies stored at the site.

Two physical operations *conflict* if at least one of them is a *write* and they both access the same physical copy. An execution history H containing the physical operations for a set T of transactions is *conflict-serializable* if there is a serial history H_s containing the same operations such that any two conflicting operations appear in the same order in both H and H_s. (A serial history is one in which operations from different transactions are not interleaved). The *conflict graph* (CG) corresponding to H is a directed graph $(T, \rightarrow)$

in which there is an edge $T_a \rightarrow T_b$ whenever T_a and T_b contain conflicting operations op_a and op_b, respectively, and op_a precedes op_b in H. H is conflict-serializable if and only if its CG is acyclic [3].

We consider the topology of our network to be its virtual communication topology. That is, if two nodes can communicate with each other, then we consider the graph to have an edge between these two nodes. We assume that a failed attempt to communicate with another node will be reported to the requesting node by the communication subsystem. We do not assume that the cause of the failure is reported.

4 Algorithm

4.1 Partition Identifiers and Connection Vectors

Each site maintains a copy of the partition identifier (PID) and the connection vector (CV) for its partition. The PID consists of two parts – higher order bits which are increasing over time for any given site, and lower order bits assigned by the site which initiates the partition. Since these lower order bits are different for different sites, PID's are unique system-wide. CV and PID are considered data items of a special type, called control data (CD), and accesses to their copies are governed by the concurrency control algorithm. Three types of transactions are executed by the DDBS – user transactions, copier transactions, and control transactions. All user and copier transactions read local copies of CV and PID, but only control transactions may write control data items. We assume that PID and CV are fully replicated at all n sites. Following the convention described in section 3, the copies of PID and CV at site i are denoted by pid_i and cv_i, respectively. The values of pid_i and cv_i give the status of site i's partition as currently perceived by site i.

The only type of control transaction we will describe in detail is the RECONFIGURE transaction, which is used to determine a new partition. Other types of control transactions may be useful for efficiency reasons, but they are not necessary for the correctness of our algorithm. The use of other types of control transactions is discussed in subsection 4.3. A reconfiguration of the system is indicated whenever a change in the communication topology of the network is detected. A RECONFIGURE transaction which carries out this reconfiguration may be triggered either by a user transaction which is unable to complete or by the communication subsystem. The best method of triggering a RECONFIGURE transaction is a topic for further research.

A site i which executes a RECONFIGURE transaction requests PID's from all other sites. It determines a new PID by setting the higher order bits to be greater than the maximum of all those received from other sites and setting the lower order bits to its unique site ID. CV contains a 1 entry for each site with which site i is able to communicate and a 0 entry for all other sites. The RECONFIGURE transaction writes the PID and CV of every member of the new partition.

4.2 Distinguished Partitions

Data items are grouped into domains as described in section 3. Each domain can be accessed in at most one partition, called the distinguished partition (DP) for that domain. In addition to setting a new PID and CV, the RECONFIGURE transaction determines for which domains the new partition is the DP. We assume some method is given for making this determination. Different methods may be used for different domains. Associated with each domain name is stored information that is needed by the method. For example, for the static quorum method, read and write quorum thresholds are stored with the domain name. A partition meets a quorum requirement for a domain if the number of sites containing a copy of some item in the domain is greater than or equal to the given quorum threshold. The new partition is the DP for the domain if it meets the requirements for both read and write quorums. As another example, for the dynamic voting method [9], an integer giving the cardinality of the set of sites having up-to-date copies of all data items in the domain is stored with the domain name. In this case, the new partition is the DP for the domain if it contains a majority of the sites that have up-to-date copies.

When a new partition is formed, there may be sites in the partition that are out-of-date with respect to a particular domain for which the new partition is the DP. If a site did not participate in the immediately previous DP for that domain, then the domain should be marked as unreadable at that site. These ideas have also been used in [4]. We explain how this marking is done in the next subsection.

4.3 Control Transactions

The RECONFIGURE transaction may be initiated whenever a change in the communication topology is detected. A RECONFIGURE transaction executes as follows: It first broadcasts read requests for CV and PID and the associated domain names and information to all sites. Let R denote the set of sites that reply. The transaction determines a new PID as described in subsection 4.1. Entries in CV are set to 1 for all sites in R and to 0 for all other sites. Using the prescribed methods, the transaction determines for which domains the new partition is the DP. For a given domain Π associated with the new partition, let PID_Π be the maximum of all PID's (returned by sites in R) which listed Π as an associated domain. For any site which returned a PID different from PID_Π, the domain Π should be considered unreadable. Finally, the RECONFIGURE transaction writes the new values for CV, PID, and the associated domain names and information to all sites in R, and marks outdated domain copies as unreadable. If any of the write requests cannot be completed due to concurrent failures, the RECONFIGURE transaction is aborted to avoid the possibility of more than one DP being formed for a given domain.

Although a site that is recovering from a failure could initiate a RECONFIGURE transaction, it may be more efficient to provide a RECOVERY transaction by means of which the site can join the current partition. A RECOVERY transaction executes at site i as follows: The transaction first issues read requests for CV and PID and the domain names associated with the partition. Since the local copies of CV and PID are considered unreadable, these read requests trigger a copier transaction which refreshes the local copies. The transaction then writes a 1 entry to $CV[i]$ at every site in the current partition, itself included. It marks local copies of data items in the domains associated with the partition as unreadable. If any of the write requests cannot be completed due to failures, the RECOVERY transaction is aborted.

Control transactions are executed concurrently with all other transactions, and they are governed by the same concurrency control algorithm and commit protocol.

4.4 User Transactions

Each user transaction reads the local copies of CV and PID before executing any other operations. The transaction is tagged with the value read for PID. The strategy used for processing read and write operations on objects within a given domain can depend on the DP method used for that domain. For example, if the quorum method is used, read and write quorum numbers may be specified for the partition which are consistent with the global read and write thresholds for determining the DP, as in [1]. If the DP is determined by means of the dynamic voting method, then a read-one/write-all strategy should be used.

Each request for reading or writing a physical copy at site k includes the PID of the transaction issuing the request. If this number does not agree with pid_k, the request is rejected. Note that this access to pid_k is considered to be a $read(pid_k)$ operation for purposes of concurrency control. If a write request is rejected or cannot be carried out because of a failure, the transaction is aborted. The transaction may or may not be aborted if a read request is rejected, since the read can be retried at another site.

4.5 Copier Transactions and Unreadable Copies

For a data copy marked as unreadable, a write operation on it removes the mark when the transaction which issued the write commits, while a request for reading it triggers a copier transaction that renovates the physical copy. The user transaction may either be blocked until the copier finishes or may read some other copy instead.

A copier transaction is responsible for refreshing a particular unreadable data copy of a data item X. It reads the local copies of CV and PID, locates a readable copy of X, uses the contents of the readable copy to renovate the local copy, and removes the unreadable mark. If version numbers are used, then it is necessary to actually copy the data only if the version numbers are different. If the copier cannot find a readable copy in the current partition, the copier transaction is aborted.

Copier transactions may be initiated by a site as part of a recovery procedure or triggered on demand by read requests. They are executed concurrently with all other transactions and are governed by the same concurrency control algorithm and commit protocol.

5 Proof of Correctness

5.1 Correctness Concepts

In this subsection, we briefly define the fundamental concepts that are needed for the correctness proof presented in the next subsection. These concepts are based on the theory developed in [12].

An *execution history* H for a set of transactions $T = \{T_a, T_b, ...\}$ is a partially ordered set $(\sigma, <)$ containing all the physical operations interpreted from the logical operations of these transactions. Note that σ may contain read and write operations corresponding to control and copier transactions as well as to the transactions in T. An *augmented execution history* is a history with an initial transaction that writes to all data copies and a final transaction that reads from all data copies. To simplify our arguments, we consider only augmented execution histories.

A transaction T_b *reads-x_i-from* T_a, denoted $T_a \Rightarrow_{x_i} T_b$, in H if $w_a[x_i] \in \sigma$, $r_b[x_i] \in \sigma$, $w_a[x_i] < r_b[x_i]$, and there is no transaction T_c such that $w_c[x_i] \in \sigma$ and $w_a[x_i] < w_c[x_i] < r_b[x_i]$. A (non-copier) transaction T_b *READS-X-FROM* a (non-copier) transaction T_a, denoted $T_a \Rightarrow_X T_b$, in H if either there is a copy $x_i \in X$ such that $T_a \Rightarrow_{x_i} T_b$ (T_b *READS-X-FROM* T_a directly), or there are copies x_i, x_j and a copier transaction T_c such that $T_a \Rightarrow_{x_j} T_c$ and $T_c \Rightarrow_{x_i} T_b$ (T_b *READS-X-FROM* T_a indirectly via the copier transaction T_c, similarly defined for a sequence of copier transactions). A *logical serial* history for T is a totally ordered set containing the logical operations from T such that operations from different transactions are not interleaved. We consider only augmented logical serial histories that have an initial transaction that writes to all logical data items and a final transaction that reads from all data items. A logical serial history defines its $READ - FROM$ relations from the total order.

Two augmented execution histories for the same set of transactions are *logically equivalent* if they define the same $READ-FROM$ relations. A history H is *logical-serializable* if there exists a logical serial history H_s that is logically equivalent to H.

A *logical-serializability testing graph* (LSTG) of a history H is a directed graph $(T, \rightarrow)$ with the following properties:

  (i) If $T_a \Rightarrow_X T_b$, then there exists an edge $T_a \rightarrow T_b$ (called a WR edge or a $READ - FROM$ edge);

  (ii) There is an edge between any two non-copier transactions that write to copies of the same logical object X (called a WW edge, denoted $\rightarrow_X$);

  (iii) If $T_a \Rightarrow_X T_b$ and $T_a \rightarrow_X T_c$, then there is an edge $T_b \rightarrow T_c$ (called an RW edge).

The main result of logical-serializability theory can be stated as follows:

Theorem 1. [12] *A history H is logical-serializable if and only if H has an acyclic LSTG.*

If we modify the definition of LSTG by replacing the word "edge" by "path", the notation $\rightarrow$ by $\rightarrow^*$, and $\rightarrow_X$ by $\rightarrow^*_X$, Theorem 1 remains correct.

For purposes of our proof of correctness, we consider two categories of data: user data (UD) and control data (CD). CD items include CV and PID, as well as the domain names and attributes. Note that with respect to CD, user transactions are read-only transactions. To simplify our arguments, the only type of control transaction we consider is the RECONFIGURE transaction. Our arguments can be extended to prove that the algorithm is still correct if other types of control transactions are also used.

5.2 Correctness Proof

We assume that the DDBS runs a correct concurrency control algorithm that ensures conflict-serializability with respect to $UD \cup CD$, but what we need to prove is logical-serializability with respect to UD. The conflict graph with respect to $UD \cup CD$ is insufficient to prove logical-serializability since it may not contain all the necessary write-order and read-before paths. Hence, we add edges to the conflict graph so as to obtain these paths while still preserving acyclicity of the resulting graph.

We assume that the algorithm provided for determining the DP for a particular domain guarantees that there is at most one DP at any given time and that the current DP has a nonempty intersection with the previous DP (i.e., at least one site in common). We say that a RECONFIGURE transaction that associates a domain Π with a new partition *activates* Π. The activations of a particular domain can be numbered consecutively, starting with 1.

We make use of the following two lemmas which follow from the fact that the execution history is conflict-serializable.

Lemma 1. If $T_a \Rightarrow_Y T_b$, $Y \epsilon UD \cup CD$, then there is a path in CG from T_a to T_b.

Proof. If T_b READS-Y-FROM T_a directly, then there is a copy y_i such that T_b reads-y_i-from T_a and hence an edge $T_a \rightarrow T_b$ in CG. If T_b READS-Y-FROM T_a indirectly via copier transactions, then there is a path $T_a \rightarrow^* T_b$ in CG.

Lemma 2. There is a path in CG between any two control transactions which activate a common domain.

Proof. (by induction)

Let T_c and T_d be RECONFIGURE transactions which both activate a common domain Π with corresponding activation numbers A_c and A_d, respectively, for Π. Assume without loss of generality that $A_c < A_d$. If $A_d = A_c + 1$, let site k be common between the two activations. Then since T_c and T_d both write cv_k and pid_k, there is an edge $T_c \rightarrow T_d$ in CG. If $A_d > A_c + 1$, let T_e be the RECONFIGURE transaction that forms the DP corresponding to $A_e = A_d - 1$. Again, there is an edge $T_e \rightarrow T_d$ in CG. By induction there is a path $T_c \rightarrow^* T_e$ in CG. Thus, there is a path $T_c \rightarrow^* T_d$ in CG.

Lemma 2 implies a total ordering on the control transactions that activate a particular domain.

Theorem 2. Based on the algorithm stated in section 4, the conflict graph (CG) with respect to $UD \cup CD$ can be augmented to form an acyclic graph G which contains an LSTG with respect to UD.

Proof. Form graph G by adding edges to CG as follows: For each domain Π and each control transaction T_c that activates Π, for any non-control transaction T_a such that $T_c \Rightarrow_{CV} T_a$, add an edge from T_a to the control transaction T_d (if any) that immediately follows T_c in the total order, if this edge does not already exist (the edge already exists if T_d writes $home(T_a)$). The resulting graph G is clearly still acyclic (since if there is a path in CG from T_d to T_a, then T_a does not READ-CV-FROM T_c).

For a given domain Π, we consider the subgraph G_Π of G consisting of user and copier transactions that access objects in Π and of control transactions that activate Π. The edges in G_Π define a partial order on these transactions in general and a total order on the control transactions (by Lemma 2). The non-control transactions which fall between two consecutive control transactions execute during a particular activation of Π. We claim that logically conflicting operations on a data item X in Π are totally ordered by edges in G. Let $op_1[X]$ and $op_2[X]$ be two such logically conflicting operations. If op_1 and op_2 occur during the same activation, then we assume op_1 and op_2 physically conflict and thus are ordered in CG according to the concurrency control algorithm. If op_1 and op_2 occur during different activations, then there is a path in G between the corresponding transactions of which they are a part, and we take the direction of this path to be the ordering. We assume that the method given for determining the DP with respect to Π, together with the strategy given for processing read and write operations on objects in Π, guarantees that if a transaction T_b READS-X, then T_b READS-X-FROM T_a, where T_a is the most recent transaction in the total order for conflicting operations on X which writes X.

We now prove that G contains an LSTG with respect to UD.

(i) Suppose $T_a \Rightarrow_X T_b$. By Lemma 1, there a path $T_a \rightarrow^* T_b$ in G.

(ii) Suppose T_a and T_b both write to copies of X, $X \epsilon \Pi$. Then since conflicting operations on X are totally ordered (by the above argument) by edges in G_Π, either $T_a \rightarrow^* T_b$ or $T_b \rightarrow^* T_a$ in G_Π and hence in G.

(iii) Suppose $T_a \Rightarrow_X T_b$ and $T_a \to_X T_c$. Since logically conflicting operations on X are totally ordered by edges in G_Π, either $T_b \to^* T_c$ or $T_c \to^* T_b$ in G_Π. Suppose $T_c \to^* T_b$. Then T_b does not $READ\text{-}X\text{-}FROM\ T_a$, a contradiction. Thus, $T_b \to^* T_c$ in G.

6 Conclusions and Future Work

One of the main ideas in this paper is the grouping of data into domains so that a suitable partition processing strategy can be applied separately to each domain. By adjusting the granularity of the data domains, we can attempt to provide maximum data availability. If all user data are members of a single domain, then transaction processing can occur only in the DP for this domain. Even if some other partition contains quorums for all the data items which a transaction initiated in that partition needs to access, the transaction will be blocked. On the other hand, if a DP is established separately for each data item, then the DP's for two different data items may be different so that a transaction that needs to access both data items cannot be executed in either partition. For example, in a banking application, DP's for checking account information and savings account information may be different, and transactions that need to access both cannot execute. By grouping logically related data items together, greater availability may be achieved. Domains can be dynamically adjusted by means of control transactions, provided that a control transaction making such an adjustment is executed in the DP for all the domains concerned. To minimize the reduction in data availability that can occur when transactions are blocked during the commit process because of failures, a generalization of the quorum-based commit and termination protocols presented in [8] should be used.

Our algorithm guarantees correctness by imposing the following conditions on the submethods used:

(1) Any two logically conflicting operations on some domain that occur during a single activation of that domain should physically conflict.

(2) In the total order imposed on logically conflicting operations for a particular data item X, a read operation always reads the value written by the most recent write operation in the total order.

For example, a quorum-based method used within a partition for processing read and write operations together with a correct concurrency control algorithm guarantees (1). A static or dynamic voting scheme for determining the DP for a domain together with (1) should ensure (2).

Thus, the burden of proving the algorithm correct is reduced to the problem of proving that the above conditions are satisfied for each method used.

One of our goals was to provide efficient recovery from failures. When a site recovery or network merge occurs, we would like for normal transaction processing to proceed as soon as possible, without having to wait for data copies to be brought up-to-date. We provide for efficient recovery by marking out-of-date copies as unreadable and allowing copier transactions which refresh such unreadable data copies to run concurrently with user transactions. By providing a special-purpose RECOVERY transaction, our algorithm achieves the same efficiency in the case of site failures as other algorithms which deal only with site failures.

For future work, we wish to incorporate optimistic and semantic approaches into our general method, allowing different approaches to be used with different domains. We plan to establish conventions that must be followed and conditions that must be satisfied by the given methods to maintain consistency of the replicated data. We also plan to explore various means of initiating control and copier transactions, perhaps having them be initiated by supporting subsystems rather than triggered by user transactions. We intend to implement our partition processing methods in the prototype RAID distributed database system so as to be able to simulate failure scenarios under various conditions and evaluate the performance of our algorithms.

References

[1] A. E. Abbadi and S. Toueg. Availability in partitioned replicated databases. In *Proc. Fifth ACM SIGACT-SIGMOD Symp. on Principles of Database Systems*, pages 240–251, March 1986.

[2] P. Bernstein and N. Goodman. An algorithm for concurrency control and recovery in replicated distributed databases. *ACM Trans. Database Syst.*, 9(4):596–615, Dec. 1984.

[3] P. Bernstein, V. Hadzilacos, and N. Goodman. *Concurrency Control and Recovery in Database Systems.* Addison-Wesley, 1987.

[4] B. Bhargava and P. Ng. A dynamic majority determination algorithm for reconfiguration of network partitions. *to appear in International Journal of Information Science*, Sep. 1988.

[5] B. Bhargava and Z. Ruan. Site recovery in replicated distributed database systems. In *Proceedings of the 6th Intl. Conf. on Distributed Computing Syst.*, May 1986.

[6] S. Davidson, H. Garcia-Molina, and D. Skeen. Consistency in partitioned networks. *Computing Surveys*, 17(3):341–370, Sep. 1985.

[7] D. K. Gifford. Weighted voting for replicated data. In *Proc. Seventh Symposium on Operating Systems Principles*, pages 150–162, ACM, Dec. 1979.

[8] C. Huang and V. Li. A quorum-based commit and termination protocol for distributed database systems. In *Proc. Fourth International Conference on Data Engineering*, pages 136–143, IEEE Computer Society Press, Feb. 1988.

[9] S. Jajodia and D. Mutchler. Dynamic voting. In *Proc. ACM SIGMOD 1987 Annual Conference*, pages 227–238, May 1987.

[10] S. Jajodia and D. Mutchler. Integrating static and dynamic voting protocols to enhance file availability. In *Proc. Fourth International Conference on Data Engineering*, pages 144–153, IEEE Computer Society Press, Feb. 1988.

[11] K. Ramarao. Transaction atomicity in the presence of network partitions. In *Proc. Fourth International Conference on Data Engineering*, pages 512–519, IEEE Computer Society Press, Feb. 1988.

[12] Z. Ruan. *File replication in distributed systems.* PhD thesis, Purdue University, Aug. 1986.

[13] D. Skeen and M. Stonebraker. A formal model of crash recovery in a distributed system. *IEEE Transaction on Software Engineering*, SE-9(3):219–227, May 1983.

[14] R. Thomas. A majority consensus approach to concurrency control for multiple copy databases. *ACM Trans. Database Syst.*, 4(2):180–209, June 1979.

INDEX OF AUTHORS

C Arbib   123
B Awerbuch   286
A Beauvieux   455
P Bellot   270
B Bhargava   509
P C P Bhatt   143
K S H S R Bhatta   400
B B Bhattacharya   88
S Biswas   211
S Browne   509
R Burstall   250
J Cheriyan   30
C Chou   122
M Crochemore   80
A Datta   108
J Desharnais   304
K Ekanadham   377
J Fiadeiro   469
K Furukawa   364
S K Ghosh   18
I S Gopal   122
M C Henson   329
F Honsell   250
G F Italiano   123
J M Janas   487
V Jay   270
J Kamper   193
S Kaplan   419
D Kapur   435
H Karnick   400
S N Khadilkar   211
S Khuller   67

W W Kirchherr   240
L M Kiruosis   286
E Kranakis   286
S V Krishnan   49
K Krithivasan   108
V Kumar   161
C Levcopoulos   154
N H Madhavji   304
S N Maheshwari   30
D Musser   435
V Nageshwara Rao   161
P Narendran   435
P Panangaden   348
A Panconesi   123
C Pandu Rangan   49
O Petersson   154
K Pingali   377
V C Prasad   143
F P Preparata   1
C A Rich   225
S Saxena   143
A Sernadas   469
C Sernadas   469
S Seshadri   49
V Shanbhogue   348
G Slutzki   225
J Stillman   435
S Sur-Kolay   88
R Turner   329
K Ueda   364
H Venkateswaran   175
P M B Vitanyi   286

RAYMOND H. FOGLER LIBRARY
DATE DUE

BOOKS ARE SUBJECT TO
RECALL AFTER TWO WEEKS

JAN 1 3 1989